The Year
in Television, 2008

The Year in Television, 2008

A Catalog of New and Continuing Series, Miniseries, Specials and TV Movies

VINCENT TERRACE

McFarland & Company, Inc., Publishers

Jefferson, North Carolina, and London

LIBRARY OF CONGRESS CATALOGUING-IN-PUBLICATION DATA

Terrace, Vincent, 1948–
    The year in television, 2008 : a catalog of new and continuing
series, miniseries, specials and TV movies / Vincent Terrace.
      p.   cm.
    Includes index.

    ISBN 978-0-7864-4391-8
    softcover : 50# alkaline paper ∞

    1. Television series — United States — Catalogs.   2. Television
specials — United States — Catalogs.   3. Television mini-series —
United States — Catalogs.   4. Made-for-TV movies — United
States — Catalogs.   I. Title.
PN1992.8.S4T485   2009
016.79145'750973090051— dc22   2009006686

British Library cataloguing data are available

Cover image ©2009 Shutterstock

Manufactured in the United States of America

McFarland & Company, Inc., Publishers
  Box 611, Jefferson, North Carolina 28640
   www.mcfarlandpub.com

TABLE OF CONTENTS

PREFACE

The Year in Television, 2008 is the only source that chronicles all the first run entertainment programs broadcast from January 1, 2008 through December 31, 2008. Included are series, specials, TV movies, pilots, miniseries and internet series. All the broadcast networks are represented (including syndication) as are cable networks (including specialized outlets like the gay and lesbian channels Here! and Logo).

Each of the alphabetically arranged entries contains a storyline, performer/character casts, credits, month/day/year broadcast dates, and genre. A full index concludes the book. Where possible, reviews are included with programs that premiered in 2008.

From the obscure to the well known to the one episode wonders, everything, entertainment wise, is presented in a concise, easy to use guide that presents a look at what happened in 2008 — for convenience now or in the future.

PART I

. . . .

New Shows — Debuted in 2008

1 **The A List Awards.** (Special; Awards; Bravo; June 12, 2008)

A celebration of the creative process covering the fields of beauty, design, fashion, food and pop culture.

Host: Kathy Griffin. **Presenter:** Margaret Cho, Tamara Barney, Tyson Beckford, Lu Ann de Lesseps, Simon Doonan, Vicki Gunvalson, Bethenny Frankel, Rachel Dratch, Billy Eichner, Molly Simms, Alex McCord, Ramona Singer, Jerry Springer, Jeana Tomasina, Lauri Waring, Jill Zarin.

Credits: *Producer:* Todd Chambers, Jason Uhrmacher, Eric Cook.

2 **Abby in Wonderland.** (Pilot; Children; PBS; November 27, 2008)

The pilot presentation for a proposed series featuring Jim Henson's Muppet characters in fanciful adaptations of classic fairy tales. *Abby in Wonderland*, adapted from *Alice in Wonderland*, tells the story of a young girl (Abby) who loves fairy tales and hopes to grow up and have her own fairy tale. One day, as Abby's friend Elmo reads the classic *Alice in Wonderland*, Abby falls asleep and dreams she is Alice and experiences the adventures Alice found in Wonderland.

Voices: Carroll Spinney, Kevin Clash, Chris Knowings, Nitya Vidyasagar, Pam Alciero, Rickey Boyd, Fran Brill, Tyler Bunch, Jerry Nelson, Carmen Osbahr, Lara MacLean, John Kennedy, David Rudman.

Credits: *Executive Producer:* Carol-Lynne Parente. *Co-Executive Producer:* Kevin Clash. *Coordinating Producer:* April Chadderdon. *Senior Producer:* Melissa Dino. *Producer:* Tim Carter, Benjamin Lehmann. *Director:* Kevin Clash. *Writer:* Christine Ferraro.

3 **ABC's the List.** (Special; Variety; ABC; December 23, 2008)

A look back at 2008 with lists covering the top five items in pop culture, entertainment and celebrities (for example, in the category "Dishing the Stars" [celebrities who provide their own dirt] the "winners" were Valerie Bertinelli, number 5, for her book *Losing It*; Lance Bass, number 4, for his book *Out of Sync*.; Maureen McCormick, number 3, for her book, *Here's the Story*; Tori Spelling, number two for her book, *Story Telling*; and, in the number one position, Tony Curtis, who, at 83 years of age, penned his memories in the book *American Prince*. Other categories include: "Naughty and Nice," "Odd Baby Names" and "Rejected Roles."

Host: Rove McManus.

Credits: *Executive Producer:* Lee Hoffman. *Supervising Producer:* Jennifer Joseph. *Producer:* Gail Deutsch, Donna Hunte, Ira Robinson, Myrna Toledo. *Director:* Jeff Winer. *Writer:* Scott Jacobson, Lee Hoffman.

4 **The Academy Awards.** (Special; Variety; ABC; February 24, 2008)

The 80th annual presentation that honors the best in the movie industry.

Host: Jon Stewart. **Guests:** Colin Farrell, Josh Brolin, Renee Zellweger, Nicole Kidman, Denzel Washington, Helen Mirren, Owen Wilson, Patrick Dempsey, John Travolta, Forest Whitaker, Keri Russell, Jack Nicholson, Tom Hanks, Martin Scorsese, Cameron Diaz, Jessica Alba, George Clooney, Harrison Ford, Hilary Swank, Miley Cyrus, Jennifer Garner, Katherine Heigl, Penelope Cruz. **Music Performers:** Kristin Chenoweth, Amy Adams, Glen Hansard, Jamia Simone Nash.

Credits: *Executive Producer:* Gilbert Cates. *Producer:* Don Scotti, Seth Kienberg, Dennis Doty, Adam Lowitt. *Associate Producer:* Michael B. Seligman, Susan M. Baker. *Director:* Louis J. Horvitz. *Writer:* Buz Kohan.

5 **An Accidental Friendship.** (TV Movie; Drama; Hallmark; November 15, 2008)

Fact-based story about a police officer

(Tami) and a homeless woman (Yvonne), each of whom share similar emotional pasts, who form an unlikely friendship — and how they help each other out in trying times.

Cast: Kathleen Munroe (Tami Baumann), Chandra Wilson (Yvonne), Ben Vereen (Wes), Gabriel Hogan (Kevin Brawner), Taylor Trowbridge (Gloria), Jean Yoon (Lila Jones).

Credits: *Executive Producer:* Rich Rosenberg, Bob Christiansen, Lorraine Toussaint, Irene Litinsky. *Producer:* Michael Prupas, Steve Solomos. *Director:* Don McBrearty. *Writer:* Anna Sandor.

Reviews: "*Accidental Friendship* almost serves a near-political metaphor while working as pick-yourself-up by the bootstraps inspiration" (*Variety*).

"*Friendship* should hit home with women viewers. There is hardly anything in it to offend, doubt or to refute; on the other hand, there is hardly anything to set a spark" (*The Hollywood Reporter*).

6   Aces 'n Eights. (TV Movie; Western; Ion; March 15, 2008)

Somewhat violent tale of ranchers battling the railroads for control of land and the efforts of government agent Luke Rivers to settle the dispute.

Cast: Casper Van Dien (Luke Rivers), Bruce Boxleitner (D.C. Cracker), Ernest Borgnine (Thurmond Prescott), Jeff Kober (Tate), Deirdre Quinn (Jo Tanner), Rodney Scott (Monty), Jack Noseworthy (Riley).

Credits: *Executive Producer:* Larry Levinson. *Producer:* Matt Fitzsimons, Michael Moran, James Wilberger. *Music:* Gary Chang. *Writer:* Ronald M. Cohen, Dennis Shryack. *Director:* Craig R. Baxley.

7   The Adult Entertainment Expo 2008. (Special; Variety; HD-TV; January 13, 2008)

Specialized program in which the adult entertainment industry displays the latest in movies, gadgets and related adult entertainment items. The industry's most gorgeous female stars, clothed in skimpy bikinis and sexy but slinky gowns, showcase the various venders' goods.

Host: Olivia Munn, Kevin Pereira. **Guests:** Stormy Daniels, Ashlynn Brooke, Naomi Cruz, Anna David, Jessica Drake, Carmen Hart, Logan James, Sunny Lane, Regina Lynn, Michelle McLarren, McKenzie Miles, Marlie Moore, Tera Patrtick, Megahan Perry, Mia Presley, Kristen Price, Faye Reagan, Sunset Thomas, Sofia Valentine, Erika Vultion, Tera Wray. **Porno Fire Place Segment Cast:** Ron Jeremy, Zach Selwyn, Meghan Perry, Erik Palladino, Liam Kyle Sullivan. **Sexual Harassment Training Sketch Cast:** Summer Herrick, Brad Stevens, Matthew Taylor.

Credits: *Executive Producer:* Michael Danahy. *Supervising Producer:* Mark Tye Turner. *Producer:* Yaniv Fituci, Bobbi Conway. *Director:* Jesse Selwyn. *Writer:* Zach Selwyn, Brad Stevens, Boyd Vico.

8   The AFI Achievement Award — A Tribute to Warren Beatty. (Special; Tribute; USA; June 25, 2008)

A tribute to actor Warren Beatty from his friends and colleagues.

Guest of Honor: Warren Beatty. **Guests:** Halle Berry, Molly Ringwald, Barbra Streisand, Faye Dunaway, Dyan Cannon, Julie Christie, Elaine May, Robert Downey, Jr., Diane Keaton, Harvey Kitel, Robert Towne, Jack Nicholson, Mike Nichols, Goldie Hawn, Gene Hackman, Jane Fonda, Don Cheadle, Quentin Tarantino.

Credits: *Announcer:* Gina Tuttle. *Executive Producer:* Gary Smith. *Producer:* Chris Merrill, Louis J. Horvitz. *Director:* Louis J. Horvitz. *Writer:* Jon Macks.

9   The AFI's 10 Top 10. (Special; Variety; CBS; June 17, 2008)

A look at the top ten films in ten genres as chosen by members of the American Film Institute.

Appearing: Jessica Alba, Tim Allen, Kirk Douglas, Clint Eastwood, Jane Fonda, Harrison Ford, Michael J. Fox, Brad Garrett, Ben Gazzara, Gene Hackman, Jennifer Love Hewitt, Nathan Lane, Robert Loggia, Andie McDowell, Amy Madigan, Rob Reiner, Susan Sarandon, Talia Shire, Steven Spielberg, Quentin Tarantino, Lesley Ann Warren, Sigourney Weaver, Vanessa Williams, James Woods.
Credits: *Executive Producer:* Gary Smith, Frederick S. Pierce. *Producer:* Dann Netter. *Director:* Gary Smith.

10   All Girl Getaways. (Series; Reality; Fine Living Network; Premiered: October 16, 2008)

Cameras follow various groups of women as they plan and execute mini vacations.
Host: Stephanie Oswald.
Credits: *Executive Producer:* Nancy Glass, Joanne Cossrow, Cindy Connors. *Producer:* Shannon McManus, Cyndi Haas, Danette Kubanda, Christine Long, Natalie Feldman.

11   The Alma Awards. (Special; Awards; ABC; September 12, 2008)

A celebration of Latino performers in the arts and entertainment world.
Host: Eva Longoria. **Appearing:** America Ferrera, Wynonna Judd, Sergio Mendes, Roselyn Sanchez, Charlie Sheen, Jessica Alba, Cheech and Chong, Edward James Olmos, Selena Gomez, Ryan Seacrest, The Cheetah Girls, Kiely Williams, Terrence Howard.
Credits: *Executive Producer:* Michael Levitt. *Producer:* Mick McCullough, Gary Tellalian. *Director:* Alan Carter.

12   Amazing Wedding Cakes. (Series; Reality; WE; Premiered: September 7, 2008)

A behind-the-scenes look at the making of wedding cakes — from the designers to "the over-the-top personalities who create them."

Credits: *Executive Producer:* Joseph Correll, Judy Lyness. *Producer:* Kimberly Prince.

13   American Chopper. (Series; Reality; TLC; March 1, 2008 to October 30, 2008)

A profile of a volatile father (Paul Teutul, Sr.) and his timid son (Paul, Jr.), the owners of Orange County Choppers, the world's most successful custom motorcycle shop.
Stars: Paul Teutul, Sr., Paul Teutul, Jr., Michael Teutul.
Credits: *Announcer:* Mike Rowe. *Executive Producer:* Craig Piligian, Hank Capshaw. *Co-Executive Producer:* Rob Hammersley, C. Russell Muth. *Supervising Producer:* Scott Popjes, Sara Reddy, Scott Feeley, Steve Nigg. *Music:* Jason Brandt, Matt Koskenmaki.

14   American Gladiators. (Series; Game; NBC; January 6, 2008 to August 4, 2008)

A revised version of the 1980s syndicated series of the same title. Two six member teams, the male vs. the female are pitted against same gender gladiators (athletes) in a series of athletic contests. Each program pits two men and two women against the gladiators (male vs. male; female vs. female). The two poorest performers, one man and one women, are eliminated. The winners of each of these three weekly contests move into the final competition where additional contests are held. The last male and female contestants standing split $100,000.
Hosts: Hulk Hogan, Laila Ali. **Gladiators Cast:** Gina Carano (Crush), Alex Castro (Militia), Robin Coleman (Hellga), Beth Horn (Vermon), Tanji Johnson (Stealth), Jamie Kovac (Fury), Mike O'Hearn (Titan), Tanonia Reed (Toa), Justice Smith (Justice), Romeo Williams (Mayhem), Valerie Waugman (Siren), Don Yates (Wolf).
Credits: *Executive Producer:* David

Hurwitz, Mark Koops, Howard Owens, Claire O'Donohoe. *Co-Executive Producer:* J. Rupert Thompson. *Producer:* Edison Layne, Tom Herschko. *Director:* J. Rupert Thompson.

Reviews "Granted, someone may break a leg (in a literal sense, not the showbiz one) along the way. But in the world of *American Gladiators* no pain, no fame" (*Variety*).

"The producers have updated the show with all the usual reality bells and whistles: flashing lights, dramatic music, two tons of product placement and a studio audience warmed up with loco weed" (*The Hollywood Reporter*).

15   The American Mall. (TV Movie; Comedy; MTV; August 11, 2008)

Tween musical comedy about Ally, the daughter of a mall store owner and her efforts to impress Joey, one of four night janitors who is also in a rock band.

Cast: Nina Dobrev (Ally), Rob Mayes (Joey), Autumn Reeser (Madison), Brenda Webb (Penny), Yasmin Aleis (Erin), Brooke Lyons (Dori), Al Sapienza (Max), Bianca Collins (Mia), Rodney To (Ben), Neil Haskell (Drew).

Credits: *Executive Producer:* Barry Rosenbush, Arata Matsushima. *Producer:* Bill Borden, Terry Spazek. *Music:* David Lawrence. *Choreographer:* Bonnie Story. *Director:* Shawn Ku. *Writer:* Margaret Oberman, Tomas Romero, P.J. Hogan.

16   The American Music Awards. (Special; Variety; ABC; November 23, 2008)

The 36th annual American Music Association awards presentation honoring the best in all fields of music (from Pop and Rock to Alternative Rock to Country and Western). Broadcast live from the Nokia Theater in Los Angeles.

Host: Jimmy Kimmel. **Performers:** Taylor Swift, The Pussycat Dolls, The New Kids on the Block, Rihanna, Ne-Yo, Annie Lennox, Beyonce, Christina Aguil-

era, Alicia Keyes, Natasha Bedingfield, Miley Cyrus, Cold Play, Sarah McLachlan.

Credits: *Executive Producer:* Orly Adelson. *Producer:* Larry Kelin. *Associate Producer:* Don Harary. *Writer:* Harris Wittels.

17   America's Favorite Mom. (Special; Variety; NBC; May 11, 2008)

A Mother's Day special that pays tribute to mothers from all walks of life and in the following categories: working mom, military mom, single mom, the non-mom and the C.O.E. (Chairman of Everything) mom.

Hosts: Donny Osmond, Marie Osmond.

18   America's Prom Queen. (Series; Reality; ABC Family; March 17, 2008 to April 7, 2008)

Ten teenage girls compete for the title of "America's Prom Queen." Each episode places the girls in beauty pageant–like challenges with the weakest performers being eliminated. The one girl who shows the best overall talent and personality is crowned Prom Queen.

Host: Susie Castillo.

Credits: *Executive Producer:* Krishnan Menon, Patty Ivins Specht, Julie Pizzi. *Talent Producer:* Havva Eisenbaum.

19   America's Toughest Jobs. (Series; Reality; NBC; August 25, 2008 to October 25, 2008)

Thirteen ordinary people compete in rather dangerous challenges wherein they have to perform occupations that are considered really difficult — from logging to bridge inspector to crab fishing. People associated with the jobs being tackled act as judges and eliminate the weakest performers (as the host would say, "I'm sorry, you weren't tough enough").

Host: Josh Temple.

Credits: *Executive Producer:* Thom Beers, Gail Berman, Philip D. Segal. *Producer:* Bryan O'Donnell, Barry Hennessy, Devon Platte.

Reviews: "It's tough turning innovative reality premises into derivative drones but somebody's got to do it" (*The Hollywood Reporter*).

"Premiering as soon as the Olympics torch flickers out, the series will test whether NBC can sustain any momentum or will tumble back to reality once swimmer Michael Phelps and those little gymnasts dispense" (*Variety*).

20 **Amnesia**. (Series; Game; NBC; February 22, 2008 to April 11, 2008)

Players must answer questions based on incidents in their lives in return for money. "You in 60 Seconds," the first round, awards players $1,000 for each correctly answered question. The remaining rounds have the player answering personal questions based on information acquired from interviewing people associated with the player. Additional cash is awarded for each question he answers correctly.

Host: Dennis Miller.

Credits: *Executive Producer:* Mark Burnett, Adam Cohen, Cara Tapper, Joanna Vernetti. *Co-Executive Producer:* Jeff Krask, Jim Roush. *Supervising Producer:* Evelyn Warfel. *Producer:* Derek Che, Nate Hayden, Stacey Margetts, Mary Morelli, Sascha Rothchild.

Reviews: "The show is silly and harmless... Think of it as *This Is Your Life* for someone you have never met or obviously have no interest in" (*Variety*).

"Billed as a comedy quiz show, it will sink or swim on the shoulders of a comic genius whose bemused expression reveals a man who can't quite believe he's doing this" (*The Hollywood Reporter*).

21 **Anaconda 3: The Offspring**. (TV Movie; Horror; Sci Fi; July 26, 2008)

Sequel to the *Anaconda* feature films. Here, a mercenary (Hammett) attempts to capture a large, mutated (and dangerous) snake whose venom could provide a cure for terminal illnesses.

Cast: David Hasselhoff (Hammett), Crystal Allen (Amanda), John Rhys-Davies (Murdock), Anthony Green (Captain Grozny), Patrick Regis (Nick), Serban Celea (Professor Kane).

Credits: *Producer:* Alsion Semenza, Bryan Sexton. *Co-Producer:* Vlad Paunescu. *Music:* Peter Meisner. *Writer:* Nicholas Davidoff, David C. Olson. *Director:* Don E. Faunt.

22 **The Andromeda Strain**. (Miniseries; Science Fiction; A&E; May 26 and 27, 2008)

Reporter Jack Nash seeks the facts behind a deadly accident when a U.S. military satellite crashes in the small town of Piedmont and unleashes a deadly plague called Andromeda. Based on the novel by Michael Crichton.

Cast: Eric McCormick (Jack Nash), Benjamin Bratt (Dr. Jeremy Stone), Christa Miller (Dr. Angela Noyce), Daniel Dae Kim (Dr. Tsi Chou), Viola Davis (Dr. Charlene Barton), Justin Louis (Col. Ferrus), Barry Flatman (Chuck Beeter).

Credits: *Executive Producer:* Ridley Scott, Tony Scott, Tom Thayer, David W. Zucker. *Producer:* Clara George, Mikael Salomon. *Writer:* Robert Schenkkan. *Director:* Mikael Salomon.

23 **Animalia**. (Series; Cartoon; PBS; Premiered: January 6, 2008)

Animalia is a world where intelligent animals rule and live in peace due to the power of words. Suddenly their core of power, a glowing gold-like globe of energy, begins to crack, releasing core spores into the atmosphere and turning Animalia into a dark, forbidding land. Human teenagers Zoe and Alex are in a library doing research on animals when they are magically transported to Animalia. Here they meet Livingston T. Lion, the animal leader, and are asked to help restore the sunshine to Animalia. Stories follow their efforts to find and return the missing spores to the core of power.

Voices: Brooke "Mikey" Anderson,

Dean O'Gorman, Kate Higgins, Christopher Hobbs, Peta Johnson, Robert Mark Klein, Katie Leigh.

Credits: *Executive Producer:* Evan Bennett, Graeme Base, Murray Pope, Bruce Johnson, Tom Ruegger. *Producer:* Ewan Bennett, Murray Pope. *Music:* Christopher Elves.

24   Ashley Paige's Bikini or Bust. (Series; Reality; TLC; July 11, 2008 to August 9, 2008)

Ashley Paige is famous for designing sexy and skimpy bikinis for women. Although popular with A-list celebrities, the company really never took off. Now, at near rock bottom, Ashley is attempting to reestablish her company. Cameras follow her efforts to do just that.

Star: Ashley Paige.

Credits: *Executive Producer:* Rob Worsoff. *Producer:* Patrick Bachmann.

25   Ask Aida. (Series; Advice; Food Network; Premiered: August 2, 2008)

Meal preparation coupled with responses to viewers culinary questions (received through e-mails).

Host: Aida Mollenkamp. **Assistant:** Noah Starr (her "tech guy").

Credits: *Executive Producer:* Matt Sharp. *Co-Executive Producer:* Irene Wong. *Producer:* Jenni Gilroy.

26   Ax Men. (Series; Reality; History Channel; March 9, 2008 to June 15, 2008)

A look at the dangerous work faced by loggers as they cut and prepare trees for shipment to wood mills.

Host-Narrator: Thom Beers.

Credits: *Executive Producer:* Dolores Gavin, Thom Beers. *Co-Executive Producer:* Jeff Conroy. *Supervising Producer:* Sarah Whalen. *Music:* Bruce Hanifan.

27   The Baby Borrowers. (Series; Reality; NBC; June 25, 2008 to July 30, 2008)

Five teenage couples who feel they are adult enough to have children are given a dose of reality. Each of the couples takes care of someone else's baby. After three days, the infants are replaced by toddlers (the toddlers are then replaced by pre-teens; the pre-teens by teenagers and the teenagers by very elderly people). There are no prizes and no eliminations — just real life experience.

Narrator: Craig Zimmerman.

Credits: *Executive Producer:* Richard McKerrow, Tom Shelly. *Co-Executive Producer:* Kevin Harris. *Supervising Producer:* Jen McClure-Metz. *Producer:* Dave Brown, Johnny Petillo, Emily Sinclair. *Music:* David Vanacore.

28   Backwoods. (TV Movie; Adventure; Spike; June 8, 2008)

Survival epic about a group of camping executives for Global Gamming who are stalked by an unknown killer while on retreat.

Cast: Haylie Duff (Lee), Jonathan Chase (Peter), Willow Geer (Gwen), John Hemphill (Ranger Ricks), Ryan Merriman (Adam Benson), Deborah Van Valkenburgh (Ruth).

Credits: *Producer:* Michael Moran, Albert T. Dickerson III. *Co-Producer:* Tony Romanz, Traceigh Scottel. *Director:* Marty Weiss. *Writer:* Anthony Jaswinski.

29   Baisden After Dark. (Series; Talk; TV One; Premiered: June 21, 2008)

Radio personality Michael Baisden oversees a nightly talk show in which controversial topics are often discussed.

Host: Michael Baisden. **Co-Host:** George Willborn.

Credits: *Executive Producer:* Michael Baisden. *Producer:* Carl Cray, Rikki Hughes, Calvin Brown, Jr. *Music:* Morris Day.

30   Ballet Shoes. (TV movie; Drama; PBS; December 25, 2008)

Professor Matthew Brown, called "Gum," is an eccentric paleontologist who travels the world seeking fossils. He lives with his niece, Sylvia Brown and, during the course of his travels he found and unofficially adopted three orphaned girls (each from a different mother). He gave the girls (Pauline, Petrova and Posey) the last name Fossil and left their upbringing to Sylvia (who raised them as if they were real sisters). London, England, during the 1930s is the setting (when the girls are teenagers). The times are difficult and money is tight and the story follows the girls as they struggle to fulfill their dreams: Pauline to become an actress; Petrova, an aviator; and Posy, a ballerina. A 2007 British TV movie based on the classic children's story by Noel Streatfield.

Cast: Emma Watson (Pauline Fossil), Yasmin Paige (Petrova Fossil), Lucy Boynton (Posy Fossil), Emilia Fox (Sylvia Brown), Richard Griffiths (Matthew Brown), Victoria Wood (Nana), Eileen Atkins (Madame Fidolia), Gemma Jones (Dr. Jakes), Marc Warren (Mr. Simpson), Peter Bowles (Sir Donald Houghton).

Credits: *Executive Producer:* Michele Buck, Patrick Stone, Heidi Thomas, Damien Timmer. *Producer:* Piers Wenger. *Music:* Kevin Sargent. *Director:* Sandra Goldbacher. *Writer:* Heidi Thomas.

31 **Bananas**. (Series; Comedy; Syn.; Premiered: September 2008)

"Are you ready for *Bananas*? It's the comedy show that takes you inside and behind the mind of a comic." Guest comics are profiled and perform on a weekly basis.

Host: Thor Ramsey.

Credits: *Executive Producer:* Steve Howard. *Producer:* John Jackson. *Associate Producer:* Rob Dixon. *Director:* John Jackson.

32 **Barbara Walters Presents the 10 Most Fascinating People of 2008**. (Special; Interview; ABC; December 4, 2008)

Newswoman Barbara Walters's annual event wherein she chats with the most prominent names in entertainment, sports, politics and pop culture.

Host: Barbara Walters. **Guests:** Miley Cyrus, Tom Cruise, Tina Fey, Will Smith, Frank Langella, Mark Phelps (Olympic swimming champion), Sarah Palin (Alaska Governor), Thomas Beatiel (transgender man who gave birth).

Credits: *Executive Producer:* Barbara Walters, Bill Gedde. *Director:* Bill Gedde.

33 **The Barbara Walters Special**. (Special; Interview; ABC; February 24, 2008)

A pre–Academy Awards program in which Barbara Walters interviews celebrities.

Host: Barbara Walters. **Guests:** Miley Cyrus, Ellen Page, Harrison Ford, Vanessa L. Williams.

Credits: *Executive Producer:* Don Mischer. *Producer:* Joann Goldberg, Beth Polson, Daniel Wilson.

34 **Batman: The Brave and the Bold**. (Series; Cartoon; Cartoon Network; Premiered: November 14, 2008)

Millionaire Bruce Wayne, alias the mysterious caped crusader Batman, teams with heroes from across the universe (the Blue Beetle, Red Tornado and Plasticman) to battle the forces of evil. The Blue Beetle is a teenager who battles villains with his armored blue suit. Red Tornado is an android with super speed and incredible strength that can create tornado force winds. Plasticman is an ex-con with the ability to stretch his body into any shape or size, then snap back into a normal looking person.

Voice Cast: Diedrich Bader (Batman), Corey Burton (Red Tornado), Will Friedle (Blue Beetle), Tom Kenny (Plasticman).

Credits: *Executive Producer:* Sam Register. *Producer:* Linda Steiner, James Tucker. *Music:* Andy Sturmer, Michael McCusstion, Kristopher Carter.

Review: "The premiere, frankly, doesn't put the show's best foot forward, in as much as, Blue Beetle is seemingly the least interesting of Batman's rotating champions, nor will child-free adults be as tempted to tune in as they are for harder-edged animated fare" (*Variety*).

35 Battle of the Bods. (Series; Reality; Fox Reality Channel; January 19, 2008 to October 19, 2008)

Late night reality competition (1:00 A.M.) in which five very sexy women compete against each other for cash prizes based on just how sexy they can be. A panel of male judges are situated behind a one-way mirror. The women are presented with challenges involving attractiveness and sexuality and are judged based on the outcome of the performance. The women who live up to the predictions made by the judges receive cash.

Host: Olivia Lee.

36 Battle 360. (Series; Reality; History Channel; February 29, 2008 to March 7, 2008)

Computer animation and special effects are used to detail the *USS Enterprise*, an air craft carrier that is dispatched to the world's most troublesome situations.

Host: Wally Kurth.

Credits: *Executive Producer:* Douglas Cohen, Louis Tarantino. *Producer:* Sam Dolan, Brian Thompson. *Music:* Eric Amdahl.

37 Battlestar Galactica: The Face of the Enemy. (Series; Science Fiction; Internet; December 10, 2008 to January 12, 2009)

A ten episode web series that is actually an extension storyline not broadcast on the Sci Fi channel's *Battlestar Galactica* (see program 659). The story focuses primarily on Felix Gaeta, a lieutenant on *Galactica* as he and several crew mates (Col. Tigh and Lieutenants Hoshi and Edmondson), confined to a small space craft (a Raptor) with a group of strangers, engage in a psychological war to discover who or what is systematically killing the passengers.

Cast: Alessandro Juliani (Lt. Felix Gaeta), Michael Hogan (Col. Saul Tigh), Brad Dryborough (Lt. Hoshi), Leah Cairns (Lt. Margaret Edmondson), Grace Park (Number 8), William C. Vaughn (Finn), Jessica Harmon (Esrin), Michael Rogers (Brooks).

Credits: *Executive Producer:* Michael Rogers, Ronald D. Moore, Jane Espenson. *Producer:* Harvey Frand, Ron French. *Co-Producer:* Maris Davis, Paul M. Leonard. *Music:* Bear McCreary.

38 Ben 10: Alien Force. (Series; Cartoon; Cartoon Network; Premiered: April 18, 2008)

A sequel to *Ben 10* (which dealt with ten-year-old Ben Tennyson's battle against aliens). Ben, now 15, and his cousin, Gwen Tennyson, once again become a team to battle aliens (the DNAliens) when they kidnap Ben's Grandpa Max and begin an unprovoked attack on Earth. Kevin Levin, Ben's former nemesis, joins them as stories relate their battle.

Voice Cast: Yuri Lowenthal (Ben Tennyson), Ashley Johnson (Gwen Tennyson), Paul Eiding (Grandpa Max), Greg Cipes (Kevin Levin), Dee Bradley Baker (Big Chill/Brainstorm/Chromostone/Echo Echo/Goop/Humongousaur/Jetray/Spider Monkey/Swamp Fire).

Credits: *Producer:* Glen Murokami. *Music:* Kristopher Carter, Michael McCuistion, Lolita Ritmanis.

39 The BET Awards. (Special; Variety; BET; June 24, 2008)

A celebration of African-American actors, musicians and creative personnel.

Host: D.L. Hughley. **Performers:** Alicia Keyes, Chris Brown, Kanye West, Al Green, Weezy Fo Sheezy, Usher, Rihanna, Ne-Yo, Marvin Sharp, Young Jeezy.

40 The BET Honors. (Special; Variety; BET; February 23, 2008)

An awards program that acknowledges distinguished African-American leaders.

Host: Cedric the Entertainer. **Performers:** Raheem DeVaughn, Wyclef Jean, Gladys Knight, John Legend, Brian Mc-Knight, Ne-Yo, Jill Scott, Stevie Wonder. **Credits:** *Producer:* Aaron B. Cooke, Paul Watson.

41   Beyond Loch Ness. (TV Movie; Horror; Sci Fi; January 5, 2008)

Crypto zoologist James Murphy teams with guide Josh Reilly to prove that a 60-foot plesiosaur is inhabiting the lake of Pike Island in Ashburn on Lake Superior.

Cast: Brian Krause (James Murphy), Niall Matter (Josh Reilly), Carrie Genzel (Karen Riley), Donnelly Rhodes (Uncle Sam), Amber Borycki (Zoe), Neil Denis (Chad), Sebastian Gacki (Brody).

Credits: *Executive Producer:* Kirk Shaw, Lisa Hansen. *Producer:* Lindsay Mac-Adam. *Music:* Pinar Toprak. *Writer:* Jason Bourque, Paul Ziller. *Director:* Paul Ziller.

42   The Big 4-0. (Series; Reality; TV Land; March 12, 2008 to April 16, 2008)

People who have or are just about to turn 40 are profiled.

Credits: *Executive Producer:* J.D. Roth, Todd Nelson, Adam Greener, Keith Cox. *Co-Executive Producer:* Julie Singer. *Supervising Producer:* Scott Zabielski, Lisa Singer. *Director:* Rick Pendleton.

Review: "The good news about *40* is that it's only a half-hour, so the inanity ends rather quickly ... in TV getting older really doesn't mean growing up any wiser" (*Variety*).

43   Big Medicine. (Series; Reality; TLC; January 9, 2008 to March 5, 2008)

A program about overweight people that goes beyond NBC's *The Biggest Loser* to focus on extremely obese people and the doctors who treat them. Each program follows several patients at the Methodist Weight Management Center in Houston, Texas, as they prepare for (then given) by-pass surgery.

Cast: *Surgeons:* Robert Davis, Garth Davis, John LoMonico, Norman Rappaport. *Psychologist:* Mary Jo Rapini.

Credits: *Executive Producer:* Darryl Silver, Stephen David. *Co-Executive Producer:* Brian Catalina, Robin Younie. *Associate Producer:* Mark D'Anna.

Line Producer: Laura Elizabeth. *Field Producer:* Maggie Zeltner, Larissa Matsson.

Review: "One viewing has done for me what all the diets and weight watchers never did: I may never eat again" (*New York Post*).

44   Billy Crystal: The Kennedy Center Mark Twain Prize. (Special; Tribute; PBS; November 20, 2008)

The tenth annual Kennedy Center Mark Twain Prize for Humor presentation that honors the most versatile and prolific careers in the entertainment industry. Prior winners include Steve Martin, Jonathan Winters and Neil Simon. In addition to film clips that highlight Billy's career, friends appear to pay tribute. Winners are awarded a copy of an 1884 bronze portrait bust of Mark Twain.

Guest of Honor: Billy Crystal. **Guests:** Robin Williams, Whoopi Goldberg, Rob Reiner, John Goodman, Jon Lovitz, Robert DeNiro, Jimmy Fallon, Martin Short, Barbara Walters, Bob Costas, Madeleine Peyroux.

Credits: *Executive Producer:* Bob Kaminsky, Peter Kaminsky, Mark Krantz, Cappy McGarr. *Producer:* Robert C. Pullen, Kate Hipp. *Director:* Christina Clark Badley.

45   Bingo America. (Series; Game; Game Show Network; March 31, 2008 to October 18, 2008)

A blank bingo card is placed before each of the two players who compete. The game begins when a bingo ball is released from a large air machine and its number revealed. A question is then read. The first player to buzz in receives a chance to answer. If the player responds correctly, the number (for example, C3, D14) appears in its appropriate place on the bingo card. If he is incorrect, his opponent receives a chance to answer the question and steal the number. The first player to fill his bingo card wins.

Host: Patrick Duffy, Richard Karn. **Co-Host:** Crystal Wallasch.

Credits: *Executive Producer:* Grant Julian, Lillian Lim. *Producer:* Tony Federico, Andrew Glassman. *Associate Producer:* Kevin Meister, Brent Jacoby.

46 Bizarre Foods with Andrew Zimmern. (Series; Reality; Travel Channel; September 9, 2008 to January 20, 2009)

Chef Andrew Zimmern travels the globe seeking to sample the cuisine of lands whose foods appear quite strange when compared to what Americans consume.

Host: Andrew Zimmern.

Credits: *Executive Producer:* Andrew Zimmern. *Producer:* Beth Pacunas. *Director:* Beth Pacunas, Andrew Zimmern, Chris Marino. *Writer:* Beth Pacunas, Andrew Zimmern.

47 Black Gold. (Series; Reality; Tru TV; June 18, 2008 to August 6, 2008)

A look at the work and lives of wildcatters — the people who race from location to location to be the first to tap into the Texas oil reserves.

Narrator: Thom Beers.

Credits: *Executive Producer:* Thom Beers. *Co-Executive Producer:* Philip David Segal, Jeff Conroy. *Producer:* Jan Childs, Michael Gara.

48 Blue Dragon. (Series; Cartoon; Cartoon Network; Premiered: March 28, 2008)

Nene is the alien commander of a floating fortress that brings destruction wherever it goes. When the fortress produces purple clouds over the Earth, three friends (Jiro, Kluke and Shu) find themselves becoming super heroes when they are affected by the clouds and are able to transform their shadows into blue monsters. Jiro's shadow becomes a Minotaur; Kluke, a Phoenix; and Shu, a Blue Dragon. Stories relate their adventures as they struggle to protect the Earth by defeating Nene.

Voice Cast: Sam Riegel (Jiro), Michelle Ruff (Kluke), Yuri Lowenthal (Shu), Kirk Thornton (Minotaur), Lex Lang (Blue Dragon), Karen Strassman (Valkyrie), David Lodge (Nene), Michael P. Greco (Deathray), Melissa Fahn (Bouquet).

49 Blush: The Search for the Next Great Makeup Artist. (Series; Reality; Lifetime; Premiered: November 11, 2008)

Makeup artists from around the country compete for $100,000, a contract with Max Factor cosmetics and the opportunity to become a makeup artist in an upcoming *In Style* magazine photo shoot. The contenders compete in a series of fashion industry challenges with the weakest performers being eliminated on a weekly basis. The last player standing based on the opinions of guest judges (associated with the magazine and fashion industry) wins.

Host: Vanessa Marcil.

Credits: *Executive Producer:* Laura Fuest, Scott Kramer, Rob Lee.

50 Bone Eater. (TV Movie; Horror; Sci Fi; February 9, 2008)

During the building of a resort in Sweetwater, a construction crew unearths an ancient Indian burial site and inadvertently unleashes a skeleton-like killing creature called a Bone Eater. The story follows the efforts of the town sheriff, Steve Evans, a half-breed known as Running Wolf, and the local Katonahs Indian Chief, Storm Cloud, to stop the creature by finding a ancient tomahawk that has the power to destroy evil.

Cast: Bruce Boxleitner (Steve Evans), Michael Horse (Chief Storm Cloud),

Veronica Hamel (Miss Hayes), William Katt (Doctor), Gil Gerard (Big Jim Burns), Kristen Honey (Rachel LeGrand), Paul Rae (Neil Miller).

Credits: *Executive Producer:* Stefano Dammicco. *Producer:* Lisa M. Hansen, Paul Herttzberg. *Music:* Chuck Cinno. *Director:* Jim Wynoiski.

51 The Bonnie Hunt Show. (Series; Talk; Syn.; Premiered: September 8, 2008)

Actress Bonnie Hunt hosts an informal, relaxed daytime program wherein she interviews celebrities from all facets of show business.

Host: Bonnie Hunt. **Assistant:** Holly Wortell. **Announcer:** Don Lake.

Credits: *Executive Producer:* Greg Gorden, Bonnie Hunt, Don Lake, Jim Paratore. *Supervising Producer:* Jason Kurtz. *Producer:* David Perler, Stacie Nice. *Music:* Nicholas Pike.

Reviews: "The first two days of ... *The Bonnie Hunt Show* makes it instantly clear that Hunt was born for this deceptively difficult gig but may not entirely know it" (*The Hollywood Reporter*).

"Bonnie Hunt seems well equipped to the task with a genuinely funny style that exudes a certain sisterly charm. So far, however, the laughs aren't long enough nor the concept as compelling as it needs to be to make viewers want to tune in daily" (*Variety*).

52 The Boot. (Series; Reality; BET; April 21, 2008 to May 19, 2008)

A dating show geared to African Americans. Six singles are brought together with the object being to find a perfect match between two of them. Those that are deemed incompatible are given "the boot" and must leave.

Hostess: MC Lyte.

Credits: *Executive Producer:* David Garfinkle, Jay Renfroe. *Supervising Producer:* Bryan Shields, Tim Morton. *Producer:* Jamala Garther, Matt Waldon.

53 The Boston Pops Fireworks Spectacular. (Special; Variety; CBS; July 4, 2008)

The 35th annual presentation of the fireworks display from the Charles River Esplande in Boston; music is provided by the Boston Pops Orchestra.

Host: Craig Ferguson. **Guest:** Rascall Flatts.

Credits: *Announcer:* John Pleisse. *Supervising Producer:* Richard MacDonald, Pamela Picard. *Producer:* Mike Mathis, Ricky Kirshner, Glenn Weiss, Sheryl Bursik. *Director:* Glenn Weiss. *Writer:* Eugene Pack. *Boston Pops Orchestra Conductor:* Keith Lockhart.

54 Breaking Bad. (Series; Drama; AMC; Premiered: January 20, 2008)

Walter White is a chemistry professor with a wife (Skyler), a physically challenged child (Walter, Jr.) and a short time to live (inoperable lung cancer). To provide for his family's future, Walter teams with a former student (Jesse) and together become criminals: Jesse sells the drugs (crystal meth) Walter produces. Stories follow Walter's efforts to provide for his family while remaining just one step ahead of the law.

Cast: Bryan Cranston (Walter White, Sr.), Ann Gunn (Skyler White), Aaron Paul (Jesse Pinkham), R.J. Mitte (Walter White, Jr.), Dean Norris (Hank Schrader), Betsy Brandt (Marie Schrader), Max Arcinicega (Krazy-8), John Koyama (Emilio).

Credits: *Executive Producer:* Vince Gilligan, Mark Johnson. *Producer:* Karen Moore. *Co-Producer:* Melissa Bernstein. *Music:* Dave Porter.

Reviews: "...as polished as *Breaking Bad* is, in terms of long-term potential (or however long Walter has left), it's the sort of front-loaded affair that invites skepticism as to whether the idiosyncratic tone can be maintained" (*Variety*).

"There is good chemistry all around in

this darkly humorous tale of desperation" (*The Hollywood Reporter*).

55 Bridal Fever. (TV Movie; Comedy; Hallmark; February 2, 2008)

Romance novelist Dahlia Marchand seeks story material by attempting to find the perfect mate for Gwen Green, an unlucky in love editor.

Cast: Delta Burke (Dahlia Marchand), Andrea Roth (Gwen Green), Vincent Walsh (Mark), Melinda Deines (Sandra), Richard Fitzpatrick (Burt), Nigel Bennett (Ben).

Credits: *Executive Producer:* Orly Adelson, Jonathan Esjenas, Frank Siracusa. *Producer:* Ian McDougall. *Writer:* Karen McClellan. *Director:* Ron Oliver.

56 Britney Spears: For the Record. (Special; Documentary; MTV; November 30, 2008)

A profile of Britney Spears, the beautiful but troubled rock star, as she prepares for a comeback, putting her hectic public life behind her to concentrate on a new album and her appearance on *The MTV Video Music Awards* program.

Star: Britney Spears.

Credits: *Executive Producer:* Larry Rudolph, John Kamen, Frank Scherma, Maria Suro, Justin Wilker, Steve Bilchik, Robert Friedman, Heather Olander. *Producer:* Andrew Ford, Adam Leber, Phil Griffin. *Director:* Phil Griffin.

57 Britz. (TV Movie; Drama; BBC America; November 30 and December 1, 2008)

Two-part British produced TV movie that tracks the lives of two British Muslims prior to the terror attacks of 9/11. Sohail and his sister, Nasima, are the principal focus. Part one deals mainly with Sohail, a law student whose anger toward Islamic extremism prompts him to join MI-5 (British Intelligence) to help bring down terrorist cells. Nasima, the focus of part two, is a medical student who, like her brother, has been assimilated into British society but rebels against the government's repressive policies toward her people.

Cast: Riz Ahmed (Sohail), Manjinder Virk (Nasima), Zahra Ahmadi (Sabia), Mary Stockley (Tess), Chinna Woda (Jude).

Credits: *Executive Producer:* David Aukin, Hal Vogel. *Producer:* Steven Clark-Hall. *Writer-Director:* Peter Kosminsky.

58 Bromantic. (Series; Reality; MTV; Premiered: December 29, 2008)

Bromance is a term used to indicate a brotherly bond that makes two buddies virtually inseparable. Reality TV star Brody Jenner (of *The Hills*) is seeking one special guy to join his elite entourage. Nine "regular guys" are gathered to compete for that opportunity. Contestants live together in a frat house and, because it is difficult to find a genuine friend in Hollywood, the "bros" compete in various challenges to prove they are the right man to become Brody's best friend. Brody judges each performance and those that fail to show "who's got game, who's keeping it real and who's always got Brody's back no matter what" are eliminated on a weekly basis. The one who proves, to Brody's satisfaction, to "have the complete package," joins Brody's entourage. While the format sounds like it's a gay affair, it is not. There are girls, lingerie parties, romantic (boygirl) dinners, emotional breakdowns and bar brawls. And let's not leave out the back stabbing; it's all so "bromantic."

Host: Brody Jenner.

Credits: *Executive Producer:* Ryan Seacrest, Eric Podwall, Brody Jenner. *Co-Executive Producer:* Kathy Sutula, Jason C. Henry, Eliot Goldberg, Vince Rotonda. *Producer:* Tim Andrew, Melissa A. Bohman, Ken Snow, Frankie Delgado.

59 Brooke Knows Best. (Series; Reality; VH-1; July 13, 2008 to October 5, 2008)

Brooke Hogan, the daughter of wrestling super star Hulk Hogan (and his wife Linda), leaves the family nest to make it on her own. Cameras follow her efforts as she attempts to make her mark in the music world.

Stars: Brooke Hogan, Hulk Hogan, Linda Hogan.

Credits: *Executive Producer:* Brad Abramson, Jeff Olde, Shelly Tatro, Kimberly Belcher Cowin. *Supervising Producer:* Susan Janis-Mashayekhi. *Producer:* Lauren Rickles, Kristy Wampole, Amy Fiskum.

60   Bulging Brides. (Series; Reality; WE; January 10, 2008 to February 17, 2008)

"Last Minute Squeeze," "Two Sizes Too Big" and "Worried in White" are some of the episode titles for a series that looks at overweight brides that have to go from "flab to fab" just in time for their walk down the isle. A "Dream Team" attempts to help brides who are unable to fit into their wedding dresses get in shape within six weeks (in a female only version of NBC's *Biggest Loser*).

Host: Nadeem Boman, Tommy Europe, Jean Okada.

Credits: *Executive Producer:* Blair Reekie. *Producer:* Stan Feingold.

61   Busty Beauties. (Series; Erotica; Playboy Channel; 2008)

A soft core version of the adult film industry's hard core *Bra Busters, Natural Wonders* and *Big Busty Babes* made-for-video series wherein girls with large breasts first strip then showoff their assets before engaging in (most cases) sexual activity.

Girls: Savannah Gold, Brittany Burke, Brooke Haven, Riley Evans, Trina Michaels, Eve Lawrence, Carly Parker, Camella Bing, Heather Lee, Jerica Fox, Rachel Love, Wendy Whoppers, Devin DeRay.

62   Buzzin'. (Series; Reality; MTV; July 23, 2008 to August 10, 2008)

A behind-the-scenes look at the launching of a new album, "Buzzin'," by Suretone Records and featuring the ensemble of musical artist Shwayze.

Cast: Shwayze (himself), Cisco Adler (producer), Warren Gumpel (tour manager), Jordan Schur (record company manager).

63   Camp Rock. (TV Movie; Musical; Disney; June 20, 2008)

Mitchie Torres is a teenage girl who works as a cook at a rock camp. One day she is heard (but not seen) singing by teen pop star Shane Gray. The story follows Shane as he sets out to find the mysterious girl and launch her on the road to musical stardom.

Cast: Demi Lovato (Mitchie Torres), Joe Jonas (Shane Gray), Maria Canals-Barrera (Connie Torres), Meaghan Jette Martin (Tess Tyler), Nick Jonas (Nate), Paul Kevin Jonas (Jason), Alyson Stoner (Caitlyn).

Credits: *Executive Producer:* Alan Sacks. *Producer:* Kevin Lafferty. *Writer:* Karin Gist, Regina Hicks, Julie Brown, Paul Brown. *Director:* Matthew Diamond.

64   Canterbury's Law. (Series; Drama; Fox; March 10, 2008 to April 18, 2008)

Canterbury and Associates is a prestigious Providence, Rhode Island, law firm. Elizabeth Canterbury is the firm's founder, a woman who strongly believes in justice and will go to virtually any lengths to defend her clients. While pretty, Elizabeth has a hard look about her. She is all work and totally dedicated to doing what needs to be done to win in the courtroom. Murder cases are her specialty and she knows when someone is lying to her. Elizabeth needs her clients to trust her and she sometimes feels her courtroom performances are like a vaudeville act. Russell Krauss is her assistant, a former prosecutor with the attorney general's office. Zach Williams is the district attorney; Chester Grant is a lawyer with the firm; Molly McConnell is Elizabeth's receptionist; Frank Angstrom is Elizabeth's legman; Matt Furey is Elizabeth's ex-husband.

Cast: Julianna Margulies (Elizabeth Canterbury), Aidan Quinn (Matt Furey), Trieste Kelly Dunn (Molly McConnell), James McCaffrey (Frank Angstrom), Terry Kinney (Zach Williams), Keith Robinson (Chester Grant), Ben Shenkman (Russell Krauss).

Credits: *Executive Producer:* Denis Leary, Jim Serpico, Mike Figgis. *Co-Executive Producer:* Dave Erickson. *Supervising Producer:* Tom Sellitti. *Producer:* Julianna Margulies, Don Kurt. *Co-Producer:* Katie O'Hara. *Music:* Danny Lux.

Reviews: "Julianna Margulies ... is convincing as a lawyer ... she is under a black cloud that threatens to burst ... and overwhelm the show" (*The Hollywood Reporter*).

"The challenge of casting a series around a character like Canterbury should hardly be a surprise ... if this latest litigator has any chance, it's entirely predicated on the audience buying into Margulies' character — a woman who's smart, sexy but profoundly unhappy" (*Variety*).

65　A Capitol Fourth. (Special; Variety; PBS; July 4, 2008)

The twenty-eighth annual presentation celebrating the birth of America with music, songs and a fireworks display from Washington, D.C.

Host: Jimmy Smits. **Guests:** Scott Hamilton, Taylor Hicks, Brian Stokes Mitchell, Harolyn Blackwell, Hayley Westenra, Huey Lewis and the News.

Credits: *Producer:* Jerry Colbert. *Director of the National Symphony Orchestra:* Ernie Kunkel.

66　The Capture of the Green River Killer. (TV Movie; Crime Drama; Lifetime; March 30, 2008)

Fact based film, based on the book *Chasing the Devil: My Twenty Year Quest:*

The Capture of the Green River Killer by Sheriff David Reichert, that recounts his efforts to capture the Washington State serial killer.

Cast: Thomas Cavanagh (David Reichert), Michelle Harrison (Julie Reichert), Amy Davidson (Helen Remus), Bret Anthony (Bram Seton), Paige Bannister (Colleen Brockman), Trisha Benjamin (Marsue Haller), John Fasano (Joe Jakes), Currie Graham (Captain Norwell), Sharon Lawrence (Fiona Remus), James Marsters (Ted Bundy).

Credits: *Executive Producer:* Stanley M. Brooks, Juliette Hagopian. *Producer:* Scott Anderson. *Writer:* John Pielmeier. *Director:* Norma Bailey.

67　Carlos Mencia: Performance Enhanced. (Special; Comedy; Comedy Central; May 18, 2008)

A concert by comedian Carlos Mencia.

Host: Carlos Mencia.

Credits: *Executive Producer:* Carlos Mencia, Lee Kernis. *Producer:* Robert Morton, Tim Sarkes. *Writer:* Carlos Mencia.

68　Cashmere Mafia. (Series; Drama; ABC; January 6, 2008 to February 20, 2008)

Caitlin, Juliet, Mia and Zoe are four gorgeous women who have been friends since their Ivy League educations. They live in Manhattan and each has become a successful businesswoman. Mia is a publisher for Barnstead Media; Caitlin is the senior vice president of Lily Parish, Inc.; Juliet works for Stanton Hall Hotels and Resorts; Zoe is managing director for Gorham-Sutter, Inc.

The women are driven, determined to make it in a man's world and are there for each other in the good times as well as the bad times. They confide in each other and use each other's strengths and resources to help them overcome problems. Stories follow the personal and professional lives of four women who call themselves "The

Cashmere Mafia." Davis is Juliet's husband; Father David is Caitlin's brother, a priest; Sasha and Luke are Zoe's children; Clive is Mia's boss; Catherine is Zoe's secretary.

Cast: Lucy Liu (Mia Mason), Frances O'Connor (Zoe Burden), Miranda Otto (Juliet Draper), Bonnie Somerville (Caitlin Dowd), Peter Hermann (Davis Draper), Peyton List (Sasha Burden), Nicholas Art (Luke Burden), Darren Pettie (Father David), Daniel Gerroll (Clive), Kete Levering (Catherine).

Credits: *Executive Producer:* Darren Star, Gail Katz, Kevin Wade. *Co-Executive Producer:* Susie Fitzgerald. *Producer:* Jane Rabb. *Co-Producer:* Cathy M. Frank.

Reviews: "The only real difference between *Cashmere Mafia* and ABC's already-on *Women's Murder Club* is the lack of murders... The Alphabet web trots out another uninspired show about women attempting to balance lives and careers with romantic, but other than a lesbian liaison, it feels as fresh as *That Girl*" (*Variety*).

"These women might still be fun to watch if only writer-creator Kevin Wade had provided them with wittier, smarter dialogue... For a series like *Cashmere Mafia* to survive, there would have to be practically no other dramas to watch" (*The Hollywood Reporter*).

69 **Cat Dancers**. (Special; Documentary; HBO; December 15, 2008)

Compelling look at the lives of Ron Holiday, his wife Joy and their protégé, Chuck Lizza, a Las Vegas–like act wherein the three danced with tigers. Ron is the only surviving member (Joy and Chuck were killed by the same white tiger in tragic accidents five weeks apart). His hosting and narration, coupled with home movies and archival footage, also presents a seldom seen and engrossing look at an act that few people even knew about (Ron's recollections also reveal his Joy and Chuck's private lives — where each lusted for the other — as well as other unnecessary intimate details).

Host: Ron Holiday.

Credits: *Executive Producer:* Josh Braun, Julie Goldman, Krysanne Katsoolis, Silas Weir Mitchell, Sheila Nevins, Caroline Stevens. *Producer:* Harris Fischman, Nancy Abraham, Amanda Micheli. *Director:* Harris Fischman. *Music:* Peter Salett, String Theory.

Reviews: "*Cat Dancers* is the best TV documentary of the year — so interesting you won't be able to turn way for a second" (*New York Post*).

"*Cat Dancers* is a side show. He's [Ron] the barker. For our time and attention, we get the creeps. But the tigers are beautiful" (*New York Daily News*).

70 **Catch 21**. (Series; Game; Game Show Network; Premiered: July 21, 2008)

Three players compete. A question is read by the host. The first player to correctly answer receives $100 and a card from a deck of 52 playing cards. He can keep the card or pass it to one of his opponents. The game continues in this manner with the object being for a player to score an exact 21 or stop when he feels safe (at which time the opponent must continue to play to beat the established score). Players who surpass 21 lose.

Host: Alfonso Ribeiro. **Dealer:** Mikki Padilla.

Credits: *Executive Producer:* Merrill Heatter, Scott Sternberg. *Producer:* Todd Barton.

71 **Celebracadabra**. (Series; Reality; VH-1; April 27, 2008 to June 12, 2008)

Seven celebrities are teamed with seven professional magicians to determine which celebrity has the potential to become the best magician. The celebrities are mentored by the magicians and compete in the following categories: Children's Magic, Street Magic, Comedy Magic, Cabaret Magic, Strolling Magic and Phobia Magic. The best celebrity performer receives a crown ("The Ultimate Celebrity Sorcerer") and $100,000.

Host: Jonathan Levitt. **Celebrities:** C. Thomas Howell, Kimberly Wyatt, Hal Sparks, Ant, Lisa Ann Walter, Carnie Wilson, Chris "Kid" Reid.

Credits: *Producer:* Chris Martin, Karia Hidalgo, Shelly Tatro.

72 Celebrity Apprentice. (Series; Reality; NBC; January 3, 2008 to March 28, 2008)

An all-star version of *The Apprentice* franchise that uses celebrities (as opposed to non-celebrity business men and women). Here 14 hopefuls face a series of challenges to win money for their favorite charities. The celebrities must compete against each other in various business-like challenges with the best performers continuing on while the weakest performers must leave the competition. Each is awarded a cash amount for his or her charity but the last celebrity standing receives a substantial cash award. Returned for a new cycle on March 1, 2009.

Host: Donald Trump. **Co-Hosts:** Ivanka Trump, Donald Trump, Jr. **Celebrities:** Marilu Henner, Carol Alt, Nadia Comeneci, Tiffany Fallon, Stephen Baldwin, Piers Morgan, Trace Adkins, Gene Simmons, Jennie Finch, Lennox Lewis, Tito Ortiz, Vinnie Pastore, Omarosa Manigault-Stallworth, Nely Galan.

Credits: *Executive Producer:* Donald Trump, Mark Burnett. *Co-Executive Producer:* Page Feldman, Eden Gaha. *Producer:* Brian Spoor, Peter Woronow. *Talent Producer:* Chuck LaBella. *Line Producer:* Elizabeth Schulze.

73 Celebrity Circus. (Series; Reality; NBC; June 11, 2008 to July 16, 2008)

Seven celebrities perform "death-defying circus acts." Each celebrity has been trained by a professional circus trainer and each act is judged by a professional panel (whose scores count as 50 percent of the total vote; home audience votes determine the second half). Celebrities with the lowest scores are eliminated on a weekly basis; the last celebrity standing wins. Stacey Dash and Antonio Sabato, Jr., were the two finalists; Antonio won the competition.

Host: Joey Fatone. **Judges:** Aurelia Cats, Mitch Gaylord, Louie Spence. **Celebrities:** Antonio Sabato, Jr., Rachel Hunter, Wee Man, Stacey Dash, Blu Cantrell, Christopher Knight, Janet Evans.

Credits: *Executive Producer:* Matt Kunitz. *Co-Executive Producer:* Rick Ringback. *Supervising Producer:* Michael Brooks. *Producer:* Don Harary.

74 Celebrity Family Feud. (Series; Game; NBC; June 24, 2008 to August 5, 2008)

Celebrity families compete against each other in a game based on the syndicated *Family Feud.* Questions, based on a survey of 100 people are posed. Points are awarded based on the number of people who responded to the answer given by the team at play. The first team to score 300 or more points is the winner and donates money (up to $50,000) to their favorite charity.

Host: Al Roker. **Announcer:** Burton Richardson.

Credits: *Executive Producer:* Gaby Johnston, Toby Gorman. *Supervising Producer:* Kristen Bjorklund. *Producer:* Simon Lythgoe, Elizabeth Haas. *Director:* Ken Fuchs.

Review: "Ultimately it's harmless but at best tepid fun that makes one long for the Richard Dawson [1970s *Family Feud* host] drollness over Roker's ebullience" (*Variety*).

75 Celebrity Rehab. (Series; Reality; VH-1; January 10, 2008 to March 5, 2008)

Eight celebrities who have fallen on hard times (through drinking and/or drugs) are put before the cameras to face their addiction and hopefully, through treatment, walk away from the program clean and sober.

Host: Dr. Drew Pinsky. **The Celebrities:** Daniel Baldwin, Jeff Conaway, Mary Carey (adult film star), Chyna (wrestler), Jessica Sierra (*American Idol* finalist), Jaimee Foxworth (*Family Matters* co-star), Seth "Shift" Binzer (Crazy Town lead singer), Brigitte Nielsen. **Resident Technician:** William Smith, Inez Randall. **Nurse:** Sasha Kusina.

Credits: *Executive Producer:* Brad Kuhlman, Jill Osmon-Modabber, Jeff Olde, Michael Hirschorn, Damian Sullivan, Drew Pinsky, John Irwin, Noah Pollack, Howard Lapides. *Associate Producer:* Beatriz Flores.

Reviews: "VH-1 may have another success here, but let's not kid ourselves: if this works, the channel has simply demonstrated it's possible to have your cake and snort it too" (*Variety*).

"An incredibly earnest series about the nature of addiction and the nearly superhuman efforts required to overcome it" (*The Hollywood Reporter*).

76 Celine Dion: That's Just the Woman in Me. (Special; Variety; CBS; February 15, 2008)

Singer Celine Dion performs some of her greatest hits.

Host: Celine Dion. Guests: Josh Groban, Will.i.a.m. **Dancers:** Amanda Balen, Zac Brazenas, Dominic Chaiduang, Aaron Foeiske, Melissa Garcia, Miguel Perez, Kemba Shannon, Addie Yungmee. **Announcer:** Rebecca Riedy.

Credits: *Executive Producer:* Ken Ehrlich, Rene Angelli, Dave Piatel, Paul Faberman. *Producer:* Renato Basile, Robb Wagner. *Associate Producer:* Sergio Alfano.

77 Celtic Woman. (Special; Variety; PBS; December 2, 2008)

Celtic Woman is a talented female recording group composed of five vocalists and one fiddler (Mairead). The women, all from Ireland, have produced several albums and two prior PBS specials: *Celtic Woman: A New Journey* (2006) and

Celtic Woman: A Christmas Celebration (2007). *The Greatest Journey* (their 2008 special) features the women performing their favorite songs from the album and TV specials.

Chloe Agnew, Olra Fallon, Lisa Kelly, Meav Ni Mhaolchatha and Mairead Nesbitt comprised the original group. Deirdre Shannon replaced Meav during her pregnancy in 2005. Meav returned in 2006. Hayley Westenra joined the group in August of 2006 (to make it five vocalists). In 2007, Meav left the group to concentrate on a solo career. Lynn Hilary replaced her and in 2008, Alex Sharpe replaced Lynn during Lynn's maternity leave.

Celtic Woman: Chloe Agnew, Orla Fallon, Lynn Hilary, Lisa Kelly, Alex Sharpe, Maired Nesbitt, Meav Ni Mhaolchatha, Deidre Shannon, Hayley Westenra. **Choir:** Ann Myler, Mary O'Sullivan, Daire Halpin, Yvonne Weeds, Julie Fenney, Julian Edwards, Andrew Nangle, Sean Loftus, Jeremy Moran. **Credits:** *Executive Producer:* Peter Brady, Dave Kavanagh. *Producer:* Scott Porter. *Music Director:* David Downes. *Director:* Russell Thomas.

78 Charlie and Me. (TV Movie; Drama; Hallmark; January 5, 2008)

Heartwarming tale about an elderly man (Charlie) who wants to make things better for his granddaughter (Casey) and her hard working widowed father (Jeffrey) before his time runs out.

Cast: Tom Bosley (Charlie), Jordy Benattar (Casey), James Gallanders (Jeffrey), Hannah Fleming (Jenna), Barclay Hope (Dr. Robert Graham), Cara Pifko (Dr. Fran Gilford).

Credits: *Executive Producer:* Gerald W. Abrams, Tom Wertheimer. *Producer:* Susan Murdoch. *Writer:* Karen Struck. *Director:* David Weaver. *Music:* Ron Ramin.

79 Charlie Jade. (Series; Science Fiction; Sci Fi; June 6, 2008 to August 26, 2008)

Within our world three parallel worlds exist: Alphaverse (a futuristic Earth), Betaverse (like present day Earth) and Gammaverse (an idyllic world). On Alphaverse, which is controlled by mega corporations, Vexcor, one such company, is attempting to open a doorway to Gammaverse to exploit its natural resources. Gammaverse terrorists Bern and Reena are attempting to stop Vexcor when an explosion occurs at the site of the portal. The force of the explosion propels Reena into Betaverse where she meets Charlie Jade, a rogue detective from Alphaverse who, during his pursuit of a woman, had stumbled upon the Alphaverse portal in the desert.

Vexcor is a deceptive company out to become ruler of the universe. Reena knows this and is now a threat as she can expose them. To stop her, Vexcor assigns 01 Boxer to dispose of her (01 Boxer has the ability to travel between universes by dousing himself with water). Stories follow Reena as she, Charlie and Karl Lubinsky, an ex patriot, attempt to stop Vexcor before their highly unstable experiments destroy Betaverse. Essa is the CEO of Vexcor.

Cast: Jeffrey Pierce (Charlie Jade), Patricia McKenzie (Reena), Tyrone Benskin (Karl Lubinsky), Michael Filipowich (01 Boxer), Michelle Burgers (Essa Rompkin).

Credits: *Executive Producer:* Izidore Codron, Guy Mullally, Jacques Pettigrew, Robin Spry, Robert Wertheimer. *Producer:* Adam J. Shully. *Music:* FM LeSiew.

80   Chase. (Series; Game; Sci Fi; November 11, 2008 to December 16, 2008)

Players, called Runners, compete in a video game come to life wherein they must avoid capture by Hunters to win money. Specific areas around Los Angeles (for example, the harbor, the Universal Theme Park) comprise the "game board." An amount of time is established and the Runners must accomplish a series of tasks while at the same time avoid being caught (and disqualified) by the Hunter. The player (or players) who accomplish the game's goals and avoid capture win (or split) $50,000. Hunters are identified only as Amazon, Grant, Icey, Scott, Vazquez, Wong, Kim and T-Bo.

Host: Trey Farley.

Credits: *Senior Producer:* Mike DiMaggio, Danny Kon. *Producer:* Phil Mark, Brian Heller.

Review: "As human video games go, not terribly shabby... Most ... have been exceedingly lame. But *Chase* at least follows through in its concept and never varies from the formula, even if we could spend all day picking holes in it" (*The Hollywood Reporter*).

81   Cheech and Chong: Roasted. (Special; Comedy; TBS; November 30, 2008)

Cheech Marin and Tommy Chong, better known as Cheech and Chong, are comically roasted by their celebrity friends.

Host: Brad Garrett. **Roasted:** Cheech Marin, Tommy Chong. **Guests:** Tom Arnold, Geraldo Rivera, Andy Dick, Steve Carell, Al Sharpton, Wilmer Valderrama, Ralphie May, Shelby Chong, Penn and Teller.

Credits: *Executive Producer:* Robert Morton, Ben Feigin, Joshua Klein. *Producer:* Michael Ferrucci, Tom Gianas, Quinn Monahan. *Director:* John Moffitt. *Writer:* Mike Rowe, Chris McGuire, Tom Gianas, Michael Ferrucci.

82   The Cheetah Girls: One World. (TV Movie; Musical Comedy; Disney; August 22, 2008)

Chantel, Aqua and Dornida are the Cheetah Girls, a musical group hoping to take the world by storm. They appeared (with Raven Symone as Galleria) in two prior movies (*The Cheetah Girls* and *The Cheetah Girls II*) and in this third film (without Raven) the girls travel to India to appear in a musical only to find that the producer requires only one of the girls.

The story follows their efforts to compete for the role.

Cast: Adrienne Bailon (Chantel), Sabrina Bryan (Dorinda), Kiely Williams (Aqua), Lori Anne Alter (Juanita), Deepti Daryanani (Gita), Rupak Ginn (Rahim), Kunal Sharma (Amar), Michael Steger (Vikram).

Credits: *Executive Producer:* Debra Martin Chase. *Producer:* Mitch Engel. *Music:* David Lawrence. *Director:* Paul Hoen. *Writer:* Nisha Ganatra.

83   The Cho Show. (Series; Reality; VH-1; August 21, 2008 to September 25, 2008)

A look at the life of comedienne Margaret Cho — from her daily activities, her club work and her adventures with friends and family.

Star: Margaret Cho.

Credits: *Executive Producer:* Margaret Cho, Rico Martinez, Don Lindau. *Producer:* Christy Spitzer.

Review: "As a comic, Cho almost seems too successful for VH-1's talent profiles, but the latest showcase suffers from an increasingly reality TV deficiency: it's too staged to be convincing and too unscripted to be reliably funny" (*Variety*).

84   Chocolate News. (Series; Comedy; Comedy Central; Premiered: October 15, 2008)

Risque sketches that lampoon anything and everything related to mostly the African-American experience (much like the series *In Living Color*).

Host-Star: David Alan Grier. **Regulars:** Tanea Brooks, Jennifer Dyal, Willie Garson, J.T. Jackson, Brent Jennings, Juline Leflore, Alika Ray, Arthur Roberts, Mar'Sheila Price, Oth'Than Burnside.

Credits: *Executive Producer:* David Alan Grier, Robert Morton, Fax Bahr, Adam Small, Peter B. Aronson, Jordan Levin. *Producer:* Jim Ziegler, David Nickoll. *Music:* Greg O'Connor. *Director:* Liz Plonka.

Reviews: "*Chocolate News* is a moderately tasty, low nutrition snack — the kind that, with apologies to perhaps the next ethnic frontier, will leave you hungry a half-hour later" (*Variety*).

"If you've never gotten over the cancellation of *In Living Color* or ... *Chappelle's Show* ... *Chocolate News* ... seals a void left by those shows and fills the, er, black hole in satirical pop culture" (*New York Post*).

85   Chop Socky Chooks. (Series; Cartoon; Cartoon Network; Premiered: March 7, 2008)

Wasabi World is a city built like a shopping mall. It is ruled by Dr. Wasabi, an evil chicken who strives to keep its citizens under his rule. Protecting the citizens are Chick P., KO Joe and Chuckie Chan, three martial arts chickens who encounter more mishaps than danger battling Dr. Wasabi.

Voice Cast: Shelley Longworth (Chick P.), Joseph Pateson (KO Joe), Rob Racstraw (Chuckie Chan), Paul Kaye (Dr. Wasabi).

Credits: *Executive Producer:* Miles Bullough. *Producer:* Ben Lock. *Line Producer:* Elena Adair.

Series Producer: Jacqueline White. *Music:* Lou Pomanti.

86   Chris Rock: Kill the Messenger. (Special; Comedy; HBO; September 27, 2008)

A concert by comedian Chris Rock that encompasses material from three live performances (in New York, London and South Africa).

Host: Chris Rock.

Credits: *Executive Producer:* Marty Callner, Chris Rock. *Producer:* Randall Gladstein. *Director:* Marty Callner. *Writer:* Chris Rock.

87   *A Christmas Choir*. (TV Movie; Drama; Hallmark; December 6, 2008)

Factual account about a man (Peter Andrews) who volunteers at a homeless shelter and then organizes its residents into a choir.

Cast: Jason Gedrick (Peter Andrews), Rhea Perlman (Sister Agatha), Cindy Simpson (Jill), Tyrone Benskin (Bob), Marianne Farley (Marilyn Stone), Claudia Ferri (Rita), Luis Oliva (Juan). **Credits:** *Executive Producer:* Joel S. Rice, Lisa Towers. *Producer:* Michael Prupas. *Music:* James Gelfand. *Director:* Peter Svatek. *Writer:* Donald Martin.

88   The Christmas Clause. (TV Movie; Comedy; Ion; December 19, 2008)

Sophie Kelly is a working mother. Her husband, David, is an out of work architect, and her three children, Nikki, Anna and Jay Jay, constantly crave all her time, little of which she has to spare on them. Sophie, a lawyer, is overworked and overwhelmed with family problems. As Christmas day approaches and Sophie is standing in line for her children to see Santa Claus, she idly wishes she had a different life. The mall Santa Claus (an angel in disguise) grants her wish — and the story follows Sophie as she sees what her life would be like if she never met David and had children. When Sophie realizes she misses her old life and exclaims "All I want for Christmas is my life back," it is returned to her.

Cast: Lea Thompson (Sophie Kelly), Andrew Airlie (David Kelly), Megan Charpentic (Anna Kelly), Rick Ravenello (Jake), Rachel Hayward (Marcia), Doug Abrahams (Santa), Christina Jastrzembska (Margaret), Fiona Marinelli (Silvia), Jill Morrison (Claire). **Credits:** *Executive Producer:* Kirk Shaw, Jeffrey Schneck, Robyn Messinger, Glen Hartford, Daniel Toll, Cord Doughlor, Douglas Price, Breanne Hartley, Lindsay MacAdam, George Erschbamer, Sheri Elwood. *Producer:* Kirk Shaw. *Writer:* Sheri Elwood. *Director:* George Erschbamer. *Music:* Stu Goldberg.

89   Christmas in Rockefeller Center. (Special; Variety; NBC; December 3, 2008)

The eleventh annual national broadcast (originally aired locally in New York) that heralds the arrival of the holiday season with the lighting of the world's most famous Christmas tree at Rockefeller Center in Manhattan (the 2008 event marked the 76th tree lighting ceremony).

Host: Al Roker. **Guests:** Tony Bennett, Beyonce, Neil Boyd, The Jonas Brothers, Harry Connick, Jr., David Cook, Rosie O'Donnell, Faith Hill, The Broadway Kids, Solange Knowles. **Credits:** *Executive Producer:* Bob Holmes. *Producer:* Steve Mayer, Heidi Kelso. *Associate Producer:* Kathleen Widden. *Director:* Jeff Margolis.

90   Christmas in Washington. (Special; Variety; TNT; December 17, 2008)

Name guests perform holiday songs from the National Building in Washington, D.C.

Host: Dr. Phil McGraw, Robin McGraw. **Performers:** Kristin Chenoweth, Julianne Hough, Darius Rucker, Casting Crowns, Straight No Chaser. **Credits:** *Executive Producer:* George Stevens, Jr. *Producer-Director:* Michael M. Stevens.

91   Christmas with the Mormon Tabernacle Choir. (Special; Variety; PBS; December 24, 2008)

A Christmas Eve celebration featuring holiday songs performed by the Mormon Tabernacle Choir and the King's Singers, England's premier male vocal choral ensemble. The song, "The Twelve Days of Christmas," is given a lavish production number.

Credits: *Executive Producer:* John Howe. *Producer:* Edward J. Payne. *Director:* Lee Wessman. *Music Conductor:* Craig Jessop, Mark Wilberg. *Organists:* Richard Elliott, Clay Christiansen, Andrew Linsworth. *Dance Coordinator:* Yvonne West, Terry West.

92 The Circuit. (TV Movie; Drama; ABC Family; June 8, 2008)

Rookie stock car racer Kylie Shines finds herself competing against her estranged father, Al, a former racing legend, when he re-enters her life.

Cast: Michelle Trachtenberg (Kylie Shines), Bill Campbell (Al Shines), Drew Fuller (Kid Walker), Paul Rae (Robin Cates), Maurice Dean Wint (Andy "Crash" Davis), Loretta Yu (Deanne), Jeremy Akerman (Charlie).

Credits: *Executive Producer:* Frank von Zerneck, Robert M. Sertner, William S. Gilmore, Charles Lenhoff. *Producer:* Randy Sutter. *Writer:* Bill Hanley, Quinton Peeples. *Director:* Peter Werner.

93 The City. (Series; Reality; MTV; Premiered: December 29, 2008)

A spin off from *The Hills* wherein Whitney Port leaves her home town of Los Angeles to begin a new life in New York City. Stories follow Whitney as she begins work in the fashion industry (the fashion house of Diane von Furstenberg), makes new friends and struggles to succeed in a city that can easily shatter dreams. Also cast, but only identified by first names are Olivia, the Upper East Side socialite; Erin, Whitney's long time friend; Samantha, a buyer at Bergdorf-Goodman; Jay, Whitney's friend; and Adam, Jay's best friend.

Star: Whitney Port.

94 The Cleaner. (Series; Drama; A&E; Premiered: July 15, 2008)

William Banks is a former drug addict who swore an oath to God that if he overcame his drug addiction he would help others facing the same situation.

William is married (to Melissa) and the father of Ben and Lula. He has two assistants (Akani and Arnie) and stories follow William as he becomes sort of a guardian

angel, seeking to help addicts before time runs out.

Cast: Benjamin Bratt (William Banks), Amy Price-Francis (Melissa Banks), Grace Park (Akani Cuesta), Esteban Powell (Arnie Swenton), Brett Delbuono (Ben Banks), Liliana Mumy (Lula Banks), Kevin Michael Richardson (Darnell McDowell).

Credits: *Executive Producer:* Jonathan Prince, Robert Munic, David Semel. *Co-Executive Producer:* Warren Boyd, Jay Silverman. *Producer:* Cliff Rogers. *Music:* David Lawrence.

Reviews: "Bottom Line: Intervention is needed if this show is ever to become a viewing habit" (*The Hollywood Reporter*).

"A&E bet heavily on *The Sopranos* reruns to brand the channel but its grit and blue language not with standing, *The Cleaner* doesn't represent the kind of show destined to build on that foundation" (*Variety*).

95 Click and Clack's As the Wrench Turns. (Series; Cartoon; PBS; July 9, 2008 to August 13, 2008)

Click and Clack Tappet are brothers who host a radio show (*Car Talk*) and own a garage at Car Talk Plaza, a fictional building in Harvard Square in Cambridge, Massachusetts. The series, based on the National Radio program *Car Talk* follows Click and Clack as they attempt to fix cars, deal with disgruntled customers and find ways to goof off. Beth is their show producer; Sal is the garage receptionist; Crusty (a former Harvard professor), Fidel and Stash are mechanics; Zu Zu is the garage dog.

Voice Cast: Tom Magliozzi (Click Tappet), Ray Magliozzi (Clack Tappet), Kelli O'Hara (Beth Totenbag), Cornell Loomack (Crusty), Barbara Rosenblat, Garrison Keillor, Juan Hernandez, Paul Christie, Manu Narayan.

Credits: *Executive Producer:* Howard K. Grossman, Robert Harris, Bill Kroyer.

Supervising Producer: Scott Brewninger. *Music:* Carl Finch, Brave Combo.

96   The CMA Awards. (Special; Variety; ABC; November 13, 2008)

The 42nd annual Country Music Association Awards presentation that honors the best in country and western music. Broadcast live from Nashville, Tennessee.

Host: Carrie Underwood, Brad Paisley. **Guests:** Miley Cyrus, Billy Ray Cyrus, George Strait, Trace Adkins, Reese Witherspoon, Vince Gill, Martha McBride, Kellie Pickler, Nicole Kidman, Sugarland, Kid Rock, Keith Urban, Toby Keith, Kenny Chesney, Tim McGraw, LeAnn Rimes, Faith Hill.

Credits: *Executive Producer:* Walter C. Miller. *Producer:* Robert Deaton. *Director:* Paul Miller.

97   Coco Chanel. (TV Movie; Drama; Lifetime; September 13, 2008)

The rags-to-riches story of fashion designer Coco Chanel from her youth in an orphanage outside of Paris, France, to her struggles to achieve fame.

Cast: Shirley MacLaine (Coco Chanel), Barbora Bobulova (Young Coco Chanel), Malcolm McDowell (Marc Bouchier), Brigitte Boucher (Madame de Rochefort), Valentina Carnelutti (Sister Therese), Robert Dawson (Lord Fry), Anny Duperey (Madame Desboutins).

Credits: *Executive Producer:* Daniele Passani. *Producer:* Matilde Bernabei, Sophie Ravard, Nicholas Traube. *Director:* Christian Duquay. *Writer:* Ron Hutchinson, Enrico Medioli, Lea Tafuri.

Reviews: "Sensuous and watchable, this sometimes truthful account of Coco Chanel's life is a delight" (*The Hollywood Reporter*).

"Fashion is in fashion all over TV these days but Lifetime's international co-production *Coco Chanel* has less to do with haute couture than high melodrama, recounting a life story so insanely frothy and pulpy that those who don't cry will be laughing their eyelashes off" (*Variety*).

98   A Colbert Christmas: The Greatest Gift of All. (Special; Comedy; Comedy Central; November 25, 2008)

A spoof of Christmas specials (like those hosted by Perry Como, Andy Williams and Bing Crosby in the 1970s and 80s) wherein *Colbert Report* host Stephen Colbert is tapped to host as Christmas special but is trapped in his mountain cabin by a murderous (prop) bear and unable to escape. However, his friends (guest stars) manage to drop by to provide the yuletide cheer by performing original, satirical Christmas songs.

Host: Stephen Colbert. **Guests:** Elvis Costello, Toby Keith, Willie Nelson, Jon Stewart, John Legend, Leslie Feist.

Credits: *Executive Producer:* Stephen Colbert, Allison Silverman. *Co-Executive Producer:* Meredith Bennett, Richard Dahm. *Producer:* Matt Lappin. *Music:* Adam Schlesinger. *Director:* Jim Hoskinson. *Writer:* Michael Brumm, Stephen Colbert, Richard Dahm, Peter Gwinn.

Reviews: "*A Colbert Christmas* is not only a fabulously zany hour long ad for the *A Colbert Christmas* DVD but also reinforces what a truly remarkable talent the host is... Nation, you are in for a treat" (*Variety*).

"Last week an envelope from Comedy Central arrived with something called *A Colbert Christmas* ... inside... Not only was it still six weeks before Christmas, but worse, the special airs before Thanksgiving... I decided to review this one five full days early, I'm still laughing" (*New York Post*).

99   Comanche Moon. (TV Movie; Western; CBS; January 13, 15, 17, 2008)

A prequel to Larry McMurty's *Lonesome Dove* that, set from 1858 to 1865, tells of the war between the Comanche Indians (led by Chief Buffalo Hump) and the

Texas Rangers (led by Captain Inish Scull and assisted specifically by Rangers Gus McCrae and Woodrow F. Call).

Cast: Val Kilmer (Inish Scull), Steve Zahn (Gus McCrae), Linda Cardellini (Clara Forsythe), Elizabeth Banks (Maggie), Karl Urban (Woodrow Call), Ryan Merriman (Jake Spoon), Wes Studi (Chief Buffalo Hump), Adam Beach (Blue Duck), Melanie Lynskey (Pearl Coleman), Sal Lopez (Ahumand).

Credits: *Executive Producer:* Paul Frank, Larry McMurty, Diana Ossana, Julie Yorn. *Producer:* Dyson Lovell. *Writer:* Diana Ossana, Larry McMurty. *Director:* Simon Wincer. *Music:* Lennie Niehaus.

Review: "Lighter moments of romance and horseplay are woven into CBS's six-hour miniseries, but they too often feel farcical... These false notes, however, are eased by simple, stirring scenes" (*Entertainment Weekly*).

100 Comedy Central Roast of Bob Saget. (Special; Comedy; Comedy Central; August 17, 2008)

A comical salute to comedian Bob Saget by his show business friends, in particular, his co-stars from the series *Full House* (John Stamos, Jodie Sweetin, Dave Coulier).

Roast Master: John Stamos. **Roasted:** Bob Saget. **Guests:** Jodie Sweetin, Dave Coulier, Don Rickles, Gilbert Gottfried, Cloris Leachman, Jon Lovitz, Sarah Silverman, Alan Thicke.

Credits: *Executive Producer:* Elizabeth Porter. *Producer:* Joel Gallen. *Music:* Noah Lifschey. *Director:* Joel Gallen. *Writer:* Whitney Cummings.

101 Comedy Gumbo. (Series; Comedy; Internet; 2008)

Brief skits "for people who do not have time to watch" the half-hour and sixty minute sketch shows on television.

Cast: Sean Becker, Payman Benz, Fiona Gubelmann, Adam Shapiro, Greg Benson, David Hussey, Sarah French, Kim Evey, Ryan Smith.

Credits: *Executive Producer:* Dan Halstead. *Producer:* Sean Becker, Payman Benz, Chris Darnell. *Music:* Eanan Patterson.

102 Comics Without Borders. (Series; Comedy; Showtime; September 11, 2008 to October 30, 2008)

A weekly showcase for stand-up comedians who perform their material for sold out audiences at the WAMU Theater at Madison Square Garden.

Host: Russell Peters.

Credits: *Executive Producer:* Clayton Peters, Gary Binkow, Jeff Goldenberg. *Producer:* Scott Montoya, Russell Peters, Michael Green.

103 The Complete Jane Austen. (Miniseries; Drama; PBS; January 13, 2008 to April 6, 2008)

Six adaptations of novels by Jane Austen (plus one original drama [*Miss Austen Regrets*]) that depict the adventures of young ladies seeking love at the turn of 19th century England. Listed in broadcast order.

1. Persuasion (1-13-08). A young woman (Anne Elliot) tries to rekindle a lost love when a chance meeting reunites her with Captain Frederick Wentworth, a man she once loved but was persuaded by her family to reject when he proposed marriage.

Cast: Sally Hawkins (Anne Elliot), Rupert Penry-Jones (Frederick Wentworth), Anthony Head (Sir Walter Elliot), Julia Davis (Elizabeth Elliot), Amanda Hale (Mary Elliot), Sam Hazeldine (Charles Musgrove), Alice Krige (Lady Russell). **Credits:** *Producer:* David Snodin. *Director:* Adrian Shergold.

2. Northanger Abbey (1-20-08). Jane Austen's parody of gothic fiction wherein an ordinary girl (Catherine Morland) finds a new world of elaborate dances and handsome men when she meets a man and becomes involved with the intrigue of his family estate, Northanger Abbey.

Cast: Felicity Jones (Catherine Morland), Julia Dearden (Mrs. Morland), Gerry O'Brien (Mr. Morland), Desmond Barrit (Mr. Allen), Sylvestra LeTouzel (Mrs. Allen), Geraldine James (Voice of Jane Austen). **Credits:** *Executive Producer:* Andy Harris, Charles Elton. *Producer:* Keith Thompson. *Director:* Jon Jones. *Writer:* Andrew Davies.

3. Mansfield Park (1-27-08). Following the death of her parents, a young girl (Fanny Price) is saved from a life of poverty when she is taken in by rich relatives at Stately Mansfield Park. The story is set years later when, as a young lady, Fanny finds herself the object of many suitors but in search of the one she feels is her true love.

Cast: Billie Piper (Fanny Price), Julia Joyce (Young Fanny), Jemma Redgrave (Lady Bertram), Douglas Hodge (Sir Thomas Bertram), Blake Ritson (Edmund Bertram), James D'Arcy (Tom Bertram), Michelle Ryan (Maria Bertram). **Credits:** *Executive Producer:* George Faber, Charles Pattinson. *Producer:* Susan Harrison. *Director:* Iain B. MacDonald. *Writer:* Maggie Wadey.

4. Miss Austen Regrets (2-3-08). A sentimental story, based on the life and letters of Jane Austen that examines why the romance novelist never married or even met the man of her dreams.

Cast: Olivia Williams (Jane Austen), Greta Scacchi (Cassandra Austen), Samuel Rouken (Harris Bigg), Pip Torrens (Edward Austen Knight), Tom Hiddleston (John Plumptree), Harry Gostelow (Rev. Charles Papillon). **Credits:** *Producer:* Anne Pivcevic, Jamie Laurenson. *Writer:* Gwyneth Hughes. *Director:* Jeremy Lovering.

5. Pride and Prejudice (2-10, 2-17, 2-24-08). The effect two handsome and eligible bachelors (Mr. Bingley and Mr. Darcy) have on the impressionable Bennett sisters (Jane and Elizabeth).

Cast: Susannah Harker (Jane Bennett), Jennifer Ehle (Elizabeth Bennett), Crispin Bonham Carter (Mr. Bingley), Colin Firth (Mr. Darcy), Benjamin Whitrow (Mr. Bennett), Alison Steadman (Mrs. Bennett), Julia Sawalha (Lydia Bennett), Lucy Briers (Mary Bennett), Polly Maberly (Kitty Bennett). **Credits:** *Executive Producer:* Michael Wearing. *Producer:* Sue Birtwistle. *Director:* Simon Langton. *Writer:* Andrew Davies.

6. Emma (3-23-08). Light hearted story of a matchmaker (Emma Woodhouse) who, despite her imperfect success rate, attempts to find her own Mr. Right.

Cast: Kate Beckinsale (Emma Woodhouse), Raymond Coulthard (Frank Churchill), Mark Strong (Mr. Knightley), Samantha Morton (Harriet Smith), Dido Miles (Isabella Knightley), Ray Coulthard (Frank Churchill), Olivia Williams (Jane Fairfax). **Credits:** *Producer:* Sue Birtwistle. *Associate Producer:* Joy Spink. *Director:* Diarmuid Lawrence. *Writer:* Andrew Davies.

7. Sense and Sensibility (3-30, 4-6-08). A look at two sisters (Elinor and Marianne Dashwood) and their different approaches to love. Elinor is tempered and rational; Marianne is impulsive and full of youthful passion.

Cast: Hattie Morahan (Elinor Dashwood), Charity Wakefield (Marianne Dashwood), Dan Stevens (Edward Ferrars), David Morrisey (Colonel Brandon), Janet McTeer (Mrs. Dashwood), Lucy Boynton (Margaret Dashwood), Mark Williams (Sir John Middleton), Tabitha Wady (Charlotte Palmer). **Credits:** *Producer:* Anne Pivcevic. *Director:* John Alexander. *Writer:* Andrew Davies

104   Confessions of a Go Go Girl. (TV Movie; Drama; Lifetime; August 16, 2008)

Jane McCoy is a young woman who, after graduating from college, abandons her plans to attend law school to follow her dream of becoming an actress. Along the way she acquires a job as a go go dancer to make ends meet. The story follows the problems Jane faces as her job becomes all consuming and begins to alienate her from her friends and family.

Cast: Chelsea Hobbs (Jane McCoy), Karen Kruper (Grace McCoy), James D. Hopkin (Jim McCoy), Sarah Carter (Angela Kolodoros), Corbin Bernsen (Nick), Rachel Hunter (Donna), Graeme Black (Jamie McCoy).

Credits: *Executive Producer:* Michael Frisley, Philip Kleinbart. *Co-Executive Producer:* Lenore Kletter. *Producer:* Chad Oakes, Michael Frisley. *Director:* Grant Harvey. *Writer:* Lenore Kletter.

105 Cooking for Real. (Series; Cooking; Food Network; Premiered: April 6, 2008)

Chef Sonny Anderson provides the recipes for people with limited time to spend in the kitchen.

Host: Sonny Anderson.

106 Coolio's Rules. (Series; Reality; Oxygen; October 28, 2008 to November 25, 2008)

A look at the mostly home life of Coolio (a.k.a. Artis Leon Ivey, Jr.), the Grammy Award–winning rap artist, as he struggles to cope with his not-so-average family. Coolio, a bachelor, is the father of six children, four of whom are featured (Artisha, Brandi, Artis and Jackie). He is also a musician, entrepreneur and a man who is looking for a woman to share his life. Artisha, the first born child (20 years old), loves "fashion, shopping and boys"; nineteen year-old Brandi is a college freshman (studying fashion and business); Artis, 18, is an aspiring rapper; and Jackie, 15, is focusing on all the problems associated with high school.

Star: Coolio.

Credits: *Executive Producer:* Andrew Hoegl, Jonathan Singer, Coolio, Susan Haber, Chris Coelen, Greg Goldman, Amy Introcaso-Davis, Kristen Connolly Vadas. *Co-Executive Producer:* Scott Cooper, Mike Duffy. *Supervising Producer:* Sonja Schenk. *Music:* Chris Horvath.

Review: "Instead of playing characters, Coolio and his family ... are characters. Exposing your kids to obvious ridicule on a national platform might be unthinkable to most parents but not to Compton-born Coolio" (*The Hollywood Reporter*).

107 Copperhead. (TV Movie; Science Fiction; Sci Fi; June 28, 2008)

Thriller about a small town in the Old West that is terrorized by a swarm of deadly copperhead snakes.

Cast: Billy Drago (Jesse Evans), Todd Jensen (Sheriff Mercer), Brad Johnson ("Wild" Bill Longley), Nathan Bautista (Henry), Wendy Carter (Jane), Nick Harvey (Tannen).

Credits: *Executive Producer:* T.J. Sakasegawa. *Producer:* Philip J. Roth. *Writer:* Rafael Jordan. *Director:* Todor Chapkanov. *Music:* Nathan Furst.

108 Country Fried Planet. (Series; Reality; CMT; March 14, 2008 to April 11, 2008)

A sequel to *Country Fried Home Videos* that showcases the home videos of people from around the world performing before a camera.

Host: Bill Engvall.

Credits: *Executive Producer:* Bradley Anderson, Mack Anderson. *Co-Executive Producer:* Steve Lavapies. *Producer:* Kari Killion.

109 Coupling. (Series; Comedy; BBC America; 2008)

A look at the lives of six friends: lovers Susan and Steve; Patrick and his girlfriend, Sally; Jane, a girl seeking Mr. Right; and Oliver, "a lifetime loser in love." The basis for the short-lived American series of the same title.

Cast: Jack Davenport (Steve Taylor), Sarah Alexander (Susan Walker), Ben Miles (Patrick Maitland), Kate Isitt (Sally Harper), Gina Bellman (Jane Christie), Richard Mylan (Oliver Morris).

Credits: *Executive Producer:* Beryl Vertue, Sophie Charles-Jervoise, Geoffrey Perkins. *Producer:* Sue Vertue. *Music:* Simon Brint.

110 Crash. (Series; Drama; Starz; Premiered: October 17, 2008)

An adaptation of the 2005 movie *Crash* that takes a tamer look at a group of young people living in Los Angeles: Christine Emory, a Brentwood wife caring for an ailing father while her husband, Peter, struggles as a real estate developer; Eddie Choi, an ex-gang member, still haunted by his past, turned EMT; Ben Cendars, an unstable record producer; Anthony Adams, an aspiring musician who works as Ben's driver; and Bebe Arcel and Axel Finet, less than honorable police officers.

Cast: Dennis Hopper (Ben Cendars), Clare Carey (Christine Emory), D.B. Sweeney (Peter Emory), Brian Tee (Eddie Choi), Jocko Sims (Anthony Adams), Arlene Tur (Bebe Arcel), Nick E. Tarabay (Axel Finet), Michael Fairman (Christine's father).

Credits: *Executive Producer:* Glen Mazzara, Bob Yari, Bobby Moresco, Paul Haggis. *Co-Executive Producer:* Don Cheadle, Tom Nunan, Mark R. Harris, Jorg Westerkamp, Thomas Becker, Frank Renzulli, Ted Mann. *Producer:* Stacy Rukeyser, John B. Moranville.

Review: "Messy at best, the two episode premiere suffers from wildly uneven performances, beginning with Dennis Hopper at his manic worse" (*Variety*).

111 Crash and Burn. (TV Movie; Crime Drama; Spike; March 30, 2008)

Violent tale of a tough FBI agent (Kevin) who goes undercover to break up a clever gang of car thieves.

Cast: Erik Palladino (Kevin), Heather Marie Marsden (Penny), Mirelly Taylor (Lucia Mendez), Owen Beckman (Tommy), Rebeka Montoya (Mareya), Vanessa Villalovos (Lily), Peter Jason (Manny).

Credits: *Producer:* Lincoln Lageson, Michael Moran. *Director:* Russell Mulcahy. *Writer:* Frank Hannah, Jack LoGiudice.

112 Crime 360. (Series; Reality; A&E; Premiered: March 6, 2008)

A reality series version of *Law and Order* that presents a real crime from the first 911 call to its conclusion (capture of the culprit; the courtroom case is not presented nor is the fate of the culprit in the presented case revealed).

Credits: *Supervising Producer:* Rob Dorfman. *Producer:* Kymber Lim, Ian Mallahan. *Field Producer:* Jonathan Jones. *Senior Field Producer:* Chris Voos.

Reviews: "*Cops* with a community college degree" (*The Hollywood Reporter*).

"*Crime 360* ... is one of the most amateurish programs about professional homicide detectives you'll see this year ... and it's not because of content but because of over-the-top graphics and sound effects" (*New York Post*).

113 Crusoe. (Series; Adventure; NBC; Premiered: October 17, 2008)

"Hell is wherever a man is if it keeps him from what he loves," laments Robinson Crusoe, an Englishman who has been separated from his wife, family and friends as the result of a shipwreck (caught in a storm at sea) that has marooned him on a remote island in South Africa (17th century). As the only survivor, and with no apparent hope of escape, Crusoe establishes a home in a tree and forges an array of ingenious contraptions designed to protect him and his fortress (it is assumed his dog, Dundee, also survived the shipwreck). At an unspecified time thereafter, Crusoe acquires a companion, a cannibal that he names Friday ("Because I found him on a Friday") when he saves him from a group of cannibals that came to the island to offer him as a sacrifice. Friday, who can speak 12 languages, immediately bonds with his savior and now the two look out for each other. Stories relate their efforts to survive while at the same time seek a way off the island. Flashback sequences are used to detail Robinson's life in England as a child, with his fiancée, then wife, Susannah, and his mentor, the mysterious Jeremiah Blackthorne.

Several episodes feature the character of Olivia, a woman knowledgeable in medicine, who, to survive a mutinous takeover of the ship on which she is traveling, disguises herself as a man (Oliver) and becomes a nurse to the ship's doctor. When the mutineers use Crusoe's island as a site to fix their damaged ship, Olivia meets and befriends Crusoe and Friday and each helps the other through a series of adventures that eventually defeat the mutineers but to protect Friday from a captain who wants to sell him as a slave, Crusoe elects not to join Olivia on her voyage back to England. Based on the book by Daniel Defoe.

Cast: Phillip Winchester (Robinson Crusoe), Tongayi Chirisa (Friday), Mia Maestro (Olivia/Oliver). **Flashback Cast:** Anna Walton (Susannah), Sam Neill (Jeremiah Blackthorne), William Cooke (Young Robinson, age 6), Luke Gellard (Young Robinson, age 8), Barbara Bielecka (Young Susannah), Emma Barnett (Mary Crusoe).

Credits: *Executive Producer:* Justin Bodie, Jeffrey Hayes, Genevieve Hofmeyer, Michael Prupas, Stephen Greenberg, Jean Bureau, Philip Key. *Co-Executive Producer:* Chris Philip. *Music:* James Brett.

Reviews: "Handsomely shot and offering old fashioned end-of-the-week escapism, albeit with a character unable to escape his own Purgatory. That said, this would work better as a limited series than an open-end one" (*Variety*).

"Here's what it is like to be marooned with little hope of rescue and have to get by with few resources. No, it's not about NBC, but it's on NBC" (*The Hollywood Reporter*).

114   Cupid's Funniest Moments. (Special; Comedy; My Network TV; February 13, 2008)

A look at romantic mishaps that were caught on tape — from wedding woes to not-so-romantic proposals to "goofy relatives."

Host: Charles Shaughnessy.

Credits: *Executive Producer:* Paul Sharratt, David McKenzie. *Producer:* John Ross. *Associate Producer:* Heather Biggins. *Director:* David McKenzie. *Writer:* John Ross, Heather Biggins.

115   The Cutting Edge. (TV Movie; Drama; ABC Family; March 16, 2008)

Ice skating themed film about Zach and Alexandra, skating partners attempting to put their differences (and romance) aside to win an important competition by performing the dangerous Pamchecko jump.

Cast: Matt Lanter (Zach Conroy), Francia Raisa (Alexandra Delgado), Ben Hollingsworth (Jason Bright), Christy Carlson Romano (Jackie Dorsey), Stefano Colacitti (Bryan Hemmings), Alycia Purrott (Misha Pressel).

Credits: *Executive Producer:* Sara Berrisford, Hudson Hickman. *Producer:* Craig Roessler, Irene Litinsky. *Writer:* Randall M. Badar. *Director:* Stuart Gillard.

116   Cyclops. (TV Movie; Horror; Sci Fi; December 6, 2008)

Ancient Roman tale of a gladiator (Marcus), a beautiful barbarian warrior (Barbara) and a monster-like Cyclops (captured and befriended by Marcus) as they team to defeat and evil emperor (Tiberius) who rules the land with an unjust iron fist.

Cast: Kevin Stapleton (Marcus), Frida Farrell (Barbara), Eric Roberts (Emperor Tiberius), Craig Archibald (Falco), Dimitar Masiarski (Cyclops), Dan Golden (Master of Games), DeMorge Brown (Voice of Cyclops).

Credits: *Producer:* Roger Corman, Julie

Corman. *Music:* Tom Hiel. *Director:* Declan O'Brien. *Writer:* Frances Doel.

117 Dad's Funniest Moments.
(Special; Comedy; My Network TV; June 19, 2008)

A pre–Father's Day special that looks at comical moments involving fathers that were caught on tape by family members.

Host: Erik Estrada, Laura McKenzie.

Credits: *Executive Producer:* Paul Sharratt, David McKenzie. *Producer:* John Ross. *Associate Producer:* Heather Biggins. *Director:* David McKenzie. *Writer:* Heather Biggins, John Ross.

118 Dana Carvey: Squatting Monkeys Tell No Lies. (Special; Comedy; HBO; June 14, 2008)

Comedian Dana Carvey pokes fun at current topics, including global warming, safe sex, permissive parenting and the government. Taped before a live audience in Santa Rosa, California.

Star: Dana Carvey.

Credits: *Executive Producer:* Dana Carvey, Marc Gurvitz. *Supervising Producer:* John Moffitt, Pat Tourk Lee. *Writer:* Dana Carvey. *Director:* John Moffitt.

Reviews: "If you're looking for some laughs ... then I suggest you give Dana Carvey a try ... it's all good — and parts of it are pretty great" (*New York Post*).

"Time is not on Dana Carvey's side. No, age isn't the problem ... the problem is that tonight's hour-long HBO special ... features too many jokes that have timed out" (*New York Daily News*).

119 Dance Machine. (Series; Reality; ABC; June 27, 2008 to July 25, 2008)

Six amateur dancers compete against each other for $100,000 and the title: "Dance Machine." Each of the contestants performs several dance routines that are judged by the studio audience. The vote total at the end of each program determines the winner of that week's competition.

Host: Jason Kenndy.

Credits: *Executive Producer:* Greg Goldman, Chris Coelen, Brian Veskosky. *Producer:* Steven Russo, Matt Laesch. *Writer:* Frank Thompson. *Director:* Michael Simon.

120 Dance on Sunset. (Series; Reality; Nickelodeon; March 29, 2008 to May 31, 2008)

Six teenagers appear for the opportunity to perform with Nick 6, a group of six talented dancers. Each of the six contestants is mentored by choreographer Tony Testa and then competes in various dance style competitions. The studio audience then selects the best performer (a Sunset V.I.P.) to appear with Nick 6.

Choreographer: Tony Testa. **Nick 6:** Karen Chuany, Johnny Erasme, Ashley Galvan, Shane Harper, Quddus Phillippe, Hefa Leone Tuita.

Credits: *Executive Producer:* Dan Cutforth, Bryan Lader, Frederick Levy, Jane Lipsitz, Kay O'Connell. *Producer:* Ryan Cooper.

121 Dance War: Bruno vs. Carrie Ann. (Series; Reality; ABC; January 7, 2008 to February 10, 2008)

Dancing with the Stars spin-off with *Dancing* judges Bruno Tonioli and Carrie Ann Inaba mentoring a team of dancers. The teams perform in weekly contests with home viewers determining who stays and who goes (lowest votes). The last team standing receives the opportunity to tour with a major recording artist.

Host: Drew Lachey. **Captains:** Carrie Ann Inaba, Bruno Toniolo.

Credits: *Executive Producer:* John Hesling. *Co-Executive Producer:* Moisa Posi. *Supervising Producer:* Barry Egen. *Live Series Producer:* Ann Meadows.

Reviews: "'Dancing' judges Carrie Ann Inaba and Bruno Tonioli pluck the familiar chords for all they're worth, but inasmuch as everybody has seen these steps before, there is a war with a flawed battle plan" (*Variety*).

"What we have here is derivative, repetitive and unimaginative — the perfect six episode vehicle to keep the viewing public stupopously sated" (*The Hollywood Reporter*).

122 Daniel's Daughter. (TV Movie; Drama; Hallmark; January 26, 2008)

A journey of self discovery for a woman (Cate Madighan) when she honors the last request of her late father and returns to her Massachusetts hometown to spread his ashes.

Cast: Laura Leighton (Cate Madighan), Derek McGrath (Jim Cavanaugh), McKenzi Scott (Marie Madighan), Sebastian Spence (Connor Bailey), London Angelis (Seamus).

Credits: *Executive Producer:* Gerald W. Abrams, Susan Murdoch. *Producer:* David Till. *Writer:* Tracy Rosen. *Director:* Neill Fearnley. *Music:* Ian Thomas.

123 Date My Ex. (Series; Reality; Bravo; July 21, 2008 to September 22, 2008)

A spin off from *The Real Housewives of Orange County* that spotlights Jo De La Rosa and what happened to her after leaving the show (moving to Los Angeles and making an album). Jo's former fiancé, Slade Smiley is present to help her adjust to a new lifestyle and help her find a new boyfriend.

Star: Jo De La Rosa. **Jo's Roommates:** Slade Smiley, Mayia Ingoldsby and Kay Metz.

Credits: *Executive Producer:* Greg Stewart, Kathleen French, Douglas Ross. *Supervising Producer:* Larry Grimaldi. *Producer:* Shoshanna Ezra.

124 David Blaine: Dive of Death. (Special; Reality; ABC; September 24, 2008)

Street magician David Blaine performs his established illusions then attempts, but fails on live TV, to accomplish a death-defying feat (diving off a building).

Star: David Blaine.

Credits: *Executive Producer:* Mary-Jane April, David Blaine, Nancy Stern. *Co-Executive Producer:* Denise Albert. *Producer:* Kathy Welch, Bill Kalush. *Director:* Roger Goodman. *Writer:* James Spector.

125 The Daytime Emmy Awards. (Special; Variety; ABC; June 20, 2008)

The 35th annual presentation that honors the best in daytime television.

Host: Cameron Mathison, Sherri Shepherd. **Appearing:** Tyra Banks, Peter Bergman, Carson Brown, David Canary, Crystal Chappell, Jeanne Cooper, Ellen DeGeneres, Portia de Rossi, Anthony Geary, Regis Philbin, Greg Rikaart, Michelle Stafford, Heather Tom.

Credits: *Executive Producer:* Ricky Kirshner, Glenn Weiss. *Supervising Producer:* Jim Mullen. *Producer:* Mark R. Leed, Ann R. Jones. *Director:* Glenn Weiss. *Music:* Glen Roven. *Writer:* Dave Boone.

126 DEA. (Series; Reality; Spike TV; April 2, 2008 to May 7, 2008)

A look at the work of DEA (Drug Enforcement Administration) agents as seen through the activities of the agents attached to the Detroit Division.

Credits: *Executive Producer:* Al Roker, C. Russell Muth, Hank Capshaw. *Co-Executive Producer:* Alex Eastburg.

127 Dead at 17. (TV Movie; Drama; Lifetime; May 31, 2008)

A mother (Alyssa), assisted by her daughter (Danni) seeks to uncover the mysterious circumstances that forced her 17-year-old son to commit suicide.

Cast: Barbara Niven (Alyssa), Danielle Kind (Danni), Cynthia Preston (Julie), John Bregar (Cody), Justin Bradley (Gabe), Kyle Switzer (Ty), Catherine Mary Stewart (Holly), Odessa Rae (Shari), Linden Ashby (Curt Masterson), Benz Antoine (Det. Reese).

Credits: *Executive Producer:* Tom Berry, Pierre David, Ashley Jones, Louis A. Massicotte. *Producer:* Neil Bregman, Stefan Wodoslawsky. *Music:* Richard Bowers.

128 The Deadliest Lesson. (TV Movie; Drama; Lifetime Movie Network; November 8, 2008)

Tense drama about a high school teacher (Gloria) who witnesses a gang-related murder then finds herself fighting for her life when the gang seeks to keep her from contacting the police by declaring war on her and her small group of troubled students during a special Saturday detention session.

Cast: Penelope Ann Miller (Gloria), Jeremy Luc (Benny), Alison Brie (Amber), Yancey Arias (Daniel), Jason Gretch (Mo), Christian Monzon (Leo), Peter Pasco (Dwayne Evert), Carlos Sanz (Larry Keillor), Alex Solowitz (Christian).

Credits: *Executive Producer:* Robert Halmi, Jr., Larry Levinson, Kevin Mocarde. *Co-Executive Producer:* Michael Moran. *Producer:* Brian Martinez, Erik Olsen. *Director:* Harry Winer. *Writer:* Rachel Stuhler.

129 Deal or No Deal. (Series; Game; Syn.; Premiered: September 8, 2008)

A syndicated daytime version of the NBC primetime series (see program 740). Changes: Twenty-two studio audience members appear on stage, each of whom holds a case containing an unknown amount of money. A wheel containing 22 numbers is spun. The contestant pinpointed by the wheel when it stops plays for a chance to win $500,000. The case the player holds becomes his case for the duration of the game. From this point on the game is played in the same manner, with players choosing cases, hoping to keep the large amounts ($50,000 to $500,000) in play while selecting the smaller amounts (one cent to $25,000) for large offers from the banker to buy their case and what money amount it contains. The player continues (risking loss of large

cash offers if he opens the top amounts) or can quit and sell his case at any offer.

Host: Howie Mandel. **Wheel Models:** Tameka Jacobs, Patricia Kara.

Credits: *Executive Producer:* Scott St. John. *Supervising Producer:* David Floyd, Brian Veskosky. *Producer:* Judy C. Helm.

130 Dear Prudence. (Pilot; Crime Drama; Hallmark; August 23, 2008)

"Dear Prudence" is a newspaper advice column (household tips) written by Prudence McCoy, a Martha Stewart–like woman who also hosts a New York based how-to television program. Prudence, famous for her "Pru Points" (anything from removing stains to getting rid of squeaks), is also an amateur sleuth who has a knack for stumbling upon crimes. Although Prudence can determine foul play, she cannot solve a crime alone. She acquires the assistance of Nigel Forsythe III, a genius who heads her TV lab. The proposed series was to follow Prudence and Nigel as they set out to solve crimes in a most unusual way — combining household knowledge with the technical wizardry provided by Nigel.

Cast: Jane Seymour (Prudence McCoy), Ryan Cartwright (Nigel Forsythe III), Jamey Sheridan (Sheriff Eddie Duncan)

Credits: *Executive Producer:* Tom Cox, Jordy Randall, Murray Ord, Rob Gilmer, Les Alexander, Jonathan Mitchell. *Producer:* Andrew Baynes. *Music:* Andrea Saparoff.

Reviews "As a murder mystery, *Dear Prudence* leaves a lot to be desired, including here, for example, suspense" (*The Hollywood Reporter*).

"*Dear Prudence* ... is mild entertainment in the tradition of the Saturday night TV movie that works because it leans on the charisma of its star" (*Variety*).

131 Deion and Pilar: Prime Time Love. (Series; Reality; Oxygen; April 15, 2008 to June 3, 2008)

Deion Sanders is a wealthy athlete who played in both major league baseball and football. He is married to Pilar and they are the parents of five children, ages 3 to 16. Deion is now retired and cameras follow Deion and his family as they go about living their daily lives.

Stars: Deion Sanders, Pilar Sanders, Deiondra Sanders.

Credits: *Executive Producer:* Kevin Lee, Rob Rollins, Deion Sanders, Sam Sokolow. *Associate Producer:* Paul Baker, Mindy Davis. *Segment Producer:* John Vidas.

Review: "What they (Deion and Pilar) cannot do, unfortunately, is convincingly play themselves ... instead they find themselves at the center of a bad reality-based sitcom ... the show is many things, but ready for prime time isn't one of them" (*Variety*).

132   Denise Richards: It's Complicated. (Series; Reality; E!; May 26, 2008 to June 7, 2008)

A look at the life of actress Denise Richards (divorced from Charlie Sheen), the mother of two girls (Samantha and Lola Rose), and the owner of numerous pets — ten dogs, four house-pet pigs and three cats. Cameras follow Denise as she goes about her daily activities. Also featured are her father (Irv), Michelle (her married sister), Trish and Kim (her longtime friends) and Sho Shingu (her personal assistant).

Cast: Denise Richards, Samantha Sheen, Lola Rose Sheen.

Credits: *Executive Producer:* Ryan Seacrest, Kevin Lee. *Co–Executive Producer:* Vince Rotonda, Eliot Goldberg. *Supervising Producer:* Jeff Oliver. *Producer:* Amy Loeber. *Director:* Melissa Bidwell.

Reviews: "Richards joined the growing conga line of personalities who have sought image redemption by welcoming reality producers into the extended family, only to reveal more about how messed up they are then intended ... and we are the voyeurs" (*Variety*).

"For those of you who actually care about the drama surrounding former Bond girl and star of 1997's *Starship Troopers* ... this show will give you half the story" (*Entertain Your Brain*).

133   Depth Charge. (TV Movie; Drama; Spike; September 1, 2008)

Action drama about Raymond Ellers, a doctor aboard a U.S. nuclear submarine, as he struggles to stop the sub's deranged commander (Krieg) from destroying Washington, D.C. if he doesn't get a $1 billion ransom within 24 hours.

Cast: Jason Gedrick (Raymond "Doc" Ellers), Ric Roberts (Commander Krieg), Barry Bostwick (President Taylor), Corbin Bernsen (Captain Richards), Bridgit Ann White (Katie McCallister), Chris Warren, Jr. (James Piersall).

Credits: *Executive Producer:* Robert Halmi, Jr., Richard Levinson. *Co–Executive Producer:* Nick Lombardo, H. Daniel Gross, Michael Moran. *Producer:* Kyle Clark, Stephen Niver. *Director:* Terrence O'Hara. *Music:* Stephen Graziano. *Writer:* Dennis Pratt.

Reviews: "The good news — perhaps even the shocking news is that the Spike flick *Depth Charge* is not only tolerable, but surprisingly good" (*The Hollywood Reporter*).

"The movie is pretty clear about its slacker mentality... Yet a bit more care could have been envisioned before shoving *Depth Charge* into the torpedo tubes" (*Variety*).

134   Descendants of Darkness. (Series; Cartoon; Sci Fi; Premiered: July 28, 2008)

Shinigami are supernatural detectives who have only one mission: make sure deceased souls move on. The Shinigami are unique in that they are also dead but have been granted special "alive" status to make up for unsettled incidents in their past lives. Particular focus is on Asato Tsuzki and his partner, Hisoka Kurasaki. Stories follow their case assignments as they attempt to return souls to their proper realms. Hindering their efforts is Dr. Kazutaka Muraki, a deranged serial killer. Produced in Japan.

Voice Cast: Dan Green (Asato), Liam O'Brien (Hisoka), Edward MacLeod (Kazutaka), Chunky Mon (Chief Konoe).

Credits: *Executive Producer:* John O'Donnell. *Producer:* Stephanie Shalofsky.

135   Dick Clark's New Year's Rockin' Eve 2009. (Special; Variety; ABC; December 31, 2008 to January 1, 2009)

ABC's annual New Year's Eve event that rings in the new year with performances by the top names in show business coupled with reports from Times Square in New York City as the ball drops and the seconds count down to 2009.

Host (New York): Dick Clark, Ryan Seacrest. **Host (Los Angeles):** Fergie. **Times Square Correspondent:** Kellie Pickler. **Guests:** Natasha Bedingfield, Jesse McCartney, The Pussycat Dolls, Robin Thicke, Solange Knowles, Fall Out Boy, Ne-Yo.

Credits: *Executive Producer:* Dick Clark, Ryan Seacrest, Orly Adelson. *Producer:* Larry Klein. *Director:* Barry Glazer, Bruce Gowers. *Writer:* Barry Adelman, Fred Bronson.

136   Di Gatti Defenders. (Series; Cartoon; Fox; September 13, 2008 to December 27, 2008)

Adam, Erik, Kara, Melosa and Seth are the Di Gatta Defenders, teenagers who are dedicated to protecting the Realm of Rados from the Order of the Infinis, evil beings seeking absolute power. Professor Alnar is the teen's mentor. The evil Lord Nazmul and his co-horts Brackus, Malco and Flinch are the principal villains of the Order of Infinis.

Voice Cast: Jeremy From (Adam), Stephanie Beard (Kara), Martha MacIssac

(Melosa), Dan Petronijevic (Erik), Noah Cappe (Seth).

137   The Dish. (Series; Talk; Style Network; Premiered: August 16, 2008)

Actress Danielle Fishel (*Boy Meets World*) presides over a lively series that looks at aspects of beauty, fashion and pop culture.

Host: Danielle Fishel.

Credits: *Producer:* Edward Boyd, K.P. Anderson.

138   Disney Channel Games. (Series; Game; Disney; July 20, 2008 to August 17, 2008)

An annual summer event (began in 2006) that has fifty Disney Channel stars competing in various physical challenges for the coveted Disney Channel Games Cup. Taped at Walt Disney World in Orlando, Florida.

TV Host: Brian Stepanek. **Online Host:** Meaghan Jette Martin.

Credits: *Executive Producer:* Skot Bright, Sascha Penn. *Music:* Scott Clausen, Christopher A. Lee.

139   Do Not Disturb. (Series; Comedy; Fox; September 10, 2008 to September 24, 2008)

The Inn is a hotel located next to Radio City Music Hall in New York City. It is overseen by Rhonda, the Human Resources chief, and managed by the woman-chasing Neal Danner. Nicole, the front desk supervisor, is a gorgeous but ditzy blonde who yearns to become a model. Billy is the head of security (replaced by Darren); Tasha is the reservations clerk; Molly, a plus-size model, works the switchboard. Austin is the bartender; Gus is the bellman and Larry, another employee, is a gay who feels that having a steady boyfriend (Victor) is hindering his ability to flirt. Stories focus on the antics of the staff as they go about running a hotel that appears to have few or no guests.

Cast: Jerry O'Connell (Neal Danner), Nicey Nash (Rhonda), Molly Stanton (Nicole), Jesse Tyler Ferguson (Larry), Jolene Purdy (Molly), Taylor Cole (Tasha), RonReaco Lee (Billy), Dave Franco (Gus), Alex Quijano (Darren), Blake Hood (Austin).

Credits: *Executive Producer:* Abraham Higginbotham, Howard Owens, Carolyn Bernstein, Paul Young, Peter Principato, E. Brian Dobbins. *Co-Executive Producer:* Kirk Rudell, Sally Bradford. *Producer:* John Quaintance, Kevin Slattery. *Music:* Paul Buckley.

Reviews: "They say sitcoms are just one hit away from making a comeback to their previous glory. Maybe so, but *Do Not Disturb* isn't it. This is a show that could bury the genre altogether" (*The Hollywood Reporter*).

"For comedy scribes and those who love them, be disturbed. Be very disturbed" (*Variety*).

140 **Dr. Horrible's Sing-a-Long Blog.** (Series; Comedy; Internet; Premiered: July 15, 2008)

Dr. Horrible is a would-be super villain who has applied (by mail) for acceptance into the Evil League of Evil. Unfortunately, Dr. Horrible is not yet evil enough to join and must prove his evilness to become a member. As Dr. Horrible plots villainous deeds he also breaks into song to musically detail his plans. Penny is the girl Dr. Horrible loves, but is too shy to approach her; Captain Hammer is the law enforcer seeking to end Dr. Horrible's reign.

Cast: Neil Patrick Harris (Dr. Horrible), Felicia Day (Penny), Nathan Fillion (Captain Hammer).

Review: "It's a fantastic plot rooted in our odd cultural moment — the mushroom like blooming of celebrity video blogs, or vlogs and our collective fascination with super heroes — and it's very good" (*The Hollywood Reporter*).

141 **Dr. Jekyll and Mr. Hyde.** (TV Movie; Drama; Ion; May 17, 2008)

Contemporary adaptation of the classic story about a respected physician (Dr. Jekyll) whose experiments produce an evil alter ego (Mr. Hyde).

Cast: Dougray Scott (Dr. Jekyll/Mr. Hyde), Claire Wheaton (Krista Bridges), Tom Skerritt (Gabe Utterson), Danette MacKay (Mrs. Poole), Ellen David (Det. Newcombe), Cas Anvar (D.A. McBride).

Credits: *Executive Producer:* Robert Halmi, Jr., Robert Halmi, Sr. *Producer:* Irene Litinsky. *Writer:* Paul B. Margolis. *Director:* Paolo Barzman. *Music:* FM Le Sieur.

Review: "Robert Louis Stevenson's strange tale of split personality has long fascinated film makers, but the translation has seldom been quite as limp and boring as this European production... Despite the story's enduring allure, something is clearly a miss with this latest potion" (*Variety*).

142 **The Doctors.** (Series; Talk; Syn.; Premiered: September 8, 2008)

A spin-off from *Dr. Phil* that incorporates a group of medical professionals who discuss health related topics and questions submitted by home viewers.

Doctors: Travis Stork (also the host), Lisa Masterson, Andrew Ordon, Jim Sears.

Credits: *Executive Producer:* Phil McGraw, Jay McGraw, Carla Pennington. *Co-Executive Producer:* Andrew Scher. *Supervising Producer:* George Davilas, Jeff Hudson.

Review: "Despite promising 'a brand new way to talk about medicine,' *The Doctors* ... actually recycles several old ways, all of them daytime TV or radio staples" (*Variety*).

143 **Dorm Life.** (Series; Comedy; Internet; June–July 2008)

Brief incidents in the lives of a group of college students who seem to encounter mishap before, after and during classes.

Cast: Jim Brandon (Gopher Reed), Jack DeSena (Shane Reilly), Pancho Morris (Josh Morgan), Jordan Riggs (David Benjamin), Brian C. Singleton (Michael Adame), Chris W. Smith (Mike Sanders), Jessie Hannah Pearl Utt (Brittany Wilcox), Anne Lane (Abigail Constance Brown), Nora Kirkpatrick (Courtney Cloverlock).
Credits: *Executive Producer:* Garrett Law, Peter White. *Producer:* Brian C. Singleton, Chris W. Smith. *Music:* Jeff Toyne.

144   A Double Shot at Love. (Series; Reality; MTV; Premiered: December 9, 2008)

If one bisexual woman (Tila Tequila) can seek a mate on the series *A Shot at Love with Tequila*, why not gorgeous bisexual twins (Rikki and Vikki Ikki)? With that thought in mind, *A Double Shot at Love* literally places Rikki and Vikki against each other as they are introduced to both male and female singles who compete in challenges to win the affections of the twins. The first episode however does not reveal to the contestants that the "girl" they seek is actually twins. In sequences reminiscent of the adult film *The Good Girls of Godiva High* the twins seduce the singles as one girl (each taking a turn and letting the subjects believe it is the same girl. While one twin seduces, the other watches the action via closed circuit TV). "Shock" is expressed when the contestants learn that Rikki and Vikki are twins and the program proceeds to hit rock bottom as it allows viewers to see the "action" as Rikki and Vikki battle each other for their perfect mate.
Stars: Rikki Ikki, Vikki Ikki.
Credits: *Executive Producer:* Sally Ann Salsano, Scott Jeffrees. *Supervising Producer:* Pam LaLima. *Producer:* Amy Griggs.
Review: "MTV generally doesn't send programs out for review, and absorbing an utterly mindless exercise like *A Double Shot at Love* ... it's clear why" (*Variety*).

145   Down and Dirty with Jim Norton. (Series; Comedy; HBO; Premiered: October 3, 2008)

A weekly program that features uncensored performances by up and coming as well as established stand-up comics.
Host: Jim Norton.
Credits: *Executive Producer:* John Irwin, David Steinberg. *Producer:* Mason Steinberg, Tina Magnuson.

146   Down Home with the Neelys. (Series; Cooking; Food Network; Premiered: February 2, 2008)

Chefs Gina and Pat Neely, assisted by their children (Tony, Mark, Gaelin, Shelbi and Lorine) prepare meals from their home in Memphis, Tennessee.
Hosts: Gina Neely, Pat Neely.
Credits: *Executive Producer:* Gordon Elliott, Mark Schneider. *Supervising Producer:* Aimee Rosen. *Producer:* Sara Porter.

147   The Drinky Crow Show. (Series; Cartoon; Cartoon Network; Premiered: November 19, 2008)

A not for kids animated program, broadcast on the Adult Swim block of the Cartoon Network, that adapts the *L.A. Weekly* comic strip ("Maakies") to television. A rather dark (and offensive to some) look at the pitiful lives of two friends: Drinky Crow and Uncle Gabby. Drinky, like his name implies, lives on alcohol as it provides him with the only sunshine in his depressing life. Uncle Gabby, a drunken sailor, has a life that revolves around booze, food, sleep and sex.
Voice Cast: Dino Stamatapoulos (Drinky Crow), David Herman (Uncle Gabby/Captain), Becky Thyre (Captain's Daughter)
Credits: *Executive Producer:* Tony Millionaire, Nick Weidenfeld, Eric Kaplan. *Producer:* Raduca Kaplan. *Music:* Brass Castle, Charles Sydnor.
Review: "It's violent, uncouth, vulgar and consistently funny, though in the

morning you might hate yourself for laughing" (*The Hollywood Reporter*).

148 Easter's Funniest Moments. (Special; Comedy; My Network TV; April 19, 2008)

A springtime special in which comical Easter Sunday mishaps caught on tape are presented.

Host: Erik Estrada, Laura McKenzie. **Credits:** *Executive Producer:* Paul Sharratt, David McKenzie. *Producer:* John Ross. *Associate Producer:* Heather Biggins. *Director:* David McKenzie. *Writer:* Heather Biggins, John Ross.

149 Easy Money. (Series; Comedy; CW; October 5, 2008 to November 23, 2008)

In the small Southwestern town of South Nile there exists the Prestige Pay Day Loans Company. It is run by the Buffkin family. It's motto is "Credit a wreck? We've got your check." And for people desperately in need of money, they can get it with a twenty-five percent weekly interest rate.

Bobette is the brains behind the business. Roy, her husband, supervises operations. Their children, Cooper, Brandy and Morgan, assist. Cooper handles the computers; Morgan is the enforcer (goes after dead beats); Brandy runs the office. Cherise is Cooper's wife; Julia is Morgan's girlfriend, a genetics grad student; Mike is Brandy's husband; Shep is the wheelchair bound friend of the family; Barry is the rather seedy ex-cop Morgan uses for help when needed. Stories follow the Buffkins as they deal with the various people who come to them for a fast loan.

Cast: Laurie Metcalf (Bobette Buffkin), Nick Searcy (Roy Buffkin), Jeff Hephner (Morgan Buffkin), Katie Lowes (Brandy Buffkin), Jay R. Ferguson (Cooper Buffkin), Marsha Thompson (Julia), Kimberly Estrada (Cherise Buffkin), Gary Farmer (Shep), Judge Reinhold (Barry), Joe Peracchio (Mike Klink).

Credits: *Executive Producer:* Diane Frolov, Jimmy Mulville, Andrew Schneider. *Co-Executive Producer:* Brandon Hill. *Producer:* Bobby Gaylor.

Reviews: "Extremely topical, well acted and surprisingly touching, *Easy Money* is a promising new entry... The series has that quirky, character-driven appeal that resonates well with viewers" (*Variety*).

"An engaging series like this should pay off for the CW" (*The Hollywood Reporter*).

150 Easy to Assemble. (Series; Comedy; Internet; Premiered: September 22, 2008)

Fed up with her life as an actress, Illeana Douglas impulsively decides to quit and begin a new career as a clerk at a local IKEA in Hollywood. Stories follow Illeana's still hectic life as former aspects of her life — from agents to gossip columnists to adoring fans — still plague her.

Cast: Illeana Douglas (Herself), Rebecca Lord (Amber), Michael Valdsgaard (Bjorn), Jane Lynch (Gjorn), Alan Havey (Stalker).

151 Edgar and Ellen. (Series; Cartoon; Cartoon Network; Premiered: October 7, 2008)

Edgar and Ellen are a brother and sister who live in a mansion on the edge of the town of Nod's Limbs. Edgar and Ellen however, are not your normal twins: they have a Charles Addams drawn look to them and they are quite mischievous. They have a hairy, one -eyed pet called Pet and stories relate their endless efforts to find excitement by pulling pranks on the hopeless citizens of Nod's Limbs.

Voice Cast: Kathleen Barr (Edgar/Berenice), Jillian Michaels (Ellen/Cassidy), Ashleigh Ball (Stephanie/Pepper/Principal Mulberry), Ian James Corlett (Poe/Slug).

Credits: *Executive Producer:* Trish Lindsay, Delna Bhesania, Barry Ward, Barbara Ferro. *Supervising Producer:* Rose Ann Tisserand, John Bush.

152 **The 808**. (Series; Reality; Fuel TV; 2008)

A look at the lives, struggles and ambitions of the professional surfers who swarm to Hawaii's North Shore of Oahu each winter.

Featured Surfers: Kala Alexander, Alexander DaHu, Eddie Rothman, Makua Rothman, Andy Irons, Bruce Irons, Kai Garcia, Kamalei Alexander.

153 **Eleventh Hour (British)**. (Series; Science Fiction; BBC America; 2008)

The British series on which the American series of the same title is based. Ian Hood is a former physics professor who is recruited by the British government to investigate a new problem that has arisen: human disasters and tragedies caused by modern medical experimentation. Rachel Young assists Ian and stories follow their efforts to stop those who exploit the new technologies despite what dangerous results occur.

Cast: Patrick Stewart (Prof. Ian Hood), Ashley Jensen (Rachel Young).

Credits: *Executive Producer:* Andy Harries. *Producer:* Stephen Smallwood. *Music:* The Insects.

154 **Eleventh Hour (U.S.)**. (Series; Science Fiction; CBS; Premiered: October 9, 2008)

Dr. Jacob Hood is a brilliant biophysicist who is also a special science advisor for the U.S. government. As medical technologies advance, there are unscrupulous individuals who seek to profit from them, no matter what the cost. Dr. Hood is a man who is dedicated to protecting the substance of science from those nefarious motives. When abuse is detected and a scientific or medical crisis has arisen, Dr. Hood becomes the last line of defense (called in at the eleventh hour). Stories follow Dr. Hood as he risks his life to solve scientific crimes before unspeakable horrors are set on mankind. Rachel Young, a special FBI protection agent, assists Dr. Hood. Based on the British series.

Cast: Rufus Sewell (Dr. Jacob Hood), Marley Shelton (Rachel Young).

Credits: *Executive Producer:* Jerry Bruckheimer, Jonathan Littman, Ethan Reiff, Cyrus Voris, Danny Cannon, Mick Davis, Paul Buccieri. *Music:* Graeme Revell.

Reviews: "Less than compelling knock off [of the British series of the same title]" (*New York Post*).

"How ironic then, that the *Eleventh Hour* premiere focuses on unethical clones because if cloning were really a major crime in TV, CBS executives could have the book thrown at them" (*Variety*).

155 **Eli Stone**. (Series; Drama; ABC; January 31, 2008 to December 17, 2008)

Wethersby, Posner and Klein is a San Francisco based law firm that employs Eli Stone, a cold-hearted attorney obsessed with winning cases no matter who gets hurt. One day life changes for Eli when he begins to hear (and see) George Michael singing the song "Faith" everywhere he goes. The problem is — no one else can. Shortly after, when Eli becomes involved in a pro-bono case (helping a woman prove a drug company was responsible for her son's autism) he has a change of heart. He becomes compassionate and asks to head the firm's pro-bono division. The visions and songs, however, have not stopped. An MRI reveals that Eli has an inoperable brain aneurism that could explain the visions. With the help of his holistic doctor, Fred Lobukowski (who practices under the name Dr. Chen), Eli hopes to cope with his condition and visions. Stories follow Eli as he now fights for the little guy while at the same time trying to cope with the changes that are occurring in his life.

Jordan Wethersby is the senior law partner; Taylor is his daughter (and Eli's fiancé); Patti is Eli's secretary; Matt David is a lawyer with the firm; Nathan Stone, a doctor, is Eli's brother.

Cast: Jonny Lee Miller (Eli Stone), Victor Garber (Jordan Wetersby), Natasha Henstridge (Taylor Wetersby), Loretta Devine (Patti), James Saito (Dr. Chen), Sam Jaeger (Matt Dowd), Lauren Benanti (Beth Keller).

Credits: *Executive Producer:* Greg Berlanti, Marc Guggenheim, Chris Misiano. *Co-Executive Producer:* Andrew A. Ackerman. *Co-Producers:* Michael Cedar, Melissa Berman, Jennifer Lence. *Music:* Blake Neely.

Reviews: "The series does have an engaging star ... and a willingness to tackle spiritual issues, but ... ground Eli's journey with advocating for the little guy court cases" (*Variety*).

"Eli Stone nibbles at the corners of other series, including *Ghost Whisperer* and *Saving Grace* that will ... guide Stone from his unacceptable atheism to a more conventional belief in a divine spirit" (*The Hollywood Reporter*).

156 Ellen's Even Bigger Really Big Show. (Special; Variety; TBS; November 29, 2008)

A sequel to *Ellen's Really Big Show* (TBS, November 2007) that features comedy from Ellen DeGeneres as well as variety acts from around the world (magicians, dancers, singers and music acts). Taped at Caesar's Palace in Las Vegas and a much better effort than *Rosie Live!* (see entry) at reviving the variety series on television (although this too, as of December 31, 2008) has not produced a series.

Host: Ellen DeGeneres.

Credits: *Executive Producer:* Mary Connelly, Ed Glavin, Andrew Lasiner. *Supervising Producer:* J.P. Buck. *Producer:* Douglas C. Forbes. *Director:* Michael Dempsey. *Writer:* Alison Balian.

157 The Emmy Awards. (Special; Variety; ABC; September 21, 2008)

The 60th annual presentation that honors the best in broadcast and cable television.

Hosts: Tom Bergeron, Heidi Klum, Howie Mandel, Jeff Probst, Ryan Seacrest. **Presenters Include:** Christina Applegate, Candice Bergen, David Boreanaz, Wayne Brady, Kristin Chenoweth, America Ferrera, Tina Fey, Lawrence Fishburne, Kathy Griffin, Neil Patrick Harris, Teri Hatcher, Jennifer Love Hewitt, Felicity Huffman, Hugh Laurie, Don Rickles, Nicollette Sheridan, Kiefer Sutherland, Vanessa Williams.

Credits: *Executive Producer:* Ken Ehrlich. *Producer:* Renato Basile. *Co-Producer:* Danette Herman. *Director:* Louis J. Horvitz. *Writer:* David Wild, Jon Macks, Ken Ehrlich.

158 Estate of Panic. (Series; Reality; Sci Fi; November 12, 2008 to December 17, 2008)

Seven players (per show) compete for the opportunity to win large sums of money. A "haunted house" is the setting and players must search for money hidden in the booby-trapped house; for example, a room filled with non-poisonous snakes; rooms that fill with water. Three challenges (searches) are presented on each show and after each challenge the weakest performers are eliminated (those that became frightened and were unable to finish the room search, those that just couldn't find what the challenge called for, or those with the least amount of found money). Two players are eliminated per room challenge. The last person standing (recovering the most money) faces a final challenge in the vault room. If he can successfully complete the task he wins the available money (what ever was found in the prior challenges and which was placed in the bank).

Host: Steve Valentine.

Credits: *Executive Producer:* Richard Hall. *Co-Executive Producer:* Alex Rader. *Supervising Producer:* Barry Hennessy. *Music:* Yoav Goren.

Review: "Simple-minded players endure

a parade of silly stunts and contests, but this cheeky show is mostly an ordeal for viewers" (*Variety*).

159   Every Second Counts. (TV Movie; Drama; Hallmark; July 12, 2008)

Brooke Preston is a 17-year-old girl who dreams of becoming a veterinarian. Her father, ex-rodeo rider Joe Preston, has trained Brooke for the circuit and sees her as a way of helping his family survive financial difficulties. The story follows Brooke as she puts her dreams on hold to compete in rodeo pinning contests to help her family.

Cast: Stephen Collins (Joe Preston), Magda Apanowicz (Brooke Preston), Barbara Williams (Helen Preston), Brett Dier (Caden), Chelah Horsdal (Miss Allen), Eric Keenleyside (Dutch), Jim Shield (Ken).

Credits: *Executive Producer:* Lewis Chesler, Paulina Mielech, David Permutter. *Producer:* Elizabeth Sanchez, Robert Vaughn. *Music:* Stacey Hersh. *Writer:* Arthur Martin, Jr. *Director:* John Bradshaw.

Review: "It's down right refreshing to see a film that isn't some Technicolor teen fantasy ... as far as family dramas go, this is a summer gem" (*Variety*).

160   The Ex-List. (Series; Comedy-Drama; CBS; October 3, 2008 to October 24, 2008)

Bella Bloom is a pretty 32-year-old single woman and the owner of her own floral shop (Bloom Flowers). One day, while with a group of friends, Bella is coached into having a psychic reading. It changes the course of her life. She learns that if she doesn't marry within one year she will spend the rest of her life alone. She is also told that her future husband is someone she already dated — but who? Believing what she was told, Bella makes a list of her ex flames and sets out on a search to find her one true love. Each episode presents Bella's encounter with an ex from their first meeting (seen in a flashback) to her current efforts to discover why the relationship broke off. Daphne is Bella's sister; Vivian, a high school history teacher, Augie and Cyrus are her friends and roommates; Rufus is Bella's dog. Based on the Israeli series *The Mythological Ex*.

Cast: Elizabeth Reaser (Bella Bloom), Rachel Boston (Daphne Bloom), Alexander Breckenridge (Vivian), Adam Rothenberg (Augie), Amir Talai (Cyrus), William Russ (Bella's father), Anne Bedian (Psychic).

Credits: *Executive Producer:* Segahl Avin, Avi Nir, Mosh Danon, Jonathan Levin, Diane Ruggiero. *Producer:* Jimmy Simons. *Music:* Frankie Pine.

Reviews: "*The Ex-List* is one of those rare new surprises that constantly charms straight out of the box, boasting a clear premise ... and a disarmingly appealing lead in Elizabeth Reaser" (*The Hollywood Reporter*).

"There's a twinkle in the eye of this show ... especially in the performance of ... Elizabeth Reaser... There's enough heat to warrant a second date, but not enough sparks to guarantee one" (*Variety*).

161   Eyes on Kenya. (Special; Variety; My Network TV; December 3, 2008)

Cameras follow celebrities as they travel throughout Kenya, East Africa, taking in the breathtaking countryside, viewing animals, visiting needy children (and offering hope) and embarking on a safari. The program also features traditional African music and holiday songs.

Host: Roger Moore. **Celebrities:** Dean Cain, Shannon Elizabeth, Kyle Massey, Christopher Massey, Louis Gossett, Jr.

Credits: *Executive Producer:* David McKenzie, Paul Sharratt. *Producer-Writer:* John Ross. *Director:* David McKenzie, John Ross.

162   Fab Five: The Texas Cheerleader Scandal. (TV Movie; Drama; Lifetime; August 2, 2008)

Factual movie based on events that took place in McKinney (a Dallas, Texas suburb) about five cheerleaders (Brooke, Jeri, Lisa, Ashley and Tabitha, known as "The Fab Five") as they defy teachers, parents and school authorities to do what they want — from drinking to posting suggestive photos on the Internet.

Cast: Tatum O'Neal (Lorene Tippet), Ashley Benson (Brooke Tippet), Jessica Heap (Jeri Blackburn), Aimee Spring Fortier (Lisa Toledo), Stephanie Honore (Ashley), Ashlynn Ross (Tabitha Doering), Jenna Dewan (Emma Carr), Carissa Capobianco (Cindy Harper), Hailey Wist (Meagan Harper), Dameon Clarke (Adam Reeve), Daniel Newman (Trevor).

Credits: *Executive Producer:* Orly Adelson. *Co-Executive Producer:* Jonathan Eskenas. *Producer:* Bob Wilson, *Writer:* Teena Booth. *Director:* Tom McLoughlin.

Review: "Insane and inane and perfect for a slow Saturday night when the second most exciting choice is a visit to the late night nail joint down the street" (*New York Post*).

163 Factory. (Series; Comedy; Spike TV; June 29, 2008 to July 27, 2008)

A small town factory located in any city that could make anything (nothing is exactly identified) is the setting for a look at the life of the blue collar worker as depicted through the antics of four buffoons: Gary, Smitty, Chase and Gus.

Cast: Mitch Rouse (Gary), David Pasquesi (Smitty), Michael Coleman (Chase), Jay Leggett (Gus).

Credits: *Executive Producer:* Mitch Rouse, John D. Lynch, Dave Becky, Michael Rotenberg. *Supervising Producer:* Ken Lipman.

Reviews: "*Factory* quickly devolves into a meaningless slapstick of goofy faces and a forced awkwardness that suggests the vision of someone who has watched *Curb Your Enthusiasm* over and over but still has

not figured out what makes it so funny" (*The Hollywood Reporter*).

"While it's unlikely this *Factory* will mass-produce anytime soon, sticking with these Cro-Magnons could pay dividends down the line" (*Variety*).

164 Faith Hill: Joy to the World. (Special; Variety; PBS; December 18, 2008)

Singer Faith Hill celebrates the Christmas holiday with songs from her album "Joy to the World" (including "A Baby Changes Everything," "Have a Holly Jolly Christmas," "Winter Wonderland" and "Little Drummer Boy").

Host: Faith Hill.

Credits: *Producer-Director:* Joe Thomas. *Co-Producer:* Christine Davies. *Orchestra:* David Campbell. *Backup Vocals:* Crystal Talicfero, Penny Coleman, Wendy Moten.

165 Family Court with Judge Penny. (Series; Reality; Syn.; Premiered: September 9, 2008)

Real cases involving matters that affect families, from husbands vs. wives to parents suing their children.

Judge: Penny Brown Reynolds. **Bailiff:** Damon Ormsby. **Narrator:** Bill Fike.

Credits: *Executive Producer:* Stephanie Drachkovitch, Rasha Drachkovitch, Judge Penny Brown Reynolds, Jill Blackstone. *Co-Executive Producer:* Glenn Mehan. *Supervising Producer:* Mike Kopplin. *Producer:* Ted Bortolin, Matthew Flynn, Angela Ford.

166 Family Entertainment Awards. (Special; Variety; CW; December 12, 2008)

The annual ANA Alliance for Family Entertainment presentation that honors the shows, actors, actresses and producers that support family friendly programs. Only the winning subject in each category is revealed, followed by a short clip to illustrate the choice. Also featured is an emotional tribute to John Ritter by Kaley

Cuoco, who is brought to tears when she reflects on working with John on the series *Eight Simple Rules*. Originally aired as *The Family Television Awards*.

Host: Tyler James Williams. **Guests:** Miley Cyrus, Jennifer Love Hewitt, Leona Lewis, Taylor Swift, Blake Lively, Mario Lopez, Mary Hart, Ryan Seacrest, Jennie Garth, Julianne Hough, Chris Rock, Kaley Cuoco.

Credits: *Executive Producer:* Orly Adleson, Barry Adelman. *Producer:* Cindy Clark. *Director:* Chris Donovan. *Writer:* Barry Adelman, Matt Miller.

167   Family Foreman. (Series; Reality; TV Land; July 16, 2008 to August 20, 2008)

An intimate look at the home and working life of George Foreman, the former heavyweight boxing champion, who has reinvented himself as a businessman (inventor of the George Foreman Grill).

Cast: George Foreman, Leola Foreman, Mary Foreman, Natalie Foreman, George Foreman III, George Foreman IV, George Foreman V, George Foreman VI.

Credits: *Executive Producer:* Mark Ford, Jon Kroll, Kevin Lopez, Jim Rosenthal. *Supervising Producer:* Jen Sleeper, Jerry D'Allesandro. *Producer:* Mark Costa. *Music:* Doug DeAngelis.

Review: "The thinnest of thin plot lines aside, *Family Foreman* is a must for anyone who has followed the ... career of George Foreman ... whose sledge hammer fists ... made him the most feared fighter on the planet 35 years ago" (*New York Post*).

168   Farmer Wants a Wife. (Series; Reality; CW; April 30, 2008 to June 25, 2008)

Ten city women are brought to the Missouri farm of Matt Neustadt (who is looking for a wife). The women compete in farm related challenges (with the weakest performers being eliminated). The girl who best demonstrates her abilities on a farm has the opportunity to become

Matt's wife. The women are Amanda (student), Ashley (catering sales manager), Brooke (marketing representative), Christa (personal assistant), Josie (math and tennis teacher), Kanisha (property management), Krista (accountant), Lisa (singer/dancer), Stacey (sales and marketing), Stephanie (jeweler).

Farmer: Matt Neustadt.

Credits: *Executive Producer:* Adam Cohen, Cara Topper, Joanna Vernetti. *Supervising Producer:* Chris Carlson, Jen Rowland. *Producer:* Jack Cannon. *Senior Producer:* Jeff Kuntz, Benny Reuven.

Reviews: "...the series has some ratings potential by CW's chicken feed standards but doesn't feel distinctive or titillating enough to keep 'em down on the farm" (*Variety*).

"Picture *The Bachelor* set amongst chickens and cow chips, and you've got a pretty good idea of the CW's *Farmer Wants a Wife*" (*The Hollywood Reporter*).

169   Fashion Rocks. (Special; Variety; CBS; September 9, 2008)

A star-studded concert, taped at Radio City Music Hall, that honors the extraordinary relationship between fashion and music.

Host: Denis Leary. **Performers Include:** Mariah Carey, Justin Timberlake, Keith Urban, Kid Rock, Chris Brown, Beyonce, Black Eyed Peas, L'il Wayne, Rihanna.

Credits: *Producer-Director:* Don Mischer.

170   Fat Guy Gets Stuck in Internet. (Series; Comedy; Cartoon Network; Premiered: June 15, 2008)

Ken Gemberling is an overweight computer program designer. One night Ken pours beer on his computer. Immediately he is sucked into the internet and meets Bit and Byte, computer heroes who battle the foes of the web. When Ken learns the internet is threatened by evil he allies himself with Bit and Byte. Stories follow the trio as they begin their quest to defeat Chains, a dimwitted villain seeking to stop them. Aired as a segment of the Adult Swim series.

Cast: John Gemberling (Ken Gemberling), Liz Cackowski (Byte), Neil Casey (Bit), Curtis Gwinn (Chains).

Credits: *Executive Producer:* John Gemberling, Curtis Gwen, David Tochterman. *Producer:* Marshall Eder. *Music:* Cody Westheimer.

171　Fear Itself. (Series; Anthology; NBC; June 5, 2008 to August 21, 2008)

A thirteen episode series of horror stories featuring lesser known performers but well known movie writers and directors.

Performers Include: Cynthia Watros, Colin Ferguson, Nicole Leduc, Maggie Lawson, Sonja Bennett, Wendell Pierce, Paul Jai Parker, Briana Evigan, Elisabeth Moss, Stephen R. Hart, Russell Hornsby, Stephen Martines, Shiri Appleby, John Billingsley.

Credits: *Executive Producer:* Andrew Deane, Keith Addes, Mick Garris. *Co-Executive Producer:* Peter Block. *Supervising Producer:* Grant Rosenberg. *Producer:* Adam Goldworm, Ben Browning. *Music:* Bobby Johnston.

172　Female Forces. (Series; Reality; Biography Channel; Premiered: October 5, 2008)

Profiles of the women of the Naperville, Illinois Police Department as they patrol the streets (and arrest felons).

Credits: *Executive Producer:* Leslie Greif, Adam Reed. *Producer:* Elizabeth Herrera, Salvador Rios, Marie Joelle Rick. *Associate Producer:* Terice Wafer.

173　50 Cent: The Money and the Power. (Series; Reality; MTV; Premiered: November 6, 2008)

Curtis Jackson, alias rapper 50 Cent, earned over $150 million in 2007 and has proven himself a successful businessman. Fourteen hopeful moguls are brought together and compete in a series of business challenges with the best performing player winning $100,000. Curtis reviews the contestants performances and eliminates the weakest performers on a weekly basis.

Host: Curtis Jackson. **Judges:** LL Cool Jay, Lloya Banks, Tony Yayo.

Credits: *Executive Producer:* Michael Bloom. *Co-Executive Producer:* Gabriel Alvarez, Sacha Jenkins. *Supervising Producer:* Lennox Wiseley, Bruce Klassen. *Producer:* Matt Mays.

174　Final Approach. (TV Movie; Drama; Hallmark; May 24, 2008)

Hostage drama about extremists who take over a plane and threaten to destroy it unless their imprisoned cult leader is released.

Cast: Dean Cain (Jack Bender), Anthony Michael Hall (Greg Hilliad), Ernie Hudson (Lorenzo Dawson), Lea Thompson (Alicia Bender), Sunny Mabrey (Sela Jameson), Christopher Cousins (Vince Gilford), Tracey Gold (Lina Howren).

Credits: *Executive Producer:* Larry Levinson. *Producer:* Michael Moran. *Writer:* Adam Armus, Nora Kay Foster. *Director:* Armand Mastroianni.

175　Finish Line. (TV Movie; Adventure; Spike; April 21, 2008)

Action combined with crime about Mitch Camponella, a race car driver who becomes involved in an arms smuggling operation.

Cast: Sam Page (Mitch Camponella), Scott Baio (Frank Chase), Taylor Cole (Jessie Chase), Timilee Romolini (Agent Matthews), Dan Lauria (Joe Camponella), Lexi Baxter (Blossom), Tracy Dali (Warden Ilsa), Travis Willingham (Tommy Granger).

Credits: *Executive Producer:* Michael Moran, H. Daniel Gross, Milena Milicevic. *Producer:* Randy Pope. *Director:* Gerry Lively. *Writer:* Ron McGee.

176　Fire and Ice: The Dragon Chronicles. (TV Movie; Horror; Sci Fi; October 19, 2008)

Medieval tale of a princess (Luisa) and a knight (Gabriel) who risk their lives to save their kingdom from a dragon.

Cast: Amy Acker (Princess Luisa), Tom Wisdom (Gabriel), Arnold Voslon (King Augustin), John Rhys-Davies (Sangimel), Oana Pellea (Queen Remini), Loredana Groza (Lila).

Credits: *Executive Producer:* Angela Mancusco, Alma Sarbu. *Producer:* Andrei Boncea, Michele Greco. *Music:* Frankie Blue.

177　First Class All the Way. (Series; Reality; Bravo; Premiered: November 3, 2008)

A look at how the very wealthy indulge on lavish vacations. Sara Duffy, the founder of the Los Angeles–based Travel Concierge, SRD International, arranges the trips for her high-end clients as they traverse the globe.

Host: Sara Duffy.

Credits: *Executive Producer:* Scott A. Stone, Lori Kaye, David Osper. *Co-Executive Producer:* Omid Kahangi, Amy Elkins, Jennifer Herschko. *Music:* David Vanacore.

Reviews: "Bravo's lineup sounds increasingly tone deaf—pushing ... caviar dreams to a nation in the throes of 401(k) nightmares" (*Variety*).

"Will a debt-riddled nation devastated by a ravaged economy ... and a looming credit crisis flock to watch a show that details how the richest of the rich splurge while on holiday?" (*The Hollywood Reporter*).

178　Flashpoint. (Series; Crime Drama; CBS; July 11, 2008 to September 18, 2008)

Gregory Parker is a sergeant with the SRU (Strategic Response Unit) of the Toronto, Canada, Police Department, a unit whose duty is to defuse explosive standoff situations. Jules, Sam, Ed, Kevin and Mike assist him; Dr. Amanda Luria is the unit's psychiatrist. Episodes begin with a standoff situation; flashbacks are used to detail the circumstances that led to it and how the team resolves it (hopefully through negotiations rather than deadly force). The second season premiered January 9, 2009.

Cast: Enrico Colantoni (Gregory Parker), Amy Jo Johnson (Jules Callaghan), Hugh Dillon (Ed Lane), Daniel Paetkau (Sam Braddock), Ruth Marshall (Dr. Amanda Luria), Michael Cram (Kevin Wordsworth), Sergio DiZio (Mike Scarlatti), Janaya Stephens (Sophie Lane; Ed's wife).

Credits: *Executive Producer:* Anne Marie La Traverse, Bill Mustos, Jessie Cameron. *Producer:* Tracy Boulton. *Music:* Ron Proulix.

Reviews: "*Flashpoint* is a perfectly competent police procedure right down to its convincing weapons and tactics. However, based on the pilot, it isn't particularly fresh or inventive" (*The Hollywood Reporter*).

"...as a viewing experience, the series itself possesses so little flash ... that it's difficult to see the point" (*Variety*).

179　Flirting with 40. (TV Movie; Drama; Lifetime; December 6, 2008)

Jackie Laurence is a divorcee and the mother of two children (Jessica and William). She is also about to turn 40. Kyle Hamilton is a twenty-something surf instructor based in Hawaii. To take a break from her hectic life, Jackie vacations in Hawaii, meets Kyle and soon after, begins a promising relationship with him. The story follows the problems that ensue for both as they become involved in an older woman, younger man situation.

Cast: Heather Locklear (Jackie Laurence), Robert Buckley (Kyle Hamilton), Vanessa L. Williams (Kristine), Connor Bancroft (Daniel Laurence), Jamie Bloch (Jessica Laurence), Anne Hawthorne (Claire), Sam Duke (William Laurence).

Credits: *Executive Producer:* Frank von Zerneck, Robert M. Sertner, Judith Verno.

Co-Executive Producer: Lucy Mukerjee. *Producer:* Lynn Raynor. *Director:* Mikael Salmon. *Writer:* Julia Dahl.

Reviews: "*Flirting with 40* is ... a frothy girls night in of the 'I am cougar: Hear me purr' variety — one that should seduce a femme audience hungry for white sand beaches and well toned abs" (*Variety*).

"This is a terrific couch and cake, girls only story that could have been anything but a TV movie" (*New York Post*).

180   The Florence Henderson Show. (Series; Talk; Retirement Living TV; Premiered: January 17, 2008)

A look at Hollywood, past and present, via interviews with celebrities who were a part of that glorious era (like Lindsay Wagner, Bob Newhart, Monty Hall and Carol Burnett).

Host: Florence Henderson.

Credits: *Executive Producer:* Jim Downs, Peter M. Green. *Producer:* Connie Magana, Jennifer Wojnar, Anne Hill, Daresha Kyi.

181   Flu Bird Horror. (TV Movie; Horror; Sci Fi; August 23, 2008)

Man vs. bird saga about townspeople battling mutant birds carrying a deadly virus.

Cast: Sarah Butler (Ava), Bill Posley (Derrick), Brent Lydie (Gordan), Tarri Markell (Dr. Giovanna Thomas), Clare Carey (Dr. Jacqueline Hale), Rebekah Kochan (Lola), Lance Guest (Garrett).

Credits: *Executive Producer:* Kenneth Badish. *Music:* Alan Howarth. *Director:* Leigh Scott. *Writer:* Tony Daniel, Brian D. Smith.

182   Food Detectives. (Series; Reality; Food Network; Premiered: July 29, 2008)

Culinary experts explore then unravel the mysteries and myths behind food.

Host: Ted Allen.

183   For the Love of Grace. (TV Movie; Drama; Hallmark; August 30, 2008)

Romance drama focusing on the relationship between a how-to book writer (Grace) and a reckless fire fighter (Steve).

Cast: Chandra West (Grace), Mark Consuelos (Steve Lockwood), Corbin Bernsen (Captain Washington), Ennie Esmer (Frank Lockwood), Cara Pifko (Jen).

Credits: *Executive Producer:* Frank Siracusa, Orly Adelson, Amy Goldberg. *Co-Executive Producer:* Mark Consuelos. *Producer:* Ian McDougall. *Writer:* Paul Reuhl, Ramona Barckart. *Director:* Craig Pryce.

Review: "*For the Love of Grace* is one of those unfortunate made-for-television movies that can't find its way to taking off and flying right. It stays grounded in the humdrum of the ordinary, and that's not good for anyone involved, especially the viewer" (*The Hollywood Reporter*).

184   Foreign Body. (Series; Drama; Internet; Premiered: May 27, 2008)

On August 5, 2008 a book called *Foreign Body* was released. To promote sales, a 50 episode daily series based on the book was produced prior to the book's release. The program attempts to make viewers aware of the dangers of seeking medical treatment in foreign countries. To demonstrate this, United Medical Heath Care trains a gorgeous Indian woman (Veena) to prove their point by killing patients who leave the U.S. for medical treatment overseas.

Cast: Pranidhi Varshney (Veena Chandra), Terasa Livingstone (Petra Danderoff), Rachna Khatau (Samira Patel), Cal Morgan (Wes McGee), Keith Arthur Bolden (Durell Williams), Jennifer Dorogi (Sam Ramos), Lisha Yakub (Supriya), Ranjit Johal (Amala), Charles Pacello (Dr. Owen Tomlinson).

Credits: *Executive Producer:* Douglas Cheney, Michael Eisner, Chris Hampel, Chris McCaleb. *Producer:* Jim Stoddard. *Music:* Jim McKeever.

185   Forensic Files. (Series; Reality; Tru TV; Premiered: January 1, 2008)

Crimes are reenacted to show how the science of forensics played a pivotal role in allowing police to solve the case.

Narrator: Peter Thomas.

Credits: *Executive Producer:* Paul Dowing, Lori Siegel. *Supervising Producer:* Ed Hersh. *Producer:* Ed Freedman, Vince Sherry, William J. Floyd. *Music:* Alan Ett Music Group.

186   *4 Real.* (Series; Reality; CW; October 5, 2008 to November 23, 2008)

Celebrity guests travel to various cities and countries around the world to connect with young adults who are affecting real changes in their particular environment. Episodes are inspirational as cameras capture "the real heroes of our time."

Host: Sol Guy.

Credits: *Producer:* Sol Guy.

187   Fringe. (Series; Drama; Fox; Premiered: September 9, 2008)

Olivia Dunham, a former U.S. Marine investigator, and Mark Valley are FBI agents. However, unlike others in their field, they investigate cases involving fringe science — situations that are not only puzzling but seemingly beyond all that is currently known by science (such as reanimation, mind control, unknown toxins and astral projection). They are assisted by Walter Bishop, a somewhat crazy scientist involved with cutting edge research and Peter, his rebellious, genius ne'er-do-well son. Phillip Broyler is Olivia's superior; Nina Sharp is the manipulative corporate executive; and FBI agents Charlie Francis and Astrid Farnsworth are the other members of the team.

Cast: Anna Torv (Olivia Dunham), John Scott (Mark Valley), John Noble (Walter Bishop), Joshua Jackson (Peter Bishop), Lance Reddick (Phillip Broyler), Blair Brown (Nina Sharp), Jasika Nicole (Astrid Farnsworth).

Credits: *Executive Producer:* J.J. Abrams, Alex Kurtzman, Roberto Orci, Jeff Pinner, Bryan Burk, Alex Graves. *Producer:*

Robert M. Williams. *Music:* Michael Giacchino.

Reviews: "What really makes *Fringe* so promising is that it is potentially reminiscent, in a small way, of the battle-of-the-sexes charm of that once made *Moonlighting* the best show on TV of its time" (*The Hollywood Reporter*).

"Being derivative isn't necessarily a condemnation in television, but given the auspices and hype, *Fringe* disappoints... The title should do a reasonably good job of describing the show's audience" (*Variety*).

188   From G's to Gents. (Series; Reality; MTV; July 15, 2008 to October 1, 2008)

Fourteen rough-around-the-edges men compete to become gentlemen and a cash prize of $100,000. Each competes in challenges that include style, grace, chivalry and etiquette. The weakest performer each week is denied entrance into the Gentleman's Club. The one diamond-in-the-rough who shows the most potential wins.

Host: Fonzworth Bentley.

Credits: *Executive Producer:* Jamie Foxx, Jaime Rucker King, Marcus King. *Producer:* Ryan Crow, Allison Schermerhorn.

189   *Front* of the Class. (TV Movie; Drama; CBS; December 7, 2008)

A *Hallmark Hall of Fame* presentation based on the autobiographical book by Brad Cohen. Brad was born with Tourette syndrome (involuntary tics and noises like a dog bark) and has only one dream: to become a teacher. The emotionally charged story relates the hardships Brad had to overcome to achieve his goal.

Cast: Jimmy Wolk (Brad Cohen), Patricia Heaton (Ellen Cohen), Dominick Scott Kay (Young Brad), Treat Williams (Norman Cohen), Molly Sullivan (Molly), Kathleen York (Diane), Sarah Drew (Nancy Lazarus), Lori Beth Edgeman (Deborah).

Credits: *Executive Producer:* Timothy

Shriver, Brent Shields. *Producer:* Cameron Johnson, Andrew Gottlieb. *Director:* Peter Werner. *Writer:* Tom Rickman.

Review: "*Hallmark Hall of Fame* hits a dramatic bulls-eye with a tale of courage and perseverance" (*The Hollywood Reporter*).

190   The Funniest Commercials of the Year. (Special; Comedy; TBS; December 23, 2008)

A look at the most humorous television commercials broadcast during 2008 (including national, regional and local).

Host: Kevin Nealon.

Credits: *Executive Producer:* Robert Dalrymple. *Producer:* Tony Lonni. *Co-Producer:* Rachel Costa. *Associate Producer:* Steve Zoslavsky. *Writer:* Tony DeSena.

191   Gadget or the Girl. (Series; Reality; Playboy Channel; Premiered: September 1, 2008)

A somewhat unusual take on the traditional TV dating programs. Here a straight guy is introduced to three gorgeous females "with sizzling bodies." After a short session in which the guys question the girls (to learn compatibility), he chooses the two he feels most comfortable with. The three are sent out on a date with cameras capturing the activities that follow. After the date, the guy selects the one girl he would like to date on a one-to-one basis. However, after the girl is chosen, the guy is offered a deal: a weekend excursion with the girl or give her up for an expensive "gadget" (for example, a plasma television. The girl can also win a prize if she persuades the guy to pick her. If she is successful, she wins whatever the guy would have received). Surprisingly (or not?) the gadgets are sometimes chosen over "a hot babe."

Host: Iliza Schlesinger.

192   Gary Unmarried. (Series; Comedy; CBS; Premiered: September 24, 2008)

Gary Brooks is recently divorced (after 15 years of marriage) and the owner of Gary House Painting. He is the father of Louise and Tom and is hoping to start a new life without the constant interference of his ex-wife (Allison).

Gary is a free spirit; Allison is compulsive; their relationship led to a divorce. Now, three months later, Gary feels it is time to find another mate (as does Allison). Gary has chosen Vanessa, a single mother with a young son (Parker); and Allison, Walter Krandall, her and Gary's marriage counselor (the author of the book, *Rules of the Perfect Divorce*). Stories follow Gary and Allison as they each try to begin new lives despite the complications that ensue as Allison still feels she needs to control Gary's life. Eleven-year-old Louise is a very pretty girl who is fascinated by Al Gore; Tom is 14 years old and fine with his friends but terrified of girls. Dennis works for Gary; Charlie and Connie are Allison's parents; Jack is Gary's father. Originally titled *Project Gary*.

Cast: Jay Mohr (Gary Brooks), Paula Marshall (Allison Brooks), Jaime King (Vanessa Flood), Ed Begley, Jr. (Walter Krandall), Kathryn Newton (Louise Brooks), Ryan Malgarin (Tom Brooks), Al Madrigal (Dennis Lopez), Charles Henry Wyson (Parker Flood), Martin Mull (Charlie), Jane Curtin (Connie), Max Gail (Jack Brooks).

Credits: *Executive Producer:* Ed Yeager, James Burrows, Ric Swartzlander. *Co-Executive Producer:* Janae Bakken, Ira Ungerleider. *Producer:* Dionne Kirscher.

Reviews: "It has some genuinely funny lines ... CBS will be thrilled if the series can hold most of the audience from *The New Adventures of Old Christine* but even that might be asking a lot" (*The Hollywood Reporter*).

"Boiled down to a personal ad... *Gary Unmarried* would read 'Divorced white male seeks audience. Those looking for anything fresh, new or consistently amusing need not apply.' CBS shouldn't stay home waiting by the phone" (*Variety*).

193   Gavin and Stacey. (Series; Comedy; BBC America; Premiered: 2008)

Stacey is a 26-year-old woman who lives on Barry Island in South Wales, with her mother, Gwen. Gavin, also 26, lives in Billericay, Essex, with his parents, Mick and Pam. Gavin and Stacey are also romantically involved, although it is a long distance love. Stories follow their ups and downs as they try to make their relationship work despite the problems they encounter with friends who feel the relationship will not work. Smithy is Gavin's friend; Nessa is Stacey's best friend, a 40-year-old who works in the arcade on Barry Island.

Cast: Matthew Horne (Gavin), Joanna Page (Stacey), Ruth Jones (Nessa), James Corden (Smithy), Melanie Walthers (Gwen), Larry Lamb (Mick), Alison Steadman (Pam).

Credits: *Executive Producer:* Lindsay Hughes, Henry Normal. *Producer:* Ted Dowd. *Associate Producer:* Ruth Jones.

194   Gemini Division. (Series; Science Fiction; Internet; August 18, 2008 to October 16, 2008)

Anna Diaz is a streetwise undercover detective with the N.Y.P.D. She is engaged to Nick Korda and drawn into a dangerous mystery when Nick is killed and Anna discovers he was involved with the Gemini Division, a secret and sinister organization involved with covert military operations and simulated humanoid life forms. The fifty episode web cast follows Anna as she seeks to learn why Nick was eliminated and stop Gemini Division from assimilating its simulated life forms into society.

Cast: Rosario Dawson (Anna Diaz), Justin Hartley (Nick Korda), Elizabeth Bogush (Dr. Elizabeth Gavillan), Francois Chau (Dr. Martin Ng), Daz Crawford (The Cleaner), Matt Bushell (Det. Pete Vacarella), Allison Scagliotti (M+M), Peter

Jason (Colonel Black), Raphael Sbarge (Corporal Ryder).

Credits: *Executive Producer:* Rosario Dawson, Stan Rogow, Brenda Friedman. *Producer:* John Alexander. *Web Content Producer:* Deric A. Hughes.

195   Generation Gap. (TV Movie; Drama; Hallmark Channel; October 25, 2008)

Tale of a troubled teenager (Dylan) who is sent by his mother (Veronica) to live with his grandfather (Bart) in an effort to change his wayward ways.

Cast: Edward Asner (Bart Cahill), Alex Black (Dylan Statlan), Catherine Mary Stewart (Veronica Statlan), Rue McClanahan (Kay), Ralph Waite (Chick), Hal Williams (Mac), Danielle Savre (Jenny).

Credits: *Executive Producer:* Kevin Bocarde. *Producer:* Kyle A. Clark, Stephen Niver. *Music:* Roger Bellon. *Director:* Bill L. Norton. *Writer:* Sean King, Ray Starmann.

Review: "A solid veteran cast more than offsets an otherwise unremarkable film" (*The Hollywood Reporter*)

"The acting is smooth ... the script professional and polished, if not soaring" (*New York Daily News*).

196   Generation Kill. (Miniseries; Drama; HBO; July 13, 2008 to August 24, 2008)

Seven part adaptation of Evan Wright's gritty first person account that details the experiences of U.S. Marines during the first 40 days of the Iraq invasion.

Cast: James Ransone (Josh Ray Person), Alexander Skarsgard (Brad Colbert), Lee Tergesen (Evan Wright), Jon Huertas (Antonio Espera), Stark Sands (Nathaniel Fick), Billy Lush (Harold Trombley), Jonah Lotan (Robert Bryan), Pawel Szajda (Walt Hasser), Wilson Bethel (Evan Stafford).

Credits: *Executive Producer:* David Simon, Ed Burns, Anne Thomopoulos, Charles Patterson. *Producer:* Andre Calderwood. *Writer:* David Simon, Ed Burns. *Director:* Susanna White.

Review: "If *John Adams* was something of an expensive misfire, HBO nails the target with *Generation Kill*, a raw, gritty, so real you'll forget it's a dramatic miniseries" (*Variety*).

197 Getting Away with Murder. (Series; Comedy; Internet [IFC.com]; 2008)

Seth Silver is a 25-year-old man who leads a double life. He lives with his neurotic mother, Rhonda (who believes he is a veterinary technician) and his pretence to be a slacker covers for his actual job as a killer for hire. Stories follow Seth as he struggles to cope with the situations that arise when his professional hit man skills constantly interfere with his other life. Lily is Seth's girlfriend; Rex is Seth's best friend; Kip is the man "who reared Seth in the death business"; Pinkie is one of Kip's killers; The Spook is the unnamed government agent bent on bringing down Kip's death ring. Rhonda hosts a TV cooking show called *Ronnie's Kitchen*.

Cast: John Gilbert (Seth Silver), Misti Traya (Lily), Gina Hecht (Rhonda Silver), Kian Mitchum (Rex), Eric Beck (Kip), John Kerry (The Spook), Justin Cotta (Pinkie).

198 Ghost Adventures. (Series; Reality; Travel Channel; October 17, 2008 to December 6, 2008)

Three ghost hunters explore supposed haunted locations armed with only their hand held cameras to discover if said locations are really haunted. Each episode also includes a history of the site being investigated.

Ghost Hunters: Aaron Goodwin, Nick Groff, Zak Bagans.

Credits: *Executive Producer:* Zak Bagans. *Supervising Producer:* Katy DaSilva. *Producer:* Anthony DiDonato.

199 Ghost Hunters International. (Series; Reality; Sci Fi; Premiered: January 9, 2008)

A spin-off from *Ghost Hunters* that moves away from the U.S. and its haunted houses to search for ghosts in the most eerie places in countries around the world. Once a site is chosen, a team sets up its special audio and video equipment to capture the sights and sounds of the spirits that are allegedly haunting it.

Narrator: Mike Rowe. **Team:** Robb Demarest, Shannon Sylvia, Brian Harnois, Donna LaCroix, Andy Andrews, Barry Fistgerald.

Credits: *Executive Producer:* Alan David, Rob Katz, Craig Piligian, Tom Thayer. *Supervising Producer:* Mark Marinaccio. *Producer:* Matthew Hobin.

Reviews: "There are many moments meant to scare the pants off the audience. Sometimes it works, sometimes it doesn't" (*The Hollywood Reporter*).

200 Ghost Voyage. (TV Movie; Science Fiction; Sci Fi; January 26, 2008)

Chiller about a haunted ship and the efforts of its passengers to battle the evil forces that command it.

Cast: Antonio Sabato, Jr. (Michael), Seanna Russo (Serena), Cary-Hiroyuki Tagawa (Steward), Julian Berlin (Jessica), Nicholas Irons (Nicholai), P.J. Marino (Raymond), Zhasmina (Seductive Ghost), Tanya Kozhuharova (Junkie Ghost).

Credits: *Producer:* Jeffrey Beach, Philip J. Roth. *Co-Producer:* T.J. Sakasegawa. *Writer:* Rob Mecarini. *Director:* James Oxford. *Music:* Nathan Furst.

201 Ghouls. (TV Movie; Horror; Sci Fi; July 12, 2008)

A seemingly normal college student (Jennifer) finds her life turned upside down when she discovers her family's dark secret: they are, in reality, unearthly creatures called Ghouls.

Cast: Kristen Renton (Jennifer), Erin Gray (Liz), William Atherton (Stefan), James DeBello (Thomas), Don Badarau (Vlad), Lucien Maier (Draga), Ivana Abur (Jennifer's mother), Marian Iacob (Alexa).

Credits: *Executive Producer:* Ewehard Engels. *Producer:* Kenneth Badish. *Music:* Alan Howarth. *Writer:* Brian D. Young. *Director:* Gary Jong.

202   Giada at Home. (Series; Cooking; Food Network; Premiered: October 18, 2008)

Chef Giada DeLaurentis shows viewers how to prepare meals for special occasions and gatherings with friends and family.

Host: Giada DeLaurentis.

Credits: *Executive Producer:* Rachel Purnell. *Supervising Producer:* Olivia Ball. *Producer:* Carl Green.

203   Gimme My Reality Show! (Series; Reality; Fox Reality Channel; Premiered: October 9, 2008)

A reality competition to find a star to host their own reality program. The candidates compete in a series of challenges to test their abilities to handle the chores of a reality show host. The winner receives a shot at his or her own series on Fox Reality ("All reality all the time").

Host: George Gray. **Contestants:** Traci Bingham (actress), A.J. Benzal (gossip columnist), Gretchen Bonaduce (opportunist), Susan Olsen (Cindy on *The Brady Bunch*), Ryan Starr (*American Idol* contestant), Bobby Trendy (*Anna Nicole Smith Show* queen), Kato Kaelin (O.J. Simpson trial witness). **Announcer:** Bill Lloyd.

Credits: *Executive Producer:* Carol Sherman, Jeff Androsky. *Producer:* Christine Blake.

Review: "...if this isn't the biggest waste of human DNA in television history, it must be awfully close" (*The Hollywood Reporter*).

204   Girl's Best Friend. (TV Movie; Comedy; Lifetime; February 2, 2008)

Lighthearted tale of a young woman (Mary) who begins a cross country road trip with her dog, a Jack Russell terrier named Binky, to find herself after she becomes frustrated with her job as a music critic.

Cast: Janeane Garofalo (Mary), Nicholas Wright (Ethan), Kristen Holden-Ried (Jake), Sara Bradeen (Elaine), Noah Bennett (Gary), Felicia Shulman (Gertie), Allison Graham (Susan), Claire Brosseau (Erica).

Credits: *Executive Producer:* Michael Jacobs, Harry Winer, Michael Prupas. *Producer:* David Patterson, Jesse Prupas. *Music:* Luc St. Pierre. *Writer:* Muffy Marracco. *Director:* Peter Svatek.

205   The GLAAD Media Awards. (Special; Variety; Bravo; June 27, 2008)

The 19th annual event that honors the gay, lesbian, bisexual and transgender community in media and entertainment.

Host: Graham Norton. **Appearing:** Kevin Bacon, Jennifer Beals, Candis Cayne, Cindy Crawford, Ellen DeGeneres, Kathy Griffin, Janet Jackson, Jay Manuel, Kyra Sedgwick, Sharon Stone, Sofia Vergara, Paul James.

Credits: *Executive Producer:* Frances Berwick, Neil Giuliano, Nadine C. Licostie. *Producer:* Diana Rodriquez, Dave Serwatka. *Director:* Nadine C. Licostie.

206   Gladiators. (Series; Reality; BBC America; Premiered: November 1, 2008)

A revised version of a 1990s British series of the same title that was based on the 1980s U.S. series *American Gladiators*. Six men and six women are pitted against a group of Gladiators in athletic contests designed to determine the better of the two.

Host: Kristy Gallacher, Ian Wright. **Commentator:** Alan Parry. **Referee:** John Anderson IV. **Gladiators:** Sam Bond (Atlas), Roderick Bradley (Spartan), Du'aine Ladejo (Predator), David McIntosh (Tornado), Nicholas Aldis (Oblivion), Damar Martin (Destroyer), Lucy Boggis (Tempest), Kara Nwidobie Sharpe (Panther), Jemma Palmer (Inferno), Caroline Pearce (Ice), Jenny Pacey (Enigma), Shirley Webb (Battleaxe), Donna Williams (Cyclone).

Credits: *Executive Producer:* Robin Ash-brook, John Pollak, Karen Smith, Richard Woolfe, Steve Jones. *Producer:* Marc Bassett, Louise Whalley. *Games Producer:* Andrew Norgate.

207   Glam God with Vivica A. Fox. (Series; Reality; VH-1; August 21, 2008 to October 16, 2008)

Stylists compete in various challenges for the opportunity for a career as a celebrity stylist and a cash prize of $100,000. Each of the challenges is judged by a panel and the weakest performers are eliminated on a weekly basis.

Host: Vivica A. Fox. **Judges:** Philip Bloch, Melanie Bromley, Vivica A. Fox.

Credits: *Executive Producer:* Cris Abrego, Vivica A. Fox, Lita Richardson. *Supervising Producer:* Kristen Kelly, Jill Osmon Modabber, Jeff Olde.

208   Go Go Rikki. (Series; Cartoon; CW Kids; Premiered: September 13, 2008)

Nine circle-shaped characters, who are each a different color and representative of different cultures, interests and temperaments, are the stars of a comedy accented animated program aimed primarily at tweens. Here their differences are secondary as the characters are always there for each other as they learn about life and help each other overcome the problems they encounter. Characters: Bigoriki, Boboriki, Chikoriki, Docoriki, Olgariki, Ottoriki, Pogoriki, Rosariki, Wolliriki.

Voices: Emlyn Tyler, Dave Wells, Jason Griffith, Bella Hudson, Heather Donahue, Dan Green, Wayne Grayson.

Credits: *Executive Producer:* Norm Grosfield, Alfred Kahan. *Producer:* Kathy Borland. *Music:* Marian Lande.

209   The Golden Globe Awards. (Special; Awards; NBC; January 13, 2008)

The Hollywood Foreign Press Association honors achievements in film and television. Originally scheduled as a three-hour event that was affected by the 2007 writer's strike. When most actors refused to cross picket lines, the event was retooled as a sixty minute news conference wherein the winners were announced and a picture of said winner shown in the background.

Announcer: Shawn Parr.

Credits: *Producer:* Don Harary.

210   Gone Country. (Series; Reality; CMT; Premiered: January 25, 2008)

Performers from various facets of the entertainment industry learn the ins and outs of the country music industry in an attempt to become a country and western entertainer.

Host: John Rich.

Credits: *Executive Producer:* David Garfinkle, Marc Oswald. *Producer:* Bob Kusbit, Jay Renfroe, Melanie Moreau.

211   The Gong Show. (Series; Variety; Comedy Central; July 17, 2008 to August 21, 2008)

A revised version of the 1970s program of the same title wherein amateur variety acts perform seeking a cash prize and hoping to avoid hearing a large gong sound (which disqualifies them).

Host: Dave Attell. **Prize Girl:** Heidi Van Horne. **Judges:** Julia Lea Wolov, Ron White, J.D. Smoove, Jim Norton, Diandra Newline, Dana Goodman, Steve Schirripa, Triumph the Insult Comic Dog (a puppet).

Credits: *Executive Producer:* Zoe Friedman. *Co-Executive Producer:* Jennifer Heffler. *Producer:* Bryce Eckhaus, Hedda Musket.

Reviews: "The new *Gong Show* will doubtless draw some curiosity seekers. The question is how long they'll stick around. The more disturbing question is why" (*New York Daily News*).

"Totally tasteless. Horribly embarrassing. Filled with filthy-mouthed morons. Don't you just love summer TV?... Yes, it's the return of *The Gong Show*, smaller and worse than ever. And just as funny" (*New York Post*).

212 Good Morning Internet. (Series; Comedy; Internet [IFC.com]; 2008)

A daily program that presents "all things Internet" with co-hosts Quinn Morgan, Colby Honeycutt, Chip Stockley, Devon Shiloh and man-on-the-street reporter Devon Shiloh.

Cast: Maggie Ross, Ryan Hunterm, Ryan Hall, Taige Jensen, Jennifer Lyon.

Credits: *Executive Producer:* Colin Moore, Craig Parks, Jennifer Caserta. *Producer:* Tyler Jackson. *Director:* Karrie Crouse. *Writer:* Ryan Hunter.

213 The Good Witch. (TV Movie; Comedy-Drama; Hallmark; January 19, 2008)

Small town sheriff Jake Russell becomes involved in a controversy when he falls in love with Cassandra Nightingale, a newcomer to town whose actions cause the citizens to believe she is a witch.

Cast: Catherine Bell (Cassandra Nightingale), Chris Potter (Jake Russell), Catherine Disher (Martha), Peter MacBeill (George O'Hanrahan), Allan Royal (Walter Cobb), Hannah Endicott-Douglas (Lori), Paula Boudreau (Nancy).

Credits: *Executive Producer:* Orly Adelson, Frank Siracusa. *Producer:* Ian McDougall. *Writer:* Rod Spence. *Director:* Craig Pryce.

214 The Governor's Wife. (TV Movie; Drama; Lifetime Movie Network; September 21, 2008)

A young newlywed (Hayley Danville) seeks to prove that her husband's mother (Ann) is plotting to kill her.

Cast: Marilu Henner (Ann Danville), Scout Taylor-Compton (Hayley Danville), Matt Kessler (Nathan Danville), Deborah Van Valkenburgh (Jill Quigley), Timothy Bottoms (Carl Lovett), Wendy Glenn (Mandy Paulson).

Credits: *Executive Producer:* Michael Moran. *Producer:* Albert T. Dickerson III. *Music:* Lawrence Schragge. *Director:* David Burton Morris. *Writer:* Edithe Swenson.

215 The Grammy Awards. (Special; Variety; CBS; March 6, 2008)

The 50th annual presentation in which performers from the music world are honored.

Guests: Cyndi Lauper, Tony Bennett, Aretha Franklin, Alicia Keyes, Jerry Lee Lewis, Ringo Starr, Burt Bacharach, Beyonce Knowles, Cher, Quincy Jones, Herbie Hancock, Tina Turner, Andy Williams, Miley Cyrus, Carrie Underwood, Taylor Swift, Little Richard, Carole King, Andrea Bocelli, Lyle Lovett, Cab Calloway, Jason Bateman, Tom Hanks, Natalie Cole, Roselyn Sanchez, Chris Brown.

Credits: *Announcer:* Rebecca Reidy. *Executive Producer:* John Cossette, Ken Ehrlich. *Producer:* Quincy Jones, Walter C. Miller, Pierre Cossette. *Director:* Walter C. Miller.

216 The Grammy Nominations Concert Live!—Countdown to Music's Biggest Night. (Special; Variety; CBS; December 3, 2008)

A live program (the first presentation) that announces the Grammy nominations for the scheduled February 2009 telecast of the music industry's most coveted event.

Host: Taylor Swift, LL Cool J. **Guests:** Christina Aguilera, Mariah Carey, Celine Dion, Foo Fighters, B.B. King, John Mayer.

Credits: *Executive Producer:* John Cossette, Ken Ehrlich.

217 Grave Misconduct. (TV Movie; Mystery; Lifetime; September 6, 2008)

Julia London is a struggling mystery novelist and librarian of the Mystery Writer's Workshop. Following the death of a member, Julia finds his manuscript, *Grave Misconduct* and, claiming it as hers, finds a publisher. Later, Julia finds herself becoming a detective to uncover the culprit who is committing murders based on incidents described in the book.

Cast: Crystal Bernard (Julia London), Michael Cole (Jason Connelly), Dorian

Harewood (Baxter Kyle), Mercedes Colon (Cricket Jones), Fran Bennett (Mrs. Crutch), John Fleck (Billy Speck), Roxanne Hart (Margo Lawrence), Joanna Miles (Catherine Hallow).

Credits: *Executive Producer:* Larry Levinson. *Producer:* Susan McGuire, Brian Gordon. *Director:* Armand Mastroianni. *Writer:* Matthew Chernov, David Rosiak.

218   Greatest American Dog. (Series; Reality; CBS; July 10, 2008 to September 10, 2008)

Twelve people and their pampered dogs are brought together and placed in a mansion called Canine Academy. Each week the dogs are placed in a physical competition with the weakest dog performer causing him and his master to leave. The last owner standing wins $250,000 and has his or her pooch crowned "The Greatest American Dog."

Host: Jarod Miller. **Judges:** Wendy Diamond, Allan Reznick, Victoria Stillwell.

Credits: *Executive Producer:* R.J. Cutler, Stu Schreiber, Stephen Kroopnick. *Co-Executive Producer:* Jamie Canniffe, Jim Buss, Lenid Rodov. *Supervising Producer:* Drew Brown. *Producer:* Mary Lisio.

Reviews: "As much as people love their pooches, there's something beyond silly about shoehorning them into a mastermutt reality elimination game ... feels like old reheated kibble" (*Variety*).

"If you are a dog person, have I got a show for you. It's like dog camp but done as a reality show" (*New York Post*).

219   Greatest Holiday Moments: Holiday Home Video Countdown. (Special; Comedy; NBC; December 25, 2008)

Comical Christmas season moments, captured on video tape by viewers, are showcased.

Announcer: Nolan North.

Credits: *Executive Producer:* Robert Horowitz, Lewis Fenton. *Co-Executive Pro-*

ducer: Emily Sinclair. *Producer:* Carrie Vanover.

220   Greatest Holiday Moments: Songs of the Season Countdown. (Special; Variety; NBC; December 12, 2008)

A look at the "top" twenty Christmas songs of "all" time. The countdown begins with number twenty ("It's the Most Wonderful Time of the Year" performed by Andy Williams) to the number one song ("White Christmas" by Bing Crosby and Frank Sinatra). Other selections that are true to the title are "Feliz Navidad" (number 13, by Charo), "Jingle Bells" (number 12, by Sonny and Cher), "Santa Claus Is Coming to Town" (number 9, by Tony Bennett), "All I Want for Christmas Is You" (number 3, by Mariah Carey) and "The Christmas Song" (number 2, by Nat King Cole). Each of the selected songs is shown via an incomplete clip; however, many songs that are true to the season are not used or even mentioned. These include "Silver Bells," "Rudolph, the Red Nosed Reindeer," "Home for the Holidays" and "I'll Be Home for Christmas."

Announcer: Nolan North.

Credits: *Executive Producer:* Robert Horowitz, Lewis Fenton. *Co-Executive Producer:* Emily Sinclair. *Producer:* Carrie Vanover.

221   Greatest Holiday Moments: TV and Film Countdown. (Special; Variety; NBC; December 5, 2008)

A countdown of the 25 "greatest" moments from film and television Christmas themed productions (with number 1 being the film *It's a Wonderful Life* and number 25 being the film *Home Alone*). Other "classics" include the TV show *The Office* (number 22), *The Simpsons* (19), the film *Planes, Trains and Automobiles* (13), *Saturday Night Live* (8) and *National Lampoon's Christmas Vacation* (4). The selections presented are, for the most part, ridiculous, as they are not representative of truly great

TV and movie Christmas moments (missing, for example, are *The Honeymooners, I Love Lucy* and *Father Knows Best* TV shows and such movies as *The Bishop's Wife, Christmas in Connecticut* and *A Tree Grows in Brooklyn* which presented what the program missed).

Announcer: Nolan North.

Credits: *Executive Producer:* Robert Horowitz, Lewis Fenton. *Co-Executive Producer:* Emily Sinclair. *Producer:* Jeanne Bremer.

222   The Guinness Book of World Records: The Top 100. (Special; Reality; NBC; January 27, 2008)

A look at the 100 most unusual entries found in *The Guinness Book of World Records.*

Credits: *Executive Producer:* Al Berman, Glenda Hersh, Shari Solomon. *Producer:* Laurie Pekich, Gregory Fein, Liz Sterbenz. *Director:* Liz Plonka.

223   A Gunfighter's Pledge. (TV Movie; Western; Hallmark; July 5, 2008)

During a gunfight with outlaws, Sheriff Matt Austin accidentally shoots an innocent Californo (a Californian of Mexican descent). Before the man dies, he asks Matt to help his family defeat the town villain (Lamar Horn) seeking his land. The story follows Matt as he encounters love (with Amaya) and trouble attempting to defeat Horn.

Cast*:* Luke Perry (Matt Austin), C. Thomas Howell (Lamar Horn), Jaclyn DeSantis (Amaya), Kim Coates (Tate), Nicholas Guest (Vaughn), James Keane (Preacher), Francesco Quinn (Sheriff Montero), Johann Urb (Lars Anderson).

Credits: *Executive Producer:* Larry Levinson, Robert Halmi Jr. *Co-Executive Producer:* H. Daniel Gross. *Producer:* Albert T. Dickerson III. *Writer:* Jim Byrnes. *Director:* Armand Mastroianni. *Music:* Nathan Furst.

Reviews: "The only thing that separates Hallmark Channel's *A Gunfighter's Pledge*

from being a top-notch Western is its far-fetched story, questionable casting, misleading title and stereotyped characters. The scenery is terrific, though and the costumes are perfect" (*The Hollywood Reporter*).

"The *Pledge* ... adorns itself with a few pieces of genre cliché, a few recognizable scenarios and nothing else ... it provides Western fans with exactly what they want, then wraps up and heads home. B pictures used to work like this, and now too, does the *Pledge*" (*DVD Talk*).

224   Gym Teacher: The Movie. (TV Movie; Comedy; Nickelodeon; September 12, 2008)

Dave Stewie, a disgraced Olympic gymnast working as a middle school physical education teacher, seeks to redeem himself by winning a gym teacher of the year award.

Cast: Christopher Meloni (Dave Stewie), Amy Sedaris (Abby Hofmann), Nathan Kress (Roland Waffle), Benna O'Brien (Morgan), Chelah Horsdal (Winnie Bleeker), Alexia Fast (Susie Salisbury).

Credits: *Executive Producer:* Stanely M. Brooks, Jim Head, Lauren Levine. *Producer:* Scott McAboy. *Music:* Daniel Licht. *Director:* Paul Dinello. *Writer:* Daniel Altiere, Steve Alticere.

Review: "Put the words *Law and Order: SVU* [referring to the show's star, Christopher Meloni] and gym teacher together in the same sentence and your first thought is likely to be 'this can't read well.' But put those few words in Nickelodeon's hands and you've got yourself a TV movie that the whole family can enjoy" (*New York Post*).

225   H20: Just Add Water. (Series; Comedy; Nickelodeon; Premiered: March 14, 2008)

Cleo, Emma and Rikki are three 16-year-old girls who live on the Australian Gold Coast. One day, while cruising the water, the boat in which the girls are riding runs out of gas and strands them in mid-ocean. With only the mysterious Mako Island in sight, the girls paddle their way to the nearest shore. With evening approaching the girls take refuge in a cave. There, they discover a pool that Emma believes could lead to the ocean. (While it is not shown, it is assumed that the girls' parents have become worried over their daughters' disappearance and have called the Water Police.)

Emma swims the length of the pool and discovers that it does lead to the ocean. She convinces Cleo and Rikki to swim the underwater channel to safety.

As the girls swim through the channel, a mysterious glow from a full moon engulfs them. The girls escape from the island and are rescued by the Water Police.

The girls appear to be fine. The next day, however, life changes for each of them. When Emma goes swimming a startling metamorphous occurs: ten seconds after entering the water she turns into a beautiful mermaid; Cleo has just stepped into a bathtub when she becomes a mermaid; Rikki, walking across a lawn, is sprinkled with water and she too becomes a mermaid. While not shown, when the water evaporates from their mermaid scales, they return to normal.

The girls quickly adjust to the fact that water has changed their lives. They do acquire the power over water but must avoid unnecessary contact with it to keep their secret safe.

Stories follow events in the lives of Cleo, Emma and Rikki as they struggle to cope with and conceal their true identities while at the same time facing the everyday problems teenage girls face.

Lewis is their friend, a scientist, who seeks a way to reverse the process; Kim is Cleo's sister; Elizabeth is Emma's brother; Miss Chatham is a teacher; Angela is Cleo's cousin; Lisa and Neil are Emma's parents; Bev and Don are Cleo's parents. Produced in Australia.

Cast: Cariba Heine (Rikki Chadwick), Claire Holt (Emma Gilbert), Phoebe Tonkin (Cleo Sertori), Angus McLaren (Lewis McCartney), Annabelle Stephenson (Miriam), Burgess Abernathy (Zane Bennett), Cleo Maskey (Kim Sertori), Trent Sullivan (Elliot Gilbert), Jada Paskins (Angela), Caroline Kennison (Lisa Gilbert), Jared Robinsen (Neil Gilbert), Deborah Coulls (Bev Sertori), Alan David Lee (Don Sertori).

Credits: *Executive Producer:* Jonathan M. Shiff, Ben M. Rad. *Producer:* Jonathan M. Shiff. *Theme Vocal:* "No Ordinary Girl" by Ellie Henderson. *Music:* Danny Beckerman, Ric Formosa.

Reviews: "It's a quality piece of Australian children's television. It looks good; the three female leads are engaging and there's some lovely underwater photography" (*The Sydney Morning Herald*, Australia).

"It isn't exactly every young girl's dream escape, but *H20* comes pretty close to carrying away its target viewers on a magical mystery ride" (*The Hollywood Reporter*).

226 Hallmark Heroes with Regis Philbin. (Special; Tribute; Hallmark; December 25, 2008)

Moving special about people whose acts of kindness and charity have affected many other lives. The recipients are interviewed and presented with a check for $5,000 to help them with their future good endeavors. The recipients are: Katy Hatfield who, with her sister, Nancy, started a web site (www.KnowAlz.com) to help people facing the same problems in caring for people affected with Alzheimer's disease; Murray Hernandez, who established a non-profit organization (http://diabetes handsfoundation.org) to help people with diabetes and people without the disease understand it; Hal Honeyman, who established Project Mobility: Cycles for Life, which seeks special bicycles that can be used by children with Cerebral Palsy; and

John Beltzer, the founder of the Songs of Love Foundation, which creates uplifting, personalized songs for children and teens struggling with life-threatening illness or lifetime disabilities. Performers like Nancy Sinatra, Michael Bolton, Billy Joel and David Lee Roth have donated their talents. A very special tribute is also paid to actress Jane Seymour for her extensive work with the American Red Cross and their Measles Initiative.

Host: Regis Philbin. **Special Guest:** Jane Seymour.

Credits: *Executive Producer:* Colby Gaines, Brent Montgomery. *Producer:* Courtney Napurano, Clare O'Donohue, Helen Tierney. *Director:* Brad Garfield.

227   Head Case. (Series; Comedy; Starz; January 23, 2008 to March 12, 2008)

Spoof of psychiatry-based television shows in which Dr. Elizabeth Goode, a therapist who dispenses judgmental advice to her patients — actual Hollywood celebrities (who appear with scripted problems).

Cast: Alexandra Wentworth (Dr. Elizabeth Goode), Sally Kirkland (Elizabeth's mother), Sam McMurray (Elizabeth's father), Michelle Arthur (Lola Buckingham), Steve Landesberg (Dr. Myron Finkelstein), Rob Benedict (Jeremy Berger).

Credits: *Executive Producer:* Robert Bauer, Jason Farrand, Alexandra Wentworth, Eric Bonniot. *Producer:* William Butler-Slosi, Rachel North. *Music:* H. Scott Salinas.

228   Heat Stroke. (TV Movie; Science Fiction; Sci Fi; May 31, 2008)

A soldier (Steve) teams with an ex-model (Caroline) to foil alien plans to accelerate the global warming process to make the Earth habitable for their race.

Cast: D.B. Sweeney (Capt. Steve O'Bannon), Danica McKelllar (Caroline), Kelly Rice (Jillian Grange), Chris Cleveland (Waters), Francesca Buller (Dr. Taggert), Charlotte Dias (Rahela), Kimberly Nault (Brooke).

Credits: *Executive Producer:* John Ching, Christian Arnold-Beutel, Jeffrey Hayes, David Kemper, John F.S. Laing, Deborah U. Lau, Jason K. Lau. *Producer:* David Macaione, Tim McGrath. *Music:* Mike Verta. *Writer:* Richard Manning. *Director:* Andrew Prowse.

229   Her Only Child. (TV Movie; Drama; Lifetime; March 22, 2008)

A lonely, deeply disturbed woman (Inez) plots to keep her daughter (Lily) by her side by destroying her relationships with men.

Cast: Nicholle Tom (Lily Stanler), Gwynth Walsh (Inez Stanler), Cameron Daddo (Larry Nowack), Craig Thomas (Roger), Kim Bubbs (Joanna).

Credits: *Executive Producer:* Tom Berry, Louis Massicotte. *Producer:* Neil Bregman. *Music:* Richard Bowers. *Writer:* Christine Conradt, Mary Weinstein. *Director:* Douglas Jackson.

230   Here Come the Newlyweds. (Series; Reality; ABC; March 2, 2008 to April 6, 2008)

Seven newlywed couples appear. Each couple was chosen for a specific reason (for example, together since high school; Barbie and Ken clones; four times married and divorced) and the program, a more athletic version of *The Newlywed Game*, puts trust to the test by subjecting the couples to answering personal questions and competing in challenging stunts designed to test compatibility.

Host: Pat Bullard.

Credits: *Executive Producer:* Jay Blumenfield, Tony Marsh. *Co-Executive Producer:* Alex Campbell. *Producer:* Jeff Anderson. *Supervising Producer:* Shannon Keenan. *Show Producer:* Jeff Nucera. *Director:* Tony Sacco.

Reviews: "*Here Come the Newlyweds* has a strong concept but suffers from poor execution and casting, including a vote-off element that generates absolutely zero suspense" (*Variety*).

"For the most part, though, this is dull, unimaginative and sleep inducing. The most successful part of this show will be guessing if it stays on for its six-week run" (*The Hollywood Reporter*).

231   The Hero Awards. (Special; Variety; My Network TV; July 4, 2008)

An awards show, subtitled "Heroes Among Us," that honors everyday heroism — exceptional individuals and organizations "who work to make our world a better place." These include celebrities and individuals for their acts of charity, firemen and emergency response personnel.

Host: Dean Cain. **Guests:** Gloria Gaynor, B.J. Thomas, Ace Young, Farrah Fawcett, Nicholas Cage, Louis Gossett, Jr., Joan Lunden, Paul Williams.

Credits: *Executive Producer:* James Romanovich. *Producer:* Carlos Aguila.

232   High School Confidential. (Series; Reality; WE; March 10, 2008 to April 28, 2008)

A series that is actually four years in the making. In 2002, filmmaker Sharon Liese chose 12 girls from a Kansas high school to document their high school years from freshmen to seniors. Two girls are profiled on each program (including interviews with her parents and siblings) The interviews are quite frank and can make one wonder why people appear on national television to air their dirty laundry.

Narrator: Wendy K. Gray.

Credits: *Executive Producer:* Jon Kroll, Sharon Liese, Sydney Levin, Jim Rosenthal. *Supervising Producer:* Mary Belton. *Producer:* Suzanne Ali, Mark Costa.

Review: "*High School Confidential* has something to say about the social pressures felt by teenage girls whose biggest worry in this intensely dramatic period of their lives is what other people think of them" (*New York Post*).

233   High School Musical: Get in the Picture. (Series; Reality; ABC; July 20, 2008 to September 8, 2008)

An audition series to find a teenager to star in a music video that will be shown during the closing credits of the fall 2008 feature film *High School Musical 3: Senior Year.* Twelve teenagers compete in music and dance challenges for the music video and a contract with ABC and Disney Records. The teens are guided by a professional faculty to hone their acting, singing, dancing and performing skills.

Host: Nick Lachey. **Faculty:** Tiana Brown (dancer), Regina Williams (actress), Rob Adler (actor), Chris Prinzo (Broadway star).

Credits: *Executive Producer:* Tony Marsh, Jay Blumenfield. *Supervising Producer:* Trevor Baierl, Dean Ollins. *Producer:* Jeff Anderson-Munkres, Alex Campbell. *Music:* Jeff Lippencott, Mark T. Williams.

Review: "What distinguishes *Musical* is its breathtaking cross-platform promotion of Disney properties, from the upcoming movie [*High School Musical 3*] to the studio theme parks to the animated Disney movies whose songs are belted out as calling cards" (*Variety*).

234   High School Reunion. (Series; Reality; TV Land; March 5, 2008 to April 9, 2008)

Sixteen former high school students are gathered in Maui, Hawaii, for a twenty year reunion that is captured by cameras. The graduates are from J.J. Pearce High School in Richardson, Texas, and include the bully, the class beauty, the popular girl, the nerd, the stud, etc. They meet again — most for the first time in many years and reminisce about their past and present experiences. Returned for a new cycle on February 18, 2009.

Credits: *Executive Producer:* Mike Fleiss, Lisa Levenson. *Co-Executive Producer:* Drew Hoegl, Jonathan Singer. *Supervising*

Producer: Scott Cooper. *Senior Producer:* Walt Amiecinski. *Producer:* David Price. *Director:* David Sullivan.

Review: "It's a rather uninspiring journey, boiling it with denizens down to archetypes (the stud, the popular girl, the bully) before turning them loose on what amounts to 'Temptation Island: Almost 40 Edition'" (*Variety*).

235   Hip Hop Honors. (Special; Tribute; VH-1; October 6, 2008)

A tribute to the luminaries who pioneered the cultural phenomenon of hip hop music.

Host: Tracy Morgan. **Guests:** Big Boi, Biz Markie, Bun B, Ghostface, Killah, Kid Rocko, McLyte, Lil' Jon, Lil' Wayne, Q-Tip, Scarface, Wyclef Jean, Cheech and Chong, Sanaa Latham.

Credits: *Executive Producer:* Jae Benson II, Lee Rolontz. *Co-Executive Producer:* Fab 5 Freddy, Nelson George. *Director:* Louis J. Horvitz.

236   The Hive. (TV Movie; Horror; Sci Fi; February 17, 2008)

Reminiscent of the old time radio play *Lenningen vs. the Ants*, the story follows a team of specialized agents as they attempt to stop armies of ants, being controlled by alien forces, from ravaging an island.

Cast: Elizabeth Healey (Claire), Tom Wopat (Bill), Jessica Reavis (Debbie), Mark Ramsey (Cortez), Kal Weber (Len).

Credits: *Executive Producer:* Robert Halmi, Sr., Robert Halmi, Jr. *Producer:* Charles Salmon. *Music:* Charles Olms, Mark Ryder. *Director:* Peter Manus. *Writer:* T.S. Cook.

237   Hole in the Wall. (Series; Game; Fox; Premiered: September 7, 2008)

Two three member teams compete in a silly game wherein they must make themselves into the right shape to fit through a shape cut out in a Styrofoam wall. Round one has each individual member of each team face the wall. As the wall approaches, the player must position himself and run toward the wall and pass through the cutout. Success earns one point; failure results in a dip in the water under the wall. Round two has two players, working as a team, attempting to jump through cutouts; round three encompasses all three members and a wall with three cutouts. The team with the highest score wins $25,000.

Hosts: Brooke Burns, Mark Thompson. **Lifeguard:** Laila Odom.

Credits: *Executive Producer:* Stuart Krasnow. *Co-Executive Producer:* Kevin Williams. *Producer:* Jon Peper.

Review: "Despite being harmless nonsense, it's another me-too effort for Fox, whose recent reality formula has mostly consisted of over producing under whelming concepts that ape an exciting show" (*Variety*).

238   A Holiday Celebration on Ice. (Special; Variety; Syn.; December 21, 2008)

Ice skating stars dance to Christmas songs performed by guests or to recordings. Taped in Nashville, Tennessee.

Host: Nancy Kerrigan. **Singers:** Billy Ray Cyrus, Sherri Austin, Sawyer Brown. **Ice Skaters:** Nancy Kerrigan, Tania Kwatakowski, Isabelle Braussevy, Lloyd Isler, Sirila Bonaly, Elvis Stojko.

Credits: *Executive Producer:* Jerry Solomon, Alonzo Monk, Brian Hughes. *Producer:* Mike Long. *Director:* Meg Streeter.

239   Hollywood Residential. (Series; Reality; Starz; 2008)

A spoof of home repair programs that spotlights an accident-prone celebrity home makeover expert. Tony King is the "expert" and stories follow Tony as he and his crew attempt to wreck as little havoc as possible while remodeling the homes of celebrities (like Paula Abdul, Carmen Electra, Jamie Kennedy, Beverly D'Angelo and Cheryl Hines).

Cast: Adam Paul (Tony King), Lindsay Stoddart (Lila Mann, his co-host), David Ramsey (Don Merritt, crew member), Eric Allan Kramer (Pete, crew member), Carrie Clifford (Carrie, crew member).
Credits: *Executive Producer:* Cheryl Hines, Andy Lerner, Peter Principato, Paul Young. *Producer:* Sean K. Lambert, Terry Crotzer. *Music:* Sheldon Mirowitz.

240 Hollywood Singing and Dancing: A Musical Tribute. (Special; Variety; PBS; March 1, 2008)
A clip rich look at the history of the Hollywood musical beginning with the era of the Bubsy Berkley dance spectaculars of the 1930s.
Host: Shirley Jones. **Appearing:** Pat Boone, Leslie Caron, Marge Champion, Rhonda Fleming, Betty Garrett, Tab Hunter, Shirley MacLaine, Joan Leslie, Patti Page, Janis Paige, Rita Moreno, Liza Minnelli.
Credits: *Producer:* Mark McLaughlin, Jane Shayne, Julie Antepli. *Associate Producer:* Philip Dye, Randy Gitsch, Denise Hamilton. *Writer:* Philip Dye, Denise Hamilton, Tasha Lowe-Newsome, Mark McLaughlin. *Director:* Mark McLaughlin.

241 A Home for the Holidays with Faith Hill. (Special; Variety; CBS; December 23, 2008)
The tenth annual presentation wherein country music star Faith Hill and her guests present holiday songs and touching stories about foster care adoption (to raise awareness of the social issue).
Host: Faith Hill. **Guests:** Melissa Etheridge, Tim McGraw, Gavin Rossdale, Jamie Foxx, Kristin Chenoweth, Rene Russo, Martin Short, Patricia Heaton.
Credits: *Executive Producer:* Karen Mack, Stu Schreiber, Marilyn Seabury. *Supervising Producer:* Kimberly Steer. *Producer:* Kelly Block. *Director:* Michael Simon.

242 Hopkins. (Series; Reality; ABC; June 26, 2008 to August 7, 2008)
Compelling, true series that focuses on the doctors, nurses and patients at John Hopkins Hospital in Baltimore. Cameras capture everything — from the operations to staff personal problems to the hopes and despair of the patients.
Credits: *Supervising Producer:* Brad Herbert, Alex Piper. *Producer:* Erica Baumgart, Ken Chu, Monica Dela Rosa, Sarah Fogel, Sarah Namias, Ali Sargent.
Review: "Watching *Hopkins* ... you get the feeling this is about as close as we're ever going to get to truly capturing a measure of unfettered honesty in a prime-time medium that typically wields manipulation like a machete" (*The Hollywood Reporter*).

243 Hotel Babylon. (Series; Drama; BBC America; 2008)
A British version of *Hotel* that relates incidents in the lives of guests who check into the elegant Hotel Babylon in England. Rebecca Mitchell is the hotel director; Charlie Edwards is her assistant. Jackie Clunes is the head of housekeeping; Tony Casemore is the concierge; Anna Thornton-Wilton is the lobby receptionist. Like the American series, stories also focus on the efforts of the hotel staff to help patrons overcome their problems.
Cast: Tamzin Outhwaite (Rebecca Mitchell), Emma Pierson (Anna Thornton-Wilton), Max Beesley (Charlie Edwards), Dexter Fletcher (Tony Casemore), Natalie Mendoza (Jackie Clunes).
Credits: *Executive Producer:* Gareth Neame, Laura Mackie, Lucy Richer. *Producer:* Christopher Aird. *Music:* John Lunn, Jim Williams.
Reviews: "More controversial than the best BBC [British Broadcasting Corporation] the series gets by on an attractive cast and its high style, serving up a trifle that's not compulsive enough initially to demand an extended stay" (*Variety*).

"It's been nearly 20 years since ... *Hotel* closed its doors on ABC. For those who waited for a grand re-opening, you're in luck. Check out and check into *Hotel Babylon* on BBC America" (*The Hollywood Reporter*).

244 House of Saddam. (TV Movie; Biography; HBO; December 7 and 14, 2008)

Two-part "dramatization based on certain facts" that charts the rise and fall of Iraqi leader Saddam Hussein and his family beginning in 1979 when Saddam deposed the then president and quickly established his rule as a powerful and feared leader.

Cast: Igal Naor (Saddem Hussein), Shohreh Aghdashlon (Sajida), Philip Arditti (Uday Hussein), Said Taghmaoui Samira (Barzan Ibrahim), Christine Stephen-Daly (Shalbano), Amr Waked (Hussein Kamel).

Credits: *Executive Producer:* Alex Holmes, Hilary Salmon. *Producer:* Steve Lightfoot. *Director:* Alex Holmes, Hilary Salmon. *Writer:* Alex Holmes, Stephen Butchard.

Reviews: "*House of Saddam* is too episodic to be fully engaging, providing a sporadically interesting glimpse into how cheap life was under Hussein's brutal rule" (*Variety*).

"*House of Saddam* fills in enough details for a complete picture of the devious dictator to emerge but here's the catch. You've got to be willing to put aside four hours, which is asking a lot when the subject is a dead, savage, cold-hearted brutal megalomaniacal tyrant" (*The Hollywood Reporter*).

245 Housecat House Call. (Series; Reality; Animal Planet; June 7, 2008 to August 30, 2008)

Programs devoted to dogs have aired on various networks over the years, but cats have not seen the same glory. While not the drama of *Lassie*, it is a look at cats and their owners — and the problems the felines cause. Helping to resolve the problem is Dr. Katrina Warren, an Australian veterinarian, who visits people with problem cats with the object being to allow the family to rule the house, not the pet. Produced in association with Purina Cat Chow.

Host: Dr. Katrina Warren.

Credits: *Producer:* Jason Pyne, Steve Jones.

246 How to Look Good Naked. (Series; Reality; Lifetime; Premiered: January 14, 2008)

Women with poor self-esteem and poor body image are the subjects — to help them realize there is potential for improvement without the need for plastic surgery.

Host: Carson Kressley.

Credits: *Executive Producer:* Riaz Patel, Alex Fraser, Jim Sayer, Jo Rosenfelder, Chris Coelen. *Co-Executive Producer:* David Garfield. *Associate Producer:* Atousa Hojat Panah.

Reviews: "Unlike reality shows that tout themselves as a social experiment, this series feels like the real thing — or, at the very least, good water cooler material" (*The Hollywood Reporter*).

"The message is clear: no matter who you are, or what your size, you're beautiful and you should know it. This works" (*Variety*).

247 Hulk Hogan's Celebrity Championship Wrestling. (Series; Reality; CMT; October 18, 2008 to December 7, 2008)

Ten celebrities are brought together and trained in the art of wrestling to compete in challenges and eventually master the ring to become professional-quality wrestlers.

Host: Hulk Hogan. **Judges:** Hulk Hogan, Eric Bischoff, Jimmy Hart. **Celebrities:** Danny Bonaduce, Todd Bridges, ButterBean, Trishelle Cannatella, Dustin Diamond, Erin Murphy, Dennis Rodman, Frank Stallone, Nikki Ziering, Tiffany

Ziering. **Ring Announcer:** Todd Keneley. **Referee:** Anthony Rosas.

Credits: *Executive Producer:* Eric Bischoff, Jason Hervey, Hulk Hogan, Brian Smith, Bob Kusbit, Melanie Moreau. *Supervising Producer:* Todd Hurvitz. *Co-Executive Producer:* Mark Herwick.

248   Husband for Hire. (TV Movie; Comedy; Oxygen; January 19, 2008)

In order to retain her share of the family inheritance, a perfectionist Latina woman (Lola), must marry. Unable to find a man who meets her standards, she hires a local workman (Bo) to pose as her suitor. The story relates the complications that ensue as she struggles to not only transform him but convince her skeptical family that she has found the perfect man.

Cast: Nadine Velazquez (Lola), Mark Consuelos (Bo), Rosa Arredondo (Simona), Jayce Bartok (Bread), Tempsett Bledsoe (Nian), Hugh Elliot (Manchita), Erik Estrada (Victor Diaz).

Credits: *Executive Producer:* Lauren Dale, Howard Gertler, Robert O. Green. *Producer:* Susan Kirr. *Writer-Director:* Kris Isacsson. *Music:* David Derby, Michael Kotch.

249   I Can't Believe I'm Still Single. (Series; Comedy; Showtime; June 22, 2008 to September 21, 2008)

Eric Schaeffer is 35 years old and single. He thought, as a teenager, that when the time was right, he could easily find a girl with whom to settle down. Unfortunately, as he grew older, he found this to be a myth. He has searched and searched but to no avail. Stories follow Eric as he goes to extremes — from hookers to internet dating — to find that one elusive girl.

Star: Eric Schaeffer.

Credits: *Executive Producer:* Eric Schaeffer, Terence Michael. *Producer:* Michael Levine. *Associate Producer:* Em Sinick.

250   I Do! (Series; Reality; NBC; July 26, 2008 to August 2, 2008)

A look at the planning stages of the weddings of ordinary people. Produced in association with *The Knot* (a wedding magazine).

Host: Carley Roney (editor-in-chief, *The Knot*).

Credits: *Executive Producer:* Morgan Hertzan. *Producer:* Justin Goldberg, Jordana Starr, Grace Kim. *Associate Producer:* Pamela Kirkland.

251   I Know My Kid's a Star. (Series; Reality; VH-1; April 10, 2008 to May 8, 2008)

Former child star Danny Bonaduce (*The Partridge Family*) hosts a reality series that seeks to find the next child star. The children appear with their parents and must compete in a series of weekly challenges (like voicing a cartoon character) with the weakest performers facing elimination. The one child left standing wins the competition and the opportunity to star on a television series.

Host: Danny Bonaduce. **The Kids:** Melissa Brasselle, Helene Kress, Gian Di Franco, Alai Divinity, Devon Goocher, Kevin Goocher, Cheyenne Hayness, Gigi Hunter, Mackenzie Knapps, Ivan Kraljevic, Austin Parker, Jonathan Parker, Hayley Sanchez, Cameron Vanderwerf, Mary Jo Wold.

Credits: *Executive Producer:* Jeff Collins, Adam Greener. *Supervising Producer:* Todd Radnitz. *Producer:* Danny Bonaduce.

252   I Love Money. (Series; Reality; VH-1; July 6, 2008 to October 5, 2008)

Contestants from former VH-1 series (*Flavor of Love, I Love New York* and *Rock of Love*) are brought together on Huatulco Beach in Mexico to compete against each other in a series of challenges wherein the best performer wins $250,000.

Host: Craig Jackson. **Contestants:** Heather Chadwell, Brandi Cunningham, Joshua Gallander, Megan Hauseman, Frank Maresca, Lee Marks, Destiney Moore, Torrey Samuels, Cindy Steele.

Credits: *Executive Producer:* Matt Odgers, Cris Abrego, Mark Cronin. *Supervising Producer:* Fred Backhead, Michelle Brando, Scott Teti. *Producer:* Seth Frye, Ryan Smith.

253 I Love the New Millennium. (Special; Variety; VH-1; June 23, 2008 to June 26, 2008)

A look at the good, bad, funny and sad times of the years 2000 through 2007.

Hosts: Regan Burns, Rachel Quaintance, Keith Powell.

Credits: *Executive Producer:* Karla Hilalgo, Meredith Ross. *Producer:* Pat Twist, Jill Solz.

254 I Survived. (Series; Reality; Biography Channel; Premiered: December 1, 2008)

People who were confronted and survived situations that looked like the end, appear to tell their harrowing experiences and how they overcame them.

Credits: *Producer-Director:* Sally Howard. *Music:* Plan 9.

255 I Survived a Japanese Game Show. (Series; Game; ABC; June 24, 2008 to August 5, 2008)

Ten Americans are sent to Japan to compete against each other in outrageous (as well as hilarious) stunt challenges. The ten players live together in a large residence for the duration of the contest. The weakest performers are eliminated on a weekly basis. The one player left standing not only wins the grand prize ($250,000) but receives the opportunity to exclaim, "I Survived a Japanese Game Show."

Host: Tony Sano. **Master of Ceremonies:** Rome Kanda.

Credits: *Executive Producer:* Kent Weed, Karsten Bartholin, Tim Crescenti, David Sidebottom, Arthur Smith. *Supervising Producer:* Rick Brown, Jonathan Chinn, Amy Jacobson, Blake Levin. *Producer:* Dave Oliver.

256 I Want to Work for Diddy. (Series; Reality; VH-1; August 4, 2008 to October 6, 2008)

Apprentice-like program in which hip hop mogul Sean "P. Diddy" Combs seeks an assistant by putting 13 young hopefuls through a series of challenges. The weakest performers are eliminated on a weekly basis with the best performer receiving the job as Sean's business assistant.

Host: Sean "P. Diddy" Combs. **Winners:** Suzanne Siegel, Mic Barber.

Credits: *Executive Producer:* Sean "P. Diddy" Combs. *Co-Executive Producer:* Mark S. Jacobs. *Producer:* Bill Gaudsmith.

257 Imagination Movers. (Series; Children; Disney; Premiered: September 6, 2008)

Imagination Movers, a New Orleans based music group, oversees a program that encourages children to utilize their creative skills to solve everyday problems.

Stars: Wendy Calio, Frank Crim, David Poche.

Credits: *Executive Producer:* Skot Bright, Richard Gitelson, Sascha Penn. *Producer:* Kati Johnston. *Music:* Stuart Kollmorgen.

258 In Harm's Way. (Series; Reality; CW; October 5, 2008 to November 23, 2008)

Documentary-like program that chronicles the stories of brave people who risk their lives in life-threatening jobs (e.g., hurricane chasers, rodeo bull riders, oil well cappers, Coast Guard rescue swimmers, avalanche hunters).

Host: Hunter Ellis.

Credits: *Executive Producer:* Hunter Ellis

259 In Plain Sight. (Series; Crime Drama; USA; June 1, 2008 to August 17, 2008)

Mary Shannon is a U.S. Marshal attached to WITSEC (the Federal Witness Protection Program). She is based in Albuquerque, New Mexico and is partners with Marshall Mann. Mary's job is to protect and manage relocated federal witnesses (people who are relocated to the Southwest to begin a new life under a new name for helping authorities collar criminals). Stories follow Mary and Marshall as they risk their lives to keep federally protected witness safe.

Mary, who must keep the true nature of her job secret, lives with her mother, Jinx, and her younger sister, Brandi. To help the people she is assigned to protect, Mary (and Marshall) must often pretend to be somebody else (from marriage counselor to mother) to help witnesses make an easy transition into their new lives.

Jinx adores her daughters, but has never really been a supportive mother. She appears to be adverse to work but loves to drink and has had many romantic interludes. Brandi is a bit more ambitious than her mother but has a tendency to use drugs and fall for the worst possible men.

Stan McQueen is Mary's superior, a chief inspector for WITSEC; Raphael is Mary's on-and-off again boyfriend.

Cast: Mary McCormack (Mary Shannon), Frederick Weller (Marshall Mann), Lesley Ann Warren (Jinx Shannon), Nichole Hiltz (Brandi Shannon), Paul Ben-Victor (Stan McQueen), Cristian DeLa Fuente (Raphael Ramirez).

Credits: *Executive Producer:* David Maples, Paul Stupin. *Producer:* Mark Piznarski, Randi Richmond.

Reviews: "After an impressive string of cable dramas ... this lighthearted female cop show feels stale and nondescript... Given the evidence, the investigation should be brief" (*Variety*).

"USA is rolling out *In Plain Sight* with a 76-minute 'limited interruption' premiere which ends up being more than enough to pass judgment. It's mediocre" (*The San Francisco Chronicle*).

"*In Plain Sight* could be viewed as the anti–*Gossip Girl*: McCormick's Mary is a loner ... she favors Western boots made for walkin' ... she deals in hard-won truths.

The more Mary hews to these traits, the better the show is" (*Entertainment Weekly*).

260   In Treatment. (Series; Drama; HBO; Premiered: January 28, 2008)

The meeting between a psychiatrist (Paul Weston) and his patients are presented as a weeknight therapy session. Each night is devoted to a different patient: Laura (Monday), Alex (Tuesday), Sophie (Wednesday), Jake and Amy Bickerson (Thursday), and Paul (Friday), who meets with his therapist (Gina) to deal with his own problems (including a troubled marriage and "losing patience with my patients"). Based on the Israeli series *Be'Tinpul.*

Cast: Gabriel Byrne (Paul Weston), Michelle Forbes (Kate Weston), Melissa George (Laura), Blair Underwood (Alex), Mia Wasikowska (Sophie), Josh Charles (Jake Bickerson), Embeth Davidtz (Amy), Dianne Wiest (Gina Toll).

Credits: *Executive Producer:* Rodrigo Garcia, Stephen Levinson, Hagel Levi, Mark Wahlberg. *Co-Executive Producer:* Noa Tishby. *Producer:* Sarah Lum, Leonard Torgan. Joanne Toll.

Reviews: "*In Treatment*'s intensity does build on the weekly progress but it's never completely absorbing and you wonder how many viewers will commit to such a demanding regimen" (*Variety*).

"It's rather impossible to imagine watching an emotionally exhausting show like *In Treatment* ... night after night ... this is a series for which TiVo was invented if there ever was one" (*The Hollywood Reporter*).

"...because it's on HBO with a therapist and a sofa, *In Treatment* is not *Tell Me You Love Me*. What *Treatment* lacks in *Tell Me* style graphic sex, it makes up for in hot-tempered neuroses" (*Entertainment Weekly*).

261   Inside the Box. (Series; Game; Syn.; Premiered: September 16, 2008)

Three players compete. One is placed

inside "the box"; two remain outside. The box player has a series of questions relating to a television show, character or actor. The outside players have only one image of the subject to whom the questions refer. Two minutes is placed on a clock and the box players ask indirect questions of the outside players, one at a time. The box players can stop the clock and attempt to guess the subject at any time. The amount of time left on the clock when an identification is made becomes the player's score. If an outside player gives an incorrect response to a question, he receives a five second penalty (which is deducted from his two minutes box time). Each player receives a chance inside the box with the highest scoring time player at the end of two rounds being declared the winner.

Host: Sam Kalilieh.

Credits: *Executive Producer:* Michael Geddes, Chris Geddes. *Supervising Producer:* Jake Werner. *Producer:* Rachel Horvath, Ann Camilleri. *Music:* Peter Warnica.

262 Into the Unknown with Josh Bernstein. (Series; Reality; Discovery Channel; August 18, 2008 to October 6, 2008)

Explorer Josh Bernstein travels from Italy to Turkey to uncover the truth about Roman Gladiators — do they resemble Hollywood's portrayal of them or where they, in actuality, something else?

Host: Josh Bernstein.

Credits: *Executive Producer:* Josh Bernstein, Beth Dietrich, Bernadette McDail.

263 The IT Crowd. (Series; Comedy; IFC; September 30, 2008 to December 22, 2008)

Reynholm Industries is a large corporation in England. While the company employs many people, the entire focus is on three workers in the computer division: Jen, Roy and Moss, young people who lack not only social skills but, for Jen, also the ability to actually use a computer for business. Jen lied about her qualifications and has to pretend to know what she is doing. Roy is an Irishman who thinks he's a ladies' man; Moss is a genius who is also a goof off. Produced in England.

Cast: Katherine Parkinson (Jen Barber), Chris O'Dowd (Roy), Richard Ayoade (Moss)

Credits: *Producer:* Ash Atalia, Derren Schlessinger. *Music:* Neil Hannon. *Writer-Director:* Graham Linehan.

Reviews: "An entertaining American influenced British workplace comedy finds a U.S. outlet ... if the show gains any buzz on IFC, look for an American adaptation within a couple of years" (*The Hollywood Reporter*).

"While the concept for *The IT Crowd* is extremely clever and benefits from its series broad, loopy execution, it only sporadically fulfills that promise" (*Variety*).

264 It's Me or the Dog. (Series; Reality; Animal Planet; Premiered: July 11, 2008)

Tips on training dogs — from unruly mutts to pampered poodles from ten year dog training expert Victoria Stilwell. Based on the British series of the same title.

Host: Victoria Stilwell.

Credits: *Producer:* John Magennis.

265 Jacked: Auto Theft Task Force. (Series; Reality; A&E; August 21, 2008 to October 30, 2008)

A look at the officers of the Auto Theft Task Force (better known as "The Wolf Pack") of the Northern New Jersey Police Department. Episodes show how the unit tracks down and recovers stolen cars.

Credits: *Executive Producer:* Joey Allen, Kevin Bachar, Andy Berg, Robert Sherenon. *Producer:* Brian McAllister, Rob Greene.

266 Jamie at Home. (Series; Cooking; Food Network; Premiered: January 12, 2008)

Chef Jamie Oliver prepares meals focusing on fresh garden ingredients.

Host: Jamie Oliver.
Credits: *Executive Producer:* Ben Galen, Rachel Purnell, Lindsay Bradbury. *Producer:* Sophie Seiden.

267 Janice and Abbey. (Series; Reality; Oxygen; February 19, 2008 to March 27, 2008)

Abbey Clancy is a potential model who became the runner up on the British TV series *Britain's Next Top Model*. Supermodel Janice Dickinson sees potential in Abbey and sets out to train her. Stories follow Abbey as she travels to Los Angeles to begin the regime of modeling chores with the hope of becoming a super model.

Stars: Janice Dickinson, Abbey Clancy.
Credits: *Executive Producer:* Rachel Arnold, Janice Dickinson, Clare Hollywood. *Producer:* Heather Langone.

268 Jeffrey Ross: No Offense Live from New Jersey. (Special; Comedy; Comedy Central; August 22, 2008)

Stand-up comedian Jeffrey Ross satirizes life in the Garden State, the home of his birth.

Host: Jeffrey Ross.
Credits: *Executive Producer:* Jeffrey Ross, Brian Volk-Weiss, Barry Katz. *Producer:* Jay Chapman. *Writer:* Jeffrey Ross. *Director:* Jay Karas.

269 Jekyll. (Series; Drama; BBC America; August 4, 2008 to September 8, 2008)

A modern adaptation of the Robert Louis Stevenson novel, *Dr. Jekyll and Mr. Hyde*. It is the present (2007) when Tom Jackman learns that he is the only known living descendant of the 19th century physician, Dr. Henry Jekyll, the man who was plagued by an evil alter ego named Edward Hyde. Henry's medical experiments cursed him to become two people living in the same body. Like his ancestor, Tom has inherited a dark side — his own alter ego, Mr. Hyde. While the two share the same body, Mr. Hyde is unaware that Tom has a family (a wife, Claire, and two children, Harry and Eddie). Through the use of modern technology, Tom has found a way to keep Mr. Hyde from overtaking him; Mr. Hyde, however, grows stronger each day and seeks to get out and becomes increasingly persistent. Stories follow Tom as he struggles to suppress his evil side and avoid capture by a secret, ancient organization that seeks to harness Mr. Hyde for their own sinister purposes. Produced in England.

Cast: James Nesbitt (Tom Jackman/ Mr. Hyde), Gina Bellman (Claire Jackman), Christopher Day (Harry Jackman), Andrew Byrne (Eddie Jackman), Meera Syal (Miranda), Michelle Ryan (Nurse Katherine Reemer), Paterson Joseph (Benjamon), Fenella Woolgar (Min), Denis Lawson (Peter Syme).

Credits: *Executive Producer:* Beryl Vertue, Steven Moffat. *Producer:* Elaine Cameron, Jeffrey Taylor. *Writer:* Steven Moffat. *Director:* Douglas MacKinon, Matt Lipsey.

270 The Jerry Lewis MDA Labor Day Telethon. (Special; Variety; Syn.; August 31 to September 1, 2008)

The 43rd annual presentation wherein Jerry Lewis, National Chairman of the Muscular Dystrophy Association, hosts an entertainment extravaganza to raise research money for children (Jerry's Kids) suffering from the disease. Aired on 190 stations and broadcast live from Las Vegas; $65 million was raised.

Host: Jerry Lewis. Co-Hosts: Jann Carl, Nancy O'Dell, Tony Orlando, Tom Bergeron, Allison Sweeney. Announcer: Ed McMahon.

Credits: *Executive Producer:* Richard Burgio. *Producer:* Lisa Nann, Chris Lopez. *Music:* Dan Rosengard. *Director:* Debi Gelman.

271 Jimmy Kimmel's Big Night of Stars. (Special; Interview; ABC; September 21, 2008)

A special that aired prior to *The Emmy Awards* telecast in which Jimmy Kimmel interviews personalities from the world of television, film and music.

Host: Jimmy Kimmel. **Guests:** Selma Hayek, Tracy Morgan, Michael Phelps, Tom Bergeron, Heidi Klum, Howie Mandel, Jeff Probst, Ryan Seacrest.

Credits: *Executive Producer:* Jimmy Kimmel. *Producer:* Doug DeLucca.

272   John Adams. (Miniseries; Drama; HBO; March 16, 2008 to April 27, 2008)

Seven-part adaptation of the David McCullough autobiography about John Adams, the second president of the United States.

Cast: Paul Giamatti (John Adams), Laura Linney (Abigail Adams), David Morse (George Washington), Sarah Polley (Abigail "Nabby" Adams), Rufus Sewell (Alexander Hamilton), Justin Theroux (John Hancock), Tom Wilkinson (Benjamin Franklin), Danny Huston (Samuel Adams), Stephen Dillane (Thomas Jefferson).

Credits: *Executive Producer:* Gary Goetzman. *Producer:* David Coatsworth, Tom Hanks. *Writer:* Kirk Ellis, Michelle Ashford. *Director:* Tom Hooper. *Music:* Robert Lane, Joseph Vitarelli.

Reviews: "It is the small moments more than the soaring themes that are the real triumph here, and which lifts *John Adams* out of the realm of ordinary biopics and *Birth of the Nation* dramas" (*The Wall Street Journal*).

"And there's the production itself, which completely lives up to HBO's high standards for period dramas. I only wish I could say the same for *Adams* himself" (*USA Today*).

"You'd have to be a heartless Commie bastard not to enjoy HBO's seven-part miniseries *John Adams*" (*Entertainment Weekly*).

273   Journey to the Center of the Earth. (TV Movie; Adventure; Ion; January 27, 2008)

An anthropologist (Jonathan Brock) embarks on an expedition to the earth's center to find a scientist (Edward Dennison) who vanished years earlier. Based on the novel by Jules Verne.

Cast: Rick Schroder (Jonathan Brock), Victoria Pratt (Martha Dennison), Peter Fonda (Edward Dennison), Steven Grayhm (Abel Petkov), Jonathan Brewer (Wakinta), Elyse Levesque (Emily), Richard Side (Solomon Smith).

Credits: *Executive Producer:* Robert Halmi, Jr., Robert Halmi, Sr., Lisa Richardson. *Producer:* George Hories. *Writer:* Thomas Baum, William Gray. *Director:* T.J. Scott. *Music:* Rene Dupere.

274   Judge Jeanine Pirro. (Series; Reality; CW; Premiered: September 22, 2008)

Former Westchester County (New York) district attorney and judge, Jeanine Pirro, presides over real small claims cases.

Judge: Jeanine Pirro.

Credits: *Executive Producer:* Bo Banks. *Co-Executive Producer:* Jill Olsen. *Supervising Producer:* Melissa Porter.

Review: "The show is a little different from *Judge Judy* and *The People's Court.* Lower class people — or at least those who don't mind embarrassing themselves on national television — appear seeking money or trying to hide from responsibility" (*The Hollywood Reporter*).

275   Judge Karen. (Series; Reality; Syn.; Premiered: September 9, 2008)

Daily program of actual small claims cases presided over by Judge Karen Mills-Francis.

Judge: Karen Mills-Francis. **Bailiff:** Christopher Gallo.

Credits: *Executive Producer:* Rich Goldman. *Co-Executive Producer:* Susan Sobocinski Puckert. *Supervising Producer:* Margot Foley, Trenny Stovall. *Producer:* Tracey Slates.

276   Jurassic Fight Club. (Series; Documentary; History Channel; July 29, 2008 to October 13, 2008)

A look at how dinosaurs battled based on recent evidence uncovered by archeologists. CGI Animation is used to create the very realistic looking dinosaurs and each episode details how a specific species struggled to survive and how and who they fought.

Host: George Blasing.

Producer: Dolores Gavin.

Review: "So good and so exciting, *Jurassic Fight Club* should be compulsory viewing for every kid over 10, not to mention their parents" (*New York Post*).

277 Kath and Kim. (Series; Comedy; NBC; Premiered: October 9, 2008)

Kimberly "Kim" Day is a beautiful young woman who believes she was meant for the finest things life has to offer. She is the daughter of Kathleen "Kath" Day, a single mother (a hairdresser) who has just found romance with Phil Knight, the owner of a fast food store (Phil's Sandwich Island) in the mall. All appears to be progressing well until Kim leaves her husband of six weeks (Craig) and moves back home to live with Kath. Kim became disillusioned living with Craig ("I didn't sign up for cooking or caring about how anybody's day was. I'm a trophy wife") and is now seeking to find herself but also putting a damper on Kath's new romance.

Kath is shallow and self-absorbed and admits that she is a high maintenance girl. Kim is a self-obsessed woman-child (a spoiled brat who wants things her way or no way at all). Craig, an electronics store employee (at Circuit Surplus Electronics), loves Kim and is trying to make the marriage work, but he can never seem to say what Kim wants to hear). Stories follow Kath as she tries to begin a new life and Kim as she wallows in self-pity with no apparent ambition but to find someone to treat her like she believes she should be. Based on the Australian series of the same title.

Cast: Selma Blair (Kim Day), Molly Shannon (Kath Day), John Michael Higgins (Phil Knight), Mikey Day (Craig Baker).

Credits: *Executive Producer:* Michelle Nader, Gina Riley, Jane Turner, Rick McKenna. *Co-Executive Producer:* Will Calhoun, Liz Astrof. *Producer:* Patrick Kienlen.

Reviews: "What is hard to understand is why NBC thought this particular adaptation would work. It lacks the charm of the original [Australian]. Worse, the characters on the NBC show are so exaggerated that the whole thing feels like a skit. A very long skit" (*The Hollywood Reporter*).

"*Kath and Kim* will likely have American audiences scratching their heads, wondering what Australians saw in the concept or if something was seriously lost in the translation" (*Variety*).

"The big difference between the show in Australia and its dish water copy here is that the Australian producers know how to make fun of themselves. American TV people prefer to make fun of everything else" (*New York Post*).

278 The Kennedy Center Honors. (Special; Awards; CBS; December 30, 2008)

The 31st annual presentation, taped at the Kennedy Center Opera House stage, that honors people in the entertainment industry for their lifetime contributions to American culture through the performing arts.

Host: Caroline Kennedy. **Special Guests:** President George Bush, First Lady Laura Bush. **Honorees:** Barbra Streisand (singer-actress), George Jones (singer), Morgan Freeman (actor), Twyla Tharp (choreographer), Pete Townshend (Musician), Roger Daltry (musician). **Guests:** Jack Black, Lily Tomlin, Denzel Washington, Glenn Close, Clint Eastwood, Brad Paisley, Shelby Lynne, Luciana Paris.

Credits: *Executive Producer-Writer:* George Stevens. *Producer-Director:* Michael M. Stevens.

Review: "The show itself remains a delightfully mixed bag, from rock to country to dance. There are surely worse ways to spend two hours between Christmas and New Year's" (*Variety*).

279 Keyshia Cole: The Way It Is. (Series; Reality; BET; Premiered: November 11, 2008)

Keyshia Cole is a young woman who struggled to make her mark in the music world (a singer with A&M Records). She yearns to be an inspiration for young people, especially those growing up "in the hood" as Keyshia herself had a difficult childhood and struggled to become a success. Keyshia believes everyone has goals to realize and through her series she attempts to relate the problems she had and does encounter with family, friends and business associates. The title, "The Way It Is," reflects her first album for A&M Records.

Star: Keyshia Cole.
Credits: *Executive Producer:* James DuBose. *Supervising Producer:* Tracey Finley. *Producer:* Kanika Utley.

280 A Kiss at Midnight. (TV Movie; Drama; Hallmark; December 27, 2008)

Susan Flowers, the owner of a match making service (Hearts and Flowers) appears to have great success in matching clients, but has not yet found her Mr. Right. Widower Josh Sherman is the CEO of Romance.com, an Internet dating service. Believing the Internet site will hurt her business, Susan creates a profile and posts it on the site with the intention of proving that the Internet cannot provide true love. Unknown to Josh, his daughters (Cassie and Jennifer) have posted his profile, hoping to acquire a new mother. The site matches Susan with Josh — a seemingly perfect match until each discovers what the other does for a living and each believes the other is out to destroy their business. The story relates their bickering — until they come to realize that each has found their true love.

Cast: Faith Ford (Susan Flowers), Cameron Daddo (Josh Sherman), Dyan Cannon (Kay Flowers), Lorna Scott (Carla Walsh), Jadin Gould (Cassie Sherman), Abigail Mavity (Jennifer Sherman), Kim Rhodes (Maureen O'Connor), Hal Linden (Arthur Wright).

Credits: *Executive Producer:* Larry Levinson. *Producer:* Mary Church, Lincoln Lageson. *Director:* Bradford May. *Writer:* Anna Sandor.

Review: "If you loved the Tom Hanks–Meg Ryan romance *You've Got Mail* so much that you would watch anything with even the vaguest resemblance, then make a date tonight to watch *A Kiss at Midnight*" (*New York Daily News*).

281 Knight Rider. (Series; Adventure; NBC; Premiered: September 24, 2008)

An update of the 1980s series of the same title (about Michael Knight, a lone crusader who battled crime with the help of KITT, a Knight Industries 2000 car).

It is the present time and a new KITT (Knight Industries 3000) has been developed. It has many improvements, including the ability to change shape and color, artificial intelligence and a super computer capable of hacking virtually any system. The morphing cars are KITT Hero (a Ford Mustang Shelby GT 500 KR) that appears as an ordinary car; KITT Attack is a high speed version of the prior car that transforms into attack mode with the help of air ride technology and specialized body parts. The third vehicle, KITT Remote is a driverless version of Hero.

In the original series, Wilton Knight created KITT. Here, scientist Charles Graiman makes the improvements needed to bring KITT into the 21st century. His daughter, Sarah, a 24-year-old PhD. candidate at Stanford University, is following in his footsteps. Mike Tracer, a 23-year-old ex–Army Ranger (a childhood friend of Sarah's) is chosen to drive KITT. Carrie

Rivai is the FBI agent Knight Industries helps (and vice versa) to bring criminals to justice. Stories follow Michael and Sarah as they use KITT's unique abilities to solve complex criminal situations. Michael later takes the name Michael Knight when the FBI arranges his "death" to keep Mike Tracer's past from catching up with him. Alex heads the unit; Zoe and Billy assist at headquarters. The pilot film aired on NBC on February 17, 2008.

Cast: Justin Bruening (Mike Tracer/ Michael Knight), Deanna Russo (Sarah Graiman), Sydney Tamiia Poitier (Carrie Rivai), Bruce Davison (Charles Graiman), Val Kilmer (Voice of KITT), Smith Cho (Zoe Chase), Paul Campbell (Billy Morgan), Yancey Arias (Alex Torres).

Credits: *Executive Producer:* Glen A. Larson, Doug Liman, David Bartis, Gary Scott Thompson. *Co-Executive Producer:* Steve Shill. *Supervising Producer:* Dave Andron, Sean Ryerson. *Music:* Christopher Tyng.

Reviews (Pilot): "The two hours mostly amount to watching two people that once dated drive around together in a conspicuously product-placed Ford Mustang [KITT]. And yes, that's just about as much fun as it sounds" (*Variety*).

"The revival of *Knight Rider* ... should gladden the heart of viewers ... employed by Ford ... for the rest of us ... an elaborate commercial around which bits of story are sprinkled" (*The Hollywood Reporter*).

Reviews (Series): "Everything that made the original unique and fun has effectively been scrubbed away from this new edition ... an hour devoid of soul" (*The Hollywood Reporter*).

"The *Knight Rider* revival movie set the bar low in terms of expectations, and damned if the series premiere still doesn't go skidding under it" (*Variety*).

282   Kung Fu Killer. (Miniseries; Crime Drama; Spike TV; August 17 and 18, 2008)

Two-part violent martial arts saga about White Crane, an aging kung fu master who battles evil wherever he finds it. In part one, Crane seeks a psycho killer who plans to enslave the country. Part two finds Crane battling a former classmate seeking revenge. Filmed in China and set in the 1930s.

Cast: David Carradine (White Crane), Daryl Hannah (Jane), Jimmy Taenaka (Bingo), Osric Chau (Lang Hu), Kay Tong Lim (Khan), Pei-Pei Cheng (Myling), Rosalind Pho (Tong Ho), Nolan Willlard (Young Crane), Karen Bergan (Crane's mother).

Credits: *Executive Producer:* Robert Halmi, Sr., Robert Halmi, Jr. *Producer:* Matthew O'Connor, Shan Tam. *Music:* Jim Guttridge.

283   Ladies of the House. (TV Movie; Drama; Hallmark Channel; October 16, 2008)

Three women (Rose, Elizabeth, and Birdie) pool their talents (and resources) to refurbish a run down house so that it can be sold and its profits used to keep a local day care center in operation.

Cast: Florence Henderson (Rose), Donna Mills (Elizabeth), Pam Grier (Birdie), Lance Hendriksen (Frank), Richard Roundtree (Stan), Michael Ensign (Pastor Wesley), Judith Baldwin (Amelia), Nicole DuPont (Tracy).

Credits: *Executive Producer:* Robert Halmi, Jr., Larry Levinson. *Co-Executive Producer:* Michael Moran, Matt Fitzsimons. *Producer:* Brian Gordon. *Music:* Alex Wilkinson. *Director:* James Contner. *Writer:* Karen Struck.

Reviews: "Even a script asleep at the wheel can't stop Florence Henderson, Donna Mills and Pam Grier from shining in this sugary story" (*The Hollywood Reporter*).

"It's a joy to watch these pros [Florence, Donna, Pam] pull out all the stops and make even mediocre material fly" (*New York Post*).

284 Laffapalooza. (Special; Comedy; TBS; November 30, 2008)

An annual TBS event wherein top comedians perform their material.

Host: Tracy Morgan. **Comedians:** Mark Curry, Sheryl Underwood, Corey Holcomb, Lavelle Crawford, Earthquake.

Credits: *Executive Producer:* Jamie Foxx, Marcus King, Stu Schrieberg, Ron Wilson, Stephen Kroopnick, Marilyn Seabury. *Producer:* Myrna Byrne. *Director:* Chuck Vinson.

285 Larry the Cable Guy's Star Studded Christmas Extravaganza. (Special; Comedy; CMT; November 21, 2008)

A comical pre–Thanksgiving romp with Christmas overtones that features performances by an array of guest stars.

Host: Dan Whitney (Larry the Cable Guy). **Guests:** Tony Orlando, Fred Willard, Toby Keith, Lewis Black, Jeff Foxworthy, Charlie Callas, Jennifer Aspen, Angela Little, Joey Fatone, Terry Bradshaw, Kellie Hudson, Bill Engvall.

Credits: *Executive Producer:* J.P. Williams, Stella Stolper, Dan Whitney, Tom Forrest, Chris Choun. *Producer:* Ben Tyson, Jennifer Novak, David Higby.

286 Legally Blonde The Musical: The Search for Elle Woods. (Series; Reality; MTV; June 2, 2008 to July 21, 2008)

A talent search to find an actress to play the role of Elle Woods, the pampered blonde, in the Broadway musical *Legally Blonde*. Ten girls are brought together in New York City. The girls are mentored by professionals then tested in acting, singing and dancing challenges. A panel of judges rates the performances with the weakest performer being eliminated on a weekly basis. The one girl who proves to be the best wins the role of Elle Woods (replacing the current actress, Laura Bell Bundy).

Mentor: Haylie Duff. **Judges:** Heather Hatch, Paul Canaan, Bernard Telsey, Jerry Mitchell.

Credits: *Executive Producer:* Steve Kroopnick, Eugene Peck, Stu Schreiberg. *Producer:* Jennifer Stander. *Music:* Jim Parker.

287 Legend of the Seeker. (Series; Adventure; Syn.; Premiered: November 1, 2008)

In a time that has long since been forgotten, a book called *The Book of Counted Shadows* was composed by unknown beings to record the secrets of power. A being called the Seeker used the book to defeat evil. A society of women called Confessors were chosen to protect the book and risk their lives to ensure the safety of the Seeker.

The series is set many centuries later (in a medieval-like era) when an evil ruler, Darken Rahl, is seeking to rule the world and enslave mankind. He requires *The Book of Counted Shadows* to ensure that power.

In an area called the Midlands, a baby boy, destined to become a Seeker, is born to a woman. To protect the baby from Rahl (who seeks to kill it), the wizard Zeddicus Zul Zorander (called Zedd) takes the baby and gives him to a young couple, George and Mary Cypher, to raise. The baby grows to become the woodsman Richard Cypher.

It is thirty-three years later when Richard comes to know his true calling. Kahlan, a Confessor, has been assigned to find Richard, present him with the book and have Zedd proclaim him as the next Seeker. Rahl has sensed the presence of a new Seeker and has dispatched soldiers to destroy the Seeker and retrieve the sacred book for him.

Zedd has not revealed his true nature to Richard. They are friends, but Richard believes he is a crazy old man who talks to his chickens. When Kahlan finds Zedd, Zedd reveals his true nature to Richard and presents him with the Sword of Truth — forged metal to ordinary men, but a magical means to destroy evil for the true Seeker. Richard questions what he has been told until Rahl's soldiers attack them. The ensuing battle, in which Richard finds a strength he has never known before, convinces him that what he has been told is the truth. He then learns from Kahlan about Darken Rahl and his mission: to destroy Rahl and save mankind. Stories follow Richard, Kahlan and Zedd as they set out on a dangerous quest to find Rahl and stop him before he can accomplish his goal. Hindering them is Rahl, who has issued wanted posters for Richard's capture (one thousand gold pieces as a reward). Richard destroyed the book in the third episode (his way of acquiring the secrets of power). Rahl's soldiers have informed him of this and now Rahl must capture Richard in order to acquire the power. Michael is Richard's brother; Chase is Richard's friend.

Cast: Craig Horner (Richard Cypher), Bridget Regan (Kahlan Amnell), Bruce Spence (Zedd), Craig Parker (Darken Rahl), David de Latour (Michael Cypher), Jay Laga'aia (Chase).

Credits: *Executive Producer:* Sam Raimi, Robert Tapert, Joshua Donan, Ned Nalle. *Co-Executive Producer:* Barry Schkolnick, Stephen Tolken. *Supervising Producer:* Mike Sussman, Chad Fiveash, James Stoteraux. *Producer:* Chloe Smith, David Roessell, Mark Beesley. *Music:* Joseph Lo-Duca.

Reviews: "There is nothing howlingly bad here ... but nothing particularly distinctive either. Rather *Legend of the Seeker* feels like a hodgepodge of better sci fi/fantasy fare" (*Variety*).

"Big on style but more challenged in terms of substance, *Seeker* demonstrates much production savvy but at the same time too little provocative/evocative interaction aside from the ultra violet kind" (*The Hollywood Reporter*).

288 **Legend of the Seeker: The Making of a Legend.** (Special; Documentary; Syn.; October 18, 2008)

A behind-the-scenes look at the making of the syndicated TV series *Legend of the Seeker* (see prior title), a much anticipated fall 2008 series.

Host: Lucy Lawless.

Credits: *Executive Producer:* Gary Holland, Gary Lsiter, Blake Bryant. *Producer:* Skip Robinson, Joshua Levine, Jeff Diner, Ryan Moore. *Director:* Gary Lister.

289 **Lesbian Sex and Sexuality.** (Series; Reality; Here!; Premiered: 2008)

A very specialized series (aired on the gay channel Here!) that takes an extremely frank look at what it means to be a lesbian in today's world. The program explores lesbian sexuality through interviews with "sexperts" as well as by visiting erotic dance clubs, lesbian owned adult film companies and sex shops.

Credits: *Executive Producer:* Katherine Linton, Paul Colichman, Stephen P. Jarchow, Meredith Kadlec. *Producer:* Desireena Almoradie, Tracy Izact. *Writer:* Katherine Linton. *Director:* Katherine Linton.

290 **Leverage.** (Series; Drama; TNT; Premiered: December 7, 2008)

Nate Ford is an insurance company investigator with an impressive record of recovery (reclaiming millions of dollars in stolen goods for his company). When Nate's son becomes ill and his company refuses to pay the medical bills (that cost his son's life), Nate quits in disgust but soon finds himself descending into alcoholism. He is literally saved by an aeronautics executive who hires him to recover an exclusive airplane design that was stolen by a rival company. To help him accomplish his goal are less than honorable friends he met while working at the insurance company: Alec Hardison, a specialist in Internet and computer fraud; Parker, an expert thief; Eliot Spencer, a retrieval specialist; and Sophie Devereaux, a grifter who is also a talented actress. Once accomplishing his mission Nate forms a unique organization — recover what has been stolen. Stories follow the team's case assignments as they incorporate their unique skills to return stolen objects to their rightful owners.

Cast: Timothy Hutton (Nate Ford), Beth Riesgraf (Parker), Aldis Hodge (Alec Hardison), Christian Kame (Eliot Spencer), Gina Bellman (Sophie Devereaux).

Credits: *Executive Producer:* Dean Devlin, Chris Downey, John Rogers. *Co-Executive Producer:* Marc Roskin, Kearie Peak. *Co-Producer:* Amy Berg, Rachel Olschen.

Reviews: "There's someone besides accident-chasing legal firms to put the law on your side" (*The Hollywood Reporter*).

"...aside from an easygoing quality and mild comic flair, there's not much here to steal the hearts of viewers; instead it's another lightweight addition to TNT's dinner-style menu of comfort food for a weary nation" (*Variety*).

291 Lewis Black's Root of All Evil.
(Series; Comedy; Comedy Central; March 12, 2008 to October 1, 2008)

A parody of the reality court programs wherein a judge (comedian Lewis Black) presides over cases involving celebrities and pop culture figures he deems as being "the root of all evil."

Host: Lewis Black. **Regulars:** Patton Oswalt, Greg Giraldo, Andrew Daly, Matt Price, Shaun Russell.

Credits: *Executive Producer:* David Sacks, Scott Carter, Lewis Black. *Co-Executive Producer:* Jo Anne Astrow, Mark Lonow. *Supervising Producer:* Michael Addis. *Producer:* Alicia Good, Allison Dykstra. *Music:* Stephen Phillips.

292 The Librarian: Curse of the Judas Chalice.
(TV Movie; Adventure; TNT; December 7, 2008)

The third of two prior *Librarian* movies

about Flynn Carsen, a brilliant student at the Metropolitan Library who uses his intellect to find lost treasures and outwit those who seek the library's collection of magical and mythical artifacts. The story finds Flynn seeking a Judas chalice that has the power to revive the undead (in this instance, the infamous Count Dracula). Charlene and Judson are Flynn's superiors. *The Librarian: Quest for the Spear*, the first film, aired in 2004; it was followed by *The Librarian: Return to King Solomon's Mines* in 2006.

Cast: Noah Wyle (Flynn Carsen), Bob Newhart (Judson), Jane Curtin (Charlene), Bruce Davison (Professor Lazlo), Stana Katic (Simone), Dikran Tulaine (Kubichek).

Credits: *Executive Producer:* Dean Devlin, Marc Roskin, Kearie Peak. *Co-Executive Producer:* Phillip M. Goldfarb. *Producer:* Noah Wyle, John Rogers. *Director:* Jonathan Frakes. *Writer:* Marco Schnabel.

Reviews: "This third installment of TNT's *The Librarian* movies benefits from nifty special effects and a wholehearted embrace of the modern-day *National Treasure*–type swashbuckler status" (*Variety*).

"For the *Librarian* movie franchise, it turns out that the third time really is the charm. The latest (and last) in the series ... packs more humor, suspense and adventures into two hours than either of its two predecessors" (*The Hollywood Reporter*).

"It's a fun ride and Wyle has gotten a little better each time. That's why it's a shame there apparently won't be another" (*New York Daily News*).

293 The Life and Times of Tim.
(Series; Cartoon; HBO; September 28, 2008 to November 30, 2008)

Tim is a young man who lives and works in New York City. He has a girlfriend (Amy) and very serious problems: he is self conscious and extremely prone to making the worst decisions each day. Stories, which are adult in nature, follow Tim as he struggles to get through the trying times of each day. Debbie, a prostitute, is Tim's friend; Stu is Tim's friend and co-worker.

Voice Cast: Steve Dildarian (Tim), Mary Jane Otto (Amy), Nick Kroll (Stu), Peter Giles (Boss), Edie McClurg (Amy's grandmother), Kari Wahlgren (Amy's mother), Bob Morrow (Debbie).

Credits: *Executive Producer:* Tom Werner, Mike Clements, Steve Dildarian. *Co-Executive Producer:* Leynete Carrapa.

Reviews: *Tim* holds some genuine promise with its dry with and understated sensibility" (*The Hollywood Reporter*).

"Viewed alone, in small doses, the show is pretty damn funny ... a mix of minimalist animation, wildly absurd situations and understated voice work" (*Variety*).

294 The Life and Times of Vivienne Vyle. (Series; Comedy; Sundance; September 8, 2008 to October 13, 2008)

A British produced spoof of daytime talk shows that focuses on the hectic on camera and behind the scenes life of Vivienne Vyle, the screaming, always harassed host of *The Vivienne Vyle Show*. Helena is her producer; Jared is her husband; Jonathan is her psychotherapist.

Cast: Jennifer Saunders (Vivienne Vyle), Miranda Richardson (Helena de Wend), Conleith Hill (Jared), Jason Watkins (Dr. Jonathan Fowler), Helen Griffin (Carol), Dave Lamb (Des).

Credits: *Executive Producer:* Jon Plowman. *Producer:* Jo Sargent. *Music:* Dilly Fox.

295 Life on Mars (British). (Series; Crime Drama; BBC America; 2008)

The British series on which the American series of the same title is based (ran on BBC-One, 2006–2007). Sam Tyler is a Detective Chief Inspector with the Manchester Police Department in England. One day, during a case investigation, Sam is hit by a car and awakens in 1973 as a member of the Manchester and Salford Police Department as Detective Inspector (his sudden presence is explained as being a transfer from another precinct). Sam quickly adjusts to the fact that he is no longer in 2006 and stories follow his efforts to follow the police procedures of the 1970s world but supplement those techniques with those he learned in the 21st century. Gene Hunt is his superior, an old fashioned cop who will break the rules to get results. Ray Carling, Chris Skelton and Annie Cartwright (also Sam's romantic interest) work with Sam. The final episode shows Sam awakening from a coma. Believing his experiences in 1973 were real, but now feeling out of place in 2007, he climbs to the top of the police station and jumps off. He appears to return to the past, but the episode is confusing as it can also indicate that Sam may not have returned to the present. Overall, it really doesn't tell the viewer if Sam was insane, in a coma and if he really traveled back in time.

Cast: John Simm (Sam Tyler), Philip Glinster (Gene Hunt), Liz White (Annie Cartwright), Dean Andrews (Ray Carling), Marshall Lancaster (Chris Skelton).

Credits: *Executive Producer:* Matthew Graham, Jane Featherstone, Claire Parker. *Producer:* Marcus Wilson. *Music:* Edmund Butt.

296 Life on Mars (U.S.). (Series; Crime Drama; ABC; Premiered: October 9, 2008)

"I had an accident and woke up 35 years in the past. Now that either makes me a time traveler, a lunatic or I'm lying in a hospital bed in 2008 and none of this is real," says Sam Tyler, a detective with the N.Y.P.D. 125th Precinct (called 1-2-5) in 2008 who is now a detective with the 1-2-5 in 1973.

In 2008 Sam is romantically involved with fellow detective Maya Daniels. While investigating a case involving a kidnapper-murderer, Maya appears to have been kidnapped and Sam is hit by a car. The viewer sees a brief dream-like sequence as Sam awakens to find himself in 1973 — as a member of the 1-2-5 in Manhattan. His identification also reflects 1973 and he finds himself working on a case that is identical to the one he was working on in 2008. Sam believes that if he solves this case he can save Maya and return to 2008 (while Sam does solve the case, he is not transported back to his time). Sam's sudden appearance at the 1-2-5 is accepted because he is believed to be a transfer from upstate New York.

Sam quickly adjusts to the fact that he is where he is. At the precinct Sam meets his team: Gene Hunt, his superior, a rather uncouth lieutenant who believes in rough tactics; Annie Norris, a police woman (at a time when such personnel were part of the Police Woman's Bureau and not permitted to assist on cases as men do). She has a psychology degree from Fordham University in the Bronx and lives with her parents in Queens. She is the only one who sympathetic to Sam's plight. Chris Skelton is the rookie detective; Ray Carling is the tough, sexist detective with a chip on his shoulder.

At the end of the first episode, Sam hears Maya's voice over his car radio telling him that she is okay and asking him to come home. But how? Stories follow Sam as he seeks that answer and his efforts to incorporate the technologies of 2008 police science in an era where such things as forensic science and finger print analysis and even computers were a far-fetched dream. Based on the British series (see prior title).

Cast: Jason O'Mara (Sam Tyler), Gretchen Mol (Anne Norris), Harvey Keitel (Gene Hunt), Michael Imperioli (Ray Carling), Jonathan Murray (Chris Skelton), Lisa Bonet (Maya Daniels).

Credits: *Executive Producer:* Josh Applebaum, Andre Nemec, Scott Rosenberg, Jane Featherstone, Stephen Garrett. *Co-*

Executive Producer: David Wilcox, Michael Katleman. *Supervising Producer:* Adele Lim, *Producer:* Jane Rabb. *Music:* Peter Nashel.

Reviews: "An inexplicable trip through time injects life into the police drama genre ... if it holds its own against the final season of *ER*, *Mars* might be orbiting the schedule for years" (*The Hollywood Reporter*).

"Every year ABC rolls the dice on one truly first rate pilot that breaks the usual mold. *Life on Mars* is the latest gamble... *Mars* offers fine performances, some intriguing images, sly satire and a terrific song score" (*Variety*).

297 The Lifetime Achievement Award: A Tribute to Warren Beatty. (Special; Tribute; USA; June 25, 2008)

A tribute to actor Warren Beatty.

Guest of Honor: Warren Beatty. **Guests:** Faye Dunaway, Dustin Hoffman, Halle Barre, Diane Keaton, Barbra Streisand, Don Cheadle, Angela Lansbury, Steven Spielberg, Goldie Hawn, Dyan Cannon, Annette Bening.

Credits: *Executive Producer:* Gary Smith. *Producer:* Chris Merrill. *Associate Producer:* Aaron B. Cooker. *Director:* Louis J. Horvitz. *Writer:* Jon Macks.

298 The Line. (Series; Comedy; Internet; Summer 2008)

Seven part satire about a young man and his friend and the problems they face when they become first in line for a popular science fiction movie — weeks before it opens.

Cast: Bill Hader, Simon Rich, Joe LoTruglio, Paul Scheer, Miriam Tolan.

Credits: *Producer:* Jack Sullivan, Erin David, Dina Holmes, Nick Mallardi. *Writer:* Bill Hader, Simon Rich. *Director:* Seth Meyers.

299 Lingerie Secrets Revealed. (Special; Reality; WE; February 14, 2008)

A makeover program geared to women

that offers advice on how to purchase lingerie that is the perfect fit for her figure and change a "so so to so so sexy." Ten women are involved and each is given a makeover for style (by Rachel Zalis), lingerie (Amanda Diaz), hair (Kellye Garbner) and makeup (Tasha Reiko Brown).

Host: Rachel Zalis.

Credits: *Executive Producer:* Kerri Zane. *Segment Producer:* Samantha Day, Natalia Baldwin Leon.

300 Lipstick Jungle. (Series; Drama; NBC; February 7, 2008 to January 9, 2009)

A look at the lives of three women who are the tops in their field: Wendy Healy (movie executive at Parador Pictures), Nico Reilly (called Nico, is editor-in-chief of the fashion magazine *Bonfire*) and Victory Ford (is a fashion designer and owner of Victory Ford Fashions).

Cast: Brooke Shields (*Wendy Healy*), Kim Raver (*Nico Reilly*), Lindsay Price (*Victory Ford*), Andrew McCarthy (*Joe Bennett*), Paul Blackthorne (Shane Healy), Sarah Hyland (Maddie Healy), Mary Tyler Moore (Joyce; Wendy's mother).

Credits: *Executive Producer:* Oliver Goldstick, Timothy Busfield, Candace Bushnell. *Producer:* James Bigwood. *Music:* W.G. Snuffy Walden.

Reviews: "With the premiere of *Lipstick Jungle*, it seems safe to say that if someone is going to have a hit based on three female friends in the cutthroat business world, it isn't going to happen this season" (*The Hollywood Reporter*).

"*Lipstick Jungle* is the superior product of this winter's career-woman pals trying to have it all dramedies ... there are shreds of humanity to latch onto here if the network can lure enough young women in to respect the merchandise" (*Variety*).

301 Lisa Williams: Voices from the Other Side. (Pilot; Reality; Lifetime; October 27, 2008 to October 31, 2008)

A five episode test for an attempt by Lifetime to see if it can break away from the clutter of talk and judge shows that occupy daytime television. Here, British psychic Lisa Williams seeks to help real people, suffering a loss (friend, lover, family member) find some closure by contacting the spirits of those they lost.

Host: Lisa Williams.

Credits: *Executive Producer:* Robert Pritchard, Ronnie Ward, Roy Bank, Yann Debonne. *Producer:* Terence Michael. *Music:* Matthew Puckett.

302 Little Britain. (Series; Comedy; BBC America; 2008)

An exaggerated look at the British Isles (from Scotland to Wales) with a focus on the quirky characters that inhabit the countryside of the United Kingdom (for example, Sebastian Love, the Prime Minister's gay assistant; Vicky Pollard, the teenage troublemaker; Ray McLooney, the eccentric Scottish hotel manager; and Marjorie Dawes, a dietician who makes fun of fat people).

Cast: Matt Lucas, David Walliams, Anthony Head, Paul Putner, Joann London, Stephen Furst, Stirling Gallacher, Leelo Ross, Ruth Jones. **Narrator:** Tom Baker.

Credits: *Executive Producer:* Jon Plowman.

Producer: Geoff Posner. *Music:* David Arnold.

303 Little Britain, U.S.A. (Series; Comedy; HBO; September 28, 2008 to November 2, 2008)

Raunchy, fast-paced skit comedy wherein the male leads, portraying an array of character (including females) spoof American culture. Based on the British series *Little Britain*.

Stars: Matt Lucas, David Walliams.

Credits: *Executive Producer:* Matt Lucas, David Walliams, Simon Fuller, Larry Brezner, David Steinberg, Michael Patrick James. *Producer:* Stephanie Laing.

Reviews: "*Britain U.S.A.* is mostly just

crude, reveling in mock condescension toward American stereotypes" (*Variety*).

"Rude humor and outrageous characters combine to make delightful comedy" (*The Hollywood Reporter*).

304 Little Girl Lost: The Delimar Vera Story. (TV Movie; Drama; Lifetime Movie Network; August 17, 2008)

Fact based story about Luz Cuevas, a young mother who begins a seemingly fruitless search to find her daughter (Aaliyah)—said to have been killed in an apartment fire but whom Luz believes was kidnapped.

Cast: Judy Reyes (Luz Cuevas), A Martinez (Angel Cruz), Ana Ortiz (Valerie Valleja), Hector Luis Bustamante (Pedro Vera), Jillian Bruno (Delimar Vera/Aaliyah), Marlene Forte (Tatita).

Credits: *Executive Producer:* Paul A. Kaufman, Harvey Kahan, Joey Plager, Larry Thompson. *Director:* Paul A. Kaufman. *Writer:* Christopher Canaan, Maria Bation.

Reviews: "Representing the kind of ripped-from-the headlines melodrama the networks used to make, *Little Girl Lost* telegraphs where its going—but you'd still have to be a pretty heartless bastard to resist becoming a little choked up at the end" (*Variety*).

"Even by Lifetime standards, the original telepic ... is wrenching, heavy-duty stuff that largely honors a real life tale with earnestness and realism" (*The Hollywood Reporter*).

305 Little Spirit: Christmas in New York. (Special; Cartoon; NBC; December 10, 2008)

Leo is a young boy who has just moved with his family from the Midwest to New York City. Christmas is approaching and Leo feels displaced and only finds comfort with his dog Ramona. Shortly after, while walking his dog, Ramona escapes his grasp and runs off. A magical creature called Little Spirit appears to Leo with a mission:

help him find Ramona. As Leo and Little Spirit search through the various Manhattan neighborhoods, they meet people of various nationalities, religions and ages — all meant to teach Leo to embrace his new home as a warm and inviting place. The computer animated program is filled with product placement to accommodate a Macy's Department Store tie-in.

Voice Cast: Danny DeVito (Cabbie/Narrator), Michael Hall D'Addario (Leo), Fred Newman (Little Spirit/Ramona/Squirrel). **Additional Voices:** Lisa Liu, Freddy Rodriquez, Rachel Scheer, Brian Williams, Brenda Song, Sally Winters.

Credits: *Executive Producer:* Chet Fenster, Leopoldo Gout, Susan Holden, Jon Paley. *Producer:* Lorne Orleans, Kris Greengrove. *Music:* Duncan Sheik. *Director:* Leopoldo Gout, Susan Holden. *Writer:* Andy Rheingold.

Review: "It's too bad the Grinch isn't able to steal Christmas specials" (*The Hollywood Reporter*).

306 Living Hell. (TV Movie; Horror; Sci Fi; February 23, 2008)

A hazmet specialist (Carrie) teams with a school teacher (Frank) to stop an escaped military secret experiment (an organism that feeds on light and power) from reaching its target: a nuclear bomb. Frank's father helped create the organism and Frank has an unusual connection to the creature; he is literally the only one capable of stopping it.

Cast: Jonathan Schaech (Frank Sears), Erica Leerhsen (Carrie Freeborn), Jason Wiles (Glenn Freeborn), James McDaniel (Col. Eric Maitland), Terrence Jay (Sgt. Arbogast), Judy Herrera (Una Fernandez).

Credits: *Producer:* Deborah Del Prete, David Greathouse. *Co-Producer:* Linda McDonough. *Music:* Terrence Jay. *Director-Writer:* Richard Jefferies.

307 Living Lohan. (Series; Reality; E!; May 26, 2008 to July 27, 2008)

Dina Lohan (divorced from Michael) is

the single mother of Lindsay and Ali Lohan. Lindsay, the troubled (at the time) mega star does not appear on the program. The focus is on Ali, her 14-year-old sister whom stage mother Dina is hoping to launch on a singing career. The program showcases Dina's professional and home life as well as Ali's cutting a record in Las Vegas.

Cast: Dina Lohan, Ali Lohan, Michael Lohan.

Credits: *Executive Producer:* Phil Maloof, Laura Korkoian, Jeff Jenkins, Andrew Jameson, Jonathan Murray. *Producer:* Christine Reed.

Reviews: "Half-hour infomercial for the less-famous members of the [Lindsay] Lohan clan, which Ma [Dina] uses to humanize both herself and her brood ... it's a tedious experience ... with limited appeal" (*Variety*).

"It's ... not one that I can see watching over the long run, basically because I don't care about the evolution of Ali's career" (*Entertain Your Brain*).

308   Living Proof. (TV Movie; Drama; Lifetime; October 18, 2008)

Compelling drama bout a doctor's (Denny Slamon) total dedication to finding a cure for breast cancer.

Cast: Harry Connick, Jr. (Dr. Denny Slamon), Angie Harmon (Lily Tartikoff), Bernadette Peters (Barbara Bradfield), Amanda Bynes (Jamie MacGraw), Swoosie Kurtz (Elizabeth Aldridge), Paula Cale (Donna), Regina King (Ellie Jackson), Tammy Blanchard (Nicole Wilson), Amy Madigan (Fran Visco), Jennifer Coolidge (Tish), John Benjamin Hickey (Blake Rogers).

Credits: *Executive Producer:* Neil Meron, Vivienne Radkoff, Craig Zadan, Renee Zellweger. *Producer:* Cathy Frank. *Director:* Dan Ireland. *Writer:* Vivienne Radkoff.

Reviews: "Ernest, emotional and cast to the hilt with cameos for actresses, *Liv-*

ing Proof rises above most Lifetime movie fare" (*Variety*).

"A true and absorbing tale about L.A. oncologist Dennis Slamon and the celebrities who helped him save lives" (*The Hollywood Reporter*).

309   The Locator. (Series; Reality; WE; September 6, 2008 to October 25, 2008)

Troy Dunn is a real life locator (a person who finds missing people). Emotionally charged episodes follow Tony as he reunites people who have drifted apart and now need to be reunited (from lost loves to childhood friends to adopted children seeking their birth mothers).

Host: Troy Dunn. **Chief Investigator:** Katie Dunn.

Credits: *Executive Producer:* Jonathan Koch, Kelly Hefner, Steven Michaels. *Supervising Producer:* David Berrent. *Co-Executive Producer:* Ted Haimes. *Producer:* Taylor Humphries.

310   Lone Rider. (TV Movie; Western; Ion; April 12, 2008)

Following the Civil War, Bobby Hattaway returns to Texas to find his family ranch and general store in debt and the town being sought by the greedy Stu Croker. The story follows Bobby as he becomes the town's lone hope to stop Croker.

Cast: Lou Diamond Phillips (Bobby Hattaway), Angela Alvarado (Serena Sanchez), Stacy Keach (Robert Hattaway), Vincent Spano (Stu Croker), Cynthia Preston (Constance), Robert Baker (Vic), Timothy Bottoms (Gus), Terry Maratos (Curtis), Tom Scanley (Mike Butler).

Credits: *Executive Producer:* Robert Halmi, Jr., Larry Levinson. *Co-Executive Producer:* Matt Fitzsimons, Nick Lombardo, Michael Moran. *Producer:* Albert T. Dickerson III. *Music:* Joe Kraemer. *Director:* David S. Cass, Sr. *Writer:* Frank Sharp.

311   Long Way Down. (Series; Reality; Fox Reality Channel; Premiered: August 2, 2008)

Cameras follow two friends, Ewan Mc-Gregor and Charley Boorman, as they undertake an 85-day, 15,000 mile motorcycle trek across Africa.

Stars: Ewan McGregor, Charley Boorman, Eve Mavrakis (Ewan's wife).

Credits: *Producer-Director:* David Alexanian, Russ Malkin. *Producer:* Lucy Trujillo.

***312*　Lost City Raiders.** (TV Movie; Science Fiction; Sci Fi; November 22, 2008)

In a futuristic time (2048) the Polar Ice Caps begin to melt, causing massive death and destruction. Surviving members of the human race establish new civilizations on existing land masses. As the new cities become overcrowded, a group of salvage specialists (Lost City Raiders) emerge with one goal: to find the old relics and treasures from submerged cities to connect an uncertain future with the past.

Cast: James Brolin (Pa Kubiak), Ian Somerhalder (Jack Kubiak), Jamie Thomas King (Thomas Kubiak), Bettina Zimmerman (Giovanna Becker), Flodie Frenck (Cara), Ben Cross (Nicholas Filminov), Dan Hurst (Alexi), Michael Mendl (Cardinal Battaglia).

Credits: *Executive Producer:* Jonas Bauer, Rola Bauer, Tim Halkin. *Co-Executive Producer:* Christopher Morgan. *Producer:* Brigid Olen. *Director-Writer:* Jean de Segonzac.

Reviews: "Bruce Springsteen fans know "The Rising" as a song of hope... Fans of tonight's made-for TV-movie *Lost City Raiders*, a group likely to be more modest in number, will know the Rising as something less hopeful" (*New York Daily News*).

"*Lost City Raiders*, a combination of two of the worst movies in recent history, melded into *the* worst TV movie is recent and probably even future history" (*New York Post*).

***313*　Lost Treasure of the Grand Canyon.** (TV Movie; Horror; Sci Fi; December 20, 2008)

Susan Jordon, the daughter of a Smithsonian research professor (Dr. Samuel Jordon), seeks a way to rescue her father and his team of researchers when they unearth an ancient Aztec city and release an evil spirit (a flying serpent) that threatens to kill them.

Cast: Shannen Doherty (Susan Jordon), Duncan Fraser (Dr. Samuel Jordon), Michael Shanks (Jacob Thain), J.R. Bourne (Marco Langford), Toby Berner (Stewart Dunbar), Heather Doerksen (Hildy Wainwright), Peter New (Isaac Preston).

Credits: *Executive Producer:* Karen Bailey. *Producer:* Harvey Kahn. *Associate Producer:* Nadia Mear. *Music:* Michael Neilson. *Director:* Farhad Mann. *Writer:* Clay Carmouche.

***314*　The Love of Her Life.** (TV Movie; Comedy; Lifetime; March 1, 2008)

Allison is a gorgeous 30-year-old woman whose extreme jealousy keeps her from maintaining a steady relationship with men. When her latest love leaves her for 41-year-old Kathryn Brown, Allison decides to get even by stealing the heart of Scott, Kathryn's 17-year-old son. The story follows Allison's efforts and Kathy's attempts to keep Scott from falling in love with Allison.

Cast: Cynthia Preston (Allison), Brandy Ledford (Kathryn), Alex House (Scott Brown), Paula Jean Hixson (Joy), Catie Campo (Young Allison), Nick Baillie (Ian Matthews).

Credits: *Executive Producer:* Tom Berry, Pierre David, Ken Sanders. *Producer:* Stefan Wodoslawsky. *Writer:* Christine Conradt. *Director:* Robert Malenfant.

***315*　Love Sick: Secrets of a Sex Addict.** (TV Movie; Drama; Lifetime; March 1, 2008)

True story based on Sue Williams book about her addiction to and successful attempts to overcome sexual addiction.

Cast: Sally Pressman (Sue Williams), Peter Flemming (Andrew Silverman),

Roger Haskett (Dr. Robert Gardiner), Medina Hahn (Jill), Jill Morrison (Linda), Ken Kramer (Irwin Silverman), Sandra Timuss (Fay Silverman), Samantha Coughlan (Joannie).

Credits: *Executive Producer:* Jean Abounader, Tim Johnson. *Producer:* Kirk Shaw. *Music:* Peter Allen. *Writer:* Maria Nation. *Director:* Grant Harvey.

316   Luke's Parental Advisory. (Series; Reality; VH-1; August 4, 2008 to September 22, 2008)

Luther "Luke" Campbell of the group 2 Live Crew, and his fiancé, Kristin (an attorney) are featured as cameras follow events in their daily lives, focusing mostly on Luke's efforts to deal with his children (Lacresha and Luke, Jr.) from a prior marriage.

Stars: Luke Campbell, Lacresha Campbell, Luther Cambell, Jr.

Credits: *Executive Producer:* Brad Abramson, Tone Boots, Kimberly Belcher Cowin. *Supervising Producer:* Warren Cohen. *Producer:* Shelly Tatro, James Rosemond, John Ehardt.

317   The Macy's Fourth of July Fireworks Spectacular. (Special; Variety; NBC; July 4, 2008)

Fireworks displays coupled with music and songs from New York City.

Host: Natalie Masters, Tiki Barber. **Guests:** Katherine McPhee, Jordin Sparks, Kenny Chesney, Natasha Bedingfield.

Credits: *Executive Producer:* Bob Holmes. *Producer:* Heidi Kelso. *Associate Producer:* Gregory Scamici. *Director:* Louis J. Horvitz.

318   The Macy's Thanksgiving Day Parade. (Special; Variety; NBC; November 27, 2008)

Macy's Department Store's 82nd annual event (first broadcast on TV in 1945) that features stars, character balloons and elaborate floats to signify the start of the 2008 Christmas season. Broadcast live from New York (beginning at 77th Street and Central Park West and winding down Broadway).

Host: Meredith Vieira, Matt Lauer, Al Roker. **Guests:** Miley Cyrus, David Archuleta, Trace Adkins, Ashanti, Adrienne Bailon, Sabrina Bryan, Cedric the Entertainer, Kristin Chenoweth, The Cheetah Girls, John Lequizamo, Idina Menzel, The Radio City Rockettes, Darius Rucker, James Taylor, Steve Whitmire, Andy Williams, Kiely Williams.

Credits: *Executive Producer:* Brad Lachman, Bill Bracken. *Macy's Executive Producer:* Robin Hall. *Music Director:* Milton DeLugg. *Director:* Gary Halvorson. *Writer:* Mark Waxman. *Announcer:* Joel Goddard.

319   Magic's Biggest Secrets Finally Revealed. (Series; Reality; My Network TV; October 6, 2008 to November 24, 2008)

A masked, unknown magician reveals the secrets behind magic tricks and illusions. The illusion is performed then recreated to show how it was accomplished.

Masked Magician: Val Valentino. **Narrator:** Mitch Pileggi.

Credits: *Executive Producer:* Bruce Nash, Don Weiner, Andrew Jebb. *Producer:* Val Valentino. *Music:* Danny Lux.

320   Mail Order Bride. (TV Movie; Drama; Hallmark; November 8, 2008)

Old West tale of a beautiful con artist (Diana McQueen) who poses as a mail order bride to escape from her ruthless boss (Tom Rourke) and begin a new life with an unsuspecting groom (Beau Canfield) on the frontier.

Cast: Daphne Zuniga (Diana McQueen), Greg Evigan (Tom Rourke), Cameron Bancroft (Beau Canfield), Karin Konoval (Mrs. Vaughn), Michael Teigen (Joe), William MacDonald (Sheriff), Kathleen Isabelle (Jen).

Credits: *Executive Producer:* Ira Pincus, Noreen Helpern, Dori Weiss. *Producer:*

Randolph Cheveldave. *Director:* Anne Wheeler. *Writer:* Tippy Dobrofsky, Neal Dobrofsky.

Review: "Most of the movie seems to be walking through molasses. The characters are static ... and not given much in the way of dialogue that is believable or any where near original" (*The Hollywood Reporter*).

321   Make Me a Super Model. (Series; Reality; Bravo; January 10, 2008 to April 17, 2008)

Fourteen hopeful models (both male and female) compete for a $100,000 modeling contract with New York Model Management. Each of the models competes in various photo shoots and modeling challenges with the weakest candidates being eliminated.

Host: Nicki Taylor. **Co-Host:** Tyson Beckford.

Models: Katy Caswell, Stephanie Bulger, Ben DiChiara, Frankie Godoy, Jacki Hydock, Holly Kiser, Ronnie Kroell, Aryn Livingston, Jay McGee, Shannon Pallay, Casey Skinner, Perry Ullmann.

Credits: *Executive Producer:* Jamie Munro, Lisa Perrin, Andrew Zein. *Producer:* Jillian Horgan, Makario Sarsozo.

Reviews: "The geniuses at Bravo came to the conclusion that what TV viewers need most is yet another show about becoming a model. Not mention this is a great way to fill an hour with young, sexy bodies, so I won't" (*The Hollywood Reporter*).

322   Making Mr. Right. (TV Movie; Comedy; Lifetime; February 9, 2008)

A young woman (Hallie) attempts to transform a rough-around-the-edges man (Eddie) into the man of her dreams — a handsome, mannerly bachelor.

Cast: Christina Cox (Hallie Galloway), Dean Cain (Eddie), Jocelyne Loewen (Christine), David Lewis (Bobby), Greg Rogers (Angelo), Tom Butler (Paul Gottman).

Credits: *Executive Producer:* Tim Johnson, Wendy Kram, Kirk Shaw. *Producer:* Rob Lycar. *Music:* Peter Allen, John Sereda. *Writer:* Dan Beckerman, Julie Saunders, Guy Mann. *Director:* Paul Fox.

323   Man and Wife. (Series; Reality; MTV; Premiered: September 30, 2008)

Fatman Scoop and his wife, Shanda, the first married couple in the hip-hop genre, frankly discuss sex, relationships, jobs, politics and marriage. Scoop and Shanda are fierce advocates of safe sex and they encourage this along with responsibility and monogamy.

Stars: Fatman Scoop, Shanda.

324   Manhunters: Fugitive Task Force. (Series; Reality; A&E; Premiered: December 9, 2008)

"The best of the best, hunting down the worst of the worst" is the tag line for a series that showcases the work of the U.S. Marshal's Fugitive Task Force as they track down wanted felons.

Credits: *Executive Producer:* Gary Tarpinian, Stuart Goodman, Vincent Scarza. *Supervising Producer:* Sonia Slutsky, Siobhan Walshe.

Reviews: "Getting bad guys off the street is good. *Manhunters* is not" (*New York Daily News*).

"In short, *Manhunters* doesn't even marginally advance the ball beyond the cinema-verite standard *Cops* established" (*Variety*).

325   Martha Speaks. (Series; Cartoon; PBS; Premiered: September 1, 2008)

Martha is a friendly dog who, after eating a bowl of alphabet soup, finds that she suddenly has the ability to speak English. With her new found ability, Martha finds a new meaning to life and through her activities introduces various aspects of life to children.

Voice Cast: Tabitha St. Germain (Martha), Vanessa Tomasino (Carolina), Alex Ferris (T.D.).

Credits: *Executive Producer:* Chris Bartleman, Carol Greenwald. *Producer:* Sarah Wall. *Music:* Daniel Ingram.

326   The Marvelous Misadventures of Flapjack. (Series; Cartoon; Cartoon Network; Premiered: June 5, 2008)

Flapjack is a young boy who was lost at sea and raised by Bubbie, a talking whale. Captain K'Nuckles is a crusty old pirate whose life was saved by Flapjack and Bubbie. Now, as a team, the trio searches for the magical Candied Islands and its treasures of lollipop trees and lemonade springs.

Voice Cast: Thurop Van Orman (Flapjack), Brian Doyle Murray (Captain K'Nuckles), Roz Ryan (Bubbie).

Credits: *Executive Producer:* Brian A. Miller, Jennifer Pelphrey, Thurop Van Orman. *Producer:* Pernelle Hayes.

327   The Mary Van Note Show. (Series; Comedy; Internet; 2008)

Comedian Mary Van Note is described as "a cross between Sarah Silverman and Pee Wee Herman." She is intimate yet rude and "strangely innocent." The ten episode web series explores Mary's inner mind as she searches for the man of her dreams. Mary is also seen speaking directly to the camera as well as performing in real and imagined skits.

Cast: Mary Van Note, Moshe Kasher, Alex Koll, Brent Weinbach.

Credits: *Executive Producer:* James Web. *Associate Producer:* Juan Marmol. *Writer-Director:* Mary Van Note.

328   Master of Dance. (Series; Reality; TLC; June 9, 2008 to July 14, 2008)

Dance competition show with a twist: competing players must be flexible and be able to adapt to a new routine when a song is changed in mid-routine. Dancers unable to adapt quickly enough are eliminated. The most accomplished dancer wins the $50,000 first prize.

Host: Joey Lawrence. **Judges:** Lucinda Dickey, Loni Love, Keith Diorio.

Credits: *Executive Producer:* Craig Piligian. *Co-Executive Producer:* Dan Funk. *Supervising Producer:* Ron Muccianti. *Producer:* Lisa Sichi.

329   Matched in Manhattan. (Series; Reality; Lifetime; January 4, 2008 to February 14, 2008)

A dating game type of series combined with the elements of a makeover program. Host Matt Titus is a relationship expert who is said "to specialize in helping straight women and gay men find Mr. Right rather than Mr. Right now." Each program is devoted to the makeover of a relationship challenged woman. The subject is given a complete makeover. Following the change, the subject is counseled on relationships and dating and given a fresh chance to find her Mr. Right.

Host: Matt Titus. **Co-Host:** Tamsen Fadal, Eddie Varley.

Credits: *Executive Producer:* Mark Efman, Sara Chazen-Leand. *Co-Executive Producer:* Amy Kohan. *Supervising Producer:* Richard Van Meter. *Producer:* Gil Ilam, Jordana Starr. *Associate Producer:* Iraida Gomez, Melissa Hunter.

Reviews: "*Matched in Manhattan* is basically *Sex in the City* meets *The Dating Game* and the concept is somewhat promising, but the execution is as painful as trolling through chat rooms on a Saturday night" (*Variety*).

"A word of advice to the lovelorn: Television is not going to provide the key that unlocks a lifetime of future bliss — only the Internet can do that" (*The Hollywood Reporter*).

330   Maui Chopper. (Series; Reality; Tru TV; Premiered: December 8, 2008)

A look at the work of the helicopter pilots attached to Windward Aviation (based at Hawaii's Kahului Airport) as they assist the Maui County Fire and Ocean Safety Departments as well as state and federal agencies.

Credits: Executive Producer: Al Edgington, Mark Koops, Robert Williams. *Producer:* Rita Doumar. *Music:* The Newton Brothers.

331   Me, Mom, Dad and Her. (TV Movie; Drama; Lifetime; May 10, 2008)

A troubled teen (Sydney) attempts to ease into a new family when her single mother sends her to live with her father (Ben) and his new wife (Emma) in the hope of straightening her out.

Cast: Melora Hardin (Emma), Britteney Wilson (Sydney), Paul McGillion (Ben), Dorla Bell (Robin), Sarah Deakins (Lynn).

Credits: *Executive Producer:* Anne Hopkins, Tim Johnson, Marian Rees, Kirk Shaw. *Music:* Graeme Coleman. *Writer:* Anna Sandor. *Director:* Anne Wheeler.

332   The Memory Keeper's Daughter. (TV Movie; Drama; Lifetime; April 12, 2008)

Twins are born to a doctor (David) and his wife. The boy is healthy but the girl has Down syndrome. The story follows the events that develop years later when the wife (Nora) discovers that David kept the girl a secret from her (telling her that she died during delivery) and had placed her up for adoption.

Cast: Dermot Mulroney (Dr. David Henry), Gretchen Mol (Nora Henry), Owen Pattison (Paul Henry, age 6), Tyler Stentiford (Paul, age 13), Jamie Spilchuk (Paul, age 18–22), Emily Watson (Caroline Gil), Lita Llewellyn (Ruby), David Gibson McLean (Duke), Kerry McPherson (Kay).

Credits: *Executive Producer:* Michael Jaffe. *Producer:* Howard Braunstein, Michael Mahoney. *Writer:* John Pielmeier. *Director:* Mick Jackson. *Music:* Daniel Licht.

333   The Mentalist. (Series; Crime Drama; CBS; Premiered: September 23, 2008)

"My name is Patrick Jane, I'm here to help you" is what a victim of crime will hear when Patrick Jane becomes involved in a case. Patrick himself is a victim of crime (his wife and daughter were shot by a serial killer) and thus feels for victims and takes a personal interest in their plight.

Patrick is an independent consultant for the California Bureau of Investigation (CBI). He pays attention to details at a crime scene and notices the little things that can easily be overlooked. He can read people and his past experiences, pretending to be a psychic (to help people) has given him an edge in that some people actually believe he is psychic. Teresa Lisbon is the head of the CBI; Kimball, Wayne and Grace are the other team members. Stories follow the team, in particular Patrick's somewhat unconventional methods, to solve crimes.

Cast: Simon Baker (Patrick Jane), Robin Tunney (Teresa Lisbon), Tim Kang (Kimball Cho), Owain Yeoman (Wayne Rigsby), Amanda Righetti (Grace Van Pelt).

Credits: *Executive Producer:* Bruno Heller, David Nutter. *Producer:* Charles Goldstein. *Music:* Blake Neely.

Reviews: "Although USA's *Psych* merely hints at the possibility that some psychics could be frauds, CBS's *The Mentalist* argues forcefully that self-proclaimed seers ... are as supernaturally gifted as pet rocks" (*The Hollywood Reporter*).

"The show's lone distinguishing characteristic stems from the casting of Simon Baker as a latter-day Sherlock Holmes — albeit one who winds up squabbling in tiresome fashion with his gender-switched Dr. Watson" (*Variety*).

334   The Meow Mix Think Like a Cat Game Show. (Series; Game; Game Show Network; Premiered: November 15, 2008)

Cat owners appear with their pets to compete in question and answer rounds (based on their knowledge of cats) as well as in challenges that involve their pet's ability to perform specific tasks. Money is awarded based on the cat's performance as well as how his master scored in the question and answer session. Sponsored by Meow Mix cat food.

Host: Chuck Woolery.

Credits: *Executive Producer:* John P. Cordero, David Doyle, Matthew Glass. *Co-Executive Producer:* Keith Fernbach. *Supervising Producer:* Steve Ochs. *Producer:* Margo Kent.

335 The Metal Show. (Series; Documentary; VH-1; Premiered: November 14, 2008)

A review of Heavy Metal music that has been performed over the last 40 years.

Host: Jim Florentine, Don Jamieson, Eddie Trunk.

336 The Middleman. (Series; Science Fiction; ABC Family; June 16, 2008 to September 2, 2008)

A super secret organization called 02STK has been established to battle comic book-like villains seeking to wreck havoc on the world. Middleman, the unit's top agent, is a mysterious figure who loves a cool glass of milk and uses high tech weaponry to battle evil. Wendy Watson is a struggling artist who assists Middleman (on her prior job, she encountered a grotesque experiment that escaped from a lab beneath her building. Although Wendy showed great courage by attempting to battle the creature, she was unable and grabbed. She was saved when Middleman seemed to appear from out of nowhere and disposed of the creature. Wendy's bravery so impressed Middleman that he brought her into the agency). Stories relate their efforts to battle creatures nightmares are made of. Lucy is Wendy's friend, an activist and conceptual artist; Ida is Middleman's cantankerous robotic girl Friday ("a soulless android from outer space who masquerades as a librarian"). Nose is Wendy's eccentric friend, a musician.

Cast: Natalie Morales (Wendy Watson), Matt Keestar (Middleman), Bret Morgan (Lucy Thornfeild), Mary Pat Gleason (Ida), Jake Smollet (Nose).

Credits: *Executive Producer:* Javier Grillo-Marxuach, John Ziffren. *Co-Executive Producer:* Hans Beimler. *Supervising Producer:* Jeremiah Chechik, Tracey Stern. *Producer:* Ron McLeod. *Music:* Tree Adams.

Review: "*The Middleman* manages the increasingly rare feat of being knowing but snide. It's a show ... for people who love ... TV. By that standard, it's far from middle, but rather rises straight to the top" (*Variety*).

337 The Mighty B! (Series; Cartoon; Nickelodeon; Premiered: April 26, 2008)

Ten-year-old Bessie Higgenbottom dreams of two things: acquiring every merit badge the Honeybees have to offer and becoming a super hero (the Mighty B!). As she strives to acquire those badges, her flights of super hero fancies are also seen.

Voice Cast: Amy Poehler (Bessie Higgenbottom), Andy Richter (Ben Higgenbottom), Dee Bradley Baker (Happy), Grey DeLisle (Portia), Dannah Feinglass (Penny), Jessica DiCicco (Gwen).

Credits: *Executive Producer:* Amy Poehler, Cynthia True, Erik Wiese. *Producer:* Amy Poehler. *Writer:* Cynthia True, Amy Poehler, Jessica Chaffin, Jessica Gao.

Reviews: "Imaginative and frenetic, this ... series ... has the kind of crazed energy and inventiveness that isn't associated often enough with girl oriented children's fare" (*Variety*).

"Nickelodeon's ... series ... has what every kid needs in order to grow up strong and self-sufficient in today's adult world. Violence, nonsensical verbage and, most importantly, a built-in idea that you rule the universe" (*The Hollywood Reporter*).

338 Million Dollar Password. (Series; Game; CBS; June 1, 2008 to August 24, 2008)

A revised version of *Password*. Two teams compete, each composed of one celebrity and one non-celebrity contestant. The object is for one player (the giver) to get his partner (the guesser) to identify a key word through one word clues (five key words are used for each of the four 30 second rounds that are played). The player with the highest score is the winner and receives the opportunity to play for $1 million.

A board with six money amounts is shown. The player is teamed with the celebrity with whom he scored the most points. He can choose to be the giver or guesser. In round one ($10,000) he must get five out of ten passwords; round two ($25,000), five out of nine; round three ($50,000), five out of eight; round four ($100,000), five out of seven; round five ($250,000), five out of six; round 6 ($1 million), five out of five. The player risks loss of everything if he fails to complete a round (he can quit at any time and leave with what money he has won). Returned for a second season on December 18, 2008.

Host: Regis Philbin.

Credits: *Executive Producer:* Vincent Rubino. *Supervising Producer:* Rich Sirop. *Producer:* Chris Ahearn, Graham Shaw.

339   The Millionaire Matchmaker. (Series; Reality; Bravo; January 29, 2008 to September 15, 2008)

Patti Stanger is a real life matchmaker. Her clients are millionaires who are unable to find a mate. These millionaires, however, are not your Donald Trump; they are "millionaire losers — men who want Madonna in the bedroom, Martha Stewart in the kitchen and Mary Poppins in the nursery — and they need help." The viewer is "treated" to the client, the women and the matches Patti tries to establish.

Host: Patti Stanger. **Guest Host:** Shannon Fox. **Featured Women:** Holly Sherman, Natalie Gray, Cassie Fliegel, Carolyn Cannon, Dawn Ashley Cook.

Credits: *Executive Producer:* Rob Lee, Kevin Dill, Mechelle Collins. *Co-Executive Producer:* Bill Hochhauser. *Supervising Producer:* Thomas Jaeger, Rob Worsoff. *Producer:* Mark Cole, Hollie Labosky. *Co-Producer:* Lennox Wiseley. *Associate Producer:* Sonia Garcia Clyne.

Reviews: "Just when you think TV can't get any worse along comes *The Millionaire Matchmaker*, a show so demeaning to women — and so ugly to everyone else" (*New York Post*).

"If the way men view women is getting shallower and scarier — and ditto for the way women view men — here's the best proof: a wildly entertaining series about how superficial we've all become" (*The Hollywood Reporter*).

340   Minute Men. (TV Movie; Comedy; Disney; January 25, 2008)

The mischief caused by two teens (Virgil and Charlie) when Charlie invents a machine that can rewind time.

Cast: Jason Dolley (Virgil Fox), Luke Benward (Charlie Tuttle), Chelsea Staub (Stephanie Jamson), Kara Crane (Jeanette), Dexter Darden (Chester), Steven R. McQueen (Derek Beauregard), Nicholas Braun (Zeke Thompson).

Credits: *Executive Producer:* Andrew Gunn, Ann Marie Sanderlin, Doug Sloan. *Producer:* David Diamond, David Weissman. *Writer:* John Killoran. *Director:* Lev L. Spiro

341   A Miser Brother's Christmas. (Special; Cartoon; ABC Family; December 13, 2008)

A sequel to *The Year Without a Santa Claus* (ABC, December 10, 1974) about Santa's disenchantment over the lack of holiday spirit and his threat to cancel his Christmas Eve sleigh ride. While testing a new high tech sleigh, the North Wind sabotages Santa's ride, hoping to take his place on Christmas Eve. Santa injures his back and the North Wind blames the bickering Miser Brothers (Snow and Heat) for the accident. The North Wind's plans are foiled, however, when Mother Nature steps in and persuades the Miser Brothers to put their differences aside and fill in for Santa on Christmas Eve. Filmed, like the original, in stop-motion photography.

Voice Cast: Mickey Rooney (Santa Claus), George S. Irving (Heat Miser), Juan Chioran (Snow Miser), Catherine Disher (Mrs. Claus).

Credits: *Executive Producer:* Howard Schwartz, Adam Shaheen, Linda Steiner. *Producer:* Lynda Craigmyle, Christine Davis. *Director:* Dave Barton Thomas. *Writer:* Eddie Guzelian.

342 The Miss America Pageant. (Special; Contest; TLC; January 26, 2008)

The 83rd presentation, broadcast live from the Theater of the Performing Arts in Las Vegas (making this only the third time in pageant history, that it was not held in Atlantic City, New Jersey). Fifty women, each representing a state, compete in specific challenges (beauty, swimsuit, poise, interview, talent, evening gown) for the title of Miss America 2008.

Host: Mark Steines. **Presenter:** Lauren Nelson (Miss America 2007). **Winners:** Kirsten Hagland (Miss America 2008; from Michigan), Nicole Rash (Miss Indiana, First Runner-Up), Elyse Umemoto (Miss Washington, Second Runner-Up), Hannah Kiefer (Miss Virginia, Third Runner-Up), Jessica Jacobs (Miss North Carolina, Fourth Runner-Up).

Credits: *Executive Producer:* Anthony Eaton, Angela Shapiro. *Producer:* Sam Brenzel. *Director:* Kathy Fortine.

343 Miss America: Reality Check. (Series; Reality; TLC; January 4, 2008 to January 24, 2008)

Contestants for the Miss America Pageant are profiled and compete in actual beauty pageant challenges as they prepare for the actual event.

Host: Michael Urie.

Credits: *Executive Producer:* Patty Ivins

Specht, Julie Pizzi. *Supervising Producer:* Benjamin Greenberg. *Producer:* Christine Reed. *Associate Producer:* Pamela Welch.

344 Miss Guided. (Series; Comedy; ABC; March 20, 2008 to April 3, 2008)

Rebecca "Becky" Freeley is a graduate of Glen Ellen High School. She was an underachiever at the time but has changed and has returned to her school to become its guidance counselor. Stories provide an inside look at the lives of the students and faculty who populate the school as seen through Becky's eyes.

Cast: Judy Greer (Becky Freeley), Brooke Burns (Lisa Germain), Kristopher Polaha (Tim O'Malley), Earl Billings (Principal Phil Huffy), Chris Parnell (Vice Principal Bruce Terry).

Credits: *Executive Producer:* Mark Hudis, Gabrielle Allan, Karey Burke, Todd Holland, Ashton Kutcher. *Co-Executive Producer:* Caroline Williams. *Producer:* Jeffrey Morton. *Associate Producer:* Megan Gaspar.

Reviews: "The idea that we never outgrow high school is hardly new but Judy Greer's quirky vulnerability of this stunted emotional development helps elevate *Miss Guided* slightly above its familiar and predictable formula" (*Variety*).

"*Miss Guided* evokes memories of several school-based sitcoms including the fractured idealism of *Welcome Back, Kotter* and the persistence of *Our Miss Brooks*" (*The Hollywood Reporter*).

345 Miss Teen U.S.A. (Unaired Special; Contest; 2008)

The 26th Miss Teen U.S.A. Pageant was held at the Atlantis Resort in the Bahamas on August 16, 2008. Normally, the event would have been televised by NBC; however, NBC's failure to renew its contract coupled with its non-stop coverage of the 2008 Summer Olympics resulted in a blackout for the pageant, the first in its 25-year history. Here, teenage girls, representing the 50 states, compete in contests of beauty, poise, swimwear, evening gown and personality for the title Miss Teen U.S.A. 2008.

Presenters: Shelley Henning, Seth Goldman. **Winners:** Stevi Perry (Miss Teen U.S.A. 2008; representing Arkansas), Brittany Pjetraj (First Runner-Up, South Carolina), Julia Dalton (Second Runner-Up, North Carolina), Lindsay Evans (Third Runner-Up, Louisiana), Shareece Pfeiffer (Fourth Runner-Up, Idaho).

346   The Miss U.S.A. Pageant. (Special; Contest; NBC; April 11, 2008)

The 57th annual presentation wherein contestants representing the fifty states, compete against each other in various categories (from swim wear to evening gown) for the title "Miss U.S.A. 2008."

Hosts: Donny Osmond, Marie Osmond. **Winner:** Crystie Stewart (Miss U.S.A. 2008). **Judges:** Kristian Alfonso, Joey Fatone, Rob Schneider, Robert Earl, George Wayne, Heather Mills, Amanda Beard, Christian Siviano.

Credits: *Executive Producer:* Philip Gurin. *Supervising Producer:* Mariana Ferraro. *Producer:* Morenike Evans. *Director:* Glenn Weiss. *Writer:* Eugene Pack.

347   The Miss Universe Pageant. (Series; Contest; NBC; July 14, 2008)

The 57th annual event, broadcast from the Crown Convention Center (Diamond Bay Resort) in Nha Trang, Vietnam. Eighty women from around the world compete in various contests (from swimwear to evening gown) for the coveted title of Miss Universe 2008. The special marks the first time a major U.S. based TV program was broadcast from Vietnam since the end of the war as well as being held in a contemporary Communist state for the first time.

Host: Jerry Springer, Melanie Brown. **Winners:** Davana Mendoza (Miss Universe 2008, representing Venezuela), Taliana Vargas (First Runner-Up, Colombia), Marianne Cruz (Second Runner-Up, Do-

minican Republic), Vera Krasova (Third Runnr-Up, Russia), Elisa Najera (Fourth Runner-Up, Mexico).

Credits: *Executive Producer:* Philip Gurin. *Supervising Producer:* Mariana Ferraro. *Producer:* Erica Gardner, Shayna Weber. *Director:* Glenn Weiss. *Writer:* Eugene Pack.

348   The Mr. Men Show. (Series; Cartoon; Cartoon Network; February 4, 2008 to March 12, 2008)

An animated sketch show that features Mr. Men and Little Misses characters in various themed situations geared to children.

Voice Cast: Phil Lollar (Mr. Lazy/Mr. Small/Mr. Strong), Susan Ballboni (Little Miss Scary), Jeff Stewart (Mr. Tickle), Peter Mitchell (Mr. Messy), Alicyn Packard (Little Miss Sunshine/Little Miss Whoops/Little Miss Naughty).

Credits: *Executive Producer:* Kate Boutilier, Eryk Casemire, Kurt Mueller, Ashley Postewaite, Darrel Van Citters. *Producer:* Peggy Regan. *Music:* Jared Faber.

349   Mitzi Gaynor Razzle Dazzle: The Special Years. (Special; Variety; PBS; November 14, 2008)

A nostalgic, clip-rich look at the television specials singer-actress-dancer Mitzi Gaynor made during the 1970s and 80s. Mitzi's reminisces are accompanied by those of her show business friends.

Cast: Mitzi Gaynor, Carl Reiner, Rex Reed, Kristin Chenoweth, Randy Doney, Bob Mackie, Kelli O'Hara, Aston Huff.

Credits: *Executive Producer:* Sal Scamardo. *Producer:* David Stern, Annette Jolles, Rene Reyes. *Director:* David Stern. *Writer:* Annette Jolles, Jennifer Matson, Rene Ryes, Shane Rosamonda, David Stern.

350   The Mole. (Series; Reality; ABC; June 2, 2008 to August 11, 2008)

Twelve players compete in various athletic challenges for money. One of the participants, however, is a mole and has been assigned to prevent players from winning money by sabotaging the challenges. Each week the players are quizzed about the mole and the player with the least knowledge about the mole is eliminated; the winner is the one player left standing with the mole.

Host: Jon Kelley.

Credits: *Executive Producer:* Scott A. Stone, Clay Newbill. *Co-Executive Producer:* Leslie Garvin, Rabin Gholam, Jeff Krask. *Supervising Producer:* David Finklestein, Tess Gamboa, Bill Hochhauser.

Review: "In essence, *The Mole* borrows from the best, combining the traveling component of *The Amazing Race* with the challenges and squabbling of *Survivor...* Given how rarely reality feels nowadays, there's something to be said for simply making it here" (*Variety*).

351 The Moment of Truth. (Series; Game; Fox; January 23, 2008 to April 2, 2008)

Prior to the broadcast, players are hooked up to a lie detector and asked a series of personal questions. The polygraph results, however, are not revealed to them. On stage, a player is seated opposite friends and family members and asked selected questions that were previously answered. Money is awarded for each question the player answers that agrees with his polygraph results (if the player responds differently, he is eliminated). If questions become too personal (fearing to offend a friend or family member) he can quit and walk away with the money he has won up to that point. A wrong answer at any point costs a player his winnings.

Host: Mark L. Walberg.

Credits: *Executive Producer:* Howard Schwartz, Mike Darnell. *Senior Producer:* Jeff Rosenthal. *Associate Producer:* Talia Frankel. *Music:* William Anderson.

Review: "Finally, someone manages to give honesty a bad name. Thanks, Fox!" (*The Hollywood Reporter*).

352 Momma's Boys. (Series; Reality; NBC; December 16, 2008 to January 19, 2009)

Dating show with a slight twist: 32 beautiful single women not only have to win the heart of one of three eligible bachelors — but that of the boy's mother — who helps him choose the right girl. The bachelors and their mothers live together in a large house throughout the six episode run. The program relates the conflicts between a mother's wishes and a son's desires as the sons seek the perfect woman (for him and his mother) and the woman of choice's efforts to prove herself to the boy's mother.

Bachelors: JoJo Bojanowski, Robert Kluge, Michael Sarysz. **Mothers:** Khalood Bojanowski (JoJo's mother), Esther Kluge (Robert's mother), Lorraine Sarysz-Nichols (Michael's mother). **The Women:** Morgan Albertus, Vita Alexander, Meghan Allen, Misty Alli, Amanda Myers, Madeleine Aseron, Julie Bornemann, Jessica Brown, Donna Coffee, Jessica Crider, Payton Ellington, Erica Ellyson, Mindy Finney, Natalie Flores, Amy Forth, Brittany Fuchs, Stacy Fuson, Maisha Gainer, Liz Gasinski, Simonen Hopson, Rana Lyn Kaidbey, Michelle Kopasz, Lynette McKinney, Nikki O'Connell, Camilla Poindexter, Lauren Potter, Cara Quici, Jamie Rapp, Callie Stilwell, Myaa Thompson, Rochelle Torgman, Carina Whitcomb.

Credits: *Executive Producer:* Ryan Seacrest, Andrew Glassman. *Co-Executive Producer:* Elliot Goldberg, Grant Julian. *Supervising Producer:* Carrie Franklin, Rebecca Shumsky, Lisa Knapp, Dan Zimmerman. *Music:* Russ Landau.

Reviews: "All told, it's the most familiar of reality concepts with all the usual tricks — barely deviating from established programs" (*Variety*).

"*Momma's Boys* ... follows the same tired ... formula of every other dopey dating show... Except here we have three embarrassing men instead of one" (*New York Post*).

353   Mom's Cooking. (Series; Cooking; Lifetime; Premiered: December 1, 2008)

Cooking combined with reality as mothers teach their daughters how to prepare favorite family dishes. There is no competition and no prizes — just real people sharing real life experiences.

Host: Joe Corsano.

Credits: *Executive Producer:* Michael Morrisay. *Producer:* Mean Isenstadt, Andy Stewart.

Review: "It's pure comfort TV. Anyone who doesn't think there's a place for this in the TV mix should take a look at what else is playing. *Divorce Court* anyone?" (*New York Daily News*).

354   Mom's Funniest Moments. (Special; Comedy; My Network TV; May 7, 2008)

A pre–Mother's Day special in which mothers are caught on tape in embarrassing situations.

Host: Erik Estrada, Laura McKenzie.

Credits: *Executive Producer:* Paul Sharratt, David McKenzie. *Producer:* John Ross. *Associate Producer:* Heather Biggins. *Director:* David McKenzie. *Writer:* Dan Goldman, Heather Biggins, John Ross.

355   Monster Ark. (TV Movie; Horror; Sci Fi; August 9, 2008)

A group of archeologists attempt to uncover the mysterious and deadly secret behind the remnants of a ship found in a remote desert.

Cast: Amanda Crew (Joanna), Renee O'Connor (Ava), Tim DeKay (Nicholas), Tommy "Tiny" Lister (Gentry), Richard Gnolfo (Wilson), Bill Parks (Russell), Tommy Nohilly (Coles), Mike Straub (Hutch).

Credits: *Producer:* Jeffrey Beach, Philip J. Roth. *Writer-Director:* Declan O'Brien. *Music:* Claude Foisy.

356   Monster Buster Club. (Series; Cartoon; Jetix; Premiered: June 9, 2008)

Single Town is an Earth city that is plagued by trouble-making aliens. In an effort to protect Single Town, Cathy Smith, a girl who appears to be 10 years old, and her grandfather, Mr. Smith, travel from their planet (Rhapsodia) to Earth and establish the Monster Buster Club. Cathy, who is actually 7,000 years old, recruits three Earth children (Samantha, Danny and Chris) and together they set out to stop the alien rampage.

Voice Cast: Andrea Libman (Cathy), Anna Cummer (Samantha), Matt Hill (Danny), Sam Vincent (Chris), Sonja Ball, Ian James Corlett, Rick Jones, Matt Hill, Tabitha St. Germain, Michael Yarmush.

Credits: *Producer:* David Michel, Vincent Chalvon-Demersay.

357   Moonlight and Mistletoe. (TV Movie; Drama; Hallmark; November 29, 2008)

Santaville was a once thriving business in Chester, Vermont, that celebrated Christmas year round. Recently, however, the business has fallen on hard times and owner Nick Crosby fears he will have to shut down operations. Hope beckons when Nick's daughter, Holly, returns home for the holidays and with the help of Nick's master carpenter, Peter, seeks a way to bring prosperity back to Santaville.

Cast: Candace Cameron (Holly Crosby), Tom Arnold (Nick Crosby), Christopher Wiehl (Peter), Barbara Niven (Ginny).

Credits: *Executive Producer:* Craig Anderson. *Producer:* Karen Mayeda Vianek. *Music:* Lawrence Shragge. *Director:* Karen Arthur. *Writer:* Joany Kane, Duane Poole.

358   The Most Wonderful Time of the Year. (TV Movie; Drama; Hallmark; December 13, 2008)

Jennifer Cullen is a single mother who finds the Christmas holiday season becoming a chore as she struggles to provide a happy holiday for her six-year-old son (Brian). As feelings of depression threaten a happy holiday, two men enter her life: Morgan, an acquaintance of her Uncle Ralph, and Richard, a successful businessman. The story follows Morgan and Richard as they compete for Jennifer's affections.

Cast: Brooke Burns (Jennifer Cullen), Henry Winkler (Uncle Ralph), Warren Christie (Morgan), Woody Jeffreys (Richard), Teach Grant (Lanny), Connor Levins (Brian Cullen).

Credits: *Executive Producer:* Dan Wigutow, Harvey Kahn, Michael M. Scott. *Producer:* Caroline Moore. *Music:* Philip Giffin. *Director:* Michael M. Scott. *Writer:* Bruce Graham.

Review: "The producers and performers here deserve an extra sugarplum in their stockings for taking a story with no visible suspense or surprise and making it watchable, charming and even a bit fresh" (*New York Daily News*).

359 The Movie Awards. (Special; Awards; My Network TV; May 26, 2008)
The 16th annual presentation that honors the best in movie trailers (the previews movie studios use to promote their films as TV commercials).

Host: Sinbad.

Credits: *Executive Producer:* Evelyn Brady. *Producer:* Mike Nagle. *Director:* John Pritchett.

360 The MTV Movie Awards. (Special; Variety; MTV; June 1, 2008)
MTV's annual presentation wherein Golden Popcorn awards are presented to the winners in such film categories as best film, best male and female performers, best kiss, best fight.

Host: Mike Myers. **Musical Guests:** The Pussycat Dolls, Coldplay.

Credits: *Executive Producer:* Mark Bur-

nett, Audrey Morrissey. *Producer:* Jane Mun. *Associate Producer:* Evan Matthews. *Writer:* Jordan Allen-Dutton, Peter Karinen, Corinne Marshall, Melissa Wong. *Director:* Mark Burnett.

361 MTV's Top Pop Group. (Series; Reality; MTV; Premiered: September 11, 2008)
A search to find a new music group. Nine groups, chosen from open auditions, are mentored (from stage presence to harmony and style) then compete in various music challenges with the weakest performers being eliminated. The one group that proves to be the best wins $100,000 and the title of "MTV's Top Pop Group."

Host: Mario Lopez. **Judges:** Michelle Williams, Brian Friedman, and, as credited, Eve, Taboo.

Credits: *Executive Producer:* Richard Hopkins, Allison Wallach. *Supervising Producer:* Lauren Dolgen, Liz Gateley. *Producer:* Eric Salat. *Music:* District 78.

362 A Muppets Christmas: Letters to Santa. (Special; Children; NBC; December 17, 2008)
It is Christmas Eve and while waiting in a post office line to mail their Christmas cards, the Muppets mistakenly advert three letters from making their way to Santa Claus and the North Pole. Realizing that three children's wishes will not be granted, Kermit the Frog, Fozzie Bear, Beaker and Rizzo the Rat begin a trek to the North Pole to deliver the letters to Santa before his annual sleigh ride.

Voice Cast: Steve Whitmire (Kermit the Frog/Beaker/Rizzo the Rat), Eric Jacobson (Miss Piggy/Fozzie Bear/Sam the Eagle), Kevin Clash (Clifford), Richard Griffiths (Santa Claus), Whoopi Goldberg (Cab Driver), Dave Goelz (The Great Gonzo/Waldorf/Zoot/Dr. Bunsen Honeydew), Madison Pettis (Claire), Jane Krakowski (Claire's mother), Uma Thurman (Joy), Paul Williams (Elf), Nathan Lane (Officer Meany).

Credits: *Executive Producer:* Brian Hanson. *Producer:* Martin G. Baker, Anthony Katagas. *Director:* Kirk R. Thatcher. *Writer:* Hugh Fink, Scott Ganz, Andrew Samson. *Songs:* Paul Williams.

363 Murder in Black and White. (Series; Reality; TV One; Premiered: October 5, 2008)

Documentary-like presentation that looks at — and attempts to solve — cold cases from the Civil Rights era.

Host: Al Sharpton.

Credits: *Executive Producer:* Keith Beauchamp. *Supervising Producer:* Robyn Greene, Federico Negri. *Producer:* Barnard Jaffier. *Music:* Fred McFarlane.

364 Murder on Her Mind. (TV Movie; Drama; Lifetime; October 12, 2008)

Psychological drama about Sally Linden, a troubled young woman who bonds with an accused killer (Theresa) then seeks to have the case reopened when she believes Theresa is innocent.

Cast: Annabeth Gish (Sally Linden), Chandra West (Theresa Nichol), Hugh Dillon (Vincent Nichol), Maury Chaykin (John Emory), Kristen Hager (Aimee Linden), Gabriel Hogan (Danny), Matthew Edison (Peter Kahane).

Credits: *Executive Producer:* Sami Chelias, Ilana Frank, Daniel Iron. *Producer:* Victoria Woods. *Director:* David Wellington. *Writer:* Sami Chelias.

365 M.V.P. (Series; Drama; Soap Opera Network; January 18, 2008 to March 11, 2008)

Intimate glimpses into the private lives of the team members (and their "puck bunny women") of the Mustangs, a Canadian hockey team. Gabe is the team center; Trevor is the number one draft pick; Malcolm is the team CEO; Damon is the team's enforcer; Connie is Gabe's romantic interest; Tabbi is Trevor's girlfriend; Evelyn is the widow of late team captain Adam McBride; Molly is Evelyn's daughter; Megan is Connie's friend.

Cast: Lucas Bryant (Gabe McCall), Dillon Casey (Trevor Lemonde), Matthew Bennett (Malcolm LeBlanc), Kristin Booth (Connie Lewis), Anastasia Phillips (Tabbi), Peter Miller (Damon Trebuchet), Natalie Krill (Molly McBride), Amanda Brugel (Megan Chandler), Olivie Wadruff (Grace Morris).

Credits: *Executive Producer:* Mary Young Leckie, Heather Haldane, Lena Cordina, T.W. Peacocke. *Writer:* Kent Staines, Sherry White. *Director:* T.W. Peacocke

Reviews: "Ignore those funky Canadian accents and *M.V.P.* is passable night time soap ... using hockey (!) as a slick backdrop to its bed-hopping shenanigans" (*Variety*).

"Do you spend more time basking in the warm glow of the TV when the nights turn long and cold? The CBC [Canadian Broadcasting Corporation] knows you do and hopes to capitalize on couch-bound Canadians cocooning instincts by tantalizing them with a winter season of slick and sometimes salacious new programming" (*The National Post*, Canada).

366 My Big Redneck Wedding. (Series; Reality; CMT; January 11, 2008 to November 22, 2008)

Real weddings, that are all but glamorous, are showcased as mud fights, square dances and monster trucks take center stage.

Host: Tom Arnold.

Credits: *Executive Producer:* Lewis A. Bogach, Bob Kusbit. *Producer:* Anna Goodman-Herrick, Sara Hoff, Kristy Wampole, Josh Barnett, Elizabeth McDonald.

367 My Dad Is Better Than Your Dad. (Series; Game; NBC; February 18, 2008 to April 7, 2008)

Four father and son (or father and daughter) teams compete. A series of various physical contests are held in which the fathers perform the most strenuous part of the stunt with the son or daughter coaching or assisting in aspects that will not cause them any harm. Each competition eliminates the weakest team. In the final round, the two remaining teams compete for a chance to win $50,000.

Host: Dan Cortese.

Credits: *Executive Producer:* Mark Burnett, Howard T. Owens, Mark Koops, Jon Hotchkiss, Mike Nichols. *Co-Executive Producer:* Jim Roush, Jared Tobman. *Director:* Michael Simon.

368 My Fair Wedding. (Series; Reality; WE; October 26, 2008 to November 30, 2008)

Misguided brides are set on the right path to a happy wedding day with a complete makeover from dress to décor.

Host: David Tutera (celebrity event planner).

369 My Family's Got Guts. (Series; Reality; Nickelodeon; Premiered: September 15, 2008)

Real families (most with some athletic abilities) challenge professional athletes in various sports challenges.

Host: Ben Lyons, Asha Kuerten.

Credits: *Supervising Producer:* Christine Woods. *Producer:* Jeff Sutphen.

370 My Music: Love Songs of the 50s and 60s. (Special; Variety; PBS; November 29, 2008)

A look back (through film clips) at the music and performers of love songs from the 1950s and early 1960s (including Connie Stevens, Petula Clark, Patti Paige, the Eberly Brothers).

Host: Connie Stevens.

Credits: *Executive Producer:* J.T. Lubinsky. *Producer:* Jim Pearson. *Announcer:* Mike Frazier.

371 My Own Worst Enemy. (Series; Drama; NBC; October 13, 2008 to December 15, 2008)

A secret government organization with subterranean headquarters located beneath a building at 5210 S. Grand Avenue in Los Angeles plays a key role in protecting the U.S. from her enemies. It operates under the guise of the Janus Corporation. Edward Albright is a decorated war hero, a man who can speak 13 languages and hold his breath underwater for five minutes. He believes to prove the existence of free will a person must do something he does not want to do. When he learns of an experiment that will test his beliefs, he volunteers. What results is a split personality ("We manifested a diver gate identity dormant in a small portion of the medial temporal lobe, creating a split personality," says Mavis Heller, the head of Janus). Henry Spivey is the result, a part of Edward, but a man who leads a separate life (married to Angie; the father of Ruthy and Jack; and strategic consultant for Janus). Henry, "born" at the facility on March 16, 1969, has no knowledge of Edward although they share the same body (when Henry is asleep Edward functions; when Henry awakens, he is Henry. His disappearances to become Edward when needed are explained as business trips).

All is progressing well until a system malfunction makes Henry aware that something is not right and he soon realizes that he is two different people, but the same person. Although the two can never physically meet, they communicate with each other (through recorded messages each makes and views over a computer). Stories follow Henry and Edward as they thrust into unfamiliar territory where each man is dangerously out of his element. Tom Grady is Henry's friend and co-worker (at Janus) but also an agent named Raymond (for Mavis); Tony is the systems operator responsible for maintaining the balance between Henry and Edward; Norah is Henry's psychiatrist ("who is in tune with the inner workings of both Edward and Henry").

Cast: Christian Slater (Henry Spivey/ Edward Albright), Alfre Woodard (Mavis Heller), Madchen Amick (Angie Spivey), Bella Thorne (Ruthy Spivey), Mike O'Malley (Tom Grady/Raymond), Taylor Lautner (Jack Spivey), Saffron Burrows (Dr. Norah Skinner), Omid Abtahi (Tony).

Credits: *Executive Producer:* Jason Smilovic, David Semel. *Co-Executive Producer:* John Eisendrath. *Supervising Producer:* Kim Clement. *Producer:* Michael Hissrich. *Music:* John McCarthy.

Reviews: "Slater delivers the goods with helpings of magnetism along with his trademark quirky intensity, portraying two men trapped in a single man's body with a measure of credibility" (*The Hollywood Reporter*).

"*My Own Worst Enemy* holds our interest despite its utter preposterousness because if there is anything Slater knows how to do, it's present a believable head case" (*Variety*).

372 The NAACP Image Awards.
(Special; Variety; Fox; February 14, 2008)

A program honoring people and projects that promote diversity in the performing arts.

Guests: Hill Harper, Kate Walsh, Lance Gross, Tom Joyner, LaVan Davis, Tyler Perry, America Ferrera, Masi Oka, Jessica Lucas, Taye Diggs, Holly Robinson-Peete, Tichina Arnold, Ruby Dee, Anthony Anderson, Tracy Morgan, Janet Jackson, Cassi Davis, Sidney Poitier, Angela Bassett, Wayne Brady, Audra McDonald, Kimberly Elise. **Performers:** Kim Burell, Tak 6, Jordin Sparks, Ziggy Marley, Sounds of Blacknell, Stevie Wonder.

Credits: *Executive Producer:* Vicangelo Bulluck. *Producer:* Marilyn Seabury. *Co-Prodcuer:* Royce Osborn, Ricky Minor. *Music:* Ricky Minor. *Director:* Jonathan X. *Writer:* Royce Osborn.

373 Nashville Star. (Series; Reality; NBC; June 9, 2008 to July 14, 2008)

Amateur singers compete for a chance to become the next great country and west-

ern music star. Each program is broadcast live and viewer votes determine who goes and who they feel is worthy of staying and eventually winning the coveted title.

Host: Billy Ray Cyrus. **Judges:** Jewel, John Rich, Jeffrey Steele.

Credits: *Executive Producer:* Jeff Boggs. *Co-Executive Producer:* Mark Kopps, Todd Lubin. *Producer:* Gordon Cassidy.

374 NBC's New Year's Eve with Carson Daly. (Special; Variety; NBC; December 31, 2008 to January 1, 2009)

A program that rings in 2009 with variety performances and live reports from Times Square in New York City as the seconds tick down to the new year. Broadcast in prime time from 10:00 P.M. to 11:00 P.M. and late night (after a break for local station news) from 11:35 P.M. to 12:35 A.M.

Host: Carson Daly. **Guests:** Elton John, Katy Perry, 50 Cent, Ludacris. **Times Square Reporter:** Amy Robach. **Events Reporter:** Luke Russert.

Credits: *Executive Producer:* Carson Daly, David Friedman. *Co-Executive Producer:* Guy Oseary. *Director:* Steve Paley. *Writer:* Brian Brown.

375 Never Cry Werewolf. (TV Movie; Horror; Sci Fi; May 11, 2008)

Loren is a teenage girl with an inquiring mind. When she becomes suspicious of her new neighbor (Peter Stebbings) and begins spying on him, she believes he is a werewolf and responsible for a series of murders. Figuring no one will believe her, she decides to act alone. At the local sporting goods store, where Loren is seeking a weapon to kill a werewolf, she arouses the suspicions of Redd Tucker, a big game hunter, who agrees to help her when he questions her. The story follows their dangerous quest to uncover the truth.

Cast: Nina Dobrev (Loren Hansett), Kevin Sorbo (Redd Tucker), Jared Martin (Peter Stebbings), Melanie Leishman (Angie Bremlock), Sean O'Neill (Steven Kepkik), Billy Otis (Charles Pope).

Credits: *Executive Producer:* Eric Gozlan, Mike Greenfield, Daniel Grodnik, Gary Howsam, Jacqueline Kelly, Barbara Sacks, Brenton Spencer. *Producer:* Wendy Kay Moore, Martin Scharf, Aaron Barnett. *Music:* Michael Richard Plowman. *Director:* Brenton Spencer. *Writer:* John Sheppard.

376 New Amsterdam. (Series; Crime Drama; Fox; March 4, 2008 to April 14, 2008)

In the 1640s when New York was known as New Amsterdam, John Amsterdam was a soldier in the Dutch army. During a battle with a Native American tribe, John stepped in front of a sword to save the life of a young Indian girl. The girl brought John to a place of refuge and saved his life by casting an ancient spell that made him immortal. John will never age and the spell can only be broken (to make him mortal again) when he finds his one true love. The centuries pass and John has devoted his life to upholding the law. It is 2008 when viewers are introduced to John Amsterdam. He lives in Manhattan and is a detective with the N.Y.P.D. John has seen New York grow from its colonial beginnings to its present day metropolis. He and Manhattan are a part of each other and his 400 years of experiences have made him an invaluable addition to the police department. Only one man, Omar, the owner of a jazz club and his life-long friend, knows John's secret. Over the course of time, John has met and known and lost many women — but none have been the one that can change his life.

This happens one day while chasing a suspect and John suffers a heart attack and nearly dies. He realizes that during that pursuit he must have crossed paths with his one true love. He now realizes that his life has changed forever. Stories follow John as he not only upholds the law, but seeks the mysterious woman the Indian girl spoke of in her prophecy. Eva Marquez is John's partner.

Cast: Nikolaj Coster Waldau (John Amsterdam), Zuleikhla Robinson (Eva Marquez), Stephen Henderson (Omar), Alexie Gilmore (Dr. Sarah Dillane), Robert Clohessy (Detective Santori).

Credits: *Executive Producer:* Allan Loeb, David Manson. Steven Pearl. *Co-Executive Producer:* John David Coles. *Supervising Producer:* Ashley Gable. *Producer:* Margo Myers. *Music:* Mychael Danna.

Reviews: "Life's a bitch, and then you don't die. Having an *American Idol* lead-in can keep the grim reaper at bay (justified or not)" (*The Hollywood Reporter*).

"Easy to dismiss at first glance, the series does exhibit some possibilities in its second episode, though it's still a relatively uninspired time killer for those of us with just one life to live" (*Variety*).

377 New York Goes Hollywood. (Series; Reality; VH-1; August 4, 2008 to September 22, 2008)

Tiffany Pollard, known as New York on *The Flavor of Love* and *I Love New York*, leaves Manhattan to pursue her dream of becoming an actress. Cameras chart those efforts.

Star: Tiffany Pollard.

Credits: *Executive Producer:* Cris Abrego, Mark Cronin, Matt Odgers, Ben Samek.

378 Newlywed — Nearly Dead. (Series; Reality; Fine Living Network; Premiered: June 19, 2008)

Therapist Gary Direnfeld attempts to help newlyweds on the verge of a breakup overcome their differences and rekindle the spark that brought them together in the first place.

Host: Gary Direnfeld. **Narrator:** Paul Ackerley.

Credits: *Executive Producer:* Guy O'Sullivan. *Supervising Producer:* Jessica Wright. *Producer:* Rebecca Ruddle. *Associate Producer:* Meredith Veats.

379 Ni Hao, Kai-Lan. (Series; Cartoon; Cartoon Network; Premiered: February 7, 2008)

An attempt to introduce children to the Chinese culture and the Mandarin language through Kai-Lan Chow, a preschooler who shares colorful adventures and story telling with other children her age. The title translates as "Hello, Kai-Lan."

Voice Cast: Jade-Lianna Peters (Kai-Lan Chow), Beverly Duan (Lulu), Angie Wu (Ho Ho), Laura Marano (Mei Mei), Zachary Gordon (San San), Clem Cheung (Ye Ye), Tommy Nightingale (Fluffy), Jack Samson (Rintoo).

Credits: *Executive Producer:* Mary Harrington. *Supervising Producer:* Dave Marshall. *Producer:* Debby Hundman.

380 The Nickelodeon Kids Choice Awards. (Special; Variety; Nickelodeon; March 29, 2008)

The annual presentation that honors the best in children's programming.

Host: Jack Black. **Appearing:** Hayden Panettiere, Jessica Alba, Drake Bell, Miranda Cosgrove, Miley Cyrus, Cameron Diaz, Harrison Ford, Jennette McCurdy, Shia Le Beouf.

Credits: *Executive Producer:* Bob Bain. *Supervising Producer:* Gregory Sills. *Producer:* Paul Flattery. *Director:* Beth McCarthy-Miller. *Writer:* Sam Maccarone.

381 Nigella Express. (Series; Cooking; Food Network; Premiered: January 12, 2008)

Chef Nigella Lawson teaches viewers how to prepare meals in record time.

Host: Nigella Lawson.

Credits: *Executive Producer:* Lindsay Bradbury, Ben Galen, Rachel Purnell. *Producer:* Sophie Seiden.

382 Nightmare at the End of the Hall. (TV Movie; Drama; Lifetime Movie Network; June 22, 2008)

Eerie tale about a young teacher (Courtney Snow) who meets a student (Laurel) she feels may be the reincarnation of a friend who committed suicide years earlier.

Cast: Sara Rue (Courtney Snow), Jacqueline MacInnes Wood (Laurel), Amber Borycki (Young Courtney), Kavan Smith (Brett), Christine Danielle (Emory), Sebastian Gacki (Young Brett), Duane Keogh (Chester).

Credits: *Executive Producer:* Joseph Lawlor, Kirk Shaw. *Producer:* Jamie Goehring. *Writer:* Nora Zuckerman. *Director:* George Mendeluk. *Music:* Clinton Shorter.

383 90210. (Series; Drama; CW; Premiered: September 2, 2008)

An updated version of the Fox series *Beverly Hills, 90210.* Life in fashionable Beverly Hills, especially West Beverly Hills High School, as seen through the eyes of Annie Wilson and her adopted brother, Dixon, the new kids at school (having just relocated from Kansas with their parents, Harry and Debbie, to be closer to their grandmother [Harry's mother], Tabitha, a former television star and a charter member of the Betty Ford Clinic).

Annie is sweet and friendly and has a passion for the theater; Dixon is the star athlete. Their father is the school's new principal. Naomi is the spoiled, rich girl; Ethan is the popular jock; Navid is the aspiring journalist; Silver is the rebel student who produces a You Tube Internet blog. Kelly Taylor (a student on the original series) is now the school's guidance counselor; Ryan is a teacher; Nat owns the local hangout, the Peach Pit.

Cast: Shenae Grimes (Annie Wilson), Tristan Wilds (Dixon Wilson), Rob Estes (Harry Wilson), Lori Loughlin (Debbie Wilson), Jessica Walter (Tabitha Wilson), Anna Lynne McCord (Naomi Clark), Dustin Milligan (Ethan Ward), Jennie Garth (Kelly Taylor), Jessica Stroup (Silver), Michael Steger (Navid Shirazi), Ryan Eggold (Ryan Matthews), Joe E. Tata (Nat Bussichio), Shannen Doherty (Brenda Walsh).

Credits: *Executive Producer:* Gabe Sachs, Jeff Judah. *Producer:* Michael Pendell. *Music:* Marc Dauer, Evan Frankfort, Liz Phair.

Reviews: "The stage is set for a slick and sharply crafted teen soap that pays homage to the first *90210* without wallowing in past glory" (*The Hollywood Reporter*).

"This spin off, eight years after the first ended, is a pallid copy of the original fish out of water story, only with shinier cars, fancier clothes and Botox aplenty" (*Variety*).

384 Novel Adventures. (Series; Drama; Internet; Premiered: November 3, 2008)

Lizzie, Amy, Laura and Joanna are four Los Angeles women who belong to a book club. As the sessions become boring to them, they decide to ditch the club and live the adventures they would normally only read about. Stories relate their experiences as they transform their ordinary lives into once in a lifetime experiences.

Cast: Daphne Zuniga (Laura French), Ashley Williams (Lizzie McKenzie), Jolie Jenkins (Amy Pierson), Paola Turbay (Joanna Ruiz).

385 Now and Then, Here and There. (Series; Cartoon; Sci Fi; Premiered: July 28, 2008)

While attempting to rescue a mysterious girl with strange eyes (Lala-Ru) a young Japanese boy (Shu) is magically transported to her desert world and into the midst of a battle between her people and the evil ruler General Hamdo. Stories follow Shu and Lala-Ru, who possesses the power to create water, as the battle the cruelties of Hamdo.

Voice Cast: Eddie Paulson (Shu), Lisa Ortiz (Lala-Ru), Jack Taylor (Hamdo), Dana Halsted (Abelia), Henry Tenney (Captain), Dan Green (Nabuca), Crispio Freeman (Tabool).

Credits: *Producer:* Shorchi Kumabi, Kazuaki Morijiri.

386 The Nutcracker. (Special; Ballet; PBS; December 17, 2008)

San Francisco, 1915 is the setting for this adaptation of the E.T. Hoffman classic story of a wooden nutcracker that comes to life. It is Christmas Eve and a young girl (Clara) receives a nutcracker dressed as a Royal soldier, as a gift from her grandfather. As the grandfather tells Clara the story of how the nutcracker came to be, she imagines herself in magical adventures where she becomes a princess in an enchanted winter wonderland. The ballet concludes with Clara awakening but not sure if her experiences where real or imagined. Performed by the San Francisco Ballet Company; based on the music by Peter Ilyich Tchaikovsky.

Host: Kristi Yamaguchi. **Cast:** Elizabeth Powell (Clara), Davit Karapetyas (Nutcracker Prince), Yuan Yuan Tan (Snow Queen), Damian Smith (Uncle Drosselmeyer), Pierre Francois-Vilanoba (Snow King), Vanessa Zahorian (Sugar Plum Fairy), Sarah Van Patten (Genie).

Credits: *Executive Producer:* Michael Isip. *Producer:* Judy Flannery. *Music Director:* Martin West. *Director:* Matthew Diamond. *Choreographer:* Helgi Thomasson.

387 N.Y.C.: Torpedo Terror. (TV Movie; Science Fiction; Sci Fi; June 14, 2008)

Disaster film in which electrical tornadoes, sparked by global warming, descend on New York City.

Cast: Nicole de Boer (Cassie Lawrence), Sebastian Spence (James Lawrence), Jerry Wasserman (Mayor Leonardo), Tegan Moss (Lori), Jennifer Copping (Maggie Flynn), Matthew Harrison (Dr. Quinn).

Credits: *Producer:* Cheryl Lee Fast. *Associate Producer:* Kelly-Ruth Mercer. *Director:* Tibor Takacs. *Music:* Clinton Shorter. *Writer:* T.S. Cook.

388 Ocean Force. (Series; Reality; True TV; Premiered January 12, 2008)

The work of real life guards (here representing Huntington Beach in California) are depicted in a more serious light than on the series *Baywatch*. While *Baywatch* did show that beach rescues can be dangerous, *Ocean Force* relates the real life rescues with all the hazards such rescues involve.

Lifeguards: Michael Bartlett, Eric Dieterman, Jon Elser, Matthew Norton.

Credits: *Supervising Producers:* Stephanie Griffin. *Producer:* Nate Harrington, Chad Horning, Laurie Pekich.

389 The Office (British). (Series; Comedy; BBC America; 2008)

The British series on which the American series (see program 994) of the same title is based. Documentary style presentation that follows the staff of the Wernham Hogg Paper Company. David Brent is the office manager; Gareth Keenan, the workers team leader; Tim, the sales rep; Dawn, the receptionist; Neil and Jennifer are the bosses.

Cast: Ricky Gervais (David Brent), Mackenzie Crook (Gareth Keenan), Martin Freeman (Tim Canterbury), Lucy Davis (Dawn Tinsley), Patrick Baladi (Neil Godwin), Stirling Gallacher (Jennifer Taylor-Clarke).

390 An Old Fashioned Thanksgiving. (TV Movie; Drama; Hallmark Channel; November 22, 2008)

Bittersweet holiday tale, set in New Hampshire just after the Civil War, about an estranged mother (Isabella), her daughter (Mary) and their efforts to heal emotional wounds and become a family again.

Cast: Jacqueline Bissett (Isabella), Helene Joy (Mary Bassett), Tatiana Massiany (Mathilda Bassett), Gage Munroe (Solomon Bassett), Vivien Endicott Douglas (Prudence), Ted Atherton (Mr. Hopkins), Paula Boudreau (Mrs. Hopkins), Kristopher Turner (Gad Hopkins).

Credits: *Executive Producer:* Michael Prupas. *Producer:* Steve Solomon. *Music:*

James Gelfand. *Director:* Graeme Campbell. *Writer:* Shelley Evans.

Review: "Hallmark's new Thanksgiving movie is even weepier than usual. But the characters are so gosh-darned likable that you stay with them, and in the end, they even go a few places you may not have expected" (*New York Daily News*).

391 On Surfari. (Series; Reality; Fuel TV; 2008)

A look at the world of surfing as seen through the travels of the McIntyre family as they go to "all the weird places to surf."

Host: Shannon McIntyre, Shayne McIntyre, Banyan McIntyre.

392 100 Million B.C. (TV Movie; Horror; Sci Fi; December 27, 2008)

During the late1940s, a professor (Dr. Frank Reno) conducted a time traveling experiment called the Rainbow Project that sent a team of scientists back in time. A glitch in the system prevented a return trip and the team became stranded in the Cretaceous Period. In 2008 evidence is uncovered (a message found inscribed on a rock in a cave) that the team survived the trip. With advance technology now available, Frank organizes a team of Navy SEALS to rescue the marooned scientists. They are successful but during the return trip, a Tyrannosaurus Rex–like creature is brought back to Los Angeles. The story relates the team's efforts to dispose of the beast before it wrecks havoc on the city.

Cast: Michael Gross (Dr. Frank Reno), Christopher Atkins (Erik Reno), Greg Evigan (Ellis Dorn), Wendy Carter (Betty), Stephen Blackehart (Lt. Robert Peet), Marie Westbrook (Ruth), Dean Kreyling (Chief "Bud" Stark), Phil Burke (Stubbs).

Credits: *Executive Producer:* David Rimawi. *Producer:* David Michael Latt. *Associate Producer:* Paul Bales. *Director:* Griff Furst. *Writer:* Paul Nales. *Music:* Ralph Rieckermann.

393 Opportunity Knocks. (Series; Game; ABC; September 22, 2008 to October 14, 2008)

A game show where the stage is set up on the street opposite the home of the family chosen to be the contestants. Friends and neighbors are the "studio audience" and each member of the chosen family are asked questions that refer to how well they know each other (compiled from interviews with family and friends). Correct answers earn the family cash (up to $250,000 if each member can answer each of the questions correctly).

Host: J.D. Roth.

Credits: *Executive Producer:* Ashton Kutcher, Jason Goldberg, Karey Burke, J.D. Roth. *Co-Executive Producer:* Kathy Satula. *Supervising Producer:* Jason Gabel. *Producer:* Claudia Magre, Daba David. *Music:* Jeff Lipencott.

Reviews: "The lights are on but nobody's home" (*The Hollywood Reporter*).

"It's harmless but pretty stupid, which generally describes most of actor-producer Ashton Kutcher's forays into prime time" (*Variety*).

394 Oprah's Big Give. (Series; Reality; ABC; March 2, 2008 to April 20, 2008)

Ten ordinary people compete in challenges that test their ability to be generous and help people who are less fortunate. Each do-gooder is judged by a panel and the weakest performers are eliminated. The most charitable person, chosen on the last episode, receives $500,000 for himself and an equal amount for his charity.

Host: Nate Berkus.

Judges: Jamie Oliver, Tony Gonzalez, Malaak Compton-Rock.

Credits: *Executive Producer:* Oprah Winfrey, Ellen Rakieten, Harriet Seitler, Bertram Van Munster, Elsie Doganieri. *Supervising Producer:* Jonathan Sinclair, Shannon McGinn, Fred Pichel. *Producer:* Barry Hennessy, Maren Patterson.

Review: "[Oprah] Winfrey insists that "America will ... love the heart of this show." That organ does appear to be in the right place. It's just the surrounding parts and pieces ... that seem to have been rather haphazardly stitched together" (*Variety*).

395 The Orange Bowl Parade. (Special; Variety; CBS; January 1, 2008)

Elaborate floats coupled with celebrity guests and marching bands that celebrates (and airs prior to) the annual telecast of the Orange Bowl football game in Florida.

Grand Marshal: Don Shula. **Cast:** Victoria Rowell, Pat O'Brien, Tito Puente, Tito Puente, Jr., Bryan White.

Credits: *Executive Producer:* Mike Gargiulo. *Producer:* Phil Arone. *Director:* Brian Glazer.

396 The Osmonds 50th Anniversary Reunion. (Special; Variety; PBS; March 2, 2008)

Singers Marie Osmond and her brothers reunite for a nostalgic look back at the family now (who perform songs) and as they were years earlier when they were regulars on *The Andy Williams Show* in the 1960s.

Stars: Marie Osmond, Donny Osmond, Wayne Osmond, Jay Osmond, Jimmy Osmond, Alan Osmond, Merrill Osmond.

Credits: *Producer:* Jimmy Osmond.

Review: "There's nothing wrong with *The Osmonds 50th Anniversary Show* ... the problem is there isn't that much that's right about it... For Osmond fans, it delivers ... but music can and does have more substance than this" (*New York Daily News*).

397 The Other Woman. (TV Movie; Drama; Lifetime; June 21, 2008)

Jill and Derek Plumley are a happily married couple. Derek is a successful lawyer and Jill gave up her career as a TV news producer to support him. Problems arise when Derek's boss is murdered in his sleep and his wife confesses, claiming it was self defense. The story follows Jill as she and her journalist friend (Peter) seek to uncover what really happened.

Cast: Josie Bissett (Jill Plumley), Ted Whittall (Derek Plumley), Graeme Black (Barry), Jason Priestley (Peter Henderson), Lisa Marie Caruk (Nicole), MacKanzie Porter (Lauren Plumley), Joseph Allan Sutherland (Cole), Travis Milne (Tyler).

Credits: *Executive Producer:* Joy Fielding, Michael Frisley, Chad Oakes. *Producer:* Jay Daniel. *Music:* Zack Ryan. *Writer:* Dave Schultz. *Director:* Jason Priestley.

398 Our First Christmas. (TV Movie; Drama; Hallmark; December 20, 2008)

Cindy and Tom, divorced parents with children from previous marriages, marry. All appears to be progressing well until the Christmas season approaches and Cindy's children become reluctant to give up their traditions to accommodate Tom's children and vice versa. The story relates Cindy and Tom's efforts to solve their respective problems by starting new family traditions.

Cast: Julie Warner (Cindy), Steven Eckholdt (Tom), John Ratzenberger (Joe), Katerina Graham (Bernie), Dixie Carter (Evie Baer), Cassi Thompson (Tory), Grace Fulton (Lilly), Maxim Knight (Jacob), Marian Antonieta Vazquez (Barista).

Credits: *Executive Producer:* Larry Levinson. *Producer:* Erik Olson, Brian Martinez. *Director:* Armand Mastroianni. *Writer:* Edithe Swensen.

399 Outsider's Inn. (Series; Reality; CMT; August 15, 2008 to October 3, 2008)

Former *Brady Bunch* star Maureen McCormick (Marcia) takes on the challenge to run a bed and breakfast in rural East Tennessee. Episodes relate her progress (a lack of it in some cases) as she and her show business friends, Bobby Brown and Carnie Wilson, struggle to succeed.

Stars: Maureen McCormick, Bobby Brown, Carnie Wilson.

Credits: *Executive Producer:* David

Garfinkle, Jay Renfroe. *Producer:* John Hamlin, Bob Kusbit, Claire McCabe.

400 Pam: Girl on the Loose. (Series; Reality; E!; August 3, 2008 to September 15, 2008)

An-depth profile of the vivacious Pamela Anderson as an actress, mother, business woman and animal activist.

Star: Pamela Anderson. **Featured:** Peter Archer, Hugh Hefner, Elton John, David LaChapelle.

Credits: *Executive Producer:* Pamela Anderson, Fenton Bailey, Randy Barbato, Tom Campbell. *Producer:* Julio Kollerbohm, Jeff Pollack.

Reviews: "The *Baywatch* babe demonstrates undeniable savvy regarding how to leverage fame" (*Variety*).

"*Pam* ... carefully crafts an image of Anderson as an appreciative and approachable sex symbol, a doting mother, a tireless crusader for animals and a celebrity who's just as down to earth as you and me" (*The Hollywood Reporter*).

401 The Paper. (Series; Reality; MTV; April 14, 2008 to May 26, 2008)

The daily activities of a group of teenagers at Cyprus Bay High School in Weston, Florida, who put out the school newspaper, *The Circuit*.

Cast: Rhonda Weiss (Advisor), Amanda Lorber (Editor), Alex Angert (Managing Editor), Cassia Laham (Entertainment Editor), Trevor Ballard (Layout Editor), Geana Pacinelli (News Editor), Dan Surgan (Staff Writer), Adam Brock (Advertising Manager).

Credits: *Executive Producer:* Lindsey Bannister, Jessica Chesler, Marshall Eisen, Sam Simmons, Dave Sirulnick. *Producer:* Josh Haygood. *Music:* Joshua Myers.

Reviews: "The first thing any journalist will notice about *The Paper* is that it doesn't sound real ... these high schoolers have grown up with reality TV and know ... that over-the-top characters stand out" (*New York Post*).

"In execution, the show is like any other MTV reality show, using its setting to cover up the lack of plot ... it's entertaining ... because it is such a nerdy train wreck" (*The Daily Beacon*, University of Tennessee).

402   Paradise Hotel. (Series; Reality; My Network TV; January 4, 2008 to May 19, 2008)

Paradise Hotel is a luxurious, secluded beachside resort. Here eleven singles are brought together in the hope of sparking a romance. The singles are urged to pair up or be replaced by a new single. The singles that are not compatible are eliminated. Cameras follow the activities of the singles as they become intimate with each other.

Host: Amanda Byram. **The Singles:** Charla Pihlstrom, Tara Gerard, Toni Ferrari, Amanda Dominguez, Holly Pastor, Melanie Barger, Kavita Channe, Amy Toliver, Keith Cuda, Dave Kerpen, Beau Wolf, Scott Hanson, Kristin Ellis, Zack Stewart, Alex Van Camp, Matthew Chei, Andon Guenther, Tom Rodriquez.

Credits: *Supervising Producer:* Rick Ringback, Rob Bagshaw. *Producer:* Bill Pruitt. *Associate Producer:* Thomas Loureiro.

403   Paris Hilton: My New BFF. (Series; Reality; MTV; September 30, 2008 to December 2, 2008)

Paris Hilton, called "America's Number One It Girl," seems to gain popularity wherever she goes and whatever she does. Paris is a party girl and loves to shop. Her inner circle are normally A-list celebrities but, for a change, Paris has decided to seek a non-show business figure to join her entourage.

Fourteen "tabloid ready" women and two "flamboyant guys" compete in various society-based challenges for the honor of becoming Paris's new BFF (Best Friend Forever). Paris oversees the competition and chooses who goes and who stays based on performance.

Host: Paris Hilton.

Credits: *Executive Producer:* Chris Choun, Tony DiSanto, Paris Hilton, Liz Gateley, Michael Hirschorn, Douglas M. Wilson. *Producer:* Kira Bosak, Sean Jennings, Audrey Kim.

404   Parking Wars. (Series; Reality; A&E; January 8, 2008 to March 4, 2008)

Cameras follow members of the Philadelphia Parking Authority as they ticket, boot and tow cars.

Officers: Frannie Esposito, Steve Garfield, Keith Hevener, Bill Kurtis.

Credits: *Executive Producer:* Daniel Elias, Bill Kurtis, Robert Sharenow, David Houts. *Supervising Producer:* Dan Flaherty, Laura Fleury, Po Kutchins. *Senior Producer:* Andrew Dunn. *Producer:* Wei Ling Chang, Liz Fine, Danny Alias. *Associate Producer:* Laurissa James, Kendall E. Canner.

405   Party Monsters: Cabo. (Series; Reality; E!; Premiered: December 2, 2008)

Nine party planners compete in various challenges to be the last one standing to produce the ultimate party (at the luxurious L.G. Villa in Cabo, called "The Mexican Riviera") for a group of A-List celebrities.

Host: Michele Merkin. *Judges:* Michele Merkin, Brian Worley.

406   The People's Choice Awards. (Special; Variety; CBS; January 8, 2008)

The annual presentation that honors the film, television and music personalities chosen by fans.

Host: Queen Latifah.

Credits: *Executive Producer:* Carol Donovan. *Producer:* Chris Cohoun, Liz Sterbenz. *Director:* Bruce Gowers.

407   Phineas and Ferb. (Series; Cartoon; Disney; Premiered: February 1, 2008)

It's summer vacation and step brothers Phineas and Ferb have 104 days off from school. To fill the time, they decide to do whatever they can for fun. Hampering their good times is Candace, Phineas's obnoxious older sister, who finds pleasure in tattling and getting them in trouble. Joining in their outrageous adventures is Perry, a platypus who is actually an agent and secretly battles the evil Dr. Doofenshmirtz.

Voice Cast: Vincent Martella (Phineas Flynn), Thomas Sangster (Ferb Fletcher), Ashley Tisdale (Candace Flynn), Dee Bradley Baker (Perry the Platypus), Dan Povenmire (Dr. Doofenshmirtz), Caroline Rhea (Linda Flynn-Fletcher), Richard O'Brien (Lawrence Fletcher).

Credits: *Executive Producer:* Dan Povenmire, Jeff Marsh. *Producer:* Walt Disney Television. *Director:* Dan Povermire, Zac Moncrief.

Reviews: "Infused with a refreshing sense of wit and irreverence, *Phineas and Ferb* is that rare modern animated series for kids that even adults without a frontal lobotomy can sit through" (*Variety*).

"...the show is fast and furious enough to keep today's sophisticated tween (and older and younger) viewers tuned in" (*The Hollywood Reporter*).

408   Picture This. (TV Movie; Comedy; ABC Family; July 13, 2008)

The problems that befall an unpopular teenage girl (Mandy) when she lands a date with the school hunk (Drew) and encounters a jealous girlfriend determined to sabotage the date and an overprotective father who feels Drew is not right for his daughter.

Cast: Ashley Tisdale (Mandy), Robbie Amell (Drew Patterson), Cindy Busby (Lisa Cross), Lauren Collins (Alexa), Shenae Grimes (Cayenne), Marie-Marguerite Sabongui (Blair), Maxim Roy (Marsha Gilbert), Justin Bradley (Mickey), Kevin Pollak (Tom Gilbert).

Credits: *Executive Producer:* Ronald Gilbert, Ashley Tisdale. *Producer:* Patrick Hughes, Brian Reilly. *Music:* Richard Mar-

vin. *Writer:* Temple Matthews. *Director:* Stephen Herek.

409   Pinocchio. (TV Movie; Fantasy; Ion; December 14, 2008)

Nineteenth century Italy is the setting. Shortly after childbirth claims the life of his wife and son, Geppetto, a lonely wood craftsman, fashions a puppet he names Pinocchio from a block of wood. The magical Blue Fairy transforms the wooden boy into a real boy as a companion for Geppetto and the story follows Pinocchio's various adventures as he learns about life. Based on the novel by Carlo Collodi.

Cast: Bob Hoskins (Geppetto), Robbie Kay (Pinocchio), Alessandro Gassman (Carlo Collodi), Margherita Buy (Maestrina), Violante Placido (Fata Turchina), Luciana Littizzetto (Grillo Parlante), Joss Ackland (Mastro Ciliegia), Toni Bertorelli (La Volpe).

Credits: *Executive Producer:* Justin Bodie, Daniele Passani. *Producer:* Luca Bernubei. *Music:* Jan A.P. Kaczmarek. *Director:* Alberto Sironi. *Writer:* Ivan Cotronco, Carlo Mazzotta.

410   The Pioneers of Television. (Special; Documentary; PBS; January 2, 2008 to January 23, 2008)

A four-part special that explores, with representative guests and film clips, comedy, variety, game and talk shows from the early years of television.

Narrator: Harlan Saperstein.

Credits: *Producer:* Steve Boettcher, Mike Trinklein. *Writer:* Mike Trinklein. *Director:* Steve Boettcher.

411   Power Rangers: Jungle Fury. (Series; Science Fiction; ABC; Premiered: March 29, 2008)

Mighty Morphin Power Rangers spin-off wherein the new Power Rangers (Lily, Casey and Theo), endowed with the ability of jungle cats, battle the evil alien, Dai Shi and his assistant, Camille, who plan to dominate the Earth.

Cast: Anna Hutchison (Lily), Aljin Abella (Theo), Jason Smith (Casey), Holly Shanahan (Camille), David de Lautour (R.J.), Bede Skinner (Dai Shi/Jarrod), Sarah Thomson (Fran), Nathaniel Lees (Master Mao).

Credits: *Executive Producer:* Koichi Sakanoto, Bruce Kalish. *Producer:* Sally Campbell. *Co-Producer:* Jackie Marchand. *Music:* Wayne Jones, Gad Emile Zeitune, Leigh Roberts. *Theme:* Gabriel Moses, Leigh Roberts, John Ehrlich.

412   Prairie Fever. (TV Movie; Western; Ion; March 28, 2008)

Former Sheriff Preston Briggs risks his life to escort three beautiful mail order brides (Abigail, Blue and Lettie) across rugged and lawless territory to Carson City, Kansas, during the 1880s.

Cast: Kevin Sorbo (Preston Briggs), Dominique Swain (Abigail), Jamie Anne Allman (Olivia Thibodeaux), Jillian Armenante (Lettie), Felicia Day (Blue), Silas Weir Mitchell (Frank), Caryn Mower (Mary Biggs), Lance Henriksen (James Monte), Chris McKenna (Sheriff Logan).

Credits: *Executive Producer:* Robert Halmi, Jr., Larry Levinson. *Supervising Producer:* Lincoln Lageson. *Producer:* Jeff Kloss. *Writer:* Steven H. Berman. *Director:* David S. Cass, Sr.

413   The Price Is Right Million Dollar Spectacular. (Series; Game; CBS; April 30, 2008 to July 9, 2008)

Prime time version of the daytime series *The Price Is Right* that plays in the same manner (players attempting to guess the list price of merchandise items) with the change occurring during the final game, the Prize Showcase. Here, if a player can guess, within one thousand dollars, the selling price of an extravagant merchandise showcase, he wins $1 million.

Host: Drew Carey. **Models:** Brandi Sherwood, Rachel Reynolds, Gabrielle Tuite.

Credits: *Announcer:* Rich Fields. *Producer:* Roger Dabkowitz, Philip W. Rossi.

414   Primeval. (Series; Science Fiction; BBC America; Premiered: August 7, 2008)

Nick Cutter is a professor of Paleontology at the Center Metropolitan University in London. He is called an "evolutionary zoologist" and investigates gaps in the evolutionary record. Eight years earlier, Nick's wife, Helen (his assistant), mysteriously disappeared in a time-ripping anomaly. Then, suddenly she reappeared in the present day — as do prehistoric creatures who cross the corridors of time via the unexplained anomalies. Helen holds the key to the riddle of the anomalies and stories follow Nick and his team as they struggle to protect society from the past as it threatens not only the present, but the future. Stephen is Nick's assistant; Abby is the reptile expert; Connor is the college intern with an interest in dinosaurs; Claudia is the government's (Ministry of Science and Technology) agent who oversees Nick's investigations; James is the government official who seeks to keep the public in the dark about what is happening.

Cast: Douglas Henshall (Nick Cutter), Juliet Aubrey (Helen Cutter), Andrew Lee Potts (Conner Temple), Lucy Brown (Claudia Brown), James Murray (Stephen Hart), Hannah Spearritt (Abby Maitland), Ben Miller (James Lester).

Credits: *Executive Producer:* Tim Haines. *Producer:* Cameron Allister. *Music:* Dominick Schenner.

Review: "A crackling good BBC America sci fi series thriller that's packed with vivid CGI prehistoric predators galore and a story line that's almost plausible" (*The Hollywood Reporter*).

415   Princess. (TV Movie; Fantasy; ABC Family; June 20, 2008)

Fantasy-like tale about a Jack of all tradesman (William Humphrey) who tries to win the heart of Ithaca, a mysterious self-titled princess.

Cast: Nora Zehetner (Ithaca), Kip Pardue (William Humphrey), Deborah Grover (Nana), Mallory Margel (Phoenix), Mayko Nguyen (Sophie Baxter), Shileen Paton (Mermaid), Matthew Edison (Louis Baxter).

Credits: *Executive Producer:* Craig Berenson. *Producer:* John Calvert. *Writer:* Heidi Ferrer. *Director:* Mark Rosman.

416 The Principal's Office. (Series; Reality; Tru TV; Premiered: August 21, 2008)

A behind-the-scenes look at the role of a school's principal — from dealing with students and parents to overseeing operations and meetings with school board officials.

Credits: *Executive Producer:* Brent Montgomery, Colby Gaines, Chris Bry. *Supervising Producer:* Augi Jakovac.

Review: "Nothing here is dramatic enough to be genuinely or consistently interesting ... the result is a high school version of *The People's Court* seeking to elevate the humdrum to operatic levels" (*Variety*).

417 Privileged. (Series; Drama; CW; Premiered: September 9, 2008)

Megan Smith is a college graduate with a journalism degree from Yale University. She wants to write about people that matter, people who make a difference, but is instead working for a New York tabloid magazine. Through a connection with her editor, Megan receives a chance to fulfill that dream. She moves to Palm Beach, Florida, and meets with Laurel Limoges, a widow who turned a small company (Limoges Cosmetics) into a mega enterprise. She is also appointed the guardian of Laurel's two beautiful, 16-year-old twin granddaughters, Sage and Rose (orphaned when their parents were killed in a plane crash).

Sage and Rose are rich and spoiled. Laurel wants them to attend Duke University, but the girls have little interest in school work (they attend Cielo Prep;

Megan receives $1500 a week and if she can succeed, Laurel will pay off her student loans). As Megan begins she finds Rose is interested in attending Duke but Sage, a free spirit, sees Megan as a threat. Rose means a great deal to Sage and she feels Megan is trying to steal her away — something she means to see not happen. Stories follow Megan as she struggles to fulfill Laurel's wishes. Lily is Megan's sister, a hair dresser; Marco is Laurel's gourmet chef; Will is Laurel's neighbor; Artie is Megan's father (operator of Captain Artie's Boat Tours).

Cast: JoAnna Garcia (Megan Smith), Anne Archer (Laurel Limoges), Lucy Kate Hale (Rose Baker), Ashely Newbrough (Sage Baker), Kristina Apgar (Lily Smith), Allan Louis (Marco Giordello), Brian Hallisay (Will Phillips), David Giuntoli (Jacob Cassidy), John Allen Nelson (Artie Smith).

Credits: *Executive Producer:* Rina Mimoun, Michael Engler, Leslie Morgan Stern, Bob Levy. *Producer:* Peter Burrell. *Music:* Joey Newman.

Reviews: "This show wants to be *Ally McBeal*–esque broad piece of serio comedy but hasn't really the slightest idea how to pull it off... It makes do ... with something that's really neither animal or vegetable" (*The Hollywood Reporter*).

"Trying to build upon the over-hyped non phenomenon that is *Gossip Girl,* the CW follows up with another literary hour that's smart, breezy and glossy" (*Variety*).

418 Prototype This. (Series; Reality; Discovery Channel; October 15, 2008 to January 7, 2009)

Four technical geniuses test proposed inventions — from road rage proof cars to life size boxing robots. The results (the good and the bad) are shown.

Geniuses: Joe Grand (electrical engineer), Zoz Brooks (MIT researcher), Mike North (nanotechnology expert), Terry Sandin (animatronics expert). **Narrator:** John Guidry.

Credits: *Executive Producer:* John Luscombe. *Supervising Producer:* John Tessier. *Music:* Colin Bayley.

Review: "Unfortunately, the four dweebs at the center of *Prototype This* seem to be having considerably more fun than the audience is apt to" (*Variety*).

419 Psychic Kids: Children of the Paranormal. (Series; Reality; A&E; June 16, 2008 to July 21, 2008)

Children, aged eight to twelve (and who live in remote sections of the country) are profiled as they use their psychic abilities to communicate with the spirits of deceased children. The children meet with professional psychologists (to help them understand what is happening) but credibility is questioned by bad camera work (extreme close-ups of the children's eyes) and eerie music to suggest something is happening when nothing is.

Host: Lisa Miller. **Narrator:** Chip Coffey.

Credits: *Executive Producer:* Betsy Schechter, George Plamondon, Robert Shorenow, Elaine Fontain-Bryant. *Producer:* Kyle McCabe, Chris Mozak. *Director:* David Miller

Reviews: "*Psychic Kids* edits its subjects in a way that makes their ... interactions with the dead feel like badly conceived science fiction" (*Variety*).

"It's disturbing to see kids channel the dead people's spirits to predict the future, but it's also tedious to watch" (*Entertain Your Brain*).

420 Pulling. (Series; Comedy; Sundance; October 19, 2008 to November 23, 2008)

Donna and her fiancé Karl have been a couple for many years and are planning to marry. Donna has lived a life that was basically carefree. As the big day approaches it dawns on Donna that what she has been doing will soon end. Impulsively she calls off their wedding days before the event to continue living a life she loves. She moves in with her friends Karen (a party girl) and the man-hungry Louise, and stories follow events in the lives of the three women. Produced in England and somewhat difficult to understand due to thick British accents.

Cast: Sharon Horgan (Donna), Tanya Franks (Karen), Rebekah Staton (Louise), Cavan Clerkin (Karl).

Credits: *Executive Produer:* Daisy Goodwin. *Producer:* Phil Bowker.

421 Pushing Twilight. (Series; Drama; Internet; 2008)

Reality-like program in which a group of disenchanted young people dare each other to complete a series of tasks that cause them to go places and accomplish feats they never thought they were capable of doing.

Cast: D.C. Douglas (Host), Adam Edgar (Mason Marks), Jamie Anderson (Layla Marks), Jonathan Beran (Dominic Moss), Daniel Robaine (Jacob Wright), Eric Emmanuel (Cole Edwards), Jackie Seldan (Avery Ward), Lacy Phillips (Madison Price), Makinna Ridgeway (Paige Gray).

Credits: *Producer:* Paul Tarantino.

422 The Pussycat Dolls Present Girlicious. (Series; Reality; CW; February 18, 2008 to April 23, 2008)

Fifteen girls compete for the opportunity to form a new three-girl singing group called Girlicious. Robin Antin, creator the Pussycat Dolls, oversees the competition in which the girls must display talent, sexuality and star quality. The weakest performers are eliminated on a weekly basis. The final episode changed the concept that had originally been established when the judges, faced with four very talented girls (Natalie Mejia, Tiffanie Anderson, Nichole Cordova, Chrystina Sayers) in the final elimination chose to make Girlicious a four girl group instead of the original three. Girlicious performed a song from their first album "Like Me" to close out the series.

Host: Mark McGrath. **Hostess-Judge:** Robin Antin. **Judges:** Kimberly "Lil Kim" Jones, Ron Fair. *Choreographer:* Mickey Minden. **Vocal Coach:** Kenn Hicks.

Credits: *Executive Producer:* Robin Antin, Ken Mok. *Producer:* Anna Mastro. *Senior Producer:* Tess Gamboa. *Associate Producer:* Michael Nelson, Laura Flanagan. *Music:* Jeff Lippencott, Mark T. Williams. **Music Director:** Dave Aude.

423   Quarterlife. (Series; Drama; NBC; Premiered/Ended: February 26, 2008)

A network adaptation of the Internet series of the same title that focuses on the lives of a group of friends who are in their twenties. Principal focus is on Dylan Krieger, a writer for *Attitude* magazine who relates her feelings about herself and her friends on the Internet blog site *Quarterlife*. The series was cancelled the same night it premiered. Had the series continued (six episodes were produced) serial-like stories would have followed the young adults as they faced the daily challenges of life.

Cast: Bitzie Tulloch (Dylan Krieger), Maite Schwartz (Lisa), Scott Michael Foster (Jed Burlin), David Walton (Danny Franklin), Michelle Lombardo (Debra), Kevin Christy (Andy), Barrett Swatek (Brittany).

Credits: *Executive Producer:* Marshall Herskovitz, Ed Zwick. *Co-Executive Producer:* Joshua Gummersall. *Associate Producer:* Mickie Reuster. *Music:* W.G. Snuffy Walden.

Reviews: "Its success or failure ultimately depends on how well these characters play in their journey from Net to network. The two episodes screened ... make for surprisingly promising prospects" (*The Hollywood Reporter*).

"The producers joyfully report that *Quarterlife* ... goes on without the 'network even seeing the scripts beforehand' ... if they had a first look, they might not have had a second look. I, for sure won't" (*New York Post*).

424   Queen Bees. (Series; Reality; Nickelodeon; July 13, 2008 to August 31, 2008)

Teenage girls who epitomize meanness are brought together in an attempt to change their attitudes and become nice to others. Each of the girls competes in a series of challenges and the one girl who changes for the best wins $25,000 for her school.

Host: Dr. Michelle R. Callahan. **The Girls:** Gisabelle Castillo, Yoanna House, Kiana Jenkins, Shavon Jovi, Brittany Keiffer, Camille Lopez, Michelle Madonna, Stassi Schroeder.

Credits: *Executive Producer:* Lamar Damon, James Rowley. *Supervising Producer:* Julie Choi. *Producer:* Justin Medeiros.

425   Queen Sized. (TV Movie; Drama; Lifetime; January 12, 2008)

Fact-based story about an overweight teenage girl (Maggie) who is nominated as her high school homecoming queen as a cruel practical joke.

Cast: Nikki Blonsky (Maggie), Annie Potts (Joan), Lily Holleman (Casey), Liz McGeever (Liz), Kimberly Matula (Tara), Jackson Pace (Will), Kelsey Schultz (Camille), Brandi Coleman (Lucy Phillips).

Credits: *Executive Producer:* Robert M. Sertner, Frank von Zerneck. *Producer:* Judy Cairo. *Writer:* Rodney Johnson, Nora Kletter, Richard Kletter. *Director:* Peter Levin.

426   The Rachel Zoe Project. (Series; Reality; Bravo; September 8, 2008 to October 20, 2008)

A behind-the-scenes look at fashion stylist Rachel Zoe as she attempts to expand her business empire.

Stars: Rachel Zoe, Rodger Berman, Brad Goreski, Taylor Jacobson.

Credits: *Executive Producer:* Charles Corwin, Jamie Patricof. *Co-Executive Producer:* Clara Markowicz, Andrew Perry. *Supervising Producer:* Lamar Damon. *Producer:* Zach Pritchett, Jen Rivera.

Review: "Stylist Rachel Zoe frets, frowns and dresses her clients, and all we can do is watch" (*The Hollywood Reporter*).

427   Racing for Time. (TV Movie; Drama; Lifetime; February 16, 2008)

True story about a guard (Cleveland Stackhouse) at a Texas correctional youth center who changes the lives of female offenders by organizing them into a multiracial track team to teach them responsibility, self-esteem and team work.

Cast: Charles S. Dutton (Cleveland Stackhouse), Yaya DaCosta (Vanessa), Aunjanue Ellis (Officer Baker), Shanna Forrestall (Sgt. Jane Daniels), Douglas M. Griffin (Braylon Nash), Tiffany Haddish (Denise), Zulay Henao (Carmen), Sara Jane Henriques (Maria).

Credits: *Executive Producer:* Rocky Lang, Diane Nabatoff, Peter Sadowski, Frank von Zerneck. *Producer:* Christopher Morgan. *Writer:* Glenn German, Adam Rodgers. *Director:* Charles S. Dutton. *Music:* The Angel.

428   A Raisin in the Sun. (TV Movie; Drama; ABC; February 25, 2008)

A TV adaptation of the Lorraine Hansberry play about an African-American family's efforts to deal with poverty, racism and inner conflict on Chicago's South Side.

Cast: Sean "P. Diddy" Combs (Walter Lee Younger), Sanaa Latham (Beneatha Younger), Audra McDonald (Ruth Younger), Phylicia Rashad (Lena Younger), Emily Swiss (Priscilla), David Oyelowo (Asagai), Ron C. Jones (Willy).

Credits: *Executive Producer:* Susan Batson, David Binder, Sean "P. Diddy" Combs, Neil Meron, Carl Rumbaugh, Craig Zadan. *Producer:* John M. Eckert, Vivek J. Tiwary. *Music:* Mervyn Warren. *Director:* Kenny Leon. *Teleplay:* Paris Qualles.

Review: "Director Kenny Leon discreetly opens up the play to street and bar scenes, and what appear to be handheld-camera close-ups never mar the delicacy of the performances. Indeed, the whole production is a model of subtle adaptation" (*Entertainment Weekly*).

429   Raising the Bar. (Series; Drama; TNT; September 1, 2008 to November 3, 2008)

Jerry Kellerman is an idealistic young lawyer who cares about people, especially those accused of a crime but do not have the means to hire a lawyer. Though well respected and financially secure, Jerry looks anything like a brilliant attorney — rumpled clothes, disorderly hair and frayed collar edges on his shirt. He is with the Manhattan Public Defenders Office and stories relate his and fellow defense attorneys (Roberta and Richard) court cases. Rosalind Whitman is the Chief Public Defender; Nick Baico is the cunning D.A.; Trudy Kessler is the judge who hears their cases; Michelle and Marcus are prosecutors; Charlie is the judicial clerk.

Cast: Mark-Paul Gosselaar (Jerry Kellerman), Gloria Reuben (Rosalind Whitman), Currie Graham (Nick Baico), Jane Kaczmarek (Trudy Kessler), J. August Richards (Marcus McGrath), Melissa Sagemiller (Michelle Emhardt), Natalia Cigliuti (Roberta Gilardi), Teddy Sears (Richard Woolsley), Jonathan Scarfe (Charlie Sagansky).

Credits: *Executive Producer:* Steven Bochco. *Co-Executive Producer:* Jesse Bochco. *Supervising Producer:* David Feige. *Producer:* Daynna Bochco. *Music:* James S. Levine.

Reviews: "This legal drama doesn't so much raise the bar as nudge it" (*The Hollywood Reporter*).

"Steven Bochco has been associated with a glittering array of ensemble dramas, but this producer's latest doesn't so much raise the bar on courtroom series as gently limbos under it" (*Variety*).

430   Ramsay's Kitchen Nightmares. (Series; Reality; BBC America; 2008)

The British series on which *Kitchen Nightmares* is based. Gordon Ramsay, called "The Sultan of Scary," is a tough talking chef who seeks perfection. Here, he travels to various British restaurants to expose unacceptable conditions and improve on them.

Host: Gordon Ramsay.

Credits: *Executive Producer:* Becky Clarke, Patricia Llewellyn. *Producer:* Paul Ratcliffe, Christine Hall. *Music:* Jonathan Gunton.

431   Randy Jackson Presents America's Best Dance Crew. (Series; Reality; MTV; January 26, 2008 to August 21, 2008)

Hip hop dance groups compete for money and a touring contract to perform across the U.S. Each dance challenge is judged by a panel and the weakest performers are eliminated on a weekly basis.

Host: Mario Lopez, Rachelle Leah. **Judge:** Lil Mama, J.C. Chasez. **Correspondent:** Layla Kaykleigh.

Credits: *Executive Producer:* Karen Schwartz, Howard Schwartz, Harriet Sternberg, Randy Jackson, Joel Gallen, Abe Hoch, Rob Lee. *Co-Executive Producer:* Josh Greenberg. *Supervising Producer:* Dan Sacks. *Consulting Producer:* Jordan Allen-Dutton, Eric Weiner. *Music:* Dylan Berry.

432   Rate My Space. (Series; Reality; HGTV; Premiered: June 15, 2008)

Designer Angelo Summelis takes to the road to help couples remodel their homes.

Host: Angelo Summelis. **Assistant:** Jared Dostie.

Credits: *Producer:* Dan Coffey, John E. Sykes.

433   Real Chance of Love. (Series; Reality; VH-1; November 3, 2008 to January 12, 2009)

A spin off from *I Love New York* wherein Real (Ahmad Givens) and his brother Chance (Kamal Givens), the self-pro-claimed "Stallionaires," were first introduced (the series attempted to match men with a girl named New York). Real and Chance fell in love with New York and it appeared she would select one of them. She rejected both and they were sent home. Real, a gentleman with a soft romantic side, and Chance, a player, made such an impression with viewers that they were given a chance to find the woman of their dreams. Fifteen young ladies are the contestants and each vies to win the brothers' hearts. Real and Chance date each of the women and send those home whom they feel are not right for them. The brothers have the final decision and pick the girl each would like to begin a relationship with.

Stars: Ahmad Givens, Kamal Givens.

Credits: *Executive Producer:* Cris Abrego, Mark Cronin, Ben Samek, Jeff Olde, Kristen Kelly. *Supervising Producer:* Michelle Brando, Chris Miller, Zach Kozek. *Producer:* Anthony Zaldivar, Sam Berns, Joseph Ruzer.

434   The Real Exorcist. (Series; Reality; Sci Fi; October 30, 2008)

People who believe they are possessed by demons receive help from Bob Larson, a TV and radio evangelist who has performed over 6,000 exorcisms. His wife Linda assists him. Each episode examines one case of demonic possession to expel the evil that the person believes exists inside of him. The series, produced in England, was broadcast with back-to-back episodes on the above date.

Stars: Bob Larson, Linda Larson.

Credits: *Supervising Producer:* Will Ehbrecht. *Producer:* Amanda Ross.

435   The Real Hustle. (Series; Reality; True TV; Premiered: January 22, 2008)

The first program produced for True TV (formally known as Court TV) that attempts to expose con artists and the tricks they use to take your money. A trio of scam artists are employed to pull cons on unsuspecting people to show, through hidden cameras, how con artists operate.

The Trio: Apollo Robbins (expert pick pocket), Dani Marco (actress whose specialty is distraction), Ryan Oakes (magician). **Narrator:** Phil Tanzini.

Credits: *Executive Producer:* Anthony Owen, Matt Crook, Andrew O'Connor. *Producer:* Jon Richards. *Director:* Justin Gorman.

Reviews: "Like so much reality TV, this show is over produced, from repeated shots of the leads posing for the camera to the 'Jaws'-like music that accompanies each operation" (*Variety*).

436   Real Simple Real Life. (Series; Reality; TLC; Premiered: October 24, 2008)

A makeover program in which everyday women are the subjects. Each chosen woman is evaluated and shown how to improve her appearance without spending a small fortune (by incorporating simple, low cost solutions).

Host: Kit Hoover.

Credits: *Executive Producer:* Fernando Mills, Jude Weng. *Producer:* Seth Laderman. *Associate Producer:* Aaron Schurman.

437   Real Vice Cops. (Series; Reality; Spike; Premiered: August 6, 2008)

The work of vice squad officers (with the Florida and Tennessee Police Departments) are profiled as a TV crew patrols with the officers as they crack down on prostitution, gambling and drugs.

Credits: *Executive Producer:* David McKenzie, James Romanovich, Paul Sharratt. *Producer:* Bryan Albright. *Music:* John Ross.

438   Reality Binge. (Series; Reality; Fox Reality Channel; Premiered: July 11, 2008)

A comical reality series that pokes fun at the genre by spoofing the various formats that have been seen on television since the premiere of *Survivor*.

Host: Eric Toms.

Credits: *Executive Producer:* Robb Weller, Gary Grossman. Co-Executive Producer: Barbara Wellner, Peter Carlin. *Senior Producer:* Laura Chambers.

439   Reality Bites Back. (Series; Comedy; Comedy Central; July 17, 2008 to September 4, 2008)

A parody of reality programs in which ten comics compete against each other in a series of challenges patterned after actual reality shows (for example, "So You Think You Can Drive?," "Extreme Manipulation: House Edition," and "Hunting with the Stars").

Host: Michael Ian Black. **Regulars:** Kyle Cease, Chris Fairbanks, Jeffrey Garcia, Red Grant, Tiffany Haddish, Bert Kreischer, Mo Mandel, Donnell Rawlings, Amy Schumer, Theo Vonkuinatowski.

Credits: *Executive Producer:* J.D. Roth, Todd Nelson, Adam Greene. *Co-Executive Producer:* Matt Assmus, Tom Johnson. *Supervising Producer:* Michael Dugan.

440   Recount. (TV Movie; Drama; HBO; May 25, 2008)

Documentary-like film that chronicles the week of the 2000 U.S. Presidential election and the necessary Florida recount that followed.

Cast: Kevin Spacey (Ron Klain), Bob Balaban (Ben Ginsberg), Ed Begley, Jr. (David Boies), Denis Leary (Michael Whouley), John Hurt (Warren Carpenter), Laura Dern (Katherine Harris), Bruce McGill (Mac Stipanovich), Jayne Atkinson (Theresa LePore).

Credits: *Executive Producer:* Len Amato, Sydney Pollack, Jay Roach, Paula Weinstein. *Producer:* Michael Hausman. *Writer:* Danny Strong. *Director:* Jay Roach. *Music:* Dave Grusin.

441   Redemption Song. (Series; Reality; Fuse; Premiered: October 29, 2008)

Eleven women with checkered pasts compete in a talent competition that borrows its format from *American Idol*. The contestants here, however, "are banged-up drunken female singers with tremendous talent." The women, from madam to stripper to petty thief, are addicted to drugs, sex and rampage. Keeping the reality in reality (more so than any other such show) the women drink before each performance, fight with each other, complain about the songs they are asked to sing, and worst of all, degrade each other's performances. Weakest performers are eliminated on a weekly basis and the girl with the most talent receives a recording contract.

Host: Chris Jericho. **Judge:** Ron Fair (head of Geffen Records, plus two record company guests). **Vocal Coach:** Mauli B.

Credits: *Executive Producer:* Ron Fair. *Supervising Producer:* Steve Joachim. *Producer:* Matthew Hobin, Chris Smith.

442   Rediscovered. (Special; Variety; ABC; December 23, 2008)

A unique special, also a backdoor pilot for a potential series, that gives former child actor hopefuls a second chance at stardom some twenty years later as adults. Casting director Matt Casella has discovered such stars (when they were kids) as Christina Aguilera, Britney Spears, Justin Timberlake, Keri Russell and Ryan Gosling (whose audition footage for *The New Mickey Mouse Club* is seen for the first time). With each success there are ten times as many children who never achieve show business success. With a large library of child audition tapes, Matt and his staff tracked down five then aspiring child actors to give them a second chance at stardom with a call back many years following that original audition.

The "chosen few" are flown to Los Angeles and perform live in front of a studio audience (who choose the best performer to receive $50,000 and a special surprise from the hosts: the opening act for one night for "The Donny and Marie Show" at the Flamingo Hotel and Casino in Las Vegas).

The five call backs are Heidi Elliott (from 1988, now a waitress), John DuPree (1990, life insurance training agent), Natalie DeLucia (1992, dance teacher), J.D. Stelljes (1992, heath care products seller) and Dion McIntosh (1989, real estate developer). Dion was chosen as the winner.

Host: Marie Osmond, Donny Osmond. **Co-Host:** Matt Casella.

Credits: *Executive Producer:* Dave Broome, Donny Osmond, Marie Osmond. *Co-Executive Producer:* Elayne Cilic. *Supervising Producer:* Rob Wolsoff. *Producer:* Matt Casella. *Music:* Ricky Minor. *Director:* Ryan Polito.

443   The Return of Jezebel James. (Series; Comedy; Fox; March 14, 2008 to March 21, 2008)

Successful children's book editor Sarah Thompkins decides, after devoting all her energies to work, to become a single mother. Her hopes are shattered when she discovers she is unable to conceive. Although devastated, Sarah comes up with a plan: ask her sister, Coco, to carry her baby. Sarah is a perfectionist; Coco is rather untidy and stories follow the sisters as Coco moves in with Sarah and tries to not only deal with an upcoming pregnancy, but Sarah's endless rules and regulations. The title is derived from Coco's imaginary childhood friend — whom Sarah used as an inspiration for a children's book. Ronald and Talia are Sarah's parents.

Cast: Parker Posey (Sarah Tompkins), Lauren Ambrose (Caroline "Coco" Tompkins), Scott Cohen (Marcus Sonti), Ron McLarty (Ronald Tompkins), Dianne Wiest (Talia Tompkins), Dana Ivey (Molly), Savannah Stehlin (Zoe).

Credits: *Executive Producer:* Amy Sherman-Palladino, Daniel Palladino. *Producer:* Michael Petok. *Music:* Grant Lee Phillips.

Reviews: "The stories are exaggerated, the premise is incredible and the chemistry is almost non-existent" (*The Hollywood Reporter*).

"...the mismatched sisters at the center of *Jezebel James* do little more than bicker, with the few sedate moments offering a welcome respite from a project that's otherwise painfully predictable" (*Variety*).

444   Ricky Gervais: Out of England — The Stand-Up Special. (Special; Comedy; HBO; November 15, 2008)

Comic Ricky Gervais's spoof of nursery rhymes, obscenity, fame, Nazis and fund raising.

Host: Ricky Gervais.

Credits: *Executive Producer:* Ricky Gervais. *Producer:* John Moffitt, Pat Tourk Lee. *Writer:* Ricky Gervais. *Director:* John Moffitt.

Reviews: "This special is pure British mean. Where else can anyone get away with making fun of diseases and their fund raisers?... You'll laugh till your butt falls off— the couch that is" (*New York Post*).

"The adult entertainment starts early tomorrow night on HBO with Ricky Gervais delivering 75 minutes of stand-up comedy that will melt any remaining obscenities in your insulation" (*New York Daily News*).

445   Riddles of the Sphinx. (TV Movie; Horror; Sci Fi; September 27, 2008)

An astronomer (Robert Parr) and his daughter (Karen), a cryptographer, accidentally unleash a deadly Sphinx then seek to return it to its resting place by solving a series of seven ancient, complex riddles.

Cast: Dina Meyer (Jessica), Lochlyn Munro (Robert Parr), Emily Tennant (Karen Parr), Donnelly Rhodes (Thomas), Mackenzie Gray (Ryder), Donovan Cerminara (Corporal Evans).

Credits: *Producer:* Kirk Shaw, Richard D. Titus. *Associate Producer:* Oliver De Caligny. *Director:* George Mendeluk.

Writer: Brook Durham, Jacob Eskander, Kevin Leeson.

446   Ring of Death. (TV Movie; Drama; Spike TV; October 17, 2008)

Brutal story of a man (Burke Wyatt) who infiltrates a prison to expose a warden (Golen) who oversees a fight to the death ring with his prisoners.

Cast: Johnny Mesner (Burke Wyatt), Stacy Keach (Warden Golen), Derek Webster (Steven James), Charlotte Ross (Mary Wyatt), Uriah Shelton (Tommy Wyatt), Jonathan Chase (Lancer), Meredith Giangrande (Nova), Sam McMurray (Wheaton).

Credits: *Executive Producer:* Larry Levinson. *Co-Executive Producer:* Matt Fitzsimons, Nick Lombardo, Michael Moran. *Producer:* Randy Pope. *Director:* Bradford May. *Writer:* Matthew Chernov, David Rosiak.

447   Rita Rocks. (Series; Comedy; Lifetime; Premiered: October 20, 2008)

Rita Clemens is a housewife and mother facing an identity crisis ("My needs come last and I make time for everyone else but not for myself. My kids don't listen to anything I say. My husband is off in his own world"). Rita is married to Jay and is the mother of Shannon (nine years old) and Hallie, a teenager who can't wait to become a woman. Rita is very attractive and now knows her life is in a rut (she works as a towel folder at a Bed and Bath Max and has just been passed over for a promotion). As she begins to reflect on how much better her life was when she was younger and worked as a musician (played guitar with the Bangles), she becomes inspired to change her situation. She dusts off her old guitar and forms a garage band with her friends Patty, a postal letter carrier, and Owen, her unemployed neighbor. Rita now hopes to recapture the happy times of her youth to lighten up her present day life. Stories follow Rita as she seeks fulfillment in her drab life. Hallie is totally self-absorbed and knows she is a beautiful girl (so much so that she was punished for posting pictures of her self in her bra and panties on her cell phone). Shannon's life appears to revolve around her eagerness to become a karate master. Kip is Hallie's boyfriend.

Cast: Nicole Sullivan (Rita Clemens), Richard Ruccolo (Jay Clemens), Natalie Dreyfuss (Hallie Clemens), Kelly Gould (Shannon Clemens), Tisha Campbell-Martin (Patty), Ian Gomez (Owen), Ravir Ullman (Kip).

Credits: *Executive Producer:* James Berg, Michael Hanel, Mindy Schultheis, Stan Zimmerman. *Producer:* Sylvia Green, Franco Bario.

Reviews: "The best part of *Rita Rocks* ... is when they let Rita actually rock. Unfortunately, when Rita isn't rockin', what's left is as funny as reading sheet music" (*New York Post*).

"Utterly conventional. The series plays a tired old tune ... the jokes here are often flatly predictable or improbable" (*Variety*).

448 Road Tasted with the Neelys. (Series; Reality; Food Network; Premiered: July 22, 2008)

Patrick and Gina Neely, owners of Neely's Bar-B-Que in Memphis, take to the road to find the tastiest bites and best stories behind foods that can be home delivered.

Hosts: Patrick Neely, Gina Neely.

Credits: *Executive Producer:* Gordon Elliott, Mark Schneider. *Supervising Producer:* Aimee Rosen. *Producer:* Sara Porter.

449 Robin Hood. (Series; Adventure; BBC America; 2008)

British produced version of the Robin Hood legend about the 11th century hero who opposed the evil Sheriff of Nottingham (working for the evil Prince John) to save England for its rightful king (Richard). Robin of Locksley (and the Earl of Huntingdon), and his group of Merry Men have established a base of operations in Sherwood Forest: Alan-A-Dale, Little John, Djag, Much, Will Scarlett and Friar Tuck. Maid Marian is Robin's romantic interest; Sir Guy is the Sheriff's evil right-hand man.

Cast: Jonas Armstrong (Robin Hood), Lucy Griffiths (Marian Fitzwalter), Keith Allen (Sheriff of Nottingham), Richard Armitage (Guy of Gisborne), Gordon Kennedy (Little John), Joe Armstrong (Alan-A-Dale), Sam Troughton (Much), Harry Lloyd (Will Scarlett), Anjali Jay (Dhag), Toby Stephens (Prince John), David Harewood (Friar Tuck), Michael Elwyn (Edward Fitzwalter).

Credits: *Executive Producer:* Foz Allan, Dominic Minghella, Greg Brenman. *Producer:* Jane Hudson, Richard Burrell. *Music:* Andy Price.

450 Rocco Gets Real. (Series; Reality; A&E; Premiered: October 4, 2008)

People (mostly women) who could be classified as "clueless in the kitchen" are the subjects. Rocco DiSpirito is a celebrity chef whose goal is to solve cooking dilemmas. Once a subject is chosen, Rocco comes to her home and literally takes over the kitchen with the goal being to help the challenged chef overcome her fears of cooking and "embrace the process of feeding the ones they love."

Host: Rocco DiSpirito.

Credits: *Producer:* Margit Ritz.

451 Rock Monster. (TV Movie; Horror; Sci Fi; March 22, 2008)

While backpacking through Central Europe, a teenager (Jason) pulls a sword from a stone that he finds in the woods. The action awakens an ancient rock-formed monster with an appetite to kill. The story finds Jason and his friend (Toni) attempting to destroy the creature he awoke.

Cast: Chad Collins (Jason), Alicia Lagano (Toni), Natalie Denise Sperl (Cassandra), David Figlioli (Dimitar), Jon Polito (The Colonel).

Credits: *Executive Producer:* T.J. Sakasegawa. *Producer:* Jeffrey Beach, Philip Roth. *Writer:* Berkeley Anderson, Ron Fernandez. *Director:* Declan O'Brien. *Music:* Tom Hiel.

Review: "Tonight's offering — as bad as they come — is truly so horrible it should be a collector's item before it even airs. I loved every terrible minute of it" (*New York Post*).

452 Rock of Love Charm School with Sharon Osbourne. (Series; Reality; VH-1; October 7, 2008 to December 19, 2008)

Fourteen "rude, crude and frequently naked" girls from seasons one and two of *Rock of Love* are brought together for one purpose: attend charm school and refine their rough ways. Sharon Osbourne, the wife of Ozzy Osbourne ("the Godfather of Heavy Metal music") is the school's headmistress and episodes relate her efforts "to strip the girls of their former rebellious and wild ways." The girls compete in various charm and etiquette challenges with the one girl proving herself the most capable winning $100,000.

Host: Sharon Osbourne.

Credits: *Executive Producer:* Matt Odgers, Cris Abrego. *Supervising Producer:* Kevin Thomas. *Producer:* Sheri A. McGee.

453 Ron Howard: 50 Years in Film. (Special; Documentary; TCM; December 29, 2008)

A look at the acting and film directing career of Ron Howard. Ron, 54, talks about his own career which began with early acting appearances in 1959 on *The Many Loves of Dobie Gillis*, progressing to co-starring roles on *The Andy Griffith Show*, *Happy Days* and *The Smith Family* to his film directing roles (which include *Cocoon*, *Splash*, *The Paper*, *The DaVinci Code* and *Far and Away*).

Host: Richard Schickel.

Credits: *Producer-Writer-Director:* Richard Schickel. *Co-Producer:* Doug Freeman.

Review: "Clips are meticulously cho-sen. In terms of penetrating Howard's cinematic *Cocoon* though, this *Splash*-free exercise remains pretty *Paper* thin" (*Variety*).

454 Rookies. (Series; Reality; A&E; October 21, 2008 to December 2, 2008)

A look at the training periods of rookie police officers attached to the Louisiana and Tampa, Florida, police academies.

Rookies: Amy Hess, Tommie Tolbert, Rebecca Webster, Henry Conravey, Elton Johnson, April Levine, Josh Norris, Dennis Cooper, Mark Monson, Jefferson Parish, A.J. Cafaro.

455 Rosie Live! (Special; Variety; NBC; November 26, 2008)

A special that doubles as a pilot and is an attempt to revive the variety series format. The program, broadcast live, features celebrity guests, musical performances, comedy skits and new talent discoveries.

Host: Rosie O'Donnell. **Guests:** Liza Minnelli, Gloria Estefan, Rachael Ray, Jane Krakowski, Clay Aiken, Kathy Griffin, Alex Baldwin, Alanis Morrissatte, Ne-Yo.

Credits: *Executive Producer:* Rosie O'-Donnell, David Friedman. *Supervising Producer:* Janette Barber. *Producer:* Alison Sandler. *Director:* Alan Carter. *Music Producer:* Lori E. Seid. *Writer:* Janette Barber, Eric Kornfeld, Seth Rudetsky, Hunter Foster.

Reviews: "NBC's misguided special/series trial balloon doubtless tested the loyalty of even O'Donnell's most ardent fans and had anyone outside that category praying for commercials" (*Variety*).

"There's nothing like a good holiday variety show and this was nothing like one" (*The Hollywood Reporter*).

456 Roxy Hunter and the Horrific Halloween. (TV Movie; Mystery; Nickelodeon; October 26, 2008)

Nine-year-old Roxy Hunter, a girl with a knack for stumbling upon mysteries, lives with her widowed mother, Susan, in the town of Serenity Falls. The story follows Roxy as she seeks to uncover the truth about Stefan, a classmate who hails from Transylvania and whom Roxy believes is a vampire.

Cast: Aria Wallace (Roxy Hunter), Robin Brule (Susan Hunter), Demetrius Joyette (Max), Yannick Bisson (Jon Steadman), Vik Sahay (Rama), Connor Price (Stefan), Joe Pingue (Deputy Potts), Tara Shelley (Jill), Devon Bostick (Drew), Juan Chioran (Vlad), Roger Dunn (Sheriff Tom).

Credits: *Executive Producer:* Michael Espensen, Bill O'Dowd, Barry Tropp. *Producer:* Sarah Soboleski, Anthony Leo. *Music:* Nathan Furst. *Writer:* Robin Dunne, James Kee. *Director:* Eleanor Lindo.

457   Roxy Hunter and the Mystery of the Moody Ghost. (TV Movie; Mystery; Nickelodeon; June 25, 2008)

Roxy Hunter is a nine-year-old girl with the mind of Sherlock Holmes. She lives in the small town of Serenity Falls with her widowed mother, Susan, and has an uncanny knack for stumbling upon mysteries. The story finds Roxy and her genius friend, Max, attempting to solve the mystery of a ghost that is supposedly haunting the house she and her mother have just moved into.

Cast: Aria Wallace (Roxy Hunter), Robin Brule (Susan Hunter), Demetrius Joyette (Max), Yannick Bisson (Jon Steadman), Vik Sahay (Rama), Jayne Eastwood (Mabel Crabtree), Stephanie Mills (Rebecca), Sebastian Pigott (Ted Caruthers), Tara Shelley (Jill).

Credits: *Executive Producer:* Michael Espensen, Bill O'Dowd, Barry Tropp. *Producer:* Sarah Soboleski, James Jackman. *Music:* Nathan Furst. *Writer:* Robin Dunne, James Kee. *Director:* Eleanor Lindo.

458   Roxy Hunter and the Myth of the Mermaid. (TV Movie; Mystery; Nickelodeon; July 13, 2008)

Roxy Hunter, a pretty nine-year-old girl who lives in the small town of Serenity Falls with her widowed mother Susan, possesses the uncanny knack of stumbling upon mysteries. In the story, Roxy and her friend Max, try to learn the true identity of a young woman who appears to be unfamiliar with everything that surrounds her (Roxy discovers the girl is actually a mermaid whom she must help find her way back home).

Cast: Aria Wallace (Roxy Hunter), Robin Brule (Susan Hunter), Demetrius Joyette (Max), Bik Sahay (Rama), Yannick Bisson (Jon Steadman), Jayne Eastwood (Mable Crabtree), Joe Pingue (Deputy Potts), Ashleigh Rains (Mermaid).

Credits: *Executive Producer:* Michael Espensen, Bill O'Dowd, Barry Tropp. *Producer:* Anthony Leo, Sarah Soboleski. *Music:* Nathan Furst. *Writer:* Robin Dunne, James Kee. *Director:* Eleanor Lindo.

459   Roxy Hunter and the Secret of the Shaman. (TV Movie; Mystery; Nickelodeon; June 18, 2008)

Roxy Hunter is an adorable nine-year-old girl who lives in the town of Serenity Falls with her widowed mother, Susan. She is resourceful and determined and has a knack for stumbling upon mysteries. Roxy also considers herself an amateur detective and here she attempts to prove that a vagrant, whom Roxy believes is a Shaman, is innocent of a theft.

Cast: Aria Wallace (Roxy Hunter), Robin Brule (Susan Hunter), Demetrius Joyette (Max), Yannick Bisson (Jon Steadman), Vik Sahay (Rama), Richard McMillan (Shaman), Roger Dunn (Sheriff Tom Dawson), Joe Pingue (Deputy Martin Potts), Tara Shelley (Jill).

Credits: *Executive Producer:* Michael Espensen, Bill O'Dowd. *Producer:* Sarah Soboleski, Barry Tropp. *Music:* Nathan Furst. *Writer:* Robin Dunne, James Kee. *Director:* Eleanor Lindo.

460   Ruby. (Series; Reality; Style Network; Premiered: November 9, 2008)

A not pleasing to the eye look at a woman's desperate efforts to lose weight. The subject, Ruby Gettinger, lives in Savannah, Georgia, and weighs 480 pounds. Cameras show what restrictions on life such weight problems cause, followed by her efforts to get the help she needs to slim down (which she does with the help of friends who encourage her).

Credits: *Executive Producer:* Gay Rosenthal, Paul Barrosse, Tim Puntillo, Sarah Weideman. *Co-Executive Producer:* Nicholas Caprio, Victor Zielinski. *Producer:* Allison Hilliard, Lisa Bellomo. *Music:* Mark Strand.

461   The Russell Girl. (TV Movie; Drama; CBS; January 27, 2008)

Sensitive drama about a medical student (Sarah Russell) who returns to her home town to make peace with her past (settle an old conflict) to enable her to plan her future.

Cast: Amber Tamblyn (Sarah Russell), Tim DeKay (Tim Russell), Paula Barrett (Fran), Daniel Clark (Daniel Russell), Max Morrow (Rick Morissey), Ben Lewis (Jon Morrisey), Richard Fitzpatrick (Ray).

Credits: *Executive Producer:* Brent Shields. *Producer:* Stefanie Epstein, Andrew Gottlieb. *Writer:* Jill E. Blotevogel. *Director:* Jeff Bleckner. *Music:* Jeff Beal.

462   Samurai Girl. (Miniseries; Adventure; ABC Family; September 5, 2008 to September 7, 2008)

A female infant, nicknamed Heaven by the press (because "it seemed she had fallen from the sky") was the only survivor of a plane crash. She was adopted by the powerful Kogo family and grew up in a life of luxury. Nineteen years later, on her wedding day, Ninjas attack the reception (seeking to kill her father) but instead kill her brother. Heaven's life is suddenly changed and she is plunged into a world of danger when she discovers her family has ties to the Japanese mob, the Yakuza. Heaven, a martial arts champion, has vowed to find her brother's killers. Her quest brings her in contact with Jake Stanton, a ninja master who once worked for the Yakuza crime syndicate, who joins in her quest. Cheryl is Heaven's friend; Karen is the mysterious woman from Jake's past; Otto is Cheryl's roommate; Tasuke Kogo is Heaven's father — and the sinister head of the Kogo family; Severin is the government agent seeking to bring down the Kogo family.

Cast: Jamie Chung (Heaven Kogo), Brendan Fehr (Jake Stanton), Saige Thompson (Cheryl), Anthony Wong (Tasuke Kogo), Steven Brand (Severin), Stacy Keible (Karen).

Credits: *Executive Producer:* Bob Levy. *Music:* Stephen Endelman, Michael Wandmacher.

Reviews: "Loaded with adventure... *Samurai Girl* doesn't stop for a minute in an all out effort to entertain the senses. The intellect is another story altogether" (*The Hollywood Reporter*).

"It's the sort of production rife with plenty of action but nothing that's remotely stirring, putting far too much pressure on petite Jamie Chung to carry the drama" (*Variety*).

463   Sanctuary. (Series; Science Fiction; Sci Fi; October 3, 2008 to January 9, 2009)

Dr. Helen Magnus is a seemingly young woman who has devoted her life to cutting edge medical science. She was one of the first female doctors at Royal College in Victorian England and today, at age 157, heads Sanctuary, a mysterious world (protected by a force field) where a group of special (some terrifying) beings live but roam among humans. Helen has made it her goal to unlock the mysteries of their existence while at the same time battling the dangerous phenomena of the paranormal that also exists. Assisting Helen are her strong-willed daughter, Ashley, who grew up in Sanctuary; Will Zimmerman, a forensic psychiatrist; and Ryan Robbins, a weapons designer and computer expert. John Druitt is an enemy of Helen's, a being who is able to appear and disappear at will. The series is shot using green screen (actors perform on bare sets; virtual effects and visual effects are added later).

Cast: Amanda Tapping (Dr. Helena Magnus), Emilie Ullerup (Ashley Magnus), Robin Dunne (Dr. Will Zimmerman), Henry Foss (Ryan Robbins), Christopher Heyersahl (John Druitt).

Credits: *Executive Producer:* Damian Kindler, Sam Egan, Amanda Tapping, Martin Wood, Keith Beedle, N. John Smith. *Producer:* George Hories. *Music:* Ian Browne.

Reviews: "If ... things that go bump in the night are ... up your dark alley then *Sanctuary* is perfect for you. Otherwise, there's little to recommend" (*Variety*).

"Scary moments and humans who convince us they're worth caring about ... make for a sci-fi drama that doesn't yet suck" (*The Hollywood Reporter*).

464   Sandhogs. (Series; Reality; History Channel; Premiered: September 7, 2008)

A look at the work of sandhogs — the men who risk their lives to build subway systems, bridge footings and waste and sewage tunnels.

Credits: *Executive Producer:* Edward Barbini, Craig Piligian, Edward Rosenstein. *Producer:* John Scott.

465   Santa's Funniest Moments. (Special; Comedy; My Network TV; December 10, 2008)

A collection of Christmas holiday mishaps caught on tape by amateur photographers (mostly families opening gifts and/or preparing for the holiday).

Host: Erik Estrada. Laura McKenzie.

Credits: *Executive Producer:* David McKenzie, Paul Sharratt. *Producer:* John Ross. *Associate Producer:* Heather Biggins. *Director:* David McKenzie. *Writer:* Heather Biggins, Dan Goldman, John Ross.

466   The Sarah Jane Adventures. (Series; Science Fiction; Sci Fi; April 11, 2008 to May 30, 2008)

A spin-off from *Doctor Who* wherein Earth girl Sarah Jane Smith was depicted as one of the companions of the time traveling Doctor Who, a Time Lord from the planet Gallifrey. In 1985, Sarah Jane left the Doctor to resume her life as a journalist in England. The Doctor gave her his mechanical dog, K-9, and a pilot was produced called *K-9 and Company* that was to depict Sarah Jane's adventures as she and K-9 battled evil. The pilot aired in the U.S. (Produced in England) but a series never materialized.

In 2006, the BBC reprised the Sarah Jane Smith character (casting Elisabeth Sladen, the original Sarah Jane, as the new Sarah Jane). Sarah Jane is still a journalist. She is single and lives at 30 Banneman Road in England. K-9 is still her dog, but he is on assignment — protecting the Earth from an approaching black hole. Sarah Jane also has an alien computer named Mr. Smith and wrist bracelets that can detect alien presences. Sarah Jane prefers to be alone as it is the only way of keeping what she does secret.

Her life changes when a new neighbor, Maria Jackson, accidentally discovers her secret. It is 2:37 in the morning when a glowing light awakens Maria. She sees Sarah Jane with a fairy-like alien (who is lost. Sarah Jane is helping her find her way back home). Sarah Jane spots Maria and is a bit upset but later finds Maria and her friend, Kelsey (whom Maria told about the incident) a big asset when they help her stop an alien invasion by an enemy called the Bane (who planned to control humans through a soft drink called Bubble Shock. The drink contained Bane DNA that when absorbed would make humans slaves to the Bane). In addition to Maria and Kelsey, Sarah Jane also acquires another helper — a genetically engineered boy called an archetype (created by the Bane in an attempt to replicate humans). To protect the boy (who learns by observing) Sarah Jane secretly "adopts" him and names him Luke. Stories follow Sarah Jane as she and her assistants battle aliens (according to Sarah Jane, some aliens are friendly and only seeking help in reaching a destination). Produced in England.

Cast: Elisabeth Sladen (Sarah Jane Smith), Yasmin Paige (Maria Jackson), Tommy Knight (Luke Smith), Porsha Lawrence-Mavour (Kelsey), Joseph Millson (Alan Jackson, Maria's divorced father), Alexander Armstrong (Voice of Mr. Smith, Sarah's computer).

Credits: *Executive Producer:* Phil Collinson, Russell T. Davies, Julie Gardner. *Producer:* Matt Bouch, Susie Liggat. *Music:* Sam Watts.

Reviews: "Broadly aimed at kids, with cheesy monsters and two youthful protagonists joining in the world-saving exploits, the series may be modestly entertaining for the moppet crowd but will test the patience of adults in this dimension or any other" (*Variety*).

467 Saturday Night Live Presidential Bash 2008. (Special; Comedy; NBC; November 3, 2008)

A primetime, 2008 election eve satire that spoofs presidential elections and politics in general.

Cast: Tina Fey, Fred Armisen, Will Forte, Bill Hader, Darnell Hammond, Seth Meyers, Amy Poehler, Andy Samberg, Jason Sudeikis, Kenan Thompson, Kristen Wiig, Casey Wilson.

Credits: *Executive Producer:* Lorne Michaels. *Producer:* Steve Higgins, Marci Klein, Michael Shoemaker. *Director:* Don Roy King. *Head Writer:* Seth Meyers.

468 Saturday Night Live Weekend Update Thursday. (Series; Comedy; NBC; October 9, 2008 to October 23, 2008)

A three episode *Saturday Night Live* extension series that incorporates that show's "Weekend Update" segment to spoof the 2008 Presidential campaign and the topical issues of the week preceding the broadcast.

Anchors: Seth Meyers, Amy Poehler.

Credits: *Executive Producer:* Lorne Michaels, Michael Shoemaker. *Supervising Producer:* Ken Aymong. *Producer:* Steve Higgins, Marci Klein.

469 School of Sex. (Series; Erotica; Playboy Channel; Premiered: December 6, 2008)

Gorgeous adult film star Tera Patrick appears as a sex instructor to teach her willing students how to better enjoy sex. To help illustrate Tera's discussions, sexually explicit demonstrations are conducted (sometimes crossing the line between "R" and "X" rated).

Host: Tera Patrick.

470 Scream Queens. (Series; Reality; VH-1; October 20, 2008 to December 8, 2008)

Virtually unknown actresses (with the exception of Shawnee Smith, who has appeared on several TV series) are brought together for the opportunity of appearing in a horror movie to be produced by Lionsgate Films. The actresses compete in various acting challenges (including the ability to scream and react to scary situations) with the best performer receiving a movie contract.

Host: James Gunn. **Actresses:** Sarah Agor, Lindsay Felton, Kylah Kim, Jo-Anne Krupa, Jessica Palette, Marissa Skell, Shawnee Smith, Lina So.

Credits: *Executive Producer:* Jim Ackerman, Dave Hamilton, Biagio Messina, Jeff Olde. *Producer:* John Slaughter, Peter Spoerri. *Associate Producer:* Scott Martin.

471 The Screen Actors Guild Awards. (Special; Variety; TBS and TNT; January 27, 2008)

The 14th annual presentation that

honors the best in motion picture and television production.

Appearing: Kate Beckinsale, Josh Brolin, Steve Carell, Marion Cottillard, Tom Cruise, Eric Dane, Ruby Dee, Zac Efron, Tina Fey, Ben Foster, Hal Holbrook, Kate Hudson, Holly Hunter, Tommy Lee Jones, Denis Leary, Debra Messing, William Petersen, Burt Reynolds, Mickey Rooney, John Travolta, Vanessa Williams.

Credits: *Supervising Producer:* Gloria Fujita O'Brien, Mike McCullough. *Producer:* Kathy Connell. *SAG Producer:* Yale Summers, Jo Beth Williams, Paul Napier, Daryl Anderson, Shelley Fabares. *Writer:* Stephen Pouliot. *Director:* Jeff Margolis.

472   The Scripps National Spelling Bee. (Special; Reality; ABC; May 30, 2008)

Top spellers, aged eight to fifteen, compete in the final championship rounds for the honor of becoming the nation's best speller.

Host: Tom Bergeron.

Credits: *Executive Producer:* Jed Drake. *Co-Executive Producer:* Robert Liano, Sammy Silver, David Winner. *Director:* Doug Holmes, Danny Silver.

473   Secret Diary of a Call Girl. (Series; Comedy-Drama; Showtime; June 16, 2008 to July 30, 2008)

Hannah Baxter is a 27-year-old woman who leads a double life. By day she is Hannah Baxter, a legal secretary. By night, she is Belle, a high-priced call girl. At first Hannah is able to keep her two lives separate. As time passes she finds her two worlds increasingly difficult to maintain. Hannah's voice-overs and direct to the camera observations highlight each episode which are built around a specific type of client Belle encounters as an escort. Stephanie is Belle's employer; Ben is Hannah's ex-boyfriend; Gail and Niall are Hannah's parents. The series is produced in England. Second season episodes premiered January 18, 2009.

Cast: Billie Piper (Hannah/Belle), Cherie Lunghi (Stephanie), Iddo Goldberg (Ben), Toyah Willcox (Gail), Stuart Organ (Niall).

Credits: *Executive Producer:* Greg Brenman, Avril Macrory, Michael Foster. *Producer:* Chrissy Skins, Rebecca de Souza, Rosanna Benn. *Writer:* Lucy Prebble. *Director:* Yann DeMange.

Reviews: "It's eye opening stuff, at least some of it, and yet not as titillating as you might suppose. Considering the subject matter, there's surprisingly little nudity and practically nothing graphic" (*The Hollywood Reporter*).

"Skein is shot nudity free in a way that puts titillation on the back burner ... there's no glamour here other than the way Hannah goes about her day, living two lives that are split neatly and maintained impeccably" (*Variety*).

474   The Secret Life of the American Teenager. (Series; Drama; ABC Family; July 1, 2008 to September 9, 2008)

A look at the personal lives of several teenagers who attend Grant High School in Southern California: Amy, Adrian, Grace, Ricky, Ben and Gregg. Particular focus is on members of the school's marching band and its cheerleaders. Amy, who plays French horn, is 15 years old and pregnant; Adrian, the school's bad girl, is a gorgeous majorette; Ricky is a free-spirited rebel and known womanizer; Grace is the beautiful cheerleader; Jack is Grace's boyfriend; Ben is Amy's would-be boyfriend; Ashley is Amy's rebellious 13-year-old sister; Anne and George are Amy's parents; Marshall and Kathleen are Grace's parents; Tom, who is suffering from Down syndrome, is Grace's brother. The series returned for a new season on January 5, 2009.

Cast: Shailene Woodley (Amy Juergens), Francia Raisa (Adrian Lee), Megan Park (Grace Bowman), Daren Kagasoff (Ricky Underwood), India Eisley (Ashley Juergens), Molly Ringwald (Anne Juergens), John Schneider (Marshall Bowman), Josie Bissett (Kathleen Bowman), Mark Derwin (George Juergens), Greg Finley (Jack Poppos), Luke Zimmerman (Tom Bowman), Kenny Bauman (Ben).

Credits: *Executive Producer:* Brenda Hampton. *Producer:* Lindsley Parsons III. *Music:* Dan Foliart.

Reviews: "...teen pregnancy, especially on a youth oriented network — is too important a subject matter for such shallow, ham-fisted treatment... *The Secret Life of the American Teenager* should probably stay a secret" (*Variety*).

"ABC Family, which hardly ever disappoints, is holding true form with their newest series ... a top flight series about a group of high school students, most of whom I liked immediately" (*New York Post*).

475 Secret Millionaire. (Series; Reality; Fox; December 3, 2008 to December 18, 2008)

The basic premise attempts to show America's wealthiest individuals just how bad it has gotten for some people. Each program takes the millionaire away from his lavish lifestyle and places him as "an undercover agent" to experience life in an impoverished area. The millionaires are challenged to live on minimum wage and must immerse themselves in situations they have never experienced. Cameras capture their experiences as they work with community members and befriend those in need. At the end of the experience, millionaires reveal who they really are and award $100,000 of their own money to those of whom they feel are the most deserving.

Credits: *Executive Producer:* Chris Coelen, Greg Goldman, Bruce Toms, Jean-Michel Michenaud. *Co-Executive Pro-*

ducer: Megan Estrada, Danielle King, Lauren Alvarez. *Supervising Producer:* Patrick Higgins. *Producer:* Hope Moore.

Reviews: "In *Secret Millionaire's* world, the rich are benevolent if slightly detached and the poor are simply hard luck cases helped by angels on earth, without shades of gray" (*Variety*).

"This ... series ... is awash with tears and sadness, happiness, gratitude, you name it ... come on admit it, you checked out the show ... and bawled like a baby. You didn't? Then I suggest you ... see a cardiologist because you must have a heart of stone" (*New York Post*).

476 The Secret Saturdays. (Series; Cartoon; Cartoon Network; Premiered: October 10, 2008)

Solomon Saturday, his wife Drew and their son, Zak are no ordinary family. They carry a powerful secret: they are the guardians of Cryptids, legendary creatures that exist, but ordinary scientists refuse to acknowledge them. The Saturdays, who operate as secret scientists, track down and protect Cryptids before they fall into the hands of evil beings, in particular V.V. Argost, who seeks them for his own sinister purposes.

Solomon, called Doc, is a scientific genius and inventor who spent his life studying Cryptids. His weapon: a high tech power glove. Drew, raised by Gypsies, believes in the power of the supernatural. She battles evil with her Tibetan Fire Sword. Zak has the ability to bond with Cryptids. Fiskerton, who resembles a large cat, is the family pet; Komodo is another pet, a 250 pound dragon with chameleon-like abilities; Zon, a thought to be extinct prehistoric bird, also assists the Saturdays. The dim-witted Munya assists V.V.

Voice Cast: Nicole Sullivan (Drew Saturday), Phil Morris (Doc Saturday), Sam Lerner (Zak Saturday), Diedrich Bader (Fiskerton), Corey Burton (V.V. Argost), Fred Tatasciore (Komodo/Zon/Munya).

Credits: *Supervising Producer:* Fred Schaefer. *Producer:* Scott Jeralds.

477   Secret Talents of the Stars. (Series; Variety; CBS; Premiered/Ended: April 8, 2008)

Sixteen B-list celebrities appear to display a hidden talent (for example, singer Clint Black as a standup comedian; former *Star Trek* regular George Takei performing as a country and western entertainer). Viewers vote, via the internet (CBS.com/vote) to determine who goes and who stays. A winner was not chosen as the series was cancelled the same night it premiered.

Host: John O'Hurley. **Judges:** Debbie Reynolds, Brian McKnight, Gavin Polone (producer). **Celebrities:** Clint Black, Danny Bonaduce, Sasha Cohen, Sheila E, Ric Flair, Joe Frazier, Roy Jones, Jr., Marla Maples, Bridget Marquardt, Cindy Margulies, Jo Dee Messina, Joshua Morrow, Mya, Ben Stein, George Takei, Malcolm-Jamal Warner.

Credits: *Executive Producer:* Robyn Nash, Don Weiner. *Co-Executive Producer:* Dan Funk. *Supervising Producer:* Laurie Howarter, Jonathan Karsh. *Coordinating Producer:* Tim Gaydos. *Co-Producer:* Allen Cody. *Music:* Doug Angelos. *Director:* Don Weiner.

Reviews: "For the most part, the secret talents of the stars continue to remain so" (*The Hollywood Reporter*).

"Any series that claims to feature 16 of America's most talented stars and counts Danny Bonaduce and Marla Maples among them at least deserves some credit for generosity of spirit, bordering on false advertising" (*Variety*).

478   Secrets of a Restaurant Chef. (Series; Cooking; Food Network; Premiered: July 29, 2008)

Restaurant chef Anne Burrell shares practical techniques for creating delicious meals at home.

Host: Anne Burrell.

Credits: *Producer:* Geoffrey Campbell, Jenni Gilroy.

479   Secrets of the Summer House. (TV Movie; Horror; Sci Fi; January 6, 2008)

Nikki and George Wickersham are a happily married couple who are expecting their first child. When George inherits a centuries-old family summer home, Nikki learns that it is supposedly cursed and affects male heirs with strange behavior and sometimes death. When George's personality begins to change, Nikki believes that not only is her husband in danger, but their unborn child. The story follows Nikki as she seeks a way to break the curse and save her family.

Cast: Lindsay Price (Nikki Wickersham), David Jones (George Wickersham), Emma Stevens (Virginia Roberts), Sadie LeBlanc (Margie Mancuso), Susan Bain (Celia Calvert), Macha Grenon (Jill Ambrose), Frank Schorpron (Jebidah Wickersham).

Credits: *Executive Producer:* Justin Bodie, Jean Bureau, Anne Carlucci, Stephen Greenberg. *Producer:* Serge Denis, Josie Mauffette. *Music:* James Gelfand. *Director:* Jean-Claude Lord. *Writer:* Donald Martin, John Martin.

480   7 Things to Do Before I'm 30. (TV Movie; Comedy-Drama; Lifetime; January 26, 2008)

In her teens, Lori Madison made a list of things to accomplish before she reached the age of 30. Now, with her thirtieth birthday approaching, Lori realizes she never fulfilled her dreams and sets out on a mission to finalize the list.

Cast: Amber Benson (Lori Madison), John Reardon (Dan Hart), Julia Duffy (Vanessa Madison), Christopher Jacot (Michael Chapman), Haig Sutherland (Will Madison), Tegan Moss (Meredith Vargas).

Credits: *Executive Producer:* Amy Goldberg, Stephen P. Jarchow, Paul A. Kaufman.

Producer: Harvey Kahn. *Music:* James McVay. *Writer:* Duane Poole. *Director:* Paul A. Kaufman.

481   Sex and Lies in Sin City: The Ted Binion Scandal. (TV Movie; Drama; Lifetime; October 25, 2008)

Fact based story that recounts the incidents surrounding the mysterious death of Ted Binion, heir to the Horseshoe Casino in Las Vegas.

Cast: Matthew Modine (Ted Binion), Mena Suvari (Sandy Murphy), Jonathan Schaech (Rick Tabish), Peter Haskell (Ian Miller), Michelle Greathouse (Rhonda Samuels), Mark Sivertsen (Jay Green), Kiira Arai (Bonnie Binion), Chris Ashworth (Frank Lipjanic).

Credits: *Executive Producer:* Frank Konigsberg. *Producer:* David Rosemont. *Director:* Peter Medak. *Writer:* Teena Booth.

Reviews: "Lifetime does the low life story proud" (*New York Post*).

"Scoring an impressive titling trifecta that includes "Sex," "Sin" and "Scandal," this Lifetime movie simply doesn't live down to its sleaze-mongering name" (*Variety*).

482   Sex Change Hospital. (Series; Documentary; WE; October 14, 2008 to November 18, 2008)

A rather graphic look at the patients of a hospital in Trinidad, Colorado, where people face the final step in their transition from one gender to another. Dr. Marci Bower, a transgender woman, counsels her patients and is seen performing all the surgeries (quite bloody and unsettling; not for the squeamish).

Surgeon: Dr. Marci Bowers.

Credits: *Executive Producer:* Fenton Bailey, Randy Barbato, Jeremy Simmons. *Producer:* Chris McKim. *Music:* David Benjamin Steinberg.

483   Sex ... with Mom and Dad. (Series; Reality; MTV; Premiered: September 29, 2008)

A deceiving title for a program in which Dr. Drew Pinsky offers relationship advice to help parents and their teenage children deal with the problems they will face as their children become curious about the opposite sex.

Host: Drew Pinsky.

Credits: *Executive Producer:* Bryan Scott, Lisa Tucker. *Co-Executive Producer:* Lesley Goldman. *Supervising Producer:* Gil Ilam, Jordana Starr.

484   Shaken Not Stirred: A Comedy Roast. (Series; Comedy; My Network TV; October 29, 2008 to November 19, 2008)

A somewhat misleading title as the program is not a celebrity roast in the typical sense (wherein friends of a celebrity guest comically insult him). Here a guest joins the four comic hosts for a round table discussion that covers mostly, aspects of the guest's life (for example, Pamela Anderson, who appeared in a very skimpy pink dress, was asked questions regarding her home and business life, her association with protecting animals, her on-and-off relationship with Tommy Lee and, which gathered the biggest audience reaction, her decision to have breast implants and then have them removed). The hosts, as well as the guest, are permitted to smoke or have a glass of wine as they talk.

Host: Anthony Anderson, D.L. Hughley, Paul Rodriquez, John Salley.

Credits: *Executive Producer:* Walter Latham, Sue Fellows. *Co-Executive Producer:* Robert Stein, Chuck Vinson. *Producer:* Beth Einhorn, Devon Shepard, Xavier Cook. *Music Director:* Robert Brookins. *Director:* Walter Latham.

485   Shame to Fame. (Series; Reality; Fuse; Premiered: October 29, 2008)

Ten women with checkered pasts (from former drug addicts to those with criminal records) compete in various challenges for the opportunity to achieve musical stardom — a record contract and a video to be played on the Fuse Music Network.

Host: Chris Jericho.

486 Shark Swarm. (TV Movie; Drama; Hallmark; May 25, 2008)

Fisherman Daniel Wilder leads the battle to save Full Moon Bay, a quaint seaside town, from man-eating sharks, chemically enhanced by real estate tycoon Hamilton Lux, to destroy marine life, drive the fishermen out and allow him to develop the land.

Cast: John Schneider (Daniel Wilder), Daryl Hannah (Brooke), Armand Assante (Hamilton Lux), F. Murray Abraham (Bill Girdler), Marco Assante (Barry), Darcy Rose Byrnes (Heather), Gene Davis (Sheriff Dexter Murray), Elisa Donovan (Brenda).

Credits: *Executive Producer:* Kevin Bocarde. *Producer:* Stephen Niver, Kyle Clark. *Writer:* Matthew Chernov, David Rosiak. *Director:* James A. Contner. *Music:* Nathan Furst.

487 Sharpshooter. (TV Movie; Adventure; Spike; January 27, 2008)

A CIA sharpshooter (Dillon) seeks to uncover the reason why he has been targeted for assassination during his final assignment before retiring.

Cast: James Remar (Dillon), Mario Van Peebles (Flick), Catherine Mary Stewart (Amy), Bruce Boxleitner (Sheriff Garner), Stacey Hinnen (Carson), Nick Hermz (Bhan), John Braver (Cing), Al Sapienza (Phillips).

Credits: *Producer:* Kevin Bocarde, Nick Lombardo, Michael Moran. *Co-Producer:* Nick Lombardo, James Wilberger. *Director:* Armand Mastroianni. *Writer:* Steven H. Berman. *Music:* Stephen Graziano.

488 Shatner's Raw Nerve. (Series; Talk; Biography Channel; Premiered: November 28, 2008)

Actor William Shatner in a new spin on talk shows — interviewing fellow actors with the object being "to hit a raw nerve"

and reveal a side of a guest you really never knew existed.

Host: William Shatner.

Credits: *Executive Producer:* Scott Sternberg, Rob Sharenow Michael Morrison. *Supervising Producer:* Tracy Whittaker. *Talent Producer:* Susan Gold.

Reviews: "William Shatner takes his career where it has never gone before. And it works" (*The Hollywood Reporter*).

"*Shatner's Raw Nerve* ... proves neither raw nor nervy enough to be consistently interesting — essentially plopping the host on one comfy chair, his guest in another and letting them chat until 30 minutes elapse" (*Variety*).

489 The Shell Seekers. (TV Movie; Drama; Hallmark; May 3, 2008)

Adaptation of the Rosamunde Pilcher book about a 60-year-old woman (Penelope Keeling) who, after suffering a mild heart attack, travels to the Mediterranean to visit with her daughter (Olivia) and reflect on her life.

Cast: Vanessa Redgrave (Penelope Keeling), Victoria Smurfit (Olivia Keeling), Maximilian Schell (Lawrence Sterne), Maisie Dimbleby (Young Penelope), Victoria Hamilton (Nancy), Sebastian Koch (Cosmo), Charles Edwards (Noel), Toby Fisher (Ambrose).

Credits: *Executive Producer:* Verena von Heeremann, Rikolt von Gagern. *Producer:* Alexander Ollig, David Cunliffe. *Writer:* Brian Finch. *Director:* Piers Haggard.

490 She's Got the Look. (Series; Reality; TV Land; June 4, 2008 to July 9, 2008)

Hopeful female models, thirty-five to forty years of age, compete for a contract with the Wilhelmina Modeling Agency and a spread in *Self* magazine. Twenty finalists' are chosen from open auditions (ten of whom are eliminated after the first photo shoot). The remaining women compete in various modeling challenges with the weakest performers being eliminated on a weekly basis. The one woman who best shows modeling potential wins.

Host: Kim Alexis. **Judges:** Beverly Johnson, Sean Patterson, Robert Verdi.

Credits: *Executive Producer:* Allison Grodner, Keith Cox, Sal Maniaci, Sean Patterson, Corey Preston. *Co-Executive Producer:* Fernando Hernandez. *Supervising Producer:* Stephanie Jenz. *Producer:* Brandon Panoligan.

Reviews: "Host Kim Alexis proclaims '*She's Got the Look* is a modeling competition like no other,' which is flat out balderdash. It's rather a competition like *every* other, the only distinction being this aspires to models 35 and over" (*Variety*).

"The good thing about this show is that if it lasts, then the losers of the CW's *America's Next Top Model* will have a place to go for a second chance" (*Entertain Your Brain*).

491 A Shot at Love 2 with Tequila. (Series; Reality; MTV; April 22, 2008 to July 8, 2008)

Tila Tequila (real name Tila Nguyen) is a bi-sexual woman who is looking for a new lover. Fifteen men and fifteen women compete against each other vying to be that one special person. Each episode places the contenders in challenges that test their dedication to falling in love with Tequila. The final program has Tequila choosing the man or woman she would most like to be with. A spin-off from *A Shot at Love with Tequila*.

Host: Tila Nguyen.

Credits: *Executive Producer:* Sally Salsano. *Co-Executive Producer:* Joel Zimmer. *Supervising Producer:* Ben Hatta, Mark Allen. *Producer:* Brian Spoor, Damon Epps, Christopher Roach, Krista Van Nieuwburg, Kyle Simpson.

Reviews: "To even write a review for this show is to deign it with a credibility it little deserves, for it's essentially a transparent gimmick in the guise of a legitimate concept" (*New York Daily News*).

"At last! A reality show about a bisexual Playboy model that can be enjoyed by kids and young adults alike!" (*New York Post*).

492 Sid the Science Kid. (Series; Cartoon; PBS; Premiered: September 1, 2008)

Sid is a very curious pre-schooler. He wants to know everything about everything and will not rest until his curiosity is satisfied. The computer animated series from the Jim Henson Company, introduces children to the wonders of the world as Sid seeks to find the answers to the questions that fascinate him.

Voice Cast: Misty Rosas (Sid), Jesse Springer (Voice-Overs).

Credits: *Executive Producer:* Brian Henson, Lisa Henson, Joyce Campbell, Bradley Zeweig, Halle Stanford. *Producer:* Chris Plourde.

493 Simply Delicioso. (Series; Cooking; Food Network; Premiered: January 1, 2008)

Latin inspired meals are prepared for viewers by chef Ingrid Hoffman.

Host: Ingrid Hoffman.

Credits: *Executive Producer:* Brooke Badley Johnson. *Producer:* Ingrid Hoffman.

494 The Singing Office. (Series; Reality; TLC; June 29, 2008 to August 17, 2008)

A search to find the best singer from office staff workers. Each contestant is chosen by his or her fellow workers then competes with others chosen in the same manner. The weakest performers are then eliminated during performance contests. The one who proves to be the best wins. Alan Thicke hosted the unaired pilot version.

Host: Joey Fatone, Melanie Brown.

Credits: *Executive Producer:* Laurie Girion. *Producer:* Karri-Leigh Mastrangelo. *Associate Producer:* Jeff Girion, Caroline Self, Matt Sims. *Director:* Brad Kreisberg, Tony Sacco.

495   6Teen. (Series; Cartoon; Cartoon Network; Premiered: November 6, 2008)

Events in the lives of six sixteen-year-old friends who, through their activities, learn from one another. Jen, Nikki, Jonesy, Caitlin, Wyatt and Jude are the teens who are seen mostly attempting to cope with life at the shopping mall where each has a job.

Jen Masterson still carries her tomboyish ways and loves sports. She is energetic and works at a sports store called The Penalty Box. Nikki Wong is a realist, somewhat defiant and has a tough exterior. She is an individualist and hates mass consumerism. Unfortunately, her inability to abide by authority finds her working in a tacky clothing store called The Khaki Barn (the only business that would hire her). Jonesy Garcia appears to be interested in only two things — hockey and girls, but not necessarily in that order. He is irresponsible and goes from job to job. Caitlin Cooke like to have things go her way although she will go out of her way to help a friend. She works in a lemon costume at a juice bar called The Big Squeeze. She hopes to become a cheerleader at school. Wyatt Williams is the intellectual member of the group and works at a music store called Spin. He would like to become a musician and relishes in the fact that he is different. Jude Lizowski is a fun-loving guy who appreciates the little things in life — like his job at Stick It (a fast food store that serves a different food each day on a stick). He feels this is the job he was born to have.

Voice Cast: Megan Fahlenboch (Jen Masterson), Stacey DePass (Nikki Wong), Brooke D'Orsay (Caitlin Cooke), Jesse Gibbons (Wyatt Williams), Christian Potenza (Jude Lizowski), Terry McGurrin (Jonesy Garcia), Jamie Watson (Coach Halder), Lauren Lipson (Kristen).

Credits: *Executive Producer:* Brian Irving. *Producer:* Wendy Errington, Jaelyn Galbraith, Tom McGillis, Jennifer Pertsch. *Music:* Don Breithaupt, Anthony Vanderburgh.

496   69 Sexy Things to Do Before You Die. (Series; Reality; Playboy Channel; Premiered: March 10, 2008)

Real people allow cameras to record their erotic adventures as they expose themselves to sexual situations that, for the most part, most people have never attempted (or even heard of; for example, a couple experiencing the activities of the risqué Montreal, Canada, nightlife; a woman experiencing the Japanese performance art called "Naked Sushi" ["female body arrangement"]).

Credits: *Supervising Producer:* Kira Reed. *Producer:* Christopher Bavelles, Andrew Nock.

497   Ski Patrol. (Series; Reality; Tru TV; October 20, 2008 to November 26, 2008)

The work of ski patrol teams as they struggle to keep the slopes safe for skiers. Teams from Crystal Mountain in Washington and Blue Mountain in Pennsylvania are featured.

Ski Patrol: Jim Dailey, Ben Moran, Brian Hohenshilt, Chas Bloxsome, Ed Kupillas, Glenn Amery, Hans Buckley, Jenna Blanchard, Joe Urbans.

Credits: *Executive Producer:* Anthony Horn, Jeff Jenkins, Jonathan Murray, Jason Morgan. *Co-Executive Producer:* Gil Goldschein. *Supervising Producer:* Russell Jay. *Producer:* Kasey Barrett, Jack Reifert.

498   Skins. (Series; Drama; BBC America; August 17, 2008 to December 19, 2008)

Bristol, England, is the setting for a look at a group of teenagers, most freshmen at Roundview College, as they face the daily pressures of life — at home, at school and with their friends. Tony, the most popular kid in town, is a ladies' man and dating the most gorgeous girl in town — Michelle (whom he calls "Nips") — who knows she is not only sexy but sultry. Cassie, described as "completely bonkers," is anorexic and has a very low self-esteem. Sid is Tony's "best bud," a 16-year-old who longs for a girl like Michelle. Chris is the class clown; Maxxie is a gay male who is struggling to cope with his sexuality; Anwar is Maxxie's friend, a Muslim trying to break away from the strict traditions of his family and find independence; Jal believes she is the best clarinet player in the country and is best friends with Michelle.

Cast: Nicholas Hoult (Tony Stonem), April Pearson (Michelle Richardson), Hannah Murray (Cassie), Mike Bailey (Sid Jenkins), Dev Patel (Anwar), Larissa Wilson (Jal), Joe Dempsie (Chris), Mitch Hewer (Maxxie Oliver).

Credits: *Executive Producer:* Bryan Eisley, George Faber, Charles Pattinson. *Producer:* George Clough.

Review: "Teenagers, sex and drugs are ... a controversial mix... *Skins* lacks ... a compelling point of view, other than ... the shock value of seeing British youths smoke pot and sleep around" (*Variety*).

499 Smile! You're Under Arrest.
(Series; Reality; Fox Reality Channel; Premiered: December 27, 2008)

An innovative concept: capture actual wanted felons through comical stings. Criminals with outstanding warrants are the unsuspecting subjects as a real life sheriff and a team of improvisational actors ban together to plot a comical prank, then lure the criminal out of hiding and into the arms of the law. Cameras capture the hijinks as the criminal becomes part of the sting not realizing that his minutes as a fugitive from justice are numbered.

Sheriff: Joe Arpaio. **Actors:** Diana Terranova, David Storrs, Tori Meyer, Dave Sheridan.

Credits: *Producer:* Scott Satin.

500 The Smoking Gun Presents The World's Dumbest Criminals.
(Series; Reality; Tru TV; Premiered March 13, 2008)

"Real Videos. Real Stupid. Real Awesome" is the tagline for a program that spotlights "brain-deficient" criminals who were so clueless in their approach to committing a crime that stupidity cost them their capture. Celebrities and crime experts appear to introduce the actual caught-on-tape segments.

Celebrities: Danny Bonaduce, Tonya Harding, Amy Fisher, Leif Garrett, Todd Bridges.

Credits: *Executive Producer:* Jason Cilo. *Producer:* John Petro. *Associate Producer:* Julie K. Morris, Paul Kaup

501 Snoop Dogg's Fatherhood.
(Series; Reality; E!; Premiered: November 30, 2008)

A profile of rapper Snoop Dogg as he attempts to balance his life as a music artist, husband to wife Shante and father to his children Corde, Cori and Cordell.

Star: Snoop Dogg.

Credits: *Executive Producer:* David Roma, Constance Schwartz, Snoop Dogg, Ted Chung. *Supervising Producer:* Derrick Speight. *Producer:* Jordan Allen-Dutton, Eric Weiner. *Music:* Shawn K. Clement.

502 Snow 2: Brain Freeze.
(TV Movie; Comedy; ABC Family; December 14, 2008)

A sequel to the 2004 ABC Family TV movie *Snow*. It is three days before Christmas and Nick Snowden, a.k.a. Santa Clause, and his wife, Sandy, begin arguing over last minute preparations. To clear his mind, Nick steps through his magic mirror (which allows him to leave the North Pole). But the experience lands him in the hospital with amnesia. With Christmas now in jeopardy, Sandy struggles to help Nick remember who he is in time for his legendary Christmas Eve sleigh ride. Hindering Sandy is Buck Seger, Nick's nemesis, who is seeking Santa's magical secrets.

Cast: Thomas Cavanagh (Nick Snowden), Ashley Williams (Sandy Snowden), Patrick Fabian (Buck Sinclair), David LeReaney (Chris), Rebecca Toolan (Marilyn), Jake Church (Young Nick Snowden), Irena Karas (Nurse).

Credits: *Executive Producer:* Phil Kruener, Craig McNeil. *Producer:* Tom Cox, Jordy Randall, Murray Ord. *Director:* Mark Rosman. *Writer:* Rich Burns.

503   Somebodies. (Series; Comedy; BET; September 9, 2008 to October 28, 2008)

BET's first scripted series. Scottie is a young man who is undecided about his future. He is attending college (University of Georgia) and has settled into a role as a professional student. One day, as his friends begin to move on in the real world, Scottie realizes that he must also move on. Stories follow Scottie as he begins a journey of self discovery.

Cast: Hadjii (Scottie), Kaira Akita (Diva), Nard Holston (Marlo), Anthony Hyatt (Tory), Quante Strickland (Six), Corey Redding (Jelly), Tyler Craig (the Reverend Hill).

Credits: *Executive Producer:* Hadjii, Peter Aronson, Warren Hutcherson. *Producer:* Pamela Kohn. *Writer-Director:* Hadjii. *Music:* Stanley A. Smith.

504   Son of the Dragon. (TV Movie; Adventure; Hallmark; September 14, 2008)

A karate master (Bird) and a young thief (D.B.) who idolizes Bird, team to steal the royal jewels of India.

Cast: David Carradine (Bird), John Reardon (D.B.), Desiree Ann Siahaan (Princess Li Wei), Theresa Lee (Ting Ting), Eddy Ko (Lord Shing), Rupert Graves (Lord of the North), Kay Tong Lim (Governor)

Credits: *Executive Producer:* Robert Halmi, Sr., Robert Halmi, Jr. *Producer:*

Matthew O'Connor, Shan Tam. *Music:* Lawrence Shragge. *Director:* David Wu. *Writer:* Jacqueline Feather, David Seidler.

505   Sons of Anarchy. (Series; Drama; FX; September 3, 2008 to November 26, 2008)

Charming is a small, sheltered community that in addition to its police department, has the added protection of the Sons of Anarchy, a motorcycle gang that appears to have only one purpose: safeguarding Charming from drug dealers, corporate developers and over zealous cops. Their real purpose, however, is to use their protection status as a guise for their thriving illegal arms business. Jackson "Jax" Teller appears to be the leader of the gang; in actuality, his ruthless mother (Gemma) and stepfather (Clay) control operations. Stories follow the gang's activities as they deal arms and protect Charming.

Cast: Charlie Hunnan (Jackson "Jax" Teller), Katey Sagal (Gemma Teller Morrow), Ron Perlman (Clarence "Clay" Morrow), Drea de Matteo (Wendy; Jax's ex-wife), Johnny Lewis (Kid "Half Stack" Epps), Stevie Long (Long John), Emilio Rivera (Marcus Alvarez), Dendrie Taylor (Luannae), Sprague Grayden (Donna Lerner), Mark Boone Jr. (Bobby Munson), Kim Coates (Alex Trager).

Credits: *Executive Producer:* Kurt Sutter, Arti Linson, John Linson, Jack Lo Giudice. *Producer:* Kelly Manners.

Reviews: "The series features an intriguing cast and introduces a bleak new world. Once that's accomplished, though, there's not much momentum to the story" (*Variety*).

"*The Sopranos* meet *Hell's Angels on Wheels*— awesome! Here's hoping *The Sons of Anarchy* have a long run" (*Viewpoints*).

506   Sordid Lives: The Series. (Series; Comedy; Logo; Premiered: July 23, 2008)

An adaptation of the 2000 feature film *Sordid Lives* that continues to depict outrageous events in the lives of a dysfunctional family and their friends who reside in a trailer park in a small Texas town. Ty Williamson is gay but has not yet revealed the fact to his mother (Latrelle) fearing that she will not be able to handle it. Brother Boy, institutionalized for being gay and a transvestite, impersonates singer Tammy Wynette (his female psychiatrist, Dr. Eve, is trying to change his ways for her book on "de-homosexualizing men"). Bitsy Mae is the local saloon singer; Sissy is Latrelle's sister; Noleta is Sissy's friend; Granny is Latrelle's senile mother; G.W. is Latrelle's legless neighbor; Jacob, an actor (as is Ty) is Ty's boyfriend.

Cast: Bonnie Bedelia (Latrelle Williamson), Jason Dottley (Ty Williamson), Beth Grant (Sissy Hickley), Leslie Jordan (Earl "Brother Boy" Ingram), Caroline Rhea (Noleta), Olivia Newton-John (Bitsy Mae Harling), Rue McClanahan (Grandma Peggy), Rosemary Alexander (Dr. Eve), David Stein (G.W. Netherscott), Ted Detwiler (Jacob), Georgette Jones (Tammy Wynette).

Credits: *Executive Producer:* Stanley M. Brook, Rob Eric, Damian Ganczewski, Dave Mace, Pamela Post, Del Shores. *Producer:* Iddo Lampton. *Music:* Joe Patrick Ward.

Review: "*Sordid Lives* has great stars ... great characters ... what *Sordid Lives* doesn't have is genuine fun. It's like watching a drag show — you know when you're supposed to laugh because we're conditioned to laugh on cue. But in reality, it's forced and gaiety" (*New York Post*).

507 Spaced. (Series; Comedy; BBC America; 2008)

To solve their frustrations seeking the right apartment as singles, Tim Bisley, a love sick skateboarder, and Daisy Steiner, a hopeful journalist, pretend to be a couple and rent a room in a home owned by the alcoholic Marsha Klein. Also residing at the rooming house are Brian, a dis-

turbed painter; Tim, Brian's best friend; Twist, Daisy's friend, a fashion designer; and Mike, a war fanatic. Stories relate "the agony and ecstasy" of the residents of the house as they interact with each other.

Cast: Simon Pegg (Tim Bisley), Jessica Hynes (Daisy Steiner), Julie Deakin (Marsha Klein), Kathy Carmichael (Twist Morgan), Mark Heap (Brian Topp), Nick Frost (Mike Watt).

Credits: *Executive Producer:* Lisa Clark, Humphrey Barclay, Tony Orston. *Producer:* Gareth Edwards. *Music:* Guy Pratt.

508 Spain ... On the Road Again. (Series; Reality; PBS; Premiered: October 2, 2008)

A look at various aspects of Spain — from its people, cuisine and customs as experienced by actress Gwyneth Paltrow and her traveling companions (Claudia, Mario and Mark).

Stars: Gwyneth Paltrow, Claudia Bassols, Mario Batali, Mark Brittman.

Credits: *Executive Producer:* Charles Pinsky. *Co-Executive Producer:* Angel Diaz, Eduardo Garcia. *Producer:* Eric Rhee.

509 Special Delivery. (TV Movie; Drama; Lifetime Movie Network; December 21, 2008)

Bounded courier Maxine Carter faces her worst assignment: Deliver a bratty 15-year-old girl (Alice Vanlen) to her mother — a task that becomes complicated and dangerous when Maxine learns that Alice's parents are involved in a bitter custody battle and each will stop at practically nothing to possess Alice.

Cast: Lisa Edelstein (Maxine Carter), Brenda Song (Alice Vanlen), Michael Cowell (Bill Devane), Robert Gant (Nate Spencer), Stan Egi (Danny Wong), Ned Van Zandt (Alan Cantwell), Milan Tresnak (Rudd Weathers), Alana Brennan (Fran).

Credits: *Executive Producer:* Marc B. Lorber, Fernando Szew, Roy Tijoe, Richard S. Galindez. *Producer:* Michael Jacobs. *Associate Producer:* Angela Laprete. *Music:*

Philip Giffin. *Director:* Michael Scott. *Writer:* Matt Dearborn.

510 **Spectacle: Elvis Costello With…** (Series; Interview; Sundance; Premiered: December 3, 2008)

The program, produced in England, features musician Elvis Costello chatting with fellow musicians. In addition to performances by the host, musical clips are presented to represent a guest's work.

Host: Elvis Costello.

Credits: *Executive Producer:* Elton John, David Furnish, Steve Hamilton Shaw, Jordan Jacobs, Martin Katz, Steve Warden, Elvis Costello. *Co-Executive Producer:* Alex Coletti.

Review: "The program has little direction and almost no flow. Segments leap from song to interview to video clips and back with nearly a segue or logical progression. The stage is too dark and a secondary proscenium flanked by velvet drapes hems everyone in" (*The Hollywood Reporter*).

511 **The Spectacular Spider-Man**. (Series; Cartoon; Kids WB; Premiered: March 15, 2008)

After being bitten by a radioactive spider, Peter Parker acquires the proportionate powers of a living spider. Designing a costume to conceal his true identity, Peter becomes Spider-Man, a mysterious crusader who battles villains in New York City.

Voice Cast: Josh Keaton (Peter Parker/ Spider-Man), Deborah Strang (Aunt May), Lacey Chabert (Gwen Stacy), Joshua LeBar (Flash Thompson), Ben Diskin (Eddie Brock), Dee Bradley Baker (Dr. Curt Connors), Kath Soucie (Martha Connors).

Credits: *Executive Producer:* Craig Kyle, Stan Lee, Eric S. Rollman. *Supervising Producer:* Greg Weisman, Victor Cook. *Producer:* Diana A. Crea. *Music:* Kristopher Carter, Michael McCuistion.

512 **Speeders Fight Back**. (Series; Reality; Tru TV; Premiered: October 16, 2008)

An extension series based on *Speeders* (see program1087) wherein those ticketed or arrested for speeding appear in court to plead their cases (mostly trying to convince a judge they are innocent).

Narrator: Alex Verde, David Staniszewski.

Credits: *Executive Producer:* Barry Poznick, Diane Best, John Stevens. *Supervising Producer:* Jennifer Tyson, Cynthia Bruck. *Prodcuer:* Michael Wilder, Josette Perrone. *Producer:* Tiffany Dickerson, Sergio Coronado, Matteo Borghese, Kyle Fulmer, Molly Fitzgerald.

513 **The Spirit of Christmas**. (Special; Variety; My Network TV; December 16, 2008)

A soul music celebration of the Christmas season coupled with stories of inspiration.

Host: Robert Wagner. **Performers:** Bo Bice, Natalie Cole, James Ingram, Al Jerreau, Christopher Massey, Kyle Massey, Brian McKnight, Jeffrey Osborne, Tiffany, The Greater Los Angeles Gospel Choir.

Credits: *Executive Producer:* James Romanovich. *Director:* Mark Mardoyan. *Writer:* Steve Jarczak.

514 **Split Ends**. (Series; Reality; Style Network; Premiered: November 22, 2008)

People associated with the hair salon business are the subjects. Each episode features two such people (from owners, to managers to employees) but from different salons. The subjects exchange places and go to work for a day at the other's salon with the object being for each individual to learn from the other and possibly incorporate techniques in their own business.

Credits: *Executive Producer:* Stephanie Drachkovitch, Glenn Meehan, Rasha Drachkovitch. *Supervising Producer:* Andrew Greenberger. *Producer:* Nicole Dunn,

Mark Herwick. *Associate Producer:* Joanna Malino, Chase Mattew, Lori Denil.

515 The Stagg Party. (Series; Documentary; Internet; 2008)

A look at the personal and professional life of Ellen Stagg, a photographer based in Brooklyn, New York. Episodes relate aspects of her work (including shooting nudes), her dating life, relationships with her family and how she balances her erotic work with her mainstream life (like shooting a travel catalogue).

Star: Ellen Stagg. **Models:** Justine Jolie, Joanna Angel, Jelena Kensen, Asa Akira.

Credits: *Executive Producer:* Colin Moore, Craig Parks. *Producer-Writer-Director:* Joe Swanberg.

516 Stand Up to Cancer. (Special; Variety; ABC, CBS, NBC; September 5, 2008)

Commercial free, three broadcast network attempt to raise money for cancer research. Sixty celebrities appear and donate their time for the benefit.

Host: Katie Couric, Charles Gibson, Brian Williams. **Performers Include:** Miley Cyrus, Jessica Alba, Jennifer Aniston, Meryl Streep, Dakota Fanning, Jack Black, Keanu Reeves, Kirsten Dunst, Christina Ricci, Christina Applegate, Halle Berry, Neil Patrick Harris, Jennifer Garner, Dana Delany, Sally Field, Angie Harmon, Marg Helgenberger, Rob Lowe, Fran Drescher, Mariah Carey, Lauren Bacall, Olivia Newton-John, Jimmy Smits, Carrie Underwood, Sarah Silverman.

Credits: *Executive Producer:* Laura Ziskin. *Producer:* Michael B. Seligman. *Music:* Ricky Minor. *Director:* Louis J. Horvitz. *Writer:* Laura Ziskin, Jon Macks, Dave Boone.

517 Star Wars: The Clone Wars. (Series; Cartoon; Cartoon Network; Premiered: October 3, 2008)

Three dimensional computer animation is encompassed to chronicle the further adventures of *Star Wars* characters that covers the period between the fifth and sixth films (*Attack of the Clones* and *Revenge of the Sith*). The series itself focuses on the heroic Jedi Knights of the Republic as they battle the evil Separatists. Anakin Skywalker leads the Clone Army of the Republic. Ahoska Tano is a teenage Padawtan who assists Anakin and, though she often deviates from a plan set by Anakin, she is eager to impress him. Obi-Wan Kenobi is a Jedi Master and a general in the Clone Army. Yoda, a 900-year-old species from an unknown race, sides with the Galactic Republic. General Grievous (from the planet Kalee) is a war lord who allied himself with the Separatists after he failed to become a Jedi Knight (lacked force sensation).

Voice Cast: Matt Lanter (Anakin Skywalker), Ashley Eckstein (Ahsoka Tano), James Arnold Taylor (Obi-Wan Kenobi), Tom Kane (Yoda), Dee Bradley Baker (Captain Rex/Clones), Ian Abercrombie (Chancellor Palpatine), Matthew Wood (General Grievous), Nika Futterman (Asajj Ventress), Corey Burton (Count Dooku).

Credits: *Executive Producer:* George Lucas, Catherine Winder. *Producer:* Sarah Wall, Mary Maffei.

Reviews: "*Clone Wars* ... wants to blow anyone away. Somehow the characters and the action just don't capture our hearts and enthusiasm like the original *Star Wars* trilogy did. Never-the-less, *Clone Wars* has plenty of action ... to keep fans coming back" (*Inside the Box.com*).

"Impressively rich animation to mount big, splendidly realized battle sequences ... the half-hour episodes are so jam-packed with action, the clunky dialogue flies by ... and the irritating characters have less time to annoy" (*Variety*).

518 The Starter Wife. (Series; Drama; USA; October 10, 2008 to December 12, 2008)

A continuation of the 2007 miniseries of the same title (which told the story of Molly Kagan, a woman who faces a different life style after she and her husband, Kenny, an ambitious Hollywood movie executive, divorce). Now, facing a life as a single woman, Molly has adjusted to the fact that she is no longer a part of the high profile life she once lived. Molly has begun a search for self in a self-absorbed society (she hopes to become a writer) and stories relate how she does so — without the prestige, less money and fewer designer clothes (she later turns her tell-all journal into a screenplay called *Wife Moves On*). Jaden is Molly's daughter; Zach, a has-been novelist, is Molly's romantic interest; Joan, a recovering alcoholic, and Rodney, a gay interior designer, and Liz, are Molly's best friends; Lou is Molly's ex-lover.

Cast: Debra Messing (Molly Kagan), Brielle Barbusca (Jaden Kagan), Judy Davis (Joan McAllister), Chris Diamantopoulas (Rodney), David Alan Bashe (Kenny Kagan), Danielle Nicolet (Liz Marsh), Joe Mantegna (Lou).

Credits: *Executive Producer:* Debra Messing, Gigi Levangie Grazer, Josann McGibbon, Sara Parriott, Stephen Davis, Howard Klein, Molly Madden. *Producer:* Todd Himmel. *Co-Producer:* Howard Morris, Connie Burge, Dan Lerner.

Reviews: "If you ever wondered why Hollywood is identified with dirty dealings, hypocrisy, moral bankruptcy, over indulged children and a ceaseless preoccupation with status, check out *The Starter Wife*" (*The Hollywood Reporter*).

"While the characters here haven't yet had the chance to become as interesting as Carrie Bradshaw and company, this great adaptation of Gigi Levangie Grazer's story should help fill the gap left by *Sex and the City*" (*Variety*).

519 Step It Up and Dance. (Series; Reality; Bravo; April 3, 2008 May 29, 2008)

Twelve dancers compete for the title of "The Ultimate Dancer" and $100,000 in cash. Each of the contestants competes in a weekly challenge designed to test their ability to perform specific dance styles. Three judges rate the performances and the weakest dancers are eliminated. The last dancer standing wins.

Hostess: Elizabeth Berkley. **Judges:** Nancy O'Meara, Vincent Paterson, Jerry Mitchell. **Dancers:** Nicole Berrong, James Alsop, Michelle Aguilar Camaya, Tovah Collins, Nick Drago, Miguel Angel Zarate, Michael Silas, Cody Green, Janelle Ginestra, Jessica Feltman.

Credits: *Executive Producer:* Jane Lipsitz, Gunnar Wetterberg, Dan Cutforth. *Producer:* Bill Gaudsmith. *Associate Producer:* Damien Breen. *Field Producer:* Jordan J. Mallari.

Reviews: "The main problem with Bravo's *Step It Up and Dance* is its really stupid; not just a little stupid but world class idiotic" (*Variety*).

520 Stephen King's the N: An Original Series. (Series; Cartoon; Internet; August 4, 2008 to August 29, 2008)

Comic book-like adaptation (pan and scan of drawn panels) of Stephen King's short story *N* about a psychiatrist who becomes obsessed with a mission that he must save the world. Resembles the 1949 series *The Telecomics* (which used the same format) but with much more sophisticated art work (by Alex Maleer).

Voices: Ben Shenkman.

521 Storm Cell. (TV Movie; Adventure; Hallmark; April 22, 2008)

A storm chaser (April Saunders) attempts to help the people of an unsuspecting town who are in the path of a deadly tornado.

Cast: Mimi Rogers (April Saunders), Robert Moloney (Sean Saunders), Elyse Levesque (Dana Saunders), Ryan Kennedy (Ryan Laswell), Andrew Airlie (Travis), Michael Ironside (James), Kristy Dinsmore (Young April), Tracy Trueman (Molly Saunders).

Credits: *Executive Producer:* Lindsay MacAdam, Kirk Shaw, Lisa Hansen. *Producer:* Oliver DeCaigny. *Music:* Corey A. Jackson. *Writer:* Michael Konyves. *Director:* Steven R. Monroe.

522   Storm Chasers. (Series; Reality; Discovery Channel; October 17, 2008 to December 8, 2008)

A team of storm chasers, led by Josh Wurman, attempts to track storms (especially tornados) then get as close as possible to photograph what they are seeing.

Storm Chasers: Josh Wurman, Mara McFalls, Herb Stein, Justin Walker.

Credits: *Executive Producer:* Charles Corwin. *Producer:* Lisa Block, Chris Voos. *Assistant Producer:* Andrew Fitzgerald. *Music:* Didier Ranchone.

523   Street Patrol. (Series; Reality; My Network TV; January 8, 2008 to October 21, 2008)

Story: A rather graphic series (parental warning issued before the program begins) that follows the actual police officers in various U.S. cities and towns as they patrol the streets.

Narrator: William T. Cole.

Credits: *Executive Producer:* John Langley. *Supervising Producer:* Douglas Waterman. *Producer:* Morgan Langley. *Music:* John Lee

524   Student Body. (Series; Reality; Nickelodeon; July 13, 2008 to August 31, 2008)

A youngster's version of *The Biggest Loser* wherein overweight teenagers compete against each other in various challenges that will hopefully help them lose weight. The teen who loses the most weight wins a $25,000 grant for his school.

Host: Laila Ali.

Credits: *Executive Producer:* Mark Koops, H.T. Owens, Dave Broome, Benjamin Silverman. *Co-Executive Producer:* Kate Hall.

Supervising Producer: Jarrod Harlow, Kirk Darham. *Producer:* Kate Kopser, Ken Snow.

525   Studio DC: Almost Live. (Series; Children; Disney; Premiered: October 6, 2008)

Muppet characters Kermit the Frog and Miss Piggy appear to present performances by Disney Channel kid stars (for example, Miley Cyrus, The Jonas Brothers, Ashley Tisdale, Cole and Dylan Sprouse). Also featured are the backstage antics of various Muppet characters.

Voice Cast: Steve Whitmire (Kermit the Frog), Eric Jacobson (Miss Piggy/Fozzie Bear), Dave Goelz (Gonzo), David Rudman (Various Voices), Paul McGinnis (Various Voices).

Credits: *Executive Producer:* Martin G. Baker. *Producer:* Ritamarie Pergggi. *Music:* Bud'da.

526   Style by Jury. (Series; Reality; Syn.; Premiered: September 8, 2008)

An unsuspecting individual is brought to a studio under the assumption they are going to appear on a makeover show. As the subject sits with the host, a jury of nine ordinary people view her (most often a female) through a one way mirror. The subject is then told she has been evaluated by the jury (whose observations are then seen by the subject). The subject is then given a real makeover — the results of which are seen a week later.

Host: Bruce Turner. **Stylist:** Francesca Fontana, David Clemmer.

Credits: *Executive Producer:* Romann D'Andrea, Carolyn Meland, Jeff Preyra. *Producer:* Kim Kuhteubhl, Susan Posner. *Music:* Rohan Staton.

527   Stylista. (Series; Reality; CW; October 23, 2008 to December 17, 2008)

Eleven fashion hopefuls compete for the opportunity for a dream job with *Elle* magazine, the industry's leading fashion magazine. The contenders compete in groups or as singles in various assistant challenges (fashion and editorial) with the poorest performers, based on the opinions of *Elle* editors, disqualified from the competition. The one player who is best able to "live and breathe fashion" receives her dream job (junior editor) and a Manhattan apartment for one year.

Host: Anne Slowey (*Elle* fashion editor).

Credits: *Executive Producer:* Tyra Banks, Ken Mok, Eli Holzman, Desiree Gruber, Jane Cha. *Co-Executive Producer:* Omid Kahangi, J. Paul Buscemi. *Supervising Producer:* Louis Boyd. *Producer:* Matt Cabral, Bradford Sisk.

Reviews: "Benefits from its choice of drama-queen contenders, from the spoiled rich girl ... to the emotional diva with heaving cleavage. Consider this the saving grace" (*Variety*).

"The show is a lot of fun. Like playing dress-up when you were a kid — and about as realistic" (*New York Post*).

528   Suburban Secrets. (Series; Reality; Tru TV; Premiered: 2008)

A behind-the-scenes look at the crime and corruption that plagues small and medium-sized American towns (how it's caused and how it is stopped).

Credits: *Executive Producer:* Rebecca Difenbach, Valerie Haselton. *Supervising Producer:* Jack Laufer. *Producer:* Carolyn Day, David Erickson. *Associate Producer:* James Mazzella. *Music:* Craig Sharmat.

529   Sugar Rush. (Series; Drama; Logo; 2008)

Kim Daniels is a beautiful British high school student struggling to come to terms with the fact that she is a lesbian. Maria Sweet, called Sugar, is a gorgeous straight girl on whom Kim has a secret crush. While Kim cannot reveal her feelings for Sugar, viewers do see her fantasies about making love to her. Sugar is into boys, drinking and sex and Kim's complete opposite. Stories follow Kim as she attempts to overcome the troublesome situations she encounters with Sugar. Stella is Kim's flirtatious mother; Nathan is her father (unaware of Stella's unfaithfulness); Matt is Kim's younger, cross-dressing brother; Saint is Kim's lesbian friend (a bartender at the Clit Club); Dale is the handyman with whom Stella is having an affair.

Cast: Olivia Hallinan (Kim Daniels), Lenora Crichlow (Maria "Sugar" Sweet), Sara Stewart (Stella Daniels), Richard Lumsden (Nathan Daniels), Kurtis O'Brien (Matt Daniels), Sarah-Jane Potts (Saint), Neil Jackson (Dale), Anna Wilson-James (Anna).

Credits: *Executive Producer:* Julian Murphy. *Producer:* Johnny Capps, Lowri Glain.

530   The Suite Life on Deck. (Series; Comedy; Disney; Premiered: September 26, 2008)

A spin off from *The Suite Life of Zack and Cody* that takes the mischievous teenage twins, Zack and Cody, from the luxurious Tipton Hotel to the posh cruise ship *S.S. Tipton* for a semester at sea (at Seven Seas High School). Stories depict their adventures as they travel to exotic ports, cause numerous problems with their antics, and attempt to get an education. London, Mr. Tipton's daughter, has also been assigned to the cruise in the hope that it will provide her with a better education; Mr. Moseby, the hotel's manager, has been given the responsibility of caring for the trio; Bailey is London's roommate; Woody is Cody's roommate (Zack has his own room). Miss Tutweiler is the featured teacher.

Cast: Cole Sprouse (Cody Martin), Dylan Sprouse (Zack Martin), Brenda Song (London Tipton), Phill Lewis (Mr. Moseby), Erin Cordillo (Emma Tutweiller), Debby Ryan (Bailey Pickett), Matthew Timmons (Woody).

Credits: *Executive Producer:* Pamela Eels, Danny Kallis, Jim Geoghan, Irene

Dreayer. *Producer:* Walter Barnett, Kelly Sandefur. *Music:* John Adair, Steve Hampton, Gary S. Scott.

531   Summer Heights High. (Series; Comedy; HBO; November 9, 2008 to December 28, 2008)

A "mockumentary" that follows three main characters, mixes actors with real students and teachers, to look at a year in the life of a public high school in Australia. Australian comedian Chris Lilley portrays Mr. G., Jonah and Ja'mie. Mr. G. is a drama teacher at Summer Heights High School who is more interested in writing a musical based on a school tragedy rather than instructing his students (his biggest fear is that the special education students may ruin his play). Jonah is a Pacific Island brat with a nasty attitude; Ja'mie is unsettling — a spoiled 16-year-old girl (played in drag by 33-year-old Lilley) who is recent transfer from a private school and feels superior to everyone. Produced in Australia.

Star: Chris Lilley.

Credits: *Producer:* Bruce Kane. *Co-Producer:* Laura Waters, Chris Lilley. *Music:* Bryony Marks.

Reviews: "Cultural distinctions not withstanding, *Summer Heights High* seldom rises above silliness and mostly proves plain irritating" (*Variety*).

"You won't get too high on this Aussie import" (*New York Daily News*).

532   The Summit. (TV Movie; Drama; Ion; June 15, 2008)

A grieving mother (Ellie Bruckner) seeks justice for her son, the victim of drugs manufactured by a corrupt pharmaceutical company.

Cast: Wendy Crewson (Ellie Bruckner), Rachelle Adderly (Leonie Adderly), Mark Thomas (Lawrence Slingsby), Christopher Plummer (P.J. Aimes), Bruce Greenwood (Richard Adderly), James Purefov (Thom Lightstone), Lisa Ray (Rebecca Downy).

Credits: *Executive Producer:* Justin Bodle, Scott Garvie, Christina Jennings. *Producer:* Robin Neinstein, Adam Haight, Robert Cohen. *Writer:* John Krizanc. *Director:* Nick Copus.

533   Swamp Devil. (TV Movie; Horror; Sci Fi; October 12, 2008)

A young woman (Melanie) attempts to clear her father of a series of grisly murders by proving they were committed by a creature that lives in the swamps of their small American town in the deep south.

Cast: Cindy Sampson (Melanie Blaime), Bruce Dern (Howard Blaime), Mari-Pier Gaudet (Lisa), Allison Graham (Deputy Jolene Harris), Nicholas Wright (Jimmy Fuller), James Kidnie (Sheriff Nelson Bois).

Credits: *Executive Producer:* Robert Halmi, Sr., Robert Halmi, Jr., Michael Prupas. *Producer:* Irene Litinsky. *Music:* James Gelfand. *Writer:* Gary Dauberman, Ethile Ann Vare. *Director:* David Winning.

534   Sweet Nothing in My Ear. (TV Movie; Drama; CBS; April 20, 2008)

Laura and Dan Miller are a happily married couple with a young son (Adam). Laura is deaf; Dan has normal hearing. The controversial story relates what happens when Adam suddenly loses his hearing and Laura opposes Dan's efforts to hopefully restore his hearing through a cochlear implant.

Cast: Marlee Matlin (Laura Miller), Jeff Daniels (Dan Miller), Noah Valencia (Adam Miller), Sonya Walger (Joanna Tate), Phyllis Frelich (Sally), Ed Waterstreet (Max), Rosemary Forsyth (Louise Miller), Bradford English (Henry Miller), Deanne Bray (Dr. Walters), Coleen Flynn (Priscilla Scott), Steve Cell (Jerry Scott).

Credits: *Executive Producer:* Marian Rees, Brent Shields. *Producer:* Joseph Sargent. *Writer:* Stephen Sachs. *Director:* Joseph Sargent. *Music:* Charles Bernstein.

535   Swingtown. (Series; Drama; CBS; June 5, 2008 to September 5, 2008)

A look at the seedier side of the mid 1970s (from drugs to open marriages) as seen through Susan and Bruce Miller, a monogamous married couple with two children (Laurie and B.J.) who are introduced to a new world of sex and drugs when they move into a lakeside town in Chicago and befriend their new neighbors, Trina and Tom Decker, swingers who believe in everything from threesomes to high priced coke.

Cast: Molly Parker (Susan Miller), Jack Davenport (Bruce Miller), Lana Parrilla (Trina Decker), Grant Show (Tom Decker), Shanna Collins (Laurie Miller), Aaron Christian Howles (B.J. Miller), Miriam Shor (Janet Thompson), Josh Hopkins (Roger Thompson), Brittany Robertson (Samantha Saxton), Kate Norby (Gail Saxton), Michael Rady (Doug Stephens).

Credits: *Executive Producer:* Mike Keley, Alan Powl, Robert DelValle. *Co-Producer:* Rick Tunell. *Associate Producer:* Blake McCormick, Jori Adler. *Music:* Liz Phair, Marc "Doc" Dauer, Evan Frankfort.

Reviews: "*Swingtown* manages to be about sex without showing much of it ... [it] has the making of a series that will earn a small but loyal following only to leave them disappointed" (*Variety*).

"*Swingtown* has a chance to shine during a time when few provocative programs are introduced" (*FilmStew.com*).

536   Sybil. (TV Movie; Drama; CBS; June 7, 2008)

Adaptation of the book by Flora Rheta Shreiber about a psychiatrist (Cornelia Wilbur) and her efforts to help Sybil Dorset, a young woman suffering from multiple personality disorders as a result of childhood abuse.

Cast: Jessica Lange (Dr. Cornelia Wilbur), Tammy Blanchard (Sybil Dorset), Jo Beth Williams (Hattie Dorset), Ron White (Dr. Atcheson), Liam McNamara (Tommy), Fab Filippo (Ramon).

Credits: *Executive Producer:* Mark Wolper, Norman Stephens. *Producer:* Michael Mahoney. *Writer:* John Pielmeier. *Director:* Joseph Sargent.

Review: "A strong performance by Jessica Lange goes largely to waste in this remake of the 1976 Joanne Woodward–Sally Field movie *Sybil.* The main problem ... is why someone felt a good movie needed to be remade in the first place" (*New York Daily News*).

537   Tabatha's Salon Takeover. (Series; Reality; Bravo; August 21, 2008 to October 9, 2008)

Australian-born hair stylist Tabatha Coffey attempts to help faltering salons in Los Angeles and New York regain their footing in the business world.

Host: Tabatha Coffey.

Credits: *Executive Producer:* Howard Owens, Mark Koops, Jonas Larsen. *Co-Executive Producer:* Heather Schuster. *Producer:* Jennifer Stander, Michael Webster, Jennifer White.

538   Take Home Chef. (Series; Reality; TLC; Premiered: June 16, 2008)

Unsuspecting super market shoppers are approached by chef Curtis Stone and asked "What's for dinner?" When he discovers what it is he accompanies the shopper home to see how the family eats and offers cooking advice.

Host: Curtis Stone.

Credits: *Executive Producer:* Mike Mathis. *Supervising Producer:* Brian Puterman. *Producer:* Alicia Gargaro. *Music:* Henri Yonet.

539   Take Home Nanny. (Series; Reality; TLC; July 21, 2008)

Parents with unruly children receive help from Emma Jenner, a professional nanny who comes to their homes to discipline the children and create harmony in the family once again.

Star: Emma Jenner.

Credits: *Executive Producer:* Gerry

McKean. *Supervising Producer:* Rich Hansil. *Producer:* Jamie Alberti, Keira Brings. *Director:* Rich Hansil.

540   A Teacher's Crime. (TV Movie; Drama; Lifetime; May 3, 2008)

Tale of a high school teacher (Carrie) who finds herself being blackmailed by an ex-convict (Bill) when she tries to help his troubled son (Jeremy).

Cast: Ashley Jones (Carrie Ryans), Claudia Besso (Patti Meyers), Larry Day (Detective Chay), Ellen Dubin (Anne Libby), James Gallanders (Dean Ryans), Art Hindle (David McMillian), Erik Knudsen (Jeremy Rander), Chris Mulkey (Bill Rander).

Credits: *Executive Producer:* Tom Berry, Pierre David. *Producer:* Neil Bregman. *Writer:* Christine Conradt, Corbin Mezner. *Director:* Robert Malenfant.

541   Teen Choice Awards. (Special; Awards; Fox; August 4, 2008)

The results of an online voting poll wherein the winners (in such categories as film, music, TV and sports) receive the Surf Board Award.

Host: Miley Cyrus. **Appearing:** Mariah Carey, Kristen Bell, Drake Bell, Chris Brown, Miranda Cosgrove, The Cheetah Girls, Josh Duhamel, Summer Glau, Brian Austin Green, Selma Gomez, Katherine McPhee, Jerry O'Connell, Hayden Panettiere.

Credits: *Executive Producer:* Bob Bain, Mike Burg. *Supervising Producer:* Gregory Sills. *Producer:* Paul Flaherty, Kelly Brock. *Director:* Bruce Gowers.

542   The Tenth Circle. (TV Movie; Drama; Lifetime; June 28, 2008)

Tense drama about the police investigation into the death that occurs after 14-year-old Trixie Stone accuses her boyfriend of raping her and he commits suicide.

Cast: Kelly Preston (Laura Stone), Brittany Robertson (Trixie Stone), Ron Eldard (Daniel Stone), Jamie Johnston (Jason

Underhill), Michael Riley (Mike), Haley Beauchamp (Zepher Santorelli).

Credits: *Executive Producer:* Stephen Furst, Scott Goldman, Michael Jaffe. *Producer:* Michael Mahoney. *Writer:* Maria Nelson, Jodi Picoult. *Director:* Peter Markle. *Music:* Velton Ray Bunch.

543   Terminator: The Sarah Connor Chronicles. (Series; Adventure; Fox; Premiered: January 13, 2008)

Television adaptation of *The Terminator* theatrical films. On April 19, 2011, the Skynet Missile Defense Program will be launched and murderous machines will declare war on mankind. Sarah Connor knows this and her son, John, is the futuristic savior of mankind. Skynet's creators are aware of John and are determined to dispose of him before he can fulfill his mission.

Cameron Phillips is a futuristic re-programmed (for good) Terminator robot that has been sent back in time to protect John. Cromartic, a deadly terminator robot, also has a mission: kill John. Sarah's race against time to destroy Skynet and stop the war before it begins is the focal point of the series (in 1984 Sarah was saved from a futuristic Terminator robot by the time traveling resistance fighter Kyle Reese. Kyle fathered John but was killed before he could stop Skynet; the mission then became Sarah's destiny).

Cast: Lena Headey (Sarah Connor), Thomas Dekker (John Connor), Summer Glau (Cameron Phillips), Richard T. Jones (James Ellison), Brian Austin Green (Derek Reese), David Kilde (Cromartie).

Credits: *Executive Producer:* John Friedman, John Writh, Mario Kassar, Andrew Vajna, Joel Michaels, David Nutter. *Producer:* Charles Goldstein. *Music:* Bear McCreary.

Reviews: "Credibly expanding the *Terminator* franchise into TV, this series faces a considerable challenge — beginning with the usual contortions of time travel logic —

to maintain its initial pace without developing into silliness" (*Variety*).

"The series, like the movie, is an action-packed explosion-filled Sci Fi variation of *The Fugitive*, though circumstances are sketchier. While it helps to have seen the movie, you can catch up with the premise in a few minutes" (*The Hollywood Reporter*).

544 **Testees**. (Series; Comedy; FX; Premiered: October 9, 2008)

Peter and Ron are thirty-year-old best friends who make a living in a most unusual way: they are human guinea pigs for Testico, a product and drug testing company. Stories follow the mishaps that occur in their lives as they struggle to deal with the various side effects that occur from testing experimental products and medications. Larry, Kate and Nugget are other brain-dead guinea pigs.

Cast: Steve Markle (Peter), Jeff Kassel (Ron), Kim Schraner (Kate), Kenny Hotz (Larry), Joe Pingue (Nugget).

Credits: *Executive Producer:* Derek Harvie, Kenny Hotz. *Supervising Producer:* Suzanne Berger. *Producer:* John Morayniss, Michael Rosenberg.

Reviews: "*Testees* lives several rungs down the evolutionary ladder from FX's once promising and now increasingly disappointing *It's Always Sunny in Philadelphia*... It's about as narrow as comedy gets" (*Variety*).

"...a combo platter for the college crowd which is probably a good programming decision — but here's hoping the ambition of *Testees* makes its premise in future episodes" (*The San Francisco Chronicle*).

545 **That's Amore**. (Series; Reality; MTV; March 2, 2008 to April 6, 2008)

A spin off from *A Shot at Love with Tequila* wherein former Tequila suitor Domenico Nesci conducts his own search for true love, seeking the right girl from 15 single women who compete in various challenges to win his heart.

Host: Domenico Nesci.

Credits: *Executive Producer:* Sally Ann Salsano. *Senior Producer:* Bradley Kell. *Producer:* Krista Van Nieuwburg, Jennifer Ryan.

546 **That's Amore: Italian American Favorites**. (Special; Variety; PBS; September 6, 2008)

A clip rich show that encompasses singers from the 1950s and 60s performing Italian accented songs. Performers include Connie Francis, Rosemary Clooney, Julius LaRosa, Johnny Desmond, Nat King Cole, Lou Monte, Frankie Laine.

Host: Danny Aiello.

Credits: *Executive Producer:* T.J. Turbelsy. *Supervising Producer:* Paul Bernstein. *Announcer:* Michael Frazer. *Director:* Jim Pearson.

547 **This American Life**. (Series; Reality; Showtime; Premiered: March 22, 2008)

The real life stories of ordinary American people are profiled from where they live and work (camera crews go to where the stories are to present an honest and homespun approach to the people they profile). Based on the long-running public radio series of the same title.

Host: Ira Glass.

Credits: *Executive Producer:* Alex Blumberg, Ken Druckerman, Julie Snyder, Banks Tarver, Christine Vachon. *Co-Executive Producer:* Christopher Wilcha. *Producer:* Nancy Updike, Jane Feltes. *Line Producer:* Kevin Vargas.

Reviews: "The radio program successfully tunes into television by making the ordinary lives of others seen extraordinary" (*The Hollywood Reporter*).

548 **The Tony Awards**. (Special; Variety; CBS; June 15, 2008)

The 62nd annual presentation that honors the best of the Broadway stage.

Host: Whoopi Goldberg.

Credits: *Producer:* Rick Kirschner,

Glenn Weiss, Jim Mullen. *Director:* Glenn Weiss.

549 The Tony Rock Project. (Series; Comedy; My Network TV; Premiered: October 8, 2008)

Candid Camera type of program wherein comedian Tony Rock plays practical jokes on unsuspecting people on the street. A "Spy Cam" segment features pranks played on celebrities.

Host: Tony Rock. **Co-Host:** Whitney Cummings.

Credits: *Executive Producer:* Claude Brooks, John Langley, Morgan Langley, Tony Rock. *Co-Executive Producer:* Galila Asres. *Producer:* Patrick DeLuca.

550 Top This Party. (Series; Reality; Lifetime; Premiered: January 4, 2008)

An inside look at how people of Orange County, California, spend money on themselves and their parties (not just ordinary parties but expensive, extraordinary parties — like a Halloween party for 500 people; a singles safari). Each party is overseen by event planner Brian Dobbin and his partner, Chef Robin, handles the food (although the viewer never gets to see the final culinary result; just its planning).

Stars: Brian Dobbin, Chef Robin.

Credits: *Executive Producer:* Mechelle Collins, Kevin Dill. *Co-Executive Producer:* Blake Levin, Jennifer Colbert. *Associate Producer:* Erin Coan, Ashley Holm.

Reviews: "*Top This Party* is replete with narcissistic and disgustingly decadent folks who fuss about how best to spend money on themselves and their parties" (*The Hollywood Reporter*).

551 Torchwood. (Series; Science Fiction; BBC America; 2008)

A spin off from *Dr. Who* about Captain Jack Harkness, a Time Agent and con man from the 51st century, who travels back in time (the 21st century) to join the Torchwood Institute, a renegade investigative organization, founded by Queen Victoria, to battle elements of the supernatural (and hostile extraterrestrials). Gwen, Owen, Toshiko and Ianto are members of Jack's team.

Cast: John Barrowman (Jack Harkness), Eve Myles (Gwen Cooper), Naoko Mori (Toshiko Sato), Gareth David-Lloyd (Ianto Jones), Burn Gorman (Owen Harper).

Credits: *Executive Producer* Russell T. Davies, Julie Gardner. *Producer:* Richard Stokes. *Music:* Ben Foster, Murray Gold.

552 The Tournament of Roses Parade. (Special; Variety; NBC; January 1, 2008)

The 119th presentation of elaborate floats that was first staged in 1890 by members of Pasadena's Valley Hunt Club. It was at this time that people turned out to watch a parade of flower-covered carriages and compete in polo matches, foot races and tugs of war. Over the years the parade expanded to include marching bands and motorized floats. In 1895 the Tournament of Roses Association was formed to handle the festivities when it became too large for the Valley Hunt Club to manage. The tradition, as it is known today (honoring football) began in 1902 when the association added the sport to enhance the day's festivities. In 1922 a stadium was built in Pasadena, California, that was dubbed the Rose Bowl by the press. On January 1, 1923, the Tournament held its first football game in the stadium. The event was first heard on radio in 1927 on NBC and the Rose Bowl was first telecast locally in Los Angeles (station KTLA) in 1948; NBC telecast it nationally for the first time in 1952.

Host: Bob Eubanks, Michaela Pereira. **Grand Marshal:** Emeril Lagasse. **2008 Rose Queen:** Dusty Gibbs. **2008 Royal Court Rose Princesses:** Zena Brown, Katie Merrill, Kelsey MacDougall, Courtney Rubin, Chloe Ghoogassian.

553 Tracey Ullman's State of the Union. (Series; Comedy; Showtime; March 30, 2008 to April 27, 2008)

A day in the life of America as interpreted by comedian Tracey Ullman (portraying virtually all characters both real and fictional). Each episode is divided into segments with Tracey satirizing a specific person (for example, newscaster, TV show character, political figures).

Star: Tracey Ullman. **Featured:** Scott Bakula. **Narrator:** Peter Strauss.

Credits: *Executive Producer:* Tracey Ullman, Allan McKeown. *Producer:* Bruce Wagner, Gail Parent, Shawn Wilt. *Director:* Troy Miller. *Writer:* Tracey Ullman, Gail Parent, Craig DiGregorio.

Reviews: "Comedy-variety isn't an easy genre to duplicate but with sitcoms in decline, Ullman's return provides a welcome jolt to the funny bone" (*Variety*).

554 Trivial Pursuit: America Plays. (Series; Game; Syn.; Premiered: September 22, 2008)

Three players compete. A randomizer pinpoints one of several subjects that are displayed. A question is asked by the person who submitted it (seen in a video clip). The first player to buzz in receives a chance to answer. If correct, he scores money (placed in the studio bank) and one of six wedges of a token is filled in. If the incorrect answer is given, the money is placed in America's bank (representing the people who submitted questions). The game continues in this manner until one player fills in his token with six correct answers. He now plays the bonus round. Several categories are revealed, worth from $500 to $5,000. Questions are asked with correct answers placing money in the studio bank; wrong answers place money in America's bank. If the player scores higher than America's bank he wins; if not, the players who submitted the questions split the money accumulated in America's bank.

Host: Christopher Knight.

Credits: *Executive Producer:* Burt Wheeler. *Producer:* Sharon Sussman.

555 Tru TV Saturday Night. (Series; Reality; Tru TV; Premiered: January 2008)

A review of the prior week's Tru TV's top crime oriented reality shows with a recap of cases and updated information on cases that were unsolved at the time of the original broadcast.

Hosts: Megan Gunning (former Miss Maryland U.S.A.), Chuck Nice (comedian).

556 True Blood. (Series; Drama; HBO; September 7, 2008 to November 23, 2008)

Sookie Stackhouse is a barmaid at Merlotte's Bar in the small town of Bon Temps, Louisiana. She is very pretty but somewhat of an outcast due to what she considers her "curse"—her ability to hear the intimate feelings of people. She and her brother, Jason, a construction worker (and a ladies' man) were orphaned as children and raised by their grandmother.

Bill Compton is a 173-year-old vampire (he, as well as others of his kind, survive on the Japanese invention of synthetic blood). He has just returned to Bon Temps, his family home to reconnect with his past. Bill, a loner, and Sookie meet and begin a relationship. Stories follow their relationship and Sookie's efforts to unravel the mystery surrounding Bill's past. Lafayette is the bar cook; Sam is the bar owner.

Cast: Anna Paquin (Sookie Stackhouse), Stephen Moyer (Bill Compton), Ryan Kwanten (Jason Stackhouse), Nelsan Ellis (Lafayette Reynolds), Sam Trammell (Sam Merlotte), Brooke Kerr (Tara Thornton), Zenoli Turner (Young Sookie), Labon Hester (Young Jason), Jim Patrick (Hoyt Fortenberry), Michael Raymond James (Rene Lemier).

Credits: *Executive Producer:* Alan Ball. *Producer:* Carol Dunn Trussell. *Co-Producer:* Bill Johnson. *Music:* Nathan Barr.

Reviews: "A difficult drama with a heroine who is more vampire player than slayer ... with its constant profanity, gore and banal cruelty, it will have limited appeal" (*The Hollywood Reporter*).

"So while the show is a trifle hokey, its soapy elements, gothic atmosphere and cliffhanger endings — coupled with Anna Paquin's knockout performance — do reel viewers in" (*Variety*).

557 True Confessions of a Hollywood Starlet. (TV Movie; Drama; Lifetime; August 9, 2008)

After a stint in rehab, party-going actress Morgan Carter moves in with her aunt (Trudy), adopts the guise of an ordinary teenage high school girl and struggles to live a life outside the spotlight.

Cast: Joanna "Jo Jo" Levesque (Morgan Carter), Valerie Bertinelli (Aunt Trudy), Shenae Grimes (Marissa), Lynda Boyd (Bianca Carter), Ian Nelson (Eli Walsh), Leah Cudmore (Debbie), Jonathan Potts (Principal Bowman), Rebecca Amare (Bethany)

Credits: *Executive Producer:* Barbara Lieberman, Jon Maas. *Producer:* Mark Winemaker. *Director:* Tim Matheson. *Writer:* Elisa Bell, Lola Douglas.

Review: "*Confessions*, which is aimed at 15-year-old divas ... cheerfully borrows Lindsay Lohan's life and the plots of three of her movies to stitch together a perfectly watchable, good-natured formula flick that's better than just about all of Lohan's movies" (*New York Post*).

558 True Jackson, V.P. (Series; Comedy; Nickelodeon; Premiered: November 8, 2008)

True Jackson is a pretty 15-year-old high school girl who makes extra spending money by selling sandwiches outside the offices of Mad Style, a top fashion label. True is totally in tune with the latest in fashion and dreams of becoming a fashion designer. One day, while selling her sandwiches, Max, the somewhat absent-minded head of Mad Style, notices True's marketable fashion sense and offers her an on-the-spot job as vice president in charge of the firm's youth apparel line. True accepts and stories follow True as she attempts to learn the ins and outs of the corporate world while at the same time being a regular kid and coping with the problems of school — from cliques to crushes to mean classmates. Amanda is True's nemesis, an ambitious fashion executive who feels working with True infuriating; Lulu is True's friend and assistant at Mad Style; Ryan is True's best guy friend; Oscar is the office receptionist. Keke Palmer wrote and sings the theme.

Cast: Keke Palmer (True Jackson), Ashley Argota (Lulu), Matt Shively (Ryan), Danielle Bisutti (Amanda Cantwell), Ron Butler (Oscar), Greg Proops (Max), Suzy Nakamura (Cricket), Robbie Amell (Jimmy).

Credits: *Executive Producer:* Andy Gordon. *Producer:* Brenda Hanes-Berg, Veronica Moti McElvoy, Judy Oseransky. *Music:* Eban Schletter.

Review: "Just as the Disney Channel has made hay with girls and tweens, this broadly pitched, undemanding but sprightly series should ... reward Nickelodeon with a loyal audience to twin with its *I Carly* franchise" (*Variety*).

559 The Trumpet Awards. (Special; Awards; My Network TV; August 27, 2008)

The sixteenth annual presentation that honors the accomplishments of men and women who have achieved success in their chosen professions, such as in entertainment, sports, medicine and business.

Host: Samuel L. Jackson. **Guests:** Peabo Bryson, India Arie, Lalah Hathaway, Marcus Johnson, Michael Phillips, Angie Stone, Teddy Riley, The O'Jays.

Credits: *Executive Producer:* Xernona Clayton. *Supervising Producer:* Philip Hack. *Director:* Ron De Moraes.

560 Turbo Dogs. (Series; Cartoon; NBC; Premiered: October 4, 2008)

Computer animated program about a group of canine friends who race cars whenever the opportunity arises. Although cars are used for speeding and the program is aimed at children, automotive safety is stressed as the Turbo Dogs find misadventure and relate learning lessons to their target audience.

Voice Cast: Lyon Smith (Dash), Stacey Depass (Mags), Dan Petronijevic (GT), Joris Jarsky (Strut), Hadley Kay (Stinkbert), Peter Cugno (Clutch/GPS), Terry Naburrin (Cam), Ron Pardo (Ump), Shakura S'Aida (Marlene).

Credits: *Producer:* Kristine Klohk, Rodney MacDonald. *Supervising Producer:* P. Jonas Diamond. *Music:* Brian Pickett, David Kelly, Graeme Cornies, James Chapple. *Theme Vocal:* Trust.

561   The TV Land Awards. (Special; Variety; TV Land; June 15, 2008)

The sixth annual presentation that pays tribute to television programs of the past. Current and veteran performers appear to announce the nominees (*The Golden Girls* and its stars Betty White, Rue McClanahan and Bea Arthur won for show and performers).

Host: Vanessa L. Williams. **Appearing:** Edward Asner, Gary Coleman, Joyce DeWitt, Sara Gilbert, John Goodman, Teri Hatcher, Sherman Hemsley, Jack Klugman, Bernie Kopell, Vicki Lawrence, Penny Marshall, Maureen McCormick, Dick Van Dyke, Dawn Wells, Henry Winkler, Jonathan Winters, Cindy Williams.

Credits: *Executive Producer:* Greg Daniels. *Supervising Producer:* Gregory Sills. *Writer:* Jon Macks, David Wild. *Director:* Jeff Margolis.

562   TV's All Time Funniest. (Special; Comedy; ABC; May 10, 2008)

A look at television's favorite sitcom characters in the following categories: mothers, fathers, kids, neighbors, bosses and co-workers.

Hosts: Edward Asner, Mary Tyler Moore, Marion Ross.

Credits: *Executive Producer:* Brad Lachman. *Supervising Producer:* Bill Bracken. *Producer:* Gary Bormet.

563   12 Miles of Bad Road. (Unaired Series; Comedy; HBO; Produced in 2008)

A proposed six episode series about the Shakespeare's, a filthy rich Texas family and the problems associated with running a real estate empire. Amelia is the head of the family; C.Z. is her sister; Jerry is Amelia's son; Juliet is Jerry's wife; Gaylor is Jerry's sister.

HBO cancelled the very expensive series ($3.6 million per episode) before it ever aired (as of 12-31-08) most likely due to the stereotyped characters (insulting to Texans) and the fact that it did not fit in with HBO's Sunday night block of original programming.

Cast: Lily Tomlin (Amelia Shakespeare), Mary Kay Place (C.Z. Shakespeare), Gary Cole (Jerry Shakespeare), Katherine LaNasa (Juliet Shakespeare), Eliza Coupe (Gaylor Shakespeare), Leslie Jordan (Kenny Kingman), David Andrews (Saxby Hall), Kim Dickens (Jonelle Shakespeare), Cameron Richardson (Mckenna Shakespeare-Hall), Cherilyn Wilson (Caitlin Shakespeare), Michael McShae (Cameron Shakespeare).

Credits: *Executive Producer:* Linda Bloodworth-Thomason, Harry Thomason. *Producer:* Douglas Jackson, Peter Barnett. *Associate Producer:* Peter Phillips.

564   24: Redemption. (TV Movie; Adventure; Fox; November 23, 2008)

A writer's strike in late 2007 caused production on the series *24* to come to a halt. Eight episodes were filmed, but the three month strike made it impossible for producers to deliver its twenty-four episode commitment in time for a January to May schedule. The series was postponed and did not air in 2008. To bridge the 18 month gap between the end of season six (May 21, 2007) and the beginning of the seventh season (January 11, 2009), a two-hour real time prequel was produced to fill that gap and update the life of Jack Bauer, the anti-terrorist whose case assignments unfold in 24 hours (each episode is one of those 24 hours).

When last seen, Jack was in Africa, standing on a hill and contemplating what he had just done: ruined his personal life to save the world (basically the premise of each season of the series). The movie opens three years later with Jack seeking solace as a missionary in Africa. This is short lived when he finds himself in a bloody coupe in the fictional nation of Sangala, where a ruthless dictator is using children as soldiers. Keeping in line with the series premise, the film represents two hours of real time (3 P.M. to 5 P.M.) as Jack defeats the dictator, saves the children and makes his way back to Washington, D.C. just as the inauguration of the first female president (Allison Taylor) is taking place (replacing President Noah Daniels). The movie is self-contained and sets up the revised series story line (the CTU [Counter Terrorism Unit] is gone and Jack and his team now work for "an off-the-books" wing of the FBI. The series setting also changes from Los Angeles to Washington, D.C.).

Cast: Kiefer Sutherland (Jack Bauer), James Cromwell (Philip Bauer), Kim Ravier (Audrey), Powers Boothe (Noah Daniels), Cherry Jones (Allison Taylor), Robert Carlyle (Carl Benton), Gregory Itzin (President Logan), Jon Voight (Jonas Hodges), Ha Kiem-Kazim (Colonel Dubaku), Peter MacNichol (Tom Lennox), Colm Feoire (Henry Taylor), Carly Pope (Samantha Roth), Sprague Grayden (Olivia Taylor).

Credits: *Executive Producer:* Brian Grazer, Howard Gordon, Evan Kaz, Jon Cassar, Kiefer Sutherland, Manny Coto, David Fury. *Co-Executive Producer:* Stephen Kronish, Brad Tucker, Alex Gansa, Brannon Braya, Juan Coto. *Producer:* Michael Klick, Paul Gadd. *Music:* Sean Callery. *Director:* Jon Cassar. *Writer:* Howard Gordon.

Reviews: "If the new season lives up to the excitement of this trailer, then you better fasten your seat belts for a bumpy ride" (*New York Post*).

"Cast like a feature, the project delivers two real time hours, though its no assurance that Baur's seventh very long day [seventh season] ... will avoid the program's recent pattern of starting like gangbusters and limping toward the dawn" (*Variety*).

"Bottom line: A two-hour preview that will make you pant for the start of a new season of *24*" (*The Hollywood Reporter*).

565 The Twister Sisters. (Series; Reality; WE; Premiered: January 2, 2008)

Melanie Metz and Peggy Willenberg are not sisters in the actual sense. They share a love of severe weather and live to chase storms (hence, dubbed "The Twister Sisters"). In 2003 they formed a tornado tour business and episodes follow Melanie and Peggy as they (and their guests) search for the most severe weather they can find.

Stars: Melanie Metz, Peggy Willenberg.

Credits: *Supervising Producer:* Dan Jackson. *Producer:* Mark Landsman, Jim Pastore. *Music:* Andy Kubizewski.

566 The Two Coreys. (Series; Reality; A&E; June 22, 2008 to August 26, 2008)

From July 29 to September 9, 2007 former teen movie idols Corey Feldman and Corey Haim reunited for a reality program that updated their lives. In the 2008 second cycle, the Coreys return to allow cameras to follow them as they struggle to get their lives back together and possibly rekindle their movie careers with the film *The Lost Boys 2* (both appeared in *The Lost Boys* in 1987).

Stars: Corey Feldman, Corey Haim, Susie Feldman (Corey's wife).

Credits: *Executive Producer:* Corey Feldman, Corey Haim, Greg Goldman, Scott Carlson, Jonathan Singer. *Supervising Producer:* Mark S. Jacobs, Kirk Shaw. *Music:* Jeff Toyne.

Reviews: "This latest look at has been Hollywood fails to strike a single convincing note in reuniting onetime teen heartthrobs Corey Haim and Corey Feldman" (*Variety*).

"As with any reality show, the critical question here is whether we care enough about the characters or the drama in their lives. At this point, frankly, the two *Lost Boys* may be losing us" (*New York Daily News*).

567 The Two Mrs. Kissels. (TV Movie; Drama; Lifetime; November 15, 2008)

Fact-based tale about brothers Andrew and Robert Kissel, a real estate mogul (Andrew) and a Wall Street banker, and how they lived the high life but met untimely deaths. Nancy is Robert's wife; Hayley is Andrew's wife; Bill is the brother's father.

Cast: John Stamos (Andrew Kissel), Anson Mount (Rob Kissel), Robin Tunney (Nancy Kissel), Gretchen Egolf (Hayley Kissel), Chuck Shamata (Bill Kissel), Michael Del Priore (Vincent Walsh), Lester Kaufman (Simon Reynolds), Rachel Wilson (Melinda), Karen Cliche (Pris).

Credits: *Executive Producer:* Dan Wigutow. *Co-Executive Producer:* Michael Scott. *Producer:* John Stamos, Terry Gould. *Director:* Ed Branchi. *Writer:* Maria Nation.

Reviews: "Racy by Lifetime's standards, the pic is exactly the kind of tawdry, sexy, strange-but true tale that makes for a juicy TV movie" (*Variety*).

"Movies based on true crime stories ... have been produced for TV for years. The good news is: This one ... represents a new high standard that will be difficult for other movies of its kind to beat" (*New York Post*).

568 2008: Today Looks Back, a Holiday Special. (Special; Review; NBC; December 22, 2008)

The news program *Today* (NBC, 7 to 11 A.M. daily) airs a prime time special in which its anchors look at the most memorable events and news breaking stories of 2008 (including the five top news stories, the top five people of the year, and the most unforgettable pop culture stories).

Anchors: Ann Curry, Matt Lauer, Al Roker, Meredith Vieira.

Credits: *Executive Producer:* Jim Bell, Phil Griffin. *Senior Producer:* Don Nash, Amy Chiaro. *Director:* Joe Michaels.

569 UFO Hunters. (Series; Reality; History Channel; Premiered: January 30, 2008)

UFO experts take to the road to investigate reports of UFO sightings to separate fact from fantasy.

Host-Investigators: Ted Acworth, William Birnes, Jeff Tominson, Pat Uskert.

Credits: *Executive Producer:* Rob Katz, Craig Piligian, Tom Thayer. *Co-Executive Producer:* Alan David. *Supervising Producer:* Jay Bluemke.

570 The Ugliest House on the Block. (Series; Reality; HGTV; January 4, 2008 to February 8, 2008)

A team of design experts tackle homes that are the eye sore of a neighborhood and, within four days, transform it into the loveliest house on the block.

Host: Chris Leary. **Design Team:** Leslie Segnete, Jeff Rolfe, James Lundy, Michael Baron, Red Barone.

Credits: *Producer:* Madeline Fuste, Thom Hinkle, Jennifer Holbach.

571 Ultimate Recipe Showdown. (Series; Reality; Food Network; Premiered: February 17, 2008)

Nine chefs (per cycle) compete in six cooking challenges (chicken, cakes, pastas, cookie, burgers and comfort foods) with the object being to prepare the best recipes for a $25,000 prize and a version of the winning recipe appearing at a TGIF Friday's restaurant.

Host: Marc Summers, Guy Fieri. Credits: *Executive Producer:* Art Edwards. *Supervising Producer:* Scott Felley.

572 Under One Roof. (Series; Comedy; My Network TV; Premiered: April 16, 2008)

Winston Hill is a wealthy San Francisco real estate businessman; his brother, Calvester (called Cali Cal) is a two-time loser struggling to avoid a third strike and life imprisonment. To help Cal, Winston allows him to live with his family (his wife Ashley and children Heather and Winston, Jr.). Stories follow Cal as he tries to live on the straight and narrow. Heather is gorgeous and totally self-absorbed; Winston, Jr., is highly intellectual but easily impressed by Cal's non-conformist ways; Ashley relishes in the high life and fears Cal's checkered past will ruin her social standing in the community. Su Ho is their housekeeper.

Cast: William "Flavor Flav" Drayton (Calvester Hill), Kelly Perine (Winston Hill, Sr.), Carrie Genzel (Ashley Hill), Marie Michel (Heather Hill), Jesse Reid (Winston Hill, Jr.), Emily Kuroda (Su Ho).

Credits: *Executive Producer:* Claude Brooks, Darryl Quarles. *Co-Executive Producer:* Galila Asres. *Supervising Producer:* Brian K. Roberts. *Producer:* Kirk Shaw. *Associate Producer:* Oliver DeCaigny. *Theme Vocal:* "Under One Roof" by Flavor Flav.

573 Unexplained with George Noory. (Series; Reality; Sci Fi; Premiered: November 16, 2008)

A daily series, based on the radio program of the same title, that explores alien abductions, paranormal phenomena, time travel, witchcraft, reincarnation and similar subjects.

Host: George Noory. Credits: *Executive Producer:* George Noory, Carol Sherman, Jeff Androsky.

574 Unhitched. (Series; Comedy; Fox; March 2, 2008 to March 30, 2008)

Jack "Gator" Gately works at Beacon Street Financial in Boston. He is about to divorce his wife, Nikki. Jack's friends are Kate, a divorce lawyer who broke off a relationship six months earlier; Tommy, who has been married and divorced three times; and Freddy, a doctor whose wife walked out on him and is clueless to everything around him. In essence all four friends are unhitched and stories relate their efforts to find new mates — but always encountering a bit of misadventure as they enter the social scene.

Cast: Craig Bierko (Jack Gately), Rashida Jones (Kate), Johnny Sneed (Tommy), Shaun Majumder (Dr. Freddy Sahgal), Erinn Bartlett (Nikki).

Credits: *Executive Producer:* Peter Farrelly, Bobby Farrelly, Bradley Thomas, Brad Johnson. *Co-Executive Producer:* Mike Bernier, Chris Pappas. *Producer:* Kevin Bartlett, Katy McCaffrey, Randy Cordray. *Director:* Bobby Farrelly, Peter Farrelly. *Writer:* Mike Bernier, Chris Pappas, Kevin Barnett. *Music:* John Nordstrom.

Reviews: "Think *Seinfeld* with a shot of tequila or a raunchy version of *Friends* ... now you're getting the idea of Fox's *Unhitched*, a standout comedy with a lousy title" (*The Hollywood Reporter*).

575 Valentine. (Series; Comedy; CW; October 5, 2008 to November 23, 2008)

Although thought to only exist in ancient Greek mythology, the gods of love are alive and living on Mount Olympus (located in California's Laurel Canyon). Grace Valentine (a.k.a. Aphrodite) is the head of the family, a woman who still believes in the power of love and strives to implement her beliefs on others. Grace and her family are also facing a difficult task. True love is disappearing and being replaced by one night stands and impersonal computer dating. If Grace cannot bring soul mates together, she and her family will lose their powers and become mortal.

Grace is assisted by her sons, Danny (a.k.a. Eros and Cupid, the God of Erotic Love), and Leo (a.k.a. Hercules), and her daughter Phoebe, who has the power of a fortune teller (by placing her hand over the Oracle of Delphi [represented by a hot tub], she can see the past, present and futures of the people they are matching). She is a Titan, a being that is reborn after each death but has no recollection of her prior lives. Grace feels this is not enough. She recruits Kate Providence, a mortal romance novelist she feels understands the human heart and can greatly assist them with her perspective of the human condition.

Valentine, Inc. is the company name by which Grace operates; the gods select the people to be matched; the Valentines (Aphrodite's family) then set out to do what it takes to make true love happen.

Cast: Jaime Murray (Grace Valentine), Christine Lakin (Kate Providence), Kristopher Polaha (Danny Valentine), Autumn Reeser (Phoebe Valentine), Robert Baker (Leo Francisco).

Credits: *Executive Producer:* Courtney B. Conte, Kevin Murphy. *Co-Executive Producer:* Kevin Lenhart, John J. Sakmar. *Supervising Producer:* Kevin Dowling. *Music:* Nathan Wang.

Reviews: "While the hour is not without its charm, it's just a tad too precious for its own good ... it destroys any chance it may have to connect with us on anything greater than a superficial level" (*The Hollywood Reporter*).

"The new comedy ... *Valentine* will certainly need divine intervention" (*Variety*).

576   The Venice Walk. (Series; Drama; Internet; March 2008)

Paco Santana is a former officer with the N.Y.P.D's Juvenile Probation Division. He is concerned about the welfare of children and has relocated to Venice Beach, California, where he becomes a Juvenile Department Probation Officer and placed in charge of a group of teenage delinquents (who attend Venice High School): Mia, Allison, Yo'Bro, Rose, Roger, Mescal and Atlas. The web series (6 to 7 minute episodes) follows Paco as he deals with the problems his charges present to him. Samantha, Paco's friend, is a teacher at the high school.

Cast: Robert Hegyes (Paco Santana), Tiffany Moretti (Samantha), Priscilla Medina (Rose), Dustin Varpness (Mescal), Garrett Plotkin (Roger), Brittany Lan Stewart (Mia), Brea Grant (Allison), Preston Davis (Yo' Bro), Richie Blair (Atlas).

Credits: *Executive Producer:* Brett Hudson, Robert Hegyes. *Producer:* Michael Nallin. *Associate Producer:* Andrea McDonald. *Writer-Director:* Robert Hegyes.

577   A Very Merry Daughter of the Bride. (TV Movie; Comedy-Drama; Lifetime Movie Network; December 20, 2008)

When Roxanne, a twenty-something wedding planner, feels her forty-something widowed mother (Rose) is making a wrong decision about marrying after a whirlwind romance, she plots to sabotage the wedding (to make her mother see she has made a mistake) but finds herself in the same predicament when she falls for an older man.

Cast: JoAnna Garcia (Roxanne), Helen Shaver (Rose), Luke Perry (Charlie), Lorette Clow (Liz Sandor), Christy Greene (Jessica), James D. Hopkin (Martin Sandor), Chantal Perron (Tish), Kenneth Welsh (Jack).

Credits: *Executive Producer:* Josanne B. Lovick, Pamela Wallace. *Producer:* Michael Frislev, Chad Oakes. *Music:* Zack Ryan. *Director:* Leslie Hope. *Writer:* Scott Eastlick, Nadine Van Der Veld.

578   The Victoria's Secret Fashion Show. (Special; Variety; CBS; December 3, 2008)

Gorgeous models (called Angels) displaying the latest in sexy lingerie from Victoria's Secret are seen in musical performances, a runway presentation, red carpet interviews and model profiles. Also presented is a behind-the-scenes look at the making of "The world's most celebrated fashion show." Taped at the legendary Fontainebleau Hotel in Miami Beach, Florida.

Host: Heidi Klum. **Models (Angels):** Alessandra Ambrosio, Selita Ebanks, Doutzen Kroes, Adriana Lima, Marisa Miller, Miranda Kerr. **Musical Guest:** Usher.

Credits: *Executive Producer:* Ed Kazek, Monica Metro, Ian Stewart. *Supervising Producer:* Ric Wanetik. *TV Producer:* Katy Mulla. *Fashion Show Producer:* Susan Schroeder. *Music Director:* Jeremy Healey. *Director:* Hamish Hamilton.

579 The Video Game Awards. (Special; Awards; Spike; December 14, 2008)

Awards program honoring the achievements in the video game industry (including animation, technology, music and performances).

Host: Jack Black. **Guests:** Alex Evans, LL Cool J, Todd Howard, Cliff Bleszinski, Hideo Kojima, 50 Cent, Weezer.

Credits: *Executive Producer:* Albie Hecht. *Supervising Producer:* Gregory Sills. *Producer:* Magda Liolis, Kari Kim. *Director:* Beth McCarthy Miller. *Writer:* Chris DeLuca.

580 Vinegar Hill. (TV Movie; Drama; CBS; May 25, 2008)

A look at the events that befall a dysfunctional family as seen through the eyes of Ellen and her husband, Jake, when they fall on hard times are forced to move in with Jake's family.

Cast: Mary Louise Parker (Ellen Grier), Tim Guinee (Jake Grier), Tom Skerritt (Fritz Grier), Betty Buckley (Mary-Margaret Grier), Larissa Laskin (Barb), Hollis McLaren (Salome), Troy Lalchun (Jake Grier, Jr.), Roberta Maxwell (Ellen's mother), Claire Stone (Amy Grier), Ty Wood (Bert Grier).

Credits: *Executive Producer:* Ira Pincus, Robert Sertner, Frank von Zerneck. *Producer:* Peter Werner, Peter Sadowski. *Music:* Richard Marow. *Writer:* A. Manette Ansay, Suzwette Couture. *Director:* Peter Werner.

Review: "*Vinegar Hill*, an original TV movie that was an Oprah book selection, stars hot property TV actors, has a searing storyline, an extremely well-written script and is directed and acted perfectly" (*New York Post*).

581 Viva Hollywood. (Series; Reality; VH-1; April 13, 2008 to May 25, 2008)

Twelve aspiring Latinas and Latinos actors compete for the opportunity for a role on a Telemundo (Spanish network) series (telenovela). Each of the actors receives guidance from Walter Mercado, an astrologist. Each episode presents an acting challenge and the weakest performers are eliminated. The twelve contenders are all attractive and have definite sex appeal (a must for a Telemundo series). The one actor who best proves his ability to conform to the demands of a telenovela wins the role.

Judges: Maria Conchita Alonso, Carlos Ponce.

Credits: *Executive Producer:* Fenton Bailey, Randy Barbato, Danny Salles. *Supervising Producer:* Tom Greenhut. *Producer:* Gary Stella. *Associate Producer:* Brenda Erazo, Talia Frankel. *Music:* Tor Hyams.

582 Walt Disney World Christmas Day Parade. (Special; Variety; ABC; December 25, 2008)

The 25th telecast of an annual event that features celebrity performances and an array of Disney characters celebrating the holiday season. Taped at the Magic Kingdom in Orlando, Florida.

Host: Regis Philbin, Kelly Ripa, Ryan Seacrest. **Guests:** Miley Cyrus, Billy Ray Cyrus, The Jonas Brothers, Corbin Bleu, David Cook, Sarah Brightman, Jose Feliciano, David Archuleta.

Credits: *Executive Producer:* Andy Perrott. *Producer:* John M. Best, Philip W. Hack, Gary Bormet. *Director:* Ron de Moraes. *Writer:* Eugene Pack.

583 Wanna Bet? (Series; Game; ABC; July 21, 2008 to September 2, 2008)

Ordinary people who claim to be able to perform extraordinary feats are the subjects. Each of the four celebrity guests who appear receive $25,000 betting money and wager any portion of it on the subject's ability to perform the stunt. Each correct prediction by the celebrity (succeed or fail) adds the bet amount to his score; an incorrect guess deducts the amount. The celebrity with the highest cash score wins that amount for his favorite charity.

Hosts: Ant McPartlin, Declow Donnelly.

Credits: *Executive Producer:* Phil Gurin, Marc Jansen, Glenn Weiss. *Co-Executive Producer:* R.A. Clark.

584 Warbirds. (TV Movie; Horror; Sci Fi; April 19, 2008)

Strange tale of Word War II, U.S. soldiers propelled to an island inhabited by prehistoric creatures.

Cast: Brian Krause (Jack Toller), Jamie Elle Mann (Max West), Tohoru Masamune (Ozu), Lucy Faust (Hoodsie Smith), David Jensen (W.R. Hamilton), Gizza Elizondo (Vicky Teeling), Stephanie Honore (Lana), John McCarthy (Sgt. Murphy), Caleb Michaelson (John Lee).

Credits: *Executive Producer:* William R. Greenblatt. *Producer:* Kevin Gendreau, Jason Hewitt. *Writer-Director:* Kevin Gendreau.

585 Watching the Detectives. (Series; Reality; Biography Channel; Premiered: September 7, 2008)

Recreations of crime cases that were investigated by actual New York City police detectives.

Credits: *Supervising Producer:* Robyn Younie, Karey Green. *Producer:* Shirley Tatum. *Associate Producer:* Bryan Ranharter.

586 Welcome to the Captain. (Series; Comedy; CBS; January 4, 2008 to February 26, 2008)

Josh Flug is a washed up Hollywood writer and director (he won an Oscar five years ago but his career hasn't progressed). Hoping to reestablish his career he takes up residence at the Captain, a fabled Hollywood hotel that is home to a group of eccentric people. Stories relate Josh's reactions to the people he befriends: Uncle Saul a former writer for *Three's Company*; Charlene Van Ark, a former soap star; Jesus, the blabbermouth desk clerk; Hope, a gorgeous girl studying Chinese medicine; and Marty, his former college roommate.

Cast: Jeffrey Tambor (Saul Fish), Fran Kranz (Josh Flug), Chris Klein (Marty Tanner), JoAnna Garcia (Hope), Raquel Welch (Charlene Van Ark), Al Madrigal (Jesus).

Credits: *Executive Producer:* John Hamburg, Andrew Riech, Ted Cohen. *Co-Executive Producer:* Liz Astrof, Sherry Bilsing, Tucker Cawley, Ellen Plummer. *Co-Producer:* Anders Barr. *Music:* Tree Adams.

Reviews: "Inserted in the midst of the CBS Monday night comedy block, the show brings a light heart and a deft comedic touch to bear on the foibles and stereotypes of Hollywood" (*The Hollywood Reporter*).

"While there's enough here to recommend checking out *Welcome to the Captain*, let's just say reservations are warranted whether the show will be checking in for an extended stay" (*Variety*).

587 The Wendy Williams Show. (Pilot; Talk; Fox; July 14, 2008 to August 22, 2008)

New York radio "shock jock" Wendy Williams hosts a live daily program that features interviews with celebrities from all walks of life. A six week test that ran on Fox stations in New York, Los Angeles, Dallas and Detroit.

Host: Wendy Williams.

Credits: *Executive Producer:* Rob Dauber, Wendy Williams, Kevin Hunter. *Supervising Producer:* Elise Silvestri. *Producer:* Joelle Dawson, Lorraine Haughton, Alia Zamel. *Director:* Deborah Miller.

Review: "The daytime talker starring the longtime New York radio fixture and shock jock ... looks uncomfortable and out of her element at the outset of a show that has six weeks to get right" (*The Hollywood Reporter*).

588   Whacked Out Videos. (Series; Reality; My Network TV; January 2, 2008 to April 2, 2008)

Clips of very bizarre videos taken from various sources from around the world.

Narrator: Mark O'Brien.

Credits: *Executive Producer:* Harley Tat, Mark O'Brien, Jon Kramer, Mark Rafalowski. *Co-Executive Producer:* Dennis Principe. *Supervising Producer:* Michel Grodner. *Music:* Devin Powers.

589   Whatever Martha. (Series; Comedy; Fine Living Network; Premiered: September 16, 2008)

Alexis Stewart, the daughter of how to diva Martha Stewart, and her friend, Jennifer Koppelman Hutt, screen old episodes of *The Martha Stewart Show* to poke fun at (with Martha's approval) what they are seeing.

Cast: Alexis Stewart, Jennifer Koppelman Hutt.

Credits: *Executive Producer:* Martha Stewart.

590   When We Left Earth: The NASA Missions. (Series; Documentary; Discovery Channel; June 8, 2008 to July 13, 2008)

The first 50 years of the NASA space program is explored beginning with the Mercury program (the first attempt to put a man in space) to the moon landings to the first un-tethered space walk by Bruce McCandless.

Narrator: Gary Sinise.

Credits: *Executive Producer:* Bill Howard, Richard Dale. *Producer:* Tyler Butterworth, Daniel Hall. *Music:* Richard Blair-Oliphant.

Reviews: "...a new look at how the moon was won ... keep in mind ... that with the focus so squarely on NASA, there is little reference to other concurrent but related events, such as domestic politics and the Cold War" (*The Hollywood Reporter*).

"Without a doubt ... the best and most important telling to one of the best and most important accomplishments of the 20th century — the race into space and to the moon" (*New York Post*).

591   When Women Ruled the World. (Series; Reality; Fox Reality Channel; March 3, 2008 to April 17, 2008)

Eighteen women and 18 men are brought together on a remote island for a role reversal test to see what will happen if women are in charge and men are subservient. A mythical society is set up and episodes relate the efforts of the women to boss and the men to obey.

Host: Judith Shekoni.

Credits: *Executive Producer:* Chris Cowan, Jean-Michel Michenaud. *Co-Executive Producer:* Scott Jeffrees. *Producer:* Missy Bania, Jeff Becko, Alison Martino. *Director:* Gary Shaffer.

592   Who Are You Wearing? (Series; Reality; TLC; August 22, 2008 to October 24, 2008)

Ordinary people with a flair for fashion are given the opportunity of a lifetime — design a dress for a celebrity for a red carpet event.

Host: Keisha Whitaker.

Credits: _Executive Producer:_ Fernando J. Hernandez. _Producer:_ Stephen Brophy. _Director:_ David Charles Sullivan.

593 Why I Ran. (Series; Reality; Biography Channel; Premiered: September 1, 2008)

A look at high speed police chases as seen from the driver's perspective with first hand accounts from the actual people involved.

Credits: _Executive Producer:_ Robert Sharenow, Elaine Bryant, Mechelle Collins, Kevin Dill. _Supervising Producer:_ Jessica Morgan.

594 Wilfred. (Series; Comedy; Internet; 2008)

A look at the life of a dog (actor in costume) named Wilfred as portrayed as if he were human and plagued by life's endless problems — from loneliness, anxiety to behavioral problems. Produced in Australia and first seen in the U.S. on IFC.com. Carol and Adam are Wilfred's human neighbors.

Cast: Jason Gann (Wilfred), Cindy Waddingham (Carol), Adam Zwar (Adam).

Credits: _Producer:_ Jenny Livingston. _Director:_ Tony Rogers.

595 Will You Merry Me? (TV Movie; Comedy; Lifetime Movie Network; December 13, 2008)

Henry Kringle, a Christian living in Los Angeles, and Rebecca Fine, a Jewish girl from Madison, Wisconsin, meet, fall in love and plan to marry. The story follows the problems that arise within their respective families when they announce their engagement just before Christmas and find themselves in a clash of religious tradition when Rebecca's parents try to observe Christmas to please Henry's parents and Henry's parents' efforts to observe Hanukah and please Rebecca's parents.

Cast: Tommy Lioutas (Henry Kringle), Vikki Krinsky (Rebecca Fine), Wendie Malick (Suzie Fine), Cynthia Stevenson (Marilyn Kringle), David Eisner (Marvin Fine), Patrick McKenna (Hank Kringle), Reagan Pasternak (Kristy Easterbrook), Richard Waugh (the Reverend Bill).

Credits: _Executive Producer:_ Fernando Szew. _Producer:_ Mary Panteldis, Marc B. Lorber. _Director:_ Nisha Ganatra. _Writer:_ Karen McClellan.

596 Wipeout. (Series; Game; ABC; June 24, 2008 to September 16, 2008)

Twenty-four ordinary men and women compete for a $50,000 grand prize by tackling an extreme obstacle course. The first three rounds eliminate the 20 weakest performers (those who run the obstacle course in the best time continue on). The four remaining players compete in the Wipeout competition. The one player who is able to run a very difficult obstacle course in the least amount of time wins $50,000.

Host: John Anderson, John Henson. **Field Host:** Jill Wagner. **Announcer:** Ellen K.

Credits: _Executive Producer:_ Matt Kunitz. _Co-Executive Producer:_ Shye Sutherland. _Supervising Producer:_ Kevin Wehrenberg. _Producer:_ Brent Jacoby.

597 Wire in the Blood. (Series; Crime Drama; BBC America; Premiered: April 6, 2008)

Dr. Tony Hill is a clinical psychologist with the ability to tap into his own dark side and place himself in the head of serial killers. Dr. Hill lives in the fictional town of Bradfield (in Yorkshire, England) and stories relate his efforts, working with vice squad detectives, to apprehend killers before they strike again. Produced in England.

Cast: Robson Green (Dr. Tony Hill), Simone Lahbib (Det. Alex Fielding), Mark Letheren (Det. Kevin Geoffries), Emma Handy (Det. Paula McIntyre), Hermoine Norris (Det. Carol Jordan).

Credits: _Executive Producer:_ Sandra Jobling, Kathryn Mitchell. _Producer:_ Philip

Leach. *Associate Producer:* Tina Murray. *Music:* The Insects.

598 Wisegal. (TV Movie; Drama; Lifetime; March 15, 2008)

Fact based tale about Patty Montanari, the single mother of two children, who becomes involved with the mob when she begins dating wiseguy Frank Russo and soon finds herself running a nightclub and laundering money across the Canadian border.

Cast: Alyssa Milano (Patty Montanari), Jason Gedrick (Frank Russo), James Caan (Salvatore Palmeri), Alessandro Costantini (Joey Montanari), Gina Wilkinson (Mary Russo), Zak Longo (Mouse Russo), Gabriel Hogan (Robert Wilson).

Credits: *Executive Producer:* Anthony Melchiorri, Daniel H. Blatt, Joseph D. Pistone, Leo Rossi. *Producer:* Terry Gould, Alyssa Milano. *Writer:* Shelley Evans. *Director:* Jerry Ciccoritti. *Music:* John Frizzell.

599 Woke Up Dead. (Series; Comedy; Internet; 2008)

A "Zombie Comedy" about a University of Southern California student who wakes up one morning underwater and in a bathtub. He suspects that he may be dead and the 50 episode series follows the student as he ponders his new existence as a zombie.

Star: John Fasano.

Credits: *Producer:* Brent V. Friedman, Stan Rogow, Jeff Sagansky. *Writer-Director:* John Fasano.

600 Women Behind Bars. (Series; Reality; WE; 2008)

A stark, true look at hardened women whose lives are now restricted to prison. Anthology-like stories are in-depth portraits of women and the crimes they committed.

Credits: *Executive Producer:* John Burrud. *Co-Executive Producer:* Richard Swindell. *Supervising Producer:* Ashley Crary.

Producer: Hillary Heath. *Music:* Craig Dobbin, Jesse Rhodes.

601 The World Magic Awards (2007). (Special; Variety; My Network TV; January 1, 2008)

The 2007 awards presentation in which the world's best magicians are honored (and who also perform their most amazing feats).

Host: Roger Moore. **Announcer:** James Romanovich.

Credits: *Executive Producer:* Gay Blackstone, David McKenzie, Paul Sharratt. *Producer:* Brad Thomas, Christian Moore, John Ross. *Director:* Mark Mardoyan, David McKenzie. *Magic Director:* Gay Blackstone.

602 The World Magic Awards (2008). (Special; Variety; My Network TV; November 26, 2008)

An awards ceremony that honors the best magicians in the following fields: Best Escape Artist, Best Classic Magic, Best Contemporary Magic, Best Original Cabaret Magic, Best Duo Cabaret Magic, Best Cabaret Male Magic, Best Cabaret Female Magic, Best Comedy Magic, Best Illusionist, Best Stage Magician, Best Teen Magician and Magician of the Year.

Host: Neil Patrick Harris. **Performers:** Ed Alonzo, Roxanne, Lance Burton, Hans Kluk, The Amazing Jonathan, Florian Zimmer. **Presenters:** Melora Hardin, Ernie Hudson, Christopher Massey, Kyle Massey, Sofia Milos, John Schneider, D.B. Sweeney, Corbin Bernsen, Traci Bingham.

Credits: *Executive Producer:* David McKenzie, Paul Sharratt, Gay Blackstone. *Supervising Producer:* Brad Thomas. *Music Director:* John Ross. *Director:* Mark Mardoyan. *Writer:* Steve Jarczak. *Announcer:* James Romanovich.

603 The World Music Awards 2008. (Special; Variety; My Network TV; November 2, 2008)

The 20th annual event that honors excellence in music (based on CD sales and legally downloaded songs from the Internet; illegal downloads are not counted). Taped in Monte Carlo.

Host: Jesse Metcalfe, Michelle Williams. **Guests:** Mariah Carey, Alicia Keyes, Chase Crawford, Ringo Starr, Laurent Wolfe, Beyonce, Kid Rock, Solange, The Killers, Ne-Yo, Kate Ryan, Anastasia.

Credits: *Executive Producer:* Melissa Corken, John Martinolli. *Producer:* Peter Baron. *Producer-Director:* Jason Shepherd. *Writer:* Jake Yapp.

604   The World of Quest. (Series; Cartoon; Kids WB; March 15, 2008 to September 27, 2008)

Prince Nestor, the son of the king and queen of Odyssia, has begun a quest: find his missing parents, who have been kidnapped by the evil Lord Spite (who wants to rule the land). Stories follow Nestor as he and his assistants, Grarer and Quest, attempt to defeat Lord Spite and free the king and queen.

Voice Cast: Landon Norris (Prince Nestor), Ron Pardo (Quest/Grarer), James Rankin (Lord Spite), Melissa Altro (Way), Kedar Brown (Gatling/General Ogun), Krystal Meadows (Anna Maht).

Credits: *Executive Producer:* Michael Hirsh, Tope Taylor, John Vandervelde, Stephen Sustoissic, Pamela Slavin. *Supervising Producer:* Tom Stevens.

605   The World's Funniest Moments. (Series; Comedy; My Network TV; Premiered: October 7, 2008)

Clip show that borrows blooper-like scenes from the Internet as well as from amateur productions from around the world.

Host: Arsenio Hall.

Credits: *Executive Producer:* David McKenzie, James Romanovich, Paul Sharratt. *Producer:* Dan Goldman.

606   Worst Week. (Series; Comedy; CBS; Premiered: September 22, 2008)

If something can go wrong it will and it will happen to Sam Briggs, a likeable young man who works as an assistant editor for a magazine called *Cap Weekly.* It appears that Sam is "blessed" with bad luck and has accepted that fact. He can't avoid it and has learned to live with it and the after-effects of each experience. Sam is engaged to Melanie "Mel" Anne Clayton, a girl who has learned to live with Sam's mishaps because she honestly loves him. Stories follow Sam as he struggles to get through each day with as little bad luck as possible. Richard "Dick" Clayton, a respected judge, is Mel's father; Angela is her mother; Chloe is Mel's sister; Scotty is Chloe's son; Paul and Sheila are Sam's parents. Based on the British series *Worst Week of My Life.*

Cast: Kyle Bornheimer (Sam Briggs), Erinn Hayes (Melanie Clayton), Kurtwood Smith (Dick Clayton), Nancy Lenehan (Angela Clayton), Brooke Nevin (Chloe Clayton), Parris Mosteller (Scotty Clayton), Fred Willard (Paul Briggs), Connie Ray (Sheila Briggs).

Credits: *Executive Producer:* Matt Tarses, Jimmy Mulville. *Co-Executive Producer:* Adam Bernstein. *Producer:* Matthew Nodella. *Music:* David Schwartz.

Reviews: "Almost certainly the most promising newcomer of the fall, *Worst Week* only tempers enthusiasm because the opener is so intricate it's difficult to envision what the series can do for an encore, much less an entire season" (*Variety*).

"...dopey new sitcom *Worst Week*, one of the worst new shows of the week" (*New York Post*).

607   Worst Week of My Life. (Series; Comedy; BBC America; 2008)

The British series on which *Worst Week* is based. Howard and Mel Steel are a happily married but unusual couple: they are "blessed" with bad luck. No matter what they do, alone or together, the unfortunate happens and stories, which are presented in seven episode cycles, represent the events of a single day in their hectic lives.

Cast: Ben Miller (Howard Steel), Sarah Alexander (Mel Steel), Alison Steadman (Angela Cook), Geoffrey Whitehead (Dick Cook).

Credits: *Executive Producer:* Cheryl Taylor, Mario Stylianider, Mark Freelane. *Producer:* Mark Bussell, Justin Sbresni. *Music:* Nina Humphreys.

608   Yeti: Curse of the Snow Beast. (TV Movie; Horror; Sci Fi; November 8, 2008)

Survival tale about a group of passengers and their efforts to defeat a murderous snow creature when they are stranded in the Himalayas after airplane crash.

Cast: Peter DeLuise (John Sheppard), Carly Pope (Sarah), Josh Emerson (Andrew), Crystal Lowe (Ashley), Elfina Luk (Kyra), Brandon Jay Laren (Rice), Kris Pope (Rafael Garcia), Marc Menard (Peyton Elway), Adam O'Byrne (James De-Ravin).

Credits: *Executive Producer:* Eric Gozlan, Dana Dubovsky, Michael Greenfield. *Producer:* Aaron Barnett, Mark Lester, Wendy Kay Moore. *Music:* Michael Richard Plowman. *Director:* Paul Ziller. *Writer:* Rafael Jordan.

609   You Must Remember This: The Warner Bros. Story. (Special; Documentary; PBS; September 23, 2008 to September 25, 2008)

A fascinating, clip rich look at the 85 year history of Warner Bros.—from the era of silent films to the contemporary films of today.

Narrator: Clint Eastwood. **Appearing:** George Clooney, Faye Dunaway, Warren Beatty, Carroll Baker, Lauren Bacall, Jane Fonda, Goldie Hawn, Dustin Hoffman, Shirley Jones, Joan Leslie, Jack Nicholson, Robert Redford, Martin Scorsese, Connie Stevens, Barbra Streisand, Joanne Woodward.

Credits: *Executive Producer:* Clint Eastwood. *Producer-Writer-Director:* Richard Schickel.

610   Young American Bodies. (Series; Documentary; Internet; 2008)

An intimate, no holds barred look at the intersecting love lives of a group of young (twenty-something) people. Contains nudity.

Cast: Nikita Wood, Kris Williams, Nathan Adloff, Mollie Leibovitz, Eve Rounds.

Credits: *Producer-Writer-Director:* Joe Swanberg. *Co-Producer-Writer:* Kris Williams.

611   Your Mama Don't Dance. (Series; Reality; Lifetime; February 28, 2008 to April 18, 2008)

Ten couples compete, each comprised of a parent and their child. Each couple receives professional coaching on the particular dance competition of the week. The poorest performing couples are eliminated on a weekly basis (based on the observations of celebrity judges). The one remaining team is awarded a cash prize.

Cast: Ian Ziering (Host), Marguerite Pomerhn-Derricks (Choreographer), Collen Fitzpatrick (Judge), Ben Vereen (Judge), Cris Judd (Judge).

Credits: *Executive Producer:* Linda Lea, Dave Noll, Bob Bain. *Co-Executive Producer:* Stephanie Chambers, Paul Flattery. *Supervising Producer:* Nate Green. *Consulting Producer:* Gregory Sills. *Senior Field Producer:* Jennifer Morton. *Field Producer:* Brandice DeVeau.

612   Z Rock. (Series; Comedy; IFC; August 24, 2008 to October 26, 2008)

Brothers Paulie and David Z and their best friend, Joey Cassata, are the rock band Z Rock. They live in New York City (born in Brooklyn) and are struggling to make the big time. To make ends meet, the group performs in clubs at night (as Z Rock) and by day (as the band Z Brothers) on the kiddie party circuit (entertaining the children of wealthy Manhattan parents). Stories, which are partly improvised, follow the group as they begin the rocky climb to musical stardom. Dina is their manager; Becky is Joey's girlfriend; Neil is their foul-mouthed gay friend.

Cast: David Z (Himself), Paulie Z (Himself), Joey Cassata (Himself), Lynne Koplitz (Dina), Allison Becker (Becky), Jay Oakerson (Neil)

Credits: *Executive Producer:* Mark Farrell, Mark Elfman, Andrew Gottlieb. *Co-Executive Producer:* Bob Held, Lynn Lendway, Stephen J. Castagnola. *Producer:* Lindsay Freed.

Reviews: "*Z-Rock* is effortlessly, genuinely hilarious. It blends reality with improv dialogue and clever shitick in a way that's never forced" (*The Hollywood Reporter*).

"The good news: the concept, which is terrific; the bad: the writing is high school Internet level" (*New York Post*).

613   Zane's Sex Chronicles. (Series; Anthology; Cinemax; Premiered: October 11, 2008)

Erotic adaptations of African-American short stories penned by Zane, a New York Times best-selling author. The adult stories feature strong sexual situations and female nudity.

Credits: *Executive Producer:* Suzanne De Passe, Zane, Madison Jones. *Producer:* Suzanne Coston. *Co-Producer:* Adam Doench, Christopher Gosch, Lelly Mendelsohn.

614   The Zula Patrol. (Series; Cartoon; NBC; Premiered: September 20, 2008)

Zula, a distant planet from the Earth, is responsible for the safety of the universe. The Zula Patrol (Bula, Multo, Zetter, Wizzy and Wiggy) are Zula agents who perform missions to insure that goodness prevails. Computer animated stories, which are geared to children, relate scientific lessons as the Zula Patrol performs missions. Each episode concludes with a "Multo Moment" (wherein Multo explains an aspect of science to children).

Voices: Tom Burns, Erik J. Anderson, Les Abell, Cathy Carlisle, Dorothy Manchester, Michelle Nichols, Gay Pettibone, Katherine Sullivan, Kathleen Swan, Michael Montgomery.

Credits: *Executive Producer:* Debroah Manchester, Beth Hubbard, Margaret Loesch, Dan Angel, Bruce Stein. *Co-Executive Producer:* Dana Tafoya-Bodton. *Music and Theme:* Jeff Dana.

PART II

....

Returning Series — Debuted Prior to 2008

615 **Access Hollywood**. (Variety; Syn.; Premiered: September 1996)

A daily entertainment series that presents the latest gossip on celebrities, movies, TV shows, music and other entertainment fields.

Host: Nancy O'Dell, Billy Bush, Larry Mendte, Giselle Fernandez, Pat O'Brien. **Credits:** *Executive Producer:* Jonathan P. Goodman, Joseph R. Lynch, David Hall, David Hedges, Rob Silverstein. *Producer:* Ann Lewis. *Music:* David Leon, Jeremy Sweet.

616 **According to Jim**. (Comedy; ABC; Premiered: October 3, 2001)

Jim (no last name) lives in Chicago and is the owner of Grounds Up Designs (a construction company). He is married to Cheryl and they are the parents of Gracie, Ruby and Kyle. Jim has his own ideas about everything and his efforts to implement them and prove himself right is the focal point of the series. Dana is Cheryl's sister; Andy is her brother; Ryan is Dana's boyfriend, later husband. The series ended its season run on May 27, 2008. When it returned with new episodes (November 2, 2008), Cheryl and Jim were now also the parents of infant twins (Gordon and Jonathan). Dana and Ryan are no longer a part of the series (characters were said to have moved to Los Angeles) and stories were revised somewhat to now focus on Jim as he attempts to deal with (and help Cheryl even more than before) raise five children. Emily is Andy's girlfriend. Tara Strong is credited as the twins crying voice.

Cast: Jim Belushi (Jim), Courtney Thorne-Smith (Cheryl), Kimberly Williams (Dana), Larry Jo Campbell (Andy), Billi Bruno (Gracie), Taylor Atelian (Ruby), Connor and Grant Sullivan (Kyle), Anthony and Brian Toro (Kyle), Connor Rayburn (Kyle), Mitch Rouse (Dr. Ryan Gibson), Mo Collins (Emily). **Credits:** *Executive Producer:* Suzanne

Bukinik, Tracy Newman, Marc Gurvitz, James Belushi, Marshall Boone, Jonathan Stark. *Co-Executive Producer:* Nastara Dibai, Warren Bell, Bob Nickman, Howard J. Morris, Jeffrey Hodes, Tracy Gamble. *Supervising Producer:* Jason Fisher. *Producer:* John D. Beck, Sylvia Green, Harry Hannigan, Robert Heath. *Music:* Jim Belushi, Jonathan Wolff, Rich Ragsdael, Scott Clausen. *Theme:* Jim Belushi and the Sacred Hearts.

617 **Ace of Cakes**. (Reality; Food Network; Premiered: August 17, 2006)

A look at extreme cake making (for example, cakes shaped like cars, buildings) with Chef Duff Goldman.

Host: Duff Goldman. **Credits:** *Executive Producer:* Lauren Lexton, Tom Rogan. *Co-Executive Producer:* Willie Goldman, Kelly McPherson. *Producer:* Michael Bouson.

618 **The Adrenaline Project**. (Reality; Fox; September 29, 2007 to April 5, 2008)

Five teenagers compete in various athletic contests for the title of "The Ultimate Adrenalite."

Host: Richard Cazeau. **Stunt Coordinator:** Boomer Phillips. **Credits:** *Producer:* Mark J.W. Bishop, Matt Hornburg. *Supervising Producer:* Roberta Pazdro. *Associate Producer:* Nicki Skinner, Nicole McKechnie.

619 **Afro Samurai**. (Cartoon; Spike; Premiered: January 4, 2007)

Vengeance themed adult cartoon about Afro, an African American samurai who must overcome numerous obstacles to defeat Justice, the man who killed his father (Rokutaro), but a man who also happens to be the number one fighter in the world. Ninja Ninja is Afro's chatty companion.

Voice Cast: Samuel L. Jackson (Afro/ Ninja Ninja), Ron Perlman (Justice), Greg Eagles (Rokutaro), Lucy Liu (Sio), Mark Hamill (Bin). **Credits:** *Executive Producer:*

Samuel L. Jackson, Takashi Okazaki, Eric Garcia, Julie Yorn. *Producer:* Alex Gartiner. *Music:* RZA.

620 Afterworld. (Science Fiction; Internet; Premiered: August 23, 2007)

Has the world ended? Russell Shoemaker, a Seattle advertising executive on a business trip to New York City, believes so. He wakes up one morning and finds that virtually the entire population has been vaporized (due to an atomic blast). Stories follow Russell as he struggles to find a way back to Seattle to learn the fate of his wife and child.

Cast: Roark Critchlow (Russell Shoemaker), Tonya Cornelisse (Amy), Stephanie Wiand (Joan), Graham Sibley (Arlen). **Credits:** *Producer:* Jon Alexander Reed, Adam Sigel.

621 Aliens in America. (Comedy; CW; October 1, 2007 to August 31, 2008)

Franny and Gary Tolchuck and their children Claire and Justin live in Medora, a conservative community in Wisconsin. Franny is a take-charge woman; Gary is an aspiring entrepreneur; Claire is a gorgeous and popular teenager; Justin is 16 years old, shy, insecure and socially awkward. In an attempt to help Justin, Claire hits on a plan to host a foreign exchange student — one she envisions as "an athletic, brilliant Nordic teen." What the family gets is Raja Mursharaff, a 16-year-old Muslim from a small Pakistan village. Raja, as foreign as foreigners can be in Medora, is thoughtful, wise and responsible — not what Franny had in mind to help Justin achieve "coolness." Justin is not too thrilled about Raja until he gets to know him and becomes his guide to introduce him to the American way of life. Stories follow Raja's experiences as he attempts to become part of a society that he finds intriguing but totally foreign to him.

Cast: Dan Byrd (Justin Tolchuck), Amy Pietz (Franny Tolchuck), Scott Patterson (Gary Tolchuck), Lindsey Shaw (Claire Tolchuck), Adhir Kalyan (Raja Mursharaff). **Credits:** *Executive Producer:* David Guarascio, Moses Port, Tim Doyle. *Co-Executive Producer:* Richard Day, Michael Glouberman. *Producer:* Michael Pendell. *Associate Producer:* Matthew Conner. *Music:* Adam Gorgoni.

622 All Grown Up. (Cartoon; Nickelodeon; Premiered: April 12, 2003)

An updated version of *The Rugrats* that advances the infants to the age of ten. The former Rugrats gang (Tommy, Chuckie, Susie, Angelica, Kimi, Betty, Phil and Lil) are as mischievous as ever and stories relate their adventures as adolescents.

Voice Cast: Elizabeth Daly (Tommy Pickles), Nancy Cartwright (Phil and Lil), Kath Soucie (Betty DeVille), Dionne Quan (Kimi Finster), Cheryl Chase (Angelica Pickles), Cree Summer (Susie Carmichael), Meagan Smith (Rachael), Lizzie Murray (Nicole Moscarelli), Shayna Fox (Savannah), Clancy Brown (Estes Pangborn), Tara Strong (Dil Pickles), Jack Riley (Stu Pickles), Melanie Chartoff (Didi Pickles), Michael Bell (Chazz Finster/Drew Pickles), Julia Kato (Kira Finster), Tress MacNeille (Charlotte Pickles), Joe Alaskey (Grandpa Lou Pickles). **Credits:** *Producer:* Sheila M. Anthony, Erin Ehrlich. *Music:* Mark Mothersbaugh, Robert Mothersbaugh.

623 All My Children. (Drama; ABC; Premiered: January 5, 1970)

Dramatic incidents in the lives of the Tyler and Martin families, residents of the community of Pine Valley.

Principal 2008 Cast: Susan Lucci (Erica Kane), David Canary (Adam Chandler, Sr./Stuart Chandler), Ray MacDonnell (Joseph Martin, Sr.), Eileen Herlie (Myrtle Fargate), Amanda Baker (Arabella "Babe"Chandler), Tamara Braun (Reese), Rebecca Budig (Greenlee Smythe), Bobbie Eakes (Krystal Carey Martin), Melissa Claire Egan (Annie McDermott Lavery), Beth Ehlers (Taylor Thompson), Cameron

Mathison (Ryan Lavery), Michael E. Knight (Thaddeus Martin), Thorsten Kaye (Zachary Slater), Vincent Irizarry (David Hayward), Ricky Paull Goldin (Joseph "Jake" Martin), Alicia Minshew (Kendall Hart Slater), Brianne Moncrief (Colby Chandler), Debbi Morgan (Angela Hubbard), Eden Riegel (Bianca Montgomery), Chrishell Stause (Amanda Dillon), Denise Vasi (Randi Morgan), Jacob Young (Adam "JR" Chandler, Jr.), Darnell Williams (Jesse Hubbard), Walt Willey (Jackson Montgomery), Aiden Turner (Aidan Devane), Sterling Sulieman (Dre Woods), Cornelius Smith, Jr. (Frank Hubbard), James Mitchell (Palmer Cortlandt), Lee Meriwether (Ruth Martin), Rebecca Levine (Jenny Martin), Jill Larson (Opal), Daniel Kennedy (Peter Cortlandt), Shannon Kane (Natalia), Cheryl Hulteen (Winifred), Joel Fabiani (Barry Shire), Elizabeth Rodriquez (Carmen "Sugar" Morales), Jennifer Bassey (Marian Colby Chandler), Jenna DiMartini (Corinna Vasquez). **Credits:** *Executive Producer:* Julie Hanan Carruthers. *Theme Music:* David Benoit. *Creator:* Agnes Nixon.

624 The Amazing Race. (Reality; CBS; September 5, 2001 to December 8, 2008)

Eleven teams, each composed of two members, race around the world to arrive at specific destinations on time or face elimination if they fail to do so. The grand prize is $1 million and teams have to overcome overwhelming challenges to come out on top. The one successful team wins the money. Returned for a new cycle on February 15, 2009.

Host: Phil Keoghan. **Credits:** *Executive Producer:* Scott Einziger, Amy Chacon, Jonathan Littman, Jon Kroll, Evan Weinstein, Hayman Washington, Allison Gardner, Don Wollman, Kathleen French, Rich Meehan, Paul Romer, Douglas Ross, Arnold Shapiro, Greg Stewart, J. Rupert Thompson. *Supervising Producer:* Alex Rader, Elsie Doganieri, Eric Wagenen,

Mark A. Vertullo, John Platt, Tracy Green, Daniel Sorseth. *Music:* Ray Colcord.

625 American Dad. (Cartoon; Fox; Premiered: February 6, 2005)

A comical look at the life of a paranoid CIA agent (Stan Smith) and his family: his wife, Francine, Steve and Hayley, their children (attend Pearl Bailey High School); Roger, an alien Stan rescued from the notorious Area 51 in New Mexico; and Klaus, a botched attempt to transplant a German man's brain into a fish.

Voice Cast: Seth MacFarlane (Stan Smith/Roger), Wendy Schaal (Francine Smith), Rachael MacFarlane (Hayley Smith), Scott Grimes (Steve Smith), Dee Bradley (Klaus). **Credits:** *Executive Producer:* Mike Barker, Seth MacFarlane, Matt Weitzman. *Co-Executive Producer:* David Hemingston, David Zuckerman, Rick Wiener, Michael Shipley, Kenny Schwartz, Jim Bernstein. *Supervising Producer:* Dan Vebber, Josh Bycel, Jonathan Fener, Carter Bays, Craig Thomas. *Producer:* Nahnatcka Khan, Brian Boyle, Karen Vallow. *Music:* Walter Murphy.

626 American Gangster. (Documentary; BET; Premiered: November 28, 2006)

Documentary-like stories that examine the lives of African-American criminals and the impact they have had on the communities in which they grew up.

Narrator: Ving Rhames. **Credits:** *Executive Producer:* Nelson George, Steven Michaels, Frank Sinton, Arthur Smith, Ken T. Weed. *Supervising Producer:* Mark Rowland. *Producer:* Henry Schipper, Shola Lynch, Yvonne Smith, Anthony Storm. *Music:* Mark Qura Ranki, Derryck Thornton.

627 American Idol. (Reality; Fox; June 11, 2002 to May 21, 2008)

Aspiring singers compete for a recording contract, fame and the title "American Idol." The contestants are judged by a panel but cannot be eliminated by them (only offered opinions). Home audience votes determine who goes and who stays and who becomes an American idol. Returned for a new cycle on January 13, 2009.

Host: Ryan Seacrest. **Judges:** Simon Cowell, Paula Abdul, Randy Jackson. Kara DioGuardi becomes a fourth judge in 2009. **Credits:** *Executive Producer:* Simon Fuller, Ken Warwick, Nigel Lythgoe, Simon Jones, Cecile Frot-Coutaz. *Supervising Producer:* David Goffin. *Producer:* Nicola Gaham, John Entz, Tarbenia Jones, Ron DeShay, Billy Cooper, Andy Meyer, Beth McNamara. *Associate Producer:* Katie Fennelly, Norm Betts, Nikki Boelle, Megan Michaels, Patrick Lynn, Jessica Kelly. *Music:* Shawn K. Clement, Cathy Dennis, Jeremy Sweet, Ricky Minor.

628 American Idol Rewind. (Reality; Syn.; Premiered: September 1, 2006)

Highlights of past seasons of *American Idol* (beginning with the first season in 2002) that excludes the viewer call-in voting segments but includes additional footage of casting calls, auditions, behind-the-scenes activity and song rehearsals.

Host: Ryan Seacrest. **Judges:** Simon Cowell, Paula Abdul, Randy Jackson. **Credits:** *Executive Producer:* Doug James. *Supervising Producer:* Shantel Klinger, Justin Hochberg. *Producer:* Missy Bania, John Petro, Ashley Edens.

629 American Justice. (Reality; A&E; Premiered: September 15, 1992)

Criminal cases are profiled with a look at the investigative methods used to bring them to successful conclusions. The program also profiles the police, witnesses, victims and perpetrators involved in each case.

Host: Bill Kurtis. **Credits:** *Executive Producer:* Jonathan Towers. *Supervising Producer:* Matt Palm, David Boodell. *Producer:* Charles Fitzgerald, Mary Boylan, Jennifer Maiotti.

630 American Masters. (Documentary; PBS; Premiered: June 23, 1986)

A tribute to American creative artists past and present. Presented as a series of specials.

Credits: *Executive Producer:* Jac Venza, Susan Lacy, Prudence Glall, Calvin Sacks. *Supervising Producer:* Julie Sacks. *Producer:* Susan Steinberg, Kirk D'Amico, James Hacker, Brian McDonald, Kenneth Bowser, Julia Schlossberg, Michael Epstein. *Music:* Thomas Wagner, Todd Boekelheidi, Joel Goodman.

631 American Princess. (Reality; WE; August 7, 2005 to October 7, 2008)

Twenty uncouth, rude, ill-mannered American women (who also lack social skills) are brought to England to master the fine art of British society. Each of the women are put through a series of tasks to find the one woman who can change her crude ways to become a dignified lady. The one woman who most improves herself receives a golden tiara and the title "American Princess."

Host: Mark Durden-Smith. **Credits:** *Executive Producer:* Rachel Ashdown, Laura Fuest, Jeff Thacker. *Supervising Producer:* David Rupel.

632 America's Ballroom Challenge. (Reality; PBS; Premiered: February 1, 2006)

Six couples compete for the title of "America's Best Ballroom Dancers." The first four programs feature the couples competing in the categories of American Rhythm, American Smooth, International Standard and International Latin. The weakest couple in each category is eliminated. The fifth and final episode features a dance-off between the two remaining couples.

Host (2006–07): Marilu Henner, Tony Meredith. **Host (2008):** Jasmine Guy, Ron Martinez. **Credits:** *Producer:* Aida Moreno.

633 America's Funniest Home Videos. (Comedy; ABC; Premiered: November 26, 1989)

A clip program that showcases the comical home videos of average people. All videos shown are comical moments that unexpectedly happen and not staged.

Host: Bob Saget, John Fugelsang, Daisy Fuentes, Tom Bergeron. **Announcer:** Ernie Anderson. **Credits:** *Executive Producer:* Vin Di Bona, Richard C. Brustein. *Co-Executive Producer:* Terry Moore, Steve Paskay, Todd Thicke, Chris Cusack. *Producer:* J. Elvis Weinstein, Gary H. Grossman, Tom Bergeron. *Music:* Dan Slider, Les Sekely, Frank Macchia.

634 America's Got Talent. (Reality; NBC; June 21, 2006 to October 1, 2008)

Everyday people with varying talents compete for the top prize of $1 million. Each act is judged by a panel but it is the home audience votes that determines the ultimate winner. Neal E. Boyd (opera singer) won the third cycle, 2008 prize.

Host: Regis Philbin (Cycle 1), Jerry Springer (Cycle 2, 3). **Judges:** David Hasselhoff, Brandy Norwood, Piers Morgan (Cycle 1), David Hasselhoff, Sharon Osbourne, Piers Morgan (Cycle 2, 3). **Credits:** *Executive Producer:* Simon Cowell, Ceceile Frot-Coutaz, Nigel Hall, Ken Warwick. *Supervising Producer:* Patrick Byrnes. *Producer:* Megan Michaels, Adam Shapiro.

635 America's Most Smartest Model. (Reality; VH-1; October 7, 2007 to January 6, 2008)

Sixteen female models, most of whom are not very bright, compete in a series of modeling challenges for a contract and the title "America's Most Smartest Model." The dumbest participants (like those who can not name round things while modeling) are eliminated on a weekly basis. The challenges are judged by a comedian (Ben Stein) and a fashion expert (Mary Alice Stephenson).

Hosts: Ben Stein, Mary Alice Stephenson. **Credits:** *Executive Producer:* Alex Demyanenko. *Supervising Producer:* Michelle Barndo. *Co-Producer:* Michael Flutie, Robert A. Flutie.

636 America's Most Wanted. (Reality; Fox; Premiered: February 27, 1988)

Hard hitting factual series that asks the viewing audience to help bring criminals to justice. A crime is covered in detail and toll free numbers are given for tips or information that is not known to authorities.

Host: John Walsh. **Credits:** *Executive Producer:* Greg Klein, Lance Heflin. *Supervising Producer:* Steve Katz. *Producer:* Pam Lewis, Kenneth A. Carlson, Alissa Collins, Cord Keller, Peter Koper, Evan A. Marshall, Cindy Miller, Sam Rath, Todd Robinson, Karen S. Shapiro, Paula C. Simpson, Sedgwick Tourison.

637 America's Next Top Model. (Reality; WB/CW; May 20, 2003 to November 19, 2008)

Twelve potential female models compete in a series of actual modeling shoots with the weakest performer being eliminated on a weekly basis. The girl who proves herself superior is crowned "America's Next Top Model" and wins a magazine fashion spread, a contract with Cover Girl cosmetics and a contract with a top modeling agency.

Host: Tyra Banks. **Judges:** Tyra Banks, Janice Dickinson, Nigel Barker, Jay Manuel, Twiggy, J. Alexander, Beau Quillian, Paulina Porizkova. **Credits:** *Executive Producer:* Tyra Banks, Ken Mok, Anthony Dominici. *Supervising Producer:* Richard M. Rothstein. *Producer:* Allison Chase, Joe Coleman, Mark Freeman, Miriam Jobiani, Justin Lacob, Sydney Levin, Rachel Loren, Sean Rankine, Maggie Zeltner. *Music:* Les Pierce.

638 America's Psychic Challenge. (Reality; Lifetime; October 12, 2007 to January 13, 2008)

Sixteen self-proclaimed psychics compete. They are put through a series of tests designed to determine their psychic abilities. Players are eliminated based on their inability to complete any of the assigned tasks. The one player who proves to be the most psychic wins.

Host: John Burke. **Credits:** *Producer:* John Vidas, George Whitman.

639   Antiques Roadshow. (Reality; PBS; Premiered: January 1, 1997)

Ordinary people appear to have their prized possessions appraised by auction house experts.

Hosts: Chris Jussel, Dan Elias, Lara Spencer, Mark C. Walberg. **Credits:** *Executive Producer:* Peter B. Cook, Aida Moreno, Marsha Bemko, *Producer:* Robert Marshall.

640   Are You Smarter Than a Fifth Grader? (Game; Fox; Premiered: February 22, 2007)

Five fifth graders (ten year olds) appear on stage as the Class. One adult, the Student, appears with the host. The Student selects one fifth grader as a classmate (a different one for each two questions). A board with 10 questions (based on first through fifth grade subjects) appears. Questions range from $1,000 to $500,000. The Student receives money based on how many questions he can answer (with help from his classmates). If a player fails to answer a question correctly before the guaranteed $25,000 question, he loses everything. Answering all 10 questions earns him $500,000 and the chance to answer the million-dollar question (which, if missed, knocks him back to $25,000).

Host: Jeff Foxworthy. **The Class (Cycle One):** Laura Marano, Alana Etheridge, Kyle Collier, Jacob Hayes, Spencer Martin, Marti Ann Meyer. **The Class (Cycle Two):** Olivia Glowacki, Mackenzie Holmes, Nathan Lazarus, Cody Lee, Sierra McCormick. **The Class (Cycle Three):** Jenna Balk, Bryce Cass, Jonathan Cummings, Olivia Dellums, Francesca DeRosa. **Announcer:** Mark Thompson. **Credits:** *Executive Producer:* Mark Burnett, Roy Bank, Barry Poznick, John Stevens. *Supervising Producer:* David Eilenberg. *Producer:* Jeff Foxworthy, Benjamin Silverman, Mark Burnett. *Director:* Don Weiner.

641   Army Wives. (Drama; Lifetime; June 3, 2007 to November 2, 2008)

A profile of the wives of the career military men attached to Delta Force. Stories focus on how they help each other overcome the sacrifices, hardships and uncertainties that the actual current wars (Iraq, Afghanistan) may place on military families. Claudia Joy Holden is the wife of Colonel Michael Holden and the self-proclaimed leader of the group of wives. Roxie Le Blanc is a bartender with two children (from different men) who is currently married to Trevor, a private. Denise Sherwood is the wife of Major Frank Sherwood and the mother of Jeremy; Pamela is a former police officer and married to Chase, a paratrooper. Pamela also has a secret that could affect Chase's military career: she "rents" herself out as a surrogate to earn money. Women are not necessarily army wives. Men can too as seen through the character of Roland Baryon, the husband of Joan, an alcoholic with post-traumatic stress syndrome after a tour of duty in Afghanistan. Roland is a psychiatrist; Denise is concealing signs that her husband abuses her; Pamela fears the money she earns as a surrogate is being squandered by her irresponsible husband.

Cast: Kim Delaney (Claudia Joy Holden), Sally Pressman (Roxy LeBlanc), Brigid Brannagh (Pamela Moran), Catherine Bell (Denise Sherwood), Wendy Davis (Joan Burton), Brian McNamara (Michael Holden), Sterling K. Brown (Roland Burton), Drew Fuller (Trevor LeBlanc), Terry Serpico (Frank Sherwood), Rhoda Griffis (Lenore Baker). **Credits:** *Executive Producer:* Katherine Fugate, Deborah Spera,

Mark Gordon. *Co-Executive Producer:* Marshall Persinger. *Producer:* Harry Bring. *Co-Producer:* Celia Hamel. *Music:* Marc Fantini, Steffan Fantini, Scott Gordon.

642 Arthur. (Cartoon; PBS; Premiered: September 2, 1996)

Eight-year-old Arthur Timothy Read (an aardvark) is fascinated by reading. Unfortunately, his quest to read is sidetracked by his obnoxious younger sister, Dora (called D.W.) and his mischievous friends, Binky, Francine, Brian and Buster. Stories follow Arthur as he seeks to read and faces the challenges of growing up.

Voice Cast: Michael Yarmush (Arthur Timothy Read), Cameron Ansell (Arthur Timothy Read), Oliver Grainger (Dora Winifred Read), Sonja Ball (Jane Read), Bruce Dinsmore (David Read), Paul Brown (Brian), Stephen Crowder (Brian), Joanna Noyes (Grandma Thora Reed), A.J. Henderson (Grandpa Dave Read), Daniel Brochu (Buster Baxter), Tracy Braunstein (Kate Read). **Credits:** *Executive Producer:* Marc Brown, Micheline Charest, Toper Taylor, Pierre Valette. *Producer:* Jacqui Deegan, Diane Dallaire, Greg Bailey, Geoff Adams, Cassandra Schafhausen, Ronald W. Weinberg. *Music:* Raymond C. Fabi.

643 As the Bell Rings. (Comedy; Disney; Premiered: August 26, 2007)

Five minute series that focuses on six high school teens (Brooke, Charlotte, Danny, Skipper, Tiffany and Toe Jam) and their experiences in the corridor between classes (before and after the bell rings). Based on the Italian series *Quelli dell'Intervallo*.

Cast: Gabriella Rodriquez (Brooke), Demi Lovato (Charlotte), Tony Oller (Danny), Colin Cole (Skipper), Carlson Young (Tiffany), Seth Ginsberg (Toe Jam) **Credits:** *Executive Producer:* Jonathan Young. *Producer:* Jim Allen.

644 As the World Turns. (Drama; CBS; Premiered: April 2, 1956)

Dramatic events in the lives of the people of fictional Oakdale, U.S.A.

Principal 2008 Cast: Elizabeth Hubbard (Lucinda Walsh), Helen Wagner (Nancy Hughes McCloskey), Don Hastings (Bob Hughes), Scott Holmes (Tom Hughes), Noelle Beck (Lily Snyder), Terri Colombino (Kate Perett Snyder), Ellen Dolan (Margo Hughes), Eileen Fulton (Lisa Grimaldi), Kathryn Hayes (Kim Hughes), Elizabeth Hubbard (Lucinda Walsh), Kelly Menighan-Hensley (Emily Stewart), Trent Dawson (Henry Coleman), Van Hansis (Luke Snyder), John Hensley (Holden Snyder), Roger Howarth (Paul Ryan), Agim Kaba (Aaron Snyder), Marie Wilson (Meg Snyder Ryan), Maura West (Carly Tenney), Marnie Schulenburg (Alison Stewart), Colleen Zenk-Pinter (Barbara Ryan), Billy Magnussen (Casey Hughes), Grayson McCouch (Dusty Donovan), Michael Park (Jack Snyder), Austin Peck (Brad Snyder), Ellery Capshaw (Natalie Snyder), Ewa da Cruz (Vienna Hyatt), Marie Masters (Susan Stewart), Anthony Herrera (James Stenbeck), Kathleen Widdoes (Emma Snyder), Sam Stone (Daniel Hughes), Deirdre Skiles (Danielle Andropoulos), Wolfe Parks (Dallas Griffin), Julie Pinson (Janet Ciccone), Chauntee Schuler (Bonnie McKechnie), Laurence Lau (Brian Wheatley), Meredith Hagner (Liberty Ciccone), Allie Gornec (Sage Snyder), Jake Silbermann (Noah Mayer). **Credits:** *Executive Producer:* Christopher Goutman. *Senior Producer:* Carole Shure. *Producer:* Vivian Gundaker. *Associate Producer:* Jennifer Maloney.

645 Ask This Old House. (Reality; PBS; Premiered: October 12, 2002)

The program responds to home repair questions by demonstrating the techniques needed to repair, build or tackle some do-it-yourself project.

Host: Kevin O'Connor. **Regulars:** Tom Silva (contractor), Roger Cook (landscaper), Richard Thretheway (plumber), Norm Abram (carpenter). **Credits:** *Executive Producer:* Russell Morash. *Producer:* Bruce Irving, David Vos, Chris Deck.

646　At the Movies. (Reviews; Syn.; Premiered: September 1982)

A weekly look at current movies with a "thumbs up" or "thumbs down" to each film that is discussed. The series began as *Sneak Previews* and aired locally in Chicago in 1975. Also known as *Siskel and Ebert at the Movies.*

Hosts: Roger Ebert (1982–2008), Gene Siskel (1982–1986), Bill Harris (1986–1988), Rex Reed (1986–1990), Dixie Whatley (1988–1990), Richard Roeper (2000–2008), Ben Lyons and Ben Mankiewicz (2008–). **Credits:** *Executive Producer:* Don Dupree. *Supervising Producer:* David Plummer.

647　A.T.O.M.—Alpha Teens on Machines. (Cartoon; Jetix; Premiered: August 27, 2005)

Mr. Lee is a mysterious scientist (head of Lee International) who has created a series of unique crime fighting vehicles. He has also organized five teens (Axel, Hawk, King, Lioness and Shark) as his team. Their mission: protect the city from Alexander Paine, an evil crime lord and his band of criminals.

Voice Cast: James Arnold Taylor (Axel Manning), Ali Mauzey (Cat "Lioness" Leone), Charlie Schlatter (Zack "Hawk" Hawkes), Alois Hooge (Crey "King" Kingston), Tom Kenny (Mr. Lee), Clancy Brown (Alexander Paine). **Credits:** *Executive Producer:* Olivier Dumont, Michael Lekes, Jacqueline Tordsman. *Producer:* Sylvie Barro, Bruno Branchi, Greg Klein, Thomas Pugsley. *Music:* Alain Garcia, Noam Kaniel.

648　Avatar: The Last Airbender. (Cartoon; Cartoon Network; February 21, 2005 to August 9, 2008)

At one point in time the Air Nomads, the Earth Kingdom, the Fire Nation and the Water Tribe ruled the Earth. Each society possessed a "bender," a man or woman who was capable of "bending" (harnessing their inborn talent to manipulate their native element). Each bender is called an Avatar and each Avatar keeps his or her society in perfect harmony. The evil leaders of the Fire Nation seek world domination and begin a quest to destroy the other nations. An Avatar has not been reborn into the Air Nomads and the Water, Earth and Air tribes are facing extinction as the Avatar cycle appears to have been broken. In the South Pole, Water Tribe members Katara and her brother Sokka, find Aang, a 12-year-old boy frozen in an iceberg. After releasing him, Katara and Sokka learn that Aang is an Air Bender and the long-lost Avatar of the Air Nomads. With a strong knowledge of the Avatar, Katara and Sokka must safeguard Aang and teach him how to master the elements of all four nations to save the world from the Fire Nation.

Voice Cast: Mae Whitman (Katara), Jack De Sana (Sokka), Zach Tyler Eisen (Aang), Mitchel Musso (Aang; later), Dante Basco (Prince Zuko), Olivia Hack (Ty Lee), Mako (Uncle Iroh) Johanna Braddy (Princess Yue). **Credits:** *Executive Producer:* Bryan Konietzko, Michael DiMartino. *Producer:* Aaron Ehasz. *Music:* Benjamin Wynn, Jeremy Zuckerman.

649　The Bachelor. (Reality; ABC; Premiered: March 25, 2002)

The basic format has one handsome bachelor attempting to choose the one girl he would like as his own from a field of 25 eligible women.

Host: Chris Harrison. **Credits:** *Executive Producer:* Lisa Levenson, Mike Fleiss. *Co-Executive Producer:* David Bohnert, Jason A. Carbone, Scott Jeffress. *Supervising Producer:* Shantel Klinger, Sam Korkis, Sally Ann Salsano, Monica Stock. *Producer:* Rebecca Eisen, Ross Breitenbach,

Tracey Finley, Tess Gamba, Tiffany Mc-Linn Lore, Alycia Rossiter. *Music:* Timothy Edwards, Danny Lux, Rob Cairns, John Carta.

650 The Bachelorette. (Reality; ABC; January 8, 2003 to July 7, 2008)

Bachelor spin off wherein one woman, introduced to 25 single men, must choose the one she would like to be with. She eliminates those she feels are not right for her and in the final episode reveals her choice (who has the option of accepting or rejecting her).

Credits: *Executive Producer:* Mike Fleiss. *Co-Executive Producer:* Lisa Levenson, Scott Jeffress, Jason A. Carbone, Sally Ann Salsano, Clay Newbill. *Supervising Producer:* Tiffany McLinn Lore, Shantel Klinger. *Producer:* Heather Adams, David Bohnert, Hayley Goggin, Dan Morando. *Music:* Danny Lux, John Carta, Rob Cairns.

651 Back to the Barnyard. (Cartoon; Nickelodeon; Premiered: September 29, 2007)

An animated series that picks up from where the theatrical feature *Barnyard* leaves off. It is the story of a cow (Otis) who would like nothing more to do than be a slacker but he must live up to his responsibilities: protecting the animals on his farm.

Voice Cast: Chris Hardwick (Otis), Wanda Sykes (Bessie), Rob Paulsen (Peck), Maria Bamford (Mrs. Beady), Steve Oedekerk (Mr. Beady), Jeff Garcia (Pip), Cam Clarke (Freddy), Toni Insani (Pig), Dom Irrera (Duke). **Credits:** *Supervising Producer:* Jed Spingain. *Producer:* Margaret M. Dean, Paul Marshall. *Associate Producer:* Kyle Jolly.

652 Back to You. (Comedy; Fox; September 19, 2007 to May 14, 2008)

Chuck Darling, a self-centered ladies' man, and Kelly Carr, an uptight know-it-all, are news anchors for WURG-TV, Channel 9 in Pittsburgh. They co-anchor the station's 6 P.M. and 10 P.M. newscasts and stories relate events in their home and work lives. Chuck and Kelly appear to have great chemistry on camera, but off camera they dislike each other and have only one thing in common — Kelly's 10-year-old daughter, Gracie (the result of a one night stand she and Chuck had on New Year's Eve). Stories also focus on the newsroom staff: Marsh McGinley, the sports anchor; Montana Diaz Herrera, the sexy weathergirl; Ryan Church, the news director; and Gary Crezyzewski (pronounced kre-shoov-ski), the field reporter who always gets the worst assignments.

Cast: Kelsey Grammer (Chuck Darling), Patricia Heaton (Kelly Carr), Laura Marano (Gracie Carr), Fred Willard (Marsh McGinley), Ayda Field (Montana Diaz Herrera), Josh Gad (Ryan Church), Ty Burrell (Gary Crezyzewski). **Credits:** *Executive Producer:* James Burrows, Steven Levitan, Christopher Lloyd. *Producer:* Tony Hicks. *Music:* Paul Buckley, John Adair, Steve Hampton.

653 The Backyardigans. (Cartoon; Nickelodeon; Premiered: October 11, 2004)

Fantasy is combined with Broadway-like music and songs to relate the adventures of a group of children whose back yard transforms into a magical fantasy land.

Voice Cast: Naelee Rae (Tasha), Gianna Bruzzese (Tasha; later), Reginald Davis, Jr. (Tyrone), Jordan Coleman (Tyrone; later) Jonah Bobo (Austin), La Shawn Jefferies (Uniqua), Zach Tyler (Pablo). **Credits:** *Executive Producer:* Scott Dyer, Doug Murphy, Robert Scull, Janice Burgess. *Co-Executive Producer:* Jonny Bell. *Supervising Producer:* Pamela Lehn, Ellen Martino, Patricia Burns. *Producer:* Ruta Cube. *Music:* Evan Lurie, Douglas Wieselman.

654 The Bad Boys of Comedy. (Comedy; HBO; Premiered: June 10, 2005)

Up and coming comedians are given a chance to entertain in front of a live audience at the Brooklyn Academy of Music in New York.

Host: Sean "P. Diddy" Combs. **Act Introductions:** Doug E. Fresh. **Credits:** *Executive Producer:* Sean "P. Diddy" Combs, Walter Latham. *Supervising Producer:* John Irwin.

655   The Bad Girls Club. (Reality; Oxygen; Premiered: December 5, 2006)

Several self professed "bad girls" are placed together in a Los Angeles house with cameras capturing the "drama" as the girls attempt to live with each other.

Girls (Cycle 1): Ty Colliers, JoAnna Hernandez, Andrea Lange, Leslie Ramsue, Jodie Howell, Kerry Harvick, Ripsi Terzian, Aimee Landi, Zara Sprankle, DeAnn. **Girls (Cycle 2):** Cordella Gitter, Darlen Escobar, Jennavecia Russo, Hanna Thompson, Neveen Ismail, Tanisha Thomas, Lyric. **Girls (Cycle 3):** Aliea, Amber B., Amber M., Kayla, Sarah, Tiffany, Whitney. **Credits:** *Executive Producer:* Jonathan Murray. *Co-Executive Producer:* Dana DeMars, Laura Korkoian. *Supervising Producer:* Maria Akl, Benjamin Greenberg. *Producer:* Robert Brehmer. *Music:* Dan Beyer, Jeff McDonough.

656   Baldwin Hills. (Reality; BET; July 10, 2007 to August 19, 2008)

The experiences of African American teenagers are chronicled as they deal with everyday issues with family and friends. Casts vary with each cycle.

Credits: *Executive Producer:* Marc Brown, Sheri Maroufkhani, Michael McNamara, Bill Rademaekers. *Supervising Producer:* Michael H. Miller, Talika Freundlich. *Music:* Rico Laurie.

657   Barefoot Contessa. (Cooking; Food Network; Premiered: November 30, 2002)

Meal preparation and cooking short cuts with chef Ina Garten. Taped at her home in the Hamptons (New York).

Host: Ina Garten. **Credits:** *Executive Producer:* Rachel Purnell. *Supervising Producer:* Olivia Ball. *Producer:* Carl Green, Sophie Selden. *Director:* Ben Warwick, Stuart Bateup.

658   Barney and Friends. (Children; PBS; Premiered: April 1, 1992)

A purple dinosaur (Barney) entertains and teaches children aspects of life, mostly courtesy and manners. Barney is surrounded by a group of children and is assisted by Baby Bop and his brother B.J.

Cast: Bob West (Barney), Dean Wendt (Barney), Carey Stinson (Barney), David Joyner (Barney), Jeff Ayres (Baby Bop), Patty Wirtz (B.J.), Jeff Brook (B.J.). **Credits:** *Executive Producer:* Dennis De Shazer, Randy A. Dalton. *Supervising Producer:* Linda Houston. *Producer:* Ben Vaughn. *Associate Producer:* Julie Hutchings, R. Shawn Kelly, Charlotte Spivey.

659   Battlestar Galactica. (Science Fiction; Sci Fi; December 8, 2003 to March 20, 2009)

A revised version of the 1978 ABC series of the same title. In a futuristic era, the inhabitants of the Twelve Colonies created intelligent robots called Cylons to work as slaves and soldiers to fight humanities wars. Over time, the Cyclons became aware of their unrealistic situation and rebelled. A war ensued between man and machine but ended in a stalemate when the Cylons retreated to a remote section of outer space. After 39 years of peace the Cyclons launched an unprovoked attack on the Twelve Colonies and destroyed billions of lives. There were survivors: those stationed aboard the *Galactica*, a giant battleship commanded by William Adama. With knowledge of a distant 13th colony (Earth) the surviving members of the Twelve Colonies seek to preserve mankind by finding Earth. Stories relate their efforts while constantly battling the pursuing Cylons who seek to destroy them. See also

Battlestar Galactica: The Face of the Enemy (program 37).

Cast: Edward James Olmos (Admr. William Adama), Katee Sackhoff (Capt. Kara "Starbuck" Thrace), Mary McDonnell (Pres. Laura Roslin), Tricia Helfer (Number 6), Grace Park (Lt. Sharon "Athena" Agathon), Jamie Bamber (Capt. Lee "Apollo" Adama), James Callis (Dr. Gaius Baltar), Aaron Douglas (Off. Galen Tyrol), Tahmoh Penikett (Lt. Karl C. "Helo" Agathon), Kandyse McClure (Off. Anastasia Dualla), Alessandro Juliani (Lt. Felix Gaeta), Nicki Clyne (Specialist Cally), Bodie Olmos (Brendan "Hot Dog" Costanza), Leah Cairns (Lt. Margaret "Racetrack" Edmonson), Luciana Carro (Lt. Louanne "Kat" Katraine), Michael Hogan (Colonel Saul Tigh), Aaron Douglas (Chief Galen Tyrol), Michael Trucco (Ensign Samuel Anders), Nicki Clyne (Specialist Cally Henderson), Donnelly Rhodes (Dr. Cottle), Lucy Lawless (D'Anna Biers), Kate Vernon (Ellen Tigh), Luciana Carro (Capt. Louanne "Kat" Katraine). **Credits:** *Executive Producer:* Ronald D. Moore, David Eick. *Co-Executive Producer:* Mark Verheiden, Toni Graphia, Michael Angeli. *Supervising Producer:* Michael Taylor. *Producer:* Harvey Frand, Michael Rymer, Mark Verheiden. *Co-Producer:* Paul M. Leonard, David Weddle, Bradley Thompson. *Consulting Producer:* Glen A. Larson. *Music:* Ben McCreary, Richard Gibbs.

660 BBQ with Bobby Flay. (Cooking; Food Network; Premiered: January 1, 2004)

Master grilling chef Bobby Flay takes to the open road to discover how Americans from New York to Alaska barbeque their favorite foods.

Host: Bobby Flay. **Credits:** *Executive Producer:* Gary H. Grossman, Steve Lange, Robb Weller. *Supervising Producer:* Amy Corral. *Producer:* Shannon Hall, Karen Juve, Aileen Martinez.

661 Beauty and the Geek. (Reality; WB/CW; June 1, 2005 to August 19, 2008)

Seven absolutely gorgeous girls and seven self-proclaimed geeks are placed together and paired up. The girls have had plenty of dating experience but the guys are lacking such skills (as well as social function abilities). Couples are assigned tasks with the weakest performers being eliminated. The one couple that outperforms the others split $250,000.

Host: Mike Richards. **Credits:** *Executive Producer:* Ashton Kutcher, John Foy, Jason Goldberg, Todd A. Nelson, J.D. Roth, Nick Santora. *Co-Executive Producer:* Brian Richardson, Eli Holzman. *Producer:* Adam Paul. *Music:* Mark T. Williams, Jeff Lippencott.

662 Behind the Bash. (Reality; Food Network; Premiered: October 1, 2006)

A behind-the-scenes look at the preparations that go into lavish parties — from New York to Las Vegas.

Host: Giada De Laurentis. **Credits:** *Executive Producer:* Bruce David Klein. *Co-Executive Producer:* Maria Lane. *Producer:* Clare O'Donohue.

663 The Best Years. (Drama; The N; Premiered: May 22, 2007)

The lives of a group of freshmen at Charles University in Boston are profiled as they begin "the best years of their lives." Particular focus is on Samantha Best, an orphan with an unstable past, as she sets out on the most important journey of her life.

Cast: Charity Shea (Samantha Best), Athena Karkanis (Dawn Vargaz), Niall Matter (Trent Hamilton), Brandon Jay McLaren (Devon Sylver), Jennifer Miller (Kathryn Klarner), Randall Edwards (Noah Jensen), Alan Van Sprang (Lee Campbell), Sherry Miller (Dorothy O'Sullivan), Ashley Morris (Shannon Biel), Ron Lea (Professor Fisher), Siu Ta (Cynthia Song). **Credits:** *Executive Producer:* Aaron

Martin, Noreen Halpern, John Morayniss. *Producer:* Bernard Bourrett, Wendy Grean, Peter Bray, Brenda Greenberg. *Music:* John Rowley.

664 Beyond the Break. (Drama; The N; Premiered: June 2, 2006)

Oahu, Hawaii provides the setting for a dramatic look at the world of surfing as seen through four girls (Birdie, Dawn, Kai, and Lacey) as they become members of Wave Sync, the local surfing circuit. **Cast:** Tiffany Hines (Birdie Scott), Suzie Pollard (Dawn Preston), Sonya Balmores (Kai Kealoha), Natalie Ramsey (Lacey Farmer), David Chokachi (Justin Healy), Michael Copon (Vin Keahi), Jim Horigan (Dale Martin), Adam T. Brooks (D.J. Reese), Jamie Elle Mann (Liz Godfrey), Ross Thomas (Bailey Reese), Jesse Williams (Eric Medina). **Credits:** *Executive Producer:* David Brookwell, Fernando Szew, Sean McNamara. *Producer:* John Scherer, Frank Merwald, Jason K. Lau. *Music:* John Coda, Julie Greaux.

665 The Big Bang Theory. (Comedy; CBS; Premiered: September 24, 2007)

Leonard and Sheldon are brilliant Cal Tech physicists and roommates whose lives revolve around their work. Life suddenly changes for them when Penny, a gorgeous, free-spirited girl, movies into the apartment across from theirs. Leonard and Sheldon rarely interact with other people, especially women, but Penny has stirred new feelings in Leonard — he now sees women as "a whole new universe of possibilities." Stories follow Leonard as he sets out to change his life by exploring a world he has never known before (much to Sheldon's objections, who feels Leonard and Penny are never meant to be together). Howard and Rajesh are Sheldon and Leonard's socially dysfunctional Cal Tech friends (who work in the Department of Applied Physics; Howard believes he is a ladies' man; Rajesh is incapable of speaking to women). Penny works as a waitress at the Cheesecake Factory Restaurant (later a bartender). She was born in Omaha and came to Los Angeles (the series setting) to become an actress. She calls Sheldon and Leonard "beautiful mind genius guys" and is constantly in a fog when they speak in highly intellectual terms. Leslie Winkle is Leonard's co-worker.

Cast: Kaley Cuoco (Penny), Johnny Galecki (Leonard Hofstedter), Jim Parsons (Sheldon Cooper), Simon Helberg (Howard Wolowitz), Kunal Nayyar (Rajesh Koothrappali), Sara Gilbert (Leslie Winkle), Courtney Henggeler (Missy Cooper, Sheldon's fraternal twin sister). **Credits:** *Executive Producer:* Chuck Lorre, Bill Prady, Lee Aronsohn. *Co-Executive Producer:* Robert Cohen. *Producer:* Steven Molaro. *Theme Vocal:* "The Big Bang Theory" by Bare Naked Ladies.

666 Big Brother. (Reality; CBS; July 5, 2000 to September 16, 2008)

Thirteen strangers are brought together and placed in a large residence (the Big Brother House) where they all become houseguests. Cameras follow their daily activities and guests must perform specific tasks in an attempt to win $500,000. A panel of judges eliminates the weakest performers and the most capable guest wins the prize.

Host: Julie Chen, April Lewis. **Announcer:** Clayton Halsey. **Credits:** *Executive Producer:* Allison Grodner, Paul Romer, Douglas Ross, Arnold Shapiro. *Co-Executive Producer:* Don Wollman, Kathleen French, Rich Meehan, Greg Stewart, J. Rupert Thompson. *Supervising Producer:* John Platt, Tracy Green, Daniel Sorseth, Ismael Soto. *Music:* Ray Colcord.

667 The Big Gay Sketch Show. (Comedy; Logo; Premiered: April 24, 2007)

A cast of mostly unknown comics spoof everything from Broadway musicals to political candidates.

Cast: Erica Ash, Dion Flynn, Stephen Guarino, Julie Goldman, Kate McKinnon, Jonny McGovern, Nicol Paone, Michael Serrato. **Credits:** *Executive Producer:* Joe Del Hierro, Dan MacDonald, Rosie O'Donnell. *Producer:* Scott King.

668   Big Love. (Drama; HBO; Premiered: March 12, 2006)

Salt Lake City, Utah, is the setting for a look at the life of William "Bill" Henrickson, the owner of a home improvement store (Home Place) who is also a polygamist. Barbara is his first wife (they are the parents of Sarah, Ben and Tancy); Nicolette is his second wife (Wayne and Raymond are their children); Margene is Bill's third wife and they are the parents of Aaron and infant Lester. Stories relate Bill's struggles to balance his life between the pressures of raising seven children, pleasing three wives and expanding his business.

Cast: Bill Paxton (Bill Henrickson), Jeanne Tripplehorn (Barbara Henrickson), Chloe Sevigny (Nicolette Henrickson), Ginnifer Goodwin (Margene Henrickson) Bruce Dern (Frank Harlow) Grace Zabriskie (Lois Henrickson) Amanda Seyfried (Sarah Henrickson) Douglas Smith (Ben Henrickson) Shawn Doyle (Joey Henrickson), Jolean Wejbe (Tancy Henrickson), Melora Walters (Wanda Henrickson), Harry Dean Stanton (Roman Grant), Mary Kay Place (Adaleen Grant). **Credits:** *Executive Producer:* Gary Goetzman, Tom Hanks, Mark V. Olsen, Will Scheffer. *Co-Executive Producer:* David Knoller. *Supervising Producer:* Jeanette Collins, Mimi Friedman. *Music:* Mark Mothersbaugh.

669   Big Shots. (Drama; ABC; September 27, 2007 to January 24, 2008)

A look at the lives of four dysfunctional CEO's: James Auster, head of Ameri-Mart Industries; Duncan Collins, CEO of Reveal Cosmetics; Brody James, senior vice president of Alpha Crisis Management;

and Karl Mixworth, head of a large pharmaceutical company. Lisbeth is Duncan's ex-wife; Cameron is Duncan's 19-year-old daughter; Wendy is Karl's wife; Marla is Karl's mistress; Katie is James's wife.

Cast: Michael Vartan (James Auster), Dylan McDermott (Duncan Collins), Christopher Titus (Brody Johns), Joshua Malina (Karl Mixworthy), Nia Long (Katie), Paige Turco (Lisbeth), Jessica Collins (Marla), Amy Sloan (Wendy), Peyton List (Cameron). **Credits:** *Executive Producer:* Jon Harmon Feldman. *Co-Executive Producer:* Michael Katleman.

670   The Biggest Loser. (Reality; NBC; Premiered: October 14, 2004)

Obese people, coached by fitness trainers and health experts, struggle to lose weight with the most successful winning $250,000.

Host: Caroline Rhea, Alison Sweeney. **Credits:** *Executive Producer:* David Droome, Al Berman, John Foy, Todd A. Nelson, J.D. Roth, Ben Silverman. *Co-Executive Producer:* Troy Searer. *Producer:* Genevieve Tackenberg, Derrick Speight, Bradford Schultze, Marla Roberta, Fred Pichel, Elayne Cilic, Elizabeth Young. *Music:* Mark T. Williams, Jeff Lippencott.

671   The Bill Engvall Show. (Comedy; TBS; July 17, 2007 to August 7, 2008)

Bill Pearson, his wife, Susan and their children, Lauren, Trent and Bryan, live at 4321 Baker Street in Denver, Colorado. Bill is a family counselor; Susan was a nurse before marrying. Bill is relaxed and casual; Susan is practical, vivacious and sassy; Lauren wants to be hip, not conservative as her parents want her; Trent is a slacker; Bryan, the youngest, is an expert on diseases. Stories follow Bill as he tries to solve family problems — like he does at the office, but can't quite accomplish at home. Paul is Bill's friend, a man who believes everything is a conspiracy.

Cast: Bill Engvall (Bill Pearson), Nancy

Travis (Susan Pearson), Jennifer Lawrence (Lauren Pearson), Graham Patrick Martin (Trent Pearson), Skyler Gisondo (Bryan Pearson), Tim Meadows (Paul DuFrayne). **Credits:** *Executive Producer:* Michael Leeson, Bill Engvall, J.P. Williams. *Producer:* Melanie Patterson. *Music:* Jonathan Flood.

672   Blue's Clues. (Cartoon; Nickelodeon; Premiered: September 9, 1996)

Each day Blue, a magical blue puppy, visits Blue's Clues Playhouse and leaves her paw prints on three clues. The host (Steve, then Joe) must figure out the clues to determine what adventures Blue has in store for them.

Cast: Traci Paige Johnson (Blue), Steve Burns (Steve) Donovan Patton (Joe), Cheryl Blaylock (Frederica), Shannon Walker Williams (Miranda), Jean Marie Castle (Paprika), Corinne Hoffman (Paprika), Cameron Bowen (Periwinkle), Jansen Panettiere (Periwinkle), Kelly Nigh (Tickety Tock), Christiana Anbri (Moona). **Credits:** *Executive Producer:* Howard Litton, Todd Kessler. *Co-Executive Producer:* Angela Santomero. *Supervising Producer:* Jennifer Twomey.

673   The Bold and the Beautiful. (Drama; CBS; Premiered: March 23, 1987)

A dramatic look at the world of fashion — its glamour, romance and intrigues, as seen through the lives of the powerful Forrester family.

Principal 2008 Cast: Leslie-Anne Down (Jacqueline Payne Marone), Susan Flannery (Stephanie Forrester), Heather Tom (Katie Logan), Robin Riker (Beth Logan), Hunter Tylo (Taylor Hayes Marone), John McCook (Eric Forrester), Ronn Moss (Ridge Forrester), Jennifer Gareis (Donna Logan Forrester), Ashley Jones (Bridget Forrester), Lesli Kay (Felicia Forrester), Katherine Kelly Lang (Brooke Logan), Mackenzie Mauzy (Phoebe Forrester), Jacqueline MacInnes Wood (Steffy Forrester), Jack Wagner (Nick Marone), Ronn Moss (Ridge Forrester), Kyle Lowder (Rick Forrester), Winsor Harmon (Thorne Forrester), Brandon Beemer (Owen Knight), Texas Battle (Marcus Walton), Drew Tyler Bell (Thomas Forrester), Darcy Rose Byrnes (Abby Carlton), Patrick Duffy (Stephen Logan), Harley Graham (Alexandra Forrester), Betty White (Ann Douglas), Ridge Perkett (R.J. Forrester), Daniel McVicar (Clarke Garrison), Dan Martin (Lt. Bradley Baker), Mykel Shannon Jenkins (Charlie Baker), Alley Mills (Pam Douglas). **Credits:** *Executive Producer:* Bradley Bell. *Producer:* Cynthia J. Popp.

674   Bone Detectives. (Reality; Discovery Channel; Premiered: December 29, 2007)

Archeologists attempt to uncover mysteries of the past through bone remnants.

Host: Scott Moore. **Credits:** *Executive Producer:* Michael Branton, Gary R. Benz. *Co-Executive Producer:* Michael Shevloff. *Supervising Producer:* Rodney Frazier, Carrie Riley-Paul. *Producer:* Brian Tanke. *Music:* Scott Hackwith, Adam Peters.

675   Bones. (Crime Drama; Fox; Premiered: September 13, 2005)

Dr. Temperance Brennan, a forensic anthropologist with the Jefferson Institute in Washington, D.C., is the author of the books *Bone Free* and *Red Tape, White Bones*. She is totally dedicated to helping authorities solve complex murders where the only evidence is skeletal remains. Seeley Booth, a former army sniper turned FBI agent (also said to be a profiler) is the law enforcement officer Temperance assists (he calls her "Bones," something she really doesn't like, but accepts). Stories follow their case investigations with Temperance encountering a new perspective on life as she becomes involved with people beneath her intellectual status. Angela, Zack, Jack and Camille work with Temperance at the Jefferson's medico-legal lab. Angela is a three dimensional artist and can reconstruct a victim's facial features from skull remains. Zack is eager to follow in Temperance's footsteps. Jack is an expert on insects, minerals and spores. Camille joined the series in the second season and replaced the team's original boss, Dr. Daniel Goodman, the lab director (his absence was explained as being on a sabbatical). Camille is a by-the-books girl and was previously with the New York City pathology unit. The series is based on real life forensic anthropologist Kathy Reichs. Rebecca is Seeley's ex-wife; Parker is his son; Max and Christina are Temperance's parents.

Cast: Emily Deschanel (Dr. Temperance Brennan), David Boreanaz (Seeley Booth), Michaela Conlin (Angela Montenegro), Eric Millegan (Dr. Zack Addy), T.J. Thyne (Dr. Jack Hodgins), Jonathan Adams (Dr. Daniel Goodman), Tamara Taylor (Dr. Camille Saroyan), Jessica Capshaw (Rebecca Stinson), Ty Panitz (Parker Booth), Ryan O'Neal (Max Brennan). **Credits:** *Executive Producer:* Barry Josephson, Stephen Nathan, Jonathan Pontell, Hart Hanson. *Co-Executive Producer:* Tony Wharmby, Scott Williams, Craig Silverstein, Gary Glasberg, Steve Beers. *Supervising Producer:* Janet Tamaro. *Producer:* Jan DeWitt, Steve Blackman, Greg Ball, Laura Wolner, Kathy Reichs, James Chory, Dana Coen. *Music:* Peter Himmelman, The Crystal Method.

676 Boston Legal. (Drama; ABC; October 3, 2004 to December 8, 2008). Spin-off from *The Practice* that focuses on a group of brilliant, high-priced but often emotionally challenged lawyers with the Boston-based firm of Crane, Poole and Schmidt.

Cast: James Spader (Alan Shore), William Shatner (Denny Crane), Candice Bergen (Shirley Schmidt), Rene Auberjonois (Paul Lewiston), Julie Bowen (Denise Bauer), Mark Valley (Brad Chase), Lake Bell (Sally Heep), Rhona Mitra (Tara

Wilson), Monica Potter (Lori Colson), Ryan Michelle Bathe (Sara Holt), Justin Mentell (Garrett Wells), Christian Clemenson (Jerry Espenson), Constance Zimmer (Claire Simms), Monica Potter (Lori Colson), John Larroquette (Carl Sack), Tara Summers (Katie Lloyd), Saffron Burrows (Lorraine Weller), Henry Gibson (Judge Clark Brown). **Credits:** *Executive Producer:* David E. Kelley, Jeff Rake, Bill D'Elia, Scott Kaufer, Janet Leahy. *Co-Executive Producer:* Mike Listo, Peter Ocko. *Supervising Producer:* Steve Robin, Jonathan Shapiro. *Producer:* Phoef Sutton, Janet G. Knutsen, Lawrence Broch, Andrew Kreisberg. *Music:* Danny Lux.

677 Bounty Girls. (Reality; Court TV/Tru TV; Premiered: August 5, 2007) Jag, Jade, Gloria and Clyde are four women who operate Sunshine State Bail Bonds, a bounty-hunting agency in Miami, Florida. Stories profile the bounty girls (as they call themselves) as they go about their business — tracking down bad guys (and girls) for their offered rewards.

Credits: *Supervising Producer:* Mark Marinaccio. *Producer:* Barbette Somellan.

678 Boy Meets Grill. (Reality; Food Network; Premiered: January 1, 2003) The ins and outs of outdoor cooking — from the grocery shelf to grill with Chef Bobby Flay.

Host: Bobby Flay. **Credits:** *Producer:* Lauren Deen, John Bergmann.

679 Bride vs. Bride. (Reality; WE; August 13, 2006 to August 6, 2008) Brides, grooms and wedding party members compete in various physical and mental challenges for the opportunity to win money for their upcoming ceremony.

Host: Evan Farmer. **Credits:** *Executive Producer:* Mark Hickman. *Producer:* Charlie DeBevoise, Molly Weiss.

680 Bridezillas. (Reality; WE; June 1, 2004 to October 26, 2008) The hectic world of brides-to-be are profiled as each strives to produce the wedding of her dreams.

Narrator: Mindy Burbano. **Credits:** *Executive Producer:* Mary Pelloni, Sam Brick, David Green. *Supervising Producer:* Ron Davis, Elisa Rothstein. *Producer:* Paul Kolsby, Jenny McGonigal, Mario Yates. *Music:* Storm Lee.

681 Brotherhood. (Drama; Showtime; Premiered: July 9, 2006)

Michael and Tommy Caffee are brothers who grew up in an area of Providence, Rhode Island called the Hill. Tommy is a family man (married to Eileen; the father of Mary Rose) and a local politician. Michael is a gangster who has returned home after a long absence to gain control of the Hill's seedy underground. Stories relate the conflict that ensues as Tommy sets out to stop Michael from accomplishing his shady goal.

Cast: Jason Clarke (Tommy Caffee), Jason Isaacs (Michael Caffee), Annabeth Gish (Eileen Caffee), Fiona C. Erickson (Mary Rose Caffee), Fionnula Flanagan (Rose Caffee), Kevin Chapman (Freddie Cork), Brian Scannell (Silent John), Frank Ridley (Terry Mulligan), Billy Smith (Kevin "Moe" Reilly). **Credits:** *Executive Producer:* Elizabeth Stephens, Blake Masters. *Co-Executive Producer:* Nicole Yorkin. *Producer:* Donna E. Bloom. *Music:* Gary Meister, Jeff Rona.

682 Brothers and Sisters. (Drama; ABC; Premiered: September 24, 2006)

Ojai Foods is a Los Angeles–based company run by the Walker family. William and Nora are the parents; Kitty, Sarah, Thomas, Justin and Kevin are their children. Each family member has their issues with the world and each other and in soap opera–like fashion — from unhappy marriages, financial woes to unfulfilled dreams — the saga of the Walker family is presented. Betty Buckley played the part of Nora in the unaired pilot film.

Cast: Sally Field (Nora Walker), Cal-

ista Flockhart (Kitty Walker), Dave Annable (Justin Walker), Balthazar Getty (Tommy Walker), Matthew Rhys (Kevin Walker), Sarah Jane Morris (Julia Walker), Rachel Griffiths (Sarah Whedon), John Pyper-Ferguson (Joe Whedon), Ron Rifkin (Saul Holden), Tom Skerritt (William Walker), Patricia Wettig (Holly Harper), Kerris Dordey (Paige Whedon), Rob Lowe (Robert McCallister), Treat Williams (David Morton), Keri Lynn Pratt (Amber Trachtenberg). **Credits:** *Executive Producer:* Jon Robin Baitz, Ken Olin. *Co-Executive Producer:* Sarah Caplan, Craig Wright, Emily Whitesell, Molly Newman. *Producer:* Michael Morris, Nicole Carrasco, Jessica Mecklenburg. *Music:* Blake Neely.

683 Burn Notice. (Drama; USA; Premiered: June 28, 2007)

While on a dangerous undercover assignment in Nigeria, highly decorated CIA agent Michael Westen receives a burn notice (services no longer required). The mission goes sour but Michael manages to escape and returns to his hometown of Miami Beach, Florida. He finds the CIA has, for reasons he cannot figure out, frozen his bank accounts, cancelled his credit cards and refuses to acknowledge that he even exists. Through a contact at the CIA, a friend who cannot answer his questions, and is not a part of the cover up, Michael is given some help. He is told to seek out a man named Sam, an alcoholic ex–military intelligence agent (and "ex–everything else" as he says). Sam has contacts and sets him up as a private detective to solve the problems of people who cannot contact the police for help. Stories follow Michael as he tries to find out why he was given the burn notice and who is responsible for turning his life upside down. Sam and Fiona, a former IRA operative, assist Michael on his cases. Madeline is Michael's hypochondriac mother.

Cast: Jeffrey Donovan (Michael Westen),

Gabrielle Anwar (Fiona), Bruce Campbell (Sam), Sharon Gless (Madeline). **Credits:** *Executive Producer:* Matt Nix, Mikkel Bondesen. *Producer:* Jeff Freilich. *Co-Producer:* David Levine.

684   Caitlin's Way. (Drama; The N; Premiered: March 9, 2000)

Caitlin Seeger is a teenager living in Philadelphia. She was orphaned at the age of eight and given up for adoption. She grew up with an attitude and learned well the way of the streets. As she matured, she found herself in trouble with the law. After a series of petty thefts, she was arrested but given a chance to avoid jail by living with relatives, the Lowes, the owners of a ranch in Montana. Stories follow Caitlin as she struggles to shed her criminal ways and adjust to a life that is totally strange to her.

Cast: Lindsay Felton (Caitlin Seeger), Cynthia Belliveau (Dori Lowe), Jeremy Foley (Griffen Lowe), Ken Tremblett (Jim Lowe), Jason McSkimming (Will Findlay), Stephen Warner (Brett Stevens), Tania Saulnier (Taylor Langford). **Credits:** *Executive Producer:* Jay Firestone, Adam Haight, John Lynch, Tommy Lynch. *Producer:* Helene White, Jana Veverka, Ray Sager, Gary L. Stephenson, Tony Thatcher, Victoria Woods. *Music:* Reg Powell.

685   Cake. (Children; CBS; Premiered: September 16, 2006)

A program geared to teenage girls that encourages them to be creative through the activities of Cake, a girl who hosts the cable access show *Cake TV*. Miracle and Amy are her assistants (on craft projects); Benjamin is their producer.

Cast: Christa B. Allen (Cake), Anna Maria Perez De Tagle (Miracle), Emily Everhard (Amy Foster), Keegan McFadden (Benjamin Turner). **Credits:** *Executive Producer:* Andy Heyward, Michael Milliani, Sean McNamara, David Brookwell. *Co-Executive Producer:* Laura Keats. *Producer:* Pixie Wespiser. *Co-Producer:* Frank Merwald. *Music:* Ron Wasserman.

686   Californication. (Comedy; Showtime; Premiered: August 13, 2007)

When his book, *God Hates Us All* is sold for movie rights, Hank Moody moves from New York to Los Angeles. The film is produced as a comedy called *A Crazy Little Thing Called Love* and Hank, who feels the system has let him down, develops a serious case of writer's block. He retreats into his own little world and refuses to listen to his agent (Charlie) or publisher. Self-pity and unemployment now seem to suit him. He has also let his appearance go (perpetually unshaven) but (in accord with the title) he does manage to attract beautiful women. Karen is Hank's ex-girlfriend; Becca is his teenage daughter (by Karen); Bill is Karen's current love interest; Mia is Bill's teenage daughter from a prior marriage. Stories follow Hank as he struggles to live with the inner turmoil that haunts him.

Cast: David Duchovny (Hank Moody), Natascha McElhone (Karen), Madeleine Martin (Becca), Madeline Zima (Mia), Danian Young (Bill), Evan Handler (Charlie). **Credits:** *Executive Producer:* Tom Kapinos, David Duchovny, Stephen Hopkins. *Co-Executive Producer:* Melanie Greene. *Producer:* Anne Kindberg. *Music:* Tyler Bates.

687   Camouflage. (Game; Game Show Network; Premiered: July 2, 2007)

A board with scrambled letters appears on stage. A clue is given by the host that informs two players of the word or words that must be found. Puzzles begin at $200 (then increase to $300) but decrease by $10 for each letter that has to be removed before one of the players guesses the word. The highest scoring player wins.

Host: Roger Lodge. **Credits:** *Executive Producer:* Jonathan Barry, Terrence McDonnell. *Producer:* John Alexander. *Music:* Scooter Pietsch.

688   Camp Lazlo. (Cartoon; Cartoon Network; July 8, 2005 to March 27, 2008)

The adventures of a group of talking animals that attend Camp Kidney, a summer camp in the Pimpleback Mountains. Lazlo, a Brazilian Monkey, Raj, an Indian elephant and Clam, a pygmy rhino are the main characters.

Voice Cast: Carlos Alazraqui (Lazlo/ Clam), Glenn Bennett (Raj), Jill Tilley (Nina/Gretchen), Jodi Benson (Patsy Smiles/Jane Doe), Tom Kenny (Lumpus/ Slinkman). **Credits:** *Executive Producer:* Brian A. Miller, Joe Murray. *Supervising Producer:* Jennifer Pelphrey. *Producer:* Shareena Carlson, Mark O'Hare.

689 The Captain and Casey Show. (Reality; Fuel TV; Premiered: August 16, 2004)

Comedy mixed with reality as sports anchormen Casey and the Captain present the worst (amateurs) and the best the skateboarding world has to offer.

Cast: Chris Casey (Casey), Jeff Carlson (The Captain). **Credits:** *Producer:* John Layne, Matt Solomon. *Segment Producer:* Keith Davidson, Jordan Bloch, Dave Bergthold, Mike Kathman. *Music:* Robb Williamson.

690 Captured. (Reality; Oxygen; October 7, 2007 to June 2, 2008)

A shocking event — anything from a disappearance to a murder is revealed. To help solve the case, a strong female protagonist (from police officer, to D.A. to friend of the victim) is profiled as she pieces together the facts to bring the case to a successful conclusion.

Narrator: Mason Pettit. **Credits:** *Executive Producer:* Stephen Land, Geoffrey Proud. *Co-Executive Producer:* Zak Wesfield. *Supervising Producer:* Deborah Dawkins. *Producer:* Brian O'Connor. *Director:* Jeffrey S. Woods.

691 The Carol DuVall Show. (Talk; HGTV; Premiered: January 1, 1996)

Daily program of craft and decorating tips.

Host: Carol DuVall. **Credits:** *Executive Producer:* Steve Lange, Robb Weller, Gary H. Grossman. *Supervising Producer:* Kelly Ehrlich. *Producer:* Laura Brown-Fulp, Bob Levitan.

692 Carpoolers. (Comedy; ABC; October 2, 2007 to March 4, 2008)

Simplistic comedy about the incidents that befall four friends (Aubrey, Dougie, Gracen and Laird) who use the carpool lane to work each day.

Cast: Faith Ford (Leila), Jerry O'Connell (Laird Holcomb), Fred Goss (Gracen), Jerry Minor (Aubrey), Tim Pepe (Dougie), Allison Munn (Cindy), T.J. Miller (Marmaduke). **Credits:** *Executive Producer:* David Miner, Darryl Frank, Justin Falvey, Bruce McCulloch, Marsh McCall. *Producer:* Emily Cutler, Dan Kaplow, Steve Leff. *Music:* David Schwartz.

693 Cash Cab. (Game; Discovery Channel; Premiered: December 5, 2005)

A game show that is played in a moving taxicab. Passengers are the contestants. As the taxi begins its journey, the driver asks the passenger a series of questions worth from $25 to $100 each. A player wins what money he can until he reaches his destination.

Host: Ben Bailey. **Credits:** *Executive Producer:* Ron Deutsch, Tom Cohen. *Supervising Producer:* John Bertholon. *Producer:* Fred Grinstein. *Music:* Matt Anthony, Stephen O'Reilly.

694 Cathouse. (Erotica; HBO; Premiered: June 16, 2005)

The Moonlite Bunny Ranch is a legal brothel in Carson City, Nevada. The frank series focuses on the legal prostitutes (called Bunnies) and their dealings with customers (including sexual activity). While not an X-rated feature, the program is quite explicit and also attempts to shed light on the ins and outs of running a brothel. The concept began in 2002 as an HBO documentary called *Cathouse*. It was followed by another special, *Cathouse: Back in the Saddle* in 2005. In addition to the series, five additional specials aired in 2008: *Cathouse: The Musical*, *Cathouse: Come to the Party*, *The Best of Cathouse:*, *Cathouse: Menage a Trois* and *Cathouse: What's on the Menu* (a "real hot cooking show" that demonstrates how the sizzling Bunny Ranch delicacies are served). Cast and credits are the same for the series and specials.

Host: Dennis Hof, Madam Suzette. **Bunnies:** Brook Taylor, Sunset Thomas, Bridget Powers, Isabella Soprano, Monica Morris, Tiffany Taylor, Shy Love, Shelley Dushell, Melody Lane. **Credits:** *Executive Producer:* Dennis Hof, Sheila Nevin. *Supervising Producer:* George Ciccarone. *Producer:* Patti Kaplan. *Co-Producer:* Laissa Bills, Michael Goldfine. *Associate Producer:* Marni Rothman.

695 Celebrity Expose. (Reality; My Network TV; October 1, 2007 to September 15, 2008)

In-depth celebrity profiles that expose the good and bad aspects of a subject's life.

Host: Tony Potts. **Announcer:** Ryan Henry. **Credits:** *Executive Producer:* Rob K. Silverstein. *Supervising Producer:* Mike Marson, Adam Jordan. *Producer:* Cara Petry, David Shapiro.

696 Celebrity Fit Club. (Reality; VH-1; Premiered: January 9, 2005)

Eight celebrities who are a bit overweight appear and are divided into two teams. They must perform various exercise challenges in an attempt to lose weight. The day after each challenge the celebrities weigh in and are judged by a panel of experts on their progress (or lack of it).

Judges: Dr. Ian Smith, Dr. Linda Papadoupolos, Dr. Stacey Kaiser, Harvey Walden, Maria Peer. **Celebrities Include:** Tina Yothers, Erika Eleniak, Maureen McCormick, Daniel Baldwin, Erin Moran, Dustin Diamond, Willie Aames, Kim

Coles, Jackee Harry, Gary Busey, Victoria Jackson. **Credits:** *Executive Producer:* Jonas Larson, Dagmar Charlton, Curt Northrup. *Supervising Producer:* Greg Heller, Scott Cooper. *Producer:* Rebecca Dienno, Todd Modisett.

697 Celebrity Rap Superstar. (Reality; MTV; Premiered: August 30, 2007)

Personalities from the world of music, film, TV and sports compete for the opportunity to become "The Celebrity Rap Superstar." Celebrities are mentored by acclaimed rappers and judged by rapper Da Brat — who eliminates the weakest performers and selects the best as the Celebrity Rap Superstar.

Host: Liz Hernandez, Kevin Hart. **Credits:** *Executive Producer:* Joel Gallen, Pamela Kohl, Kim Rickabaugh, Mark Schulman, Giuliana DePandi. *Co-Executive Producer:* Aaron Lee. *Producer:* Josh Greenberg. *Music:* Dylan Berry.

698 Charlie and Lola. (Cartoon; Disney; Premiered: March 1, 2005)

Charlie is a very responsible eight-year-old. Lola is his mischievous five-year-old sister. Charlie feels obligated to take Lola under his wing and guide her through life by showing her right from wrong. Stories follow Charlie as he helps Lola out of the situations her eagerness gets her into.

Voice Cast: Jethro Lundie-Brown (Charlie), Maisie Cowell (Lola). **Credits:** *Executive Producer:* Andrew Zein, Michael Carrington. *Producer:* Claudia Lloyd, Nikki Chaplin.

699 Chefography. (Profile; Food Network; Premiered: March 13, 2006)

A profile of the home and working lives of chefs who have appeared on the Food Network.

Narrator: J.V. Martin. **Chefs Include:** Rachael Ray, Sandra Lee, Emeril Lagasse, Bobby Flay, Paula Deen, Giada De Laurentis, Wolfgang Puck, Tyler Florence. **Credits:** *Executive Producer:* Gary H.

Grossman, Steve Lange, Robb Weller. *Supervising Producer:* Nancy Gimbrone.

700   Chelsea Lately. (Comedy; E!; July 16, 2007 to December 5, 2008)

Comedian Chelsea Handler interviews ordinary people on random subjects as well as spoofing everything from movies and TV to news and politicians.

Host: Chelsea Handler. **Co-Host:** Chuy Bravo. **Regulars:** Carrie Keagan, Sarah Colonna, Michael Yo, Brad Wollack. **Credits:** *Executive Producer:* Corin Nelson, Mark Schulman, Brent Zacky. *Supervising Producer:* Peter Johansen, Sue Murphy, John Axelson. *Producer:* Adam Kleid. *Associate Producer:* John Milford, John Paparazzo.

701   Chowder. (Cartoon; Cartoon Network; Premiered: November 2, 2007)

Events in the hectic life of Chowder, an apprentice boy chef at a catering company in Marzipan City.

Voice Cast: Nicky Jones (Chowder), Dwight Schultz (Mung Daal), John DiMaggio (Schnitzel), Liliana Mumy (Panini), Tara Strong (Truffles), Dana Snyder (Gazpacho), Will Shadley (Gorgonzola). **Credits:** *Executive Producer:* C.H. Greenblatt. *Producer:* Louis J. Cuck. *Music:* Zac Pike, Dan Boer.

702   Chuck. (Comedy; NBC; Premiered: September 24, 2007)

Intersect, a U.S. government computer that stores the nation's most vital information, is compromised by a rogue CIA agent (Bruce). Before he is caught, Bryce destroys the computer but downloads all its information into an e-mail that he sends to his former college friend, Chuck Bartowski. Chuck, a computer geek, works at the Nerd Herd, an electronics store in the Buy More Mall in Los Angeles. When Chuck sees that he has an e-mail from Bryce, he opens it. The sublimely encoded message down loads the entire computer file into his brain. Immediately, Chuck becomes the concern of both the CIA and the NSA as the fate of the world now rests in his hands. To protect Chuck, now a living "computer" whose brain contains sensitive information, the government assigns two agents to watch over him: NSA agent John Casey (who works undercover as a salesman at the Nerd Herd) and CIA agent Sarah Walker (who, while working as a waitress at the hot dog stand Weinerlicious, pretends to be Chuck's girlfriend). Chuck must now live a dual life — computer geek and the government's most valuable agent. Stories follow Chuck's reluctant efforts to perform missions required by the government. Ellie is Chuck's sister; Morgan is his best friend; Devon is Ellie's boyfriend.

Cast: Zachary Levi (Chuck Bartowski), Adam Baldwin (Major John Casey), Yvonne Strahovski (Sarah Walker), Sarah Lancaster (Ellie Bartowski), Joshua Gomez (Morgan Grimes), Ryan McPartland (Devon), Mark Christopher Lawrence (Big Mike) Bonita Friedericy (General Beckman). **Credits:** *Executive Producer:* Josh Schwartz, McG. *Co-Executive Producer:* Chris Fedak. *Producer:* Paul Marks. *Music:* Tim Jones.

703   Cities of the Underworld. (Reality; History Channel; Premiered: April 23, 2007)

An exploration of various buildings in cities around the world to uncover the hidden engineering feats that enabled their construction at a time when such feats were thought too difficult or impossible.

Host: Eric Geller, Don Wildman. **Credits:** *Executive Producer:* Dolores Gavin, Lauren Lexton, Tom Rogan, Sarah Wetherbee, Marlene Braga. *Supervising Producer:* Chris Bray. *Producer:* Alison Hynes, Thea Bergeron, Katarina Parks. *Music:* Adam Small.

704   The Closer. (Crime Drama; TNT; Premiered: June 13, 2005)

Brenda Johnson is a first rate interrogator who can obtain confessions and close a case. She was trained by the FBI and first worked as a detective with the Atlanta Police Department before being recruited by the L.A.P.D. to head a department as a Deputy Police Chief. Brenda is tough-minded and the only female in a squad of male detectives (some of whom resent her for her quick move up the departmental ladder). Brenda is totally focused on her career and does what she has to obtain a confession. In times of stress her will power tends to desert her. Stories are quite realistic and focuses on Brenda and her team as they investigate crimes.

Cast: Kyra Sedgwick (Brenda Johnson), J.K. Simmons (Chief Will Pope), Corey Reynolds (Sgt. David Gabriel), Anthony John Dennison (Det. Andy Flynn), Jon Tenney (Agent Fritz Howard), G.W. Bailey (Det. Lt. Provenza), Robert Gossett (Captain Taylor), Barry Corbin (Clay Johnson; Brenda's father), Frances Sternhagen (Willie Ray Johnson; Brenda's mother). **Credits:** *Executive Producer:* James Duff, Michael M. Robin, Greer Shepherd. *Supervising Producer:* Alan Belanoff, Wendy West. *Co-Executive Producer:* Nancy Miller. *Producer:* Andrew J. Sacks. *Music:* James S. Levine.

705   Co-ed Confidential. (Comedy; Cinemax; Premiered: November 2, 2007)

The Omega Fraternity House of a college campus is the setting for a look at the sexual activities of the students as Ophelia, the housemother, and her on-and-off boyfriend, James, attempt to maintain a respectable frat house despite its party reputation.

Cast: Hanna Harper (Ophelia), Kevin Patrick (James), Michelle Maylene (Karen), Olivia Alana May (Emmanuelle), Sandra Luesse (Lisa), Andre Boyer (Freddy), Eric Aston (Royce), Oskar Rodriquez (Jose). **Credits:** *Executive Producer:* Marc L. Greenberg. *Producer:* Denise Roberts, Gabrielle McGinty, Marc Lawrence. *Music:* Herman Beeftink.

706   The Colbert Report. (Comedy; Comedy Central; Premiered: October 17, 2005)

Satirical views of contemporary issues as interpreted by comedian Stephen Colbert.

Host: Stephen Colbert. **Credits:** *Executive Producer:* Stephen Colbert, Jon Stewart, Allison Silverman. *Co-Executive Producer:* Meredith Bennett. *Supervising Producer:* Allison Silverman, Rich Dahm. *Producer:* Samantha Scharff.

707   Cold Case. (Crime Drama; CBS; Premiered: September 28, 2003)

Unsolved cases are labeled "Cold Cases" by police departments and usually placed in their basement morgues. One Philadelphia police woman, Lily Rush, has taken an interest in such cases and has vowed to see that these people see closure just as the victims of active cases do. For Lily and her team, a piece of evidence emerges from the past that requires going back in time — to the cold case files and finding witnesses who are still alive. Lily feels that even though her cold cases will not generate headlines, they deserve to be solved. Then and now footage is used to highlight Lily's case investigations.

Cast: Kathryn Morris (Lily Rush), John Finn (Det. John Stillman), Jeremy Ratchford (Det. Nick Vera), Justin Chambers (Det. Chris Lassing), Thom Barry (Capt. Will Jeffries), Tracie Thoms (Det. Kat Miller), Nicki Lynn Aycox (Christine Rush, Lily's sister). **Credits:** *Executive Producer:* Jerry Bruckheimer, Jonathan Littman, Meredith Stiehm, Shaun Cassidy. *Co-Executive Producer:* Greg Plageman, Andrea Newman. *Supervising Producer:* Tyler Bensinger, Sean Whitesell, David Barrett. *Producer:* Perry Husman, Merri D. Howard, Tim Matheson. *Music:* Michael A. Levine.

708   Cold Case Files. (Reality; A&E; Premiered: January 1, 1999)

When a criminal case is unable to be

solved it is labeled a cold case with all known evidence placed in a box and stored. The program explores such cases when new evidence is found and the case is reopened for investigation. In some instances, the crime is solved; in others, it still remains a cold case.

Host: Bill Kurtis. **Credits:** Producer: Michael West. *Music:* Patrick Yacono.

709 Cold Squad. (Crime Drama; Syn.; Premiered: September 2006)

The Cold Squad is a Canadian task force (specifically, a unit of the Vancouver Police Department) that reopens cases to investigate mostly short-term unsolved murders. Particular attention is on Ali McCormick, a homicide sergeant who is considered the best cop on the force. Ali, hand picked to head the squad, is stubborn and impulsive and determined to solve every cold case that comes her way. Stories follow Ali as she, like Lily Rush on America's *Cold Case* strives to close the files on previously unsolved murders.

Cast: Julie Stewart (Sgt. Ali McCormick), Michael Hogan (Det. Tony Logozzo), Jill Teed (Laura), Linda Ko (Christine Liu), Peter Wingfield (Insp. Simon Ross) Adrian Holmes (Dr. Ben Wilson), Joy Tanner (Jill Stone). **Credits:** *Executive Producer:* Marlene Matthews, Matt McLeod, Anne Marie Latrabetse, Julie Keatley. *Producer:* Richard Davis. *Music:* Graeme Coleman.

710 Comics Unleashed. (Comedy; Syn.; Premiered: September 2007)

Three guest comics join the host for a comical discussion on anything and everything.

Host: Byron Allen. **Credits:** *Executive Producer:* Byron Allen, Carolyn Folks. *Producer:* Jennifer Lucas. *Music:* D.J. A One.

711 Control Room Presents. (Variety; Syn.; Premiered: September 2007)

Performances by music entertainers form around the world (for example, En-

rique Iglesias, Smashing Pumpkins, Avril Lavigne, Maroon 5).

Credits: *Executive Producer:* Aaron Grosky, Kevin Wall. *Senior Producer:* Nicholas Jacobovitz. *Poducer:* Pierre Lamoureux, Francois Lamoureux.

712 Cops. (Reality; Fox; Premiered: March 11, 1989)

Real life police officers (in various states) are followed as they patrol the streets to serve and protect.

Announcer: Burt Lancaster (pilot episode), Harry Newman (series). **Credits:** *Executive Producer:* Malcolm Barbour, John Langley. *Supervising Producer:* Douglas Waterman. *Producer:* Paul Stojanovich, Jim Langley, Andrew Thomas, Jack Walworth, Steve Kiger, Murray Jordan.

713 Cory in the House. (Comedy; Disney; Premiered: January 12, 2007)

A spin-off from *That's So Raven*. When Raven Baxter, the older sister of Cory Baxter begins college and her mother registers for law school, Cory and his father, Victor, move to Washington, D.C. (from San Francisco) to live in the White House when Victor, a chef, acquires the job as cook for the President of the U.S. (Richard Martinez). Cory enrolls in Washington Prep Academy and stories focus on Cory as he runs amuck in the White House.

Cast: Kyle Massey (Cory Baxter), Rondell Sheridan (Victor Baxter), John D'Aquino (Pres. Richard Martinez), Madison Pettis (Sophie Martinez), Maiara Walsh (Meena Parooa), Lisa Kushell (Samantha Samuels), Lupe Ontiveros (Mama Martinez), Jason Dolley (Newt Livingston III), Jake Thomas (Jason Stickler). **Credits:** *Executive Producer:* Dennis Rinsler, Marc Warren. *Co-Executive Producer:* Patty Gary. *Producer:* Julie Tsutsui, Josh Greene. *Music:* Scott Clausen, Christopher A. Lee.

714 Country Fried Home Videos. (Reality; CMT; Premiered: June 30, 2006)

Home videos of ordinary people show-ing Americans "what real Americans do"—from acting to telling corny jokes.

Host: Bill Engvall. **Credits:** *Executive Producer:* Mack Anderson, Bradley Anderson. *Co-Executive Producer:* Steve Lavapies. *Producer:* Bill Engvall, Kimberly Austin, David T. Steckler. *Music:* Jim Parker.

715 **Criminal Minds**. (Crime Drama; CBS; Premiered: September 22, 2005)

"To catch a criminal, you have to think like one" is the philosophy of Jason Gideon, a top profiler who heads the FBI's Behavioral Analysis Unit in Quantico, Virginia. He is assisted by Aaron Hotchner, Elle Greenway, Dr. Spencer Reid, Derek Morgan and Jennifer "J.J." Jareau. Elle leaves after a shooting incident and is replaced by Emily Prentiss; Jason is replaced by David Rossi after he becomes disillusioned with the unit. Penelope Garcia is the unit's computer expert.

Cast: Mandy Patinkin (Jason Gideon), Thomas Gibson (Aaron Hotchner), Joe Mantegna (David Rossi), Lola Glaudini (Elle Greenway), A.J. Cook (Jennifer Jareau), Shemar Moore (Derek Morgan), Matthew Gray Gubler (Dr. Spencer Reid), Paget Brewster (Emily Prentiss), Kirsten Vangsness (Penelope Garcia), Meta Golding (Agent Jordan Todd). **Credits:** *Executive Producer:* Mark Gordon, Edward Allen Bernero. *Co-Executive Producer:* Deborah Spera, Jeff Davis, Peter Schindler, Judy McCreary. *Supervising Producer:* Aaron Zelman, Simon Mirren. *Producer:* Glenn Kershaw, Herb Adelman, Erica Messer, Debra J. Fisher. *Music:* Steffan Fantini, Marc Fantini, Scott Gordon, Mark Moncino.

716 **Criss Angel: Mindfreak**. (Reality; A&E; Premiered: July 20, 2005)

Amazing feats of magic as performed by Criss Angel, a modern-day magician who calls his extreme feats "mindfreak."

Host: Criss Angel. **Credits:** *Executive Producer:* Criss Angel, Dave Baram, Michael A. Blum, Steven Lenchner, Simon Miller, Nancy Dubuc, Rob Sharenow. *Supervising Producer:* Erich Recker. *Producer:* Will Raee, Marguerite Henry. *Music:* Criss Angel, Micky James.

717 **Cristina's Court**. (Reality; Syn.; Premiered: September 2006)

A daily series of actual small claims court cases presided over by Judge Cristina Perez.

Judge: Cristina Perez. **Credits:** *Executive Producer:* Peter Brennan. *Supervising Producer:* Lisa Lew, Hedda Musket. *Producer:* Regina St. Romano, Lisa Wilson.

718 **Crosswords**. (Game; Syn.; September 2007 to September 2008)

A crossword puzzle is revealed. The host reads a clue representing one of its positions. The first player (of two who compete) to buzz in and give the correct answer sees a letter appear in its appropriate spot and receives a chance to spell the missing word. If correct, the word appears in the puzzle and the player scores money. Three additional players, called Spoilers, stand behind these players. If the player makes a mistake (gives the wrong answer), a Spoiler can steal his spot and money by giving a correct response. This player then joins the remaining player and the defeated player becomes a Spoiler. The game continues in this manner; the player with the most money (most correct words guessed) becomes the champion and receives what cash he has accumulated. The series is created by Merv Griffin.

Host: Ty Treadway. **Announcer:** Edd Hall. **Credits:** *Executive Producer:* Merv Griffin, Raymond J. Brune, Andrew Yani, Breanna Huntington. *Producer:* Ritch Colbert, Josh Raphaelson.

719 **Crowned: The Mother of All Pageants**. (Reality; CW; December 12, 2007 to January 30, 2008)

Actual mothers and their daughters

compete in a beauty pageant for a tiara and $100,000. Twenty-two women (eleven mothers and their daughters) compete. Each week, actual beauty pageant challenges are held (like swim suit, evening gown, talent) and each week the weakest performers are eliminated by a panel of judges. The last telecast features three teams competing; the one team that prove themselves superior wins the crown.

Pageant Director: Linnea Maloney. **Judges:** Carson Kressley, Shanna Moakler, Cynthia Garnett. **Credits:** *Executive Producer:* Laurie Girion, Michael Levitt. *Co-Executive Producer:* James Canniffe. *Supervising Producer:* Chris Carlson, Heather Schuster. *Senior Producer:* George Sealy, Johnny Petillo. *Theme Vocal:* June Angela.

720 C.S.I.: Crime Scene Investigation. (Crime Drama; CBS; Premiered: October 6, 2000)

Gil Grissom is the head of the C.S.I. (Crime Scene Investigation Team) of the Las Vegas, Nevada, Police Department. He is assisted by Catherine Willows, Sara Sidle, Nick Stokes and Warrick Brown. Gil and his associates call themselves Forensic Scientists and handle each case objectively "with no regard to race, creed or bubble gum flavor... When the pieces of a puzzle just don't fit, they call us in." Gil's special skill is entomology (the study of insects). He was promoted to the head of the crime lab when his superior, Captain Jim Brass, was transferred to the department's homicide division. Catherine, Gil's senior investigator, is a blood splatter analysis specialist. She scrutinizes every crime scene, collects the evidence and recreates what happened by piecing together the evidence she has found. Sara's specialty is material and element analysis. Hair and fiber analysis is Nick's specialty. Warwick is an expert in audio and video analysis. Stories, which are quite graphic, relate the team's investigation of often gruesome crimes. In the episode of De-

cember 11, 2008 ("19 Down"), Gil announces to his team that he is leaving the unit (no specific reason given) and that his replacement will be Raymond Langston, a criminal pathologist he met while attending one of Raymond's teaching classes.

Cast: William Petersen (Gil Grissom), Marg Helgenberger (Catherine Willows), Jorga Fox (Sara Sidle), George Eades (Nick Stokes), Gary Dourdan (Warrick Brown), Paul Guilfoyle (Capt. Jim Brass), Laurence Fishburne (Raymond Langston), Lauren Lee Smith (Bryce Adams), Liev Schreiber (Michael Keppler), Wallace Langham (David Hodges), Kay Panabaker (Lindsey, Catherine's daughter). **Credits:** *Executive Producer:* Jerry Bruckheimer, Carol Mendelsohn, Ann Donahue, Anthony E. Zuiker, Jonathan Littman, William Petersen, Cynthia Chvatal, Kenneth Fink, Naren Shankar. *Co-Executive Producer:* Sam Strangis, Andrew Lipsitz, James C. Hart, Judy McCreary. *Supervising Producer:* Richard J. Lewis, Kenneth Fink. *Producer:* William Petersen, Danny Cannon, Louis Shaw Milito, Sarah Goldfinger, Henry Alonso, Bernie Laramie, Ron Mitchell, Peter Dunne. *Music:* John M. Keane.

721 C.S.I.: Miami. (Crime Drama; CBS; Premiered: September 23, 2002)

A graphic look at the grueling, often upsetting work of the Crime Scene Investigation Unit of the Miami Dade County Police Department. Horatio Caine heads the team and is assisted by Calleigh Dusquesne, Megan Donner, Eric Delko, Tim Speedle and Dr. Alexx Woods. Horatio is an expert in explosives and best when all the evidence does not point to the person he believes is the killer and must dig deeper. Calleigh is a ballistics expert and called "The Bullet Girl." Megan is a DNA expert and hates hunches — "Show me the evidence," she says. Tim is the team's chief investigator. He has street connections and believes in trusting his gut instinct. Alexx is the no-nonsense, know-it-all coroner.

Cast: David Caruso (Horatio Caine), Emily Procter (Calleigh Duquesne), Kim Delaney (Megan Donner), Adam Rodriquez (Eric Delko), Rory Cochrane (Tim Speedle), Khandi Alexander (Dr. Alexx Woods), Sofia Milos (Detective Yelina Salas), Elizabeth Berkley (Julia Winston). **Credits:** *Executive Producer:* Jonathan Littman, Danny Cannon, Jerry Bruckheimer, Anthony E. Zuiker, David Black, Ann Donahue, Carol Mendelsohn, Nancy Miller, Stephen Zito. *Co-Executive Producer:* Elizabeth Devine, Louise Mc-Carthy, Sam Strangis. *Producer:* Corey Miller, Sunil Nayar, Sina Lamar. Scott Shiffman.

722 C.S.I.: New York. (Crime Drama; CBS; Premiered: September 22, 2004)

The grueling work of the Crime Scene Investigation Unit of the N.Y.P.D. is profiled in graphic and potentially upsetting stories for some viewers. Mac Taylor heads the unit and is assisted by Stella Bonasera, Danny Messer, Lindsay Monroe, Don Flack and Dr. Sheldon Hawkes. Mac is a blood and splatter analysis expert who knows a lot about little things and uses that knowledge to impress people. Stella is an expert in chemical analysis. Don is streetwise and uses his contacts to help the team when they are in a bind. Lindsay was originally with the Montana C.S.I. before moving to New York to further her career. She is eager to do her best and will not rest until she brings a case to a successful conclusion. Sheldon, the unit's Chief Medical Examiner, prefers the peace and solitude of the coroner's office.

Cast: Gary Sinise (Mac Taylor), Melina Kanakaredes (Stella Bonasera), Carmine Giovinazzo (Danny Messer), Anna Belknap (Lindsay Monroe), Eddie Cahill (Don Flack), Hill Harper (Dr. Sheldon Hawkes). **Credits:** *Executive Producer:* Danny Cannon, Jerry Bruckheimer, Andrew Lipsitz, Jonathan Littman, Ann Donahue, Carol Mendelsohn, Anthony E. Zuiker. *Co-Ex-*

ecutive Producer: Wendy Battles, Peter M. Lenkov, Pam Veasey, Timothy J. Lea. *Producer:* Gary Sinise, Rob Bailey, Bruce Golin, Robert D. Simon, Deran Sarafian, Vikki Williams, Eli Talbert. *Co-Producer:* Janet Tamaro, Geoffrey Hemwall, Ken Solarz. *Music:* Bill Brown.

723 Curb Appeal. (Reality; HGTV; Premiered: September 1, 1999)

A team of designers and landscape artists transform homes that may be gorgeous on the inside but have no curb appeal on the outside.

Host: Bill Duggan, Rick Spences, Sasha Andreey, Dan Schachner. **Credits:** *Producer:* Steve Edelman.

724 Curb Your Enthusiasm. (Comedy; HBO; Premiered: October 15, 2000)

Events in the life of comedian Larry David are depicted in cinema verite style. Larry appears as a producer-writer. He is married to Cheryl, has a number of good friends (played mostly by guest celebrities) and a manager (Jeff Greene). Other regulars are Susie, Jeff's foul-mouthed wife; and Richard Lewis, Larry's closest friend.

Cast: Larry David (Himself), Cheryl Hines (Cheryl David), Jeff Garlin (Jeff Greene), Susie Essman (Susie Greene), Richard Lewis (Himself), Shelley Berman (Nat David). **Credits:** Executive Producer: Larry David, Jeff Garlin, David Mandel, Larry Charles. *Co-Executive Producer:* Sandy Chanley, Erin O'Malley, Robert B. Weide. *Producer:* Tim Gibbons, Megan Murphy, Scott Butler.

725 Curious George. (Cartoon; PBS; Premiered: September 4, 2006)

George is a very curious African monkey owned by the Man in the Yellow Hat. George is naturally curious and must explore to satisfy that curiosity. Through his explorations, children are taught lessons about life.

Voice Cast: Frank Welker (George), Jeff Bennett (Man in the Yellow Hat), William

H. Macy (Narrator). **Credits:** *Executive Producer:* Ellen Cockrill, Carol Greenwald, David Kirshner, Jon Shapiro. *Producer:* Patty Jausoro, Jacqui Deegan.

726   The CW Now. (Reality; CW; September 23, 2007 to February 24, 2008)

A fast-paced program that mixes electronic gadgetry with network promos and sponsor messages to look at lifestyles here and abroad.

Hosts: Tanika Ray, Chris Balish. **Correspondents:** Chi-Lan Lieu, J. Boogie. **Credits:** *Executive Producer:* Lisa Gregorisch-Dempsey, Mike Miller. *Supervising Producer:* Steve Longo. *Producer:* Robert Willrich.

727   Cyberchase. (Children; PBS; Premiered: January 21, 2002)

Hacker is a diabolical computer genius with only one goal: conquer the virtual universe. When he begins his quest, Motherboard, the guardian of all cyberspace, endows three children (Jackie, Matt and Inez) with the ability to become the Cyber Squad and use the power of mathematics to battle Hacker.

Cast: Christopher Lloyd (Hacker), Novie Edwards (Jackie), Annick Obonsawin (Inez), Jacqueline Pillon (Matt), Kristina Nicoll (Motherboard), Gilbert Gottfried (Digit). **Credits:** *Executive Producer:* Toper Taylor, Sandra Sheppard, Kristin Laskas Martin, Michael Hirsh, Scott Dyer. *Supervising Producer:* Pat Burns, Michelle Melanson, Jocelyn Hamilton. *Producer:* Marissa Collyer, Ellen Doherty, Lynne Warner. *Music:* George Guerrette, David W. Shaw.

728   The Daily Habit. (Variety; Fuel TV; Premiered: October 3, 2005)

Daily program that highlights action sports celebrities, musicians, comedians and "cutting edge technology."

Host: Pat Parnell. **Co-Hosts:** Sandra Sanchez, Brande Roderick, Zeke Piestrup.

Credits: *Executive Producer:* Scott Paridon, C.J. Olivares. *Supervising Producer:* Jeff Tully. *Producer:* Patrick Weir.

729   The Daily Show. (Talk; Comedy Central; Premiered: July 22, 1996)

Interviews with both known and lesser known celebrities, political figures and newsmakers.

Host: Jon Stewart. **Credits:** *Executive Producer:* Madeline Smithberg, Jon Stewart, Ben Karlin, Kahane Corn. *Supervising Producer:* Rob Fox, David Janerbaum. *Producer:* Christina Santiago, Colby Hall. *Music:* John Ilansburgh, John Linnell.

730   Dallas Cowboys Cheerleaders: Making the Team. (Reality; CMT; September 29, 2006 to November 22, 2008)

A behind-the-scenes look at the selective process women endure to become one of America's Sweetheart's, a Dallas Cowboys Cheerleader. Each of the female hopefuls is tested in overall style, dance, personality, football knowledge and athletic ability. Kelli Finglass, a former Cowboys cheerleader, oversees the proceedings.

Cast: Kelli Finglass (Host), Jay Johnson (Boot Camp Drill Sergeant), Judy Trammell (Choreographer). **Credits:** *Executive Producer:* Steve Kroopnick, Eugene Pack, Stu Schreberg. *Producer:* Jennifer Stander, Leland Ingraham. *Music:* Jim Parker

731   Dallas SWAT. (Reality; A&E; Premiered: January 5, 2006)

The work of the Dallas, Texas, Police Department's SWAT Team (Special Weapons and Tactics) as they step in to resolve situations that are too dangerous for ordinary police to handle.

Host: Steve Claggett. **Credits:** *Executive Producer:* Neil A. Cohen, Laura Fleury, John X. Kim. *Producer:* Neil Laird, C. Webb Young, Xackery Irving. *Music:* Stephen O'Reilly.

732   Damages. (Drama; FX; Premiered: July 24, 2007)

Hewes and Associates is a prestigious Manhattan law firm owned by Patricia Hewes (called Patty), one of the country's most successful class-action attorneys. Although Patty will tackle a case on her own, she believes in numbers for strength. She is forceful and so persistent that the opposing legal council often just gives up (for an out-of-court settlement) rather than face her wrath in front of a jury. Ellen Parsons, an ambitious attorney just out of law school and Tom Shayes, Patty's right-hand man, are Patty's associates. Phil Grey is Patty's husband; Dr. David Connor is Ellen's fiancé; Katie is David's sister. First season recurring storyline involves Patty's efforts to get the goods on Arthur Frobisher, a CEO who bilked 5,000 employees out of their savings in an investment scam. Ray Fiske is Arthur's unethical lawyer. Second season stories focus primarily on Patty's newest client: Daniel Purcell, a researcher who has run afoul of an energy company (Ultima National Resources). Claire Maddox, a lawyer for Ultima, is Patty's principal nemesis; Wes Krulik is a member of the therapy group Ellen attends. It is also revealed that Ellen, who was attacked and nearly killed at the end of the first season, now works with the FBI; and Patty achieved her goal and stopped Arthur Frobisher.

Cast: Glenn Close (Patty Hewes), Rose Byrne (Ellen Parsons), Tate Donovan (Tom Shayes), Ted Danson (Arthur Frobisher), Zeljko Ivanek (Ray Fiske), Anastasia Griffith (Katie Connor), Noah Bean (David Connor), Michael Nouri (Phil Grey), William Hurt (Daniel Purcell), Marcia Gay Horden (Claire Maddox), Timothy Olyphant (Wes Krulik), Tom Alredge (Uncle Pete). **Credits:** *Executive Producer:* Todd A. Kessler, Glenn Kessler, Daniel Zelman. *Producer:* Allen Coulter, Mark A. Baker.

733 Dancing with the Stars. (Reality; ABC; Premiered: June 1, 2005)

Celebrities who may or may not possess dancing skills are paired with professional ballroom dancers to compete in highly styled dance competitions that are broadcast live and in front of a studio audience. A panel of experts judges each performance but can only offer opinions. Toll free numbers are provided for home viewers whose votes determine who stays and who must leave (lowest vote total). The program also presents interviews with the dancers, a behind-the-scenes look at the preparations and commentary about the style of each dance that is performed.

Hosts: Lisa Canning, Samantha Harris, Tom Bergeron. **Judges:** Len Goodman, Carrie Ann Inaba, Bruno Tonioli. **Credits:** *Executive Producer:* Richard Hopkins, Conrad Green. *Supervising Producer:* Izzie Pick. *Producer:* Topher Hopkins, Dave West, Bechara Gholam, Ashley Edens, Suzanna Ellis.

734 Dante's Cove. (Drama; Here!; Premiered: October 7, 2005)

Serial-like stories about the residents of the Hotel Dante, a secluded Caribbean resort that caters primarily to gays and lesbians. The specialized series (broadcast on the gay channel Here!) relates events in the lives of the people who frequent the resort. Supernatural overtones are also presented, mostly through the character of Grace, a gorgeous but evil witch, and her male counterpart, the sorcerer Ambrosious (who operates from a lair beneath the Dante Cove's lighthouse). Toby and Kevin are the principal gay lovers (with Ambrosious seeking to gain Kevin's love). Diana is a girl well versed in the Tresum Order of magic; Marco is the owner of the H2Eau Bar (where Toby works as the bartender).

Cast: Tracy Scoggins (Grace Neville), Charlie David (Toby), William Gregory Lee (Ambrosious Vallin), Thea Gill (Diana Childs), Jon Fleming (Adam), Nadine Heimann (Van), Gabriel Romero (Marco Laveau), Erin Cummings (Michelle), German Santiago (Kai), Josh Collins (Rex), Adrian Quinonez (Brad Diego), Dylan Vox (Colin), Tim McElwee (Josh), Rena Riffel (Tina), Stephen Amell (Adam), Fivel Stewart (Betty), Boo Boo Stewart (Stephen), Diane Davisson (Sadia), Josh Berresford (Cory), Jensen Atwood (Griffen), Jill Bennett (Michelle), Gregory Michael (Kevin Archer), Josh Berresford (Cory Dalmass), Zara Taylor (Amber). **Credits:** *Director:* Sam Irvin. *Writer:* Liz Lachman, Patrick Moore, Donna Lettwo, Michael Oblowitz, Jason Crain, Mary Feuer, Michael Costanza.

735   Date My Mom. (Reality; MTV; Premiered: November 5, 2004)

Guys seeking to date a girl are the subjects but in order to win the girl, he must first date the girl's mother. One guy is introduced to three mothers but he is not permitted to see their daughters (not in person or even in a picture). The subject literally dates each mother seeking to acquire as much information about the daughter as possible for him to decide what she looks like and how compatible he would be with her. After the dates, the subject reveals which mother's daughter he would like to date. The chosen girl is brought out and cameras capture the subject's reactions as he sees his choice for the first time.

Credits: *Executive Producer:* Kallissa Miller. *Co-Executive Producer:* H.T. Owens. *Supervising Producer:* Roy Orechio, Jennifer Stander. *Music:* Senyo Amoake.

736   Dating Brad Garrett. (Reality; Internet; September–October 2008)

Prior to the webcast, women submitted video profiles of themselves on www.crackle.com/datebrad. Ten of the submissions were judged by a panel of comedian Brad Garrett's friends and family with the object being to find those who would make suitable companions. Brad then dates each of the finalists with the object being to find a possible mate.

Star: Brad Garrett. *Executive Producer:* Brad Garrett, Kallisa Miller, Glenn Robbins, Doug Wald.

737   DaVinci's Inquest. (Crime Drama; Syn.; Premiered: September 2007)

Dominic DaVinci is a former detective with the Vancouver (Canada) Police Department turned investigator for the coroner's office. He is meticulous but not always satisfied by what he finds at a crime scene. He relies on the work of fellow detectives and doctors to find that one piece of crucial evidence he needs to bring a criminal to justice. Stories relate his efforts to solve difficult if not complex murders.

Cast: Nicholas Campbell (Dominic DaVinci), Gwynth Walsh (Dr. Patricia DaVinci), Jewel Staite (Gabriella DaVinci), Donnelly Rhodes (Leo Shannon), Venus Terzo (Angela Kosmo), Sarah-Jane Redmond (Sheila Kurtz) Ian Tracey (Mick Leary), Suleka Mathew (Sunita "Sunny" Ramen). **Credits:** *Executive Producer:* Laszlo Barna, Chris Haddock. *Producer:* Lynn Barr, Tom Braidwood, Jonathan Goodwill. *Music:* Tim McCauley, George Blondheim.

738   Days of Our Lives. (Drama; NBC; Premiered: November 8, 1965)

Dramatic incidents in the lives of the Horton, Martin, Williams and Craig families, residents of Salem, Massachusetts.

Principal 2008 Cast: Deidre Hall (Marlene Evans), Kristian Alfonso (Hope Brady), Peggy McCay (Caroline Brady), Thaao Penghlis (Andre DiMera/Anthony DiMera), Josh Taylor (Roman Brady), Nadia Bjorlin (Chloe Lane Black), Molly Burnett (Melanie Layton), Mary Beth Evans (Kayla Brady Johnson), Shelley Henning (Stephanie Johnson), Renee Jones (Dr. Lexie Carver), Lauren Koslow (Kate Roberts), Jay Kenneth Johnson (Philip), Drake Hogesty (John Black), Kevin Dobson (Mickey Horton), Bryan Dattilo (Lucas Roberts Horton), Shawn

Christian (Daniel Jonas), Darin Brooks (Max Brady), Roscoe Born (Trent Robbins), Blake Berris (Nick Fallon), Rachel Melvin (Chelsea Brady), Frances Reid (Alice Horton), Kristen Renton (Morgan Hillingsworth), Suzanne Rogers (Maggie Horton), Alison Sweeney (Sami Brady DiMera), Arianne Zucker (Nicole Walker Kiriakis), James Scott (E.J. DiMera), James Reynolds (Abe Carver), Peter Reckell (Bo Brady), Stephen Nichols (Steve Johnson), Joseph Mascolo (Stefano DiMera), Eric Martsolf (Brady Black), John Aniston (Victor Kirakis), Lauren Boles (Ciara Brady), Tanya Boyd (Celeste Perrault), Susan Seaforth Hayes (Julie Williams), Leann Hunley (Anna Bardy DiMera). **Credits:** *Executive Producer:* Ken Corday. *Supervising Producer:* Stephen Wyman. *Producer:* Sheryl Herman. *Music:* Amy Burkhard-Evans, Steve Reinhardt.

739   Deadliest Catch. (Reality; Discovery Channel; Premiered: March 15, 2005)

Documentary-like program that charts the extremely dangerous (and sometimes fatal) work of Alaskan crab fishermen.

Narrator: Mike Rowe. **Credits:** *Executive Producer:* Tracy Green. *Supervising Producer:* Lisa Tanzer, Thom Beers, Jeff Conroy. *Producer:* Chris Smith, Johnny Petillo, Chris Nee, Tim Pastore, Matt Renner, Doug Stanley. *Music:* Bruce Hanifan, Paul Hepker.

740   Deal or No Deal. (Game; NBC; Premiered: December 19, 2005)

Twenty-six beautiful models appear on stage, each holding a case that contains an unknown amount of money (from one cent to $1 million). The player selects one case, which becomes his until the end of the game. The player must now open cases with the object being to keep the larger money amounts in play. Based on how bad (opening large cash amounts) or how good (small cash amounts), the banker offers to buy the player's case for a specific amount

of money. If he refuses, it's a no deal and the player continues picking cases. A player's winnings are based on either accepting the banker's offer or holding out to see what his case holds. Jessica Robinson became the first million dollar winner on September 1, 2008. The models listed below reflect the 2008 season; each is listed with the case she holds. See also program 129.

Host: Howie Mandel. **Models:** Claudia Jordan (Case 1), Stacey Gardner (2), Lisa Gleave (3), Keltie Martin (4), Ursula Mayes (5), Megan Abrigo (6), Sara Bronson (7), Mariela Arteaga (8), Patricia Kara (9), Anya Monzikova (10), Katie Cleary (11), Lauren Shiohama (12), Leyla Milani (13), Pilar (14), Brooke Long (15), Lisa Lakatos (16), Jenelle Moreno (17), Marisa Petroro (18), Amanza Smith (19), Alike Boggan (20), Tameka Jacobs (21), Crystal Monte (22), Aubrie Lemon (23), Kelly Brannigan (24), Hayley Marie Norman (25), Lindsay Clubine (26) **Banker:** Peter Abbay. **Credits:** *Announcer:* Joe Cipriano, Townsend Coleman. *Executive Producer:* Scott St. John. *Supervising Producer:* David Floyd, Brian Veskosky. *Producer:* Judy C. Helm. *Music:* Brad Chiet.

741   Decision House. (Reality; My Network TV; September 12, 2007 to August 25, 2008)

Couples (married or living together) facing a problem (even crisis) face Judge Lynn Toler in the hope of saving their relationship.

Host: Judge Lynn Toler. **Therapist:** Dr. Tara Fields. **Credits:** *Executive Producer:* Jay McGraw, Dan Jbara. *Supervising Producer:* Nicole Dunn, David Goldman, Amanda Barrett. *Producer:* Rick Brown, Christopher D'Elie, Natalya Shneyde. *Music:* Devin Power.

742   Deep Sea Detectives. (Reality; History Channel; Premiered: April 1, 2003)

Spectacular underwater photography

details the work of salvage specialists as they seek the remains of sea going vessels that have sunk to the bottom of the ocean. **Host:** John Chatterton, Cade Courtley, Richie Kohler. **Credits:** *Executive Producer:* Kristine Sabat. *Supervising Producer:* Tracey Cuesta. *Producer:* Neil Laird, Mark Cannon, Tom Cappello, Rocky Collins, Teresa Giordana. *Music:* Michael Richard Plowman.

743   Def Comedy Jam. (Comedy; HBO; Premiered: July 1, 1992)

Up and coming comics perform before a live audience at the Wilshire Theater in Los Angeles. **Host:** Martin Lawrence, D.L. Hughley. **Credits:** *Executive Producer:* Stan Lathan, Russell Simmons. *Producer:* Suli McCullough, Royale Watkins. *Music:* Kid Capri.

744   Design Star. (Reality; HGTV; Premiered: July 23, 2006)

Ten hopeful designers compete in various home design challenges (such as creativity and ingenuity) for the opportunity to become the "HGTV Design Star." **Host:** Clive Pearse. **Judges:** Martha McCully, Cynthia Rowley, Vern Yip. **Credits:** *Executive Producer:* Sally Ann Salsano, James Bolosh, Amy Quimby. *Co-Executive Producer:* Jace Zimmer. *Supervising Producer:* Jason Hunt. *Producer:* Krista Van Nieuwburg.

745   Desperate Housewives. (Drama; ABC; Premiered: October 3, 2004)

Wisteria Lane in a city called Fairview is a seemingly peaceful, meticulous neighborhood until one of its residents, Mary Alice Young, commits suicide and secrets and truths unfold to reveal the dirty laundry of a select group of women and their families (heard through the narration of Mary Alice as she observes her former friends). Bree, Gabrielle, Lynette, Susan and Edie are the women who become the focal point of the series. Bree, originally married to a doctor (Rex), is the mother of Danielle and Andrew. Gabrielle, married to Carlos, relishes in a rich lifestyle. Lynette, a former high-powered businesswoman, is married to Tom (owner of the Scavo Pizza parlor) and the mother of Porter, Penny, Parker and Preston. Susan, a single mother (of Julie), is divorced from Carl and illustrates children's books. Edie, "the neighborhood slut," is divorced and very flirtatious. Paul was Mary Alice's husband; Zack, her son.

Cast: Marcia Cross (Bree Van De Kamp), Nicollette Sheridan (Edie Britt), Eva Longoria (Gabrielle Solis), Felicity Huffman (Lynette Scavo), Teri Hatcher (Susan Mayer), Andrea Bowen (Julie Mayer), Steven Culp (Rex Van De Kamp), Brenda Strong (Mary Alice Young), Cody Kasch (Zach Young), Doug Savant (Tom Scavo), Mark Moses (Paul Young), Ricardo Chavira (Carlos Solis), Harriet Sansom Harris (Felicia Tilman), Shane Kinsman (Porter Scavo), Charles Carver (Porter Scavo; later), Zane Huett (Parker Scavo), Joshua Logan Moore (Parker Scavo; later), Brent Kinsman (Preston Scavo), Max Carver (Preston Scavo; later), Jesse Metcalf (John Rowland), Joy Lauren (Danielle Van De Kamp), Shawn Pyfrom (Andrew Van De Kamp), James Denton (Mike Delfino), Dana Delany (Katherine Mayfair), Gale Howard (Jackson), Kendall Applegate (Penny Scavo), Neal McDonough (Dave Williams). **Credits:** *Executive Producer:* Marc Cherry, Tom Spezialy, Michael Edelstein. *Co-Executive Producer:* Kevin Murphy, Joey Murphy, John Pardee, David Grossman, Bob Daily. *Supervising Producer:* Sabrina Wind, Susan Nirah Jaffe, Bruce Zimmerman. *Producer:* Charles Skouras II, Kevin Itten, Tracey Stern, Patty Lin, Stephanie Hagen, Alexandra Cunningham, Larry Shaw, George W. Perkins.

746   Destination Truth. (Reality; Sci Fi; June 6, 2007 to October 15, 2008)

An attempt to explain supernatural

sightings or happenings through location reports and interviews with eye witnesses. **Host:** Josh Gates. **Credits:** *Executive Producer:* Michael Mandt, Neil Mandt. *Producer:* Eric Wing. *Music:* Jon Vander Griff.

747 Dexter. (Crime Drama; Showtime; Premiered: October 1, 2006)

Dexter Morgan is a blood splatter specialist for the Miami Police Department. He was an orphan raised by Harry Morgan, a street-smart police detective. At an early age Harry noticed his son had an unnatural urge to kill. Rather than suppress this urge, Harry encouraged Dexter to kill and taught him to focus on criminals (especially serial killers and how not to leave any evidence behind). Dexter, has since, honed that urge and has become a vigilante — if the cops can't catch them or a killer beats the system — Dexter makes sure they receive their just deserts, with no trace left as to who the killer was — "I'm a very neat monster," says Dexter. In addition to Dexter's killing spree as a vigilante, stories also focus on his work at crime scenes where he excels in uncovering evidence. Rita is Dexter's girlfriend, a troubled woman who was abused by her violent ex-husband (Tom); she is the mother of Astor and Cody. Sergeant Doakes is Dexter's superior; Debra Morgan, Dexter's half-sister, is with the Vice Squad. **Cast:** Michael C. Hall (Dexter Morgan), Julie Benz (Rita Bennett), Jennifer Carpenter (Debra Morgan), Lauren Velez (Lt. Maria Laquerta), Erik King (Sgt. Doakes), David Zayas (Angel Batista), Geoff Pearson (Captain Tom Astor), James Remar (Harry Morgan), Devon Graye (Dexter as a teenager), Dominic Janes (Dexter as a child). **Credits:** *Executive Producer:* John Goldwyn, Sara Collecton, Clyde Phillips, James Manos, Jr. *Co-Executive Producer:* Dancel Cerone, Michael Cuesta. *Producer:* Drew Z. Greenberg. *Music:* Dancel Light, Rolfe Kent.

748 Digging for the Truth. (Reality; History Channel; Premiered: January 24, 2005)

Survival expert Josh Bernstein travels across the world to uncover archaeological mysteries (from the ancient pyramids to King Solomon's Mines). **Host:** Josh Bernstein, Charles Ingram, Hunter Ellis, Zay Harding. **Credits:** *Executive Producer:* Margaret Kim. *Supervising Producer:* Lori Gibson. *Producer:* William Gardner, Neil Laird. *Music:* Joe Delia, Michael Richard Plowman.

749 Diners, Drive-Ins and Dives. (Reality; Food Network; Premiered: November 4, 2006)

Chef Guy Fieri travels across the country in his 1967 Chevrolet Camaro seeking the best examples 1950s and 60s style dining in the U.S. **Host:** Guy Fieri. **Credits:** *Executive Producer:* David Page. *Supervising Producer:* Pam Suchman, Christianna Reinhardt. *Producer:* Kate Gibson, Mike Morris, Brynn Levin.

750 Dinner Impossible. (Cooking; Food Network; Premiered: January 24, 2007)

Culinary Institute of America chef and restaurateur Michael Symon accepts challenges to prepare dinners under extreme circumstances. **Host:** Michael Symon. **Credits:** *Executive Producer:* Marc Summers, Brian O'Reilly. *Supervising Producer:* Julie Roberts, Natalie Feldman. *Producer:* Jeanine Pavuk, Mary Beth Anderson, Matt Berkowitz.

751 Dino Squad. (Cartoon; CBS; Premiered: September 2, 2007)

While swimming, five teens (Fiona, Victor, Buzz, Caruso and Roger) are exposed to a mysterious oceanic ooze that alters their DNA and endows them with the ability to transform themselves into dinosaurs. With their newfound power, the teens battle evil wherever they find it.

Voice Cast: Dana Donlan (Fiona), Ben Beck (Caruso), Ian Eli Lee (Max), John Michael Lee (Peter), Nils Haaland, Ian Eli Lee, Moria Mangiamelle, Vincent Michael, Kelcey Watson. Credits: *Executive Producer:* Andy Heyward, Michael Maliana. *Producer:* Jim E. Lara. *Music:* Ron Wasserman.

752 Dinosaur King. (Cartoon; Fox; Premiered: September 9, 2007)

A mad scientist (Dr. Z) has invented a time machine to go back in time, capture dinosaurs and imprison them in special metal cards. The machine, however, malfunctions, explodes and scatters the cards all over the planet. Three pre-teens (Max, Zoe and Rex) find one of the cards and release a baby dinosaur when the button on the card is pressed. Realizing what the card represents, Max, Zoe and Rex set out on a quest to save the dinosaurs despite Dr. Z's efforts to find the cards and become his envisioned dinosaur king.

Voice Cast: Veronica Taylor (Max Taylor), Amanda Brown (Zoe Drake), Sebastian Arcelus (Rex Owen), Rachael Lillis (Ursula), Darren Dunstain (Zander), David Wills (Dr. Spike Taylor).

753 Dirt. (Drama; FX; January 2, 2007 to March 11, 2008)

Lucy Spiller is a powerful ice princess who is totally committed to her job as a magazine editor. She oversees two magazines, *Dirt* and *Now* but when *Dirt* begins to flounder, she decides to devote all her energies into saving it by giving the public the scandalous celebrity stories she believes they want. Don Knokey is her chief photographer; Gibson Home is Lucy's publisher; Willa McPherson is a reporter; and Kira Klay, a young actress, is Don's romantic interest. Stories follow the mean and foul-mouthed Lucy as she uses her conniving ways, as well as every dirty trick in the book, to get the stories she feels will sell magazines.

Cast: Courteney Cox (Lucy Spiller), Ian Hart (Don Konkey), Timothy Bottoms (Gibson Home), Alexandra Breckenridge (Willa McPherson), Shannyne Sossamon (Kira Klay), Laura Allen (Julia Mallory), Jeffrey Nordling (Brent Barrow), Josh Stewart (Holt McLaren), Will McCormack (Leo Spiller), Rick Fox (Prince Tyreese), Carly Pope (Garbo). Credits: *Executive Producer:* Matthew Carnahan, Courteney Cox, David Arquette, Joel Fields. *Co-Executive Producer:* Chris Long, Dave Flebotte. *Producer:* Thea Mann. *Music:* Rick Ziegler.

754 Dirty Dancing: Living the Dream. (Reality; WE; Premiered: December 6, 2006)

Thirty hopeful dancers (15 men and 15 women) are paired and taught specific dance routines by a professional dance instructor. Each episode features the couples performing their specific routines with the weakest performers being eliminated.

Host: Cris Judd. Dance Instructor: Jonathan Curtis. Choreographer: Cris Judd, Eddie Garcia. Credits: *Executive Producer:* Don Weiner. *Co-Executive Producer:* Jeff Kopp. *Supervising Producer:* Allen Cody. *Producer:* Peter S. Alexander. *Music:* Mark Phillips.

755 Dirty Jobs. (Reality; Discovery Channel; Premiered: November 7, 2003)

A look at the less-than-desirable jobs that ordinary people perform every day (as seen through the host's becoming a part of the job he is exploring).

Host: Mike Rowe. Credits: *Executive Producer:* Craig Piligian, Mike Rowe. *Co-Executive Producer:* Hank Capshaw. *Producer:* Alec Eastburg. *Music:* Matt Koskenmaki.

756 Dirty Sexy Money. (Drama; ABC; September 26, 2007 to December 17, 2008)

The Darlings are a fabulously wealthy family, based in New York City, and the owners of homes and vineyards around the world. Tripp and Letitia run the organization. They are the parents of Patrick, Karen, Brian and twins Juliet and Jeremy. Patrick is the Attorney General of New York City; Brian is an Episcopalian minister; Karen runs the family foundation; Juliet is a hopeful actress; Jeremy feels he is a disappointment to his family and has taken up drinking. Nick George is a lawyer who protects the Darlings billions — and dirty little secrets. Stories follow events in the lives of the Darlings as they each deal with life's problems — and Nick's efforts to keep them in the public eye as "The Darling American Family."

Cast: Peter Krause (Nick George), Donald Sutherland (Tripp Darling), Jill Clayburgh (Letitia Darling), William Baldwin (Patrick Darling), Natalie Zea (Karen Darling), Glenn Fitzgerald (Brian Darling), Samaire Armstrong (Juliet Darling), Seth Gabel (Jeremy Darling), Zoe McLellan (Lisa George). **Credits:** *Executive Producer:* Greg Berlanti, Matthew Gross, Bryan Singer, Craig Wright. *Supervising Producer:* Peter Elkoff, Yahlin Chang. *Producer:* Melissa Berman, Carl Ogawa, Kelly Van Horn. *Music:* Peter Nashel.

757 Disorderly Conduct. (Reality; Spike TV; Premiered: May 26, 2006)

Reality television that goes too far, using graphic footage of horrific accidents for its shock subject matter (for example, a woman getting hit by a car — from the first impact to the even more unsettling result). Understandable (although with reservations) on pay cable, but not for a commercial cable station where access is not denied.

Narrator: Robert Patrick. **Credits:** *Executive Producer:* Cheri Brownlee. *Co-Executive Producer:* Richard Wortman. *Supervising Producer:* Steve Ligerman. *Producer:* Alan Conn.

758 Divorce Court. (Reality; Syn.; Premiered: August 30, 1999)

Real people seeking a divorce present their cases before a real judge.

Cast: Mablean Ephriam (Judge, 1999–2006), Lynn Toler (Judge, 2006–). **Announcer:** Jimmy Hodson. **Credits:** *Executive Producer:* Jill Blackstone. *Producer:* Judson Touby, Jan Silverstein, Melissa Mascari, Gina Madrid, Jennifer Hope, Georgetta Foreman, Paul Boese. *Music:* Scooter Pietsch.

759 The D.L. Chronicles. (Anthology; Here!; Premiered: 2007)

A specialty series (geared toward gays) that focuses on men of color who lead double sex lives.

Performers Include: Darren Schnase, Damian Raven, Sherilynn Wactor, Jessica Beshir, Ty Vincent, R.J. Black, Kariem Ferguson, Jason Smart, Sydolle Noel, Holly Karrol Clark. **Credits:** *Executive Producer:* Quincy LeNear, Deondray Gossett. *Co-Executive Producer:* Ahmed Best. *Supervising Producer:* Ani Williams, Hashim Williams. *Music:* Vikter Duplait.

760 Dr. Phil. (Reality; Syn.; Premiered: September 2002)

Real people with real problems appear seeking help from psychiatrist Phil McGraw.

Host: Dr. Phil McGraw. **Credits:** *Executive Producer:* Carla Pennington. *Supervising Producer:* Angie Kraus-Bell. *Senior Producer:* Kandi Amelon, Judy Rybak. *Producer:* John Perry, Lisa Steinke, David Goldman, Marsha Armstrong, Kathy Giaconia, Charlotte Graham, Julie Johnson, Gloria Paymani, Anita Pepper, Paul Rosenthal, Julie Ross, Edward Santos, Jill Skinner.

761 Dr. Steve-O. (Reality; USA; Premiered: October 7, 2007)

A man known only as Dr. Steve-O hates wimps and has taken it upon himself to "de-wussify wimps, nerds and couch potatoes." Such subjects, nominated by their friends and family, receive a visit from the good doctor and his gorgeous nurse, Trishelle, to undergo a series of "de-wussing" challenges to turn a wimp into a man.

Cast: Steve-O (Dr. Steve-O), Trishelle Cannatella (Nurse Trishelle). **Credits:** *Executive Producer:* Jonathan Murray. *Supervising Producer:* Jeff Schmidt. *Producer:* Christopher Gallivan. *Music:* Adam Small, Jason Moss.

762   Doctor Who. (Science Fiction; Sci Fi; March 26, 2005 to August 1, 2008)

A continuation of the *Doctor Who* series that began on the BBC in England in 1962 (first seen in the U.S. in 1973). A man from the planet Gallifrey and known only as the Doctor, uses his time machine, the TARDIS (Time and Relative Dimension in Space) to save not only the Earth, but other planets threatened by evil. The Doctor has a great thirst for knowledge and uses the TARDIS, which has a slight defect (it is stuck in the guise of a 1960s British telephone booth; it is supposed to disguise itself wherever it goes) to learn all he can by visiting various periods in history. The new version, produced in 2005, begins when the Doctor comes to Earth to protect it from an evil living plastic organism that seeks to destroy it. Rose Tyler, a department store salesgirl he rescues from plastic mannequins brought to life by the alien, helps him defeat the creature. Although the Doctor is an alien, he longs for human companionship and invites Rose to become his traveling companion. Rose has a hapless boyfriend, an over-bearing mother and a not-too-bright outlook for the future. She chooses to travel with the Doctor and live a life of harrowing adventures protecting the universe from evil. The third season premiere (July 6, 2007), "The Runaway Bride," finds Rose leaving the Doctor to return to her life as it was before she met him. "Smith and Jones," the following episode, finds the Doctor (who has checked into a London hospital under the name John Smith), seeking a creature called a Plasmasvore (feeds on blood) that

has taken human form. A doctor, Martha Jones, becomes suspicious of John Smith and immediately becomes involved in his quest. The Doctor's plan to find the creature fails and he becomes its victim. Martha saves the Doctor's life and allows him to complete his mission. The Doctor reveals his true nature to Martha and in return offers her a trip on the TARDIS. Martha becomes intrigued and eventually becomes the Doctor's new traveling companion. A third incarnation, thus far only broadcast in the U.S. on BBC America (as of December 31, 2008) finds the Doctor traveling with a new companion, Donna Noble (who appeared in the episode "The Runaway Bride" but mysteriously disappeared during it; to her astonishment, she reappears two years later to replace Martha as the Doctor's traveling companion when Martha returns to her former position). The new version also features the Doctor reuniting with Rose and Martha and Sarah Jane Smith [Elisabeth Sladen], his traveling companion in the 1980s, to battle evil.

Cast: Christopher Eccleston (The Doctor), Billie Piper (Rose Tyler), Freema Agyeman (Martha Jones), Catherine Tate (Donna Noble). **Credits:** *Executive Producer:* Russell Davies, June Gardner.

763   Dog the Bounty Hunter. (Reality; A&E; August 31, 2004 to August 20, 2008)

The real life exploits of a bounty hunter (Duane "Dog" Chapman) and his family as they track down wanted criminals.

Cast: Duane "Dog" Chapman, Beth Smith, Leland Chapman, Tim Chapman, Lyssa Chapman, Travis Chapman, Abby Mae Chapman, Davina Chapman, Dakota Chapman, Cobie Chapman. **Credits:** *Executive Producer:* Daniel Elias, Nancy Dubuc, Neil A. Cohen. *Supervising Producer:* Lucas Platt. *Producer:* Adriana Pacheco, Sylvia Wright. *Music:* Dan Stein, Joel Goodman, David Bramfitt.

764   Dog Whisperer. (Reality; National Geographic; Premiered: September 13, 2004)

Animal behaviorist Cesar Millan visits families with troublesome dogs to rehabilitate them and help the family establish a balanced relationship with their pet.

Host: Cesar Millan. **Credits:** *Executive Producer:* Jim Milio, Melissa Peltier. *Supervising Producer:* Colette Beoudry. *Producer:* Sue Anne Fincke, Kay Sumner. *Music:* Gregg Miner, Andrew Kereszres.

765 **Dominick Dunne's Power, Privilege and Justice**. (Reality; Court TV/Tru TV; Premiered: 2004)

Vanity Fair columnist and author Dominick Dunne presents a look at a dark side of the law — how the rich and famous, who believe they are above the law, attempt to manipulate the system to get away with criminal activities.

Host: Dominick Dunne. **Credits:** *Executive Producer:* Anthony Horn, Vincent Kralyevich. *Supervising Producer:* Christine Connor. *Producer:* Ron Marans, Todd Moss, Ted Poole, Teresa Giardano, Joe Danisi, Norman Cohen, Patrick Taulere, Shana Hilderbrand, Scott A. Friedland. *Music:* Ryan Shore, Richard Fiocca, Max Surlas, Robert Filomena, Sarah Larson, George Small.

766 **The Donald Strachey Mysteries**. (Crime Drama; Here!; Premiered: 2005)

Donald Strachey is a tough-looking private detective based in New York City. Donald is gay but his rugged appearance could portray him as either straight or gay. Stories follow Donald's case investigations, usually into crimes (murders) involving members of the gay community. Based on the book by Richard Stevenson and broadcast on the specialty gay channel Here!

Cast: Chad Allen (Donald Strachey). **Credits:** *Executive Producer:* Barry Krost, James Shavick, Kirk Shaw. *Co-Executive Producer:* Randy Zalken. *Associate Producer:* Stacy Shaw. *Music:* Bill Buckingham, Ronnie Way.

767 **Don't Forget the Lyrics**. (Game; Fox; Premiered: July 11, 2007)

A contestant, whether he has the ability to sing or not, appears on stage. Nine song categories are revealed (for example, Rock and Roll, Tom Jones Hits, Country and Western). The player chooses a category and two associated song titles appear. He then chooses one of those songs to sing. As the band plays the selected song, the lyrics are seen on a large screen. The player sings along (like in karaoke) but when a line of blank spaces appears, he must supply the missing lyrics (from four to ten words). If the player supplies the correct lyrics he wins money (from $1,000 on the first song to $1 million on the tenth song). The player can quit at any time and leave with what money he has if he is unsure about the lyrics he supplied. The safety net, however is the $25,000 song. If the player can reach this level, he is guaranteed that amount of money should he lose on an additional song.

Host: Wayne Brady. **Orchestra:** Ricky Minor **Credits:** *Executive Producer:* Brad Lachman, Jeff Apploff, Chris Coelen, Greg Goldman. *Co-Executive Producer:* Brian Veskosky. *Supervising Producer:* Bill Bracken. *Producer:* Matthew D'Acquisto.

768 **The Doodlebops**. (Children; Disney; Premiered: 2004)

Deedee, Moe and Rooney are the Doodlebops, a rock and roll band geared to pre-school children. Through the misadventures the band encounters while rehearsing, various aspects of the world are related to its target audience.

Cast: Lisa Lennox (Deedee Doodle), Chad McNamara (Rooney Doodle), Jonathan Wexler (Moe Doodle), Jackie Richardson (Jazzmin), John Catucci (Bob the Bus Driver), Kim Roberts (Mazz), Dylan Everett (Streeter), Ron Stefaniuk (Moosehead). **Credits:** *Executive Producer:*

Michael Hirsh. *Producer:* Jamie Waese. *Line Producer:* Andrew Nevitt. *Music:* Carl Lenox.

769   Dora the Explorer. (Cartoon; Nickelodeon; Premiered: September 6, 2005)

Dora is a young Hispanic girl who, with her monkey (Boots) and talking backpack share educational adventures as they explore a world set in an animated computer.

Voice Cast: Kathleen Herles (Dora), Harrison Chad (Boots), Sasha Toro (Backpack), Ashley Fleming (Isa), Esai Morales (Papi). **Credits:** *Executive Producer:* Valerie Walsh, Chris Gifford, Brown Johnson. *Producer:* Eric Weiner, Jeff DeGrandis, Helena Uszac, Steve Socki. *Music:* Billy Straus, Steve Sandberg, Jed Becker, Chris Gifford.

770   Dragon. (Cartoon; NBC; Premiered: October 5, 2007)

Simplistic animated (clay figures) series about Dragon, a friendly blue dragon as he learns various aspects of life with the help of his friends Mouse and Beaver.

Narrator and Character Voices: Frank Meschkvleit. **Credits:** *Producer:* Vivianne Monn, Helmut Fischer, Lorraine Richard. *Music:* Ray Fabi.

771   Dress My Nest. (Reality; Style; Premiered: March 28, 2007)

Selected subjects are given a home makeover by interior designer Thom Filicia based on the chosen subject's favorite article of clothing.

Host: Thom Filicia, Erika Martin. **Credits:** *Producer:* Christine Reed, Erica Ross, Kevin Maynard. *Associate Producer:* Christopher Gallivan.

772   Duel. (Game; ABC; December 17, 2007 to July 25, 2008)

One player (chosen at random from a group of twenty-four) appears on stage. He selects one opponent from the remaining players. These players stand on opposite sides of a game podium and each re-

ceives ten casino chips, each worth $5,000. The host reads a question and four possible answers (A,B,C,D) appear on screens before each player. Players select an answer by placing a chip on the one he feels is correct (if he is not sure, he can place a chip on as many as he wants). When the correct answer is revealed, chips placed on wrong answers are removed and placed in the jackpot kitty. If both players chose the correct answer, the game continues; if a player chose an incorrect answer, he is defeated and the winner receives cash based on how many remaining chips he has. The more games (called Duels) the player wins, the more money he acquires (but he risks loss of everything if he continues and chooses an incorrect answer).

Host: Mike Greenberg. **Chip Girls:** Jennifer Aguero, Olivia Fox. **Credits:** *Executive Producer:* Gail Berman, Lloyd Baum, Chris Cowan, Jean Michel Michenaud, Charles Duncombe, David Rosconval, Francis Vacher. *Co-Executive Producer:* R.A. Clark. *Producer:* Tim Brock. *Director:* Mark Gentile.

773   Easy Entertaining. (Cooking; Food Network; Premiered: October 1, 2003)

Cookbook author and chef Michael Chiarello celebrates the Napa Valley lifestyle with an on-location series taped at the Trefethen Winery.

Host: Michael Chiarello. **Credits:** *Producer-Writer:* Michael Chiarello. *Director:* Natalie Gustafson.

774   Ed, Edd and Eddy. (Cartoon; Cartoon Network; Premiered: January 4, 1999)

Three moronic boys who share the same first name (but spelled differently) experience the pains of adolescence, growing up in an area called Peach Creek Estates.

Voice Cast: Matt Hill (Ed), Sam Vincent (Edd), Tony Sampson (Eddy). **Credits:** *Executive Producer:* Danny Antonucci, Linda Simensky. *Producer:* Samantha

Daley, Christine Danzo. *Music:* Patric Caird.

775   The Ellen DeGeneres Show. (Talk; Syn.; Premiered: September 2003)

Daily celebrity interview series that is also a mix of variety acts, musical numbers and stories of real people with something to say or possessed of an extraordinary talent.

Host: Ellen DeGeneres. **Credits:** *Executive Producer:* Ellen DeGeneres, Ed Glavin. *Co-Executive Producer:* Andy Lassner. *Supervising Producer:* Mike Gibbons, *Music:* Robin Thicke, Eban Schletter.

776   Emeril Live. (Cooking; Food Network; Premiered: January 1, 1997)

A taped show in which master chef Emeril Lagasse prepares gourmet meals in front of a live audience.

Host: Emeril Lagasse. *Producer:* Patricia LaMorte. *Writer-Music:* Emeril Lagasse.

777   The Emperor's New School. (Cartoon; Disney; Premiered: January 27, 2006)

Kuzco is next in line to rule the Ku Empire. But first he must graduate from Kuzco Academy High School. He has little ambition for school and he is unaware that Yzma, his former advisor (who is now his teacher) is hoping to prevent him from acquiring the throne so she herself can become ruler. Stories follow Kuzco as he goes about his merry way, almost always oblivious to the situations that surround him.

Voice Cast: J.P. Manoux (Kuzco), Jessica Di Cicco (Malina), Eartha Kitt (Yzma), Patrick Warburton (Kronk). **Credits:** *Executive Producer:* Bob Gannaway. *Producer:* Clay Renfroe. *Music:* Michael Tavera.

778   Engaged and Underage. (Reality; MTV; Premiered: January 1, 2007)

Young people (aged 18 to 22) who are in love and plan to marry despite objections from friends and family are profiled.

Credits: *Executive Producer:* Stuart Cohn, Lauren Fruedland, Dave Sirulnick. *Supervising Producer:* Royd Chung, Lorna Thomas. *Producer:* Jerry Henry, Dave West. *Associate Producer:* Julia Engkler-Perez, Susie Moore, Ki Whelan.

779   Entertainers. (Interview; Syn.; Premiered: September 2007)

Interviews with "the world's hottest stars." Chosen subjects are profiled with clips from their films as well as a behind-the-scenes look at the making of the subject's character and/or film.

Host: Byron Allen. **Credits:** *Executive Producer:* Byron Allen, Carolyn Folks. *Supervising Producer:* Jennifer Lucas. *Producer:* Joan Robbins.

780   Entertainment Studios.com. (Variety; Syn.; Premiered: September 2006)

Entertainment news and interviews with movie, television and music personalities.

Host: Byron Allen. **Credits:** *Executive Producer:* Carolyn Folks, Byron Allen. *Associate Producer:* Terence Hill. *Co-Producer:* Joan Robbins, Mike Androsky

781   Entertainment Tonight. (Variety; Syn.; Premiered: September 1981)

A daily series that presents the latest gossip on celebrities, movies, TV shows, music and other entertainment fields.

Host: Mary Hart, John Tesh, Mark Steines, Larry Mendte, Giselle Fernandez, Pat O'Brien. **Credits:** *Executive Producer:* Rob Silverstein, David Hedges, David Hall, Joseph R. Lynch, Jonathan P. Goodman. *Producer:* Scott Mantz, Ann Lewis, Robert Jarrin. *Music:* David Leon, Jeremy Sweet.

782   Entourage. (Reality; HBO; Premiered: July 18, 2004)

Vince Chase is an actor with a promising future. His best friends, Johnny, Eric and Turtle, join him as they leave their home in Queens, New York, to help and encourage Vince, a novice, in Hollywood, learn the ropes and hopefully make the right choices. Johnny is Vince's half-brother; Eric is Vince's advisor and second agent (Ari is Vince's real agent; he is replaced by Amanda in 2007); Kristen is Eric's girlfriend.

Cast: Adrian Grenier (Vince Chase), Kevin Dillon (Johnny Chase), Jerry Ferrera (Turtle), Kevin Connolly (Eric), Jeremy Piven (Ari Gold), Monica Keena (Kristen), Carla Gugino (Amanda). **Credits:** *Executive Producer:* Mark Wahlberg, Doug Ellin, Stephen Levinson. *Co-Executive Producer:* Rob Weiss, Timothy Marx. *Supervising Producer:* Denis Biggs. *Producer:* Janace Tashjian, Brian Burns, Lori Jo Nemhauser.

783 Eon Kid. (Cartoon; CW; September 22, 2007 to September 6, 2008)

In a futuristic age, a young boy named Marty finds the Fist of Eon, a long-lost magical fist that helped humans defeat evil robots led by the General over 500 years ago. The fist endows Marty with unique powers and with his friend, Ally, battles Raymer and Black Beauty, the evil rulers of an area known as Iron Tower.

Voice Cast: Aidan Drummond (Marty), Claire Renaud (Ally), Andy Toth (Buttons), Nicole Oliver (Black Beauty).

784 ER. (Drama; NBC; September 19, 1994 to April 2, 2009)

Chicago's County General Hospital, a level one trauma center, is the setting for a look at the mostly professional lives of the doctors and nurses who face life and death situations every hour of every day.

Cast: George Clooney (Dr. Douglas Ross), Abraham Benrubi (Dr. Jerry Markovic), Laura Innes (Dr. Kerry Weaver), Goran Visnjic (Dr. Luka Kovac), Maura Tierney (Dr. Abby Lockhart), Linda Cardellini (Nurse Samantha Taggart), Parminder Nagra (Dr. Neela Rasgotra), Mekhi Phifer (Dr. Gregory Pratt), Maria Bello (Dr. Anna Del Amico), Sharif Atkins (Dr. Daniel Gallant), Shane West (Dr. Ray Barnett), Noah Wylie (Dr. John Carter), Sherry Stringfield (Dr. Susan Lewis), Monte Russell (EMS Dwight Zadro), Gloria Reuben (Jeanie Boulet [Physician Assistant]), Ming-Na (Dr. Jing-Mei "Deb" Chen), Michael Michele (Dr. Cleo Finch), Laura Ceron (Nurse Chuny Marquez), Anthony Edwards (Dr. Mark Greene), Yvette Freeman (Nurse Haleh Adams), Lyn Alicia Henderson (EMS Pamela Olbes), Alex Kingston (Dr. Elizabeth Corday), Eriq La Salle (Dr. Peter Benton), Julianna Margulies (Nurse Carol Hathaway), Lily Mariye (Nurse Lily Jarvik), Kellie Martin (Dr. Lucy Knight), Paul McCrane (Dr. Robert Romano), Kristen Johnston (Nurse Eve Peyton), Leland Orser (Dr. Lucien Dubenko), Scott Grimes (Dr. Archie Morris), Erik Palladino (Dr. Dave Malucci), Busy Philipps (Hope Bobeck), John Stamos (Dr. Tony Gates), Angela Bassett (Dr. Cate Banfield). **Credits:** *Executive Producer:* Michael Crichton, John Wells, Jack Orman, Lydia Woodward, Carol Flint, Neal Baer, David Zabel, R. Scott Gemmill, Steven Spielberg. *Co-Executive Producer:* Janine Sherman, Dee Johnson, Walon Green, Robert Nathan, Meredith Stiehm. *Supervising Producer:* Mimi Leder, Julie Hebert. *Producer:* Bruce Miller, Richard Thorpe, Chris Misiano, Christopher Chulack, Patrick Harbinson. *Music:* Marty Davich, Christopher Neal Nelson.

785 Eureka. (Science Fiction; Sci Fi; July 18, 2006 to September 23, 2008)

Eureka is a small American town that conceals a dark secret: ever since the 1940s the U.S. government has relocated geniuses there to live and work on scientific breakthroughs. The basic premise is a look at the quirky characters that inhabit the Pacific Northwest town.

Cast: Colin Ferguson (Jack Carter), Jordan Hinson (Zoe Carter), Debrah Farentino (Beverly Barlow), Matt Frewer (Jim Taggart), Salli Richardson-Whitfiled (Allison Blake), Joe Morton (Henry Deacon), Erica Cerra (Jo Lupo), Ed Quinn (Nathan Stark), Greg Germann (Warren King), Shayn Solberg (Spencer Martin), Maury Chaykin (Sheriff Cobb). **Credits:** *Executive Producer:* Andrew Cosby. *Co-Executive Producer:* Jaime Paglia, Karl Schaefer. *Supervising Producer:* Dan Fesman, Harry Victor. *Producer:* Robert Petrovicz.

786   Every Woman. (Interview; Syn.; Premiered: September 2007)

Entertaining and inspired interviews with women who reflect the diversity of women today.

Narration Host: Michelle Logan. **Credits:** *Executive Producer:* Byron Allen, Carolyn Folks. *Supervising Producer:* Jennifer Lucas. *Producer:* Joan Robbins.

787   Everybody Hates Chris. (Comedy; UPN/CW; Premiered: September 22, 2005)

The Bedford Stuyvesant section of Brooklyn, New York, is the setting (beginning in 1982 and progressing to 1986 in 2008 episodes) for a look at the childhood memories of comedian Chris Rock. Julius and Rochelle are his parents; Drew and Tanya are his younger siblings. Julius works several jobs and is very frugal. Rochelle works as a waitress (later hairdresser at Nessa's Hair Salon). Chris, 13 years old when the series begins, is the only African-American at Corleone Junior High School (he later attends Tattaglia High School). Chris tries to do everything right (but everything usually goes wrong). He works after school at Doc's Corner, the local convenience store. Tanya has a knack for letting Chris take the blame for something she did. She and Drew attend Dolimite Elementary School. Greg is Chris's friend; Mrs. Morello is a teacher at Corleone; Mr. Raymond is its principal; Louise is the Rock's neighbor; Tasha is Louise's daughter; Joey is the school bully; Mr. Omar is the Rock's upstairs neighbor; Mr. Thurman is the principal at Tattaglia;

Doc is the store owner; Vanessa owns Nessa's Beauty Parlor. Chris Rock narrates the stories of his youth.

Cast: Tyler James Williams (Chris Rock), Terry Crews (Julius Rock), Tichina Arnold (Rochelle Rock), Tequan Richmond (Drew Rock), Imani Hakim (Tanya Rock), Vincent Martella (Greg Wulger), Travis T. Flory (Joey Caruso), Ernest Thomas (Mr. Omar), Paige Hurd (Tasha), Paul Ben-Victor (Mr. Thurman), Jacqueline Mazarella (Mr. Morello), Antonio Fargas (Doc), Jackee Harry (Vanessa). **Credits:** *Executive Producer:* Chris Rock, Michael Rotenberg, Howard Gewirtz, Dave Becky. *Co-Executive Producer:* Kriss Turner, Gregory Thompson. *Supervising Producer:* Rodney Barnes. *Producer:* Jim Michaels, Alysa Fouse. *Music:* Marcus Miller.

788   Everyday Italian. (Cooking; Food Network; Premiered: September 1, 2003)

Italian chef Giada DeLaurentis prepares updated versions of old world Italian recipes.

Host: Giada DeLaurentis. **Credits:** *Producer:* Audrey Bellezza. *Segment Producer:* Rafael August, Deren Albran, Alyson Shelton, Cody Shelton, Nell O'Hara, Suzanne Schecter.

789   Exe's and Oh's. (Drama; Logo; Premiered: January 1, 2007)

Jennifer is a young woman with a vivid fantasy life and a floundering career (documentary film maker). She is also a lesbian and looking for Ms. Right. As Jennifer searches for that special girl, viewers are given a glimpse into her private life as well as the lives of her close lesbian friends: Samantha (called Sam, a bartender), Crutch (a coffee house waitress hoping to become a singer/songwriter) and Kris (with a "K") and Chris (with a "C"), lovers who own an online pet accessories business. Also known as *The Rules: A Lesbian Survival Guide*.

Cast: Michelle Paradise (Jennifer), Marnie Alton (Sam), Heather Matarazzo (Crutch), Angela Featherstone (Kris), Megan Cavanagh (Chris), Amy Dudgeon (Emmy), Stacy Grant (Elizabeth), Darby Stanchfield (Sienna). **Credits:** *Executive Producer:* Michelle Paradise, Billy Grundfest, Noreen Halpern, Dave Mace, John Morayniss, Eileen Opatut, Pamela Post. *Producer:* Jessica Driscoll. *Music:* James Jandrisch.

790   Extra. (Variety; Syn.; Premiered: September 5, 1994)

A daily series of show business related news.

Host (2008): Danya Devon, Mark Mc-Grath, Mario Lopez. **Credits:** *Executive Producer:* Sheila Sitomer, Teresa Coffino, Neil Freundilch. *Supervising Producer:* Mike Miller, Jennifer Winer, Tracy Green, Stephen Mark Saylor, Ron Rosen. *Producer:* Gay Linill, Kelly Murphy, Terry Murphy, Evan Weinstein, Larry Lauren.

791   Extreme Makeover: Home Edition. (Reality; ABC; Premiered: December 3, 2003)

Desperate or deserving families are given a chance to begin a new life with a new or completely remodeled older home.

Crew: Ty Pennington, Tracy Hutson, Paul DiMeo, Michael Moloney, Preston Sharp, Eric Ancker, Constance Ramos, Paige Hemmis, Ed Sanders, Tanya McQueen, Eduardo Xol. **Credits:** *Executive Producer:* Tom Forman. *Co-Executive Producer:* Janelle Fiorito, Jonathan Karsh, Denise Cramsey, Star Price. *Senior Producer:* Diane Korman, Conrad Ricketts. *Producer:* Christiane Kirsch, Michael Hauser, Shana Kemp, Peter Alexander, Kathryn Vaughan, Mark Rains. *Music:* Brad Chiet, Eric Allaman, Rudy Guess, Rob Cairns.

792   The Fabulous Life Of.... (Reality; VH-1; January 1, 2003 to October 2, 2008)

A look at the lives of the extremely rich and famous (sort of a new version of the 1980s series *Lifestyles of the Rich and Famous*). Each episode focuses on a particular subject and shows how the person achieved his (or her) wealth as well as how he (or she) lives "The Fabulous Life."

Narrator: Christopher Flockton. **Credits:** *Executive Producer:* Matt Sharp. *Producer:* Mark Marruccini, Matt Hanna, Kate Bernstein, Heather Feldbaum, Avi Savar, Jordana Hockman. *Associate Producer:* David Abraham, Joshua Wright.

793   Fairly Odd Parents. (Cartoon; Nickelodeon; Premiered: March 30, 2001)

Timmy Turner is a 10-year-old boy who feels his parents deprive him of everything. Wanda and Cosmo are his godparents. When Timmy wants something he wishes for it and Wanda and Cosmo give it to him and stories relate the mishaps that follow as Timmy struggles to cop with something he wasn't supposed to have.

Voice Cast: Tara Strong (Timmy Turner), Susan Blakeslee (Wanda), Daran Norris (Cosmo), Jim Ward (Chet Ubetcha), Grey DeLisle (Vicky Turner). **Credits:** *Executive Producer:* Butch Hartman, Fred Seibert. *Producer:* Bob Boyle, Steve Marmel. *Music:* Guy Moon.

794   Family Feud. (Game; Syn.; Premiered: July 1, 1976)

Two five-member families compete in a game wherein they must answer questions based on a survey of 100 people. Points are scored based the answers given and the number of people who responded to it. The first family to score 300 or more points wins.

Host: Richard Dawson, Ray Combs, Richard Karn, Louie Anderson, John O'Hurley. **Credits:** *Executive Producer:* Gabriela Johnston, Michael Canter, Joel Klein. *Supervising Producer:* Kristen Bjorklund, Bob Boden. *Associate Producer:* Laurie Chryss. *Music:* Jeremy Sweet. *Announcer:* Burton Richardson.

795   Family Guy. (Cartoon; Fox; Premiered: January 31, 1999)

An irreverent look at a not-so-typical (and not so normal) American family called the Griffins, residents of Quahog, Rhode Island. Peter, the father is extremely obese (and a total moron). He works at the Pawtucket Brewery (later Happy Go Lucky Toys) and enjoys a drink (or two) at a bar called the Drunken Clam. Peter is married to Lois, a sexy woman who accepts Peter for all his faults. They are the parents of Chris, Megan and Stewie. Chris is rather large (overweight and tall) for a 13-year-old and quite dense. Megan, called Meg, is younger than Chris and very awkward (she is approaching puberty and having a difficult time of it). Stewie is the extremely intelligent baby of the family. He has a football-shaped head and is somewhat homicidal (he appears to be planning ways to eradicate his parents). Rounding out the Griffin household is Brian, an Einstein-intelligent, talking dog who loves martinis and often provides the only common sense in the uncommon household.

Voice Cast: Seth McFarlane (Peter Griffin/Chris Griffin/Brian/Stewie Griffin), Alex Borstein (Lois Griffin), Mila Kunis (Megan Griffin), Lacey Chabert (Megan Griffin; later), Mike Henry (Cleveland Brown), Patrick Warburton (Joe Swanson), Adam West (Mayor Adam West), John G. Brennan (Mort Goldman). **Credits:** *Executive Producer:* Seth MacFarlane, David Zuckerman. *Supervising Producer:* Mike Henry, Alec Sulkin, Wellesley Wild. *Producer:* Gene Laufenberg, Allison Adler, Kara Vallow, Sherry Gunther, Matt Weitzman, Mike Barker. *Music:* Ron Jones, Walter Murphy.

796   Fashion Police. (Reality; Style Network; Premiered: September 1, 2003)

A weekly look at what is in and what's not regarding the fashion trends of Hollywood celebrities.

Host: Robert Verdi. **Credits:** *Executive Producer:* Tia Devlin. *Producer:* Heather Lanzetta. *Associater Producer:* Kate Stanley.

797   Fearless Music. (Music; Syn.; Premiered: September 2007)

Live studio performances from "five great bands"—all of which were recorded live at Fearless Music studios in New York City.

Host: Jamie Lamm. **Credits:** *Executive Producer:* Jamie Lamm. *Producer:* Gabriele Solorino. *Theme Music:* Jamie Lamm.

798   The First 48. (Reality; A&E; Premiered: July 1, 2004)

A real life version of the *C.S.I.* programs on CBS that follows actual detectives as they investigate crimes (usually homicides) within the crucial, first 48 hours of the 911 call.

Credits: *Executive Producer:* Laura Fleury, John X. Kim. *Series Producer:* Ted Bourne. *Producer:* David Felsen, Xackery Irving, Matthew Testa, Elizabeth Tracy, Steve Kantor, Alana Campbell, Wei Ling Chang.

799   Flash Gordon. (Science Fiction; Sci Fi; August 10, 2007 to February 8, 2008)

An undated version of the characters created by Alex Raymond. Stephen Gordon, nicknamed Flash for his ability to run fast, works as a car restorer. Dale Arden, Flash's former high school sweetheart, is now an investigative reporter for WIAD-TV, Channel 4. As Flash enjoys life on Earth, sinister happenings are occurring on the planet Mongo. Ming, its evil leader, has sent a bounty hunter to Earth to find Flash and retrieve a device created by Flash's father, Lawrence, called the I-Mex (which contains all the knowledge of the universe). Flash is unaware of the I-Mex. Lawrence was a physics professor who, with his assistant, Dr. Hans Zarkov developed the I-Mex. Shortly after, during an experiment with gravity, Lawrence was pulled through a mysterious space rift, transported to Mongo and captured by Ming. To cover up Professor Gordon's disappearance, a lab fire was reported wherein Lawrence perished. To condense a long series of events, Flash, Dale and Dr. Zarkov are united when the alien bounty hunter's presence becomes known. Before the alien is destroyed, Flash learns about the I-Mex and that his father is being held captive on Mongo. Flash is now determined to find his father and protect the I-Mex (which he later finds hidden in a closet in his home) from Ming. Through a space rift device Flash finds among the alien's remains, Flash, accompanied by Dale and Dr. Zarkov, is able to travel from the Earth to Mongo and vice versa. Stories follow the trio as they seek Professor Gordon and attempt to foil Ming's plans of domination. Aura is Ming's daughter; Baylin is the alien bounty hunter who sides with Flash.

Cast: Eric Johnson (Flash Gordon), Gina Holden (Dale Arden) Jody Racicot (Dr. Hans Zarkov), John Ralston (Ming), Karen Cliche (Baylin), Anna Van Hooft (Princess Aura), Jonathan Walker (Rankol; Ming's chief scientist). **Credits:** *Executive Producer:* Matthew O'Connor, Tom Rowe. *Co-Executive Producer:* James Thorpe.

800   Flight of the Conchords. (Comedy; HBO; Premiered: June 17, 2007)

Bret and Jemaine are New Zealand musicians who now live in New York City. They have a comedy musical act (Flight of the Conchords) and stories relate their antics as they chase women, break into song whenever convenient and seek that elusive big break. Murray is their manager; Mel is their only fan.

Cast: Jemaine Clement (Jemaine), Bret McKenzie (Bret), Kristen Schaal (Mel), Rhys Darby (Murray). **Credits:** *Executive Producer:* Stu Smiley, James Bobin, Troy Miller. *Co-Executive Producer:* Tracey

Baird, Jemaine Clement, Bret McKenzie. *Producer:* Anna Dokoza, Christie Morse.

801   48 Hours Mystery. (Reality; CBS; Premiered: January 19, 1988)

Detailed investigative reports on current news stories, most of which are shrouded in mystery. Originally titled *48 Hours* then *48 Hours Investigates.*

Host: Dan Rather (1988–2002), Leslie Stahl (2002–). **Credits:** *Executive Producer:* Susan Zirinsky. *Supervising Producer:* Jim Murphy. *Producer:* Paul Ryan, Michael Maloy, Katherine Davis, Reed Collins, Jr., David Schneider, Rob Hershman. *Music:* Richard Floica, Julian Harris, Max Surlas, Todd Erickson.

802   Foster's Home for Imaginary Friends. (Cartoon; Cartoon Network; Premiered: August 13, 2004)

Madame Foster is a woman who runs a home where the imaginary friends of children are placed up for adoption when they outgrow them. Bloo, the security blanket of ten-year-old Mac, is one such friend who resides at the house. Mac, however, is still attached to Bloo and stories follow Mac as he visits Bloo each day and becomes involved in the antics of the characters that inhabit the house.

Voice Cast: San Marquette (Mac), Keith Ferguson (Bloo), Phil LaMarr (Eduardo), Candi Milo (Coco), Grey De Lisle (Frankie Foster), Tom Kane (Mr. Herriman). **Credits:** *Executive Producer:* Craig McCracken, Brian Miller. *Supervising Producer:* Jennifer Pelphrey, Lauren Faust. *Producer:* Vince Aniceto, Peter Lewis. *Music:* Jennifer Kes Remington, James L. Venable.

803   Foursome. (Erotica; Playboy Channel; Premiered: 2006)

The casting call reads: "Are you cute, fun, wild and sexy? Do you have an irresistible appetite for the opposite sex? Are you wild, fun and ready for everything? If you answered yes, we are looking for you.

We are in search of fun. Single men and women (ages 21–29) who want to be on a hot Playboy show. Best of all, you'll be paid $500 for one day of shooting." *Foursome* is a dating show like no other. Four singles (two men and two women) are brought together in a Hollywood mansion and are free to do what they want. Cameras capture the candid sexual activities that occur as they get to know each other. Like most reality shows, the participants are identified by a first name only and actually serve as the hosts, as they talk directly into the camera and set the stage for what is about to transpire.

804   Frank TV. (Comedy; TBS; November 20, 2007 to December 23, 2008)

A weekly skit series that satirizes politics, TV, movies and current events with comedian-impressionist Frank Caliendo playing all the roles.

Star: Frank Caliendo. **Credits:** *Executive Producer:* Frank Caliendo, Matt Wickline, John Bowman, Barry Katz. *Producer:* Leo Clarke, Brian Volk-Weiss. *Director:* Jay Karas. *Writer:* Frank Caliendo, John Bowman, Matt Wickline, Rich Talarico, Jeff Rothpan, Rachel Duguay, Dave Polsky, Brenda Hays, Dave King.

805   Franny's Feet. (Cartoon; PBS; Premiered: January 1, 2004)

Fantoosies is a shoe repair shop owned by the grandfather of a young girl named Franny. When a customer brings in a pair of shoes for repair, Franny tries them on and is magically transported to a place associated with those shoes (to teach learning experiences to children).

Voice Cast: Phoebe McAuley (Franny), George Buza (Grandfather). **Credits:** *Executive Producer:* Beth Stevenson. *Producer:* Kym Hyde. *Co-Producer:* John Mariella. *Music:* Miero Stamm. *Theme Vocal:* "Franny's Feet" by Tajja Isen.

806   Friday Night Lights. (Drama; NBC; October 3, 2006 to February 8, 2008)

Dillon is a small West Texas town obsessed with football (specifically the Panthers, the team of Dillon High School). The team plays on Friday nights. Football dominates conversations and events in the lives of the team members as well as its obsessed fans are depicted. On October 1, 2008 (to January 14, 2009) the series aired on Direct TV with repeats airing on NBC (beginning January 16, 2009).

Cast: Scott Porter (Jason Street), Adrianna Palicki (Tyra Collette), Minka Kelly (Lyla Garrity), Gaius Charles (Brian "Smash" Williams), Zach Gilford (Matt Saracen), Connie Britton (Tami Taylor), Derek Phillips (Billy Riggins), Kyle Chandler (Coach Eric Taylor), Aimee Teegarden (Julie Taylor), Jesse Plemons (Landry Clarke), Katherine Willis (Joanne Street), Nieko Mann (Noannie Williams), Liz Mikel (Corinna Williams), Blue Deckert (Coach Mac MaGill), Kevin Rankin (Herc) Ravin Alexander (Christina), Cindy Creekmore (Missy Aubrey), Robert Parish (Phil), Whitney McCauley (Sheila Williams), Walter Perez (Bobby "Bull" Reyes), Libby Villari (Mayor Lucy Rodell), Kate Krause (Tabby Garrity). **Credits:** *Executive Producer:* Peter Berg, Brian Grazer, Jason Katims. *Co-Executive Producer:* John Cameron, Sarah Aubrey. *Supervising Producer:* Carter Harris. *Producer:* David Hudgins, Katie O'Hara, Michael Lewis. *Music:* W.G. Snuffy Walden, Julie Greaux.

807   The Game. (Comedy; CW; Premiered: September 20, 2006)

A comedic look at the lives of the women behind the men of pro football. Particular focus is on Melanie Barnett, the live-in girlfriend of Derwin Davis, a third string rookie for the San Diego Sabers. Melanie is a very beautiful girl and she fears the worse: other women falling for Derwin (and Derwin becoming unfaithful to her). Melanie, a medical student, later becomes a doctor at San Diego Hospital). Kelly Pitts, Melanie's friend, has the same fears. She is a gorgeous "white chick" who is married to Jason Pitts, a black player. Malik Wright, a single quarterback, rounds out the main characters. His problems stem from his mother, Tasha Mack, who is also his manager (the owner of Tasha Mack Management). Malik would like to quit football and become a rap star, but his mother believes he hasn't the talent and constantly persuades him to stay with football. Stories follow the heartaches, the insecurities, challenges and rivalries each faces. The wives are members of the Saber Sunbeams. A spin off from *Girlfriends* (where the pilot aired in April of 2006).

Cast: Tia Mowry (Melanie Barnett), Pooch Hall (Derwin Davis), Brittany Daniel (Kelly Pitts), Coby Bell (Jason Pitts), Wendy Raquel Robinson (Tasha Mack), Hosea Chanchez (Malik Wright). **Credits:** *Executive Producer:* Kelsey Grammer, Mara Brock Akil, Steve Stark. *Co-Executive Producer:* Chuck Ranberg, Anne Flett-Giordano, Kenny Smith, Tim Edwards. *Producer:* Dan Dugan.

808 Game Show Moments Gone Bananas. (Comedy; VH-1; Premiered: May 21, 2005)

A Series of specials that presents humorous clips from game shows coupled with segments wherein studio audience members play classic game shows (like *Beat the Clock* and *Concentration*).

Host: Ben Stein. **Announcer:** Randy West. **Credits:** *Executive Producer:* Todd Barton. *Producer:* Mandel Ilagan, Bob Stone, Aaron Solomon.

809 Gene Simmons Family Jewels. (Reality; A&E; August 7, 2006 to August 31, 2008)

Cameras follow events in the lives of Gene Simmons, former front man for the rock group KISS, his girlfriend, Shannon Tweed, and their children Sophie and Nick.

Cast: Gene Simmons, Shannon Tweed, Sophie Simmons, Nick Simmons, Tracey Tweed. **Credits:** *Executive Producer:* Adam Reed, Nancy Dubuc, Leslie Greif, Deidre O'Hearn, Gene Simmons. *Co-Executive Producer:* Chad Greulach, Adam Freeman. *Music:* Alan Ett, Scott Liggett.

810 General Hospital. (Drama; ABC; Premiered: April 1, 1963)

Intimate glimpses into the lives of the doctors and nurses attached to the Internal Medicine Division, seventh floor, of General Hospital in Port Charles, New York.

Principal 2008 Cast: Anthony Geary (Luke Spencer), Jane Elliot (Tracy Quartermaine), John Ingle (Edward Quartermaine), Julie Marie Berman (Lulu Spencer), Nazani Boniadi (Leyla Mir), Sarah Joy Brown (Claudia Zacchara), Leslie Charleson (Monica Quartermaine), Claire Coffee (Nadine Crowell), Sonya Eddy (Epiphany Johnson), Nancy Lee Grahn (Alexis Davis), Rick Hearst (Ric Lansing), Jason Cook (Matt Hunter), Tyler Christopher (Nikolas Cassadine), Steve Burton (Jason Morgan), Maurice Benard (Sonny Cortinthos), Brandon Barash (Johnny Zacchara), Bradford Anderson (Damien Spinelli), Rebecca Herbst (Elizabeth Webber), Kimberly McCullough (Robin Scorpio), Kelly Monaco (Samantha McCall), Kirsten Storms (Maxie Jones), Megan Ward (Kate Howard), Laura Wright (Caroline Jacks), John J. York (Mac Scorpio), Greg Vaughn (Lucky Spencer), Jason Thompson (Patrick Drake), Sebastian Roche (Jerry Jacks), Ingo Rademacher (Jasper "Jax" Jacks), Rick Springfield (Noah Drake/Eli Love), Kin Shriner (Scott Baldwin), Finola Hughes (Anna Devane), Carolyn Hennesey (Diane Miller), Kent King (Lainey Winters), Stephen Macht (Trevor Lansing), Lisa LoCicero (Olivia Falconeri), Minae Noji (Kelly Lee), Kali Rodriguez (Kristina Davis), Tamlyn Tomita (Giselle), Bruce Weitz (Anthony Zacchara), Jackie Zeman (Bobbie Spencer), Barbara Tarbuck (Jane Jacks). **Credits:**

Executive Producer: Jill Farren Phelps. *Creator:* Frank Hursley, Doris Hursley.

811 General Hospital: Night Shift. (Drama; Soap Net; July 12, 2007 to October 21, 2008)

Prime time cable series based on the ABC daytime serial *General Hospital.* Stories, complete in themselves, focus on the doctors and nurses who handle the night shift at General Hospital.

Cast: Alla Korot (Stacey Sloan), Josh Duhon (Logan Hayes), Jason Gerhardt (Cooper Barrett), Lindze Letterman (Georgie Jones), Natalia Livingston (Emily Quartermaine), Kent King (Dr. Lainey Winters), Minae Noji (Kelly Lee), Graham Shiels (Cody Paul), Jason Thompson (Dr. Patrick Drake), Kimberly McCullough (Dr. Robin Scorpio), Steve Burton (Jason Morgan), Bradford Anderson (Damien Spinelli), Rebecca Herbst (Elizabeth Spencer), Billy Dee Williams (Toussaint Dubois), Amanda Baker (Jolene Crowell), Julie Berman (Lulu Spencer), Kirsten Storms (Maxie Jones), Angel M. Wainwright (Regina Thompson). **Credits:** *Executive Producer:* Lisa De Cazotte, Jill Farren-Phelps. *Supervising Producer:* Richard Schilling. *Producer:* Jeanne Hurey.

812 George of the Jungle. (Cartoon; Cartoon Network; Premiered: June 29, 2007)

A revised version of the 1960s series of the same title about George, a clumsy, tree crashing prone jungle hero as he attempts to protect his domain from evil. Magnolia and Ursula are his friends; "An ape named Ape" is his guiding light.

Voice Cast: Lee Tockar (George), Tabitha St. Germain (Magnolia), Britt Irvin (Ursula), Paul Dobson (Ape), Michael Dangerfield (Narrator), Brian Drummond (Witch Doctor). **Credits:** *Executive Producer:* Evan Baily, Eric Ellenbogen, Blair Peters, Rob Simmons, Tiffany Ward, Chris Bartleman. *Producer:* Kevin Gamble, Mike Weiss. *Music:* Michael Richard Plowman.

813 Ghost Hunters. (Reality; Sci Fi; Premiered: October 1, 2004)

A program that investigates reports of paranormal happenings. Jason Hawkes and Grant Wilson, plumbers by trade, head an organization called TAPS (The Atlantic Paranormal Society) which also incorporates ordinary people with an interest in ghosts.

Cast: Jason Hawkes, Grant Wilson, Brian Harnois, Steve Gonsalves, Kristyn Gartland. **Announcer:** Mike Rowe. **Credits:** *Executive Producer:* Tom Thayer, Peter Zasuly, Craig Piligian, Rob Katz. *Supervising Producer:* Mark Marinaccio, Richard Monahan. *Producer:* Jay Bluemke, Tim Calandrello, Eric Mazer.

814 Ghost Whisperer. (Drama; CBS; Premiered: September 23, 2005)

Same As It Never Was Antiques is a store in Grandview that is owned by Melinda Gordon. Melinda is married to Jim Clancy (Melinda uses her maiden name for business) and possesses a most unusual gift: the ability to see ghosts and communicate with the dead. Melinda can sense spirits and feel what they are feeling. She believes spirits contact her so she can help them complete a mission before seeing the light and moving on. For Melinda, it began when she was eight years old and in the fourth grade. After the passing of a classmate Melinda saw her ghost (who was not aware that she was dead). Her grandmother had the ability but her mother (Beth) does not (as the gift skips a generation). Stories follow Melinda as she tries to lead a normal life while at the same time helping spirits find closure. Andrea is Melinda's partner; later replaced by Delia (who also works as a real estate agent for Sun Briar Realty); Ned is Delia's son; Richard Payne is the Rockland College University professor who assists Melinda (he is replaced by Professor Eli James, a therapist at Rockland, who can hear but not see ghosts).

Cast: Jennifer Love Hewitt (Melinda Gordon), David Conrad (Jim Clancy), Aisha Tyler (Andrea Moreno), Camryn Manheim (Delia Banks), Tyler Patrick James (Ned Banks), Christoph Sanders (Ned Banks; later), Jay Mohr (Richard Payne), Abigail Breslin (Young Melinda), Anne Archer (Beth), Jamie Kennedy (Eli James). **Credits:** *Executive Producer:* John Gray, Kim Moses, Ian Sander, John Wirth. *Co-Executive Producer:* Jed Seidel, James Van Praugh. *Producer:* Jennifer Love Hewitt, Joe Dishner, Juanita F. Diana. *Music:* Mark Snow.

815 Giada's Weekend Getaways. (Reality; Food Network; Premiered: January 12, 2007)

Chef Giada DeLaurentis takes to the road to find three-day getaways that feature delectable foods.

Host: Giada DeLaurentis. **Credits:** *Executive Producer:* Anne Fox. *Producer:* Scott Siegel.

816 Girlfriends. (Comedy; WB/CW; September 11, 2000 to February 11, 2008)

The life, loves, joys and sorrows of Joan Clayton, Maya Wilkes, Lynn Searcy and Toni Childs, four beautiful African American women struggling to find their place in the world. Joan was originally a lawyer with the Los Angeles firm of Goldstein, Sweedleston, Donaldson and Lee. She later opens a bar called The J-Spot. Maya was originally Joan's legal secretary. She turned her ability to write into a book called *Oh Hell, Yes* that offers help to others through the hardships she faced in life. Lynn is not easily motivated and not very responsible. She has five degrees from U.C.L.A. but has never been able to put any of them to work for her. She takes whatever jobs she can find — from waitress to secretary to documentary film maker. She often lives with one of her girlfriends and in 2007 she performed as the singer Indigo Style. Toni is a material girl and dreams of marrying a millionaire. She originally worked for Colonoda Realty before beginning her own company Toni Childs Realty. William Dent is a close friend to all four girls (a lawyer at Joan's former agency); Jabari is Maya's son with ex-husband Darnell; Todd Grant is a Caucasian doctor who married Toni (but their constant bickering broke up the marriage). When the series switched to the CW it is mentioned that Toni moved to New York to be with her boyfriend who had acquired a job on a make over reality TV show.

Cast: Tracee Ellis Ross (Joan Clayton), Golden Brooks (Maya Wilkes), Persia White (Lynn Searcy), Jill Marie Jones (Toni Childs), Reginald C. Hayes (William Dent), Jason Pace (Dr. Todd Garrett), Tanner Scott Richards (Jabari Wilkes), Khalil Kain (Darnell Wilkes), Flex Alexander (Darnell Wilkes). **Credits:** *Executive Producer:* Kelsey Grammer. *Co-Executive Producer:* Michael B. Kaplan, Regina Y. Hick, Mara Brock Akil. *Supervising Producer:* Lamont Ferrell, Norman Vance, Jr. *Producer:* Michael E. Stokes, Nancy Sprow, Sheldon Epps.

817 The Girls Next Door. (Reality; E!; Premiered: August 7, 2005)

An intimate look at the public and private life of *Playboy* magazine publisher Hugh Hefner (83 years old with 2008 episodes). Bridget, Holly and Kendra are three gorgeous Playmates who live with Hugh at the Playboy Mansion in California. Episodes follow the daily events that spark Hugh's life as well as his three regular companions, his brother, Keith, mansion staff and other magazine playmates (all representing the 2008 version of the series).

Cast: Hugh Hefner (Himself), Bridget Marquardt (Herself), Holly Madison (Herself), Kendra Wilkinson (Herself), Mary O'Connor (Hugh's personal secretary), Keith Hefner (Himself), Anastasia Case (Bridget's sister), Cristal Camden (Hugh's former girlfriend), Norma Maister

(Mansion staff), Kara Monaco (2006 Playmate of the Year), Victoria Fuller (January 1996 Playmate), Alison Waite (May 2006 Playmate), Giuliana Marino (April 2007 Playmate). **Credits:** *Executive Producer:* Kevin Burns. *Co-Executive Producer:* Scott Hartford. *Supervising Producer:* Mykelle Sabin. *Producer:* Rebecca Gullion, Nicole Reitman. *Music:* Randy Jones, Jeremy Sweet.

818 Globe Trekker. (Reality; PBS; Premiered: March 31, 2002)

Fascinating journeys to lands near and far with the traveler (Globe Trekker) experiencing everything from dining with the local citizens to climbing mountains to surviving a week in a rain forest.

Globe Trekkers: Megan McCormick, Ian Wright, Justine Shapiro, Christina Chang, Lavinia Tan, Shipa Mehta, Holly Morris, Nikki Grosse, Neil Gibson, Katy Haswell. **Credits:** *Executive Producer:* Dalton Dean, Carole Tomko. *Supervising Producer:* Tracey Cuesta. *Producer:* Vanessa Colossi, Leslie Wiener. *Music:* Paul Mounsey, Daniel Pemberton.

819 Glutton for Punishment. (Reality; Food Network; Premiered: July 10, 2007)

Travel combines with cooking to present chef Bob Blumer as he tackles various cooking challenges and offers tips along the way.

Host: Bob Blumer. **Credits:** *Producer:* Mona Gienier. *Writer:* Bob Blumer. *Director:* Jonas Quastel.

820 Go, Diego Go. (Cartoon; Nickelodeon; Premiered: September 6, 2005).

A spin off from *Dora the Explorer* about her cousin, Diego, a bilingual eight-year-old who runs the Animal Rescue Center in the Latin American Rain Forest. Stories revolve around Diego as he rescues and cares for animals.

Voice Cast: Jake T. Austin (Diego), Constanza Sperakis (Alicia), E. Austin Valentine (Baby Jaguar), Rosie Perez (Click), Sebastian Arcelus (Mr. Marquez). **Credits:** *Executive Producer:* Chris Gifford, Valerie Walsh. *Music:* Steve Sandberg, Jed Becker.

821 Going Tribal. (Reality; Discovery Channel; Premiered: August 9, 2005)

Bruce Parry, a former Royal Marine, seeks out then lives with the people of remote locations (for up to a month) to experience their way of life.

Host: Bruce Parry. **Credits:** *Executive Producer:* Sam Organ. *Producer:* Steve Robinson.

822 Good Deal with Dave Lieberman. (Cooking; Food Network; Premiered: April 16, 2005)

Chef Dave Lieberman offers tips and shows viewers how to prepare inexpensive but delicious meals.

Host: Dave Lieberman. **Credits:** *Senior Producer:* Laurie Buck. *Producer:* Audrey Bellezza, John Coffey, Rachel Knobelman, Suzanne Schuster.

823 Good Eats with Alton Brown. (Cooking; Food Network; Premiered: July 7, 1999)

Food and science combine to present how food is prepared and the beneficial aspects it contains.

Host: Alton Brown. **Credits:** *Executive Producer:* Deanna Brown. *Producer:* Dana Popoff. *Music:* Patrick Belden.

824 Gossip Girl. (Drama; CW; Premiered: September 19, 2007)

Social and personal events that spark the lives of a group of students at an exclusive prep school (Constance Billiard) on Manhattan's Upper East Side. It is here that Gossip Girl, a mysterious web site, claims to be all knowing and reports all the important news that the students (and viewers) need to know. Serena van der Woodsen and her close friend Blair Waldorf are the principal focus of the series (girls, addicted to Gossip Girl, who love shopping, fashion and partying at the trendiest night spots). Other regulars include students Eric, Nate, Katy, Isabel Dan and Jenny.

Cast: Blake Lively (Serena van der Woodsen), Leighton Meester (Blair Waldorf), Connor Paolo (Eric van der Woodsen), Kelly Rutherford (Lily van der Woodsen), Chace Crawford (Nate Archibald), Sam Robards (Howie Archibald), Nan Zhang (Katy), Nicole Fiscella (Isabel), Ed Westwick (Chuck), Penn Badgley (Dan), Kristen Bell (Gossip Girl), Taylor Momsen (Jenny Humphrey), Matthew Settle (Rufus Humphrey), Margaret Colin (Eleanor Waldorf), Nicole Fiscella (Isabel Coates), Michelle Trachtenberg (Georgina Sparks), Desmond Harrington (Jack Bass), John Patrick Amedori (Aaron Rose), Robert John Burke (Bart Bass). **Credits:** *Executive Producer:* Stephanie Savage, Leslie Morgantein, Bob Levy. *Co-Executive Producer:* Felicia D. Henderson, K.J. Steinberg. *Producer:* Amy J. Kaufman, Joe Lazarov, Jessica Queller.

825   Great Performances. (Anthology; PBS; Premiered: November 4, 1972)
   Television's longest running performing arts program; full length and/or excerpts of productions spanning the genres from the Broadway stage to opera. Walter Cronkite served as the host from 1988 to 2007.
   Credits: *Executive Producer:* Jac Venza, Barry Schulman, Anthony Chapman, Margaret Smilov, Pete Gelb, John Beug, Fritz Buttenstedt, Klaus Hallig, Jack Wallis, Dan Cleary, Gabielle Babin Gugenheim, Pierre-Olivier Bardet, Costa Pilavachi, Peter Maniura, Eric Ghenassia, Jeff Rowland, Fiona Morris, Robert Kotlowitz, Tony Judge, Mark Hagen. *Producer:* Michael Bronson, Niv Fichman, Dieter Melzer, Daniel Iron, Judy Flannery, Allen Newman, Mark Cooper, Chris Cohen, John Walker, James Pluta, Martin Fischer, Tiffany Hanssen Michael Heinzl, Sam Hudson, Jason Kaillor, Kathryn Slusher, John Goberman, Kim Myers.

826   Greek. (Drama; ABC Family; July 9, 2007 to October 28, 2008)
   Fictional Cypress-Rhodes University in California is the setting for a look at a group of students who want more than an education — "We want to have fun, meet people, grow up and find ourselves." In actuality, their idea of college is joining a fraternity (or sorority) and having nonstop fun. Rusty Cartwright, an anti-social freshman, and his very social friendly sophomore sister, Casey, are the focal point of the series. Rusty is a member of the Kappa Tau fraternity; Casey belongs to the prestigious Zeta Beta sorority. Rusty is a bit awkward and exceptionally intelligent and is having a difficult time fitting in. Casey is charming and gorgeous and not that actively involved with the academic aspect of the school. Dale is Rusty's roommate; Rebecca and Ashleigh are Casey's sorority sisters; Beaver is Rusty's fraternity brother.
   Cast: Jacob Zachar (Rusty Cartwright), Spencer Grammer (Casey Cartwright), Jake McDorman (Evan), Amber Stevens (Ashleigh), Dilshad Vadsaria (Rebecca), Paul James (Calvin), Clark Duke (Dale), Aaron Hill (The Beaver), Jessica Rose (Ken K), Jhoanna Flores (Libby), Zack Lively (Heath), Derek Mio (Wade), Tiffany Dupont (Frannie). **Credits:** *Executive Producer:* Shawn Piller, Lloyd Segan, Patrick Sean Smith. *Producer:* Todd Ulman.

827   Greek to Chic. (Reality; Internet; Premiered: May 4, 2006)
   Internet makeover series that travels to various colleges to transform "rumpled frat brothers into date bait." After the makeover, the former "geeks" are given advice as how to maintain their new looks and lifestyle.
   Hosts: Sandra Sanchez, Jonathan Redford.

828   Grey's Anatomy. (Drama; ABC; Premiered: March 27, 2005)
   A penetrating look at the personal and professional lives of five surgical interns at Seattle Grace Memorial Hospital: Meredith

Grey, Cristina Yang, Isobel Stevens, Alex Karev and George O'Malley. Meredith is the daughter of renowned surgeon Ellis Grey (who is suffering from a devastating illness that overshadows Meredith's ambitions). Cristina is highly competitive and driven and refuses to accept favors from anyone. Isobel, called Izzie, is a small town girl who paid for her medical education by performing as a lingerie model. She is like Cristina — determined to make it without help from anyone. George is insecure and has a knack for saying or doing the wrong thing. Alex is the most arrogant of the interns. He is ambitious and often balks at having to do jobs that he feels are beneath him. Miranda is the senior resident in charge of interns; Derek Shepherd is the flirtatious surgeon; Preston Burke is the arrogant but skilled surgeon; Richard Webber is the chief of surgery.

Cast: Ellen Pompeo (Dr. Meredith Grey), Sandra Oh (Dr. Cristina Yang), Katherine Heigl (Dr. Isobel Stevens), Justin Chambers (Dr. Alex Karev), T.R. Knight (Dr. George O'Malley), Chandra Wilson (Dr. Miranda Bailey), James Pickens, Jr. (Dr. Richard Webber), Patrick Dempsey (Dr. Derek Shepherd), Isaiah Washington (Dr. Preston Burke), Sarah Utterback (Nurse Olivia), Kate Burton (Ellis Grey), Kate Walsh (Dr. Addison Montgomery), Sara Ramirez (Dr. Callie Torres), Mare Winningham (Susan Grey), Elizabeth Reaser (Rebecca Pope). **Credits:** *Executive Producer:* Mark Gordon, Betsy Beers, Krista Vernoff, Peter Horton, Nancy Bordson, Steve Mulholland, Kent Hodder. *Co-Executive Producer:* Mark Wilding, Tony Phelan. *Supervising Producer:* Joan Rater, Kip Koenig, Gabrielle G. Stanton, Debora Cahn, Harry Werksman. *Producer:* Rob Corn, Jeff Rafner, Jenna Bans. *Music:* Danny Lux.

829   Grill It with Bobby Flay. (Cooking; Food Network; Premiered: October 10, 2006).

Chef Bobby Flay takes to the road to test the foods of both amateur and professional chefs — and then try to improve on the meals he was just served.

Host: Bobby Flay. **Credits:** *Producer:* Karen Kinney.

830   The Guiding Light. (Drama; CBS; Premiered: June 30, 1952)

The longest running program in broadcast history, premiering on CBS radio on January 25, 1937, then on television on June 30, 1952. On radio, the series focused on the people of Five Points, a suburb of Chicago (in particular on the Rev. John Rutledge [played by Arthur Peterson]). On television, the religious aspect of the series was dropped to focus on dramatic incidents in the lives of the close-knit Bauer, Spaulding and Reardon families, residents of the town of Springfield, U.S.A. (later said to be Springfield, Illinois).

Principal 2008 Cast: Kim Zimmer (Reva Shayne), Jordan Clarke (Billy Lewis II), Mandy Bruno (Marina Cooper), Crystal Chappell (Olivia Spencer), Nicole Forester (Cassie Layne Lewis), Jessica Leccia (Natalia Rivera), Marcy Rylan (Lizzie Spaulding), Gina Tognoni (Dinah Marler), Caitlin Van Zandt (Ashlee Wolfe), Justin Deas (Buzz Cooper, Sr.), Daniel Cosgrov (Bill Lewis), Bradley Cole (Jeffrey O'Neill), Jeff Branson (Shayne Lewis), E.J. Bonilla (Raphael Rivera), Robert Bogue (A.C. Mallet), Murray Bartlett (Cyrus Foley), Frank Dicopoulos (Frank Cooper, Jr.), John Driscoll (Henry Cooper Bradshaw), Kane Manera (Grady Foley), Robert Newman (Josh Lewis), Michael O'Leary (Rick Bauer), Ron Raines (Alan Spaulding), Lawrence Saint-Victor (Remy Boudreau), Tina Sloan (Lillian Raines), Jacqueline Tsirkin (Emma Spaulding), Miles Williams (R.J. Winslow), Montel Williams (Clayton Boudreau), Yvonna Wright (Melissande Boudreau), Marj Dusay (Alexandra Spaulding), Arielle Renwart (Leah Bauer), Naelee Rae (Clarissa

Marler), Maeve Kinkead (Vanessa Reardon), Elizabeth Keifer (Blake Marler), Nicholas Art (Zach Spaulding), Kim Brockington (Felicia Boudreau), Orlagh Cassidy (Doris Wolfe), Beth Chamberlain (Beth Raines), Robert Danza, Jr. (Jude Bauer). **Credits:** *Executive Producer:* Ellen Wheeler. *Producer:* Alexandra Johnson, Maria Macina. *Theme Music:* Rick Rhodes, Danny Pelfrey.

831   The Guild. (Comedy; Internet; Premiered: July 27, 2007)

Codex is a young woman who is addicted to playing video games over the Internet (specifically "The Knights of Good," where she is the Healer). Soon the game begins to affect her life when her fellow game players believe the game is real and descend upon her home. Codex knows the game is just that, a game, but to her friends, it is an addiction that has affected their outlook on life. Stories follow Codex as she struggles to deal with and solve the real life problems her friends are experiencing as the result of over playing "The Knights of Good."

Cast: Felicia Day (Cyd "Codex" Sherman), Sandeep Parikh (Zaboo), Vincent Caso (Bladezz), Jeff Lewis (Vork), Amy Okud (Tinkerbella), Robin Thorsen (Clara). **Credits:** *Producer:* Jane Selle Morgan, Kim Evey. *Writer:* Felicia Day. *Director:* Jane Selle Morgan, Greg Benson.

832   Gunslinger Girl. (Cartoon; IFC; Premiered: October 8, 2003)

A secret Italian government organization called The Public Corporation for Social Welfare has a unique but underhanded means by which to save terminally ill young girls: they cure them with cybernetic implants that strip them of virtually all their human emotions. The girls are then trained as soldiers and incorporated as assassins to do the agency's bidding. Angelica, Claes, Henrietta, Rico and Triela are five girls, skilled in the martial arts, who become the agency's top assassins.

Stories, aimed at a mature audience, are violent and follow the girls as they perform hazardous missions while at the same time trying to retain as much as their humanity as possible. Produced in Japan.

Voice Cast: Laura Bailey (Henrietta), Monica Rial (Angelica), Alese Watson (Claes), Luci Christian (Rico), Caitlin Glass (Triela), John Burgmeier (Jose), Eric Vale (Jean), Brina Palencia (Elsa), Troy Baker (Alfonso), Cynthia Cranz (Ferro), Mark Stoddard (Lorenzo). **Credits:** *Executive Producer:* Cindy Brennan Fukunaga, Gen Fukunaga. *Producer:* Barry Watson, Daniel Cocanougher. *Opening Theme Vocal:* "The Light Before We Land" by The Delgados. *Closing Theme:* "After the Dream" by Opus.

833   Guy's Big Bite. (Cooking; Food Network; Premiered: June 25, 2006)

California chef and restaurant owner Guy Fieri sets out to prove men and women have different tastes by preparing healthy, masculine meals.

Host: Guy Fieri.

834   Hannah Montana. (Comedy; Disney; Premiered: March 24, 2006)

Twelve-year-old Miley Stewart attends Seaview Middle School, has a best friend (Lily) and is full of energy. She is also Hannah Montana, a super rock star. Miley lives in Malibu, California, with her widowed father, Robbie and older brother Jackson. As Hannah, Miley dons a blonde wig (to cover her natural brunette hair) to become her other self and protect her true identity ("If I don't I'll never be Miley again"). Robbie, a former singer/songwriter known as Robbie Ray, poses as Miley's bodyguard when she is Hannah (it was Robbie who helped Miley become a singer). In later episodes, Miley finds her secret to big to hide and reveals it to Lily and their friend Oliver. Stories follow Miley as she struggles to balance her dual life and still be a kid. Second season episodes find Miley attending high school and trying (more than ever) to conceal her singing career while struggling to lead life as a freshman. Other regulars are Amber and Ashley, the school snobs; Fermine, Hannah's wardrobe master; Rico, the annoying kid who owns (on behalf of his rich father), the beach eatery, Rico's Surf Shop (where Jackson works); Heather is Lily's mother; Susan (seen is flashbacks) is Miley's mother. Miley Cyrus performs the theme, "Best of Both Worlds."

Cast: Miley Cyrus (Miley Stewart/ Hannah Montana), Billy Ray Cyrus (Robbie Stewart), Emily Osment (Lily Truscott), Jason Earles (Jackson Stewart), Mitchel Musso (Oliver Oken), Shanica Knowles (Amber Addison), Anna Maria Perez De Tagle (Ashley DeWitt), Moises Arias (Rico), Brooke Shields (Susan), Ryan Newman (Young Miley). **Credits:** *Executive Producer:* Michael Poryes, Steven Peterman. *Co-Executive Producer:* Sally Lapiduss. *Producer:* Richard G. King. *Music:* John Carter.

835   Have Fork, Will Travel. (Cooking; Food Network; Premiered: September 4, 2007)

Comedian and chef Zane Lamprey hits the road to increase his knowledge of food by visiting diners and restaurants across the country.

Host: Zane Lamprey. **Credits:** *Executive Producer:* Matt Chan. *Producer:* Mike Kelly.

836   Heavyweights. (Cooking; Food Network; Premiered: 2006)

Nutritionist author Ellie Kreiger prepares meals that are designed to increase the viewer's awareness of healthy eating.

Host: Ellie Krieger. **Credits:** *Producer:* Angela Quilala, Beth Keiran. *Music:* Jared Gutstadt.

837   Hell Date. (Reality; BET; July 9, 2007 to July 14, 2008)

What happens when two people are set up for a date and one turns out to be a nightmare from hell? That is the premise. An unsuspecting subject is matched with a date (an actor) that defies all the rules of dating. Cameras capture the reactions of the poor soul who wound up with the date from hell.

Credits: *Executive Producer:* Peter M. Cohen, James De Bouse. *Co-Executive Producer:* Rob Dames, Lesley Wolff. *Supervising Producer:* Kim McKoy.

838   Hell's Kitchen. (Reality; Fox; Premiered: May 30, 2005)

World-renowned chef Gordon Ramsay, owner of the Hollywood based Hell's Kitchen restaurant, seeks only perfection from his staff. Twelve aspiring chefs face Ramsay's often displayed anger as they compete in various cooking competitions for the honor of working as the top chef at one of his restaurants.

Host: Gordon Ramsay. **Narrator:** Jason Thompson. **Credits:** *Executive Producer:* Arthur Smith, Kent Weed, Natalka Znak, Paul Jackson, Richard Cowler. *Co-Executive Producer:* Daniel Soiseth, Andrew Scheer. *Supervising Producer:* Tony Croll, Heidi Dahmen, Sandi Johnson, Kenny Rosen, Faye Stapleton. *Producer:* Peter Tartaglia, Ben Hatta. *Music:* Matt Koskenmaki.

839   Heroes. (Fantasy; NBC; Premiered: September 25, 2006)

Complex series about a group of people who possess special powers (acquired after an eclipse) and who need to unite to save the world from destruction. The heroes are Peter, a nurse, and his brother, Nathan, a politician, who can fly; Claire, a Texas high school cheerleader with the ability to heal herself; Hiro, a Japanese office worker with the ability to bend the space-time continuum; Nikki, a single mother (of Micah) who has incredible strength; Isaac, an artist who paints pictures of future disasters; Eden, a telepathic; Matt, a police officer who can read minds; Monica, who receives her powers from what she sees on TV; Ellen, who derives her power from electricity; and Daphne, "a chick who can run at supersonic speed."

Cast: Milo Ventimiglia (Peter Petrelli), Ali Larter (Nikki Sanders), Sendhil Ramamurthy (Mohinder Suresh), Masi Oka (Hiro Nokamura), Adrian Pasdar (Nathan Petrelli), Hayden Panettiere (Claire Bennett), Greg Grunberg (Matt Parkman), Noah Gray-Cabey (Micah Sanders), Nora Zehetner (Eden McCain), Santiago Cabrera (Isaac Mendez), Kristen Bell (Ellen), Dana Davis (Monica), Brea Grant (Daphne). **Credits:** *Executive Producer:* David Semel, Tim Kring, Bryan Fuller, Dennis Hammer. *Supervising Producer:* Adam Armus, Nora Kay Foster. *Producer:* Skip Beaudine. *Co-Producer:* Lori Motyer.

840   Hey Paula. (Reality; Bravo; June 28, 2007 to January 28, 2008)

A profile of singer and *American Idol* judge Paula Abdul. **Star:** Paula Abdul. **Credits:** *Executive Producer:* Lenid Rolov. *Supervising Producer:* Tracy Whittaker. *Producer:* Paula Abdul, Scott Sternberg.

841   Higglytown Heroes. (Cartoon; Disney; Premiered: September 12, 2004)

A computer animated series, aimed at preschoolers, that celebrates everyday heroes — from police officers to mailmen as seen through the experiences of Kip, Twinkle, Wayne, Eubie and their friend, Fran, the talking squirrel.

Voice Cast: Rory Thost (Kip), Liliana Mumy (Twinkle), Taylor Masamitsu (Eubie), Edie McClurg (Fran), Frankie Ryan Manriquez (Wayne), Dee Bradley Baker (Uncle Zooter), Kevin Michael Richardson (Uncle Lemmo), Rachel York (Bitty). **Credits:** *Executive Producer:* Jeff Fino, Holly Huckins, Kent Redecker.

842   High School Stories. (Reality; MTV; Premiered: February 1, 2004)

Reenactments of actual incidents that have occurred in high schools across the nation that feature the actual students involved in the incidents (usually pranks).

Credits: *Producer:* Jenna Grobstein Yaches, Danielle Berger. *Associate Producer:* Allyson Schwartz, Stephanie Saster, Jessica Antonini. *Coordinating Producer:* Carly Colao.

843   High Stakes Poker. (Reality; Game Show Network; Premiered: January 1, 2006)

High stakes poker players compete in tournaments wherein wagers range from $100 to $1 million.

Host: Daniel Alaei. **Dealer:** Danette Morway. **Credits:** *Producer:* Summer Zemel, Guy Marks. *Music:* John Pratt.

844   The Hills. (Reality; MTV; Premiered: May 31, 2006)

Laguna Beach spin off that follows that series regular Lauren Conrad as she moves to Los Angeles after graduating from high school to attend the Fashion Institute of Design and Merchandising (while also interning for *Teen Vogue* magazine). Lauren, called "L.C.," is from a wealthy family and has decided to do something constructive with her life. That struggle is profiled as she proves she is not a spoiled rich girl.

Cast: Lauren Conrad, Whitney Port, Heidi Montag, Lisa Love, Jordan Eubanks, Audrine Partridge, Justin "Bobby" Brescia, Brian Drolet. **Credits:** *Executive Producer:* Adam Divello, Tony Di Santo, Liz Gateley. *Co-Executive Producer:* Sean Travis. *Supervising Producer:* Lenid Rolov. *Producer:* William Longworthy. *Music:* Jon Ernst.

845   Hip Hop Harry. (Children; Discovery Kids; Premiered: September 26, 2006)

Hip Hop Harry is a large, friendly bear (actor in costume) with the ability to dance and entertain children. He lives in a classroom-like setting and is surrounded by a group of children who come to his "clubhouse" to sing, dance, play games and learn various aspects of life through the songs and dances Harry teaches them.

Cast: David Joyner (Hip Hop Harry in Costume), Kelfa Hare (Hip Hop Harry in Costume), Ali Alimi (Hip Hop Harry Voice), Valerie Sheppard (Letter Carrier Carla), Ben Blair (Dr. Vinnie). **Credits:** *Executive Producer:* Claude Brooks. *Co-Executive Producer:* Gelila Asres. *Producer:* Norma Jean Straw, Jodi Smith, Josh Zaretsky. *Music:* Judi Lewinson.

846 The History Detectives. (Reality; PBS; Premiered: July 1, 2003)

Items, which may be of historic interest and owned by ordinary people, are thoroughly investigated for their authenticity by a team of experts.

Cast: Elyse Luray-Marx (Appraiser), C. Wesley Cowan (Appraiser), Tukufu Zuberi (Sociology professor), Gwen Wright (Architecture professor). **Credits:** *Executive Producer:* Tony Tackabery, Dave Davis. *Producer:* Neil Laird, Kristian Berg, Christopher Bryson, Emma Davies, Russ Tuttle, Dana Ross, Bernadette McDavid.

847 Hollywood Heat. (Reality; Court TV/Tru TV; Premiered: January 11, 2007)

A look at the crime and the pursuit of justice within the entertainment industry.

Hosts: Lynne White, Ashleigh Banfield.

848 Holmes on Homes. (Reality; TLC; Premiered: September 7, 2001)

A contractor (Mike Holmes) helps home owners overcome the trauma of work performed by amateur or inexperienced renovators by doing what should have been done right at the outset.

Host: Mike Holmes. **Producer-Director:** Mike Holmes.

849 Horseland. (Cartoon; CBS; Premiered: January 1, 2007)

The activities of five close girlfriends (Alma Rodriquez, Chloe Stilton, Zoe Stilton [Chloe's sister], Molly Washington and Sarah Whitney) are depicted as they interact with each other and share their love of horses.

Voices: Dana Donlan, Emily Hernandez, Bianca Heyward, David Kalis, Jerry Longe, Vincent Michael, Marissa Shea, Aleyah Smith, Michelle Zacharia. **Credits:** *Executive Producer:* Andy Heyward, Michael Maliana. *Producer:* Karen Lee Brown. *Music:* Ron Wasserman.

850 Hot Babes Doing Stuff Naked. (Reality; Playboy Channel; Premiered: 2007)

Gorgeous girls, naked or scantily clad, perform non sexual "stuff" as requested by viewers from a survey conducted by the Playboy Channel. Requested activities include roller skating, deep sea fishing, chicken farming, shooting guns and washing a truck. The girls, connected with *Playboy* magazine or the Playboy mansion, are identified by first names only (for example, Amber, Brooke, Andrea and Zoe).

851 House. (Drama; Fox; Premiered: November 6, 2004)

The Princeton-Plainsboro Teaching Hospital in New Jersey is a medical facility that handles, in addition to normal cases, baffling medical diseases. Gregory House, a maverick, anti-social doctor, heads a team that tackles the mysterious cases that defy medical diagnosis. House is an expert in infectious diseases and his philosophy is "We treat. If the patient gets better we're right. If not, we learn something else." While House appears to solve every medical mystery by himself, it is actually accomplished with the investigative work of his specialized team. Stories, which painstakingly depict House's efforts to cure people who appear to have no chance at all, also relate another aspect of Gregory's hospital life: his reluctance to treat people with normal medical disorders (something he balks at doing, but does). The series has the screen title *House, M.D.*

Cast: Hugh Laurie (Dr. Gregory House),

Jennifer Morrison (Dr. Allison Cameron), Omar Epps (Dr. Eric Foreman), Jesse Spencer (Dr. Robert Chase), Lisa Edelstein (Dr. Lisa Cuddy), Kal Penn (Lawrence Kutner), Peter Jacobson (Dr. Chris Taub), Olivia Wilder (Dr. Thirteen Hadley), Robert Sean Leonard (Dr. James Wilson). **Credits:** *Executive Producer:* Paul Attanasio, Katie Jacobs, Bryan Singer, David Shore. *Supervising Producer:* Matt Witten, Thomas L. Moran. *Co-Executive Producer:* David Sempel, Garrett Lerner, Russell Friend, Doris Egan. *Producer:* Gerrit van der Meer, Marcy Kaplan. *Music:* Jason Derlatka.

852 House of Payne. (Comedy; TBS; Premiered: June 21, 2006)

A daily series that focuses on the lives of three generations of one family living under the same roof. Curtis and Ella Payne are a couple who have been married 31 years. Curtis is a firefighter and they are the parents of C.J. (a firefighter). C.J. is married to Janine and they are the parents of Jasi and Malik. Originally aired in syndication.

Cast: LaVan Davis (Curtis Payne), Cassi Davis (Ella Payne), Allen Payne (C.J. Payne), Demetria McKinney (Janine Payne), China Anne McClain (Jazmine "Jasi" Payne), Larramie "Doc" Shaw (Malik Payne), Lance Gross (Calvin Payne), Denise Burse (Miss Cloretha). **Credits:** *Executive Producer:* Tyler Perry, Reuben Cannon. *Supervising Producer:* Roger Bobb. *Music:* Herb Magwood.

853 How I Met Your Mother. (Comedy; CBS; Premiered: September 19, 2005)

How did Ted and Robin, a now happily married couple, meet? Flashbacks are used to recall their first meeting, their eventual courtship and marriage. These events are relayed by an older Ted as he tells his teenage children, an unnamed boy and girl, the various pitfalls of his and Robin's courtship. Stories also focus on the lives of Ted's friends, Barney, an executive at a Manhattan company called Altrucel, a swinging bachelor who is known to have had many affairs, especially with foreign women; and his engaged friends, Marshall (a law student) and Lily, a grade school teacher. Ted is a student at the Columbia School of Law; Robin is a reporter for Metro News One in New York City; Altrucel is famous for making "the fuzzy yellow stuff on the surface of tennis balls." Marshall and Lily also marry and become an "aunt" and "uncle" to Ted and Robin's kids.

Cast: Josh Radnor (Ted Mosby), Cobie Smulders (Robin Scherbatsky), Alyson Hannigan (Lily Aldrin), Neil Patrick Harris (Barney Stinson), Jason Segel (Marshall Eriksen), Lyndsy Fonseca (Daughter), David Henrie (Son), Bob Saget (Narrator/Older Ted Mosby), Michael Gross (Albert Mosby, Ted's father). **Credits:** *Executive Producer:* Pamela Fryman, Carter Bays, Craig Thomas, Eileen Heisler, DeAnn Heline, Greg Malins. *Co-Executive Producer:* Kirsten Newman, Ira Ungerleider, Stephen Lloyd, Chris Miller, Phil Lord. *Producer:* Chris Harris, Jamie Rhonheimer, Suzy Mamann-Greenberg. *Co-Producer:* Brenda Hsueh, Kourtney Kang.

854 How It's Made. (Reality; Discovery Channel; Premiered: January 6, 2001)

Canadian produced series that explores how everyday items are made — from bubble gum to straws to car radiators.

Narrator: Brooks T. Moore, Mark Tewksbury, Tony Hirst. **Credits:** *Producer:* Bruce Glawson.

855 How to Boil Water. (Cooking; Food Network; Premiered: January 1, 2000)

A more complex format than the title suggests as master chef Tyler Florence teaches basic cooking techniques as well as preparing meals.

Host: Tyler Florence. **Assistant:** Jack Hourugan.

856 The Hungry Detective. (Reality; Food Network; Premiered: October 31, 2006)

Former L.A.P.D. detective Chris Cognac uses his experiences on the force to uncover the best "food haunts" as he travels across America.

Host: Chris Cognac. **Credits:** *Executive Producer:* Sean P. O'Malley. *Supervising Producer:* Jason Levine. *Producer:* Rick Brush.

857 I Carly. (Comedy; Nickelodeon; Premiered: September 8, 2007)

Carly Shay is a very pretty 13-year-old girl with a powerful dream: to achieve fame as the star of a web cast. She lives at the Bushwell Apartments in Seattle and attends Ridgeway Junior High School. Her widowed father is in the military and stationed overseas. She is cared for by her 26-year-old, somewhat eccentric brother, Spencer, an aspiring sculptor. Samantha, who likes to be called Sam, is Carly's mischievous best friend. Together they star on the Internet in a show called *I Carly*. Carly came up with the idea. "We can do what we want and say what we want." Sam liked the concept — but not the work involved. "Make it your show," she told Carly. "You do the work and I'll be your amusing little sidekick." Freddie, Carly's friend, handles the camera and broadcast aspects of the show. Carly has converted her loft into a studio and each week *I Carly* presents "a show about anything — something different each week." Stories follow Carly, Sam and Freddie as they produce their weekly show. Carly's website is real and viewers can log on to it to express their opinions and share messages with Carly. Mr. Franklin is the school's principal; Francine Briggs is the stern vice principal; Lewbert is the building doorman. Miranda Cosgrove and Drake Bell perform the theme, "Leave It All to Me."

Cast: Miranda Cosgrove (Carly Shay), Jennette McCurdy (Sam Puckett), Jerry Trainor (Spencer Shay), Nathan Kress (Freddie Benson), Tim Russ (Principal Franklin), Mindy Sterling (Francine Briggs), Jeremy Rowley (Lewbert), Mary Scheer (Freddie's mother). **Credits:** *Executive Producer:* Dan Schneider. *Producer:* Amber Benson.

858 I, Detective. (Reality; Tru TV; Premiered: August 30, 2001)

Originally a Court TV program that allows viewers to follow actual detectives as they uncover clues and investigate cases from start to finish.

Credits: *Supervising Producer:* Robyn Younie, Karey Green. *Producer:* Shirley Tatum. *Associate Producer:* Bryan Ranharter.

859 I Propose. (Reality; Style; Premiered: June 12, 2007)

A look at forthcoming marriages as seen through the experiences of the groom as he prepares to pop the big question. **Credits:** *Executive Producer:* Tracy Mazeur, Scott A. Stone. *Supervising Producer:* Helen Moawad. *Producer:* Danny Shaner. *Coordinating Producer:* Darren Kane. *Music:* Brad Segal.

860 Ice Road Truckers. (Reality; History Channel; Premiered: June 17, 2007)

A look at the dangerous work of truck drivers in Yellowknife, Canada, as they brave the cold conditions to haul equipment and supplies to miners in the Canadian Tundra.

Truckers: Thom Beers, Alex Debogorski, Christian Rodska, Hugh Rowland, Drew Sherwood, T.J. Tilcox, Jay Westgard, Rick Yemon. **Credits:** *Executive Producer:* Dolores Gavin, Thom Beers. *Supervising Producer:* Adam Martin, Dawn Fitzgerald. *Producer:* Sarah Bowman. *Music:* Bruce Hanifan.

861 If Walls Could Talk. (Reality; HGTV; Premiered: January 1, 1995)

A fascinating look at the secrets that

some homes conceal (usually, during reconstruction, objects are found by homeowners and the program explores what has been uncovered and their relation to the past).

Host: Philip Palmer, Grant Goodeve, Mike Siegel. **Appraiser:** Elyse Luray-Marx. **Credits:** *Executive Producer:* Jim Berger, Tom Giesen, Duke Hartman, Sonny Hutchinson, Chris Wheeler. *Supervising Producer:* Scott Paddor. *Producer:* Kathleen Boland, Elizabeth Parkins.

862   In the Motherhood. (Comedy; Internet; Premiered: May 11, 2007)

A web series that relates comical true life situations faced by mothers and their children. The episodes are written by real life mothers (submitted to the website created by sponsors Suave and Sprint) but portrayed by a professional cast. Kim, Kelly and Heather are the featured mothers. Kelly and Heather (divorced) are sisters; Ashley is Kim's daughter; Joyce is Kim and Heather's mother.

Cast: Leah Remini (Kim), Jenny McCarthy (Kelly), Chelsea Handler (Heather), Alina Foley (Ashley), Lainie Kazan (Joyce), Jane Curtin (Joyce; later), Kylee Anderson (Kelly, age 6). **Credits:** *Producer:* Kevin M. Townsend, Jack Kelly. *Director:* Gail Mancuso.

863   In Turn. (Reality; Internet; Premiered: 2006)

Ten hopeful actors must live together and compete in various acting challenges for a 13 week contract role on the CBS soap opera *As the World Turns.* Airs exclusively on CBS.com.

Cycle 3 (2008) Actors: Michael Derek, Aisha Henry, William Howard, Peyton Lee, Krista Miller, Nell Mooney, Christina Omari, Karen Quick, Justin Smith, Audra Wahhab. **Credits:** *Producer:* Richard Mansing.

864   Inside American Jail. (Reality; Court TV/Tru TV; Premiered: August 3, 2007)

A look at the work of corrections officers who watch over hardened prisoners in the country's toughest city and county prisons.

Credits: *Executive Producer:* Morgan Langley. *Producer:* Ken Kristensen, John Langley. *Supervising Producer:* Adam Rupp. *Coordinating Producer:* Bryan Jerel Collins.

865   Inside Edition. (Variety; Syn.; Premiered: January 1989)

A daily series of hard-hitting investigative reports, celebrity profiles and human interest stories.

Host: David Frost, Bill O'Reilly. **Reporters:** Marguerite Bardone, Bill O'Reilly, Jeff Cole, Rich Kirkham. **Credits:** *Executive Producer:* Michael King, Roger King. *Producer:* Jon Tomlin, Bob Young. *Supervising Producer:* Sheila Sitomer. *Music:* Ed Kalehoff.

866   Inside the Actor's Studio. (Interview; Bravo; Premiered: June 12, 1994)

In-depth interviews with top actors, writers and directors. Students and Actor's Studio alumni comprise the studio audience.

Host: James Lipton. **Credits:** *Executive Producer:* Christian Barcellos, Frances Berwick, James Lipton, Vienna Steiner. *Producer:* Alice Christian, Sabrina Fodor, Jeff Wurtz, Michael Kostel, Caroline Kaplan, Eileen Lanci, Vienna Steiner.

867   The Insider. (Reality; Syn.; Premiered: September 2004)

A daily series dedicated to reporting the stories behind the celebrity headlines.

Hosts: Pat O'Brien, Ananda Lewis, Victoria Recano. **Correspondents:** Kathie Lee Gifford, Steven Cojocaru. **Credits:** *Executive Producer:* Linda Bell Blue. *Supervising Producer:* Steve Noble. *Producer:* Cheryl Woodcock, Kristie Griffith, Angel C. Kim.

868   Instant Beauty Pageant. (Reality; Style Network; Premiered: June 2006)

Five ordinary (but very attractive) women are selected at random in a mall and participate in an instant beauty pageant. The competition begins with the women shopping for clothes then using what they just selected in contests of style, fashion, swimwear and evening gown competitions. The best performer is crowned "Ms. Instant Beauty" and receives the clothing she selected and a tiara.

Host: Debbie Matenopoulos, Rossi Morreale. **Credits:** *Executive Producer:* Jim Buss, Jerry Biederman, Christopher Dane Owens, Mark Wolper. *Producer:* Ryan Simpkins, Mitchell Rosen. *Music:* Alec Puro, Ryan Rehn.

869 Intervention. (Reality; A&E; Premiered: March 6, 2005)

People who are losing the battle to overcome drug addiction are profiled. When it appears that the subject has hit rock bottom, an intervention takes place with friends and a professional interventionist urging the subject to seek help and overcome his addiction.

Credits: *Executive Producer:* Gary R. Benz, Michael Branton, Bryn Freedman, Dan Partland. *Supervising Producer:* Nik Robinson, Sam Mettler. *Producer:* Alison Martino. *Associate Producer:* Kumiko Maemura, Jennifer Sneider.

870 The Investigators. (Reality; Court TV/Tru TV; Premiered: February 14, 2000)

A profile of the men and women who perform the investigative chores that enable prosecutors to successfully win cases.

Credits: *Executive Producer:* Michael Schlossman, Anthony Horn, Robert Kirk. *Senior Producer:* Greg Kanaan, David Cargill. *Producer:* Scott Friedland, Patrick Taulere, Susan Carney, Tom Murray, Scooter Yancey. *Music:* Matt Anthony, Stephen O'Reilly, Richard Fiocca.

871 Iron Chef America. (Reality; Food Network; Premiered: April 23, 2004)

Chefs compete in various cooking and camera skill challenges for the opportunity to star on a four-to-six episode Food Network program.

Host: Marc Summers, Bobby Flay. **Judges:** Bob Tuschman, Susie Fogelson, Bobby Flay, Gordon Elliott. **Commentator:** Alton Brown. **Floor Reporter:** Kevin Brauck. **Credits:** *Executive Producer:* Stu Schreiberg. *Producer:* John Bravaki, Steve Kroopnick. *Music:* Craig Marks.

872 It's Always Sunny in Philadelphia. (Comedy; FX; August 4, 2005 to November 20, 2008)

Paddy's Irish Pub is a bar in Philadelphia owned by four slackers: Mac, Charlie, Dennis and Dee (Charlie and Dee are brother and sister. Frank is their wealthy but blustery father). Stories follow the argumentative group's efforts to run the bar despite both personal and financial problems.

Cast: Charlie Day (Charlie Kelly), Kaitlin Olson (Deandra "Dee" Kelly), Rob McElhenney (Mac), Glenn Howerton (Dennis Reynolds), Danny DeVito (Frank Reynolds), Anne Archer (Frank's wife). **Credits:** *Executive Producer:* Daniel Atias, Jeff Luini, Charlie Day, John Foretnberg, Nick Frankel, Glenn Howerton, Rob McElhenney, Michael Rotenberg. *Producer:* Thomas Lofaro, Jeff Luini.

873 It's Showtime at the Apollo. (Variety; Syn.; Premiered: September 1987)

Performances by popular entertainers. Taped at the Apollo Theater in Harlem.

Credits: *Executive Producer:* Bob Barnes, Percy E. Sutton. *Producer:* Don Weiner, Hal Jackson, Clarence Jones. *Associate Producer:* David Harding. *Writer:* Chuck Sutton, Don Weiner. *Music:* Joey Carbone. *Director:* Don Weiner.

874 Jacob Two-Two. (Cartoon; NBC; October 5, 2007 to July 5, 2008)

Jacob is a young boy who earned the

nickname "Two-Two" for his habit of repeating words. Jacob is best friends with Renee and stories follow their adventures as the face the challenges of being kids.

Voice Cast: Billy Rosenberg (Jacob), Julie Lemieux (Renee), Janet-Laine Green (Florence), Harvey Atkin (Morty), Kaitlin Howell (Emma), Marc McMulkin (Noah), Kristopher Clarke (Beauford Pew), Duane Hill (I.M. Greedyguts), Fiona Reed (Sour Pickles). **Credits:** *Executive Producer:* Paul Robertson, Doug Murphy, Peter Moss, Michael Hirsh, Scott Dyer. *Supervising Producer:* Michelle Melanson, Patricia Burns, Jacelyn Halilton. *Producer:* Wendy Errington, Marilyn McAuley. *Music:* Martin Kucaj.

875   Jail. (Reality; My Network TV; September 11, 2007 to November 25, 2008)

A harsh look at how frightening jail time can be (seen from the capture to booking to lockup).

Credits: *Executive Producer:* John Langley. *Supervising Producer:* Douglas Waterman. *Producer:* Morgan Langley. *Coordinating Producer:* Bryan Jerel Collins. *Theme Vocal:* Lil Droopa.

876   Jane and the Dragon. (Children; NBC; Premiered: January 8, 2006)

Jane Turnkey is a 12-year-old girl with a powerful dream: to become a knight, a privilege normally only bestowed on men. The time is that of the Medieval Ages and Jane is a Lady-in-Waiting in a castle ruled by King Caradoc and his wife, Queen Gwendolyn (they are the parents of Princess Lavinia and Prince Cuthbert). Jane's life changes suddenly when a dragon kidnaps the royal prince and takes him to his cave. Jane, who had been practicing becoming a knight in secret, dons her suit of armor and sets out to rescue the prince. When Jane confronts the dragon, she finds him to be friendly and he allows Jane to save the prince. Upon her return, the King bestows upon Jane the honor of Squire (a knight-in-training). Jane and Dragon (as Jane calls him) are now friends and stories follow Jane as she trains to become a knight — helped and hindered by the 300-year-old dragon's antics. Other regulars are Pepper, the cook; Rake, the gardener; Smithy, the blacksmith; Jester, the court jester; Sir Theodore, the head knight; Sir Ivon; Gunther, a knight-in-training.

Voice Cast: Tajja Isen (Jane), Adrian Truss (Dragon), Aron Tager (Sir Theodore), Noah Reid (Gunther), Sunday Muse (Pepper), Isabel De Carteret (Queen Gwendolyn), Jill Frappier (Princess Lavinia), Will Bowes (Rake), Mark Rendell (Jester), Cameron Ansell (Prince Cuthbert), Juan Chioran (King Caradoc).

Credits: *Executive Producer:* Scott Dyer, Doug Murray, Richard Taylor, Martin Baynton. *Co-Executive Producer:* Michael McNeil. *Supervising Producer:* Andrew Smith, Patricia Burns. *Music:* Geoff Bennett, Andre Hire, Ben Johannesen. *Theme Vocal:* "Jane and the Dragon" by Tajja Isen, Mark Rendell.

877   Jane Doe. (Crime Drama; Hallmark; Premiered: March 11, 2005)

Cathy Davis, a suburban mother, works part time designing children's puzzle games. Before her marriage to Jack, Cathy was a spy for a government organization called the CSA (Central Security Agency). Unknown to her family and friends, Cathy still works for the CSA under the code name Jane Doe (Polly, Cathy's mother, also worked for the agency). Stories follow Cathy as she performs secret missions for the CSA (usually those involving threats to the national security). Susan is Cathy's daughter; Frank Darnell is Cathy's partner in the field.

Cast: Lea Thompson (Cathy Davis), William R. Moses (Jack Davis), Jessy Schram (Susan Davis), Joe Penny (Frank Darnell), Donna Mills (Polly), Nick Davis (Zack Shada). **Credits:** *Executive Producer:* Larry Levinson, Nick Lombardo, Ann

Goldberg. *Co-Executive Producer:* Amy Goldberg, Michael Moran. *Producer:* James Wilberger, Kyle A. Clark.

878 The Janice Dickinson Modeling Agency. (Reality; Oxygen; June 6, 2006 to October 21, 2008)

Twelve hopeful models compete in various modeling competitions seeking to qualify as a top model and win a contract with super model Janice Dickinson's modeling agency.

Host: Janice Dickinson. *Executive Producer:* Stuart Krasnow, Janice Dickinson. *Producer:* Kevin Williams, Nathan Buddis, Nathan Fields, David Rusky. *Music:* Scooter Pietsch.

879 Jenna's American Sex Star. (Erotica; Playboy Channel; Premiered: November 4, 2005)

Sexual reality competition in which four gorgeous women (per cycle) compete in adult film oriented sexual challenges for a contract with adult film star Jenna Jameson's film studio, Club Jenna. The girls are judged by industry performers but viewers (via the Internet at Playboy.com) determine who goes, who stays and who becomes the winner.

Host: Jenna Jameson. **Judges:** Christy Canyon, Ron Jeremy, Jim Powers, Andrew Lowell. **Credits:** *Executive Producer:* Derek Harvie. *Producer:* Alan Higbee.

880 Jeopardy. (Game; Syn.; Premiered: September 1984)

Players select a subject from a board based on its cash value. To win the money, the player must give the question to the answer that is revealed. The highest cash scorer (of three players who compete) wins.

Host: Alex Trebek. **Credits:** *Executive Producer:* Merv Griffin. *Producer:* Alex Trebek, Harry Friedman, George Vosburgh. *Co-Producer:* Gary Johnson.

881 Jericho. (Drama; CBS; September 20, 2006–March 25, 2008)

The after effects of a supposed nuclear attack are explored as Jericho, a small U.S. Kansas town, is spared destruction and its citizens struggle to cope with what has happened and what to do when they are cut off from the rest of the world.

Cast: Skeet Ulrich (Jake Green), Gerald McRaney (Jonathan Green), Pamela Reed (Gail Green), Kenneth Mitchell (Eric Green), Ashley Scott (Emily Sullivan), Sprague Grayden (Heather Lisinksi), Shoshannah Stern (Bonnie) Erik Knudsen (Dale Turner), Michael Gaston (Gray Anderson), Brad Beyer (Stanley), Lennie James (Robert Hawkins), Darby Stanchfield (April), Siena Goines (Sarah). **Credits:** *Executive Producer:* Jon Turteltaub, Stephen Chborsky, Carol Barbee. *Producer:* Bob Simon, Karim Zreik, Dan Shotz, Jon Steinberg, Josh Schaer.

882 The Jerry Springer Show. (Talk; Syn.; Premiered: September 1991)

A sensationalized talk show that uses nudity (blurred for broadcast), foul language (bleeped) and fights between guests to expose secrets between friends and family.

Host: Jerry Springer. **Credits:** *Executive Producer:* Richard Dolack, Burt Dubrow, Jerry Springer. *Producer:* Kim Wyatt, Deborah J. Whitcas, Kerry Smith, Chris Rantamaki, Mary Morelli, Julie Laughlin, Gina Huerta, Nicole Hall, Reena Friedman, Amanda Cash, Toby Yoshimura.

883 Jimmy Kimmel Live. (Talk; ABC; Premiered: January 26, 2003)

Late night talk show that goes beyond celebrity interviews to include interviews with athletes, political figures and regular people of interest.

Host: Jimmy Kimmel. **Announcer:** Dicky Barrett. **Regulars:** Sal Iacono (as Cousin Sal), Frank Potenzo (as Uncle Frank), Guillermo Diaz (Security guard). **Credits:** *Executive Producer:* Jimmy Kimmel, Jill Leiderman, Daniel Kellison. *Co-Executive Producer:* Jason Schrift, Doug

DeLuca. *Supervising Producer:* Kevin Hamburger. *Producer:* Mark Indigaro, Raelynn Tammariello Loop, Ken Crosby, Paul Cockerill, Gina Calanni.

884   Jo Jo's Circus. (Cartoon; Disney; Premiered: September 28, 2003)

Children are introduced to various aspects of the adult world through the activities of Jo Jo Tickle, a six-year-old clown who lives and plays in Circus Town. **Voice Cast:** Madeleine Martin (Jo Jo Tickle), Marnie McPhail (Peaches, Jo Jo's mother), Noah Weinberg (Jo Jo's father), Tajja Isen (Trina), Robert Smith (Goliath) Diana Peressini (Croaky). **Credits:** *Producer:* Jim Jinkins, Morghan Fortier. *Music:* Stuart Kollmorgen.

885   John Edwards Cross Country. (Reality; WE; March 17, 2006 to November 26, 2008)

Psychic John Edwards takes to the road to help families reconnect with loved ones who have passed on. **Host:** John Edwards. **Credits:** *Executive Producer:* Paul Shavelson. *Co-Executive Producer:* Elizabeth Arias. *Producer:* Lauren Bright, Nina Bhargava, Jodi Midiri. *Music:* Jack Walker.

886   Johnny and the Sprites. (Children; Disney; Premiered: January 13, 2007)

Johnny T. is a guitarist who often needs some alone time. One day he befriends a group of sprites (Muppet-like characters) in a forest. His reactions with the sprites are presented like a mini–Broadway musical and designed to relay messages and learning aspects to young children. **Cast:** John Tartaglia (Johnny T.), Leslie Carrara (Ginger), James T. Kroupa (Seymour the Schmole), Tim Lagasse (Basil). **Credits:** *Executive Producer:* John Tartaglia, Jill Gluckson. *Music Director:* Gary Adler. *Director:* Richard A. Fernandes.

887   Jon and Kate Plus 8. (Reality; TLC; Premiered: April 23, 2007)

A look at the daily lives of the Gosselin family — parents Jon and Kate and their eight children, six of whom are sextuplets; two of whom are twins. **The Gosselin Family:** Jon, Kate, Cara, Madelyn, Alex, Hannah, Aaden, Joel, Leah and Collin. **Credits:** *Producer:* Jennifer Stocks. *Music:* Scott Pearson.

888   Judge Alex. (Reality; Syn.; Premiered: September 2005)

Actual small claims court cases presided over by Alex Ferrer, a former police officer turned judge. **Judge:** Alex Ferrer. **Bailiff:** Victor Scott. **Credits:** *Supervising Producer:* Terry Powell. *Producer:* Keith Raskin. *Senior Associate Producer:* Josh Price. *Associate Producer:* Jennifer Alfaro.

889   Judge David Young. (Reality; Syn.; Premiered: September 2007)

Daily series of real small claims cases presided over by David Young, an openly admitted gay judge. **Judge:** David Young. **Bailiff:** Antonia Young. **Credits:** *Executive Producer:* Michael Rourke. *Co-Executive Producer:* Rich Goldman. *Legal Producer:* Kristan Hiildensperge. *Associate Producer:* Katya Goldberg.

890   Judge Hatchett. (Reality; Syn.; Premiered: September 2000)

Real people fighting real legal battles before a real judge in a California Municipal Court. **Judge:** Glenda Hatchett. **Bailiff:** Tom O'Riordan. **Credits:** *Executive Producer:* Michael Rourke. *Co-Executive Producer:* Michelle Mazur, John Tomlin. *Producer:* Seth Tayler, William Richards, Michelle Menendez, Lisa Faranda.

891   Judge Joe Brown. (Reality; Syn.; Premiered: September 1997)

Actual small claims courtroom cases presided over by Judge Joe Brown. **Judge:** Joe Brown. **Bailiff:** Holly Evans. **Commentator:** Jacque Kessler.

Announcer: Ben Patrick Johnson. **Credits:** *Executive Producer:* Frank Kelly, John Terenzio, Peter Brennan, Randy Doutchit. *Supervising Producer:* Karen Gruber. *Producer:* Timothy Regler, Jason Story, Kathleen Card, Margot Foley, Suzie Munson. *Music:* John E. Nordstrom.

892 Judge Judy. (Reality; Syn.; Premiered: September 1996)

A daily series of actual small claims court cases presided over by America's most famous judge, Judith Sheindlin.

Judge: Judith Sheindlin. **Bailiff:** Petri Hawkins-Byrd. **Announcer:** Jerry Bishop. **Credits:** *Executive Producer:* Peter Brennan, Randy Doutchet. *Co-Executive Producer:* Timothy Regler. *Supervising Producer:* Brad Kuhlman, Karen Gruber, Victor Jenest, Kaye Switzer, Sandi Spreckman. *Producer:* Lisa Lew, Jenny Hope, Cybil Jordan-Malachi, Tina Nicotera, Lenville O'Donnell, Richard Russakoff, Jill Wilderman, Jonathan Sebastian. *Music:* Bill Bodine.

893 Judge Maria Lopez. (Reality; Syn.; September 2006 to September 2008)

Actual small claims court cases presided over by Judge Maria Lopez.

Judge: Maria Lopez. **Bailiff:** Pete Rodriquez. **Credits:** *Executive Producer:* Michael Rourke. *Co-Executive Producer:* Rich Goldman. *Supervising Producer:* Patricia Ciano. *Producer:* Kiersten Medvedich.

894 Judge Mathis. (Reality; Syn.; Premiered: September 1998)

Daily series of small claims court cases presided over by Judge Greg Mathis.

Judge: Greg Mathis. **Bailiff:** Doyle Deveraux, Kevin Lingle, Brendan Morgan. **Credits:** *Executive Producer:* Gus L. Blackmon, Alonzo Brown, Vicangelo Bulluck, Bo Banks. *Supervising Producer:* Gretchen Kurtz. *Producer:* Michael Hart. *Music:* Timothy Andrew Edwards.

895 Jury Duty. (Reality; Syn.; Premiered: September 2007)

Real life small claims cases are brought before a real judge but in a twist on traditional judge programs, a panel of three celebrity jurors are allowed to question the plaintiff and defendant then deliberate before offering a verdict.

Judge: Bruce Cutler. **Rotating Jurors:** Charlene Tilton, Todd Bridges, Ed Begley, Jr., Phyllis Diller, Scott Hamilton, Kevin Sorbo, Shadoe Stevens, Dick Van Patten, Bruce Vilanch, Paula Poundstone, Vicki Roberts. **Credits:** *Executive Producer:* Vincent Dymon, Linda Dymon, Susan Winston. *Producer:* John Downey III, Judy C. Helm.

896 Just for Laughs. (Comedy; ABC; July 17, 2007 to April 8, 2008)

Extreme version of *Candid Camera* that pulls elaborate practical jokes on unsuspecting people.

Host: Rick Miller. **Credits:** *Executive Producer:* Troy Miller, Pierre Girard. *Co-Executive Producer:* Tracey Baird, Michael Weinberg. *Producer:* Christos Sourligas

897 Just Jordan. (Comedy; Nickelodeon; January 7, 2007 to April 5, 2008)

Jordan Lewis, a 16-year-old from Little Rock, Arkansas, must readjust to life when his single mother, Pamela, relocates the family to California to live with her father (Grant). Jordan's 1950s–like television kid adventures (wholesome and clean) are depicted with his friends Joaquin and Tony. Monica is Jordan's sister; Tangie is his cousin; Tamika is the girl on whom Jordan has a crush but is too shy to do anything but keep it a personal secret. Jordan works part time at the diner (Papa Grant's Fresh 'n Grill) owned by his grandfather.

Cast: James "Lil' JJ" Lewis (Jordan Lewis), Shana Accius (Pamela Lewis), Kristen Combs (Monica Lewis), Beau Billingslea (Grant Cunningham), Raven Goodwin (Tangie), Eddy Martin (Joaquin), Justin Chon (Tony Park), Chelsea Harris (Tamika Newsome). **Credits:** *Executive Producer:* Ken Bright, Ralph Farquhar,

L'il JJ, Alison Taylor. *Producer:* Julia Pistor. *Music:* Kurt Farguhar.

898 Kathy Griffin: My Life on the D-List. (Reality; Bravo; Premiered: August 3, 2005)

A profile of actress and stand-up comedian Kathy Griffin as she not only performs her comedy club routines but goes about her daily life; friends and family members are also featured.

Cast: Kathy Griffin, John Griffin, Maggie Griffin, Matt Moline, Jessica Zajicek, Dennis Hensley, Tony Tripoli, Cynthia Bachman, Lisa Tucker. **Credits:** *Executive Producer:* Kathy Griffin, Marcia Mule, Bryan Scott, Cori Abraham, Frances Berwick, Amy Introcasco, Rachel Smith. *Supervising Producer:* Lenid Rolov, Chris Carlson, Matthew Blaine. *Producer:* Matthew Lahey. *Music:* Douglas G. Simpson, Jason L. Mattia.

899 Keeping Up with the Kardashians. (Reality; E!; Premiered: October 14, 2007)

A real life portrait of Kim Kardashian (daughter of lawyer Robert Kardashian), "a tinsel town babe" hoping to make her mark in show business. Kim is managed by her mother, Kris Jenner (now married to Olympic decathlon champion Bruce Jenner) and she is seen with her sisters, Khloe and Kourtney. The events that befall Kim and her family are shared with the viewing audience.

Stars: Kim Kardashian, Kris Jenner, Bruce Jenner, Khloe Jenner, Kourtney Jenner. **Credits:** *Executive Producer:* Ryan Seacrest, Jon Murray, Eliot Goldberg, Jeff Jenkins. *Co-Executive Producer:* Gil Goldschien. *Supervising Producer:* Farnaz Farjam.

900 Kenny vs. Spenney. (Reality; Comedy Central; Premiered: November 2007)

Canadian series about two childhood friends (Kenny Hotz, Spencer "Spenney" Rice) who live together in Toronto in a house wired for video and sound. Each week the two dysfunctional friends challenge each other to bizarre competitions with the loser getting the raw end of the deal: perform a humiliating stunt decreed by the winner (comedy also stems from the devious Kenny as he tries to put one over on the ethical Spenney).

Stars: Kenny Hotz, Spencer Rice. **Credits:** *Executive Producer:* Trey Parker, Matt Stone, Abby Finer, Noreen Halpern, Ira Levy, John Morayniss, Spencer Rice, Peter Williamson. *Producer:* Kenny Hotz. *Music:* Richard Pell.

901 Kimora: Life in the Fab Lane. (Reality; Style; August 5, 2007 to June 15, 2008)

A look at the life of fashion superstar Kimora Lee. Cameras follow Kimora, surrounded by stylists, managers and publicists, as she goes about her daily activities (which include shopping and visiting friends).

Cast: Kimora Lee, Aja Bair, Dana Deggs, Peyton List. **Credits:** *Executive Producer:* Steven Cantor, Carmen Mitcho, Sarah Weidman. *Co-Executive Producer:* Matthew Galkin. *Supervising Producer:* Anna Boiardi. *Producer:* Kimora Lee. *Music:* Meredith Chinn.

902 King of the Hill. (Cartoon; Fox; Premiered: January 12, 1997)

The Hills are a family that live at 123 Ramsey Street in Arlen, Texas. Hank, the father, is a salesman for Strickland Propane; Peggy, his wife, is a substitute Spanish teacher (also seen as a realtor with Seizemore Realty and a reporter for *The Arlington Bystander*). Bobby is a preteen whom Hank hopes will follow in his footsteps (although he shows no interest in propane). Also living with them is Luanne Platter, Hank's gorgeous niece, who aspires to become a beautician. Stories follow events in their lives. Hank's friends are Bill, a divorced military barber; Dale, owner of Dale's Dead Bug Exterminating; and Boomhauer, who speaks gibberish that only Hank seems to understand. Joseph Gribble is Dale's son; Buck Strickland is Hank's boss; Kahn and Minh are Hank's neighbors; Nancy is Dale's wife; Connie is Minh's daughter; John Redcorn is Hank's neighbor.

Voice Cast: Mike Judge (Hank Hill/ Boomhauer), Kathy Najimy (Peggy Hill), Pamela Segall (Bobby Hill), Brittany Murphy (Luanne Platter), Brittany Murphy (Joseph Gribble, 1997–2000), Breckin Meyer (Joseph Gribble, 2000–), Johnny Hardwicke (Dale Gribble), Stephen Root (Bill Dauterive/Buck Strickland), Ashley Gardner (Nancy Gribble), Toby Hill (Kahn), Lauren Tom (Minh/Connie). **Credits:** *Executive Producer:* Richard Appel, Greg Daniels, Mike Judge, Howard Klein, Phil Roman, Michael Rotenberg. *Producer:* Murray Miller, Joseph A. Boucher, Dan Sterling, Garland Testa, Dean Young, Greg Cohen, Alex Gregory, Johnny Hardwicke. *Music:* Richard Wolf, Brian David Blush, Lance Rubin, Gary G. Wiz, Fred Edmonston, Robert Birch, Jeffrey Baxter, John O'Connor.

903 Kitchen Nightmares. (Reality; Fox; Premiered: September 19, 2007)

Hell's Kitchen spin-off wherein Chef Gordon Ramsay takes to the road to solve the kitchen nightmares of restaurants across the country. Chef Ramsay is sort of the 911 of the restaurant world and episodes relate his efforts to solve the problems restaurants are encountering.

Host: Gordon Ramsay. **Credits:** *Executive Producer:* Patricia Llewellyn, Curt Northrup. *Producer:* Arthur Smith. *Narrator:* J.V. Martin.

904 Kyle XY. (Science Fiction; ABC Family; Premiered: June 26, 2006)

A 16-year-old boy mysteriously appears in the middle of a forest. He appears to have just been born and has no idea of who he is or where he is. The boy begins to wander and is soon arrested for indecent exposure (he is naked) when he appears in the nearby town. He is sent to a juvenile holding center in Seattle, Washington. Here psychologist Nicole Trager takes an interest in him (he has no navel, appears to be very intelligent but he is like an infant and needs to learn). Nicole names him Kyle and, to help him, takes him home (where he now lives with Nicole's husband, Stephen and her children Lori and Josh). Kyle learns by watching and listening (how he learns to speak English). Stories follow Nicole's efforts to solve the puzzle of who Kyle is and where he came from. Other regulars are Amanda, the girl next door on whom Kyle has a crush; Heather, Lori's friend; Declan, Lori's boyfriend; and Tom Foss, the mysterious man who appears to know what Kyle is all about. Second season episodes explain that Kyle was an experiment (XY) based on Einstein's theory that the longer an embryo stays in the womb the smarter it will be. A man named Adam was the only survivor of the first such experiment (at this time, the surrogate mothers, who carried the child for 13 months, died in childbirth; the infants died shortly after). Adam knew his past and wanted to create a world of geniuses. He experimented and created a birth chamber with a pink fluid that could sustain life until the embryo reached an adult stage. Kyle was such an experiment — the first since Adam to survive. But Kyle is not alone. A second experiment, conducted by the visionaries of a organization called Madacorp, produced a female — XX. This experiment escapes (like Kyle did) when an explosion destroys the lab. A bounty hunter (Emily Hollander) is hired by Madacorp to find her. The girl is nude, covered in pink "goo" (from the birth tank) and like Kyle, has no navel. She is captured by Emily and brought to Madacorp. Here she is programmed to be Jessica Hollander, Emily's sister. Madacorp's plan is to use Jesse (as Jessica is called) to befriend Kyle and monitor him for Madacorp's ultimate goal — reclaim both XY and XX. But unknown to Madacorp, Kyle has a protector, Brian Taylor, the late Adam's faithful servant, who now watches over Kyle and helps him to understand his developing abilities (Adam was shot by persons and for reasons unknown).

Cast: Matt Dallas (Kyle), Marguerite MacIntyre (Nicole Trager), Bruce Thomas (Stephen Trager), April Matson (Lori Trager), Jean-Luc Bilodeau (Josh Trager), Kirsten Prout (Amanda Bloom), Chelan Simmons (Heather), Nicholas Lea (Tom Foss), Chris Olivero (Declan), Leah Cairns (Emily Hollander), Jaimie Alexander (Jesse Hollander). **Credits:** *Executive Producer:* Eric Bress, J. MacKye Gruber, Chris Bender, J.C. Spink, David Himelfarb, Eric Tuchman. *Producer:* Julie Plec, Charlie Gogolak, Curtis Kheel. *Music:* Michael Suby.

905 The L Word. (Drama; Showtime; Premiered: January 18, 2004)

An intimate look at the lives and loves of a select group of lesbians living in Los Angeles (West Hollywood). Principal focus is on Jenny Schecter, a graduate of Chicago University, who moves to Los Angeles to live with her boyfriend, Tim Haspel and begin a professional writing career. Her life changes when she attends a party and meets Bette Porter, Tim's lesbian next-door neighbor, and Bette's lover Tina Kennard. At the party Jenny has a brief romantic encounter with Maria, a lesbian who owns the local coffee house (The Planet) and is thrust into a whole new world. She begins to question her sexuality and becomes torn between her relationship with Tim and a new life-style that she enjoys. Other regulars are lesbians Dana, a pro tennis player looking for love; Alice, a magazine writer seeking the woman of her dreams; and Shane, the hairdresser who sleeps with women for her own pleasure with no commitment.

Cast: Mia Kirshner (Jenny Schecter), Jennifer Beals (Bette Porter), Erin Daniels (Dana Fairbanks), Leisha Hailey (Alice Pieszecki), Laurel Holloman (Tina Kennard), Katherine Moennig (Shane McCutcheon), Pam Grier (Kit Porter), Karina Lombard (Marina Ferrer), Eric Mabius (Tim Haspel), Rachel Shelley (Helena Peabody), Eric Lively (Mark Wayland), Sarah Shahi (Carmen de la Pica Morales), Janina Gavankar (Papi), Cybill Shepherd (Phyllis Kroll), Marlee Matlin (Jodi), Jessica Capshaw (Nadia), Dallas Roberts (Angus Partridge), Daniela Sea (Max Sweeney), Lauren Lee Smith (Lara Perkins). **Credits:** *Executive Producer:* Ilene Chaiken, Rose Lam, Steve Golin, Larry Kenner. *Co-Executive Producer:* Elizabeth Ziff. *Producer:* Elizabeth Hunter, A.M. Homes, Mark Horowitz. *Music:* Elizabeth Ziff, Damien Rice.

906 L.A. Ink. (Reality; TLC; August 7, 2007 to April 3, 2008)

Kat Van D is a tattoo artist who made a name for herself in Miami. She has given up that business and returned to her hometown of Los Angeles to open her own tattoo parlor. Cameras follow Kat as she begins her own business as well as the people and events that surround her in her personal life.

Star: Kat Van D. **Tattoo Artists:** Hannah Aitchison, Corey Miller, Pixie (as credited), Kim Saigh. **Credits:** *Executive Producer:* Pamela Deutsch, Charles Corwin. *Co-Executive Producer:* Clara Markowicz, Luis Barreto. *Supervising Producer:* Isaac Bolden. *Producer:* Cat Rodriquez, Timothy J. Hamilton.

907 Laguna Beach. (Reality; MTV; Premiered: May 31, 2006)

Incidents in the lives of a group of teenagers living in Laguna Beach, California. The teens attend Laguna Beach High School (although cameras are not permitted inside the classrooms) and stories are presented in soap opera-like dramatic vignettes.

Cast: Lauren Conrad, Taylor Cole, Kristin Cavallari, Stephen Colletti, Talan Torriero, Alex Murrel, Dieter Schmitz, Jessica Smith, Jason Wahler, Raquel Donatelli, Kyndra Mayo, Kelan Hurley, Alex Atkinson, Chase Johnson, Sam Brennan, Stephanie Moreau, Curtis Dean Harrier, Natalie Engelke, Heidi Montag, Christopher Bland, Cami Edwards, Breanna Conrad, Jennifer Bunney, Tessa Keller, Lexie Contursi, Trey Phillips, Christina Schuller, Morgan Olsen, Lauren Bosworth. **Credits:** *Executive Producer:* Tony DiSanto, Gary Auerbach, Liz Gateley, Dave Sirulnick. *Co-Executive Producer:* Wendy Riche, Mark Ford, Steve Kruger. *Supervising Producer:* Kathryn Takis. *Producer:* Jason Sands, Tina Gazzaro, Morgan J. Freeman, Paulina Williams. *Music:* Jon Ernst.

908 The Lair. (Drama; Here!; Premiered: August 1, 2007)

The Lair is a mysterious club established for a specific clientele: attractive (hunky) gay vampires — vampires who feed on equally attractive gay men. The specialized series (broadcast on the gay channel Here!) follows a journalist (Thom) as he attempts to uncover the vampire clan and solve a series of mysterious murders whose victims have been drained of blood.

Cast: David Moretti (Thom), Peter Stickles (Damian), Beverly Lynne (Laura), Dylan Vox (Colin), Jesse Cutlip (Jonathan), Brian Nolan (Frankie), Colton Ford (Sheriff Trout), Michael Von Steele (Eric), Ted Newsom (Dr. Cooper), Evan Stone (Jimmy), Arthur Roberts (Dr. Belmont). **Credits:** *Executive Producer:* Paul Colichman, Stephen P. Jarchow. *Producer:* Kimberly A. Ray. *Co-Producer:* Jeff Schenck.

909 Las Vegas. (Drama; NBC; September 22, 2003 to February 15, 2008)

The Montecito Resort and Casino in Las Vegas is the setting for a behind-the-scenes look at the inner workings of a gambling hall. Principal focus is on an elite surveillance team, headed by Ed Deline, charged with maintaining the security of the casino.

Cast: James Caan (Ed Deline), Josh Duhamel (Danny McCoy), Nikki Cox (Mary Connell), Vanessa Marcil (Samantha Marquez), James Lesure (Mike Cannon), Molly Simms (Delinda Deline), Marsha Thompson (Nessa Holt), Lara Flynn Boyle (Monica Mancuso), Cheryl Ladd (Jillian Deline, Ed's ex-wife), Tom Selleck (A.J. Cooper). **Credits:** Executive Producer: Justin Falvey, Darryl Frank, Gary Scott Thompson, Scott Steindorff, Gardner Stern. *Co-Executive Producer:* Kim Newton, Michael Berns, David Solomon, Matt Pyken, Michael Watkins. *Producer:* Howard Grigsby, David Graziano, Francis Conway, Tracey D'Arcy, Daniel Arkin, Rebecca Kirshner. *Music:* John Nordstrom, Charles Clouser.

910 Last Comic Standing. (Reality; NBC; June 10, 2003 to August 7, 2008)

Professional and up-and-coming stand-up comedians compete for an exclusive contract with NBC. The club audience judge the material and vote their least favorite off the stage. The last comic standing is the winner.

Host: Jay Mohr, Bill Bellamy. **Credits:** *Executive Producer:* Peter Engel, Barry Katz, Jay Mohr. *Supervising Producer:* Leslie Radakovich. *Co-Executive Producer:* Rob Fox. *Producer:* Javier Winnik, Brittany Lovett, Cori Fry. *Music:* Steve Hampton, John Adair.

911 Late Night with Conan O'Brien. (Talk; NBC; Premiered: September 1, 1993)

Celebrity interviews coupled with a spotlight on off-the-wall characters as well.

Host: Conan O'Brien **Announcer:** Joel Godard. **Credits:** *Executive Producer:* Gary Considine, Jeff Ross, Lorne Michaels. *Supervising Producer:* Frank Smiley, Daniel Ferguson. *Producer:* John Irwin, Maria Notaras, Conan O'Brien, Elizabeth Ockerlund, Michael Weinberg. *Band Leader:* Max Weinberg.

912 Late Night with David Letterman. (Talk; CBS; Premiered: August 30, 1993)

Comedy bits, celebrity interviews and musical numbers comprise the nightly series.

Host: David Letterman. **Credits:** *Executive Producer:* David Letterman, Peter Lassally, Rob Burnett, Jude Brennan, Maria Pope, Robert Morton, Barbara Gaines. *Supervising Producer:* Jon Beckerman, Hal Gurnee. *Producer:* Joe Toplyn, Justin Stangel, Eric Stangel, Sheila Rogers, Jerry Foley, Rodney Rothman. *Band Leader:* Paul Schaefer.

913 Law and Order. (Crime Drama; NBC; Premiered: September 13, 1990)

Two series in one. It begins with a crime and the investigations by the detectives of the N.Y.P.D. It concludes with the D.A.'s prosecution of the culprits.

Cast: Jerry Orbach (Det. Lenny Briscoe), Steven Hill (D.A. Adam Schiff), Jesse L. Martin (Det. Ed Green), S. Epatha Merkerson (Lt. Anita Van Buren), Chris Noth (Det. Mike Logan), Leslie Hendrix (Dr. Elizabeth Rodgers), Fred Dalton Thompson (D.A. Arthur Branch), Benjamin Bratt (Det. Ray Curtis), Michael Moriarty (A.D.A. Ben Stone), Elisabeth Rohm (A.D.A. Serena Southerlyn), Angie Harmon (A.D.A. Abbie Carmichael), Dann Florek (Capt. Donald Cragen), Richard Brooks (A.D.A. Paul Robinette), Jill Hennessy (A.D.A. Claire Kincaid), Carolyn McCormick (Dr. Elizabeth Olivet), John Fiore (Det. Tony Profaci), Carey Lowell (A.D.A. Jamie Ross), Dianne West (D.A. Nora Lewin), Dennis Farina (Det. Joe Fontana), J.K. Simmons (Dr. Emile Skoda), Annie Parisse (A.D.A. Alexandra Borgia), Paul Sorvino (Det. Sgt. Philip Cerreta), George Dzundza (Det. Sgt. Maxwell Greevey), Christine Farrell (Arlene Shrier; Forensics Technician)

Larry Clarke (Det. Morris LaMotte), Alana De La Garza (A.D.A. Connie Rubirosa), Jeremy Sisto (Det. Cyrus Lupo), Alicia Witt (Det. Nola Falacci), Linus Roache (A.D.A. Michael Cutter), Anthony Anderson (Det. Kevin Bernard). **Credits:** *Theme Narration:* Steven Zirnkilton. *Executive Producer:* Dick Wolf, Edwin Sherin, Rene Balcer, Michael Chernuchia, Matthew Penn, Walon Green, Nicholas Wootton, Arthur Penn, Jeffrey Hayes. *Co-Executive Producer:* Ed Zuckerman, Peter Guilano, Kathy McCormick, Lewis Gould, Roz Weinman, Arthur Forney, Wendy Battles, Lukas Reiter, Arthur Penn, Rick Eid, William N. Fordes, Joseph Stern, Eric Overmyer. *Supervising Producer:* Michael Duggan, David Black, Gary Karr, David Wilcox, Robert Nathan, Mark B. Perry, Gardner Stern. *Producer:* Kati Johnston, Jill Goldsmith, Terri Kopp, Lorenzo Carcaterra, Aaron Zelman, David Shore, Lynn Mamet, Peter Giuliano, Lois Johnson, Billy Fox, Jeffrey L. Hayes, Nick Santora.

914 Law and Order: Criminal Intent. (Crime Drama; NBC; Premiered: September 20, 1999)

The investigations of Detectives Robert Goren and Alexandra Eames as they attempt to solve (most often) murder cases — from the first call to its successful conclusion. Later episodes also focus on the investigations of Detectives Mike Logan and Carolyn Barek.

Cast: Vincent D'Onofrio (Det. Robert Goren), Kathryn Erbe (Det. Alexandra Eames), Courtney B. Vance (A.D.A. Ron Carver), Jamey Sheridan (Capt. James Deakins), Leslie Hendrix (Dr. Elizabeth Rodgers), Chris Noth (Det. Mike Logan), Annabella Sciorra (Det. Carolyn Barek), Julianne Nicholson (Det. Megan Wheeler), Samantha Buck (Det. G. Lynn Bishop), Eric Bogosian (Capt. Danny Ross), Jeff Goldblum (Det. Zach Nichols), Steven Zirnkilton (Theme Narrator). **Credits:** *Executive Producer:* Dick Wolf, Rene

Balcer, Eileen Heisler, Peter Jankowski, Fred Berner. *Co-Executive Producer:* Geoffrey Neigher, Theresa Rebeck, Norberto Barba, Marlene Meyer, Arthur W. Forney, Matt Goldman, Warren Leight, Gerry Conway. *Supervising Producer:* Roz Weinman, Michael Kewley, Stephanie Sengupta, Gerry Conway. *Producer:* John L. Roman, Eric Overmyer, Roz Weinman, Diana Son, Mary Rae Thewlis. *Music:* Mike Post.

915 Law and Order: Special Victims Unit. (Crime Drama; NBC; Premiered: October 7, 2001)

Elliot Stabler, Olivia Benson, Fin Tutuola and John Munch are members of the Special Victims Unit of the N.Y.P.D., detectives who investigate sexually related crimes that are quite gritty and often based on true incidents.

Cast: Mariska Hargitay (Det. Olivia Benson), Christopher Meloni (Det. Elliot Stabler), Richard Belzer (Det. John Munch), Dann Florek (Capt. Donald Cragen), Ice-T (Det. Odafin "Fin" Tutuola), B.D. Wong (Dr. George Huang), Tamara Tunie (Dr. Melinda Warner), Diane Neal (A.D.A. Casey Novak), Stephanie March (A.D.A. Alexandra Cabot), Caren Browning (Off. Judith Siper), Joanna Merlin (Judge Lena Petrovsky), Michelle Hurd (Det. Monique Jefferies), Isabel Gillies (Kathy Stabler), Judith Light (Chief Elizabeth Donnelly), Fred Dalton (D.A. Arthur Branch), Leslie Hendrix (Dr. Elizabeth Rodgers), Micgaela McManus (A.D.A. Kim Greylek), Steven Zirnkilton (Theme Narrator). **Credits:** *Executive Producer:* Dick Wolff, Neal Baer, Ted Kotcheff, Robert Palm, David J. Burke, Peter Jankowski. *Co-Executive Producer:* Jonathan Green, Arthur W. Forney, Jonathan Greene, Dawn DeNoon, Amanda Green, Robert Nathan, Patrick Harbinson. *Supervising Producer:* Peter Leto, Randy Roberts. *Producer:* David Declergue, Sheyna Kathleen Smith. *Music:* Mike Post.

916 Life. (Crime Drama; NBC; Premiered: September 26, 2007)

After 12 years of imprisonment for a double homicide, L.A.P.D. detective Charlie Crews is found innocent after the physical evidence is reexamined and does not match. Now, with a second chance at life, Charlie returns to the force with a new perspective on cases: making sure what happened to him doesn't happen to anyone else. Stories also relate his efforts to find out who framed him and why. Dani is Charlie's partner; Karen is their superior; Constance is the lawyer responsible for freeing Charlie; Ted is Charlie's financial consultant.

Cast: Damian Lewis (Charlie Crews), Sarah Shabi (Dani Reese), Robin Weigert (Lt. Karen Davis), Brooke Langton (Constance Griffith), Adam Arkin (Ted Early), Donal Logue (Captain Tidwell). **Credits:** *Executive Producer:* Rand Ravich, Far Shariat, Dan Sackheim, David Semel. *Producer:* George Locas.

917 Life Is Wild. (Drama; CW; October 7, 2007 to February 3, 2008)

Danny, a widower with two children (Katie and Chase) and Jo, the divorced mother of two children (Jesse and Mia) marry and establish housekeeping in Manhattan. Danny is a veterinarian; Jo, a divorce lawyer. Their children, however, have little in common and are not getting along. Realizing that his family is drifting apart, Danny hopes to bring them closer together by moving to South Africa when he learns there is an urgent need for veterinarians. The family takes up residence at the Blue Antelope, a lodge run by Danny's late wife's (Claire) father Art. Danny begins his new job as a vet; Jo has taken on the responsibility of helping Art run the lodge; and the children, though reluctant to live in Africa, slowly adjust to the prospect that they have no other choice. Stories relate the events that affect the individual members of the family. Emily and Oliver are the children of the owner of the rival Mara Lodge; Tumelo is Danny's intern. Katie, Jesse, Emily and Oliver attend the Pecan Wood International School. Mbali is the local girl Jesse falls for.

Cast: D.W. Moffett (Danny Clarke), Stephanie Niznik (Jo Clarke), Leah Pipes (Katie Clark), K'sun Ray (Chase Clarke), Andrew St. John (Jesse Weller), Mary Matilyn Mouser (Mia Clarke), David Butler (Art), Calvin Goldspink (Oliver Banks), Tiffany Mulheron (Tiffany Banks), Atandwa Kani (Tumelo), Precious Kofi (Mbali). **Credits:** *Executive Producer:* Michael Rauch, George Faber, Charles Pattinson. *Co-Executive Producer:* Dana Baratta, Sue Tenney. *Producer:* Elizabeth Hunter. *Music:* Bob Christianson, Bill Meyers.

918 Life of Ryan. (Reality; MTV; August 27, 2007 to May 19, 2008)

A docu-drama that follows Ryan Scheckler, a 17-year-old who is also a rising star on the skateboard scene. The program also relates activities in the life of his mother (Gretchen) and his younger brothers (Shane and Kane).

Star: Ryan Scheckler. **Credits:** *Executive Producer:* Jason A. Carbone. *Co-Executive Producer:* Sarah Kane. *Supervising Producer:* Shari Brooks. *Music:* David Bellochio. *Director:* Robert Sizemore.

919 Life with Derek. (Comedy; Disney; Premiered: September 18, 2005)

A blended family comedy wherein Nora MacDonald, a single mother with two daughters (Casey and Lizzie), and George Venturi, a single father with three children (Derek, Marti and Edwin) marry and merge their two families.

Cast: Michael Seater (Derek Venturi), Ashley Leggat (Casey MacDonald), Joy Tanner (Nora MacDonald), John Ralston (George Venturi), Ariel Waller (Marti Venturi), Daniel Magder (Edwin Venturi), Jordan Todosey (Lizzie MacDonald), Arnold Pinnock (Paul), Robbie Amell (Max), Shadia Simmons (Emily), Kit

Weyman (Sam). **Credits:** *Executive Producer:* Daphne Balllon, Suzanne Martin. *Producer:* Jeff Biederman, Suzanne French. *Music:* Gary Koftinoff.

920 Lil' Bush: Resident of the United States. (Comedy; Comedy Central; June 13, 2007 to May 8, 2008)

What were president George W. Bush and other members of the White House like when they were children? *Lil' Bush* takes that concept and shows, in animated form, events in the lives of Lil' George Bush as a child (with aspirations to become the president).

Voice Cast: Chris Parson (Lil' George Bush), Dave Mitchell (George Bush, Sr.), Mara Cary (Barbara Bush), Dave Mitchell (Lil' Jeb), Iggy Pop (Lil' Rummy), Ann Villella (Lil' Laura). **Credits:** *Executive Producer:* Seth Cummings, Peter Adderton, Dominick Cary. *Co-Executive Producer:* Jay Karas. *Producer:* J. Michael Mendel, Alex Stancioff, Kim Huffman Cary. *Associate Producer:* Rochelle Ponsky.

921 Lincoln Heights. (Drama; ABC Family; January 8, 2007 to November 11, 2008)

Eddie Sutton is a police officer who wants to make a difference. He leaves the relative safety of his city beat and moves his family to the inner city Los Angeles neighborhood (Lincoln Heights) where he grew up; it is now crime ridden but it holds fond memories of his youth. Stories follow Eddie as he patrols the streets and struggles to make the people of the community feel they have someone on their side. Jen is Eddie's wife; Cassie, Lizzie and Taylor are their children.

Cast: Russell Hornsby (Eddie Sutton), Nicki Micheaux (Jen Sutton), Rhyon Nicole Brown (Lizzie Sutton), Erica Hubbard (Cassie Sutton), Misgon Ratliff (Taylor Sutton). **Credits:** *Executive Producer:* Kevin Hooks, Kathleen McGhee-Anderson. *Producer:* John F. Perry, Kevin Inch. *Assistant Producer:* Mark Nasser.

922 **Little Einsteins.** (Cartoon; Disney; March 1, 2005 to October 11, 2008)

Annie, Leo, June and Quincy are musically gifted children who use their knowledge of song, dance and instruments to familiarize children with music.

Voice Cast: Erica Huang (June), Jesse Schwartz (Leo), Natalie Wojcik (Annie), Aiden Pompey (Quincy). **Credits:** *Executive Producer:* Richard Winkler, Steve Oakes, Susan Holden, Eric Weiner. *Producer:* Kris Greengrove. *Music:* Billy Straus, Matthias Gohl.

923 **Little People, Big World.** (Reality; TLC; Premiered: March 4, 2006)

A profile of the Roloffs, a family that is composed of both little and average-sized people (parents Matt and Amy and their normal-sized children: Molly, Jacob and twins Zack and Jeremy). Each episode relates an event in their daily lives.

Credits: *Executive Producer:* Paul Barrosse, Gay Rosenthal. *Co-Executive Producer:* Nicholas Caprio, Glenn Meehan. *Producer:* Billy Cooper, Matthew Lahey, Ann Suckow. *Music:* Joey Newman.

924 **Live from Lincoln Center.** (Anthology; PBS; Premiered: January 30, 1976)

A program of varying musical performances broadcast live from Lincoln Center in New York City. Beverly Sills and Dick Cavett are the most notable hosts.

Credits: *Announcer:* Martin Bookspan. *Executive Producer:* Herbert Bonis, John Gaberman. *Supervising Producer:* Marc Bauman. *Producer:* Carl Samet, Clare Avery.

925 **Live with Regis and Kelly.** (Talk; Syn.; Premiered: 2001)

An exchange of conversation between the hosts coupled with celebrity interviews.

Hosts: Regis Philbin, Kelly Ripa. **Credits:** *Executive Producer:* Regis Philbin, Michael Gelman. *Music:* Michael Karp, Irving Robbins, Shelley Palmer.

926 **Lost.** (Adventure; ABC; Premiered: September 22, 2004)

A plane (Oceanic Flight 815) is en-route from Australia to Los Angeles when it encounters unexpected turbulence. The plane is literally ripped in half and both halves crash land on an unknown island presumably in the South Pacific. While there are casualties, 48 passengers survive from the front half of the plane (it is later revealed that passengers from the rear half of the plane also survived). When all attempts at rescue fail, the survivors make the island their home (although they find their lives threatened by the mysteries that exist on the strange island). The main survivors of a large cast are Jack Shepherd, a doctor; John Locke, a cripple who can now walk; Claire, a pregnant Australian woman who later gives birth to a son (Aaron); Charlie, a low life; Kate, a woman of mystery (she was arrested in Australia and being taken back to the U.S.); Sun and Jin, a secretive Korean couple; Hurley, the mainland lottery winner who is eager to help whenever he can; Michael and his son, Walt (and Walt's dog, Vincent); and Ana-Lucia, a mysterious woman whom Jack met at the Sydney airport and survived the rear section crash.

Principal Cast: Matthew Fox (Dr. Jack Shephard), Evangeline Lilly (Kate Austen), Emilie de Raven (Claire Littleton), Naveen Andrews (Sayid Jarrah), Jorge Garcia (Hugo "Hurley" Reyes), Josh Holloway (James "Sawyer" Ford), Daniel Dae Kim (Jin Kwon), Yunjin Kim (Sun Kwon), Dominic Monaghan (Charlie Pace), Terry O'Quinn (John Locke), Harold Perrineau (Michael Dawson), Maggie Grace (Shannon Rutherford), Adewale Akinnuoye-Agbaje (Mr. Eko), Malcolm David Kelley (Walt Lloyd), Ian Somerhalder (Boone Carlyle), Michele Rodriquez (Ana-Lucia Cortez), Elizabeth Mitchell (Dr. Juliet Burke), Kiele Sanchez (Nikki), Mira Furlan (Danielle Rousseau). **Credits:** *Executive Producer:* Carlton Cuse, Bryan Burk,

Jack Damon Lindelof, J.J. Abrams. *Co-Executive Producer:* Jeff Pinkner. *Supervising Producer:* Adam Horowitz, Edward Kitsis, Joseph Loeb, Steven Maedan, Monica Breen, Alison Schapker, Drew Goddard, Leonard Dick, Craig Wright. *Producer:* Liz Sarnoff, Patricia Churchill, Sarah Caplaw, Stephen Williams, Jean Higgins. *Music:* Michael Giacchino, Damien Rice.

927   Lost Worlds. (Reality; History Channel; Premiered: July 10, 2006)

Archaeologists use modern technology to recreate life in lost civilizations through the artifacts found in ancient cultures.

Narrator: Corey Johnson, Corey Lawson. **Credits:** *Executive Producer:* Anthony Geffen. *Producer:* Stuart Elliott, Francesca Maudslay, Martin Kemp. *Music:* Sak Shariff.

928   Mad Men. (Drama; AMC; July 19, 2007 to October 26, 2008)

Sterling Cooper is a prestigious advertising agency on Madison Avenue in New York City. The time is the 1960s and the world of media advertising as it existed at the time is realistically explored. Don and Roger are senior partners; Peggy is the junior copyrighter; Pete is the account executive; Betty is Dan's wife; Joan is the firm's head secretary.

Cast: Jon Hamm (Don Draper), John Slattery (Roger Sterling), Robert Morse (Bertram Cooper), Elisabeth Moss (Peggy Olson), Christina Hendricks (Joan Holloway), Vincent Kartheiser (Pete Campbell), Maggie Siff (Rachel Menken), January Jones (Betty Draper), Rose Marie DeWitt (Midge). **Credits:** *Executive Producer:* Matthew Weiner. *Producer:* Greg Schultz, Scott Hornbacher, Jack Lechner.

929   Mad TV. (Comedy; Fox; Premiered: October 14, 1995)

Skits based on the humor found in *Mad* magazine.

Cast: Michael McDonald, Debra Wilson, Aries Spears, Mo Collins, Nicole Sullivan, Bobby Lee, Alex Borstein, Will Sasso, Stephanie Weir, Nicole Parker, Jordan Peele, Keegan Michael Key, Erica Ash, Matt Braunger, Eric Price, Bobby Lee, Johnny Sanchez, Crista Flanagan, Lauren Pritchard. **Credits:** *Executive Producer:* Adam Small, David Saltzman, Quincy Jones, Fax Bahr, Dick Blasucci. *Co-Executive Producer:* John Crane, Garry Campbell, Steven Haft, Steven Cragg, Scott King. *Supervising Producer:* Bryan Adams, Chris Cluess, Bruce Leddy, Devon Shepard. *Producer:* Tami Sagher, Jim Wise, Maiya Williams, James Jones, Rich Talarico.

930   Made in Hollywood. (Reality; Syn.; Premiered: September 2005)

Interviews with the stars and behind-the-scenes footage of current feature films. The stars of each profiled film serve as the segment host. In 2006 (to 2007) an edition geared to young adults and dealing with non-adult films aired as *Made in Hollywood: Teen Edition*.

Host (Teen Edition): Kylie Erica Mar. **Credits:** *Executive Producer:* Cleveland O'Neal III. *Producer:* Todd Szuch, Carole Mar, Jerry A. Vasilatos. *Music:* Janet Cole Valdez, Dapo Torimiro.

931   Magi-Nation. (Cartoon; Kids WB/CW; September 22, 2007 to September 6, 2008)

Tony Jones, a young Earth boy, is magically transported to Moonlands, one of eleven parallel worlds to the Earth. He meets Edyn, a girl who tells him by the special ring the wears (given to him by his grandfather) that he is the Final Dreamer, a magical champion for good. With the help of Edyn and her friend, Strag and the magic of the ring (to summon Dream Creatures), Tony battles the evil Agram and his henchmen, Korg and Zed.

Credits: *Executive Producer:* Michael Hirsh, Pamela Slavin, Toper Taylor.

932 Making News: Savannah Style. (Reality; TV Guide Channel; June 11, 2007 to September 10, 2008). A behind-the-scenes look at the news operations of two real television stations: WJCL and WTGS in Savannah, Georgia.

Credits: Executive Producer: Nick Davis. Producer: Andeep Singh, Joshua Kaufman.

933 Making the Band. (Reality; ABC/MTV; Premiered: March 24, 2000) A search to find talented singers and/or musicians. The first cycle (ABC) seeks to find five male singer-musicians for a new boy band to be called O-Town. Cycle Two (MTV, 2002) found rap artist P. Diddy seeking aspiring rappers for a new hip-hop band. MTV continued the series with Cycle Three (2005) seeking a mixed (male-female) band and Cycle Four (2008) taking to the road with P. Diddy overseeing a cross country tour with recording groups Danity Kane and Day 26, and singer Donnie Klang.

Host: Lou Perlman (Cycle 1), Sean "P. Diddy" Combs (Cycles, 2, 3, and 4). **Credits:** *Executive Producer:* Mary-Ellis Bunim, Sean "P. Diddy" Combs, Jonathan Murray. *Co-Executive Producer:* Rick de Oliveira. *Supervising Producer:* Andrew Hogel, Perry Dance, Benjamin Greenberg. *Producer:* Jonathan M. Singer, Ken Mok, Jennifer Lange, Cris Abrego, Jae Benson II, Kenny Hull.

934 Mama Mirabelle's Home Movies. (Children; PBS; Premiered: September 9, 2007) Mama Mirabelle is a wise elephant who helps three young animals (Carla, a zebra; Bo, a cheetah and Max, an elephant) understand aspects of Mother Nature through her home movies (live action wildlife footage).

Voices: Vanessa Williams, Phillipa Alexander, Julie de Jongh, Teresa Gallagher, Elly Fairman, Alan Marriott. **Credits:** *Executive Producer:* Donna Friedman Meir.

Co-Executive Producer: Tara Sorensen. *Supervising Producer:* Andy Yerkes. *Producer:* Leo Nielsen. *Music:* Lester Barnes.

935 Man vs. Wild. (Reality; Discovery Channel; Premiered: November 10, 2006) Adventurer Bear Grylis explores the most dangerous tourist attractions and environments with the object being to show viewers how to survive in them.

Host: Bear Grylis. **Credits:** *Executive Producer:* Discovery Channel. *Producer:* Mary Donahue. *Music:* Paul Pritchard.

936 MANswers. (Comedy; Spike TV; September 19, 2007 to November 11, 2008) Comical, if not at times absurd responses to questions that border on the ridiculous (for example, "Who is the richest bitch in America?," "What is the world's smallest legal bikini?" and "What country's armed forces pays for fake boobs?").

Narrator: Matt Short. **Credits:** *Executive Producer:* Adam Cohen, Cara Tapper. *Producer:* Christopher Gallivan, Charlotte Bell. *Music:* Shawn K. Clement.

937 Martha. (Information; Syn.; Premiered: November 27, 2007) Domestic Diva Martha Stewart presents how to projects, cooking segments, gardening tips, scrap booking, decoupage and hand-making gift ideas.

Host: Martha Stewart. **Credits:** *Executive Producer:* Martha Stewart, Mark Burnett, Bernie Young. *Producer:* Greta Anthony. *Director:* Alan Heydt.

938 Martin Lawrence Presents First Amendment Standup. (Comedy; Starz; Premiered: 2007) A showcase for established as well as up-and-coming standup comics (who are permitted to use "gutter language," thus explaining the title, that is not bleeped).

Host: Doug Williams. **Credits:** *Executive Producer:* Martin Lawrence, Doug Williams. *Producer:* Michael Derek Bohusz, C. Dunsean Williams.

939 The Maury Povich Show. (Talk; Syn.; Premiered: September 1991)

A sensitive talk show that tackles very controversial topics that other shows in the genre overlook.

Host: Maury Povich. **Credits:** *Executive Producer:* Maury Povich, Diane Rappaport, Amy Rosenbaum. *Producer:* David Masure-Bosco, Dominic Pupa, Keith P. McAllen. *Music:* Billy Goldenberg.

940 Maya and Miguel. (Cartoon; PBS; Premiered: October 1, 2004)

Maya and Miguel Santos are ten-year-old Hispanic twins. They are the children of Rosa and Santiago and stories, designed to familiarize children with the Spanish culture, relate the twins' adventures at home and at school.

Voice Cast: Candi Milo (Maya Santos), Nika Futterman (Miguel Santos), Elizabeth Pena (Rosa Santos), Carlos Ponce (Santiago Santos), Carlos Alazraqui (Paco), Jerod Mixon (Theo), Elizabeth Payne (Chrissy), Lucy Liu (Maggie), Lupe Ontiveros (Abuela Elena), Erik Estrada (Senor Felipe). **Credits:** *Executive Producer:* Deborah Forte. *Producer:* Helen Kalafatic, Machi Tantillo. *Music:* Jack Livesey, David Ricard.

941 McBride. (Crime Drama; Hallmark; Premiered: January 14, 2005)

McBride calls himself "A lawyer for the little guy." He has a heart of gold, is independently wealthy and money appears not to matter to him; he often takes cases based on merit. McBride has been a lawyer for eight years when the series begins (owner of McBride and Associates). He was a member of the L.A.P.D. but became disillusioned as to how easy criminals get back on the street. He quit to attend law school. That was twelve years ago. Now, as a tough but honest defense lawyer, McBride does whatever he can, within the limits of the law, to free clients of criminal charges. Roberta Hansen is a detective with the L.A.P.D. (and McBride's former romantic interest when he was a detective; they still work well together); Phil Newberry is a former public defender who now works as McBride's assistant; Jessie is McBride's dog. John Larroquette, who plays McBride, requested that his character have no first name or even an initial. But through rumors and press material, he is listed as M. McBride (the name plate on his desk) or called Mike McBride in some sources. Roberta calls him "Mac." Black and white flashback sequences are used to detail the evidence McBride has found when he questions a suspect.

Cast: John Larroquette (McBride), Marta DuBois (Sgt. Roberta Hansen), Matt Lutz (Phil Newberry). **Credits:** *Executive Producer:* Larry Levinson. *Co-Executive Producer:* Michael Moran, Amy Goldberg, Nick Lombardo. *Producer:* Brian Gordon, Erik Olson.

942 Medium. (Drama; NBC; January 3, 2005 to May 12, 2008)

Allison DuBois is a very special woman. She cannot only sense things about other people, but she can see and talk to dead people — "It's like a freaky TV show," she says. She is married to Joe and the mother of three children (Ariel, Bridget and Maria; also called Marie). Allison is studying to become a lawyer and works as an intern at the D.A.'s office in Phoenix, Arizona. Through her visions, Allison can actually see the truth. Spirits appear to tell her things. She also has dreams that come true. "How does it happen," people ask. "I don't know. Who ever made me this way didn't give me an instruction book." Stories follow Allison as she tries to help people through her visions and dreams. Joe is an aerospace engineer for Aero Dytech Labs; Ariel appears to have the same abilities as her mother but they are not as frequent. Manny Devalos is the D.A. of Mariposa County; Lee Scanlon is detective with the Phoenix P.D. who assists Allison (and knows her secret, as does

Manuel); Cynthia Keener is the missing persons investigator. Returned for a new season on February 2, 2009.

Cast: Patricia Arquette (Allison Du-Bois), Jake Weber (Joe DuBois), Sofia Vassilieva (Ariel DuBois), Maria Lark (Bridget DuBois), Miranda Carabello (Maria DuBois), Miguel Sandoval (Manuel Devalos), David Cubitt (Lee Scanlon), Anjelica Houston (Cynthia Keener). **Credits:** *Executive Producer:* Kelsey Grammer, Glenn Gordon Caron, Rene Echevarria, Steve Stark. *Co-Executive Producer:* Javier Grillo-Marxuach, Michael Angeli. *Supervising Producer:* Robert Doherty, Moira Dekker. *Producer:* Larry Teng, Debbie Hayn-Cass. *Music:* Sean Collery, Mychael Danna, Jeff Beal.

943 Meet the Barkers. (Reality; MTV; Premiered: April 6, 2005)

A look at the daily lives of Travis Barker, drummer for Blink 182, and his wife, Shanna Moakler, a former Miss U.S.A., as they attempt to live a normal life.

Cast: Travis Barker, Shanna Moakler, Mark Hoppus, Thomas DeLonge, Landon Barker, Courtney Edwards, Andrew Fiscella, Atiana De La Hoya. **Credits:** *Executive Producer:* Melanie Graham. *Producer:* Joel Conroy, Nate Hayden.

944 Mega Disasters. (Reality; History Channel; Premiered: May 23, 2006)

Computer animation is used to explore what could happen when natural disasters strike (from volcanic eruptions to tsunamis).

Narrator: J.V. Martin. **Credits:** *Executive Producer:* Simon L. Edwards. *Producer:* Vincent Lopez.

945 Men in Trees. (Drama; ABC; September 15, 2006 to June 12, 2008)

Whose Gonna Love Your Body? and *If I Can Date, So Can You* are the books written by relationship coach Marin Frist. Her books are best sellers and she is enjoying the good life. She is engaged (to Justin)

and has numerous speaking engagements. Marin also believes she knows a lot about men. However, on a speaking engagement in Alaska, Marin finds she knows very little about men and relationships. It all begins when she accidentally grabs Justin's computer and sees a slide show of him with other women. In the small town of Elmo, Alaska, where Marin is to give a lecture, she has a rude awakening. In a town where the population is ten men to every one woman, Marin realizes that what she has been writing are all lies (she cannot figure men out and cannot sensibly categorize them). She believes Elmo is the perfect place to learn about men. Stories follow Marin as she struggles to adjust to small town life, learn what men are all about and eventually write the ultimate relationship book (the series title refers to signs posted around town — "Men in Trees" [tree trimmers]). Annie is Marin's friend; Jack is the fish and wildlife environmentalist; Buzz is the owner of Buzz Airlines; Ben is the bartender at The Chieftan Pub; Patrick is the Jack of all trades; Theresa is Ben's ex-wife; and Sara is a single mother who is also a hooker.

Cast: Anne Heche (Marin Frist), Emily Bergl (Annie), Abraham Benrubi (Ben Jackson), John Amos (Buzz), James Tupper (Jack Slattery), Sarah Strange (Theresa), Derek Richardson (Patrick), Suleka Matthew (Sara), Justine Bateman (Lynn), Lauren Tom (Mai), Cynthia Stevenson (Chief Celia Bachelor), Orlando Jones (George). **Credits:** *Executive Producer:* Jenny Bicks, Cathy Konrad, James Mangold. *Producer:* Stuart Besser. *Music:* Peter Himmelman.

946 Miami Ink. (Reality; TLC; July 19, 2005 to July 31, 2008)

A behind-the-scenes look at the world of tattoos as seen through the experiences of the workers and clientele of Miami Ink, a parlor in South Beach, Florida.

Tattoo Artists: Ami James, Chris Garver, Chris Nunez, Darren Brall. **Credits:** *Executive Producer:* Pamela Deutsch, Charles Corwin. *Co-Executive Producer:* Chris Rantamaki, Clara Markowicz. *Producer:* Jodi Midiri, Jill Dickerson.

947   The Mickey Mouse Clubhouse. (Children; Disney; Premiered: May 5, 2006)

Computer animated series set at the Mickey Mouse Clubhouse where the antics of Mickey Mouse, his girlfriend, Minnie Mouse, and their friends Donald Duck and Goofy are depicted as they go about their daily lives.

Voice Cast: Wayne Allwine (Mickey Mouse), Russi Taylor (Minnie Mouse), Tony Aneslmo (Donald Duck), Bill Farmer (Goofy), Tress MacNeille (Daisy Duck). **Credits:** *Executive Producer:* Rob LaDuca, Robert Gannaway. *Producer:* Bradley Bowlen. *Director:* Rob LaDuca, Sherie Pollack.

948   Mind of Mencia. (Comedy; Comedy Central; July 6, 2005 to July 23, 2008)

A look at everyday life as seen through the eyes of comedian Carlos Mencia — from his monologues to man-in-the-street interviews to his interactions with the studio audience.

Host: Carlos Mencia. **Credits:** *Executive Producer:* Robert Morton, Carlos Mencia, Chris McGuire. *Co-Executive Producer:* Steve Lookner, Kelly D. Hommon, Krysia Plonka, Nikki Kessler. *Producer:* Pamela Ribon. *Music:* Stephen Phillips.

949   The Minor Accomplishments of Jackie Woodman. (Comedy; IFC; Premiered: August 6, 2006)

Jackie Woodman is an attractive woman with a dream: make it in Hollywood as a TV and movie writer. Ten years have passed since she left New York and her accomplishments are virtually nil (she writes for a second rate magazine called *Image*).

Realizing that perhaps the big time is not for her, she embarks on a mission to change her life by accomplishing a series of minor achievements. Stories relate those efforts. Tara is her best friend; Bobby Paterniti (who introduces himself as "Bobby P.") is a semi successful director; Mitchell is Jackie's gay assistant at *Image*; Connor is Tara's boyfriend. Based on the real life experiences of Laura Kightlinger.

Cast: Laura Kightlinger (Jackie Woodman), Nicholle Tom (Tara), Jeffrey Kramer (Bobby Paterniti), Azura Skye (Skyler), Patrick Bristow (Mitchell), Mary Kay Place (Jackie's mother), Colleen Camp (Angela Birnbaum), Butch Klein (Connor). **Credits:** *Executive Producer:* Laura Kightlinger, David Punch, Fenron Bailey, Randy Barbato, Adam Kassen, Mark Kassen. *Supervising Producer:* Andrea Fulton, John Miller-Monzon. *Producer:* Bob Balaban, Danielle Weinstock. *Music:* Randy Lee, Morris Tepper.

950   Missing. (Reality; Syn.; Premiered: September 2003)

Investigations into missing persons cases that present all the known information and asks viewers who may possess additional information to contact authorities.

Host: Alex Paen, Pamela Bach. **Credits:** *Executive Producer:* Alex Paen. *Producer:* Larry Dunn, Luis F. Gonzalez, James Allen Bradley. *Music:* Larry Brown.

951   Missing Persons Unit. (Reality; Court TV/Tru TV; Premiered: August 16, 2006)

Real life cases of people who have disappeared are chronicled. Stories are investigative in nature and attempt to uncover the reason for the disappearance and the facts that led to both successful and failed conclusions.

Host: George Deuchar. **Narrator:** Sam Fontana. **Credits:** *Executive Producer:* Carsten Oblaender, Andreas Gutzeit. *Producer:* Jacqueline Vorhauer, Libby Sallaway, Bethany McMahon. *Associate Pro-*

ducer: Al Chester, Tara Chiusano, Bryan Ranharter.

952   A Model Life with Petra Nemcova. (Reality; TLC; June 13, 2007 to August 31, 2008)

Super model Petra Nemcova is perhaps best known for miraculously surviving the 2004 tsunami in Thailand. As the host of her own series, Petra is seeking a top model. Six hopeful models are put through various tasks to test their modeling abilities. The potential models are chosen from around the world and looks take priority over everything else. The one girl Petra feels has the look to be a fashion model is awarded that golden opportunity.

Host: Petra Nemcova. **Credits:** *Executive Producer:* Jeb Brien, Dave Broome, Sara Kozak, Tommy Mottola. *Producer:* Matt Westmore. *Music:* Mark T. Williams, Jeff Lippencott.

953   Molto Mario. (Cooking; Food Network; Premiered: December 1, 2006)

Chef Mario Batali prepares old world Italian recipes for viewers.

Host: Mario Batali.

954   Monique's Fat Chance. (Reality; Oxygen; August 6, 2005 to April 23, 2008)

Ten pretty, plus size women compete in beauty contest-like challenges for the opportunity to win $50,000 in cash and the title "Miss F.A.T."

Host: Monique. **Credits:** *Executive Producer:* Don Weiner. *Producer:* Jeff Koop, Monique.

955   Monk. (Crime Drama; USA; Premiered: July 12, 2002)

Adrian Monk, a brilliant detective with the 14th Division of the San Francisco Police Department, and his wife, Trudy, an investigative reporter for *The Examiner*, live on Cole Street. In 1998, Trudy is killed in a car bombing. Was she working on a story? Did she get too close to something? These are the questions that drive Adrian to continually review the facts of the case

in the hope that he will one day find her killer. Trudy's death also affected Adrian in another way. It triggered a rare anxiety disorder that makes him germ phobic and afraid of virtually everything. The condition immediately interferes with Adrian's work and he is given a 315 temporary suspension (a psychological discharge). Adrian regularly sees a psychiatrist (Dr. Kroger) and is aided by his full time nurse, Sharona Fleming (the divorced mother a young son named Benjy). Adrian needs to keep busy, but he is still "too nuts," as people say, to return to the force, something he desperately misses. With Sharona's help, Adrian begins a private consulting business and together they set out to help people in trouble (most often police Captain Leland Stottlemeyer, Monk's former superior). Monk has an encyclopedic knowledge of strange and unusual facts. He has a photographic memory and the deductive skills of Sherlock Holmes. A person who is neat and tidy impresses Adrian. When Monk assists the police, it is on "Observer Status" only. Later episodes feature Natalie Teeger, a single mother of 13-year-old Julie, as Monk's assistant when Sharona resigns.

Cast: Tony Shalhoub (Adrian Monk), Bitty Schram (Sharona Fleming), Kane Ritchote (Benny Fleming), Ted Levine (Capt. Leland Stottlemeyer), Traylor Howard (Natalie Teeger), Emmy Clarke (Julie Teeger), Stanley Kimel (Dr. Charles Kroger), Jason Gray-Stanford (Lt. Randall Disher), Hector Elizondo (Dr. Neven Bell; replaced Dr. Kroger). **Credits:** *Executive Producer:* Andy Breckman, David Hoberman, Tony Shalhoub, David Brickman, Rob Thompson. *Co-Executive Producer:* Randall Zisk, David M. Stein. *Producer:* Fern Field, Philip M. Goldfarb, Jane Barttelme, Anthony Santa Croce. *Music:* Jeff Beal, Patrick Williams.

956   Monster Quest. (Reality; History Channel; Premiered: October 31, 2007)

Are ghosts, werewolves, vampires, Big Foot and other such legendary "monsters" real or just folklore? The program explores the lore with an attempt to distinguish fact from fiction.

Narrator: Stan Bernard. **Credits:** *Executive Producer:* Dale Bosch, Michael Stiller. *Producer:* Collin Mullahy, Beth Parsons. *Music:* Tom Hambleton.

957 **The Montel Williams Show**. (Talk; Syn.; September 1991 to May 2008)
Discussions on controversial topics.
Host: Montel Williams. **Psychotherapist:** Maria Setaro, Patricia Johnson. **Credits:** *Executive Producer:* Montel Williams, Herman Rush, Freddy Fields, Mary Duffy, Diane Rappaport. *Supervising Producer:* Vicki DeShazo, Amie Baker. *Producer:* Shantel Klinger, Tom Cestaro, Tracey Slates, Joni Cohen Zlotowitz. *Music:* Kenny Blank, Craig Sharmat.

958 **The Morning Show with Mike and Juliet**. (Talk; Fox; Premiered: January 22, 2007)
Live morning talk show that features celebrity interviews and discussions on current topics of interest.
Hosts: Mike Jerrick, Juliet Huddy. **Entertainment Reporter:** Jill Dobson. **Credits:** *Executive Producer:* Patricia Ciano. *Producer:* Elizabeth Cover, Sabina Ryman, Nicole Pulco, Lindsay Sobel, Liz Weaver. *Theme Music:* Kathryn Korniloff.

959 **Most Daring**. (Reality; Court TV/Tru TV; Premiered: September 12, 2007)
"Ordinary People in extraordinary danger" is the tag line for this series that showcases real acts of courage that were captured on tape by both law enforcement videos and those by amateur photographers.
Narrator: Mitch Lewis. **Credits:** *Supervising Producer:* David Dean. *Producer:* Andrew Schauer. *Senior Segment Producer:* Kazeem Molake. *Segment Producer:* Bernard Neto.

960 **Most Outrageous Moments**. (Reality; NBC; Premiered: February 8, 2005)
Outtakes from movies and foreign and domestic TV shows, sporting mishaps and home video accidents caught on tape.
Narrator: John Cramer. **Credits:** *Executive Producer:* Scott Satin. *Supervising Producer:* Steve Marmalstein. *Music:* Joe Mendelson.

961 **Most Shocking**. (Reality; Court TV/Tru TV; Premiered: October 4, 2006)
A violent reality series that showcases "action-packed" videos of criminal behavior culled from various law enforcement agencies from around the world.
Host: John Bunnell. **Credits:** *Executive Producer:* Bruce Nash, Debra Weeks. *Supervising Producer:* David Dean. *Senior Segment Producer:* Julie K. Morris. *Segment Producer:* Hilari Scorl. *Music:* Scooter Pietsch, Shawn Clement.

962 **Murder by the Book**. (Reality; Court TV/Tru TV; Premiered: November 13, 2006)
The author of a best selling crime novel appears as the guest. As he discusses the crime he has written about, newspaper clippings, crime scene photos and recreations are used to reconstruct the incidents that led up to and caused the murder — and how it was solved or why it still remains a mystery.
Credits: *Executive Producer:* Jessica Shreeve. *Producer:* Nino Lopez.

963 **Murder 101**. (Crime Drama; Hallmark; Premiered: January 7, 2006)
Dr. Jonathan Maxwell is a senior citizen who is brilliant when it comes to his job (criminology professor) but away from class he is a bit absent-minded and a bit of a klutz. Jonathan may forget where his next class is being held, but if the police need help to solve a baffling crime, he is there to assist (although he most often helps Mike Bryant, a former cop turned

private detective, solve crimes). Stories relate Jonathan's investigations as he and Mike solve complex crimes. Ben Manners is Mike's nephew and legman.

Cast: Dick Van Dyke (Dr. Jonathan Maxwell), Barry Van Dyke (Mike Bryant), Shane Van Dyke (Ben Manners). **Credits:** *Executive Producer:* Dean Hargrove, Robert Halmi, Jr., Larry Levinson. *Co-Executive Producer:* Nick Lombardo, Michael Moran. *Producer:* James Wilberger, Kyle Clark. *Music:* Roger Bellon.

964 My Bare Lady. (Reality; Fox Reality Channel; Premiered: December 7, 2006)

Four gorgeous U.S. adult film stars travel to London, England, to compete in a series of challenges to establish legitimate careers on the West End Stage. In cycle two of the series, *My Bare Lady: Open for Business,* four additional U.S. adult film stars compete in a series of challenges to establish themselves a legitimate businesswomen.

Host: Mike Matorazo. **The Girls (Cycle 1):** Sasha Knox, Kristen Price, Chanel St. James, Nautica Thorn. **The Girls (Cycle 2):** Brooke Haven, Casey Parker, Sunny Leone, Veronica Rayne. **Credits:** *Executive Producer:* Danny Fenton. *Producer:* David Beitchman, Noel Siegel.

965 My Boys. (Comedy; TBS; December 28, 2006 to August 7, 2008)

P.J. Franklin, a young woman in her twenties, is a sportswriter for the Chicago *Sun Times.* P.J. has mostly male friends and could be considered a tomboy. She is a low maintenance girl and the glue that keeps her friends together. P.J. does have a female friend, Stephanie (who attended journalism school with her and who, being more feminine than P.J., offers her tips on how to use her feminine wiles on men). P.J.'s male friends are Mike, a ladies' man who is afraid to make a commitment (he works for the Chicago Cubs baseball team); Brendan, a D.J. with numerous ro-

mantic heartaches; Kenny, a dating challenged sports memorabilia store owner; and Andy, P.J.'s henpecked brother. Adding spice to P.J.'s life is Bobby, a sportswriter for the rival newspaper, the *Chicago Tribune.*

Cast: Jordana Spiro (P.J. Franklin), Kellee Stewart (Stephanie), Michael Bunin (Kenny Mortitori), Jamie Kaler (Mike Callahan), Reid Scott (Brendan Dorff), Jim Gaffigan (Andy Franklin), Kyle Howard (Bobby Newman). **Credits:** *Executive Producer:* Betsy Thomas, Gavin Polone, Jamie Tarses. *Producer:* Rick Singer. *Associate Producer:* Robert J. Viseiglia. *Music:* Ed Alton.

966 My Fabulous Wedding. (Reality; WE; Premiered: July 26, 2007)

A look at the preparations that brides-to-be encounter while planning their weddings (although those profiled are rich and do not skimp and purchase what they want — from expensive wedding gowns to exotic reception locales).

Credits: *Producer:* Brooke Gaston, Kimberly Belcher Cowin, Matthew Blaine, Chris McDaniel, Maia Monasterios. *Associate Producer:* Shoshanna Ezra, Stephen Booth, Amy Bonezzi, Travis Andrews, Josh Barnett.

967 My Fair Brady. (Reality; VH-1; September 11, 2005 to March 9, 2008)

Christopher Knight is famous for playing Peter Brady on *The Brady Bunch.* Adrianne Curry is the first winner of *America's Next Top Model.* They met on the program *The Surreal Life* and fell in love. They moved in together and became an item. Cameras follow the couple as they try to live a normal life while a part of the public spotlight.

Cast: Christopher Knight, Adrianne Curry. **Credits:** *Executive Producer:* Ben Samek, Mark Cronin, Cris Abrego. *Co-Executive Producer:* Jacquie Dincauze. *Co-Producer:* Adrianne Curry, Christopher Knight. *Associate Producer:* Jonathan James.

Segment Producer: Reese Van Allen. *Music:* Dan Radlauer, Adam Zelkind.

968   My Friend Rabbit. (Cartoon; NBC; Premiered: October 5, 2007)

Rabbit is a white hare that lives in the forest. He is close friends with Mouse (a rodent) and together they share exciting adventures with the other animals of the forest.

Voice Cast: Peter Oldring (Rabbit), Robert Binsley (Mouse), Denise Oliver (Hazel), Jeremy Harris (Thunder), Milton Barnes (Jasper), Hannah Endicott-Douglas (Amber), Isabel de Carteret (Coral). **Credits:** *Executive Producer:* Scott Dyer, Paul Robertson, Douglas Murphy. *Supervising Producer:* Jocelyn Hamilton, Tracey Dodkin. *Line Producer:* Lynne Warner. *Music:* John Weisman.

969   My Friends Tigger and Pooh. (Children; Disney; Premiered: May 12, 2007)

Computer animated adventures of the residents of the Hundred Acre Woods: Winnie the Pooh, Tigger, Piglet, Rabbit, Eeyore, Kanga and Roo, Christopher Robin and new characters six-year-old Darby, Buster, her puppy and new neighbor Lumpy.

Voice Cast: Jim Cummings (Winnie the Pooh/Tigger), Ken Sansom (Rabbit), Chloe Moretz (Darby), Struen Erhlinhorn (Christopher Robin), Travis Oates (Piglet), Dee Bradley Baker (Piglet), Max Burkholder (Roo), Kath Soucie (Kanga), Peter Cullen (Eeyore), Oliver Dillon (Lumpy). **Credits:** *Executive Producer:* Jeff Kline, Brian Hohfeld. *Producer:* Angi Dyste. *Music:* Andy Sturmer.

970   My House Is Worth What? (Reality; HGTV; Premiered: August 2, 2006)

American homes are visited and evaluated by a team of experts to educate home owners as to the value of their properties.

Host: Allen Lee Haff. **Designers:** Kerri Louise, Tom Cotter, Brock Harris, Kendra Todd, Bonita Fredericy. **Credits:** *Executive Producer:* Scott Templeton, Tara Sandler, Jennifer Davidson. *Supervising Producer:* Drew Hallmann. *Producer:* Brad Hall, Jake Gibson, Amy Arthun.

971   My Name Is Earl. (Comedy; NBC; Premiered: September 26, 2005)

Earl Hickey is a guy who would steal anything that wasn't nailed down. He was mean, took advantage of others and was simply not a nice guy. One day Earl wins $100,000 on a scratch off lottery ticket but is hit by a car and loses the ticket. While recuperating in the hospital, Earl has an epiphany; he vows to improve his life by correcting every bad thing he has ever done. He makes a list of his past misdeeds and with the help of his dim-witted brother, Randy, sets out to right what was once wrong. Joy is Earl's ex-wife; Darnell owns the Crab Shack Bar; Catalina helps Earl on occasion.

Cast: Jason Lee (Earl Hickey), Jaime Pressly (Joy), Ethan Suplee (Randy Hickey), Eddie Steeples (Darnell "Crab Man" Turner), Nadine Velazquez (Catalina). **Credits:** *Executive Producer:* Marc Buckland, Gregory Thomas Garcia. *Co-Executive Producer:* Barbara Feldman, Bobby Bowman. *Supervising Producer:* Brad Copeland. *Producer:* Harry Lange, Jr., Jason Lee, Michael Pennie. *Music:* Danny Lux, Dillon O'Brian, Jeff Silbar, Mark Leggett.

972   My Partner's a Gym Monkey. (Cartoon; Cartoon Network; Premiered: December 26, 2005)

A 12-year-old boy (Adam Lyon) finds himself attending a school dedicated to educating animals (the Charles Darwin Middle School) when his last name is misspelled (as Lion) and he is placed in the animal category. Jake, the Spider Monkey, becomes his best friend; Principal Pixiefrog runs the school.

Voice Cast: Nika Futterman (Adam Lyon), Tom Kerry (Jake), Maurice La-

Marche (Principal Pixiefrog), Grey De Lisle (Ingrid Giraffe), Brian Doyle Murray (Coach Gillis), Rick Gomez (Slips Python), Nika Futterman (Miss Chameleon). **Credits:** *Executive Producer:* Tim Cahill, Julie McNally Cahill. *Producer:* Victoria McCollum. *Music:* Shawn Clement.

973 My Super Sweet 16. (Reality; MTV; Premiered: August 25, 2005)

Fifteen year old girls preparing for their Sweet 16 parties are profiled. The girls chosen, however, are the offspring of rich parents and always get what they want — including the lavish celebrations that are thrown to celebrate that special day in a teenage girl's life.

Credits: *Executive Producer:* Danielle Medina. *Supervising Producer:* Richard Burrier, Maty Buss. *Producer:* Azon Juan, Heather Walsh, Erin Shockey, Jordana Stall, David Bowles, Ira Fields, Elyse Neiman. *Music:* Toran Caudell, Shawn Clement, Wellington Lora, Jr.

974 Mystery. (Anthology; PBS; Premiered: February 5, 1980)

A weekly presentation of British mysteries based on the works of noted authors (most notably the series *Sherlock Holmes, Miss Marple* and *Hercule Poirot*).

Hosts: Vincent Price, Gene Shalit, Diana Rigg.

975 Mystery Woman. (Crime Drama; Hallmark; Premiered: June 5, 2005)

Mystery Woman is a bookstore owned by Samantha Kinsey. As a young girl, Samantha read every mystery novel she could find. Her uncle, Bob, a crime novel aficionado, would read her a detective story each night at bedtime. As the years passed Samantha became an expert at solving baffling crimes (even before she finished reading a whodunit). When her Uncle Bob passed away, Samantha inherited not only his bookstore (Mystery Man) but Ian Philby, the store's crime connois-

seur (a former CIA agent) and mysterious friend of the family. Samantha takes over the bookstore (changing the name to Mystery Woman) and soon finds herself using her expertise to solve real life baffling crimes. It seems that wherever Samantha is (or goes) murder seems to follow. Stories relate Samantha's (and Ian's) efforts to take what they only read about in books into the real world and solve real crimes. Cassie is Samantha's friend, the Assistant D.A.; Connors is the police chief. In the pilot episode, Cassie was credited as Cassie Thomas (she is Cassandra "Cassie" Hillman in the series).

Cast: Kellie Martin (Samantha Kinsey), J.E. Freeman (Ian Philby; pilot), Clarence Williams III (Ian Philby; series), Constance Zimmer (Cassie Thomas; pilot), Nina Siemaszko (Cassie Hillman; series), Casey Sanders (Chief Connors). **Credits:** *Executive Producer:* Joyce Burditt, Robert Halmi, Jr., Larry Levinson. *Co-Executive Producer:* Michael Moran, Nick Lombardo. *Producer:* Randy Pope. *Music:* Joe Kraemer.

976 Myth Busters. (Reality; Discovery Channel; Premiered: January 23, 2003)

A group of "myth busters" attempt to disprove myths, urban legends and folklore sayings by putting the chosen subject to the test. With the help of Buster, the crash dummy, the group does what it takes to debunk supposed facts.

Host: Adam Savage, Jamie Hyneman. **Myth Busters:** Tory Belleci, Kari Byron, Scotte Chapman, Christine Chamberlain, Heather Joseph-Whitman, Grant Imahara. **Narrator:** Robert Lee. **Credits:** *Executive Producer:* Judith Plavnik, Peter Rees. *Co-Executive Producer:* Rob Hammersley. *Producer:* Richard Dowlearn. *Music:* Neil Sutherland.

977 The Naked Brothers Band. (Reality; Nickelodeon; Premiered: January 27, 2007)

The Naked Brothers Band is a rock group started by Nat and Alex Wolff, the teenage sons of composer Michael Wolff. Cameras follow the brothers as they experience all the problems starting a band and journeying up the rocky road to stardom.

Cast: Alex Wolff, Nat Wolff, Michael Wolff, Polly Draper (off screen voice of Alex and Nat's mother). **Credits:** *Executive Producer:* Polly Draper, Albie Hecht, Michael Wolff. *Producer:* Ken. H. Keller. *Coordinating Producer:* Kari Kim.

978 Naked Happy Girls. (Reality; Playboy Channel; Premiered: 2007)

Gorgeous, non-professional women (models) pose nude and in erotic situations for the chance to not only appear on the Playboy Channel but in a book by photographer Andrew Einhorn (who is accompanied by a Playboy TV crew that videotape the studio shoots).

Host: Andrew Einhorn. **Credits:** *Producer:* Ross Dale, Andrew Einhorn. *Associate Producer:* Kim Reed.

979 NASCAR Angels. (Reality; Syn.; Premiered: September 2006)

Members of the NASCAR racing circuit perform good deeds for deserving people across the country.

Hosts: Rusty Wallace, Shanna Wiseman. **Announcer:** Steve Wood. **Credits:** *Executive Producer:* Bill Miller, Tom Chauncey, Phil Alvidrez, Dennis O'Neill, Beth Reynolds, David Miller. *Producer:* Melissa Thompson, Shana Fischer, Elizabeth Langford.

980 Nature. (Documentary; PBS; Premiered: October 10, 1982)

Weekly series that explores various issues that concern animals and the environment.

Narrators Include: Howard McGillin, Paul Christie, Julia Roberts, Steve Kroft, Craig Sechler, Peter Coyote, F. Murray Abraham, Patricia Clarkson, Sally Kellerman, Michael McKean, Tim Matheson, Christopher Plummer, Stockard Channing, Anthony LaPaglia. **Executive Producer:** Fred Kaufman, Michael Rosenberg, Alex Gregory, Jeremy Bradshaw, Christin Weber, Keenan Smart, Brian Donegan, Ron Devillie, Michael Gunton, Michael Bright, Tim Liversedge. **Music:** Lenny Williams, Nicholas Hooper, Will Slater, Laura Karpman, Jennie Muskett, Robert Neufeld, Mark Adler, Eddie Freeman, Daniel Mitcham, David Poore, Jeff Heffernan, Barnaby Taylar.

981 Naughty Amateur Home Videos. (Erotica; Playboy Channel; Premiered: 1999)

Real people performing sexual acts are profiled (though not as explicit as amateur videos found in the adult sections of video stores). The program's gorgeous host travels to various cities and towns to record the sexual activities of people — alone, together or in groups. Episode titles are as suggestive as the programs themselves (for example, "West Virginia Vixens," "Tennessee Teasers," "Kansas Cougars," and "Arkansas Amateurs").

Host: Jesse Jane.

982 N.C.I.S. (Crime Drama; CBS; Premiered: September 23, 2003)

The NCIS is the Navy Criminal Investigative Service, an organization that operates outside of the U.S. military to investigate crimes associated with service men and women. Stories follow Special Agent Jethro Gibbs and his specialized team as they probe incidents that could eventually embarrass the military if not discreetly handled. Anthony DiNozzo, Ziva David, Timothy McGee, Caitlin Todd and Jimmy Palmer assist Jethro in the filed; Abby Sciuto is their lab assistant; Dr. Donald "Ducky" Mallard is the unit's medical examiner. The program is a spin-off from *JAG*.

Cast: Mark Harmon (Leroy Jethro Gibbs), Sasha Alexander (Caitlin Todd), Michael Weatherly (Tony DiNozzo),

Pauley Perrette (Abby Sciuto), David Mc-Callum (Dr. Donald Mallard), Lauren Holly (NCIS Director Jenny Shepard), Joe Spano (FBI Agent T.C. Fornell), Brian Dietzen (Agent Jimmy Palmer), Sean Murray (Agent Timothy McGee), Cote de Pablo (Agent Ziva David), Rocky Carroll (Leon Vance, NCIS Director, 2008). **Credits:** *Executive Producer:* Donald P. Bellisario. *Co-Executive Producer:* Mark Horowitz, Chas. Floyd Johnson. *Supervising Producer:* Doris Egan, Don McGill. *Producer:* David Bellisario, Avery C. Drewer, Mark R. Schlitz, John C. Kelley, Frank Military.

983 The New Adventures of Old Christine. (Comedy; CBS; Premiered: March 13, 2006). Christine Campbell is the owner of 30 Minutes to Bloom, a female only health spa in Los Angeles. She is divorced from Richard and the mother of eight-year-old Richie, Jr. Christine has not dated since her divorce and becomes the "old Christine" when Richard begins dating a younger woman named Christine (who becomes "the new Christine"). The situation angers "old" Christine (who still has feelings for Richard) and her adventures as she goes about seeking love are the focal point of the series. Barb is old Christine's business partner; Marilyn and Marly are the snooty mothers old Christine runs into at Richie's school (Westbridge); Lucy is Matthew's girlfriend. "New" Christine works as a receptionist at a law firm called Schwartz, Chervin, Jacobs, Young, Loder and White.

Cast: Julia Louis-Dreyfus (Christine Campbell), Clark Gregg (Richard Campbell), Trevor Gagnon (Richie Campbell, Jr.), Emily Rutherfurd ("New" Christine), Tricia O'Kelley (Marly), Alex Kapp (Lindsay), Hamish Linklater (Matthew Kimball), Wanda Lewis (Barb), Michaela Watkins (Marilyn). **Credits:** *Executive Producer:* Kari Lizer. *Co-Executive Producer:* Jennifer Crittenden, Adam Barr, Jeff Astrof. *Supervising Producer:* Jonathan M. Goldstein.

984 The New Yankee Workshop. (Instruction; PBS; Premiered: January 7, 1989)

Step-by-step instruction on how to build various items of furniture with master carpenter Norm Abram.

Host: Norm Abram. **Credits:** *Producer:* Russell Morash.

985 Newport Harbor. (Reality; MTV; Premiered: August 15, 2007)

Laguna Beach spin off that documents (in dramatic soap opera-like style) the lives of a group of teenagers living in Newport Beach, California (the beachside community in Orange County). Also known as *Newport Harbor: The Real Orange County.*

Cast: Clay Adler, Chase Cornwell, Sasha Dunlap, Taylor Geiney, Grant Newman, Chrissy Schwartz, Allie Stockton. **Credits:** *Executive Producer:* Gary Auerbach, Tony DiSanto, Liz Gateley, Dave Sirulnick. *Co-Executive Producer:* Jennifer Lane, Drew Brown. *Producer:* Jennifer Dugan, Aaron Sandler, Libby Niles, Maxwell A. Kaufman.

986 The Next Food Network Star. (Reality; Food Network; Premiered: June 5, 2005)

Ten chefs compete in various cooking challenges for the opportunity to become the network's next star and host of his or her own cooking series. The contestants are judged by Bob Tuschman, the senior vice president of programming and production and Susie Fogelson, vice president of marketing and brand strategy, and Food Network host Bobby Flan. The executive's decision are final as they have a stake in the winner's show.

Host: Marc Summers. **Credits:** *Supervising Producer:* Donna MacLetchel, Cameo Wallace. *Producer:* Beth Paholak, Bruce Kennedy, Neil Regan. *Associate Producer:* Amanda Abel, Daniel Markell, Jennifer Piston.

987 Night Calls. (Erotica; Playboy Channel; Premiered: 1995). Live call-in program wherein female hosts answer viewers sexually based questions. During the program's run, two spin offs aired: *Night Call 411* (2000–2005) which featured sex advice and a "net nympho" who reads e-mails submitted by viewers; and *Night Calls Hot Line* (2004–2005) which also presented sexual advice. Adult film stars Christy Canyon and Ginger Lynn host *Night Calls* on Playboy Radio.

Host (*Night Calls*): Juli Ashton, Doria Rone, Tiffany Graneth, Jesse Jane, Kristen Price. **Host (*Night Calls 411*):** Crystal Knight, Flower Edwards. **Net Nympho:** Tera Patrick, Kitana Baker, Nicole Oring. **Host (*Night Calls Hot Line*):** Ashley Blue, Nautica Thorn, Ann-Marie. **Credits:** *Executive Producer:* Derek Harvie. *Producer:* Jamie Battisa, Will Robertson.

988 Nip/Tuck. (Drama; FX; Premiered: July 22, 2003)

Sean McNamara and Christian Troy are plastic surgeons based in Miami Beach, Florida. Sean is a timid family man who devotes his life to his work to avoid facing his dysfunctional family: Julia, his oversexed and vengeful wife; Matt, his rebellious teenage son; and Annie, his preteenage daughter. Christian is an arrogant ladies' man who worships money and will go to any lengths to get it (including seducing women and blackmail). Stories follow not only the events in Sean and Christian's lives but in the patients who come to them for life changing surgery. Beginning with the episode of October 30, 2007, Sean and Christian leave Miami for greener pastures in Hollywood, California. Stories, which still focus on people seeking plastic surgery to improve their looks, also detail Sean and Christian's efforts to establish a new practice. Fiona becomes their agent when the doctors also become consultants on the TV series *Hearts 'n Scalpels*. Fedddy Prune is the show's producer.

Cast: Dylan Walsh (Sean McNamara), Julian McMahon (Christian Troy), Joely Richardson (Julia McNamara), John Hensley (Matt McNamara), Kelsey-Lynn Batelaan (Annie McNamara), Roma Maffia (Dr. Liz Cruz), Bruno Campos (Dr. Quentin Costa), Valerie Cruz (Grace Santiago), Linda Klein (Nurse Linda), Rose McGowan (Dr. Theodora "Teddy" Love), Oliver Platt (Freddy Prune), Portia de Rossi (Olivia Lord), Kelly Carlson (Kimber), Joely Richardson (Julia). **Credits:** *Executive Producer:* Ryan Murphy, Greer Shepherd, Michael. Robin. *Co-Executive Producer:* Richard Levine, Lynnie Greene. *Supervising Producer:* Sean Jablonski. *Producer:* Patrick McKee, Michael Weiss, Jennifer Salt. *Music:* James. S. Levine, Bradley Buecker.

989 Noah's Arc. (Drama; Logo; Premiered: October 19, 2005)

While Showtime's *The L Word* (see entry) focuses on lesbians, Logo's *Noah's Arc* tells the story of a group of gay men living in Los Angeles. The principals are Noah Nicholson and his romantic interest Wade, both screenwriters (although Wade is an established pro and Noah is struggling to make his mark in the film industry); Alex Kirby is an HIV/AIDS counselor; Trey, an anesthesiologist; and Ricky, the owner of an exclusive clothing store.

Cast: Darryl Stephens (Noah Nicholson), Rodney Chester (Alex Kirby), Christian Vincent (Ricky Davis), Douglas Spearman (Chance Counter), Jensen Atwood (Wade), Gregory Keith (Trey), Jennia Fredeique (Brandy), Merwin Mondesir (Dre), Wilson Cruz (Junito). **Credits:** *Executive Producer:* Dave Mace, Eileen Opatut, Pamela Post, Patrik-Ian Polk. *Co-Executive Producer:* Carol Ann Shine. *Associate Producer:* Jason Pyne, Marisa Wahl. *Music:* Brent Belke.

990 Notes from the Underbelly.

(Comedy; ABC; April 12, 2007 to February 11, 2008)

Lauren, a guidance counselor at Oakmont High School in Los Angeles, and Andrew, a landscape architect, are a happily married couple despite the fact that Andrew believes Lauren is "a huge pain in the ass." Lauren and Andrew are in their early thirties and looking forward to (but facing all the obstacles of) their first pregnancy. They now look a life in a whole new light. Lauren is especially affected as she experiences the joys, frustrations and strange food cravings of her first pregnancy. Andrew does her every bidding. Sill she's a pain, she says, "but sometimes I can be a pain in the ass too." Cooper, a gorgeous divorce lawyer, is Lauren's closest friend; Julie and Eric are Andrew and Lauren's married friends (Julie is also pregnant); Danny is Andrew's friend, a slacker who plays piano near the escalator of the women's shoe department at Norstrom's. Stories follow the daily events that effect Lauren and Andrew's lives as they await the birth of their child (had the series been renewed, it would have also focused on both Lauren and Julie as they cope with the joys and sorrows of parenthood hood).

Cast: Jennifer Westfeldt (Lauren Stone), Peter Cambor (Andrew Stone), Rachael Harris (Cooper), Melanie Paxon (Julie), Sunrish Bala (Eric), Michael Weaver (Danny). **Credits:** *Executive Producer:* Kim Tannenbaum, Eric Tannenbaum, Barry Sonnenfeld, Stacy Traub. *Co-Executive Producer:* Gary Murphy. *Supervising Producer:* Steve Joe, Greg Schaffer. *Producer:* Lesley Wake Webster, Graham Place, Bari Halle Casnow. *Music:* Blake Neely.

991 Nova. (Documentary; PBS; Premiered: March 3, 1974)

A weekly in-depth look at a specific scientific or engineering project.

Narrator: David Ogden Stiers, John Lithgow, Hal Linden, Stacy Keach, Kathryn Walker, Neil Ross, Liev Schreiber, Gene Golusha, Will Lyman, Jeremiah Kissel, Lance Lewman, Richard Donat, Robert Krulwich. **Credits:** *Executive Producer:* Paula Aspell, Marty Johnson, Robert Maciver, Malcolm Clark, Matthew Barrett, Richard Sattin, Ben Fox, Stewart Carter. *Supervising Producer:* Beverly D'Angelo, Stephen Sweigait, Lisa D'Angelo.

992 NUMB3RS. (Crime Drama; CBS; Premiered: January 23, 2003)

Charlie Eppes is a professor of applied mathematics at Cal Tech University in California (he is also the author of the book *The Attraction Equation: The Power of Pi*). He believes that math can be used to analyze crimes to reveal patterns and predict behavior. It is and has always been a theory for Charlie until his brother, Don, an FBI agent with the Metro Bureau of Investigation in Los Angeles, decides to put his theory to the test to help him and his team solve baffling crimes. Armed with his knowledge of mathematics, Charlie sets out to prove that numbers can actually capture criminals. Other regulars are Alan, Charlie's widowed father (a former urban planner); Larry, Amita and Terry, Charlie's associates; and FBI agents David Sinclair and Megan Reeves.

Cast: Rob Morrow (Don Eppes), David Krumholtz (Charlie Eppes), Judd Hirsch (Alan Eppes), Peter MacNichol (Larry Fleinhardt), Alimi Ballard (David Sinclair), Sabrina Lloyd (Terry Lake), Diane Farr (Megan Reeves), Navi Rawat (Amita Ramanujan), Kathy Najimy (Dr. Mildred Finch), Dylan Bruno (Colby Granger), Aya Sumika (Special Agent Liz Warner). **Credits:** *Executive Producer:* Ridley Scott, Tom Scott, Barry Schindel, Brooke Kennedy. *Co-Executive Producer:* Doris Egan, Cheryl Heuton, Nicholas Falacci, Julie Herbert. *Supervising Producer:* John Behring. *Producer:* Carey Keeney, Christine Larson. *Music:* Charlie Clouser.

993 October Road. (Drama; ABC; March 15, 2007 to February 18, 2008)

Turtle on a Snare Drum is a best-selling book written by Nick Garrett. The book is a rather unflattering look at his friends and his hometown of Knights Ridge, Massachusetts, a small, picturesque New England community. One day, in the spring of 2007, Nick returns to Knights Ridge after a ten year absence (having relocated to New York City). He receives a cold reception from his old friends, who are bitter for his portrayal of them in the book. He finds that his former love, Hannah Daniels, is a single mother (of ten-year-old Sam); Ray "Big Cat" Cataldo is now the owner of a construction company (Catalo Builders); "Physical" Phil, the shy one of the group, hasn't stepped a foot outside of the town since 9/11; Eddie, his former best friend, feels they can no longer be friends; and Ikey, the last member of the close-knit group, feels he can still be friends with Nick (even though he is a bit angered that he wasn't represented in the book). Nick realizes he made a mistake. He knows there are a lot of unexpected adventures in town — and he is not about to leave again (he also believes that Sam is his son [although Hannah denies it] because he and Sam are allergic to any kind of nut). Stories follow Nick as he reacquaints himself with old friends — and new experiences for a follow-up book that is true to life and honest.

Cast: Bryan Greenberg (Nick Garrett), Laura Prepon (Hannah Daniels), Warren Christie (Ray Cataldo), Evan Jones (Ikey), Jay Paulson (Physical Phil), Geoff Stults (Eddie Latekka). **Credits:** *Executive Producer:* Scott Rosenberg, Gary Fleder, Andrew Nemec, Josh Applebaum, Peter Tortorici. *Producer:* Scott Shiffman.

994 The Office (U.S.). (Comedy; NBC; Premiered: March 24, 2005)

Dunder Mifflin is a paper supply company in Scranton, Pennsylvania. Michael Scott is the regional manager, an insensitive boss who seems to care for the welfare of his employees but tries to put his own spin on company policy (something that always causes him to get into trouble). Jim Halpert is the talented but easily bored salesman; Dwight Schrute is the kiss-up; Pamela Beesley is the receptionist who yearns to become an illustrator; Roger Howard is the easily exasperated temp. Stories are a tongue-in-cheek look at the nine-to-five white collar world and is based on the British series of the same title (see program 389).

Cast: Steve Carell (Michael Scott), Rainn Wilson (Dwight Schrute), John Krasinski (Jim Halpert), Jenna Fischer (Pamela Beesly), Angela Kinsey (Angela), Kate Flannery (Meredith), Phyllis Smith (Phyllis), B.J. Novak (Ryan Howard), Leslie David Baker (Stanley Hudson), Brian Baumgartner (Kevin), Mindy Kaling (Kelly), Melora Hardin (Jan Levinson), Rashida Jones (Karen Filippelli). **Credits:** *Executive Producer:* Greg Daniels, Benjamin Silverman. Ricky Gervais, Howard Klein, Ken Kwapis, Stephen Merchant. *Co-Executive Producer:* Paul Lieberstein, Kent Zbornak. *Producer:* Mindy Kaling, Michael Schur, Teri Weinberg. *Music:* Jay Ferguson.

995 One Life to Live. (Drama; ABC; Premiered: July 15, 1968)

An insight into life in contemporary America as seen through the experiences of the Lords, an established Philadelphia family (in the town of Lanview) entrenched in the dominant social and economic milieu.

Principal 2008 Cast: Erika Slezak (Vicki Lord Davidson), A Martinez (Ray Montez), Robin Strasser (Dorian Lord), Kristen Alderson (Starr Manning), Melissa Archer (Natalie Buchanan), Justis Bolding (Sarah Roberts), Beth Ann Bonner (Talia Sabid), Kathy Brier (Marcy Walsh McBain), Kassie DePaiv (Blair Cramer),

Andrea Evans (Tina Roberts), Farah Fath (Gigi Morasco), John Brotherton (Jared Banks), Brandon Buddy (Cole Thornbart), David Chisum (Miles Lurence), Kamar De Los Reyes (Antonio Vega), Michael Easton (John McBain), David Fumer (Crisian Vega), Brian Kerwin (Charles Banks), Mark Lawson (Brody Lovett), Jacqueline Hendy (Vanessa Montez), Hillary B. Smith (Nora Hanen), Tika Sumpter (Layla Williamson), Brittany Underwood (Langston Wilde), Bree Williams (Jessica Brennan), John-Paul Lavoisier (Rex Balsom), Trevor St. John (Todd Manning), Chris Stack (Michael McBain), Jason Tam (Markko Rivera), Jerry ver Doran (Clint Buchanan), Austin Williams (Shane Morasco), Robert S. Woods (Bo Buchanan), Janet Zarish (Janet Ketring), Timothy D. Stickney (Randall Gannon), Pamela Payton-Wright (Addie Cramer), Patricia Mauceri (Carlotta Vega), Ilene Kristen (Roxanne Balsom), Robert Krimmer (the Rev. Andrew Carpenter), Catherine Hickland (Lindsay Rappaport), Patricia Elliott (Renee Hesser), Thom Christopher (Carlo Hesser). **Credits:** *Executive Producer:* Frank Valentini. *Producer:* Suzanne Flynn, John Tumino. *Associate Producer:* Shelley Honigbaum, Jacqueline Van Belle. *Creator:* Agnes Nixon.

996 One Tree Hill. (Drama; WB/CW; Premiered: September 23, 2003)

A prime time serial about teenagers (later young adults) struggling to find their place in the world. Tree Hill, a small town in North Carolina, is the setting. It follows, in particular, the lives of Lucas and Nathan Scott, two young men with little in common until they learn a dark secret — they share the same father (Dan). The fifth season premiere (January 8, 2008) advances the story four years (to deal with the characters as young adults instead of teenagers). Particular focus is on Lucas (now a published novelist) and Brooke (a fashion designer).

Cast: Chad Michael Murray (Lucas Scott), James Lafferty (Nathan Scott), Paul Johansson (Dan Scott), Moira Kelly (Karen Roe), Bethany Joy Lenz (Peyton Elizabeth Sawyer), Sophia Bush (Brooke Penelope Davis), Barbara Alyn Woods (Deborah Helen Scott), Lee Norris (Marvin "Mouth" McFadden), Craig Sheffer (Keith Scott), Barry Corbin (Coach Whitey Durham), Cullen Moss (Junk), Vaughn Wilson (Fergie), Bryan Greenberg (Jake Jagielski), Brett Claywell (Tim Smith), Danneel Harris (Rachel Gatina), Craig Sheffer (Keith Scott), Bethany Joy Galeotti (Haley James Scott) Michael Copon (Felix Taggaro), Sheryl Lee (Ellie Harp), Stephen Coletti (Chase Adams). **Credits:** *Executive Producer:* Gregory Prange, Joe Davola, Brian Robbins, Michael Tollin, Mark Schwahn, Ann Lewis Hamilton. *Supervising Producer:* William H. Brown, Jennifer Cecil. *Producer:* Lynn Raynor, David Blake Hartley. *Music:* John E. Nordstrom, Mark Morgan, Mark Snow.

997 1 vs. 100. (Game; NBC; October 13, 2006 to February 22, 2008)

One player stands before a large set that seats 100 opponents ("The Mob"). A question, worth $1,000 is asked of the player. Three possible answers appear. Each member of the Mob selects one answer. The player verbally selects an answer. When the correct answer is revealed, the player, if correct, receives $1,000 for each Mob member who answered incorrectly. If the player is wrong, he is defeated and wins nothing (the remaining Mob members split his money). Further questions increase the money amount and the player can win $1 million if he defeats all the mob members.

Host: Bob Saget. **Credits:** *Executive Producer:* Scott St. John. *Supervising Producer:* Michael Binkow. *Music:* Groove Addicts. *Director:* R. Brian DiPirro.

998 The Oprah Winfrey Show. (Talk; Syn.; Premiered: September 1986)

Daily discussions of topical and controversial issues.

Host: Oprah Winfrey. **Credits:** *Supervising Producer:* Oprah Winfrey. *Senior Producer:* Alice McGee, Melissa Geiger. *Producer:* Jill Van Lokeren, Laura Grant Sillars, Katy Murphy Davis, Angie Kraus-Bell, Amy Craig, Kandi Amelon, Mollie Allen.

***999*   Out of Jimmy's Head.** (Comedy; Cartoon Network; September 14, 2007 to May 29, 2008)

To save the life of Jimmy Roberts after he is injured by the train ride at the Gollywood Theme Park, doctors give him the brain of the late Milt Appleby, a famous cartoonist. Soon afterward, Jimmy's life becomes complicated when he is able to see and speak to cartoon characters created by Milt (Tux the Penguin, Dolly and Golly Gopher and Crocco the Alligator). Louise (an astronaut) and Ken (a counselor at the Greater Burbank Middle School) are Jimmy's parents; Yancy, a green alien adopted by Louise, is Jimmy's sister; Sonny is Milt's deranged son (seeking to reclaim his father's brain). Stories follow Jimmy as he attempts to live a normal life despite the antics of the cartoon characters that only he can see.

Cast: Dominic Janes (Jimmy Roberts), Rachel Quintana (Louise Roberts), Bill Dwyer (Ken Roberts), Rhea Lando (Yancy), Matt Knudsen (Sonny Appleby), Jonathan Ethridge (Craig Wheeler). **Voices:** Tom Kenny (Tux), Ellen Greene (Dolly), Brian Posehn (Crocco), Carlos Alazraqui (Golly). **Credits:** *Executive Producer:* David Brookwell, Sean McNamara, Adam Pava, Timothy McKeon, Eric Kaplan, Bruce Hurwit. *Producer:* Pixie Wespiser. *Music:* Paul Buckley.

***1000*   Pageant Place.** (Reality; MTV; October 10, 2007 to May 29, 2008)

Viewers are taken behind the scenes of a beauty pageant to see what occurs as contestants for Miss Teen U.S.A., Miss U.S.A. and Miss Universe become housemates as they await to compete in the various competitions.

Stars: Katie Blair, Tara Elizabeth Conner, Hilary Cruz, Riyo Mori, Rachel Smith. **Credits:** *Executive Producer:* Donald Trump, Andy Litinsky, Kathleen French, Douglas Ross, Paula Shugart, Greg Stewart. *Producer:* Alex Baskin.

***1001*   Pale Force.** (Cartoon; Internet; Premiered: September 15, 2005)

Comedian Jim Gaffigan and talk show host Conan O'Brien are seen in animated form as crime fighters Jim and Conan, super heroes who are members of the Legion of Pale (an organization through which its members fight evil with the power of paleness). Stories follow Jim, the heroic, muscular hero, and his somewhat wimpy sidekick as they battle to protect the city from evil (most notably Lady Bronze and Philip Seymour Hoffman).

Voice Cast: Jim Gaffigan (Jim/Conan/Philip Seymour Hoffman), Eartha Kitt (Lady Bronze). **Credits:** *Producer:* Jim Gaffigan, Paul Noth. *Music:* Patrick Noth. *Writer:* Jim Gaffigan, Paul Noth. *Director:* Paul Noth.

***1002*   Paradise Falls.** (Drama; Here!; 2001–2008)

Paradise Falls is a small resort in a lakeside town that appears to be a quiet vacation resort. Its roadside sign reads "Welcome to Paradise Falls Where It's Hot and Steamy All Year Round." It is also unusual in that it caters to gays and lesbians. Stories relate events in the lives of the people who find romance, intrigue and lust at the exclusive resort. The specialized series airs on the gay network Here! and contains explicit gay and lesbian love scenes.

Cast: Art Hindle (Mayor Peter Braga), Chantal Quesnel (Yvonne Bernini), Tammy Isbell (Rose Bernini), Victoria Snow (Francis Hunter), Cameron Graham (Nick Braga), Dixie Seatle (Bea Sutton), Michelle Latimer (Trish Simpkin), Kim Poirier

(Roxy Hunter), Kim Schraner (Jessica Lansing), Jim Thorburn (Michael Mansfield), Robert Seeliger (Jeff Bradshaw), Andrew Gillies (Stanley Mansfield), Marni Thompson (Valerie Hunter), Joshua Peace (Samuel Sutton), Steve Cumyn (Tony Beroni), Cherilee Taylor (Pamela Harman), Allen Altman (Billy Hunter), Alan Van Sprang (Johnny Brice), Kate Trotter (Anne Sutton). **Credits:** *Executive Producer:* Ira Levy, Peter Williamson. *Producer:* Paula J. Smith. *Music:* Eric Cadesky, Nick Dyer.

1003   **Paranormal State**. (Reality; A&E; December 10, 2007 to October 27, 2008)

The Penn State Paranormal Research Society of Penn State College, headed by its founder, Ryan Buell, investigates reports of ghostly happenings (with cameras capturing what they see — and don't see).

Host: Ryan Buell. **Credits:** *Executive Producer:* Gary Auerbach, Julie Auerbach, Betsy Schechter. *Co-Executive Producer:* Drew Brown, Tina Gazzerro, Alan LaGrande, David Miller. *Producer:* Stephanie Dervan, Autumn Humphreys. *Director:* Bradley Beasley.

1004   **Parental Control**. (Reality; MTV; Premiered: February 6, 2006)

A twist on the normal dating shows wherein the parents get to choose whom their son or daughter will date. Each of the teens that appear has a date that is unacceptable to their parents. Each parent (of a son or daughter) is presented with a group of boys or girls who meet the standards of what they feel are acceptable dates for their children. When each parent makes a selection, they are brought face to face with their child and present their choices. The child can select the one chosen by the father or mother or keep the date he or she currently has.

Credits: *Executive Producer:* Michael Canter. *Co-Executive Producer:* Bruce Klas-

sen, H.T. Owens. *Producer:* Liz Givens, Ben Hatta.

1005   **Party Heat**. (Reality; Court TV/Tru TV; Premiered: October 1, 2007)

College students on spring break or summer holiday are the focus of a program that shows their reckless side and the chaos they cause mixing the sun, the beach and alcohol. Also featured is the work of the emergency personnel who intervene to save lives.

Credits: *Executive Producer:* Lee Elman. *Producer:* Mark August, Duncan Brinkhurst, David Gelbart, Christopher O'Dowd.

1006   **Party Mamas**. (Reality; WE; Premiered: March 3, 2007)

A look at out-of-control mothers who plan extravagant (if not outrageous) parties for their children.

Credits: *Executive Producer:* Laszlo Barna, Steve Silver. *Producer:* Phyllis Newman, Susan Tonna. *Music:* Jack Lenz.

1007   **Paula's Home Cooking**. (Cooking; Food Network; Premiered: November 16, 2002)

Restaurant owner and cookbook author Paula Deen prepares Southern style meals.

Host: Paula Deen. **Credits:** *Executive Producer:* Sandy Green, Gordon Elliott. *Supervising Producer:* Aimee Rosen. *Producer:* Jevon Bruh. *Music:* David Ryan.

1008   **Paula's Party**. (Cooking; Food Network; Premiered: January 12, 2006)

Chef Paula Deen prepares meals, in front of a live studio audience, that are based in Southern cuisine.

Host: Paula Deen. **Credits:** *Executive Producer:* Gordon Elliott, Mark Schneider. *Producer:* Aimee Rosen, Stacy Rader, Shari B. Lampert.

1009   **Peep in the Big Wide World**. (Children; PBS; Premiered: October 1, 2004)

Peep is a young yellow bird that is

anxious to learn about life. As he travels throughout the forest he encounters the various animals that inhabit it. Stories, which relate learning aspects to children, follow Peep as he discovers the wonders of nature.

Voice Cast: Scott Beaudin (Peep), Joan Cusack (Narrator). **Credits:** *Executive Producer:* Jessica Hanlon, Kate Taylor. *Supervising Producer:* Melinda Toporoff. *Producer:* Marissa Wolsky. *Music:* Terry Tompkins.

1010   Penn and Teller: B.S. (Comedy; Showtime; January 24, 2003 to August 22, 2008)

Magicians Penn and Teller take to the airwaves to expose services, products or ideas that are just foolish but sucker people into them.

Cast: Penn Jillette (Himself), Teller (Himself). **Credits:** *Executive Producer:* Mark Wolper, Eric Small, Randall Moldave, Star Price. *Co-Executive Producer:* Peter Adam Golden, Michael Goudeau, Jon Hotchkiss, Penn Jillette, Teller. *Producer:* Aaron Yampolski, June Molgaard. *Music:* Gary Stockdale.

1011   The People's Court. (Reality; Syn.; Premiered: September 1981)

Real people fight real legal battles before a real judge in a California Municipal Court. The series, with Judge Joseph Wapner was based in California. When the series was revised for syndication (1997) with former New York Mayor Ed Koch as the judge, the series was videotaped in New York and switched from a 30 minute to a 60 minute format.

Cast: Judge Joseph A. Wapner (Himself), Judge Ed Koch (Himself), Judge Jerry Sheindlin (Himself), Judge Marilyn Milian (Herself). **Credits:** *Executive Producer:* Stu Billett, David Scott. *Supervising Producer:* Phil Vandervort, Beth Geddes, Jill Gould. *Producer:* Liz Marley, Monique Gallo, Michelle Meyd, Ralph Edwards.

1012   Perfect Hair Forever. (Cartoon; Cartoon Network; Premiered: November 20, 2005)

A spoof of Japanese animated series (Anime) as seen through the adventures of Gerald, a young boy who, for unknown reasons, is starting to lose his hair. With the help of Rod, the Anime God and his mentor, Uncle Grandfather, Gerald begins a quest to find a cure called Perfect Hair Forever. Aired on the Adult Swim segment of Cartoon Network.

Voice Cast: Kim Manning (Gerald), Dave Willis (Uncle Grandfather), H. Jon Benjamin (Twisty), Dave Willis (Coffio). **Credits:** *Executive Producer:* Michael Lazzo. *Producer:* Dave Willis, Matt Harrigan, Dave Hughes.

1013   The Pick-Up Artist. (Reality; VH-1; August 6, 2007 to November 30, 2008)

Eight men who lack certain social skills, are brought together and taught the art of picking up girls by Mystery, a best-selling author ("A social misfit turned seducer extraordinaire"). With the help of his coaches, Matador and J Dog, Mystery seeks one man to become a woman seducer called "Master Pick-Up Artist."

Host: Master V. **Credits:** *Executive Producer:* J.D. Roth, Adam Greener, Richard Hall, Todd A. Nelson. *Producer:* Angela Molby, Annie Imhoff.

1014   Platinum Weddings. (Reality; WE; July 23, 2006 to August 17, 2008)

A look at wealthy couples who plan not only extravagant but weddings that would break the banks of small nations.

Credits: *Executive Producer:* Nancy Miller. *Supervising Producer:* Melissa Stokes. *Producer:* Amanda Crane, Krista Van Nieuwburg.

1015   The Power of 10. (Game; CBS; August 7, 2007 to January 23, 2008)

A game based on a national poll and how Americans responded to specific questions. Two players compete. The player who comes closest to predicting the national average of a question asked wins (in round one, $1,000). This amount is increased ten fold for each additional question ($10,000, $100,000, $1 million and $10 million). Players risk loss of everything if they make an incorrect prediction.

Host: Drew Carey. **Credits:** *Executive Producer:* Michael Davies. *Co-Executive Producer:* Vincent Rubino. *Producer:* Erica Walsh. *Director:* Mark Gentile. *Music:* Lewis Finn.

1016 **The Price Is Right**. (Game; CBS; Premiered: September 4, 1972)

The game varies greatly in presentation but the basic format calls for contestants to guess the manufacturer's suggested retail price for various merchandise.

Host: Drew Carey. **Announcer:** Rich Fields. **Models:** Lanisha Cole, Brandi Sherwood, Phire Dawson, Gabrielle Tuite. **Credits:** *Executive Producer:* Mark Goodson, Bill Todman, Philip W. Rossi, Frank Wayne, Syd Vinnedge, Bob Barker. *Producer:* Philip W. Rossi, Jay Wolpert, Roger Dobkowitz. *Music:* Ed Kalehoff, Sheila Cole, James Patrick Dunne, Michael Karp.

1017 **The Prince of Tennis**. (Cartoon; Cartoon Network; Premiered: October 10, 2001)

Ryoma Echizen is a 12-year-old boy and tennis prodigy. He is known for his "twist serve" and is a member of the Seishun Gakuen Middle School Tennis Team. The Japanese produced series is a coming-of-age story that follows Ryoma, called "The Prince of Tennis," as he trains and competes in tournaments.

Voice Cast: David Neil Black (Ryoma Echizen), Jack Butler (Sadoharu Inui), Kirk Thornton (Kunimitsu Tezuka), Barbara Goodson (Sumire Ryazaki), Doug Ertholtz (Takeshi).

1018 **Prison Break**. (Drama; Fox; Premiered: August 29, 2005)

Season one follows the step-by-step planning of a prison escape as structural engineer Michael Scofield attempts to free his half-brother, Lincoln Burrows (falsely accused of killing the U.S. Vice President's brother) from the Fox River State Penitentiary (he begins by getting himself arrested [attempting to rob a bank]. By luck, he is sentenced to Fox River. Suspenseful stories chart their efforts). Second season episodes, subtitled "Manhunt," follow Michael and Lincoln's efforts to avoid capture after successfully escaping from Fox River. The third season finds Michael being imprisoned for a shooting after he and Lincoln flee to Panama. Now, with the tables turned, Lincoln must find a way to free Michael from an inhumane prison (Sona) that "is a one-way street — what goes in never comes out — unless it's dead." During this time it is learned that the Company, a shadowy, heartless organization, had infiltrated the government and framed Lincoln. The fourth season does away with the prison aspect and charts Michael and Lincoln's efforts to bring down the Company.

Cast: Dominic Purcell (Lincoln Burrows), Wentworth Miller (Michael Scofield), Sarah Wayne Callies (Dr. Sara Tancredi), Amaury Nolasco (Fernando Sucre), Robert Knepper (Theodore "T-Bag" Bagwell), Wade Williams (Bradley Bellick), William Fichtner (Alexander Mahone), Paul Adelstein (Paul Kellerman), Marshall Allman (L.J. Burrows), Rockmond Dunbar (Benjamin Miles "C-Note" Franklin), Jodi Lyn O'Keefe (Gretchen Morgan), Robin Tunney (Veronica Donovan), Stacy Keach (Warden Henry Pope), Leon Russom (Gen. Jonathan Katz), Philip Edward Van Lear (Louis Patterson), Peter Stormare (John Abruzzi), Muse Watson (Charles Westmoreland), Frank Grillo (Nick Savrinn), Jason Davis (Agent Wheeler), Patricia Wettig (Vice Pres. Caroline Reynolds), Barbara Eve Harris (FBI Agent Lang), Michael Rapaport (Donald Self),

Reggie Lee (Bill Kim), Matt DeCaro (Roy Geary), Chris Vance (James Whistler), Danay Garcia (Sofia Lugo), Lane Garrison (David "Tweener" Apolsksi), DuShon Monique Brown (Nurse Katie Welch), Silas Weir Mitchell (Charles "Haywire" Patoshik). **Credits:** *Executive Producer:* Paul Scheuring, Marty Adelstein, Dawn Parouse, Matt Olstead, Brett Ratner. *Co-Executive Producer:* Michael Watkins. *Supervising Producer:* Zach Estrin. *Producer:* Garry Brown, Nick Santora. *Music:* Ramin Djawadi.

***1019* Private Practice**. (Drama; ABC; Premiered: September 26, 2007)

A spin off from *Grey's Anatomy* that focuses on Addison Forbes Montgomery, a doctor at Seattle Grace Hospital who leaves Seattle after her marriage breaks up to begin a practice in California at the Oceanside Wellness Center in Santa Monica. Here, she joins with Naomi and Sam Bennett, her friends from medical school (Naomi is a fertility and hormone specialist; Sam is an internist and medical book author — "the common man's medical guru." They are divorced but co-exist for the sake of their teenage daughter, Maya). Dr. Cooper Freedman is the center's resident physician; Dr. Violet Turner is the unit's psychiatrist; Dr. Peter Wilder is the alternative medicine specialist; William Dell Parker is the co-op receptionist; Charlotte King is the chief of staff at the nearby St. Ambrose Hospital. Stories follow the work of the doctors attached to the Wellness Center.

Cast: Kate Walsh (Dr. Addison Forbes Montgomery), Amy Brenneman (Dr. Violet Turner), Tim Daly (Dr. Peter Wilder), Audra McDonald (Dr. Naomi Bennett), Paul Adelstein (Dr. Cooper Freedman), KaDee Strickland (Dr. Charlotte King), Chris Lowell (William Dell Parker), Taye Diggs (Dr. Sam Bennett). **Credits:** *Executive Producer:* Betsy Beers, Shonda Rhimes, Mark Gordow, Mark Tinker, Marti

Noxon. *Co-Executive Producer:* Andrea Newman. *Supervising Producer:* Michael Ostrowski. *Producer:* Jenna Bans, Ann Kindberg. *Music:* Chad Fischer, Timothy Bright.

***1020* Private Sessions**. (Profile; A&E; Premiered: July 22, 2007)

Personal profiles of contemporary musicians (from pop to country and western). Each program is devoted to one performer and features in-depth interviews and exclusive performances.

Host: Lynn Hoffman. **Credits:** *Executive Producer:* Thomas Moody. *Senior Producer:* Nicholas Van Hoogstraten. *Producer:* Lilsa Lunden, Scott Kerbey.

***1021* Project Runway**. (Reality; Bravo/Lifetime; December 1, 2004 to October 15, 2008)

Up and coming fashion designers compete for a coveted spot in the New York Fashion Show. Each contestant competes in a weekly competition and is seen preparing models and associated problems as the big day approaches. The designer with the best presentation is the winner. The series moved from Bravo to Lifetime on July 8, 2008.

Host: Heidi Klum, Tim Gunn. **Credits:** *Executive Producer:* Heidi Klum, Bob Weinstein, Harvey Weinstein, Frances Berwick, Rich Bye, Jane Chan, Dan Cutforth, Desiree Gruber, Shari Levine, Jane Lipsitz, Andrew Cohen. *Co-Executive Producer:* Dwight D. Smith, Michael Agnabian, Rich Buhrman. *Supervising Producer:* Alexandra Lipsitz, Gayle Gawlowski. *Producer:* Sebastian Doggart, Noel A. Guerra, Eli Holzman, Jennifer Berman, Michael Rucker, Andrew Wallace, Benjamin Mack. *Music:* Harold Sanders III, Biff Sanders.

***1022* Prom Queen**. (Drama; Internet; Premiered: April 2, 2007)

A look at the senior class of Edward Adams High School — a class whose students are preparing for the prom but during which time secrets threaten to destroy friendships and have adverse effects on the five girls who are competing for prom queen. See also *Prom Queen: Summer Heat*.

Cast: Katy Stoll (Sadie), Sean Hankinson (Ben), Laura Howard (Danica), Alexandra French (Nikki), Haley Mancini (Lauren), David Loren (Chad), Jake Shideler (Josh), Andre Boyer (Brett), Sheila Vand (Courtney), Amy Kay Raymond (Jill), Kateland Carr (Michele). **Credits:** *Executive Producer:* Chris Hampel, Douglas Cheney, Chris McCaleb, Ryan Wise, Michael Eisner. *Producer:* Danielle Turchiano, Laura Boersma. *Associate Producer:* Matthew Besinger. *Music:* Jim McKeever.

1023 Prom Queen: Summer Heat. (Drama; Internet; Premiered: August 27, 2007)

A spin-off from *Prom Queen* that follows students from Edward Adams High School as they seek to escape the mysteries that haunted them in high school by retreating to Mexico for their summer vacation.

Cast: Katy Stoll (Sadie), Sean Hankinson (Ben), Laura Howard (Danica), Alexandra French (Nikki), Angela Arimento (Marisol), Jake Shideler (Josh). **Credits:** *Executive Producer:* Michael Eisner, Chris Hampel. *Producer:* Danielle Turchiano. *Music:* Jim McKeever.

1024 Psych. (Crime Drama; USA; Premiered: July 7, 2006)

Shawn Spencer is a man with phenomenal powers of observation. As early as he can remember, Shawn was taught how to think, act and observe like a detective. Rather than put his talents to use in a productive way, like becoming a police officer like his father (Henry), Shawn becomes somewhat of a slacker, taking random jobs to get by. Though he is not a cop, Shawn is fascinated by crime scenes and studies such scenes he reads about in the newspaper or sees on TV. When he realizes he has found something that was overlooked, he calls the police with a tip because nothing escapes his razor sharp mind. One tip, however, backfires and Shawn is arrested as the prime suspect. Although he has no actual clairvoyant abilities and cannot read the future, he convinces the police that he is a psychic. Impressed by his "abilities," the police department hires Shawn as a consultant to help them solve difficult cases (he also opens an agency called Psych to help people). Assisting Shawn is Burton "Gus" Guster, his friend, a pharmaceutical salesman (for Central Coast Pharmaceuticals) who helps Shawn keep out of trouble.

Cast: James Roday (Shawn Spencer), Dule Hill (Burton "Gus" Guster), Corbin Bernsen (Henry Spencer), Kristen Nelson (Chief Vick), Timothy Omundson (Detective Lassiter), Maggie Lawson (Juliet). **Credits:** *Executive Producer:* Steve Franks, Chris Henze, Kelly Kulchak. *Co-Executive Producer:* Mel Damski. *Producer:* Tracey Jeffrey. *Music:* John Robert Wood, Adam Cohen.

1025 Punk'd. (Comedy; MTV; Premiered: March 1, 2003)

Candid Camera–like program in which hidden cameras capture the reactions of celebrities who become the innocent victims of practical jokes.

Host: Ashton Kutcher. **Pranksters:** Ashton Kutcher, Julia Wolov, Whitney Cummings, Rob Pue, Chris Ellwood. **Credits:** *Executive Producer:* Ashton Kutcher, Billy Rainey, Gary Auerbach, Lois Curren, David Franke. *Co-Executive Producer:* Patrick Byrnes. *Supervising Producer:* Selene Hinojosa. *Producer:* Andy Weiss, Michael Polan, Rob Weiss.

1026 Pushing Daisies. (Fantasy; ABC; October 3, 2007 to December 17, 2008)

As a youngster Ned lived a mostly carefree life. He enjoyed running in the fields with his dog, Digby, and at the age of nine had a crush on eight-year-old Charlotte Charles, whom he called "Chuck." One day, Digby was hit by a truck and Ned's life would change forever. He touched the dog and, to his surprise, brought him back to life. But his special gift — which Ned cannot explain, has a serious side effect. A second touch will return the deceased back to being dead. And, if Ned keeps a deceased alive for longer than sixty seconds, someone else must take his or her place. As Ned grows, he becomes fearful of his "gift" and somewhat of a loner. He becomes a baker and establishes his own business — The Pie Hole. One night, a criminal being chased by private detective Emerson Cod, attempts to jump across a rooftop but falls to his death. Cod witnesses Ned's ability when Ned touches the criminal, brings him to life, then touches him again. Cod finds Ned very useful and the two form a business partnership — Ned can touch a victim, bring him back to life, ask who killed him, touch him again then solve the case. A short time later, while watching TV, Ned sees a report about a woman being killed on a cruise ship. When her name is revealed as Charlotte Charles, Ned makes it his business to restore her life to find out who killed her. But Ned lets Chuck live — a situation that finds Ned, who still loves Chuck, never able to touch her and she never able to touch him (it is revealed that Chuck was mistaken for a diamond smuggler and killed). Ned, Chuck and Cod become a team to solve murders by asking the victims to identify their killers. Lily and Vivian are Chuck's aunts; Olive is Ned's waitress.

Cast: Lee Pace (Ned), Anna Friel (Charlotte "Chuck" Charles), Chi McBride (Emerson Cod), Swoosie Kurtz (Lily Charles), Ellen Greene (Vivian Charles), Kristin Chenoweth (Olive Snook), Jim Dale (Narrator), Field Carter (Young Ned). **Credits:** *Executive Producer:* Barry Sonnenfeld, Brooke Kennedy, Bruce

Cohen, Bryan Fuller, Dan Jinks. *Co-Executive Producer:* Rina Mimoun, Peter Ocko. *Producer:* Adam Kane, Dylan K. Massin. *Music:* James Dooley.

1027   Queen of Clubs. (Erotica; Playboy Channel; Premiered: 2004)

A striptease competition in which gorgeous women bare all and compete for the title of "Queen of Clubs." Contestants chosen for their obvious attributes, participate in various challenges (mostly how to be alluring and sexy while disrobing) with the one girl showing how to take it off and maintain an aura of sexuality that does not become vulgar, winning the competition. The hosts are joined by celebrity guests to judge the competition.

Hosts: Crystal Knight, Gloria Velez.

1028   The Rachael Ray Show. (Talk; Syn.; Premiered: September 2006)

Cook book author and Food Network show host Rachael Ray oversees a lively program of celebrity interviews, chatter, music and cooking segments.

Hostess: Rachael Ray. **Credits:** *Executive Producer:* Janet Annino. *Supervising Producer:* Shane Farley, Marilyn Zilinski. *Producer:* Steve Cunniffi, Stephanie Gholam, Robin Hommel, Jennifer Givner-Stone, Andrew Goldman, Meredith Weintraub.

1029   Rachael Ray's Tasty Travels. (Reality; Food Network; Premiered: August 26, 2005)

Talk show host and cookbook author Rachael Ray travels across the U.S. to find the best places to eat. The series is also known as *Rachael's Vacation*.

Host: Rachael Ray. **Credits:** *Executive Producer:* Jennifer Davidson, Gary H. Grossman, Rachael Ray, Tara Sandler, Wade Sheeler. *Supervising Producer:* Wade Sheeler, Laura Metzger. *Producer:* Scott Templeton.

1030   Radio Free Roscoe. (Comedy; The N; Premiered: August 1, 2003)

Robbie (a.k.a Question Mark), Lily (Shady Lane), Ray (Pronto) and Travis (Smog) are teenagers who attend Roscoe High School. Like most people their age, they love listening to the radio. However, finding what they like becomes a chore and Robbie hits on an idea to start their own radio station RFR (Radio Free Roscoe), an underground station that broadcasts what teenagers want to hear. Stories follow the group's efforts to avoid exposure and secretly run the station.

Cast: Hugolin Chevrette Landesque (Robbie McGrath), Kate Todd (Lily Randall), Ali Mukoddam (Ray Brennan), Nathan Carter (Travis Strong), Victoria Nestorowicz (Parker Haynes), Hamish McEwan (Principal Waller), Genelle Williams (Kim Carlisle), Ashley Newbrough (Audrey Quinlan). **Credits:** *Executive Producer:* Steve DeNure, Doug McRobb, Neil Court, Will McRobb, Beth Stevenson. *Supervising Producer:* Brent Piaskoski. *Producer:* Barry Orr. *Music:* Jim Swanson, Dave Cribbs, Josh Lowe.

1031   Rap City. (Music; BET; September 1989 to October 2008)

A showcase for hip hop artists (by showcasing their music videos) that helped to establish the current popularity of rap music.

Hosts: Hans Dobson, Prime, Chris Thomas, Joe Clair, Leslie Segar, Tigger. **Credits:** *Producer:* Theron Smith, Todd 1, Malik K. Buie, Joslyn Rose Lyons.

1032   Real Housewives. (Reality; Bravo; Premiered: March 21, 2006)

A reality program that claims to present an honest look at the lives of real housewives and how they live their everyday lives. What actually results is a look at very special housewives — rich and spoiled women who are anything but representative of real American housewives. Three versions have aired: *The Real Housewives of Orange County, The Real Housewives of New York* and *The Real Housewives of Atlanta.*

Cast (Orange County): Vicki Gunvalson, Kimberly Bryant, Lauri Waring, Jeana Tomasina, Jo De La Rosa, Tamra Barney, Gretchen Rossi. **Cast (New York):** Lu Ann de Lesseps, Jill Zarin, Bethenny Frankel, Ramona Singer, Alex McCord. **Cast (Atlanta):** DeShawn Snow, Kim Zolciak, Lisa Wu Hartwell, NeNe Leakes, Sheree Whitfield. **Credits (Orange County):** *Executive Producer:* Greg Stewart, David Rupel, Douglas Ross, Patrick Moses, Scott Dunlop, Kathleen French, Kevin Kaufman, Dean Minerd. *Supervising Producer:* Peter Tartaglia. *Producer:* Brad Isenberg. **Credits (New York):** *Executive Producer:* Nick Emerson, Jennifer O'Connell. *Co-Executive Producer:* Lenid Rolov, Kirsty Robson. *Supervising Producer:* Barrie Bernstein. *Producer:* Keira Brings. **Credits (Atlanta):** *Executive Producer:* Steven Weinstock, Glenda Hersh, Shari Solomon Ledar, Kenny Hull. *Co-Executive Producer:* Lauren Eskelin. *Supervising Producer:* Alfonzo Wesson.

1033   Real Time with Bill Maher. (Talk; HBO; February 21, 2003 to November 11, 2008)

Comedian and political satirist Bill Maher and a panel of three guest celebrities discuss the current political scene. Monologues and skits are coupled with insightful conversation.

Host: Bill Maher. **Credits:** *Executive Producer:* Scott Carter, Brad Grey, Sheila Griffiths, Marc Gurvitz. *Co-Executive Producer:* Billy Martin, Dean E. Johnsen.

1034   The Real World. (Reality; MTV; Premiered: May 21, 1992)

Seven people in their twenties (and from different countries and backgrounds) are brought together to live with each other and share experiences.

Credits: *Executive Producer:* Mary-Ellis Bunim, Jonathan Murray. *Supervising Producer:* Matt Kunitz, Tracy Chaplin. *Producer:* Russell Heldt, Anthony Dominici.

Music: Damian McDonald, Christopher Brady.

1035   Reaper. (Drama; CW; September 25, 2007 to August 26, 2008)

The twenty-first birthday for Sam Oliver, a clerk at a home improvement center called The Work Bench, is anything but normal. He learns that before his birth his parents sold his soul to the Devil. At this time Sam's father was gravely ill. The Devil appeared to him and his wife and offered them a deal: his health for their unborn child's soul. They accepted and now Sam, at first reluctant to abide by what his parents did, agrees to work for the Devil as a reaper, a bounty hunter who tracks down and returns dangerous, escaped souls to Hell (if Sam had refused, the Devil would claim his mother's soul). To help Sam accomplish his missions, the Devil provides him with a vessel (for example, a super-powered vacuum cleaner) to capture the fugitives (Sam then brings the captured soul to the Department of Motor Vehicles where Gladys, a good demon, transports them back to Hell). Sam tells his friends at work, Bert (called Sock) and Ben and stories relate their efforts to do the Devil's bidding. Andi, who also works with Sam, later learns Sam's secret and joins the team. Josie is Sock's ex-girlfriend, a paralegal; Kyle is Sam's brother.

Cast: Bret Harrison (Sam Oliver), Tyler Labine (Bert "Sock" Wysocki), Missy Peregrym (Andi), Ray Wise (Devil), Valarie Rae Miller (Josie), Rick Gonzalez (Ben), Christine Willes (Gladys). **Credits:** *Executive Producer:* Tara Butters, Michele Fazekas, Mark Gordon, Tom Spezialy, Deborah Spera. *Co-Executive Producer:* David Babcock. *Supervising Producer:* Jeff Vlaming. *Producer:* Peter Lauer, Joseph Patrick Finn. *Music:* David Schwartz.

1036   Recipe for Success. (Reality; Food Network; Premiered: April 1, 2004)

People who are risking all they have to start a food-based business are profiled.

Host: Eric McLendon, Marlie Hill. **Credits:** *Executive Producer:* Al Roker. *Producer:* Victoria Bert, Nicole DeWalt.

1037   Reel Talk. (Reviews; Syn.; Premiered: September 2005)

A weekly review of current feature films and the latest information on DVD releases.

Hosts: Jeffrey Lyons, Alison Bailes. **Interviewer:** Ben Lyons. **Credits:** *Producer:* Michael Avila.

1038   Re-Genesis. (Crime Drama; Syn.; Premiered: September 2006)

C.S.I. like series about David Sandstrom, the head of NorBAC (the North American Bio-Technology Advisory Committee), a group of Canadian-based scientists who use technology to determine the how of dangerous situations that develop.

Cast: Peter Outerbridge (David Sandstrom), Mayko Nguyen (Mayko Tran), Wendy Crewson (Rachel Woods), Dimitry Chepovetsky (Bob Melnikov), Sarah Strange (Jill Langston), Greg Bryk (Weston Field), Macine Roy (Caroline Morrison). **Credits:** *Executive Producer:* Tom Chehak, Christina Jennings. *Producer:* Christina Jennings, Virginia Rankin, Scott Garvie. *Co-Producer:* Laura Harbin, Shane Kinnear. *Music:* Thom Thirx.

1039   Reno 911. (Comedy; Comedy Central; Premiered: July 23, 2003)

A mostly improvised series that takes a behind-the-scenes look at the operations of the Washow County Division of the Reno, Nevada Police Department. Crime is played for laughs as Lt. Jim Dangle finds everything but by-the-books procedures from his mayhem making officers (who include Raineesha Williams, the sassy African-American deputy; James Garcia, the hot-headed Latino deputy; Clementine Johnson, the slutty blonde officer; and Trudy Wiegel, the lonely deputy who confides her feelings to the camera and speaks directly to the audience).

Cast: Thomas Lennon (Lt. Jim Dangle), Kerri Kenney (Deputy Trudy Wiegel), Nicey Nash (Deputy Raineesha Williams), Robert Ben Garant (Deputy Travis Junior), Carlos Alazraqui (Deputy James Garcia), Wendi McLendon-Covey (Deputy Clementine Johnson), Mary Birdsong (Deputy Cheresa Kimball), Cedric Yarbrough (Deputy S. Jones), Wendi McLendon-Lovey (Deputy Clementine Johnson), Mary Birdsong (Deputy Cherisha Kimball). **Credits:** *Executive Producer:* Danny DeVito, Robert Ben Garant, Kerri Kenney, Thomas Lennon. *Co-Executive Producer:* Peter Principato, Paul Young. *Producer:* Penny Adams, Karen Thornton. *Music:* Stephen Phillips.

1040 **The Replacements**. (Cartoon; Disney; Premiered: September 8, 2006)

Todd and Riley are futuristic orphans who are rarely happy. One day they see and ad for Fleemco Replacements, a company that will replace what ever needs replacing. The children send in their money and request replacement parents. What they get are Agent K, "a super spy mom," and Dick Daring, "a daredevil dude of a dad." Stories follow Todd and Riley's adventures as they replace anything that causes them unhappiness.

Voice Cast: Nancy Cartwright (Todd), Grey DeLisle (Riley), Kath Soucie (Agent K), Daran Norris (Dick Daring), David McCallum (C.A.R.), Jeff Bennett (Conrad Fleem). **Credits:** *Executive Producer:* Jack Thomas. *Producer:* Natasha Kopp. *Music:* Jason Frederick, Darian Sahanaja.

1041 **Rescue Me**. (Drama; FX; Premiered: July 21, 2004)

A grueling, realistic series that looks at the work of the men of Engine Company 62, a division of the New York City Fire Department.

Cast: Denis Leary (Tommy Gavin), Andrea Roth (Janet Gavin), Jack McGee (Jerry Reilly), Daniel Sunjata (Franco Rivera), James McCaffrey (Jimmy Keefe),

Michael Lombardi (Mike Silletti), Steve Pasquale (Sean Garrity), John Seurti (Kenny Shea), Diane Farr (Laura Miles), Charles Durning (Tommy's father), Susan Sarandon (Alicia), Tatum O'Neal (Maggie). **Credits:** *Executive Producer:* Denis Leary, Jim Serpico, Peter Tolan. *Producer:* Kerry Orent, Alyson Evans, Salvatore Stabile, Tom Sellitti. *Music:* Christopher Tyng.

1042 **Rescue Mediums**. (Reality; WE; Premiered: September 8, 2007)

Jackie Dennison and Christine Hamlett are internationally known psychics who call themselves "Rescue Mediums" (they help people with ghostly problems). Episodes follow the mediums as they make house calls to ask spirits "to kindly leave."

Stars: Jackie Dennison, Christine Hamlett.

1043 **Restaurant Makeover**. (Reality; TLC; Premiered: October 2, 2005)

Rundown restaurants are given a makeover (to bring them back to their former glory) by a team of chefs and renovators.

Chefs: David Adjey, Lynne Crawford. **Designers:** Robin DeGroot, Meredith Heron. **Credits:** *Executive Producer:* Andrea Gorfolova. *Producer:* LeAnne Armano, Shaam Makam. *Associate Producer:* Dana Speers.

1044 **Rich Bride, Poor Bride**. (Reality; WE; Premiered: March 3, 2007)

A behind-the-scenes look at the preparations that go into producing the perfect wedding — and staying within the budget planned by each couple.

Credits: *Executive Producer:* Sean Buckley. *Supervising Producer:* Patricia Hollinger. *Producer:* Jim Kiriakakis. *Associate Producer:* Jennifer Couke, Misty Tyson. *Music:* Graeme Cornies, Dave Kelly, Brian L. Pickett, James Chapple.

1045 **The Riches**. (Drama; FX; March 12, 2007 to April 29, 2008)

The Malloys are a backwoods Louisiana

family who live in a motor home and survive on scams as they make their way across the South. Wayne, the father, is a master thief; Dahlia, his wife, is addicted to drugs; Cael, Di Di and Sam are their children. Cael, 17 years old, is a whiner; Di Di, 16, is like her mother — hot to trot (but not hooked on drugs); Sam is somewhat insecure. Life changes for the family when their RV runs a car off the road and, in the ensuing crash, the wealthy couple in the car, the Riches, are killed. Wayne hits on the idea of assuming their identities and living the good life (with Wayne assuming the role of corporate lawyer in a real estate firm). Improbable stories follow the Malloys, now the Riches, as they experience the pitfalls of the glamorous life in Edenfalls (as well as their struggles to keep their real identities a secret). Dale is Dahlia's cousin; Hugh is Wayne's boss.

Cast: Eddie Izzard (Wayne Malloy), Minnie Driver (Dahlia Malloy), Shannon Woodward (Di Di Malloy), Noel Fisher (Cael Malloy), Aidan Mitchell (Sam Malloy), Nichole Hiltz (Ginny Dannegan), Deidre Henry (Aubie McDonald), Gregg Henry (Hugh), Todd Stashwick (Dale). **Credits:** *Executive Producer:* Dawn Prestwich, Nicole Yorkin, Eddie Izzard, Mark Morgan, Guy Oseary, Michael Rosenberg, Dimitry Lipkin. *Co-Executive Producer:* Peter O'Fallon. *Producer:* Paul Kurta, Sara Morrow. *Music:* Harry Gregson-Williams.

1046 Rob and Big. (Reality; MTV; November 2, 2006 to April 15, 2008)

A comedy reality program that follows the real life antics of Rob Dyrdek, a professional skate boarder, and his best friend and bodyguard, Christopher "Big Black" Boykin. Also featured is Meaty, the bulldog that lives with them in Rob's Hollywood mansion.

Stars: Rob Drydek, Chris Boykin. **Credits:** *Executive Producer:* Rob Drydek, Jeff Tremaine. *Co-Executive Producer:* Shane Nickerson. *Producer:* Chris Boykin,

Ruben Fleischer, Michael Lang. *Music:* Benjamin Forrest Davis, Jared Gutstadt.

1047 Robotboy. (Cartoon; Cartoon Network; Premiered: December 28, 2005)

Robotboy is a cutting edge robot, designed to battle evil, that was created by Professor Moshimo. While Robotboy has the ability to destroy entire armies, he dreams of becoming a real boy. To oblige his creation, the professor sends him to Bay Area to live with his biggest fan, Tommy Turnbull. Disrupting Robotboy's dreams is Dr. Kamikazi, an evil genius who seeks to harness Robotboy's powers to rule the world. Stories follow Tommy and his best friends, Lola and Gus, as they protect Robotboy and, with Robotboy's help, defeat Dr. Kamikazi.

Voice Cast: Tara Strong (Robotboy), Lorraine Pilkington (Tommy Turnbull), Laurence Bouvard (Lola), Jason Davis (Gus), Eiji Kusuhara (Dr. Kamikazi), Togo Igawa (Prof. Moshimo). **Credits:** *Producer:* Finn Ainesen, Clement Calvert, Christian Davin, Daniel Lenard.

1048 Rock of Love with Bret Michaels. (Reality; VH-1; July 15, 2007 to April 8, 2008)

Reality-like dating show in which Bret Michaels, front man for the 1980s metal band Poison, seeks a woman to share his life.

Star: Bret Michaels. **Credits:** *Executive Producer:* Cris Abrego, Mark Cronin, Ben Samek. *Supervising Producer:* Michelle Brando, Lauren A. Stevens, Scott Teti. *Producer:* Walt Omiecinski. *Music:* Adam Zelkind.

1049 Roker on the Road. (Reality; Food Network; Premiered: January 1, 2006)

NBC Weatherman Al Roker takes to the open road to explore cuisine across America.

Host: Al Roker. **Credits:** *Executive Producer:* Al Roker. *Producer:* Connie Collins, Brooke Smiler, Virginia Diaz.

1050   **Room Raiders**. (Reality; MTV; Premiered: October 1, 2003)

A potentially embarrassing twist (for the subject) on the typical TV dating program. Singles looking for a mate do not choose their dates by looks, intelligence (or dumbness) but by how their bedroom looks. The singles chosen to become the dates are not aware that their bedroom will be the deciding factor and cameras capture not only the condition of the room but the reaction of people whose rooms are raided. It is totally up to the subject to accept or reject a date based on what he or she sees.

Credits: Executive Producer: Charles Tremayne. *Supervising Producer:* Robert Buchalter. *Producer:* Tripp Swanhaus. Joy Newkirk, Jessica Garcia, Brian Prowse-Gany. *Music:* Shawn K. Clement.

1051   **Rules of Engagement**. (Comedy; CBS; February 5, 2007 to July 7, 2008)

Three views of marriage and relationships as seen through a married couple (Jeff and Audrey), an engaged couple (Adam and Jennifer) and an obnoxious swinging bachelor (Russell). Jeff and Audrey have been married for 12 years. The marriage works because Jeff always lets Audrey have her way. Jennifer and Adam have been dating for seven months (he proposed; she accepted and now he is not sure he made the right decision). Russell believes he has it the best of all — "I do what I want. I do it when I want and I sleep with who I want." Returned for a new season on March 2, 2009.

Cast: Patrick Warburton (Jeff), Megyn Price (Audrey), Oliver Hudson (Adam), Bianca Kajlich (Jennifer), David Spade (Russell). **Credits:** *Executive Producer:* Tom Hertz, Doug Robinson, Andy Ackerman. *Producer:* Barbara Stoll. *Music:* David Schwartz.

1052   **Run's House**. (Reality; MTV; October 13, 2005 to September 3, 2008)

Joseph "Rev. Run" Simmons is a former hip-hop star (a member of Run DMC). He is married to Justine and is the father of five teenagers (Vanessa, Joseph, Angela, Daniel and Russell). Joseph is now a preacher (living in Saddle River, New Jersey) and cameras follow the family as they go about living their daily lives.

Star: Joseph Simmons. **Credits:** *Executive Producer:* Liz Gateley, Tony DiSanto, Jason A. Carbone. *Co-Executive Producer:* Russell Simmons. *Supervising Producer:* Anna Boiardi, Nick Lee.

1053   **Russell Simmons Presents Def Poetry**. (Variety; HBO; Premiered: December 1, 2001)

An unusual series in that poets (amateur, professional and celebrities with the poetic touch) share their literary efforts with a club and home audience.

Host: Mos Def (actor/hip hop artist) **Credits:** *Executive Producer:* Stan Lathan. *Co-Executive Producer:* Daniel Simmons, Deborah Pointer, Mos Def. *Supervising Producer:* Kamilah Forbes. *Producer:* Allen Kelman.

1054   **The Salt-n-Pepa Show**. (Reality; VH-1; Premiered: October 15, 2007)

Cheryl James and Sandra Denton, better known as the female hip hop duo Salt-n-Pepa, broke up in 2002. Five years later they agree to reunite for a TV special. Cameras follow Cheryl and Sandra as they renew their friendship, reminisce about their past and prepare to again perform as Salt-n-Pepa.

Stars: Cheryl Jones, Sandra Denton. **Credits:** *Executive Producer:* Matthew Ostrom, Ken DuBanks Tarver. *Co-Executive Producer:* Brian T. Flanagan. *Producer:* Kevin Vargas.

1055   **Sam Has 7 Friends**. (Mystery; Internet; Premiered: August 28, 2006)

Samantha Breslow is an aspiring actress. Patrick is her boyfriend; Willie, her ex-boyfriend; Dani, her best friend; Chivo,

Dani's boyfriend; Scott, Sam's neighbor; Vera, Patrick's new girlfriend; and Roman, Sam's agent. Unknown to Samantha, one of them is going to kill her. The last episode (12-15-06) shows Sam, fed up with Los Angeles, about to leave, when she is murdered. Who did it? The killer is never fully shown. The webisodes were still current in 2008.

Cast: Stephanie Marquis (Samantha Breslow), Michael Finn (Patrick Ballard), Moneer Yaqubi (Willie Banner), Shantelle Canzanese (Dani Price), Jaime Zevallos (Chivo Gonzalez), Tim Halling (Scott Nichols), Kristi Engleman (Vera), Keith Wright (Roman Reid). **Credits:** *Executive Producer:* Marcus Blakely, Douglas Cheney, Chris McCaleb, Ryan Wise. *Producer:* Marcus Blakely. *Co-Producer:* Oscar H. Beltran. *Music:* Jon McKeever.

1056   Samantha Who? (Comedy; ABC; Premiered: October 15, 2007)

Samantha Who is actually Samantha Newly, a beautiful young woman who was hit by a car and awoke (after eight days in a coma) with retrograde amnesia. She can function in the world but has no memory of her personal life. Samantha doesn't know whom she was, what she did or if she was even good or evil. She is a stranger to herself and this is something she cannot live with. Acting as her own detective, Samantha begins to uncover clues about her past. She learns that the former Samantha was a horrible person (vain and cold-hearted). She also discovers that her former self had many enemies and that the car accident may have been an attempted murder. She also resumes the old Samantha's job as a vice president of Chapman and Funk International, a real estate firm. For the new Samantha, all her past mistakes have been erased. She has a clean slate, but can she change who she really was? Samantha thinks she can and stories follow Samantha as she tries to fix the mistakes her former self made and reconstruct her life into one that shows a kinder, more loving woman. Todd

is Samantha's boyfriend; Andrea and Dena are her friends; Regina and Howard are her parents; and Tracey is her secretary; Frank the building doorman.

Cast: Christina Applegate (Samantha Newly), Jean Smart (Regina Newly), Kevin Dunn (Howard Newly), Jennifer Esposito (Andrea), Barry Watson (Todd), Melissa McCarthy (Dena), Tim Russ (Frank), Joy Osmanski (Tracey). **Credits:** *Executive Producer:* Peter Traugott, Donald Todd, Cecelia Ahern. *Producer:* John Amodeo. *Music:* Jan Stevens.

1057   Samurai 7. (Cartoon; IFC; Premiered: April 1, 2006)

An animated adaptation of the classic Japanese movie *The Seven Samurai* (basis of the American film *The Magnificent Seven*) about seven fearless Samurai who come to the aid of farmers in the village of Kanna who are being persecuted by a group of mechanized Samurai called Nobiser. Kambei is the leader of the Samurai Seven; his associates are Gorobei (also a gifted entertainer), Katsushiro (the youngest member who has not yet experienced true battle), Kikuchiyo (a farmer who had his body forged with a mechanized exoskeleton to become a robot-like warrior), Shichiroji (Kambei's right-hand man), Heihachi (a craftsman who forges their weapons); Kyuzo (is the mysterious man who joined with Kambei to defeat the Nobiser). Farmer Rikichi, Kirara and Mosuke are residents of Kanna.

Voice Cast: R. Bruce Elliott (Kambei), Sean Teague (Katsuchiro), Christopher Sobat (Kikuchiyo), Bob Carter (Gorobei), Greg Ayres (Heihachi), Duncan Brannan (Shichiroji), Colleen Clinkenbeard (Kiari), Kyle Hebert (Farmer Mosuke), J. Michael Tatum (Farmer Rikichi). **Credits:** *Producer:* Kazuhiko Inomata, Daisuke Ito. *Music:* Eitetsu Hayashi, Kaoru Wada.

1058   The Sarah Silverman Program. (Comedy; Comedy Central; Premiered: February 1, 2007)

A rather raunchy comedy (an "R" rated version of *Seinfeld*) that focuses on the life a Sarah Silverman, a very pretty stand-up, foul-mouthed comedian, who has little respect for anyone. Sarah is single and lives with her dog, Doug. Her best friend is her (real life) sister, Laura, and she lives next door to Brian and Steve, two unkempt and dim-witted gay lovers. Stories relate the incidents that affect Sarah in her everyday life — and how she goes about dealing with them (not using her beauty to accomplish things, but her truly nasty attitude and being as a mean as she can be. She is number one — and she let's those she deals with know it).

Cast: Sarah Silverman (Herself), Laura Silverman (Herself), Brian Posehn (Brian), Steve Agee (Steve), Jay Johnson (Officer Jay McPherson), Laura Marano (Young Sarah; flashbacks). **Credits:** *Executive Producer:* Sarah Silverman, Dan Sterling, Heidi Herzon, Rob Schrab. *Producer:* Erin O'Malley. *Music:* Adam Berry.

1059 Saturday Night Live. (Comedy; NBC; Premiered: October 11, 1975)

"Live from New York, it's Saturday Night." Musical acts coupled with topical comedy sketches.

Cast (2008): Fred Armisen, Will Forte, Bill Hader, Darrell Hammond, Seth Meyers, Amy Poehler, Maya Rudolph, Andy Samberg, Jason Sudeikis, Kenan Thompson, Kristen Wiig, Casey Wilson, Michaela Watkins, Abby Elliott.

1060 Saving Grace. (Crime Drama; TNT; Premiered: July 23, 2007)

Grace Hanadarko is a pretty, but rather uncouth detective with the Oklahoma City Police Department (she drinks, smokes, curses and does what she wants to do — like having an affair with her married partner, Ham Dewey). One night, while partying with her friend Rhetta, Grace has a bit too much to drink and although she knows better, she decides to drive herself home. Along the way she hits a man walking by the side of the road and evokes the name of God ("Dear God, please help me") when she realizes what she has done. Suddenly, an angel appears — "I'm Earl, what do you need?" (Earl's assignment is to help mortals who need one last chance to redeem themselves. Grace, being who she is, is headed for Hell but God has given her one last chance to redeem herself and assigned Earl that task). Earl explains why he appeared, but Grace believes she is having an alcoholic blackout and refuses to accept what she is seeing. Earl reveals his angelic wings, magically transports Grace to a high cliff then returns her to the scene of the accident — but what accident? All traces of what Grace did have disappeared. As Grace comes to her senses, she accepts the fact that Earl is an angel and has been sent to help her (Earl can't be there for Grace all the time and he is not permitted to help her solve crimes; he appears to guide her when he feels she is straying from a righteous path). Although Grace has accepted Earl, she has not really changed. She is still on a path of self-destruction and Earl's job to redeem her has become more difficult. Despite what she does in her private life, Grace is totally dedicated to work; somehow she manages to keep both worlds separate. Stories follow Grace as she attempts to solve crimes and Earl's efforts to make Grace see the light and turn over a new leaf. Bobby Stillwell is Grace's nephew (the son of her late sister who died in the Oklahoma City bombing); Butch Ada is a detective who also works with Grace.

Cast: Holly Hunter (Grace Hanadarko), Leon Rippy (Earl), Kenneth Johnson (Ham Dewey), Laura San Giacomo (Rhetta Rodriquez), Gregory Norman-Cruz (Bobby Stillwater), Bailey Chase (Butch Ada), Bokeem Woodbine (Leon Cooley). **Credits:** *Executive Producer:* Nancy Miller, Gary A. Randall. *Producer:* John Ryan, Artie Mandelberg, Holly

Hunter. *Associate Producer:* Katrin Goodwin. *Music:* Susan Marder.

1061   Say Yes to the Dress. (Reality; TLC; Premiered: October 12, 2007)

A look at brides to be, the clientele of Kleinfeld Bridal in Manhattan, as they attempt to find the wedding dress of their dreams.

Host: Ronald Rothstein, Mara Urshel. **Credits:** *Producer:* Nicole Sorrenti.

1062   Scare Tactics. (Reality; Sci Fi; April 1, 2003 to August 13, 2008)

Candid Camera styled series that uses hidden cameras to capture the reactions of people caught in scary situations (like haunted houses or encounters with ghosts or other supernatural creatures).

Host: Shannen Doherty, Stephen Baldwin, Tracy Morgan. **Credits:** *Executive Producer:* Scott Hallock, Kevin Healey. *Producer:* Becky Jacobus. *Music:* Damon Zwicker.

1063   Scrubs. (Comedy; NBC; October 2, 2001 to May 14, 2008)

Sacred Heart Hospital is a medical facility that appears to be staffed by doctors and nurses who appear to know what they are doing (when it comes to saving a patient's life) but at other times they look to be escapees from a mental institution as their antics are anything but normal. Particular focus is on John Dorian, called J.D., a naïve but bright and upcoming doctor who doesn't realize his own potential, a situation that causes him to encounter numerous mishaps as he learns the ins and outs of medicine in the unreal world of Sacred Heart. Switched to ABC on January 6, 2009.

Cast: Zach Braff (Dr. John Dorian), Sarah Chalke (Dr. Elliot Reid), Donald Faison (Dr. Christopher Turk), Courteney Cox (Dr. Taylor Maddox), John C. McGinley (Dr. Perry Cox), Ken Jenkins (Dr. Bob Keso), Judy Reyes (Nurse Carla Espinosa), Neil Flynn (The Janitor), Aloma Wright (Nurse Laverne Roberts), Christa Miller (Jordan Sullivan), Elizabeth Banks (Dr. Kim Briggs). Robert Maschio (Dr. Todd Quinlan). **Credits:** *Executive Producer:* Bill Lawrence. *Co-Executive Producer:* Tad Quill, Bill Callahan, Matt Tarses, Tim Hobert, Gabrielle Allan, Eric Weinberg, Neil Goldman, Garrett Donovan. *Producer:* Mychelle Deschamps, Mike Schwartz, Mark Stegemann, Deb Fordham, Janae Bakken, Randall Winston. *Music:* Jan Stevens, Chris Link, Chad Fisher, Tim Bright.

1064   Secrets of the Dead. (Reality; PBS; Premiered: May 15, 2000)

Modern-day forensic science is used to investigate historic mysteries to discover what really happened.

Credits: *Executive Producer:* Anthony Chapman, Beth Hopper, Simon Andreaem, David Dugan, Simon Berthon, Liz McLeod, Ian Duncan. *Music:* Glenn Keiles, Howard Davidson, Brian Williams, Paul Farrer.

1065   Semi-Homemade Cooking with Sandra Lee. (Cooking; Food Network; Premiered: September 1, 2003)

Cookbook author Sandra Lee prepares meals that make the use of specially selected products purchased at the super market.

Host: Sandra Lee. **Credits:** *Supervising Producer:* Jenni Gilroy. *Producer:* Julie Epstein. *Music:* Randy Lee.

1066   Sesame Street. (Children; PBS; Premiered: November 10, 1969)

Various entertainment geared to children to teach reading skills, the alphabet, counting and the ability to solve problems — all presented through the helpful (and not so helpful) Muppet creations of Jim Henson who live on anywhere street in any anywhere city or town called Sesame Street.

Principal Cast: Bob McGrath (Bob), Loretta Long (Susan), Northern J. Calloway (David), Sonia Manzano (Maria), Roscoe Orman (Gordon), Emilio Delgado (Luis), Linda Bove (Linda), Alaina Reed (Olivia), Will Lee (Mr. Hooper), Julianne Buescher (Sherry Netherlands), Tyler James Williams (Tyler), Alison Bartlett (Dr. Gina Jefferson), Miles Orman (Miles), Bill McCutcheon (Uncle Dudley). **Muppet Voices:** Carroll Spinney, Jim Henson, Frank Oz, Richard Hunt, Brian Muehl, David Rudman. **Credits:** *Producer:* Jon Stone, Dulcy Singer, Todd Broder, Eva Saks, Lewis Bernstein, Ann Burgund, Kevin Clash, David D. Connell, Joan Ganz Cooney, Robert Cunniff, Melissa Dino, Nina Elias-Bamberger, Steve Garfinkel, Karen Ialacci, Robert Kirbyson, Lynn Klugman, Henry B. Lee, Margaret Murphy, Carol-Lynne Parente, Lynn Rogoff, Edith Zornow.

1067 7 Lives X-posed. (Erotica; Playboy Channel; Premiered: October 21, 2001)

Adults only reality series in which ordinary people compete in sexually oriented challenges to become the best love-making couple. Adult film actress Devinn Lane hosts and judges which contestants go (weakest performers) and those who stay. **Host:** Devinn Lane. **Credits:** *Executive Producer:* Kelly Cauthen. *Producer:* Tom Lazarus, Adam Cianciola, Randy Rowen.

1068 Sex Court. (Erotica; Playboy Channel; Premiered: August 7, 1998)

Take off on legitimate broadcast judge programs wherein people with sexual issues present their cases to a gorgeous "judge." Verdicts do not award money; instead losers must perform some sort of sexual act. **Judge:** Julie Strain. **Bailiff:** Alexandra Silk. **Sex Therapist:** Brittany Andrews. **Bodyguard:** Stephanie Swinney. **Credits:** *Executive Producer:* Tammara Wells, Guiditta Tornetta. *Producer:* Will Robertson, Scott Cope.

1069 Sexcetera. (Reality; Playboy Channel; Premiered: 1999)

Explicit, factual series that presents (in a humorous light) reports on human sexuality (from fetishes to sex expos). **Anchor:** Crystal Smith. **Reporters:** Thomas Archer, Valerie Baber, Susanna Breslin, Hoyt Christopher, Frank Gianotti, Lauren Hays, Asante Jones, Gretchen Massey, Scott Potasnik, Kira Reed. **Announcer:** Geno Mitchelini. **Credits:** *Executive Producer:* Frank Martin, Rudy Poe, Paul Cockerill. *Supervising Producer:* Ross Duke, Perry Chasin, Aliyah Silverstein. *Producer:* Kira Reed. *Music:* Jerrold Launer.

1070 Sexy Girls Next Door. (Erotica; Playboy Channel; Premiered: 2004)

Very sexy and gorgeous young women are brought together for a chance to become a *Playboy* magazine centerfold. Cameras capture not only the competition but the private thoughts and intimate secrets of the girls as they speak directly to the camera. The girls (identified by a first name only) bare all as they compete in various challenges; the episode titles and their tag lines are just as alluring (for example, "Fast and Curious. Yummy adult-biz wannabes expose their goodies for stardom" and "Wild Things. A threesome of buxom hotties are waiting to pounce on adult fame"). The one girl who possesses the perfect figure as well as an alluring personality becomes a Playmate of the Month. **Host:** Michele Rogers.

1071 Sexy Urban Legends. (Erotica; Playboy Channel; Premiered: May 15, 2002)

Adult themed recreations of sexually based urban legends. **Host:** Darren Scott.

1072 Shark. (Crime Drama; CBS; September 21, 2006–May 20, 2008)

Sebastian Stark, called Shark, is a brilliant defense lawyer. He is divorced from Claire and the father of 16-year-old Julie.

To Stark, the legal system is a game he plays for fun and profit. After one case, however, when Stark wins the acquittal of a wife beater, his world is turned upside down when the man he freed kills his wife. Shortly after, Manuel Delgado, the mayor of Los Angeles, approaches Stark and asks him to head the High Profile Unit of the District Attorney's Office. Feeling guilty for what has just happened, Stark accepts the offer and is assigned a staff of young prosecutors by Jessica Devlin, the D.A.: Richie Casey Woodland (the son of a senator. He is charming and good with a jury but weak on facts); Billie Willis (passionate but emotion clouds her judgment); Martin Allende (great on paper [writes for the *Law Review*] but weak on his feet); Raina Troy (has major authority problems; she is, as Stark says, "a citation waiting to happen"); and Madeline Poe (a volunteer who hopes to become a lawyer). Stark, once a brilliant defense attorney is now a brilliant prosecutor with a raw staff he must nature and teach how to apply his shark-like ruthless defense tactics into shark-like prosecutions. Stories follow Stark and his team as they prosecute cases for the D.A.

Cast: James Woods (Sebastian Stark), Jeri Ryan (Jessica Devlin), Danielle Panabaker (Julie Stark), Sophina Brown (Raina Troy), Sarah Carter (Madeline Poe), Sam Page (Richie Woodland), Alexis Cruz (Martin Allende), Lindsay Frost (Claire Stark), Carlos Gomez (Manuel Delgado), Lynn Whitfield (Anita Astin), Romy Rosemont (Margaret Pool). **Credits:** *Executive Producer:* Ian Biederman, Brian Glazer, David Nevins. *Producer:* Robert Del Valle. *Music:* Sean Callery.

1073   Shear Genius. (Reality; Bravo; April 11, 2007 to August 27, 2008)

A behind-the-scenes look at the preparations that go into producing a fashion show (or other major event). A weekly competition is interwoven into the presentation wherein a group of hairstylists attempt to outdo each other for the honor of becoming the country's best hair stylist.

Host: Jaclyn Smith. **Judges:** Sally Hershberger, Michael Cail, Rene Fris. **Models:** Erin Haglund, Adam Kaloustian. **Credits:** *Executive Producer:* Mark Koops. *Producer:* Erin Haglund, Adam Kaloustian.

1074   Shelter. (Drama; Here!; Premiered: 2007)

A specialized series (geared toward gays) about a young man (Zach) who works at a dead end job but finds pleasure in surfing, drawing and hanging out with his best friend (Gabe). Love enters the picture when Zach meets Gabe's older brother (Shaun) when Shaun is drawn to Zach's selfishness and talent as an artist. Stories follow Zach's life as he begins a relationship with Shaun while struggling to help his needy sister care for her son.

Cast: Trevor Wright (Zach), Ross Thomas (Gabe), Brad Rowe (Shaun), Tina Holmes (Jeanne), Jackson Worth (Cody), Albert Reed (Billy), Katie Walder (Tori), Matt Bushell (Alan). **Credits:** *Executive Producer:* Anne Clements, Paul Colichman, Stephen P. Jarchow. *Co-Executive Producer:* Meredith Kadlec. *Producer:* J.D. Disalvatore. *Associate Producer:* Chris Panizzon. *Music:* J. Peter Robinson.

1075   The Shield. (Crime Drama; FX; March 12, 2002 to November 25, 2008)

An unconventional, graphic police drama that focuses on the less-than-honorable members of the Strike Team, an elite unit of the Los Angeles Police Department. The unit's officers are corrupt but effective cops. Detective Vic Mackey leads the team. He is considered a rogue cop as he operates under his own set of rules. David Aceveda, the captain, is seeking to advance his political ambitions. He dislikes Vic's tactics and wants him out of the unit. Claudette Wyms is a veteran detective who plays both sides of the fence.

She understands Vic and understands David. She manipulates both to achieve her goal.

Cast: Michael Chiklis (Det. Vic Mackey), Benito Martinez (Capt. David Aceveda), C.C.H. Pounder (Det. Claudette Wyms), Glenn Close (Capt. Monica Rawling), Catherine Dent (Off. Danielle Sofer), Michael Jace (Off. Julien Lowe), Kenny Johnson (Det. Curtis "Lemonhead" Lemansky), Walter Goggins (Det. Shane Vendrell), Jay Karnes (Det. Holland "Dutch" Wagenbach), Forest Whitaker (Lt. John Kavanaugh), David Rees Snell (Det. Ron Gardocki). **Credits:** *Executive Producer:* Shawn Ryan, Scott Brazil. *Co-Executive Producer:* Reed Steiner, Kevin Arkadie. *Supervising Producer:* Glenn Mazzara. *Producer:* Craig Yahata, Kurt Sutter, Dean White, Kevin G. Cremin, Adam Fierro, Paul Marks.

1076 **Simply Ming.** (Cooking; PBS; Premiered: August 1, 2003)

Cooking program devoted to showing viewers how to prepare meals with an oriental flavor.

Host: Ming Tsai. **Credits:** *Producer:* Ming Tsai, Deborah J. Hurley.

1077 **The Simpsons.** (Cartoon; Fox; Premiered: December 17, 1989)

Adult cartoon about a totally moronic father (Homer Simpson), his level-headed wife (Marge) and their children, Bart (troublemaker), Lisa (sensible) and infant Maggie.

Voice Cast: Dan Castellaneta (Homer Simpson), Julie Kavner (Marge Simpson), Nancy Cartwright (Bart Simpson), Yeardley Smith (Lisa Simpson), Pamela Hayden (Millhouse Van Houten), Hank Azaria (Chief Wiggum), Harry Shearer (Kent Brockman), Tress MacNeille (Agnes Skinner), Marcia Wallace (Edna Kranappel), Hank Azaria (Apu/Moe), Harry Shearer (Mr. Burns/Smithers/Ned Flanders), Dan Castellaneta (Krusty the Klown/Barney). **Credits:** *Executive Producer:* James L.

Brooks, Matt Groening, Sam Simon, Mike Scully, Phil Roman, David X. Cohen, Matt Selman. *Supervising Producer:* Jay Kogan, Wallace Wolodarsky, David Richardson, Harold Kimmel. *Producer:* Ron Hauge, Frank Mula, Jeff Martin, Jon Vitti, John Swartzweider, Conan O'Brien, Richard Raynis, David Silverman, George Meyer, Richard Sakai, Dominick Cary, Dennis Sirkot, Max Pross, David Mirkin, Tom Gemmill, Bonita Pietilar. *Music:* Danny Elfman, Richard Gibbs, Alf Clausen, Arthur B. Rubinstein, Patrick Williams.

1078 **Skunk Fu.** (Cartoon; CW; September 22, 2007 to September 25, 2008)

Martial arts expert Skunk Fu and his friends Rabbit, Tiger and Fox, protect their home, the Valley, from the evil Black Dragon and his army of Ninja Monkeys.

Voice Cast: Jules Dejongh (Skunk), Paul Tylands (Panda), Rod Goodall (Dragon), Tony Acworth (Bird). **Credits:** *Executive Producer:* Paul Cummins, Tom Van Waveren, Paul Young. *Producer:* Jordan Gaucher. *Music:* Chris Bemand.

1079 **Smallville.** (Drama; WB/CW; Premiered: October 16, 2001)

Events in the life of Clark Kent before he would become Superman. It begins in 1989 in Smallville Kansas. On a clear afternoon, Smallville is struck by a devastating meteor shower. A childless farm couple, Jonathan and Martha Kent, are almost killed when a meteor passes over their truck and causes them to crash. They are rescued by a three-year-old baby who emerges from a crashed rocket that had been part of the meteor shower. The unharmed baby is actually Kal-El, the lone survivor of the doomed planet Krypton. Moments before Krypton exploded, Kal-El's parents (Jor-El and Lara) placed him in an experimental rocket programmed to land on Earth. Also part of the meteor shower were fragments of Kryptonite, green remnants of the planet that can now kill Kal-El if he is exposed to it. It is 2001 when Smallville is next seen. The baby, raised by Jonathan and Martha, is now a teenager known as Clark Kent. When Clark begins to develop his powers, Jonathan tells Clark about his past and that he must keep his powers secret and only use them for good. Episodes follow Clark as he struggles to live a normal life while adjusting to the fact that he is different from everyone else. Chloe Sullivan, Lana Lang, Pete Ross and Whitney Fordham attend Smallville High School with Clark (2001; Whitney and Pete are later dropped). Lex Luthor, a few years older than Clark, was, at first his friend, the head of the Luthor Corporation Fertilizer Plant (the thought of wealth and power corrupted him). Chloe, a reporter for the school newspaper, *The Torch*, progresses to become a reporter for *The Daily Planet* in nearby Metropolis (Lois Lane, who is introduced as a reporter for a paper called *The Inquisitor*, later becomes associated with *The Daily Planet*). Lana, who runs the local hangout, The Talon, later heads the Isis Foundation (which helps people embrace their powers). Jonathan later succumbs to a heart attack and Martha, working first for Lex, becomes a State senator. Lionel Luther is Lex's ruthless billionaire father; Jimmy Olsen is the cub reporter on *The Daily Planet*; Tess Mercer becomes the acting C.E.O. of Luthor Corp. (in 2008 when Lex is believed to have disappeared in an arctic wasteland); Davis Bloom, a paramedic is battling a growing darkness in him (that causes him to become the evil Doomsday); Perry White is the editor of *The Daily Planet*. Kara is Clark's cousin (the daughter of his father's brother, Zor-El), the only other known survivor from Krypton (she was sent on a mission by her father before the planet exploded. Her ship was caught in the meteor shower and plunged into the sea. Kara was placed in a sate of suspended animation and awoke when the Smallville

dam broke and activated her ship's life support system. She managed to find Clark and is now stranded on Earth and must learn to live life as a human). On occasion, Clark (who begins work as a paperboy on *The Daily Planet* in 2008) receives help in battling crime from Bart Allen (alias The Flash), Oliver Queen (alias The Green Arrow), Arthur "A.C." Curry (alias Aquaman), Victor Stone (alias Cyborg) and, although more evil than good, Dinah Lance (alias Black Canary).

Cast: Tom Welling (Clark Kent), Kristin Kreuk (Lana Lang), John Schneider (Jonathan Kent), Annette O'Toole (Martha Kent), Michael Rosenbaum (Lex Luthor), Allison Mack (Chloe Sullivan), Sam Jones III (Pete Ross), Erica Durance (Lois Lane), Aaron Ashmore (Jimmy Olsen), Michael McKean (Perry White), Terence Stamp (Jor-El), Wendy Chmelauskas (Laura Lang), Laura Vandervoot (Kara), Cassidy Freeman (Tess Mercer), Sam Witwer (Davis Bloom/Doomsday), Alaina Kalanji (Dinah Lance/Black Canary), John Glover (Lionel Luthor), Ben Odberg (Lewis Lang), Justin Hartley (Oliver Queen), Kyle Gallner (Bart Allen), Lee Thompson Young (Victor Stone), Alan Ritchson (Arthur Curry). **Flashback Cast:** Malkolm Alburguenque (Young Clark Kent), Jade Unterman (Young Lana Lang), Connor Stanhope (Young Lex Luthor). **Credits:** *Executive Producer:* Alfred Gough, Miles Millar, Joe Davola, Michael Tolfini, Brian Robbins. *Co-Executive Producer:* Greg Beeman, Alex Taub, Ken Horton, Steven S. DeKnight. *Producer:* Doris Egan, Michael Green, Greg Walker, Philip Levens, Todd Slavkin, David Wilson, Kelly Souder. *Supervising Producer:* Mark Verheeden. *Music:* Mark Snow, Jeffrey Cain, Gregory Slay, Remy Zero, Shelby Tate. *Theme Vocal:* "Save Me" by Remy Zero.

1080   **Smash Lab.** (Reality; Discovery Channel; Premiered: December 28, 2007)

Engineers explore everyday technology with the object being to adapt it for uses other than it was intended.

Engineers: Nick Blair, Deanne Bell, Kevin Cook, Chuck Messer, Reverend Gadget. **Credits:** *Executive Producer:* Tom Brisley. *Producer:* Damon Zwicker, Korelan Cone, Philip Lott, Jason S. Edwards, Peter D. Coogan.

1081 **Snapped**. (Reality; Oxygen; Premiered: August 6, 2004)

Statistics for the FBI's Uniform Crime Reporting Program indicate that seven percent of the killings that take place are committed by females. *Snapped* explores the cases of women accused of murder (trying to present for the viewer the reason why — "From socialites to secretaries, female killers share one thing in common: at one point they all snapped").

Narrator: Sharon Martin. **Credits:** *Executive Producer:* Stephen Land, Geoffrey Proud. *Co-Executive Producer:* Zak Weisfeld. *Supervising Producer:* Deborah Dawkins. *Producer:* David Lane, Michael Rogers, Melissa May, Michael Hart, Larissa Bliss, Todd Moss, Kevin Barry. *Music:* Brian Langsbard, Justin Mellard.

1082 **So You Think You Can Dance**. (Reality; Fox; July 20, 2005 to August 7, 2008)

Contestants perform dance routines for $100,000 and a one-year contract with Celine Dion's Las Vegas nightclub show. Participants perform a specialty dance each week — one with a professional partner, the other as a solo. Home audience votes determine which teams are eliminated. The couple with the highest votes on the final episode is the winner.

Host: Lauren Sanchez, Cat Deeley. **Judge:** Cat Deeley, Nigel Lythgoe, Mary Murphy. **Credits:** *Executive Producer:* Nigel Lythgoe, Simon Fuller, Allen Shapiro. *Senior Producer:* James Breen, Jeff Thacker. *Producer:* Nicola Gaha, Bonnie Lythgoe, Simon Lythgoe. *Associate Pro-*

ducer: Norm Betts, Mike Yuichuck, Tucker Smith.

1083 **Solitary**. (Reality; Fox Reality Channel; Premiered: June 5, 2006)

A reality series with a game show-like format wherein contestants who claim to possess psychic abilities, compete in rather difficult psychological experiments for the top prize of $50,000. Contestants do not see each other and are guided by a voice identified only as "Val."

Credits: *Executive Producer:* Bob Boden. *Co-Executive Producer:* Noel Siegel. *Producer:* Andrew J. Golder, Lincoln D. Hiatt, Duke Straub. *Music:* Jason Miller, Evan Hasse.

1084 **The Soup**. (Comedy; E!; Premiered: July 1, 2004)

If comedy had a weekly news program, *The Soup* would fill the bill. Each episode is a recap of the week's most noteworthy comical events — from sports, politics, reality shows and even home shopping programs.

Host: Joel McHale. **Credits:** *Executive Producer:* Barbara Wellner, Jay James, Edward Boyd. *Co-Executive Producer:* Boyd Vico, K.P. Anderson. *Supervising Producer:* Greg Fideler. *Producer:* Kelly Andrews, Hathaway Loftus, Aaron Barrocas.

1085 **South of Nowhere**. (Drama; The N; Premiered: November 4, 2005)

Serial-like episodes that relate incidents in the lives of Spencer Carlin, her natural brother, Glen and her adopted, African-American brother, Clay as they move from a small town to Los Angeles and experience, for the first time, the fast-paced ethnically diverse life of the big city. Arthur and Paula are their parents.

Cast: Gabrielle Christian (Spencer Carlin), Chris Hunter (Glen Carlin), Danso Gordon (Clay Carlin), Maeve Quinlan (Paula Carlin), Rob Moran (Arthur Carlin), Mandy Musgrave (Ashley Davies), Aasha Davis (Chelsea Lewis), Austen

Parros (Sean Miller), Eileen April Boylan (Kyla Woods), Valery M. Ortiz (Madison Duarte), Marissa Lauren (Sherry Pena). **Credits:** *Executive Producer:* Tommy Lynch. *Co-Executive Producer:* Nancylee Myatt. *Producer:* Greg Hampson, Jonas E. Agin, Gary L. Stephenson. *Music:* Lee Wall.

1086 South Park. (Cartoon; Comedy Central; August 13, 1997 to November 19, 2008)

Eric, Kenny, Kyle and Stan are third graders who live in the small town of South Park, Colorado. They are foul-mouthed and nasty. Weird things happen in South Park and stories relate the kids' mishaps in a not-so-typical town.

Voice Cast: Trey Parker (Stan Marsh/ Eric Cartman/Randy Marsh), Matt Stone (Kyle Brofhovski/Stuart McCormick/ Kenny McCormick), Eliza Schneider (Wendy Testaburger), Grace Lazar (Wendy Testaburger), Mary Kay Bergman (Wendy Testaburger), Eliza Schneider (Liane Cartman/Sharon Marsh), April Stewart (Laine Cartman/Sharon Marsh), Isaac Hayes (Chef). **Credits:** *Executive Producer:* Anne Garefino, Matt Stone, Trey Parker, Deborah Liebling, Brian Grading. *Supervising Producer:* Frank C. Agnone. *Producer:* Kyle McCulloch, Bruce Howell, Eric Stough, Erica Rivinoja. *Music:* Adam Bery, Jamie Dunlap. Scott Nickoley.

1087 Speeders. (Reality; Court TV/ Tru TV; Premiered: June 7, 2007)

Actual videos of speeders breaking the law then facing justice as they are caught by police is the focal point of the program. See also *Speeders Fight Back* (program 512).

Narrator: Daniel Staniszewski. **Credits:** *Executive Producer:* Barry Poznick, John Stephens. *Supervising Producer:* Christine Cavalieri. *Producer:* Rachel Brill Stellar, Dan Sacks. *Associate Producer:* Heather Dreiling, Heather Manrosi.

1088 Spike's Most Amazing Videos. (Reality; Spike TV; Premiered: February 11, 2006)

A collection of shocking videos culled from both professional and amateur photographers.

Narrator: Stacy Keach, Jr. **Credits:** *Executive Producer:* Robyn Nash, Andrew Jebb, Debra Weeks, Bruce Nash. *Senior Segment Producer:* Steve Marmalstein, Tim Stokes. *Segment Producer:* Heidi Marie Paglisisotto, Brent Young, James Crite, Bernard Neto, Beth Humphreys. *Music:* Shawn Clement.

1089 SpongeBob SquarePants. (Cartoon; Nickelodeon; Premiered: May 1, 1999)

Bikini Bottom is an underwater city inhabited by a number of unusual sea creatures, most notably SpongeBob Square-Pants, a square somewhat naïve sponge who is dense to what is happening around him. He lives in a pineapple and works as a fry cook at a diner called Krusty Krab. His antics as he frolics with his friends is the premise of the series.

Voice Cast: Tom Kenny (SpongeBob SquarePants), Bill Fagerbakke (Patrick Star), Lori Alan (Pearl Krabs), Carolyn Lawrence (Sandy Cheeks), Rodger Bumpass (Squidward Tentacles), Clancy Brown (Eugene H. Krabs), Mary Jo Catlett (SpongeBob's mother), Tom Kenny (SpongeBob's father), Mr. Lawrence (Sheldon J. Plankton), Ernest Borgnine (Mermaid Man), Tim Conway (Barnacle Boy). **Credits:** *Executive Producer:* Stephen Hillenburg. *Supervising Producer:* Derek Drymon, Paul Tibbitt. *Producer:* Helen Kalafatic, Anne Michaund, Donna Castricone. *Music:* Bradley Carow.

1090 Squirrel Boy. (Cartoon; Cartoon Network; Premiered: May 28, 2006)

Rodney, an intelligent squirrel, and Andy Johnson, his best friend, share endless misadventures as Rodney involves Andy in a variety of inane schemes.

Voice Cast: Pamela Adlon (Andy Johnson), Richard Steven Horvitz (Rodney J. Squirrel), Kurtwood Smith (Mr. Johnson),

Nancy Sullivan (Mrs. Johnson), Charles Shaunghnessy (Archie the Rabbit). **Credits:** *Executive Producer:* Everett Peck. *Producer:* Pernelle Hayes. *Music:* Erik Godal, Brad Benedict, Mark Fontana.

1091   **Stag: A Test of Love**. (Reality; Cinemax; Premiered: November 3, 2007)

Raunchy late night series that showcases the antics that occur at bachelor parties. The twist: the bachelor and his intended bride are shown the party video — with the soon-to-become bride's reactions being the focal point of the program.

Host: Tommy Habeeb. **Credits:** *Executive Producer:* Tommy Habeeb. *Supervising Producer:* Knick Tran. *Producer:* Marshall Hays. *Director:* Mike Rodgers, Knick Tran.

1092   **Star Camp**. (Reality; Internet; Premiered: July 22, 2007)

A Nickelodeon-produced Internet series that attempts to create a group of talented children and turn them into "multimedia mega stars." Ten children who possess various musical abilities (from singing, rapping and dancing) are trained (with the help of music industry singers, musicians and producers) to become "the next big stars."

Host: Nick Cannon. **Credits:** *Executive Producer:* Ray A. Brown, Nick Cannon, Quincy Jones III, Sean McNair. *Co-Executive Producer:* Mack Hodges. *Producer:* Alisha Takahashi.

1093   **Stargate Atlantis**. (Adventure; Sci Fi; July 16, 2004 to January 9, 2009)

A spin off from *Stargate SG-1.* A Stargate is an alien portal that allows travel to planets that also support a Stargate. When the fabled Lost City of Atlantis is discovered on a distant planet in the Pegasus Galaxy, a military team is formed to begin an exploration. Dr. Elizabeth Weir and Major John Sheppard are chosen to head the team. Unfortunately, the trip through their Stargate is a one-way trip because Atlantis

supports no such technology for a return trip. Their mission is to investigate the secrets of Atlantis and bring back to Earth the treasures they may uncover. Now, with no support from Earth, or means of rescue, the team must find a power source to activate the Stargate and return home. In the meantime, their lives and the lives of the peace-loving aliens of Atlantis, are threatened by the Wraith, evil life-draining beings who seek to destroy the Stargate explorers — and anything else that gets in their way. Elizabeth is 35 years old and can speak five languages. John is a mathematical genius. Teyla, a native of Atlantis, is the unofficial leader of her people. Dr. Rodney McKay, an arrogant astrophysicist, is the world's leading authority on Stargate technology. Aiden is a trigger-happy lieutenant determined to destroy the Wraith. Carson is the team's doctor and possesses a rare gene that allows him to use the ancient Atlantian technology.

Cast: Torri Higginson (Dr. Elizabeth Weir), Joe Flanigan (Major John Sheppard), Rachel Luttrell (Teyla Emmagan), Paul McGillon (Dr. Carson Beckett), David Hewlett (Dr. Rodney McKay), Rainbow Francks (Lt. Aiden Ford), Jason Momoa (Ranon Dex), Robert Picardo (Richard Woolsey). **Credits:** *Executive Producer:* Paul Mullie, Brad Wright, Joseph Mallozzi, Michael Greenberg, Robert C. Cooper. *Co-Executive Producer:* Carl Binder, N. John Smith. *Supervising Producer:* Martin Gero, Martin Wood. *Producer:* John G. Lenic, Alan McCullough, Ron French. *Music:* Joel Goldsmith.

1094   **The Steve Wilkos Show**. (Talk; Syn.; Premiered: September 2007)

Jerry Springer Show spin off wherein Jerry's former security guard takes on the reigns of his own series to help guests seek justice for wrongs done to them.

Host: Steve Wilkos. **Credits:** *Executive Producer:* Richard Dominick. *Co-Executive Producer:* Jerry Springer. *Supervising*

Producer: Rachelle Consiglin. *Director:* Greg Klazura.

1095   Stone Undercover. (Crime Drama; Syn.; Premiered: September 2006). Ex-cop Tom Stone teams with Marina Di-Luzio, a corporal with the Calgary Commercial Crimes Unit (in Alberta, Canada) to help her nab people by using his ability to blend into any scene and get the evidence Marina needs to make an arrest. **Cast:** Chris William Martin (Tom Stone), Janet Kidder (Marina DiLuzio), Stuart Margolin (Jack Welch), Brian Stolley (Wally). **Credits:** *Executive Producer:* Doug MacLeod, Tom Cox, Andrew Wreggitt. *Producer:* Jordy Randall. *Music:* Tim McCauley.

1096   Storm Hawks. (Cartoon; Cartoon Network; Premiered: May 27, 2007) Atmos is a peace-loving planet that is suddenly threatened with destruction by Master Cyclonis, the evil ruler of the Cyclonia Empire. To battle the master, the Sky Knights Squadron (Aerrow, Finn, Junko, Piper, Stork and Radaar) is formed and stories relate their battle, transforming their motorcycles into flying vehicles, against the Cyclonis. **Voice Cast:** Samuel Vincent (Aeerow/Dark Ace), Chiara Zanni (Piper), Matt Hill (Finn), Scott McBeil (Stork), Lenore Zann (Master Cyclonia), Colin Murdock (Junko). **Credits:** *Executive Producer:* Ken Faier, Asaph Fipke. *Producer:* Chuck Johnson. *Music:* Robert Buckley.

1097   Stupidface. (Comedy; Fuel TV; Premiered: June 7, 2007) Late night collection of cartoons, parodies, pranks and skits. **Cast:** Ted Newsome, Brian Jarvis, Laban Pheidas, Grant Baciocco, Beth Shea, Paul Goebel, Danforth France, Josh Perry, Cozmo Johnson. **Credits:** *Producer:* Laban Pheidias, Scott Allen Perry, Allison Locke, Brian McNelt, Susannah Mills. *Co-Producer:* Bryan O'Connell, Stacey Perry, Jamie Mitchell, Josh Perry. *Music:* Davin Wood, Scott Allen Perry.

1098   The Suite Life of Zack and Cody. (Comedy; Disney; March 18, 2005 to April 24, 2008) Zack and Cody are the twin 12-year-old sons of lounge singer Carey Martin. While Carey's husband, rock star Kirk Martin is on the road, she and her sons reside at the Tipton Hotel in Boston. Stories relate Zack and Cody's antics as they cause numerous problems for all concerned. London is the spoiled daughter of the hotel owner (Mr. Tipton); Mr. Moseby is the hotel manager; Maddie is the gift shop sales girl. See also *The Suite Life on Deck.* **Cast:** Kim Rhodes (Carey Martin), Cole Sprouse (Cody Martin), Dylan Sprouse (Zack Martin), Brenda Song (London Tipton), Ashley Tisdale (Maddie Fitzpatrick), Phill Lewis (Mr. Moseby), Adrian R'Mante (Estaban), Robert Torti (Kirk Martin). **Credits:** *Executive Producer:* Danny Kallis, Irene Dreayer. *Co-Executive Producer:* Jim Geoghan. *Producer:* Walter Barnett, Adam Lapidus, Jeny Quine, Kelly Sandefur. *Music:* Gary Scott. *Theme:* "The Suite Life" by John Adair, Steve Harrington.

1099   Sunset Tan. (Reality; E!; Premiered: May 28, 2007) A look at the inner workings of a tanning salon (Sunset Tan in Los Angeles)—its employees and the people who, despite living in sunny California, are unable to tan naturally and require artificial means. **Cast:** Jeff Boz, Nick D'Anna, Holly Huddleston, Janelle Perry, Molly Shea, Keely Williams, Erin Tietsort, Alek Carrera, Katie Lohmann, Sunshine Deia Tutt. **Credits:** *Executive Producer:* Mechelle Collins, Kevin Dill. *Co-Executive Producer:* Carl Buehl. *Associate Producer:* Teresa Hsu. *Music:* Matt Vowles.

1100   Super Why. (Cartoon; PBS; September 3, 2007)

Fairy tale characters Red (from "Little Red Riding Hood"), Princess (from "Princess and the Pea") and Whyatt (the younger brother of Jack from "Jack and the Beanstalk") host a program that begins with a 3-D like tour of a bookshelf. When a book is selected, the hosts are propelled into the story to examine what they are reading. The purpose is to help children learn how to read by reinforcing word skills.

Voice Cast: Tajja Isen (Princess Pea), Siera Florindo (Red Riding Hood), Nichols Castel Vanderburgh (Whyatt), Landon Norris. **Credits:** *Executive Producer:* Wendy Harris. *Producer:* Beth Stevenson. *Music:* Steve D'Angelo, Terry Tompkins.

1101 Supernanny. (Reality; ABC; Premiered: January 17, 2005)

A real life British nanny attempts to help families with unruly children.

Nanny: Jo Frost. **Credits:** *Executive Producer:* Mark Rowland, Nick Powell, Craig Armstrong. *Co-Executive Producer:* Amanda Murphy, Nick Emerson, Tony Yates, Carl Buehl. *Supervising Producer:* Barrie Bernstein, Vince Rotonda, Ben Greenberg. *Producer:* Rich Hansil, Michael Gross, Shana Kemp, Philip Lott. *Music:* Christopher Franke

1102 Supernatural. (Drama; WB/CW; Premiered: September 13, 2005)

Dean and Sam Winchester are young men with a most unusual job: they are bounty hunters who track down and destroy demons. When Dean was six and Sam two years of age, an unknown demon killed their mother (Mary) and set their father (John) on a path of vengeance: to find and destroy that demon (which he never did). When Dean became of age, he followed in his father's footsteps; Sam, however, chose to attend college. When that demon again strikes (killing Sam's girlfriend, Jessica), Sam joins with Dean to battle the supernatural and one day find and destroy the demon that changed their

lives. John, who was later killed by a demon, left his sons his notes and a special gun, designed by the Colt manufacturing company, that is capable of killing demons (something they fear and seek to acquire). Bobby and Tamara (called "Hunters") assist Sam and Dean as do the mysterious Ellen and Ruby.

Cast: Jensen Ackles (Dean Winchester), Jared Padalecki (Sam Winchester), Jeffrey Dean Morgan (John Winchester), Samantha Smith (Mary Winchester), Jim Beaver (Bobby Singer), Katie Cassidy (Ruby), Caroline Chikezie (Tamara), Ridge Canipe (Young Dean), Colin Ford (Young Sam), Samantha Ferris (Ellen Harvelle). **Credits:** *Executive Producer:* Robert Singer, Eric Kripke, McG. *Co-Executive Producer:* Richard Hatem, John Shiban, Kim Manners. *Supervising Producer:* Philip Sgriccia. *Producer:* Cyrus I. Yavneh, Peter Johnson. *Music:* Jay Gruska, Christopher Lennertz.

1103 Survivor. (Reality; CBS; May 31, 2002 to December 14, 2008)

Sixteen average Americans compete in the most grueling series ever produced. The players are brought to a god-forsaken island somewhere in the world and divided into tribes. Here, for 39 days, the players must live off the land and in a tribe and perform challenges. Players who fail to meet expectations face elimination. When ten players are left they merge into one team with each attempting to outperform the other to win a million dollars. The new season premiered February 12, 2009.

Host: Jeff Probst. **Credits:** *Executive Producer:* Charles Parsons, Tom Shelly, Mark Burnett. *Co-Executive Producer:* Conrad Riggs, Craig Armstrong, Doug McCallie, Kevin Greene, Viki Cacciatore, Holly Wofford, Craig Piligian. *Supervising Producer:* David Pistkin, Scott Messick. *Music:* Jonathan Chen, David Vanacore, Bobby Sommerfield.

1104 Survivorman. (Reality; Discovery Channel; Premiered: June 6, 2005)

Outdoorsman Les Stroud tackles nature by attempting to survive for a week in a remote location — from deserts to rain forests — with few supplies.

Host: Les Stroud. **Credits:** *Executive Producer:* Les Stroud. *Producer:* Stavros C. Stavrides.

1105 Sushi Pack. (Cartoon; CBS; Premiered: September 1, 2007)

Ikura, Wasabi, Tako, Masuro and Maguro are pieces of raw sushi that live to battle crime in Wharf City. Heat is their only weakness; cool air sustains their powers and they ask only that you do not eat them. Their main enemies are Orleander (a chef who is seeking to prepare them as a meal) and the evil Legion of Doom.

Voice Cast: Andrew Francis (Ikura), Rick Adams (Tako), Scott McNeil (Wasabi), Tara Strong (Maguro), Adam Behr (Titanium Chef), Chiara Zanni (Kani), Vincent Tong (Toro), Jeannie Elias, Nicole Brown. **Credits:** *Executive Producer:* Andy Heyward, Michael Maliana, Jeffrey Conrad, Sean Gorman, Ryan Weisbrook. *Producer:* J.C. Cheng, Jim E. Lara. *Music and Theme:* Phofo.

1106 Tak and the Power of JuJu. (Cartoon; Nickelodeon; Premiered: August 31, 2007)

Tak is a teenage Shaman's assistant in a prehistoric world. He is destined to become a Shaman but unexpected circumstances give him the powers 150 years before his time. Stories follow Tak as he attempts to balance two worlds — the mystical powers of the Juju (which provide a Shaman with power) and that of his tribe.

Voice Cast: Hal Sparks (Tak), Kari Wahlgren (Jeera), Haylie Johnson (Jeera; later), Patrick Warburton (Lok), Maurice LaMarche (Chief), Rob Paulsen (Tlaloc). **Credits:** *Supervising Producer:* Audu Paden. *Producer:* Mitch Watson.

1107 Take Home Handyman. (Reality; TLC; Premiered: March 31, 2007)

Shoppers at Home Depot are ap-

proached by carpenter Andrew Dan-Jumbo who offers to help them with a remodeling project. If they accept, cameras show how a master tackles a job.

Host: Andrew Dan-Jumbo. **Credits:** *Executive Producer:* Craig H. Shepherd, Peter Nissen, Robin Sestero. *Producer:* Kelly Phipps, Michael Amouri.

1108 Talk Sex with Sue Johanson. (Talk; Oxygen; Premiered: November 3, 2002)

Frank discussions about sex based on topics suggested by studio audience members and from those home viewers who call during the live telecast. Originally titled *The Sunday Night Sex Show.*

Host: Sue Johanson. **Credits:** *Music:* Nicholas Schnier.

1109 Talk Show with Spike Feresten. (Comedy; Fox; Premiered: September 16, 2006)

Former *Seinfeld* and *Simpsons* writer Spike Feresten hosts a show where the guests do all the work — from delivering monologues to performing skits.

Host: Spike Feresten. **Credits:** *Executive Producer:* Spike Feresten, Stewart Baily. *Co-Executive Producer:* Michael Armow. *Supervising Producer:* Joe Furey.

1110 Taxicab Confessions. (Reality; HBO; Premiered: January 1, 1995)

Real people, who hail a taxicab, are unknowingly recorded by hidden micro cameras as they talk about their personal lives (and being on HBO, their sometimes sexual experiences to the driver). At the end of their ride, passengers are told they were recorded and, in order for the sequence to air, they are asked to sign a release.

Taxi Drivers: Chris Moriarty, Brenda Roman, Todd Phillips. **Credits:** *Supervising Producer:* Julie Anderson, Felicia Caplan, Ted Levy. *Producer:* Harry Gantz, Joe Gantz. *Music:* Don Peake.

1111 Tell Me You Love Me. (Drama; HBO; September 9, 2007 to July 30, 2008)

Intimacy is explored in rather graphic detail as three couples, facing psychological problems, attempt to overcome their differences through the counseling of their therapist, Dr. May Foster. May is happily married to Arthur; Jamie and Hugo represent a couple in their twenties; Carolyn and Palek are the thirties couple; and Katie and David represent a couple in their forties.

Cast: Jane Alexander (Dr. May Foster), Ally Walker (Katie), Tim DeKay (David), Michelle Borth (Jaime) Luke Farrell Kirby (Hugo), Sonja Walger (Carolyn), Adam Scott (Palek), David Selby (Arthur Foster) **Credits:** *Executive Producer:* Patricia Rozema, Cynthia Mort, Gavin Polone. *Producer:* Lori-Etta Taub, Kathy Landsberg. *Associate Producer:* Dauri Chase.

1112 **Temptation**. (Game; Syn.; September 2007 to September 2008)

Each of the three players who compete each receive $20 in Temptation money. A question and answer session is held wherein each correct response awards the player a cash amount. At the end of each round an expensive merchandise item is offered at a fraction of the price (the temptation). If the player takes the deal, the money is deducted from his score. The player with the highest cash score wins.

Host: Rossi Morreale. **Co-Host:** Amanda Aardsman. **Announcer:** Rhonda Watts. **Credits:** *Executive Producer:* Ginger Simpson. *Producer:* Derek Che, Rosemarie DiSalvo, Robert Gustafson, Hal Lubin. *Music:* Nadia Solomon.

1113 **10 Items or Less**. (Comedy; TBS; Premiered: November 27, 2006)

Leslie Poole is a young man with a mission: save his family business, the Green and Grains Grocery Store (which is facing stiff competition from supermarkets). Stories, which have improvised dialogue (although based on plot outlines) follow Leslie as he attempts to run the store and cope with a group of hapless employees.

Cast: John Lehr (Leslie Poole), Roberta Valderrama (Yolanda Nelson), Christopher Liam (Richard), Kristen Gronfield (Ingrid), Bob Clendenin (Carl), Greg Davis, Sr. (Buck), Chris Payne Gilbert (Todd), Kim Coles (Mercy P. Jones). **Credits:** *Executive Producer:* Nancy Hower, John Lehr, Robert Stark Hickey. *Producer:* Barbara Stoll. *Associate Producer:* Evie Peck. *Music:* Steven Argila.

1114 **30 Days**. (Reality; FX; June 15, 2005 to July 8, 2008)

Unscripted documentary-like series that explores what life changing experiences are possible within thirty days.

Host: Morgan Spurlock. **Credits:** *Executive Producer:* Jonathan Chinn, R.J. Cutler, H.T. Owens, Benjamin Silverman, Morgan Spurlock, Dave Hamilton, Marla Chapple. *Supervising Producer:* Michael Bernstein, Max Swedlow, Poppy Das, Allison Ellewood, Stacey Offman. *Producer:* Alexandra Reed, Alan La Garde, Mary Lisio, Keri Hammond, Matthew Testa. *Music:* Jeff Cardoni.

1115 **Thirty Minute Meals with Rachael Ray**. (Cooking; Food Network; Premiered: December 1, 2001)

Meal preparations that take no longer than thirty minutes with chef, cookbook author and talk show host Rachael Ray.

Host: Rachael Ray. **Credits:** *Executive Producer:* Mark Dissin. *Producer:* Bob Tuschman, Jenni Gilroy.

1116 **30 Rock**. (Comedy; NBC; Premiered: October 11, 2006)

An exaggerated behind-the-scenes look at what "really" happens before a sketch series airs as seen through the experiences of Liz Lemon, the head writer of "a show for the ladies" called *The Girlie Show* that airs on NBC and is produced at its New York headquarters at 30 Rockefeller Plaza in Manhattan (the building is nicknamed "30 Rock"). Liz is a young woman who is totally dedicated to her job and is facing a difficult challenge: breathe new life into the show, which is faltering in the ratings and could face cancellation. Jack Donaghy, a head honcho with the General Electric division of NBC (Head of East Coast Programming) has been assigned to retool Liz's show; Jeanna Maroney is the show's star; Kenneth is the eager NBC page; Tracy Jordan is the comic hired to boost the show's ratings; Pete, Cerie and Joshua are fellow writers.

Cast: Tina Fey (Liz Lemon), Jane Krakowski (Jenna Maroney), Alec Baldwin (Jack Donaghy), Tracy Morgan (Tracy Jordan), Jack McBrayer (Kenneth), Katrina Bowden (Cerie), Scott Adsit (Pete Hornberger), Lonny Ross (Josh), Judah Friedlander (Frank). **Credits:** *Executive Producer:* Lorne Michaels. Tina Fey, JoAnn Alfano, Marci Klein, David Miner. *Co-Executive Producer:* Robert Carlock, John Riggi, Jack Burdett, Brett Baer, David Finkel. *Supervising Producer:* Adam Bernstein. *Producer:* Jeff Richmond.

1117 This Old House. (Reality; PBS; Premiered: October 1, 1980)

A weekly series in which an old house is chosen for a face lift. Each aspect of the renovation is detailed with a look at how things are done and the materials used.

Hosts: Bob Vila, Steve Thomas, Kevin O'Connor. **Regulars:** Norm Abram (carpenter), Tom Silva (contractor), Richard Trethewey (plumber), Roger Cook (landscaper). **Credits:** *Executive Producer:* Russell Morash, Jeff Ruhe. *Producer:* Deborah Hood.

1118 Thomas the Tank Engine and Friends. (Children; PBS; Premiered: August 1, 2004)

The mythical island of Sodor is the setting where the railroad engines and cars of the Sodor Railway relate learning lessons to children through their daily activities. Sir Topham Hat oversees operations and principal focus is on engines Thomas, Gordon, Percy, Emily, Edward, Henry and James.

An amazingly lifelike model railroad and specially constructed trains with human-like qualities comprise the set. Adapted from the series *Shining Time Station.*

Narrator/Voices: Alec Baldwin, Michael Brandon. **Credits:** *Executive Producer:* Jocelyn Stevenson. *Producer:* Simon Spencer. *Music:* Robert Hartshorne. *Songs:* Ed Welch.

1119 3-2-1 Penguins. (Children; NBC; Premiered: September 25, 2006)

Kevin, Midgel, Zidgel and Fidgel are "four out of this world penguins" who travel around the universe in their space ship, *The X-51.* They have befriended two Earth children (twins Michelle and Jason) and stories follow their adventures as they explore the galaxy and relate learning lessons to children.

Voice Cast: Quinn Lord (Jason), Claire Corlett (Michelle), John Payne (Zidgel), Paul Dobson (Midgel), Lee Tockar (Fidgel), Michael Donovan (Kevin). **Credits:** *Executive Producer:* Mike Heap, Jane Smith. *Producer:* Sean Roche, Joe Barruso. *Theme Song:* Mike Nawrocki, Kurt Heiecke.

1120 Til Death. (Comedy; Fox; September 7, 2006 to November 5, 2008)

Eddie Stark, a history teacher at Winston Churchill High School in Philadelphia, is married to Joy and the father of Allison. Jeff Woodcock, the school principal, is a newlywed and married to Stephanie. The four are friends and stories follow Eddie, a "more experienced" married man, as he tries to teach Jeff the ins and outs of marriage.

Cast: Brad Garrett (Eddie Stark), Joely Fisher (Joy Stark), Eddie Kay Thomas (Jeff Woodcock), Kat Foster (Stephanie Woodcock), Krysten Ritter (Allison Stark). **Credits:** *Executive Producer:* Josh Goldsmith, Cathy Yuspa. *Producer:* Brad Garrett, Glenn Robbins, Doug Wald. *Co-Producer:* Annette Sahakian Davis, Erin Braun, Jim Kukucka. *Music:* Steven Cahill.

1121   Tim Gunn's Guide to Style.
(Reality; Bravo; September 6, 2007 to
November 20, 2008)

Ordinary people who are considered
"style challenged" are the subjects. Fashion
expert Tim Gunn then works his magic to
teach the subject the proper aspects of
poise, clothes and grooming.

Host: Tim Gunn. **Credits:** *Executive
Producer:* Sarah Jane Cohen, Scott A.
Stone. *Co-Executive Producer:* Karen Kunkel. *Producer:* Hassan Cidari. *Associate Producer:* Liz Alderman. *Music:* Brad Segal.

1122   TMZ on TV. (Variety; Syn.;
Premiered: September 2007)

A TV series based on the Internet's
TMZ.com, a site for the latest celebrity
news (TMZ stands for The Thirty Mile
Zone, a place where everything exciting in
entertainment happens).

Host: Harvey Levin. **Credits:** *Executive Producer:* Harvey Levin. *Supervising
Producer:* Gillian Sheldon. *Producer:* Lisa
Hudson, John McBride, Michael Hund-
gen, Sean Borg, Michael Cole Weiss, Andrew Epstein. *Music:* Timothy Andrew
Edwards.

**1123   The Tonight Show with Jay
Leno**. (Variety; NBC; Premiered: May
25, 1992)

An opening monologue, celebrity interviews, comedy skits and musical numbers.

Host: Jay Leno. **Credits:** *Executive Producer:* Debbie Vickers, Helen Kushnick.
Supervising Producer: Patti M. Grant. *Producer:* Star Price, Larry Goitia, Susan B.
Clark, Bill Royce. *Music:* Brandford Mar-
salis, Kevin Eubanks.

1124   Top Chef. (Reality; Bravo; Premiered: March 8, 2006)

Real life chefs in high tension situations
that test their abilities to deal with any and
all problems that face top chefs everyday.
The chef who proves to be the best at coping with and solving the challenges that
are presented is named Top Chef.

Host: Padma Lukshmi. **Credits:** *Executive Producer:* Shauna Minoprio, Dan
Cutforth, Jane Lipsitz. *Supervising Producer:* Scott Shatsky, Gayle Gowlowski.
Co-Executive Producer: Rich Buhrman. *Associate Producer:* Doneen Arquine.

1125   Top Design. (Reality; Bravo;
January 31, 2007 to November 5, 2008)

Hopeful interior designers compete in
various challenges wherein they vie for the
opportunity to start their own design firm.
Host: Todd Oldham.

Judges: Jonathan Adler, Kelly Wears-
tle, Margaret Russell. **Credits:** *Executive
Producer:* Cori Abraham, Andrea Cohen,
Clay Newbill, Dave Serwatka, Scott A.
Stone. *Supervising Producer:* Ryan Flynn.
Producer: Mark Perez, Tim Laurie, Susan
House, Vanessa Ballesteros. *Music:* Brad
Segal.

**1126   Tori and Dean: Home Sweet
Hollywood**. (Reality; Oxygen; March
20, 2007 to August 12, 2008)

A continuation of *Tori and Dean: Inn
Love* (wherein actress Tori Spelling and
hubby Dean Dermott purchase a bed and
breakfast [Chateau LaRue] and later became parents [of Liam]). Here, they return to Hollywood to purchase a home,
celebrate Liam's first birthday and prepare
for the birth of their first daughter.

Stars: Tori Spelling, Dean McDermott.
Credits: *Executive Producer:* Tori Spelling,
Dean McDermott, Fenron Bailey. *Super-
vising Producer:* Chris McKini. *Producer:*
Bill Watson, Michael Call, Sara Mast.
Music: Simon J. Hunter.

1127   Total Drama Island. (Cartoon; Cartoon Network; Premiered: July 8,
2007)

An animated "reality" series in which a
group of teenagers, spending the summer
at a rundown camp (Drama Island) compete in a series of physical challenges.

Voice Cast: Christian Potenza (Chris,
the host), Megan Fahlenboch (Gwen),

Sarah Gadon (Beth), Scott McCord (Owen/ Trent), Lauren Lipsen (Sadie), Julia Chatrey (Eva), Brian Froud (Harold), Drew Nelson (Duncan), Cle Bennett (Chef). **Credits:** *Producer:* Brian Irving. *Music:* James Chapple, Dave Kelly.

1128 Totally Busted. (Erotica; Playboy Channel; Premiered: July 1, 2005)

An "R" rated version of *Candid Camera* wherein the Playboy Channel's "Dirty Trick Squad" enforces their motto: "It's not a put on unless someone takes it off." Sexy practical jokes are played on real people with the object being to catch them naked or as naked as possible.

Host: Janelle Perry, Mary Carey. **Regulars:** Candice Michelle, Steve-O, Tim Bennett, Brandon Gibson. **Credits:** *Executive Producer:* Scott Cope, Dan Smith, Robert Taylor, Nicholas Thomas. *Supervising Producer:* Eddie Delbridge. *Producer:* Linda L. Miller, Geoff Bunch.

1129 Trading Spaces. (Reality; TLC; Premiered: September 1, 2000)

Neighbors are divided into two teams, given $1,000 and a team of professional designers and carpenters to transform a room in each other's home. The program shows the make over from start to finish as well as the reactions when the home owners see what has transpired.

Hosts: Paige Davis, Alex McLeod. **Designers:** Heidi Santro Tomas, Frank Bielec, Gunevieve Gorder, Laurie Hickson-Smith, Douglas Wilson, Edward Walker, Christi Proctor, Laura Day, Kia Steave-Dickerson, Vern Yip, Mario DeArmas, Lauren Makk. **Carpenters:** Thad Mills, Faber Dewar, Brandan Russell, Carter Oosterhouse, Ty Pennington, Amy Wynn Pastor. **Credits:** *Executive Producer:* Ray Murray, Stephen H. Schwartz, Susan Cohen-Dickler, Denise Cramsey. *Producer:* Jivey Rivas, Larry Blasé, Flor Siqueiros, Alyssa Kaufman, Aimee Kramer, Laura Sevalmi, Amy Van Vessem, Patrick Denzer, Michael Precheur.

1130 Trick My Truck. (Reality; CMT; February 3, 2006 to July 4, 2008)

Big rig truck mechanics "steal" the trucks of unsuspecting drivers for only one purpose: customize them and turn them into the driver's dream machine.

Mechanics: Allen Harrah, Steve Harrah, Kevin Locklear, Matt Moore, Rob Richardson, Ryan Templeton. **Credits:** *Executive Producer:* Jason Morgan. *Producer:* Melanie Moreau, Rob Zazzali.

1131 The Tudors. (Drama; Showtime; April 1, 2007 to June 1, 2008)

England in the 1500s is the setting. The life and times of Henry VIII, a king who created a new religion (defying the Catholic faith) so he could divorce his wife and sleep with his mistress. The series spans the time from Henry's marriage to Katherine of Aragon to his marriage to Anne Boleyn.

Cast: Jonathan Rhys Meyers (King Henry VIII), Maria Doyle Kennedy (Katherine of Aragon), Natalie Dormer (Anne Boleyn), Sam Neill (Cardinal Wolsey), Jeremy Northam (Sir Thomas More), Henry Cavill (Duke of Suffolk), Callum Blue (Anthony Knivert), Gabriella Anwar (Princess Margaret Tudor), Steve Waddington (Duke of Buckingham), Mark Lambert (William Cornish), James Frain (Thomas Cromwell), Perdita Weeks (Mary Boleyn), Anna Brewster (Anna Buckingham). **Credits:** *Executive Producer:* Steve Shill, Tim Bevan, Eric Fellner, Michael Hirst, Gary Howsam, Morgan O'Sullivan, Benjamin Silverman. *Co-Executive Producer:* Teri Weinberg. *Producer:* Sheila Hockin, James Flynn. *Music:* Trevor Morris.

1132 TV Land Myths and Legends. (Reality; TV Land; January 10, 2007 to November 19, 2008)

Celebrities appear to express their opinions concerning movie and television myths (for example, Did cameras capture a ghost in the film *Three Men and a Baby?*,

"Was Lucille Ball a Communist?"). Although some myths are left unanswered, the program presents a different look at Hollywood's past.

Narrator: Khandi Alexander. **Credits:** *Executive Producer:* Paul Barrosse, Gay Rosenthal, Sid Maniaci. *Supervising Producer:* Natalie Aaron. *Producer:* Robert Zimmerman. *Music:* Jon Ernst.

1133 Two and a Half Men. (Comedy; CBS; Premiered: September 22, 2003)

The "men" of the title are Charlie Harper and his brother, Alan. Ten-year-old Jake, Alan's son, is the "half." Charlie is a womanizing jingles writer whose carefree lifestyle is suddenly interrupted when Alan divorces and he and Jake move in with Charlie in his beachfront house in Malibu, California. Also complicating Charlie's life is Evelyn, his "narcissistic, emotionally toxic mother," and Judith, Alan's neurotic ex-wife. Stories relate Alan's efforts to raise Jake on the straight and narrow despite the complexities of the situations that arise living with Charlie and his endless parade of beautiful women. Berta is Charlie's housekeeper; Rose is the woman obsessed with having Charlie.

Cast: Charlie Sheen (Charlie Harper), Jon Cryer (Alan Harper), Angus T. Jones (Jake Harper), Holland Taylor (Evelyn Harper), Conchata Ferrell (Berta) Melanie Lynskey (Rose), Marin Hinkle (Judith Harper), April Bowlby (Khandi). **Credits:** *Executive Producer:* Lee Aronsohn, Chuck Lorre, Mark Burg, Oren Koules, Eric Tannenbaum, Kim Tannenbaum. *Co-Executive Producer:* Eddie Gorodetsky, Dan Foster, Jeff Abugov. *Supervising Producer:* Eric Lapidus, Mark Roberts. *Producer:* Michael Collier, Tracey Ormandy, Annette D. Sahakian. *Music:* Chuck Lorre, Grant Geissman, Dennis C. Brown, Lee Aronsohn.

1134 2 Dudes Catering. (Reality; Food Network; Premiered: October 16, 2007)

Jon Shook and Vinny Dotolo, called renegade chefs, go to outrageous lengths to impress clients and establish a Hollywood catering company.

Hosts: Jon Shook, Vinny Dotolo. **Credits:** *Executive Producer:* Matthew Levine, Max Weissman. *Producer:* Rob Muraskin, Josh Cole, Annie Dahlie.

1135 The Tyra Banks Show. (Talk; Syn.; Premiered: September 2005)

A lively (and sometimes controversial) daily series hosted by super model Tyra Banks that deals with issues that affect people in their daily lives.

Host: Tyra Banks. **Credits:** *Executive Producer:* John Redman, Tyra Banks, Kevin Applegate, Alex Duda, Benny Medina. *Supervising Producer:* Christine Cavalieri. *Producer:* Monica Moore, William Richards, Paul Storck, Jeff Thomas, Jennifer Langhield, Adam Kleid, Jen Friesen, Margot Foley, Tracey Foley, Brooke Donberg, Brian Costell, Brenton Metzler. *Music:* Timothy Andrew Edwards, Jason Brandt.

1136 Ugly Betty. (Comedy-Drama; ABC; Premiered: September 25, 2006)

Betty Suarez, the Betty of the title, is not really ugly. She is pretty but does little to make herself attractive. She was born in Queens, New York, and is a recent graduate of Queens College. She lives with her widowed father, Ignacio, her older sister, Hilda, and her young nephew, Justin. Betty is sharp, optimistic and prepared — but life is not always fair to her. She applies for a job at Meade Publications, hoping for a position on one of their magazines. Her looks do not impress Daniel Meade, the editor of *Mode* (a fashion magazine) but they do impress Daniel's father, Bradford, who hires her as Daniel's assistant. As Betty settles into her job, she becomes involved in Daniel's fight to stop Wilhelmina Slater, a stunning, but scheming woman who seeks to become the editor of *Mode*. Stories relate events in Betty's home and working life. Based on the Colombian telenovela *Yo Soy Betty, La Fea* ("I'm Betty, the Ugly One").

Cast: America Ferrera (Betty Suarez), Eric Mabius (Daniel Meade), Tony Plana (Ignacio Suarez), Ana Ortiz (Hilda Suarez), Mark Indelicato (Justin Suarez), Alan Dale (Bradford Meade), Ashley Jensen (Christina), Becki Newton (Amanda), Vanessa Williams (Wilhelmina Slater), Judith Light (Claire Meade), Debi Mazar (Leah Feldman), Rebecca Romijn (Alexis; the transsexual). **Credits:** *Executive Producer:* Benjamin Silverman, Silvio Horta, James D. Parriott, Jose Tamez, Fernando Gaitan, Jim Haymen. *Co-Executive Producer:* Sheila R. Lawrence, Teri Weinberg. *Producer:* James Bigwood, Alice West, Jack Philbrick. *Music:* Jeff Beal.

1137 Unfabulous. (Comedy; Nickelodeon; Premiered: September 12, 2004)

Addie Singer is a pretty 13-year-old girl who attends Rocky Road Middle School. She is a talented singer and songwriter and struggling to get through adolescence. Her music helps her through the troublesome situations she has a knack for encountering and stories relate her awkward journey.

Cast: Emma Roberts (Addie Singer), Molly Hagan (Sue Singer), Markus Flanagan (Jeff Singer), Tad Kelly (Ben Singer), Malese Jow (Geena Fabiano), Jordan Calloway (Zach Carter-Schwartz), Mary Lou (Mary Ferry), Dustin Ingram (Duane Ogilvy), Bianca Collins (Patti Perez), Raja Fenske (Jake Behari), Sarah Hester (Jen), Mildred Dumas (Principal Brandywine) **Credits:** *Executive Producer:* Sue Rose. *Producer:* Aaron Staudinger, Richard T. Schor, Rebecca Khan. *Music:* Jill Sobule. *Songs Performed By:* Emma Roberts.

1138 The Unit. (Adventure; CBS; Premiered: March 7, 2006)

The 303rd Logistical Studies Unit, a division of the U.S. Army, is actually the cover for a secret Special Forces Strike Unit that is designed to battle terrorism in any part of the world on a moment's notice. Colonel Tom Ryan heads the unit; Jonas Blane, Bob Brown, Hector Williams, Mack Gerhardt and Charles Grey are his principal operatives. The Unit officially does not exist and is responsible only to the President of the United States. It is based at Fort Griffith and its compound is called "The Cave." To remain top secret, the Unit never takes credit for a completed mission. They go in, do the job and allow others to take the credit. Married members of the Unit live on the army base on Maple Street. Molly is married to Jonas; Kim is Bob's wife (they are the parents of Serena); Tiffany is Mack's wife. Stories not only follow the missions of the Unit members, but the lives of the women they leave behind whose fears and concerns are a vital part of the program.

Cast: Dennis Haysbert (Jonas Blane), Scott Foley (Bob Brown), Demore Barnes (Hector Williams), Max Martini (Mack Gerhardt), Robert Patrick (Col. Tom Ryan), Michael Irby (Charles Grey), Regina Taylor (Molly Blane), Alyssa Shafer (Serena Brown), Abby Brammell (Tiffany Gerhardt), Audrey Marie Anderson (Kim Brown), Sophina Brown (Nikki Betancourt). **Credits:** *Executive Producer:* Shawn Ryan, David Mamet, Carol Flint. *Co-Executive Producer:* Eric L. Haney, Vahan Moosekian, Paul Redford, Daniel Voll, Todd Ellis Kessler. *Supervising Producer:* Lynn Mamet. *Producer:* Sharon Lee Watson. *Music:* Robert Duncan.

1139 Unwrapped. (Reality; Food Network; Premiered: June 1, 2001)

Test kitchens are explored to show viewers the secrets behind the making of all types of food (from popcorn to cereal to soda).

Host: Marc Summers. **Credits:** *Executive Producer:* Jim Berger, Jennifer Darrow, Duke Hartman, Sonny Hutchinson, John Andreae. *Supervising Producer:* Glenna

Stacer-Saylers. *Producer:* Tim McOsker, Molly Sutton, Andrea Wayland.

1140   **Veggie Tales**. (Children; NBC; Premiered: September 16, 2006)

Veggie Valley is a magical place where vegetables come to life and live like humans. Although technically not a vegetable, a fruit, Bob the Tomato, hosts a program where he and his vegetable friends present learning lessons to children as they interact with each other. Bob's principal friends are Larry the Cucumber, Archibald Asparagus, Laura the Carrot and Junior Asparagus.

Voice Cast: Phil Vischer (Bob), Mike Nawrocki (Larry), Phil Vischer (Archibald), Lisa Vischer (Junior Asparagus), Jackie Ritz (Laura the Carrot), Mike Nawrocki (Jimmy Gourd), Phil Vischer (Lunt). **Credits:** *Executive Producer:* Miles Heap, Jane Smith, J. Chris Wall. *Music:* Kert Henecke, Alan Moore, Jason Moore, Phil Vischer. *Veggie Tales Theme Song:* Phil Vischer.

1141   **The Venture Brothers**. (Cartoon; Cartoon Network; February 16, 2003 to August 24, 2008)

Dean and Hank Venture are twin brothers who thrive on adventure. They are the sons of Dr. Thaddeus Venture, a brilliant scientist and together they set out on daring missions to battle evil (from zombies to mad scientists). Brock Samson is their bodyguard.

Voice Cast: Michael Sintemiklaas (Dean Venture), Christopher McCulloch (Hank Venture), James Urbaniale (Dr. Thaddeus Venture), Patrick Warburton (Brock Samson). **Credits:** *Executive Producer:* Christopher McCulloch, Steven Yoon. *Supervising Producer:* Jeffrey Nodelman, Jeremy Rosenberg. *Producer:* David Lipson, Rachel Simon. *Music:* J.G. Thirlwell.

1142   **The View**. (Talk; ABC; Premiered: August 11, 1997)

A daily exchange of conversation wherein a panel of women discuss the politics of the day.

Moderator: Meredith Vieira. **Panel:** Barbara Walters, Joy Behar, Star Jones, Sherri Shepherd, Elizabeth Hasselbeck, Rosie O'Donnell. **Credits:** *Executive Producer:* Barbara Walters. *Producer:* Alicia Ybarbo, Ann Marie Williams-Gray, Jakki Taylor, Erin Saxton, Susan Solomon, Sue Polonetsky, Allison Klinger, Donald Berman, Rebecca Biderman, Glenn Davish.

1143   **Viva Pinata**. (Cartoon; Fox; August 26, 2006 to September 27, 2008)

Piñata Island is a picturesque island where piñatas live and dream for the day they will be chosen to entertain at a party. Stories follow the adventures of a group of piñatas (based on animals) as they encounter various misadventures.

Voice Cast: Jamie McGonnigal (Teddington Twingersnaps), Brian Maillard (Paulie Pretztail), Dan Green (Hudson Horstachio), David Wills (Fergy Fudgehog), Marc Thompson (Franklink Fizzlybear). **Credits:** *Supervising Producer:* Paul Griffin. *Producer:* Lloyd Goldfine, Norman J. Grossfeld, Carole Weitzman. *Music:* Matt McGuire.

1144   **Weeds**. (Comedy; Showtime; Premiered: August 7, 2005)

Nancy Botwin is a recent widow and the mother of two children, Silas and Shane (they live in the fictional town of Agrestic, California). Following the sudden death of her husband, Nancy finds that the only way she can support her family is by selling marijuana. Stories follow Nancy and the people close to her as she goes about selling weed to make ends meet. Celia Hodes is Nancy's friend; Doug is Nancy's accountant (and her best client); Andy is Nancy's brother-in-law; Heylia is Nancy's weed supplier; Conrad is Heylia's son. The fourth season (June 16, 2008) changes the locale to Manhattan Beach,

California as a better opportunity for Nancy to expand her illegal drug business (she is now near the Mexican border; Agrestic was destroyed by a fire in the third season finale).

Cast: Mary Louise Parker (Nancy Botwin), Hunter Parrish (Silas Botwin), Alexander Gould (Shane Botwin), Elizabeth Perkins (Celia Hodes), Justin Kirk (Andy Botwin), Kevin Nealon (Doug Wilson), Tonya Patano (Heylia James), Romany Malco (Conrad Shepard), Mary Kate Olsen (Tara Lindman), Matthew Modine (Sullivan Groff). **Credits:** *Executive Producer:* Jenji Kohan. *Co-Executive Producer:* Roberto Benabib, Craig Zisk. *Supervising Producer:* Mark A. Burley, Devon Shepard. *Producer:* Rolin Jones. *Music:* Brandon Jay, Gwen Sanford, Joey Santiago.

1145 **Weird U.S.** (Reality; History Channel; Premiered: August 1, 2005)

Mark Moran and Mark Sceurman, authors of the book *Weird U.S.*, take to the road to explore the myths, legends and folklore of the U.S.

Host: Mark Moran, Mark Sceurman. **Credits:** *Executive Producer:* Kristine Sabat, Vincent Krolyevich, Bill Hunt. *Producer:* Jessica Conway, Mark Cannon, Penny Fearon, Jason Fine, Chris Gidez, Sarah Hunt, Karina Lahni, Ted Poole, Jonathan Santos.

1146 **What Not to Wear.** (Reality; TLC; Premiered: January 18, 2003)

"Fashion Police" Stacy London and Clinton Kelly try to help a person who dresses poorly (nominated by friends and family) find the right look — including a new wardrobe and grooming tips. Cameras capture the before and after results.

Hosts: Wayne Scott Lucas, Jillian Hamilton, Stacy London, Clinton Kelly. **Makeup Artist:** Carmindy Bowyer. **Hairdresser:** Mike Arrojo, Kylee Nicole Cook. **Credits:** *Executive Producer:* Dean Slotar, Abigail Harvey, Pamela Deutsch, Sarah

Jane Cohen, Elizabeth Browde. *Producer:* Boaz Halaban, Louisa Griffith Jones.

1147 **Wheel of Fortune.** (Game; Syn.; Premiered: September 1982)

Three players stand before a large spinning wheel that contains various cash amounts. To win a cash amount after the wheel is spun, the player suggests a letter that may be contained in a puzzle displayed on stage. If it is correct, the letter appears in its appropriate space and the player receives a chance to solve the puzzle. Turns alternate and the first player to solve the puzzle wins what money he has accumulated.

Host: Pat Sajak. **Hostess:** Vanna White. **Credits:** *Executive Producer:* Harry Friedman, Merv Griffin, Bob Murphy. *Supervising Producer:* Karen Griffith, Steve Schwartz. *Producer:* Josh Weintraub, Nancy Jones, John Rhinehart. *Associate Producer:* Randy Burke, David S. Williger.

1148 **The Whitest Kids U Know.** (Comedy; Fuse; Premiered: March 20, 2007)

Skit show in which five young men satirize topical issues and sometimes controversial topics.

Cast: Sam Brown, Trevor Moore, Timmy Williams, Darren Trumeter, Zach Cregge. **Credits:** *Executive Producer:* Jim Biederman. *Producer:* Darren Trumeter, Elizabeth Belew, Abby Hoyt.

1149 **Who Wants to Be a Millionaire?** (Game; Syn.; Premiered: September 16, 2002)

A board with 15 money amounts, ranging from $100 to $1 million is shown. A question, with four possible answers, appears on a screen before a player. If the player chooses the correct answer he wins the money at play and proceeds to the next money amount question. He can quit at any time and leave with what money he has won or risk everything for a chance at the million dollar question.

Host: Meredith Vieira. **Credits:** *Executive Producer:* Leigh Hampton. *Co-Executive Producer:* Meredith Vieira. *Producer:* Rich Sirop.

1150 Wife Swap. (Reality; ABC; Premiered: September 26, 2004)

Two families with differing lifestyles are the subjects. The wives exchange places and attempt to improve situations they find troubling. After the experience, the wives are reunited with their families and discuss the outcome. Casts vary by show. **Credits:** *Executive Producer:* Michael Davies. *Co-Executive Producer:* Laurie Girion. *Supervising Producer:* Stacey Altman, Paul Davison. *Producer:* Rick Murray, Babette Pepaj, Vanessa Frances, Michael Kaufman, Anthony Sylvester.

1151 Wildfire. (Drama; ABC Family; June 20, 2005 to March 17, 2008)

Raintree is a ranch owned by the Ritters, a family who help troubled children. Eighteen-year-old Kris Furillo is one such child. As Kris adjusts to her new surroundings she learns that the Ritters are having financial troubles and in danger of losing their ranch. Kris has an uncanny knack with horses; the Ritters have a spirited horse named Wildfire. With the help of Pablo, the local horse trainer, Kris enters the world of horse racing and, with her winnings, helps the Ritters maintain their ranch. **Cast:** Genevieve Cortese (Kris Furillo), Nana Visitor (Jean Ritter), Dennis Weaver (Henry Ritter), Micah Alberti (Matt Ritter), Andrew Hoeft (Todd Ritter), Nicole Tubiola (Danielle Davis), Greg Serano (Pablo Betart), Ryan Sypek (Junior Davis). **Credits:** *Executive Producer:* Michael Piller, Marjorie David, Lloyd Segan. *Co-Executive Producer:* Sandy Isaac, Lloyd Segan. *Producer:* Dennis Stuart Murphy, Lester Berman. *Music:* Shawn Pierce, Jay Gruska.

1152 Will and DeWitt. (Cartoon; Kids WB/CW; Premiered: September 22, 2007)

Will is a young boy with a natural curiosity about life. DeWitt is a magical frog that can transform himself into any living creature. Through DeWitt's transformations Will learns about various aspects of life (further enhanced by songs sung by various animals).

Voice Cast: Connor Price (Will), Alberto Ghisi (Will; later), Richard Ian Cox (DeWitt), London Angelis (Sam), Samantha Wilson (Tricia), Linda Ballantyne (Shelley), Katie Griffin (Mom). **Credits:** *Executive Producer:* Michael Hirsh, Andrew Nicholls, Pamela Slavin, Toper Taylor, Darrell Vickers. *Producer:* Susie Grondin. *Music:* Marvin Dolgay.

1153 The Wire. (Crime Drama; HBO; June 2, 2002 to March 9, 2008)

A gritty, hard-hitting program that details a police department's efforts to curtail the illegal business of dealing drugs. Avon Barksdale is the head of the Barksdale drug operations, a crime family that is devastating the city of Baltimore. The efforts of the officers attached to the Baltimore Police Department to stop the drug cartel is seen from the viewpoint of the individual members of the force — each of whom has a sincere desire to rid the city of drugs. Detective Jimmy McNulty heads the department's Task Force Unit. Lt. Cedric Daniels is his superior; Caroline Massey, an expert wire tapper; Shakima "Kima" Greggs, a narcotics cop; and detectives William "Buck" Moreland and Lester Freamon are the other members of Jimmy's team. Rhonda Pearlman is a tough prosecutor with the Baltimore D.A.'s office; Elena is Jimmy's ex-wife.

Cast: Dominic West (Det. James McNulty), Lance Reddick (Lt. Cedric Daniels), Sonja Sohn (Det. Shakima Greggs), Domenick Lombardozzi (Det. Thomas "Herc" Haulk), Wendell Pierce (Det. William Moreland), Jim True-Frost (Det. Ronald "Prez" Pryzbylewski), Clarke Peters (Det. Lester Freamon), Seth Gilliam

(Sgt. Ellis Carver), Idris Elba (Russell "Stringer" Bell), J.D. Williams (Preston "Bodie" Broadus), Delaney Williams (Sgt. Jay Landsman), Parker Robinson (Det. Leander Sydnor), Deirdre Faison (Commissioner Ervin H. Burrell), Wood Harris (Avon Barksdale), Michael Salconi (Det. Michael Santangelo). **Credits:** *Executive Producer:* David Simon, Robert F. Colesberry. *Producer:* Nina Kostroff-Noble, Karen L. Thorson. *Associate Producer:* Simon Egleton, Leslie Jacobowitz.

1154 **Without a Trace.** (Crime Drama; CBS; Premiered: September 1, 2002)

When a person is reported missing authorities race against time, hoping to find the victim within 72 hours (which offers the greatest hope of recovery). Stories focus on the members of the New York Missing Persons Squad, an elite team of FBI agents headed by Jack Malone, as they seek people reported as missing.

Cast: Anthony LaPaglia (John Michael "Jack" Malone), Poppy Montgomery (Agent Samantha Spade), Enrique Murciano (Agent Danny Taylor), Marianne Jean-Baptiste (Agent Vivian Johnson), Eric Close (Agent Martin Fitzgerald), Roselyn Sanchez (Agent Elena Delgado). **Credits:** *Executive Producer:* Jerry Bruckheimer, Jonathan Littman, Ed Redlich, Hank Steinberg, David Nutter. *Co-Executive Producer:* Timothy Busfield, Jan Nash, Greg Walker, Jennifer Levin, Scott Williams. Jacob Epstein. *Supervising Producer:* Jose Molia. *Producer:* Steve Beers, Paul Holahan, Simon Mirren, Ethan Smith, Barr H. Waldman, Scott White, Allison Abner. *Music:* Peter Manning Robinson, Reinhold Heil, Johnny Klimek.

1155 **The Wizards of Waverly Place.** (Comedy; Disney; Premiered: October 12, 2007)

The Russo's appear to be an ordinary family living on Waverly Place in New York City (where they operate the Waverly Place Diner). There are the parents, Theresa and Jerry and they have three children, Alexandra, Justin and Max. Looks can be deceiving. Each member of the family is a wizard and descended from a long line of wizards (from Jerry's side of the family; Theresa is just a plain, pretty, ordinary human woman. However, because Jerry married a mortal, he has been stripped of his powers. He does, however, instruct his children in the art of sorcery). Stories follow events in the lives of the family, especially the children, as they attempt to control the mischief they cause by using their developing powers.

Cast: David DeLuise (Jerry Russo), Maria Canals-Barrera (Theresa Russo), Selena Gomez (Alex Russo), David Henrie (Justin Russo), Jake T. Austin (Max Russo), Amanda Tepe (Elaine), Jennifer Stone (Harper, Alex's friend). **Credits:** *Executive Producer:* Peter Murrieta, Todd Greenwald. *Music:* John Adair, Steve Hampton.

1156 **Women's Murder Club.** (Crime Drama; ABC; October 12, 2007 to May 13, 2008)

Lindsay Boxer is a San Francisco police detective with a keen ability to immediately analyze a crime scene and proceed with a plan of action. But all her efforts are often frustrating as investigating and prosecuting a case could take months, even years. To help speed the process, Lindsay devises a plan. She forms a team with three other women — Claire Washburn, Cindy Thomas and Jill Bernhardt — a medical examiner, a newspaper reporter and an Assistant District Attorney — to do what the system can't — get quick results. Stories follow the women as they pool their talents to solve homicides within the shortest time possible following the crime. The women gather at Papa Joe's Coffee House to discuss their cases. Tom Hogan is Lindsay's ex-husband; Heather is Tom's fiancé (later his wife).

Cast: Angie Harmon (Lindsay Boxer), Paula Newsome (Claire Washburn), Aubrey Dollar (Cindy Thomas), Laura Harris (Jill Bernhardt), Tyrees Allen (Det. Warren Jacobi), Rob Estes (Tom Hogan). **Credits:** *Executive Producer:* Elizabeth Craft, James Patterson, Brett Ratner, Joe Simpson. *Producer:* Ed Milkovich. *Associate Producer:* Tony Palermo. *Music:* Jay Ferguson.

1157 **Wonder Pets**. (Cartoon; Nickelodeon; Premiered: March 3, 2006)

Linny the Guinea Pig, Ming-Ming Duckling and Turtle Tuck are pre-school animals with one special goal: rescue animals in trouble in any part of the world. Real animals are used but are digitally altered to give them clothes and the ability to move and talk.

Voice Cast: Sofie Zamchick (Linny the Guinea Pig), Teala Dunn (Turtle Tuck), Danica Lee (Ming-Ming Duckling). **Credits:** *Executive Producer:* Josh Selig. *Producer:* Tone Thyne. *Music:* Larry Hochman, Billy Lopez, Robert Lopez, Martin Erskine, J. Walter Hawkes.

1158 **Word Girl**. (Cartoon; PBS; Premiered: November 10, 2006)

Becky Botsford appears to be an ordinary little girl. She has a sidekick, a monkey named Captain Huggy Face and they are, in actuality, aliens from the planet Lexicon who have made Earth their home. Becky has super intellect and when the need arises, she becomes Word Girl, a super hero who battles crime with power of words (which, in turn, relate the meaning of words to children).

Voice Cast: Dannah Feinglass (Becky/Word Girl), Chris Parnell (Narrator), Ryan Raddatz (Mr. Botsford). **Credits:** *Executive Producer:* Dorothea Gillim. *Supervising Producer:* David Trelar. *Producer:* Will Shepard. *Theme:* Steve D'Angelo, Terry Tompkins.

1159 **Word World**. (Cartoon; PBS; Premiered: April 1, 2007)

Word World is a world where letters are used to represent everything including the main animal characters (Dog, Sheep, Ant, Duck, Frog, Pig and Bear). Stories are aimed at preschoolers and designed to help them learn letters and not judge a person by the way he or she looks. The characters show how letters make words, how other words can be made from the same letters and how certain words rhyme with other words and how the letters of a word can make shapes.

Voices: George Bailey, Marc Thompson, Sean Schemmel, Willie Martinez, Becky Poole, Zoe Martin, Billy Rippy, Michele O. Loikowski, Lenore Zann, H.O. Quinn, Daryl Ekroth, Heidi Bikkenstall. **Credits:** *Executive Producer:* Don Moody, Jacqueline Moody, David Lipson. *Supervising Producer:* Sue Hollenbberg. *Producer:* Olexa Hewryk, Alex Kay. *Music:* Nick Balaban, Stuart Killmorgan.

1160 **World Poker Tour**. (Reality; Game Show Network; Premiered: March 1, 2003)

A weekly program that presents the finals action of high stakes poker tournaments from around the world. Originally aired on the Travel Channel.

Host: Vincent Van Patten, Shana Hiatt, Courtney Friel, Mike Sexton, Layla Kayleigh. **Credits:** *Executive Producer:* Steve Lipscomb. *Producer:* Dave DiGregorio, Colin Campbell, Tom Greenhut, Joseph Grimm, George Sylark, Amy Weinberg. *Music:* Gary S. Scott

1161 **The X-Effect**. (Reality; MTV; Premiered: June 6, 2007)

Lovers who have broken up but now have new mates, are brought to a romantic getaway. However, only the ex-boyfriend or girlfriend are permitted to stay while their mates are sent home (actually to a secret location to view the activities of their partners). Fidelity is tested and the people at the resort must decide if they want to go back to their "offstage" mates or be with the new boyfriend or girlfriend they met at the resort.

Host: Natalia Castellanos, Thomas Bridegroom. **Credits:** *Executive Producer:* Amy Wruble, Douglas Tirola, Mike Powers. *Supervising Producer:* Suzanne Pate. *Producer:* Susan Bedusa. *Associate Producer:* Peter S. Alexander. *Music:* Jon Ernst.

1162 **X-Mates.** (Reality; Playboy Channel; Premiered: 2005)

With the increasing popularity of extreme sports, the Playboy Channel seeks to please its male audience with gorgeous *Playboy* magazine Playmates performing the hottest extreme sports in the nude (with the exception of a helmet for protection). The girls tackle, for example, BMX bike racing, the ATV track and wakeboarding.

The Girls: Deanna Brooks, Stacy Fuson, Vanessa Gleason, Teri Harrison, Stephanie Heinrich, Echo Johnson, Divini Rae, Shannon Stewart, Jennifer Walcott.

1163 **The Young and the Restless.** (Drama; CBS; Premiered: March 26, 1973)

A look at the New Morality as seen through the lives of the upper middle class adults who reside in the fictional metropolis of Genoa City, Wisconsin. Principal focus is on Victor Newman, head of Newman Enterprises, and his family.

Principal 2008 Cast: Eric Braeden (Victor Newman), Melody Thomas Scott (Nikki Newman), Amelia Heinle (Victoria Newman Hellstrom), Joshua Morrow (Nicholas Newman), Michelle Stafford (Phyllis Summers Newman), Peter Bergman (Jack Abbott), Sharon Case (Sharon Newman Abbott), Jeanne Cooper (Katherine Chancellor/Marge), Jess Walton (Jill Abbott), Kristoff St. John (Neil Winters), Christian LeBlanc (Michael Baldwin), Emily O'Brien (Jenna Hawkes Fisher), Greg Rikaart (Kevin Fisher), Don Diamont (Brad Carlton), Judith Chapman (Gloria Fisher Bardwell), Eileen Davidson (Ashley Abbott Carlton), Tracey E. Bregman (Lauren Fenmore Baldwin), Vail Bloom (Heather Stevens), Doug Davidson (Paul Williams), Michael Graziadei (Daniel Romalotti), Christel Khalil (Lily Winters), Daniel Goddard (Ethan "Cane" Ashby), Adrienne Frantz (Amber Moore), Elizabeth Hendrickson (Chloe Mitchell), Kate Linder (Esther Valentine), Erin Sander (Eden Baldwin), Vanessa Moreno (Eden Baldwin), Michael Gross (Lowell "River" Baldwin), Bryton McClure (Devon Hamilton), Billy J. Miller (Billy Abbott), Tammin Sursok (Colleen Carlton), Chris Egan (Adam Newman), Ted Shackelford (Jeffrey Bardwell), Patty Weaver (Gina Radison), Darcy Rose Baldwin (Abby Carlton), Michael Damian (Danny Romalotti), Nia Peeples (Karen Taylor), Eval Podell (Adrian Korbel), Tonya Lee Williams (Olivia Hastings Winters), Kevin Schmidt (Noah Newman), Beth Maitland (Traci Abbott Connelly), Thad Luckinbill (J.T. Hellstrom) Vincent Irizarry (David Chow), Raya Meddine (Sabrina Costelena), Jerry Douglas (John Abbott). **Credits:** *Executive Producer:* Josh Griffith. *Supervising Producer:* Tony Morina. *Coordinating Producer:* John Fisher.

1164 **Yu Gi Oh-Gx.** (Cartoon; WB/CW; October 10, 2005 to September 27, 2008). Jaden Yuki is a young boy who attends Duel Academy, a futuristic martial arts institute owned by the Kaiba Corporation. Other students are Alexis, Bastion, Chazz, Zane and her brother Syrus. Stories follow Jaden as he and his classmates use their martial arts abilities to battle evil. Produced in Japan.

Voice Cast: Matthew Charles (Jaden Yuki), Wayne Grayson (Syrus Truesdale), Anthony Salerno (Chazz Princeton), Priscilla Everett (Alexis Rhodes), Eric Stewart (Bastion), Scottie Ray (Zane). **Credits:** *Executive Producer:* Matthew

Drdek. *Music:* Fred Sheinfeld, Elik Alvarez.

1165 Zoey 101. (Comedy; Nickelodeon; January 9, 2005 to May 2, 2008)

Zoey Brooks is a very pretty 13-year-old girl who likes to take chances and be different. She proves this when she enrolls as a student at Pacific Coast Academy, an all-male boarding school that has just become co-ed (the school her brother, Dustin, also attends). Stories follow Zoey's life as she and her friends, Dana, Lola, Quinn and Nicole struggle to fit into a school heavily populated by boys. Jamie Lynn Spears sings the theme (written by her sister, Britney Spears).

Cast: Jamie Lynn Spears (Zoey Brooks), Kristin Herrera (Dana Cruz), Victoria Justice (Lola Martinez), Alexa Nikolas (Nicole Bristow), Paul Butcher (Dustin Brooks), Sean Flynn (Chase Matthews), Matthew Underwood (Logan Reese), Christopher Massey (Michael Barrett), Erin Sanders (Quinn Pensky), Jack Salvatore, Jr. (Mark Del Figgalo), Jessica Chaffin (Coco), Christopher Murray (Dean Rivers). **Credits:** *Executive Producer:* Dan Schneider, Jan Korbelin, Bill O'Dowd. *Producer:* Leanne Moore, Debra Spidell, Joe Catania. *Music:* Eric Hester, Drake Bell, Michael Corcoran, Jason L. Mattia.

INDEX OF PERSONNEL

References are to entry numbers.